Foundations of Interior Design

FAIRCHILD
BOOKS

Foundations of Interior Design

SECOND EDITION

Susan J. Slotkis

ASID Allied Member, IDEC Educational Affiliate,
IFDA Professional

Fashion Institute of Technology

FAIRCHILD BOOKS

NEW YORK

Fairchild Books

An imprint of Bloomsbury Publishing Inc

175 Fifth Avenue   50 Bedford Square
New York   London
NY 10010   WC1B 3DP
USA   UK

www.fairchildbooks.com

First edition published 2005

Library of Congress Cataloging-in-Publication Data

Slotkis, Susan J.

Foundations of Interior Design, 2nd Edition

ISBN 978-1-60901-115-4

2012936809

ISBN: 978-1-60901-115-4

Typeset by Precision Graphics
Cover Design by Carly Grafstein
Cover Art: background image: ©iStockphoto.com/hh5800
images from left to right: ©iStockphoto.com/molotovcoketail,
©Michael Robinson/Corbis, ©iStockphoto.com/Alexey Kashin
Printed and bound in the United States of America

This book is dedicated to the memory of Evelyn Slotkis,
my mother, my buddy, and, undoubtedly,
the best teacher I ever had.
From her I learned the true meaning of home.

Contents

Extended Table of Contents

Preface to the Second Edition

Foundations of Interior Design, first edition was written to fill a gap in the introduction of the interior design profession and practice to aspiring designers. The objective of the text was to provide an underpinning for the interior design student that would serve beyond one or two semesters or courses, be relevant for continued study, and as a reference for professional practice. It appears to have met that objective. Change is inevitable and welcome. A second edition is warranted: first, to update the information presented; second, to strengthen its ability to engage and inform its readership.

The second edition of *Foundations of Interior Design* takes an essential theme of the first edition further. That is, the premise that interior design is practiced within a service model. The process is not only creative, but problem-solving. Today's interior design student requires sensitivity to and knowledge of human factors as they relate to design solutions. Expectations for interior design to foster wellness and safety have become greater since the first edition. With these higher expectations it is even more critical for beginning students to be made aware of, and to appreciate, how the choices made by interior designers affect their clients and other users of the spaces they design. A service model approach to design incorporates social responsibility, and this is imbedded throughout the text as an ethos or belief system, rather than as a topic restricted to one chapter. Critical thinking regarding future generations and resources, including human

resources, is prompted throughout the text. Sustainable products and practices permeate this edition.

Recognition is given to the importance of history, significant events, and directions that influence culturally diverse interior design styles and solutions. This edition provides a wide range of examples of design in different styles. Projects and applications designed both by individuals and as collaborative efforts locally and globally are featured, from rural America to modern Dubai.

The content is comprehensive, yet presented in a style that is approachable for students working toward a two- or four-year degree, for both recent high school graduates and career changers. Information is presented in a practical fashion, citing applications for both theory and skill sets.

The contribution of many interior designers, those who work independently or as part of larger firms, is demonstrated in the choice of illustrations, case studies, and interviews in the printed text and accompanying CD-ROM. The presentation is a balance of small and large, simple and complex, and residential and contract projects from throughout the United States and abroad.

Organization of the Second Edition

The text is divided into 14 chapters. While the content follows a logical progression from the history of the profession through the student's preparation for entry into the field, some instructors may vary the order of presentation. The first chapter introduces the profession by citing its historical origins, significant individuals in design, and presents an overview of the profession. It concludes with trends influencing interior design including legislation and sustainability. Chapter 2 emphasizes socially responsible design within the overall framework of sustainable design. The student is presented with theoretical information to develop an understanding of human factors, global connectivity, and the impact of design decisions on individuals, society, and the environment. The responsibilities of the interior designer regarding health, safety, welfare, and environmental stewardship are presented. Chapter 3 reviews the very essential basics of design theory including aesthetics and the elements and principles of design. Chapter 4 delves more specifically into the design element of color, its complexity, and its applications. The interior design process follows in Chapter 5 where the various steps are reviewed, from needs assessment to project completion, including concepts behind space planning and furniture layouts. Chapter 6 describes how interior design ideation, conceptual thinking, and solutions are translated into graphic communications including hand and computer drawing techniques.

Chapters 7 through 10 cover the broad range of materials, applications, and techniques used that compose the interior space, beginning with lighting and lighting systems, followed by the shell or building materials, the lining or surface finishes, concluding with the feathering of the nest, or the furnishings. Attention is given to the personalization of the space with a review of art and accessories and how these elements support design concepts.

New manufacturing techniques, highlighting sustainable practices, innovative materials, products, and applications, are noted and illustrated. Collaborative solutions that address housing needs are presented. Materiality is treated comprehensively to encourage critical thinking toward potential for real-life application rather than just ideas.

Chapters 11 through 13 highlight the influences on interiors throughout history, noting how various factors have shaped spaces over time. The second edition provides several examples, including case studies, of how non-Western design and events have influ-

enced Western design throughout history. Current movements influencing interior design are cited and described in Chapter 13. The chapter begins with setting forth many influencing factors ("design drivers"), and how they influence future design. The influence of fashion, the DIY (do-it-yourself) movement, and globalization are a few of the drivers analyzed.

Chapter 14 presents a down-to-earth review of business practices followed by interior designers and assists students in planning their own future careers. Tips for job-seeking including preparing résumés and portfolios are demonstrated. Various kinds of companies, employment types in both residential and contract design, and related careers are described. Given that many students may at some point consider entrepreneurial possibilities, aspects of running a business are included, such as working with suppliers and third parties, and purchasing goods and products. The chapter does not shy away from many issues facing today's interior designers, such as the complexity of the new economy and government policies.

Pedagogy

Each chapter begins with an outline of its content and concludes with a summary, a comprehensive list of vocabulary terms pertinent to the chapter's topic, and two exercises: one aimed at reinforcing the content of the chapter and new to this edition an exercise to reinforce the learning experience offered in the CD-ROM.

"In the Spotlight" includes profiles of interior designers or industry experts or a discussion of design and innovations. In addition to the numerous tables, lists, and charts throughout the text, the *FYI . . .* feature helps students understand and remember important concepts. Maps are included to orient students to historical references influencing design. Interior design is a visual field and great attention has been given to the selection of illustrations. Over 900 illustrations, most of them color photographs, are provided to enhance the concepts, materials, and projects.

Several appendices including professional and trade organizations and brief bios and lists of notable designers in interior design, design and architecture provide a substantial pool of information to explore in further study.

For each chapter, enrichment material is provided in the accompanying CD-ROM. Students respond differently to pedagogical methods; the variety in the CD-ROM provides opportunities to enhance a student's learning experience. This unique component of *Foundations of Interior Design* includes demonstrations, animated definitions, illustrated timelines, and links to useful websites. New to this edition is an introduction to using the CD-ROM with the text.

An Instructor's Guide is available that includes a number of options for organizing and teaching the course. Supplementary exercises and assignments are provided for each chapter. Questions and answers for each chapter are included to reinforce information and encourage thought and discussion. The test bank can serve as a tool for evaluating students' comprehension. A PowerPoint presentation gives instructors a visually compelling add-on for engaging and teaching students.

ACKNOWLEDGMENTS

The author is grateful to the many people who have given her encouragement, information, and suggestions. Colleagues at ASID, IFDA, and IDEC, comprising interior designers, architects, vendors and suppliers, and others related to the A&D community, have always been willing to share their knowledge and expertise. It has been rewarding to reach out to former students to offer examples of their school work to demonstrate what "A" work is all about. They continue to grow and learn in their professional and personal lives.

Perhaps more indirectly, the education, experience, and colleagues in my previous careers, those of social services and training, have provided me with an invaluable perspective, not only for teaching, but also for the practice of interior design. The work of Fairchild's family of authors in interior design has provided much inspiration, including Susan Winchip, Mark Hinchman, Ron Reed, Douglas Seidler, and Christina Scalise, to name a few.

Comments from reviewers selected by the publisher were often challenging, yet always useful. They include Rula Z. Awwad-Rafferty, University of Idaho; Paul Black, The Art Institute of Atlanta, Stephanie Clemons, Colorado State University; Amy Crumpton, Mississippi State University; Jan Cummings, Johnson County Community College; Glenn E. Currie, Art Institute of Pittsburgh; Paulette Hebert, University of Louisiana Lafayette; Susan R. Leibold, IADT–Sacramento; Keith A. McCleary, Bradley Academy; Nancy Murray, Point Loma Nazarene University; LuAnn Nissen, University of Nevada-Reno; Christopher Priest, Minnesota State University; Jihyun Song, Iowa State University; Beth K. Stokes, Jo Ellen Weingart, Illinois Institute of Art; Travis Wilson, Western Kentucky University; and Nancy L. Wolford, Cañada College.

Thanks go to the staff at Fairchild Books—Joe Miranda, Amy Butler, Jessica Katz, photo researcher Avital Aronowitz, and in particular Olga Kontzias, executive editor, whom I've worked with since the first edition was just a gleam in our eyes. Once again, she has helped turn a suggestion into a reality with her vision, expertise, and hard work.

For her collaboration on the CD-ROM, the technical expertise and innovative ideas of Katherine Ankerson are acknowledged with, not only thanks but also awe. I gratefully acknowledge the participation of everyone featured on the CD-ROM.

I am grateful to my family, friends, and colleagues who remain loyal throughout my journey of designing, teaching, and writing. Their support and understanding is essential.

Susan J. Slotkis
2012

Exploring the *Foundations of Interior Design,* Second Edition CD-ROM

The CD-ROM included with this book is an integral part of your learning experience! Within the CD-ROM, you will find materials that supplement the text and go beyond, providing links to resources, explaining concepts, providing how-to methods, and incorporating cohesive connections through animated content, video, and links to websites.

SYSTEM REQUIREMENTS

Windows

- 2.33GHz or faster ×86-compatible processor (Intel® Atom™ 1.6GHz or faster processor for notebooks)
- Microsoft® Windows® XP Home, Professional, or Tablet PC Edition with Service Pack 3; Windows Server® 2003; Windows Server® 2008; Windows Vista® Home Premium, Business, Ultimate, or Enterprise (including 64-bit editions) with Service Pack 2; or Windows 7
- 512MB of RAM (1GB recommended)
- Display with 1024×768 resolution (16-bit color) or higher

Mac OS

- Mac OS 10.4 and later
- Intel Core™ Duo 1.83GHz or faster processor
- Mac OS X v10.6 or v10.7

- 512MB of RAM (1GB recommended)
- Display with 1024×768 resolution (16-bit color) or higher

Starting the CD-ROM

Follow these instructions to begin using the *Foundations of Interior Design* CD-ROM.

Windows

1. Insert the CD into the CD-ROM drive and begin using the CD-ROM.
2. If the autorun window does not open, open the CD window by clicking the FID icon using Windows Explorer.
3. Double-click on the Start icon.

Mac OSX

1. Insert the CD into the CD-ROM drive and begin using the CD-ROM.
2. If the CD window does not open automatically, open the CD by clicking the FID icon on the desktop or in Finder.
3. Double-click on the Start MAC icon.

ORGANIZATION OF THE CD-ROM

Scrollable Table of Contents

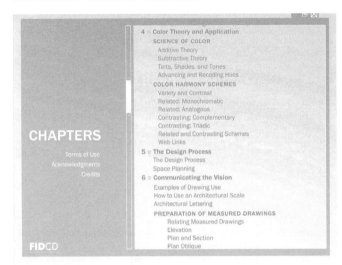

Using the vertical scroll bar, navigate up and down to the desired chapter. Mouse-clicking on a title brings up a new window with the content.

Concepts and Principles

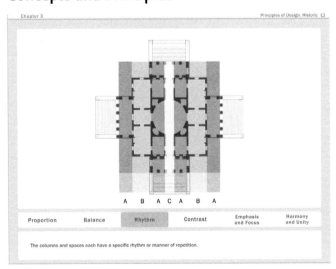

Abstract concepts are illustrated through interactive animations allowing you to select and view each.

Concepts and Principles

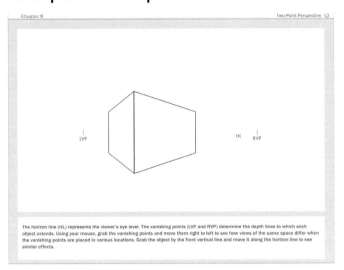

Using a mouse, each of the components of this interactive animation is movable. The vanishing points as well as the object itself may be dragged to see the effects of varying perspectives.

Demonstration of Technique

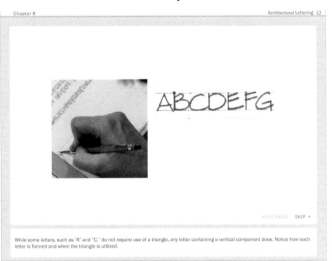

Learning to accomplish architectural lettering is enhanced by watching it being done. Strokes are highlighted, and text reinforces formation of each group of letters.

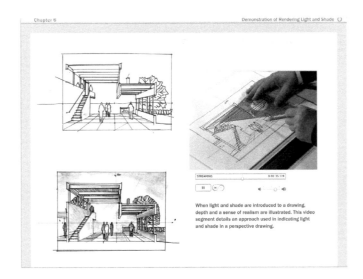

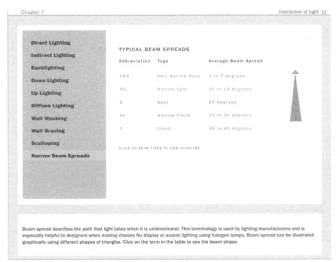

Demonstrations of techniques provide real-time video and audio to guide you through a process.

Interact with tables to see representations of the text.

Multiple Examples

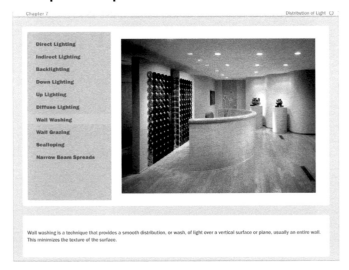

Choose the category from the list on the left to see examples of particular types of lighting.

Interactive Historical Timelines

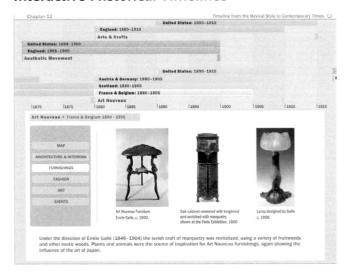

Interactive historical timelines provide a scrollable view of periods, associated countries and time frames, along with categories you may select to view for that period. This example highlights furniture from the Art Nouveau period in France and Belgium.

Active Web Links

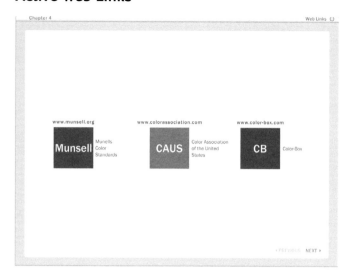

Each of the icons is a mouse-clickable link to a website containing the most current information available.

Showroom Visits

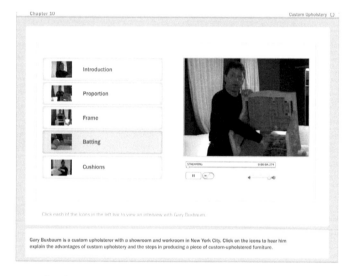

Visit the showroom of a custom upholsterer to learn firsthand the construction of a custom piece of furniture.

Student Interviews

Hear from recent graduates who give advice and relate experiences from their education, internships, and work experience.

CHAPTER 1

The Interior Design Profession

Design as a concept has its roots in the earliest experiences of humans, although it was not until the 18th century that it began to be shaped as a distinct occupational specialty. And not until the middle of the 20th century did the field of **interior design** begin to have an identity distinct from architecture and **interior decoration**. This chapter begins by discussing the origins of the practice of designing and decorating interiors and the people who undertook these activities. It then explores the growing emphasis on professionalism and the place for the **interior designer** as a collaborator within the larger architecture and design (A&D) community. The diversity of specialties available to those educated and trained in interior design is also introduced.

THE HISTORY OF INTERIOR DESIGN AND THE INTERIOR DESIGNER

Humans have occupied enclosed spaces throughout history, from prehistoric caves to present-day buildings. Design (planning based on decisions) and decoration (ornamentation) have always been a part of human history, relating not just to interiors. Detailed descriptions of the materials, furnishings, and styles used throughout history are explored in Chapters 11 and 12. A brief overview is provided here.

Ancient Civilizations

Prehistoric (prior to recorded history) civilizations were transient societies, made up of hunters and gatherers who moved about for shelter and sustenance. The mud-brick dwellings of the Sumerians, a trading people who lived in a region of Mesopotamia (now part of the Middle East) around 3500 B.C., are considered the first permanent city dwellings. Because those structures did not survive, our knowledge of the typical interior is derived from the detailed and painted models that were sometimes placed in tombs (Figure 1.1).

Interiors of the caves used by ancient primitive people served both practical and decorative purposes. Objects made for storage of everyday utensils also displayed decoration incorporating spiritual and tribal symbols.

Fifth-century B.C. Greek civilization is credited with having the most direct significant influence on the architecture of Western civilization throughout the ages. The ancient Greeks, and later the Romans, built highly structured and complex sites. These were open spaces, not enclosed interiors, and most contained civic or public buildings. These buildings, such as theaters, stadiums, baths, and temples, were constructed of marble and stone. Domestic architecture—buildings meant for residential living—were constructed less durably, primarily of mud bricks, and thus did not survive over time, as the important public buildings did. For this reason, our understanding of the interiors and domestic architecture of this era is limited. However, we know that for most citizens a simple hut was the principal domicile.

The eruption of Mount Vesuvius in A.D. 79 put a sudden end to the life of the Roman cities of Pompeii and Herculaneum. Excavations of the ruins of these cities teach us about the furnishings and decorations of ancient houses. There was little furniture, but the craftsmanship was of a high standard. Mosaic floors and wall paintings were common. Panels were painted to imitate marble or to tell the stories of mythological themes and landscapes.[1]

Figure 1.1
An opulent Mesopotamian interior is depicted, featuring elaborate wall frescoes. (*The Art Archive / Gianni Dagli Orti*)

The Greek and Roman civilizations were greatly influenced by the Egyptians, whether directly or indirectly through other cultures. Examples of this influence are seen in the Greek and Roman achievements of harmony in art, design, and architecture based on geometric principles; in the proportionate relationships of parts to a whole (see Chapter 2); and in methods of construction (see Chapter 8).

Middle Ages

In the Byzantine Empire (present-day Turkey) in the East, and England and most of Europe in the West, the period from approximately the 5th through 15th centuries A.D. is called the Middle Ages. During this period many of the refinements of the classical period disappeared as people became preoccupied with war, and survival became a way of life.

The elaborate interiors of the Middle Ages were created for the Church and aristocracy, which maintained the wealth. Arts and crafts guilds (precursors of modern trade unions), which had their heyday in feudal society in the 13th century, contributed to the decoration of interiors. There were no signature pieces (works in the distinctive style of an individual) during the Middle Ages; rather, work was categorized by the type of craft practiced by members of a group associated with a similar pursuit, called a **guild**. Artisans in guilds advanced from apprentices to masters. They might become respected by their peers for their craftsmanship, but most of these artisans were anonymous to the consumers of their goods.

Most items, although to some degree decorative, were mainly functional: for example, drinking and storage vessels, lighting fixtures, and ceramic tiles. In the later Middle Ages, merchants who attained a degree of affluence further adorned their interiors with materials such as wood paneling, as much to keep out the cold as to decorate (Figure 1.2).

Renaissance

A rebirth and patronage of the fine arts began in 14th-century Italy and spread throughout much of Europe over the next few centuries. During this period an emphasis on individualism and an appreciation for the humanities gave rise to "celebrity" artists, such as Michelangelo and Andrea Palladio. Originally trained

Figure 1.2
Middle Ages interior: Haddon Hall, Derbyshire, England (1475), shows spare furnishings and wood-paneled walls. *(Courtesy of Haddon Hall. Reproduced with kind permission of Lord Edward Manners)*

as a sculptor and stonemason, Palladio (1508–1580) became an influential architect with his published writings, *The Four Books of Architecture*, in 1570. In these books, he expounds on the architecture, both exterior and interior, for residences and churches, based on principles of the classical Greek and Roman periods. It is during the Renaissance that we see signature pieces, such as the ceiling of the Vatican's Sistine Chapel by Michelangelo (Figure 1.3).

Emerging in the latter part of the Renaissance, a style known as Baroque became popular throughout many parts of Europe. This style favored elaborate ornamentation, manifest in interiors in architectural details, furnishings, and upholstery.

Figure 1.3
Renaissance interior: ceiling frescoes of the Sistine Chapel by Michelangelo. (© Fefoff / Dreamstime.com)

Figure 1.4
Dining room interior of Monticello by Thomas Jefferson. *(Thomas Jefferson Foundation, Inc. at Monticello; Photograph by Sequoia Design)*

18th-Century Neoclassicism

It became fashionable during the 18th century to emulate the Renaissance quest for knowledge, crossing the boundaries of artistic and scientific disciplines. To attain this worldly sensibility, affluent young European men traveled and studied throughout the continent on what was called the grand tour. The term **interior architect** is still used, especially in Europe, to describe the occupation taken up by several of these neo-Renaissance men. The brothers Robert and James Adam, born in Scotland and practicing architects in England, concentrated their practice on residential interiors. They employed cabinetmakers, painters, and sculptors to execute their designs for interiors. The brothers' philosophy was that every detail must be executed from a single conception. Their supervision of large-scale projects may be thought of as similar to the general contractor of today, but with a greater emphasis on the **aesthetics**, or *beauty*, of the design.

By the end of the 18th century, Thomas Jefferson, a founder and the third president of the United States, acted as his own architect and designer for both his residence, Monticello, and the University of Virginia, in Charlottesville, Virginia. Jefferson had been greatly influenced by Palladio and the references to the classical Greek ideal of architectural order (Figure 1.4). Jefferson, an American neo-Renaissance man, had also served as ambassador to France and embraced a French approach to décor. As in earlier eras, architectural features such as the choice of materials, floors, ceilings, wall paneling, arches, columns, and woodwork constituted much of the content of interior design in the 18th century.

19th-Century Industrial Age

The Industrial Revolution, which began in the last part of the 18th century, brought about mass production of furniture and textiles for a broadening base of consumers in the cities of the United States, England, and western Europe. Queen Victoria of England, who reigned over an expansive world empire including Africa, India, and North America, influenced the style of the day and gave her name to this era (the Victorian). Many people, enthused with the myriad styles of furnishings available to them, became carried away to excess in decorating their homes. The expanse of choices available in materials, dyes, and styles from different countries created a niche for individuals with good taste who could coordinate all these options. The decorator emerged, either from the ranks of workmen, such as upholsterers, or from outside, such as antique dealers or agents, commissioning work from various craftsmen. By the end of Queen Victoria's reign in 1901, decorators aimed to return to the classical ideals of order and simplicity. However, order and simplicity are relative terms. Compared with the austerity of the modernists who followed them, the late Victorians continued to favor a more ornate style of ornamentation (Figure 1.5).

Ogden Codman Jr., one of the first to study architecture in "the colonies," decorated ten bedrooms at the Breakers, Cornelius Vanderbilt's "cottage" in Newport, Rhode Island, and Kykuit, John D. Rockefeller Jr.'s residence in Pocantico Hills, New York. With Edith Wharton, a successful American novelist, Codman cowrote *The Decoration of Houses* (1897). In their book, Wharton and Codman set forth strategies to deal with the demands of the material goods imported and accumulated by members of the emerging American upper class. In essence, they became the experts at combining the old with the new. Wharton and Codman exemplified the view that originality is found in the transfer of remembered forms that we find acceptable and desirable to new contexts (Figure 1.6).[2]

On the West Coast of the United States, another woman was achieving a different milestone. Toward the end of the 19th century, Julia Morgan was one of the first women to earn a civil engineering degree at the University of California. Although her architectural firm in San Francisco created many buildings, Morgan is best known for Hearst Castle, the grand complex she designed for publisher William Randolph Hearst (Figure 1.7).

Figure 1.5
Late-Victorian dining room. *(Photo © Rusty Reiners Photography 2003)*

Figure 1.6
Interior of Edith Wharton's home, The Mount. *(© Albert Knapp / Alamy)*

Figure 1.7
The Billiard Room at Hearst Castle, in San Simeon, California, contains billiard tables from the 1920s and Gothic tapestry completed c. 1500. *(Photograph by Victoria Garagliano/© Hearst Castle®/California State Parks)*

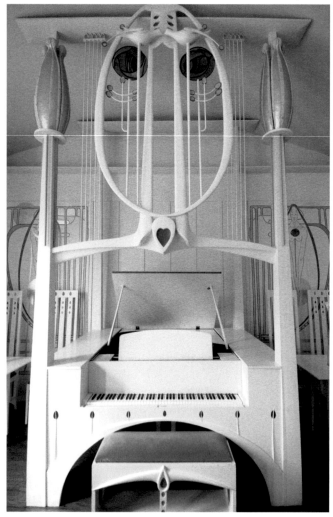

Figure 1.8
Charles Rennie Mackintosh's House for an Art Lover, Glasgow, Scotland: The architectural details and furnishings are typical of the work of this architect and designer. (© *Iain Masterton / Alamy*)

Figure 1.9
Mies van der Rohe designed the office for the director of the Bauhaus workshop with furniture designed by Walter Gropius (1923). (© *Bauhaus-Archiv Berlin*)

20th Century

To understand more fully the influence of modernists on the designs of the 20th century, it is useful to distinguish between the influences of the modern architect and the society decorator. As the 20th century began, both architects and decorators pursued the activities now called interior design. Although considerably different in style, sensibility, training, and education, they shared a common value of restraining ornamentation and limiting imitation of historical styles.

The 20th-Century Modern Architect The modern design movement was characterized by a decisive break with past traditions in the search for new forms of expression. Critical to this movement were the philosophies and practices of some key architects. Among the architects of the early 20th century famed not only for their buildings, but also for furniture and interior

design, was the American Frank Lloyd Wright (1867–1959). One principle expressed by Wright was the close relationship among nature, architecture, and interiors. This principle had a major impact on his choice of materials and colors. Another significant contributor was Charles Rennie Mackintosh (1868–1928), from Glasgow, Scotland, who considered himself both an architect and an artist. His famous commissions included residences, several tearooms, and the Glasgow School of Art. Like Wright's projects, these commissions were for the interior architecture as well as suites of furniture (Figure 1.8).

The modernist pioneers Walter Gropius (1883–1969), Ludwig Mies van der Rohe (1886–1969), and Le Corbusier (1887–1965) promoted rather austere interiors and expounded the relationship among abstract art, architecture, and interiors (Figure 1.9).

One of the few women to be recognized in the ranks of the modern pioneer architects was Eileen Gray (1879–

1976). Born in Ireland, she went to Paris in 1900 and was greatly influenced by the avant-garde modernists, including the Cubist painter Pablo Picasso. Like van der Rohe and Le Corbusier, she focused on furniture design during much of her career. Examples of the modernists' sleek leather and chrome chairs and tables are mass-produced today. However, at the time these furnishings were designed, the modernists' goal of combining good design form with new technology and materials for a broad base of consumers could not be accomplished. Production costs of these pieces remained too high.

The prosperity in the United States following World War II produced a generation of commercial skyscraper office spaces. Florence Schust (b. 1917)

trained as an architect under Mies and Eero Saarinen. After her marriage to Hans Knoll (1914–1955), in 1946, they expanded the Hans Knoll Furniture Company to include a new focus on office space design, an emerging field of commercial design. Their expanded business incorporated space-planning functions with furniture sales and changed the name of the firm to Knoll Associates (Figure 1.10). The Knolls also commissioned many other modern architects and furniture designers, who then became successful.

The 20th-Century Society Decorator As arbiters of taste, members of high society—mainly women—gained prominence for their approaches to home

Figure 1.10
Interior design sketch of Hans Knoll's New York City office by Florence Knoll, 1950. *(Florence Knoll Bassett, artist; Florence Knoll Bassett papers; Archives of American Art, Smithsonian Institution)*

décor. An 1878 publication, *Hints on Household Taste*, emphasized that "the faculty of distinguishing good from bad design in the familiar objects of domestic life is a faculty which most educated people—and women especially—conceive that they possess. How it has been acquired, few would be able to explain. The general impression seems to be, that it is the peculiar inheritance of gentle blood, and independent of all training."[3]

Following in the tradition of Edith Wharton, these new specialists were considered to be "in the know" about current and historical European styles. They also had the personal connections in society to make them influential and thus could project their taste onto others. The specialists' ideas about personal style were then broadcast through the rising number of magazines, such as *House Beautiful*.

Elsie de Wolfe (1865–1950), who wrote *The House in Good Taste* in 1913, is often considered to be the first professional decorator. De Wolfe was a stage actress before she began to pursue interior decoration as an occupation around the age of 40. She transformed the dark colors of the period to softer whites and pastels and simplified the use of ornamentation.

Dorothy Draper (1889–1969), another American society decorator, began her own company. Projects for public spaces and the interiors of commercial spaces were added to her firm's repertoire. Although American furniture manufacturers were flourishing in centers such as Grand Rapids, Michigan, and High Point, North Carolina, the society decorators continued to supply many of their clients with antiques obtained in Europe.

The British Syrie Maugham (1879–1955) established her decorating business first as an antique shop and used her frequently redecorated home as her showroom. Another self-taught decorator was the American Dorothy "Sister" Parrish (1910–1994), who founded her firm in 1933, after her husband lost money in the stock market crash of 1929. Parrish and Albert Hadley (1920–2012), who joined her firm in 1962, became known for the "undecorated look," which suggested that clients had accumulated their possessions over a lifetime. Another society decorator, Ruby Ross Wood (1880–1950), established the first decorating department in a department store (Figure 1.11).

Figure 1.11
Ruby Ross Wood interior. *(Courtesy of the Library of Congress)*

Neither a society decorator nor a modernist architect, a French contemporary of both these professionals was Jacques-Émile Ruhlmann (1879–1933). Trained as a cabinetmaker, he became known for his fine craftsmanship, using exotic materials, such as rare woods and ivory. Wealthy people, including the Rothschilds, commissioned him to execute complete luxury interior designs for them.

One of the most successful of the early decorators specifically trained in interior design was Eleanor McMillen Brown. A graduate of the Parsons School of Design in New York City, Brown founded her New York-based company in 1923. Considered the first professional full-service interior design firm in the United States, it still operates today under the management of Betty Sherrill.

21st Century

As we are just in the second decade of the 21st century, we do not have the advantage of hindsight to reflect on the changes that may eventually be described for the whole 100-year span; we can, however, definitively say that the profession continues to change and evolve. Trends that have significant impact on the 21st-century interior designer include technological advances; global connectivity; an increased role in health, safety, and welfare issues; demand for sustainable design that considers the balance of resources, including those of the environment; increased governmental regulation; greater integration of research, also called **evidence-based design**; and intra- and interdisciplinary collaboration.

Key points from leading designers are summarized in *FYI . . . "Industry Icon Perspectives"*: Contract *Magazine*.

Sometimes referred to in the media as the Great Recession, the economic downturn that began in 2008 also significantly impacted the interior design industry. Signs of recovery resulted in "controlled consumption," a term also used to describe the so-called New Economy. Traditionally, interior designer fees depended heavily on product (e.g., furniture) sales to supplement charging for design services. More than half of a typical firm's revenue came from product sales, compared with less than a third from fees for interior design services. Changes in consumer buying behavior and attitudes, as well as the popularity of lifestyle retailers, such as Restoration Hardware, Pottery Barn, and Crate and Barrel, have greatly reduced the profitability of the traditional business model. Designers have therefore had to increase the revenue they earn from fees to make up for declining profits from sales, to be discussed further in Chapters 13 and 14.

Another way to look at where we are so far in the 21st century is a snapshot view of the interior design population. It should be noted that the following statistical census information is based on self-reporting of those who describe their occupation as interior designer. No qualifications were attached to this, such

---

FYI . . . "Industry Icon Perspectives": *Contract* Magazine

In celebration of its 50th anniversary, *Contract* magazine devoted its March 2010 issue to the changes over the past five decades in contract (commercial) design. In the article "Looking Back Fifty Years," ten design practitioners reflect on the changes they have seen in the industry. Key points from the article are provided below.

Change happens more rapidly. Designers are more socially conscious and environmentally responsible, according to Stanley Felderman, a pioneer of the "total design concept," which integrates planning, architecture, interior design, and product design. It is time for designers and the future of design to broaden the scope of work.

Josephine Carmen, IIDA, CID, at Perkins+Will, sees education playing a role in change, with schools' increased allegiance to architectural thinking helping separate interior design programs from home economics departments, which taught style and decoration.

The industry itself has become much more exacting, being held accountable to more codes and to state and governmental regulations. This separates the serious designer from the hobbyist, says Andre Staffelbach, FIIDA, ASID.

Neil Frankel, FAIA, FIIDA, optimistically addresses the opportunity for the establishment of a new body of knowledge and the integration of social research to translate human needs into successful human experiences.

Lou Switzer, of The Switzer Group, in New York, the nation's largest minority-owned interior architectural design firm, happily sees a lot of diversity in the industry, with many more females and minorities as compared with when he founded his company more than 40 years ago. Today, people work in open, collaborative environments. They also specialize more, for example, project managers, designers, technicians, and so on.

Source: Ralph Mancini, "Industry Icon Perspectives: Looking Back Fifty Years," Contract, March 1, 2010, 28–39.

as academic degree or other credentials, and the interviewees were both contract (commercial) and residential designers.

According to the *U.S. Bureau of Labor Statistics, Occupational Outlook Handbook,* 2010–11 edition, interior designers number almost 72,000. About 30 percent of interior designers worked in specialized design services. Additionally, 14 percent of interior designers provided design services in architectural and landscape architectural services and 9 percent worked in furniture and home-furnishing stores. Many interior designers also performed freelance work in addition to holding a salaried job in interior design or another occupation.[4]

TODAY'S INTERIOR DESIGN PROFESSION

The profession of interior design has evolved from the earlier scope of the planning and decorating of interior spaces. Although definitions vary, certain common elements are included in most descriptions of the practice of interior design today.

The terms **interior designer** and interior decorator, both relatively new labels, are sometimes incorrectly used interchangeably. Many of today's interior designers would disagree with the comment made in the 1980s that "interior design is often undertaken without strong involvement in architecture, especially by those active in the design of residential interiors."[5] A century earlier, Wharton described the relationship of interior design to architecture as the trend toward "interior architecture" that is differentiated from the "superficial application of ornament."[6]

Sir Hugh Casson (1910-1999), architect, illustrator, and author, provides a useful way to distinguish between interior designers and interior decorators:

> Broadly speaking, for the interior designer there will be two approaches: the first is the "integrated" where the interior is indivisible from the structure and where pattern, form, texture, and lighting are part of the architecture and qualities of permanence and monumentality are sought. The second, which may be termed as "superimposed," is where the interior is required to be more

flexible, and easily modified or even transformed without mutilating the architecture in which it is temporarily contained.[7]

Another way to differentiate design from decorating is to describe interior design as the activity that plans for the necessities of a space relating to issues of safety and protection and that considers the basic function of a space and space planning. Decoration, in contrast, implies ornamentation. Simply put, a decorator works only with surface decoration, such as paints, fabrics, and furnishings. Although decoration enhances a space, adds to its individuality, and may provide psychological and symbolic comforts within the space, it is not required to meet the most basic universal human needs.

The term *interior decorator,* which first appeared in *Merriam-Webster's Dictionary* as an entry in 1867, was later followed by the term *interior design* in 1927. Interior design is described as "the art or practice of planning and supervising the design and execution of architectural interiors and their furnishings."[8] The *Encyclopedia Britannica* defines interior design as "the planning and design of man-made spaces, a part of environmental design and closely related to architecture."[9] The U.S. Bureau of Labor Statistics adds that interior design is a practical design that is conducive to a space's intended purpose, such as raising productivity, selling merchandise, or improving lifestyle.[10]

It has become increasingly important for today's designers to recognize and achieve the levels of education and training required to comply with the legal and ethical standards associated with the health, safety, welfare, and comfort of their clients; that is, the standards of professional interior design. However, it is understood that many projects that would be included in the category of interior design are carried out by segments of talented people trained in specific skills, such as those related to architecture and industrial design.

For example, Philippe Starck, a French designer (b. 1949) known for his offbeat hotel designs, studied architecture, furniture, interiors, and products. Andrée Putman (b. 1925), also French, established her Paris firm in 1978. She has received worldwide acclaim, particularly in hotel, retail, and restaurant design. Well-traveled and educated in art and music, Putman

Figure 1.12
Willard Hotel Lobby, Washington, D.C., designed by Sarah Tomerlin Lee. *(Courtesy Willard Intercontinental)*

worked as a journalist and store stylist before establishing her design firm. Sarah Tomerlin Lee (1911–2001), an American known for her contributions in the area of hotel design, studied and worked in the fields of advertising and journalism before taking over her husband's architectural firm after his death (See Figure 1.12). Clodagh, known for her concept of total design that incorporates sensitivity to the environment, was born in Ireland and began work as a fashion designer. Then, living in Spain, she became a landscape designer and architect, self-taught in all areas.

Services Performed by Today's Interior Designer

The role of interior designers in today's society is more complex and comprehensive than that of their predecessors. A major recommendation of a recent study was for the interior design community to continue to raise awareness of its distinct contributions to the interior space by recognizing its unique perspective on the humanization of space.[11] An interior designer's education emphasizes assessing the function of a space, surveying a client's needs, and involving the client in the process.

Interior designers currently provide the following services:[12]

- Help determine project goals and objectives
- Analyze a client's needs, goals, and life and safety requirements
- Formulate preliminary design concepts that are appropriate, functional, and aesthetic
- Allocate, organize, and arrange a space to suit its function
- Generate ideas for the functional and aesthetic possibilities of a space
- Develop documents and specifications relative to interior spaces in compliance with applicable building and safety codes
- Create illustrations and renderings
- Develop and present final design recommendations through appropriate presentation media
- Prepare working drawings and specifications for non-load-bearing interior construction, materials, finishes, space planning, furnishings, fixtures, and equipment[13]
- Monitor and manage construction and installation of designs
- Collaborate with other licensed practitioners in the technical areas of mechanical, electrical, and load-bearing design, as required for regulatory approval
- Prepare and administer bids and contract documents as a client's agent
- Review and evaluate design solutions during implementation
- Select and specify fixtures, furnishings, products, lighting solutions, materials, and colors
- Purchase products and fixtures
- Design and manage fabrication of custom furnishings and interior details

Specialty Segments

In addition to the numerous services professional interior designers perform, the industries and fields in which they may concentrate are diverse. In the broadest sense, interior design projects may be divided into two main categories: **residential design** and **contract,** or **commercial, design**. Each category includes many subdivisions. The following discussion outlines the many opportunities that exist for interior designers.

Residential Interior Design Residential design focuses on the planning and specifying of interior materials and products used in private residences. It implies that an interior designer is working within an environment in which an individual resides for a relatively fixed period. Most of the time, an individual person enters into a contract with a designer to design the interior of his or her family's home. An exception is the design of so-called model homes. In that instance, an interior designer creates a homelike environment but is providing services to a real estate developer or management office. Similarly, many corporations hire interior designers to create spaces for employees to live in while on temporary assignment. The area of **assisted living**, generally for senior citizens, is a bridge between residential and contract design. Although these quarters are designed to house residents in their own spaces, a managing agent contracts for the design.

Residential design includes the following sub-specializations:

- Model apartments
- Retirement housing, 55-plus or active senior housing, and independent living
- Multi-dwelling complexes
- Apartments, condominiums, cooperatives

- Home entertainment design
- Bath design
- Kitchen design (Figure 1.13a)
- Home office design
- Recreational and therapeutic design (e.g., home spa, sauna, pool, and workout areas)
- Storage design
- Children's rooms (Figure 1.13b)

Contract, or Commercial, Design The contract interior designer works within environments in which a company, rather than an individual, is contracting for the design services. The interior permanent or temporary space is where a variety of activities may be carried out, for both work and pleasure. Within this broad category are several sub-specializations, among them the following:

- *Corporate design*. Includes design for staff and executive offices, conference rooms, teleconferencing centers, workstations, computer stations, training facilities, relocation, or corporate apartments (Figure 1.14a).
- *Entertainment design*. Includes interiors, lighting, sound, and other technologies for movies, television, videos, theater, clubs, concerts, and theme and amusement parks.
- *Facilities management*. Includes the organizational management of generally large business operations. Specialists in this area

Figure 1.13
a. Kitchen design; b. Contemporary colorful room designed for a child. *(a: Photograph by Phillip Ennis; b: Photoshot/Red Cover/Nicolas Lemonnier)*

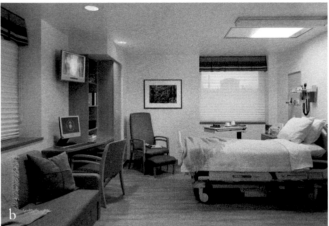

Figure 1.14

a. Corporate lobby designed by the interior design firm Carson Guest; b. Sloan-Kettering Cancer Center Inpatient Unit for Genito Urinary (New York City); c. ACCRC (Continuing Care Retirement Community) by Perkins Eastman in Japan incorporates Western programs with insights into Japanese culture; d. Hospitality design: Barcelo Raval Hotel, Barcelona, is a luxury hotel designed by Jose Maria Guillen White; e. Charym, a fitness facility/spa in Litchfield, Connecticut, by interior designer Alexandra Champalimaud; *(a: Photography by Gabriel Benzur, Designer: Carson Guest Inc.; b: Copyright Chuck Choi. Courtesy Perkins Eastman / MSKCC Design & Construction Department; c: Sun City Takatsuki, Takatsuki, Japan. Copyright Chuck Choi. Courtesy Perkins Eastman; d: Copyright: Barceló Hotels & Resorts. Photo by Pere Peris; e: Design Firm: Champalimaud, Photographer: Antony Crook)*

Figure 1.14 *continued*
f. The Althea Gibson Academy in East Orange, New Jersey; g. The Marc Jacobs store in Los Angeles; h. Trade show exhibit design at Maison & Objets, Paris, September 2010. *(f: James D'Addio, Photographer. Designed by Hiller Architecture; g: Fairchild Publications, Inc.; h: Jean Boggio for Franz, Trade show exhibit design at Maison & Objets, Paris, 2010, Image/Illustration provided by Franz Collection Inc.)*

address safety and health issues; lighting and acoustical needs; scheduling of maintenance; and coordinating of office expansions, downsizing, and relocations. This specialty relies on substantial communication among the interior designer, builders, engineers, and business decision-makers.

- *Health care design*. Includes design for hospitals, medical and dental offices, psychiatric facilities, clinics, ambulatory care centers, assisted living, halfway houses, hospices, rehabilitation centers, and nursing homes. (Figure 1.14b). A **continuing care retirement community (CCRC)** blends features of residential and health-care design. It is a concept that strives to accommodate varying needs, generally of an elderly population, in a clustered environment to ease transition from independence to a more supervised facility. It generally incorporates the following categories: independent living, assisted living, and specialized nursing or dementia units (Figure 1.14c).

- *Hospitality and restaurant design*. Includes design for hotels, motels, restaurants, country clubs, golf courses, resorts, cruise ships, bars, lounges and nightclubs, and recreational facilities (Figure 1.14d and e).
- *Institutional and governmental design*. Includes design for schools, government buildings, prisons, community centers, airports, rail stations, houses of worship, shelters, museums, stadiums, arenas, and libraries (Figure 1.14f).
- *Retail and store planning design*, which includes design for specialty and department stores, supermarkets, salons, shopping malls, showrooms, art galleries, pop-up stores, trade shows, exhibitions, and displays (Figure 1.14g and h).

Careers in both residential and contract design are driven by the economy. Currently, there is growth in the hospitality, health-care, institutional, and government sectors and in specialty facilities, such as for the senior population. Most employment opportunities also require expertise in sustainability, to be discussed further in Chapter 2.

Related Career Options Many occupations, other than becoming a practicing interior designer, are open to those who have received either a partial or complete education in interior design. Some recipients of interior design education prefer alternative uses for their skills and knowledge. Conversely, there are those who have first been educated, trained, and employed in related industries and *then* pursue additional education and training in the field of interior design. Among the related industries are historic preservation, set design, and visual merchandising (Figure 1.15).

Approaches to Interior Design

Practicing within any of the preceding sub-specialties of interior design are people who subscribe to a particular orientation, framework, or ethic in conducting business. Two of the more common approaches, described in more detail in Chapter 2, are **universal**

Figure 1.15
Historic preservation (restoration) of the Beacon Theater, built in 1929, by Beyer Blinder Belle Architects & Planners, LLP. *(Photography by T. Whitney Cox)*

design and **sustainable**, or **green**, design. Increasingly, these two approaches are presumed to be part of every designer's practice and eventually may not be considered specialties.

- *Universal design* is based on a distinct body of knowledge that relates to both human and design factors. This approach fosters opportunities for as many people as possible to have access to good design. Related to this concept is *design in the public interest*, to be discussed further in Chapter 13.
- *Sustainable design* has as its goal socially responsible design that considers the needs of future generations. Its focus is to preserve the natural environment and its resources. The notion of green design has largely been replaced by this broader concept. Many interior designers are opting to earn a credential known as **LEED** (**Leadership in Energy and Environmental Design**), a certification process managed by the **GBCI** (**Green Building Certification Institute**). More than 43,000 individuals are now LEED accredited.[14] (See Chapter 14 for additional information on LEED certification process.)

Professionalism in Interior Design

What do we mean when we speak of the profession of interior design? The interior design field, as we know it today, continues to move toward achievement of professionalism by adhering to the following standards:

- Skills are acquired through education and training based on a standardized body of knowledge.
- Services are performed in compliance with an established code of ethical standards.
- Performance is evaluated by examination, oversight, or licensing by recognized authorities.
- Members are associated with and represented by an organization whose goal is to promote affiliation, education, and practice.

Professional Interior Design Associations

One of the ways in which we categorize an occupation as a profession is by the affiliation of its members with organizations. The organizations, among other benefits, provide educational and networking opportunities for their members. The two largest interior design associations, the American Society of Interior Designers (ASID) and the International Interior Design Association (IIDA), have made attempts to merge but at present have not been able to resolve issues to accomplish this goal. Both ASID and IIDA have similar categories of membership in interior design and represent a mix of design specialties among their members.[15] Both organizations define a professional interior designer as one who is qualified through education, experience, and examination to enhance the function and quality of interior spaces.

The **American Society of Interior Designers (ASID)** evolved from a series of other organizations beginning in 1931. Today, there are 18,000 practitioner members of ASID in commercial and residential design, with 48 local chapters in the United States and Canada. An additional 18,000 members include students and industry partners. Headquartered in Washington, D.C., ASID is the largest North American professional organization for the interior design industry. Its stated purpose is to promote activities designed to maximize the profession's potential and goals. It administers a code of ethics and standards for appellation, or appropriate titles for membership categories, for example (for a complete and updated list see www.asid.org):

Professional
Practitioner
Allied Practitioner
Associate Practitioner
Industry Partner
Education Affiliate
Press Affiliate
Student

The **International Interior Design Association (IIDA)** was founded in 1994 as a result of a merger of three organizations. The goal was to create an international association with a united mission that would represent interior designers worldwide and speak on their behalf with a single voice. IIDA's 13,000 members belong to 31 chapters with members in the United States and Canda.

Membership categories are:

Professional Interior Designer
Professional Architect
Educator
Student, Affiliate
International
Industry
Student
Industry Representative

Furthering IIDA's goals for education and networking, specialty forums were created for its membership, as follows:

Corporate
Facility Planning and Management
Government
Healthcare
Hospitality
Institutional
Knowledge
Residential
Retail
Sustainability

Related Professional, Specialty, and Trade Associations

Many other associations attract interior designers, along with those employed in related fields. Among organizations that might be of interest to designers are the Institute of Store Planners (ISP), the Network of Executive Women in Hospitality (NEWH), the National Kitchen and Bath Association (NKBA), the Interior Design Society (IDS), the International Furnishings and Design Association (IFDA), the International Association of Lighting Designers (IALD), and the American Academy of Healthcare Interior Designers (AAHID). Additional information on ASID, IIDA, and these organizations can be found in Appendix A.

Interior Design Education

Many types of educational opportunities are currently available to individuals seeking to prepare for the occupation of interior designer. These include postsecondary-level academic programs; less formal courses of study, sometimes offered online; intern-

ships; and ongoing professional development through employment, professional affiliation, and self-study.

Academic Programs Several types of degree and non-degree programs refer to their programs as interior design. They range from correspondence schools and certification programs to postgraduate programs in interior design. Some courses are offered on a continuing education basis and not aimed at providing a certificate or degree.

In the United States, two-year associate degree programs, four- and five-year baccalaureate degree programs, and postgraduate programs offer interior design and related majors. Interior design programs are housed within a variety of academic school, colleges, and departments. In only about one-third of accredited programs is interior design treated as a unique discipline. It is generally considered one of a group of disciplines concerned with the interaction between humans and their environment. Increasingly, interior design education has responded to the changing nature of the industry by utilizing teaching methods that enhance student awareness and knowledge of the integrated, collaborative approach to design within a culturally diverse, global context. *FYI . . . Partial List of Interior Design Courses Offered by Various Colleges* provides a partial list of courses offered in interior design programs.

Interior designers are encouraged and sometimes required by many of the professional associations to keep their level of education and experience relevant through lifelong learning. There are many short-term courses for which designers can receive **continuing education units (CEUs)**. The **Interior Design Continuing Education Council (IDCEC)** reviews courses for approval to be counted as CEUs for these organizations. The professional associations sponsor many of these courses. Others are available at symposiums and conferences. Often, these courses deal with topical issues, such as changes in building codes, business practice issues, new products, and technology.

Associations have been formed whose aim is to advance education and practice standards. They include the Interior Design Educators Council (IDEC), the Council for Interior Design Association (CIDA), the National Association of Schools of Art and Design (NASAD), and the **National Council for Interior Design Qualification (NCIDQ)**.

FYI . . . Partial List of Interior Design Courses Offered by Various Colleges

Colleges throughout North American offer a range of interior design courses, including (order of courses does not represent specific course study or curriculum):

- Studio courses for residential, office, health-care, and hospitality design
- Historical styles of architecture, furnishings, and interiors
- Color theory and application
- Computer-aided drafting and design
- Lighting theory and application
- Textiles and materials
- Methods of construction of building and/or product

- Hand drafting and perspective drawing
- Presentation, rendering, and model-making techniques
- Human behavioral, cultural, and environmental factors
- Building codes and regulations
- Professional practice, business structures, and ethics
- Thesis and research techniques
- Portfolio development and career preparation
- Internship program

Both the **National Association of Schools of Art and Design (NASAD)** and the **Council for Interior Design Association (CIDA)** are organizations that review educational programs against established criteria in order to accredit the programs accordingly. CIDA is an independent, volunteer organization that sets standards for interior design programs, culminating in a minimum of a bachelor's degree at the postsecondary school level in the United States and Canada. Reviews are done at the request of colleges and universities that wish to achieve this high level of accreditation. Of the 350 interior design programs in the United States, 155 are accredited by CIDA. Of the 20 Canadian programs, 14 are accredited by CIDA.[16]

IDEC The membership of the **Interior Design Educators Council (IDEC)** is primarily college educators and researchers in the field of interior design. IDEC's mission is the advancement of interior design education and scholarship by promoting recognition of the contribution of interior design education, scholarship, and practice to the advancement of quality of life within the built environment. The organization strives to promote creative and critical thinking to solve problems and to expand the body of knowledge base for interior environments to improve quality of life and human performance.

Many states, jurisdictions, and Canadian provinces have moved to regulate who may use the title of interior designer and have established procedures for licensing, certification, and registration. Each state's requirements are different. Several states have included mandated continuing education requirements for recertification. The different types of legislation and requirements are discussed in Chapter 14.

Other Factors That Contribute to Professional Success

In addition to formal education in the theory and application of design, it is important for the future interior designer to consider the individual factors that can result in success. These factors include personality traits, work habits, potential and proven talents and skills, and experience.

Although a creative temperament is part of the makeup of the interior designer, it is important to real-

Harlem Hospital Center Renovation

Hellmuth Obata + Kassabaum (HOK NY), in association with Studio/JTA, devised the concept for the modernization of Harlem Hospital Center (HHC) to integrate innovative health-care planning and design excellence, with the intent to express the vibrant history and current culture of Harlem. The idea for the project grew out of a commitment toward "meaningful" design and expression of the importance of black culture and its influence on American life. From the start of the development, participants adopted a collaborative approach, with the establishment of a diverse steering committee made up of representatives of the community.

Many of the architectural and interior design decisions embraced concepts delineated by Jack Travis (FAIA, NOMAC), the principal architect of JTA/ Associates. One of these concepts was the transformation of space through art. HHC housed a number of murals painted during the Great Depression of the 1930s, many by African-American artists. These murals were slated to be demolished. It was important to this group of architects, designers, and the community to preserve and restore these historically significant murals. The largest one, *Pursuit of Happiness,* by Vertis Hayes, depicts the history of the African diaspora. The story is told through a series of vignettes, beginning with life in Africa, in an agrarian culture, and ending with life in the United States, in which African Americans hold positions in the professions, trades, and the arts. Sections of the murals were reproduced as 80-foot monuments within the building's sustainable glass façade.

Other embellishments to foster a collective memory of the culture include Heritage Hall, which traces the journey from slavery, and materials selected for many of the interior finishes. For example, the color red symbolizes the blood of the slaves who died coming over from Africa; the roughness of the wood further expresses that journey.

The expansive atrium lobby that connects buildings is also featured.

Sources: Healthcare Design. *Press release, September 2007; Nayar, Jean. "Heart and Soul."* Contract, *July 17, 2009; Papers and author's attendance at lectures on the project.*

Figures a, b, and c
Illustrations of the culturally relevant plans for the Harlem Hospital Center renovation project in New York.
a. Center's façade featuring reproduced '30s murals, *Pursuit of Happiness;* b. Heritage Hall; c. Atrium lobby. *(a, b, and c: Renderings courtesy of HOK in collaboration with Jack Travis, FAIA Architect)*

ize that much of the practice of interior design requires the direction of creative energies into problem solving. Likewise, interior design is a business and, at times, may seem more administrative than creative. And finally, interior designers have considerable responsibilities relating to the health, safety, and comfort of their clients and the public.

Along with talent and technical abilities, what are some of the personal traits needed for a satisfying career? For many careers, the following traits have been shown to foster success: enthusiasm; interpersonal skills; willingness to work hard; and the ability to manage details, time, and energy level. It is important for prospective practitioners to take personal inventory of the qualities they bring to the profession as individuals. This soul searching not only helps a prospective interior designer determine if this career is the right fit, but it also guides the individual toward a course of study that will harness the talents he or she possesses into a particular direction. One of the exercises at the end of this chapter features questions that you, as an interior design student, should continue to ask yourself throughout your education.

The results of an employer survey in 2010, a joint project of Syracuse University and ASID, concluded that 43 percent of respondents listed a positive, outgoing personality as a top consideration, followed by communication skills at 30 percent and technical design skills at 29 percent.[17] This text's concluding chapter (Chapter 14) addresses employer considerations for hiring a new designer. This first chapter has offered a taste of what lies ahead.

Summary

History tells us how, over the centuries, interior spaces have provided humankind with both temporary and permanent shelter. It also tells us how essential these primal needs are and how universal the desire is to personalize one's space.

It was not until the 18th century that the profession now known as interior design evolved as an entity unto itself. The Adam brothers, in England, were early interior architects. The 19th-century Industrial Age created a niche for individuals who could coordinate the available choices in furnishings, leading to the emergence of the society decorator. This trend flourished in the early 20th century with the work of Elsie de Wolfe, considered the first professional decorator. The early 20th century saw the impact of a few avant-garde modern thinkers, many of them architects, who strove to return to the simplicity of the classicists while making use of new technology and materials.

The current field of professional interior design is complex and varied and requires practitioners with education, skill, and experience. Increased reliance on technology, collaboration and integrated services, sustainable design, and globalization are trends impacting the 21st-century interior designer.

Among the many services an interior designer may provide are the following:

- Generating ideas for the functional and aesthetic possibilities of a space
- Organizing a space to suit its function
- Selecting and purchasing furnishings
- Creating illustrations and plans
- Developing documents in compliance with applicable codes
- Collaborating with other practitioners

A person can practice interior design in many ways and in a variety of settings. The two broadest categories of interior design are residential and contract, or commercial, design. Within those two broad categories are several sub-specialties. Increasingly, responsibility for the health, safety, welfare, and comfort of clients and the public has been added to the job of the professional interior designer. Sustainable, or green, design has been mainstreamed, and a strong knowledge base in this area is expected of the design professional of the 21st century.

The two largest professional organizations, ASID and IIDA, provide continuing educational opportunities and industry-related information to their members and the public. Organizations that aim to advance the education and practice of both the student and the practitioner include CIDA, NASAD, NCIDQ, and IDEC.

Vocabulary

aesthetics

American Society of Interior Designers (ASID)

assisted living

continuing education unit (CEU)

continuing care retirement community (CCRC)

contract (commercial) interior design

Council for Interior Design Association (CIDA)

design

evidence-based design

green

Green Building Certification Institute (GBCI)

guild

Interior Design Educators Council (IDEC)

Interior Design Continuing Education Council (IDCEC)

interior architect

interior decoration

interior decorator

interior design

interior designer

International Interior Design Association (IIDA)

Leadership in Energy and Environmental Design (LEED)

National Association of Schools of Art and Design (NASAD)

National Council for Interior Design Qualification (NCIDQ)

residential interior design

sustainable (green) design

universal design

Exercise: A Dozen Questions to Ask Yourself

Even as you begin your studies, it is helpful to take stock by asking yourself the following questions. Write your answers and save them for future reference and updating.

1. How committed am I to the intensity and cost of this formal course of study?
2. How far do I intend to go in the field? Do I see this as a full-time professional career, a pastime, or a sideline to something else?
3. What specialties, if any, have I identified that I want to pursue?
4. Am I prepared to defer financial success for the first few years of my career?
5. Am I self-motivated and self-directed?
6. Do I enjoy working with and for people?
7. Can I manage my time and have the discipline necessary to meet deadlines and other requirements?
8. Can I supervise or manage the work performed by others?
9. Do I have the creative potential to carry out innovative design solutions?
10. Can I communicate my ideas visually, orally, and in writing?
11. If necessary, will I be able to work outside a nine-to-five schedule?
12. Am I passionate about design?

Exercise: Exploring the CD-ROM

Take advantage of the contents of the CD-ROM to increase your understanding of the professional and trade organizations and their importance to the interior design profession. Follow the instructions for Starting the CD-ROM on pages xix–xx and click on Chapter One: The Interior Design Profession.

Professional and Trade Organizations: Review the websites of at least three interior design and related industry professional and trade associations. Check both the main site and the chapter listings in your area. Check their calendar of events for local activities, such as seminars or networking events. Inquire if you may attend as a prospective student member and plan to attend at least one event in the following month.

CHAPTER 2

Socially Responsible Design

More an approach to design than a specific set of standards, **socially responsible design** can be thought of as having two parallel tracks: designing for the present with current resources while anticipating and planning for the future. It is mindful of preserving natural resources, including human resources, land resources, and energy. It implies the powerful potential for design as a change agent for the public good. The concept coincides with the position taken that interior design has an impact on the health, safety, and welfare of individuals and the world we live in. Citing the unique value of the interior designer, Mary Knackstedt cites the unique ability of the interior designer to direct movement and human interaction, to enhance the senses and inspire emotion, and to make the place a better place.[1]

One way to think about this approach to design is to apply our knowledge of *human factors* to the design process. A second is to apply our knowledge of *environmental factors* to the design process. A third way is to combine both to develop safe, sound solutions for present and future clients.

In describing socially responsible design, IDEC (the Interior Design Educators Council) refers to this practice as enabling the interior designer to influence social, environmental, economic, and political systems through design interventions at the individual, societal, or global level, or a combination of these, by implementing universal design, inclusive design, and environmentally responsible design.[2] Ideally, all designers, creators, and adapters of the built environment will make this approach part of their design philosophy.

Many types of scientific research projects have demonstrated the intricate relationships between human needs and the environment (Figure 2.1). Studies in specialized fields of psychology and sociology, such as industrial relations, environmental psychology, social psychology, gerontology, and child development, have provided a wealth of information to assist designers, especially during the critical planning stages of a project.

The subject matter of this chapter is complex and thought provoking so as to encourage change. The essential objective of presenting this subject early in the text is to raise awareness. The ultimate aim is that socially responsible design be not a separate topic, but rather, a mindset, an ethos that subconsciously drives all design decisions and choices. Although some examples are noted and illustrated in this chapter, they are merely the tip of the iceberg. There are many examples of both small- and grand-scale designs throughout the text and on the CD-ROM.

Figure 2.1
Earth Day turned 40 in 2010. Since its inception it has become a symbol of the responsibility of humans to respect the earth they occupy. *(© Design Pics Inc. / Alamy)*

HUMAN FACTORS

In designing spaces, it is wise to consider the following concepts, the four As of design: *aesthetics*, *adjustability*, *adaptability*, and *affordability*. The aesthetic appeal of the space, or the pleasingness of its appearance (discussed further in Chapter 3), satisfies a need for its inhabitants but is only one of many criteria to be met. Other criteria include the design of flexible spaces that can be adjusted or adapted to meet many human needs as needs change, and enabling spaces to be accessed by many user groups, in part because they are affordable. Designing for the public good is also part of this chapter. Also referred to as design that matters, humanitarian design, and even "design like you give a damn,"[3] socially responsible design presents a challenge to the interior design student, but one that can empower him or her.

Universal Design

As defined in Chapter 1, universal design is an approach to design based on the goal that a design serves the widest range of users under the greatest number of situations. Or, as defined in 1997 by the Center for Universal Design (at North Carolina State University), universal design is "the design of products and environments to be usable by all people, to the greatest extent possible, without the need for adaptation or specialized design."[4] The center also outlined seven principles of universal design (refer to *FYI . . . The Seven Principles of Universal Design*).

Universal design is based on a body of knowledge that combines scientific findings from many vantage points, including physiology, manufacturing, and technology. Today, the general consensus in the fields relating to the built environment is that the term *universal design* is much broader than this focus on physical access. All people can be categorized in a "special user group" (discussed below) at one time or another because of the normal aging process, accident, disease, or other circumstances. Anyone who has had a broken arm or leg knows the challenges of limited mobility and accessibility. Likewise, a person who wears corrective lenses will be visually impaired without them.

Accommodating a broad range of special needs and age groups—or, put another way, *inclusivity*—is at the heart of universal design and the goal toward

FYI . . . The Seven Principles of Universal Design

1. **Equitable Use**
   The design is useful and marketable to people with diverse abilities.
2. **Flexibility in Use**
   The design accommodates a wide range of individual preferences and abilities.
3. **Simple and Intuitive Use**
   Use of the design is easy to understand, regardless of the user's experience, knowledge, language skills, or current concentration level.
4. **Perceptible Information**
   The design communicates necessary information effectively to the user, regardless of ambient conditions or the user's sensory abilities.

5. **Tolerance for Error**
   The design minimizes hazards and the adverse consequences of accidental or unintended actions.
6. **Low Physical Effort**
   The design can be used efficiently and comfortably and with a minimum of fatigue.
7. **Size and Space for Approach and Use**
   Appropriate size and space are provided for approach, reach, manipulation, and use, regardless of user's body size, posture, or mobility.

Source: The Center for Universal Design, North Carolina State University, www.ncsu.edu.

which designers should strive. In many ways, it is an ideal that may never be fully achieved, but it should serve as the basis from which all decisions are made.

Spatial Experience through the Senses

In her text *Total Design*, interior decorator Clodagh explains the way humans experience space:

> Sensory experience shapes the way you react to a space. As you move through any physical space, your eye is constantly scanning—for distance, color, light, size, the potential threat, the possible solace. You become aware of the temperature as you walk, as well as the air pressure, the vibrations, the weight and dimensions of the space. You register a spectrum of scents. Your ears filter meaning from sound. Constantly and quietly, you categorize all this sensory information, automatically adding it to your internal library, the delicate database within that stores all memory, keeps you aligned, and regulates your moods and feelings.[5]

We experience space on many levels, although not always consciously. Humans respond to sensory stimulation and strive toward **homeostasis**, a state of equilibrium and well-being. Although individuals react to their environments differently from one another, we all seek this state of being. Our sensory experience is often described as our comfort level. We are more likely to recognize our experience in a space when we are aware of a negative reaction—that is, the lack of homeostasis. This reaction may be articulated as discomfort or a poor fit. When we enter and occupy an interior space, it is through our senses that we take in much of the information, and this sensory process becomes our experience in that space.

Under normal circumstances, we have five senses available to us: sight, hearing, touch, smell, and taste. The brain processes the information taken in through the receptors of these five senses. We then have a perceptual experience, such as the visual perceptions of color and light (see Chapters 4 and 7).

If there is a deficiency in a person's ability to receive information through any one of these receptors or in the brain's ability to process the information, compensation often occurs. For example, a person who does not see may have a heightened sense of hearing or smell.

Sight Sight is the sense that most people rely on to describe the physical attributes of a space; we may describe it as beautiful or ugly. The visual sense adds to the appreciation of our surroundings. Sight is also a way in which specific information is experienced, such as the perception of one color as distinct from another color.

It is often a negative visual experience that triggers our awareness that this sense is at work. For instance, when we are blinded by glare, this is experienced through our visual sense. Glare bothers our eyes as overly stimulating colors, stripes that appear to move, or a high level of contrast. Our eyes may feel strained when several different small patterns are viewed simultaneously.

Hearing Hearing is the **auditory** experience through which our ears perceive sound, in the form of vibrations. Certain sounds or high levels of sound may be experienced as noise. In some contexts, such as in a dance club, noise may be considered desirable, but it is disturbing in other situations. It may even reach the stage of pollution, actually causing harm, for instance, when a helicopter hovers over a residential area.

Acoustics is the science that deals with the production, control, reception, and effects of sound. Interior designers pay close attention to the acoustical quality of surfaces as a means of controlling everyday sound levels, based on the needs of the occupants and the function of the space. Designers often rely on acoustical experts when planning spaces in which sound is of major importance, such as an auditorium or theater or the media room of a residence. See *FYI . . . Tips for Providing Good Sound Quality.*

White noise is a mixture of sounds in wide frequencies that are considered neutral sound. White noise has been incorporated into small electrical devices—so-called dream machines that help people relax or sleep by masking disturbing noises. This technology has expanded to include the use of more active sensory enhancements that foster a sense of well-being. For instance, calming sounds, such as those produced from the motion of water, are harnessed in the form of freestanding waterfall sculptures or used as part of the interior and exterior architecture to promote feel-

FYI . . . Tips for Providing Good Sound Quality

A designer can use auditory experiences to enhance a client's comfort level, including the following:

- Use sound-absorbing finishes, such as carpet (floors), fabrics (furniture), and draperies (windows).
- Avoid high ceilings in public areas and in common use areas, such as dining rooms.
- Plan spaces so as to separate areas for noisy activities from those for quiet ones.
- Select quiet appliances, such as choices for air conditioners and fans.

Source: Adapted from Samantha McAskill, "Designing for Acoustics, Hearing and Aging," www.asid.org/designknowledge/aa/ inplace/active/Designing+for+Acoustics_Hearing+and+Aging .htm.

ings of comfort and livability (Figure 2.2). According to Feng Shui practice, water is one of the world's five elements. (The other four are earth, metal, wood, and fire.) Water symbolizes introspection and a resolution of all things. It is a sign of abundance, promise, and positive energy.[6]

Touch Touch is our **tactile** sense, which receives perceptions of pressure or traction, usually through the skin. Touch also encompasses how we feel a surface when we make contact with it. The skin, our essential outer surface, is the end receptor as we experience texture. To express the feel of a fabric, the term *hand* may be used. For example, high-quality cotton may be described as having a "good hand." Textures are described according to how they feel against our skin, such as smooth or rough. Skin is a receptor that also transmits information deeper into the body. For instance, we have a **thermal** reaction as our skin absorbs air and as we touch objects and assess their relative temperatures.

Figure 2.2
An enhanced sensory experience in this spa is partly achieved with this expansive water feature. Harmonics Environments for SenSpa designed by TSAO Design Group. (© *Jim Roof Creative*)

The amount of moisture in the air, ranging from humid to dry, affects a person's perception of the surrounding space and sense of comfort. The amount of heat in a space is taken in by the skin receptors, among others, and translated into an experience of either comfort or discomfort, hot or cold. The sense of air circulation or ventilation is experienced through the skin as well.

Touch is also related to our muscles and joints and to body motion. This becomes the bare bones, if you will, of the field of ergonomics (see later discussion). The way in which humans and things interact effectively may be thought of as **human engineering**. Again, these interactions become more recognizable when something is wrong, either with the individual's capabilities or body mechanics or with the design. For example, a person who spends a lot of time standing or walking on a concrete floor will experience fatigue and perhaps joint pain, especially in the knees. This occurs because of a lack of resiliency in the composition of the floor,

which touches the body and is transmitted to muscles and joints. Such lack of resiliency in touch, or contact, is described as being high impact. It is easy to comprehend how an interior designer's insights into these sensory connections are vital to planning design solutions, from residences to stores, hospitals, and gymnasiums.

Smell Smell is the **olfactory** sensation delivered through the nose. Exposure to malodorous situations, such as spoiled food, garbage, chemicals, or decay, produces a negative olfactory experience. The result may even be harmful, such as when toxic odors are breathed in and affect the respiratory system. It is easy to understand why designers consider the sense of smell when planning the location of facilities such as bathrooms, food areas, and garbage disposal areas.

Today, it is becoming less acceptable to strive merely for a neutral, nonsmell environment. Our noses take in pleasurable odors, such as the smell of fresh flowers, perfumes, fragrant spices, and foods. More and more, in a broad range of applications, designers seek to provide pleasurable sensory experiences. Like the enhancement of the environment through auditory products, a designer can use olfactory experiences to modify a client's comfort level. **Aromatherapy**, an approach based on the healing potential of smell, has become an important consideration for designers, not merely those in health-care fields or healing environments, but also those designing spaces for retailers, spa owners, homeowners, and real estate developers.

Aromas often provide strong links to memories, such as the comfort of home cooking. People have individual and cultural associations with certain smells. Some scents, such as citrus fruits, are considered fresh; others, such as musk, are considered sexual.

Taste Taste is the sensation most closely connected to smell. The relationship of taste to interior spaces is less well documented than the connection to the other senses and is perhaps less direct. Both restaurant design and food presentation take into consideration how taste is perceived within the environment. A restaurant that seeks to promote a perception of hominess can help achieve this not only through a design that evokes a cozy interior, but also through a menu featuring "comfort foods" that bring to mind familiar experiences rather than thoughts of exotic or faraway lands.

Scientific Determinants of Space

In addition to understanding how individuals experience space through their senses, designers must also be aware of the ways in which our physical dimensions and mechanics interact with the technical attributes of the built environment.

Anthropometrics Simply stated, **anthropometrics** is the study of human body measurements. Data are gathered and categorized to establish dimensional norms of the body structures; these are further classified as structural and as they relate to basic activities or positions (Table 2.1). Information from these research findings is compiled into charts by category of individuals, such as adult males, adult females, and children. Dimensions for these distinct groups are then classified in several different situations, such as at rest, standing, kneeling, sitting, reaching, reclining, and viewing (Figure 2.3a and b).

These dimensions are used to establish relatively uniform standards for furniture, fixtures, and clearances, such as doors and corridors. Based on these norms, for example, most standard desks and tables will be approximately 28 inches high; counters, 36 inches above the floor; seat height, generally 18 inches high; etc. Also refer to Basic Metric Conversion Table on page 496.

These design standards can satisfactorily accommodate 90 percent of the user population. However, individuals who are either below the 5th percentile or above the 95th percentile for any particular dimension would not be accommodated. It is the goal of universal design to ensure as close to 100 percent suitability as possible. Standardized furnishings can be improved with features that provide adjustability. Such features also raise the level of comfort for those in the 90 percent average because they, too, have their own variations (Figure 2.4)

Ergonomics An applied science, **ergonomics** is concerned with designing and arranging things people use so that people and things interact most efficiently and safely. It is an approach to design that fits the environment and its equipment to the person, not vice versa. Ergonomics combines anthropometric data and an understanding of body mechanics, or physiology, with product and equipment know-how, in an effort to adapt the work or working conditions to suit the worker. These efforts relate not merely to jobs and employment, but to the various activities with which humans are involved as well.

The field of ergonomics began after World War II. At first the new field was primarily involved with improving the productivity of workers. Accident

Table 2.1
Selected Anthropometric Features of Adults

	Body Features	Male Percentiles			Female Percentiles		
		5th	50th	95th	5th	50th	95th
1.	Standing height	63.6	68.3	72.3	59.0	62.9	67.1
2.	Sitting height, erect	33.2	35.7	38.0	30.9	33.4	35.7
3.	Sitting height, normal	31.6	34.1	36.6	29.6	32.3	34.7
4.	Knee height	19.3	21.4	23.4	17.9	19.6	21.5
5.	Popliteal height	15.5	17.3	19.3	14.0	15.7	17.7
6.	Elbow-rest height	7.4	9.5	11.6	7.1	9.2	11.0
7.	Thigh-clearance height	4.3	5.7	6.9	4.1	5.4	6.9
8.	Buttock-knee length	21.3	23.3	25.2	20.4	22.4	24.6
9.	Buttock-popliteal length	17.3	19.5	21.6	17.0	18.9	21.0
10.	Elbow-to-elbow breadth	13.7	16.5	19.9	12.3	15.1	19.3
11.	Seat breadth	12.2	14.0	15.9	12.3	14.3	17.1
12.	Weight, pounds	126.0	166.0	217.0	104.0	137.0	199.0

Source: Ergonomics: A Guide to People & Productivity, prepared by SIS Human Factor Technologies, Inc., Londonderry, NH, November 1994, page 4.

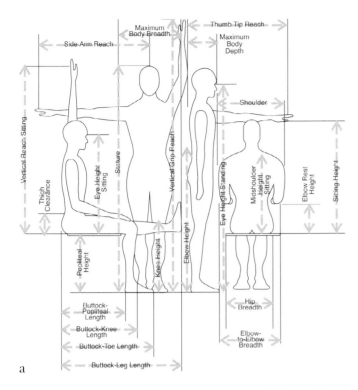

a

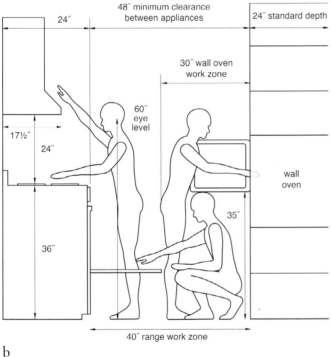

b

Figure 2.3

Anthropometrics—typical measurements of adults sitting, standing, reaching, and bending: a. various typical positions and activities; b. kitchen clearance dimensions.

FYI . . . The Arissa Collection

To better serve the needs of patients in ambulatory bariatric facilities, the Arissa Collection of seating was developed. Created for KI by designers Paul James and Dan Cramer, the series of aesthetically appealing seating adapts to the dimensions of size-challenged individuals, affording them dignity. Users can sit comfortably in several different ways.

KI Arissa Collection for Bariatric Seating. *(Courtesy of KI)*

Source: Janet Wiens, "Design Collaborative: Seating for All," Interiors and Sources, *April 10, 2010.*

Figure 2.4

The Aeron Chair designed by Herman Miller is available in three sizes to cater to users of various statures. *(Courtesy of Herman Miller)* prevention, reduced absenteeism, and increased profit margins were the main objectives. Whether because of government regulation,[7] altruism, or a combination of these, the field of ergonomics has broadened over time. Moreover, the rising number of individuals working out of their homes has expanded the concept of increasing productivity through ergonomic solutions beyond the office and factory.

Computer use in the home, school, and workplace by people of all ages has created a far greater need for more user-friendly design solutions. Recommendations based on ergonomic studies have influenced the design and position of items such as keyboards, wrist pads, monitors, desks, and chairs. Many changes were made to alleviate symptoms of health conditions known as **work-related musculoskeletal disorders (WMSDs)**. Symptoms resulting from a poor fit between humans and machines include stiff necks, fatigue, low back pain, stress on joints, and carpal tunnel syndrome. When muscles are kept in a prolonged static contraction, as occurs when sitting and working at the computer, their blood flow is inhibited. Consequently, the muscles become fatigued, resulting in a need to exercise them, and often leading to fidgety movements, poor posture, or frequent breaks away from the work site to relieve strain.

One study of productivity concluded that intermittent standing as a means of providing the required movement to relieve the buildup of fatigue is as effective as taking breaks away from the work site. This study demonstrated that workstations with stand-up capability would increase worker well-being and, therefore, organizational productivity.[8] This finding is the premise behind the Telescope series of office furniture, developed by the Danish company Omann, which features adjustable-height equipment that enables the user to alternate between sitting and standing positions (Figure 2.5).

The concepts of adjustability and flexibility are basic to ergonomics and universal design. These concepts are probably most readily identified in the plethora of task chairs designed over the past several decades. These chairs aim to prevent joint and muscle problems,

poor posture, and other stressful conditions of the body. Humanscale, a company concerned with ergonomics, describes as its corporate mission "to design and manufacture products that encourage computer users to adopt low-risk body postures—creating a healthier, more comfortable, and more productive workplace."[9] The company's founder and president, Robert King, continues his collaboration with the award-winning industrial designer Niels Diffrient to introduce new innovations in office chairs. The award-winning Freedom chair's design (Figure 2.6) eliminates the need for manual controls and maximizes the ability for natural, spontaneous movement. For instance, the gel seat is naturally load-distributing, and the backrest and armrests adjust instantly when the weight and position of the user are sensed.

Special User Groups

Disability often comes to mind first when considering groups of people with special or unique needs in relation to the built environment. The term *disabled* may be assigned to an individual with a physical or mental impairment that substantially limits one or more major life activities.

Physically impaired persons may include those with ambulation difficulties, such as poor balance. Sensory impairments include the visually impaired population, both the partially sighted and the blind. Individuals with hearing loss, like those who are visu-

Figure 2.5

Ergonomics: Telescope series table, by Omann, which adjusts by using mechanisms on both the left and right sides of the table. (*Photo provided by Omann*)

Figure 2.6
Ergonomics: Freedom task chair with headrest by Humanscale. *(Courtesy of Humanscale)*

Figure 2.7
Wheelchair-accessible kitchen designed by interior designer Cynthia Leibrock: It is part of The Green Mountain Ranch, an aging-in-place residence for the designer and her husband. It also serves as a laboratory for education. *("A Colorado Home Is Ready for the Homeowner's Old Age" by Joyce Eader,* New York Times, *February 18, 2009. Photo by Valerio Messanotti for the* New York Times*)*

ally impaired, also need special consideration, as do people with mental impairments. Age is a very important factor in defining special user groups. Children, as well as the elderly, have limitations that require an interior designer's attention.

Interior designers may choose a sector to specialize in, by designing either for specific user groups, such as the elderly, or in specific industry segments, such as health care, that cater to special user groups.

Mobility Impaired According to the U.S. Census, 1 in 5 Americans has some kind of disability, and 1 in 10 has a severe disability.[10] A person is considered to have a disability if he or she has difficulty performing certain functions or activities of daily living. If a person is unable to perform one or more activities or uses an assistive device or needs assistance from another person to perform basic activities, he or she is considered to have a severe disability. More than 68 million Americans have activity limitations, with arthritis being the most common cause.[11] The issue of accessibility is generally key to designing for individuals with mobility impairments, particularly for those who rely on wheelchairs, canes, crutches, or walkers.

Limited mobility is perhaps the most vital challenge to designing accessible, suitable, and aesthetically appealing spaces for this population (Figure 2.7). It is this special need that prompted the national legislation known as the **Americans with Disabilities Act**, commonly referred to as the **ADA**. This national law was passed by Congress and signed by former president George H. W. Bush in July 1990 after lobbying efforts by veterans of the Vietnam War and other groups called for laws mandating improved public spaces and accommodations for the disabled. The ADA first became effective in January 1992; it was amended in 2008 to clarify and reiterate who is covered under the law.

The ADA legislation is a comprehensive civil rights law that prohibits discrimination in public accommodations and guarantees opportunities in employment, transportation, state and local government services, and telecommunications for persons with disabilities.[12] The term **accessible design**, also known as **barrier-free design**, is often used to indicate compliance with the ADA. The ADA has a comprehensive set of guidelines. See *FYI . . . Key ADA Design Provisions.*

There is a growing special needs group that is challenged by the norms established by anthropometric tables relating to size; more specifically, girth, or the measurement around a person's body. The prevalence of overweight and obesity in the United States has been steadily rising; since 1962 obesity has increased from 13.4 percent to 35.1 percent of American adults.[13]

Visually Impaired More than 19 million people in the United States have visual impairments.[14] For Americans older than age 70, 1 in 6 has visual impairment. People with visual impairments require additional tactile and acoustical sensations to compensate for the lack of visual acuity. For visually impaired people who use canes, unobstructed walking spaces are critical. Braille, a form of graphics with raised dots, is used for signage

purposes for the visually handicapped, generally those blind from birth or childhood. Other innovations in signage include raised letters, symbols, and numbers to identify floors and doors. The use of auditory mechanisms to cue directions in public spaces, such as at crosswalks and for navigating in museums, is another example of efforts to modernize accessibility.

People with partial sight or color deficiency benefit from exaggerated differences in lightness between foreground and background colors. For example, the contrast between blue drapery and yellow walls is more effective than that between yellow drapery and orange walls.

The normal aging process results in twice the amount of light needed for 40-year-olds as for 20-year-olds; twice that for 60-year-olds as for 40-year-olds.

Hearing Impaired More than 34 million Americans have some degree of hearing loss.[15] A total of 1 in 4 Americans older than 70 has a hearing impairment. Nearly 32 million Americans (10 percent of the total population) indicate they have a hearing loss. The greatest increase is among baby boomers, because of noise exposure, and among those who are age 75 and older, because of aging.[16] In addition to their impaired auditory sense, many of these individuals have difficulties with balance. In the same way that visually impaired people are better served through enhancements to other sensory experiences, such as sound, the hearing impaired need to rely on enhanced visuals, such as lighting systems that provide warning signals and security.

Mentally Impaired Increasingly more attention is being given by the architectural and design community to the special needs of the other types of impairment, including neurological, cognitive, and mental conditions. One factor promoting a focus on the needs of this group has been the growing number of persons afflicted by Alzheimer's disease, a form of dementia that seriously affects a person's ability to carry out daily activities. The National Institute on Aging estimates that there are 4 million people in the United States with some degree of this disease.[17] The strain this disease puts on affected individuals and their families has spurred increased attention to finding ways to better serve this user group.

People with Alzheimer's disease have a unique combination of physical, cognitive, and psychological needs. Recent research has given interior designers some rec-

FYI . . . Key ADA Design Provisions

The following are some of the key provisions used to make a design more suitable for the physically impaired:

- A minimum door opening space of 32 inches
- Barrier-free passage, as follows: single passage that is 36 inches wide; double passage that is 60 inches wide
- A bathroom with a clear space of 60 inches to enable a wheelchair to turn around
- Doors to accessible bathrooms that swing out, not in
- A minimal slope for ramps that provides a rise of 1 foot for every 12 feet of length (1:12 ratio)
- Ramps that are 36 inches wide
- Emergency warning systems with both audible and visible signals

ommendations to follow when designing for this group. For instance, it is advisable to avoid heavily patterned and active prints. Yellow is a preferred color because it feels comforting and pleasing.[18] People with Alzheimer's disease, as well as developmentally disabled individuals, may also need extra assistance, such as proper lighting and visual cues, in finding their way through spaces.

At the other end of the continuum is the increased prevalence of autism among children. **Autism spectrum disorder (ASD)** is a range of complex neurodevelopment disorders, characterized by social impairment; communication difficulties; and restricted, repetitive, stereotyped patterns of behavior.[19] According to the Centers for Disease Control 1 out of 110 children in the U.S. are diagnosed with ASD; 1 out of 70 of boys.[20]

A condition known as **seasonal affective disorder (SAD)** is a form of depression that tends to recur as the days grow shorter during the fall and winter and the amount of daylight is reduced. Not to be confused with the so-called winter blues, the ordinary craving for sunlight most of us experience during this season, SAD is a clinically diagnosed condition thought to be related to the brain's secretion of the enzyme melatonin. Since this condition was first identified in 1985, great strides have been made in developing appropriate interventions. Full-spectrum lighting, light boxes, and other forms of **phototherapy** are now used to help alleviate this condition.

Aging Population The special user group of the elderly is a broad category. The normal aging process brings change, often accommodated by relatively simple yet effective design problem solving. However, the needs of the frail elderly raise distinctly different issues, requiring an understanding not only of the aging process, but also of the impact of illness and debilitation on the day-to-day functioning of this population.

The elderly population is growing rapidly. By the year 2030 it is projected that the percentage of those who are 65 and older will increase to almost one-fourth of the U.S. population.[21] By 2045 the global population of people 60 and older will exceed the number of children.[22]

The concept of an aging, rather than elderly, population is perhaps more appropriate because the term *aging* denotes a continual process rather than a static condition. This aging population is also living a rela-

Figure 2.8
Active elders enjoy line dancing at a senior center. *(Not Just Bingo,* New York Times, *December 6, 2009. Photo: Richard Perry, New York Times)*

tively healthier life than previously (Figure 2.8). Medical advances have brought unsurpassed longevity to a worldwide population.

The oldest members of the baby boom generation, those born between 1946 and 1964, may blanch at the term *elderly*, but would be hard-pressed to deny that they are aging.

The needs of affluent and poor elderly populations differ. Poverty continues to be an issue for many older adults, who often rely on public or charitable resources to create safer, more comfortable environments. However, the aging baby boomer population includes a significant number of people now in or approaching retirement age who are financially secure and physically active. It is members of this group who will hire interior designers to assist them in maintaining a quality lifestyle in their own homes.

The concept of **aging in place** gained prominence in the 1990s. It is defined by the National Aging in Place Council as "the ability to continue to live in one's home safely, independently, and comfortably, regardless of age, income, or ability level. It means living in a familiar environment, and being able to participate in family and other community activities."[23]

According to a survey conducted by AARP, 86 percent of the organization's members want to remain in their own homes. This was also the theme of a more recent study sponsored by the American Society of Interior Designers (ASID).[24] According to the ASID study, 83 percent of those over age 45 who were sur-

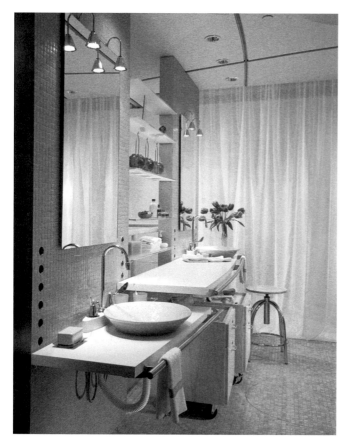

Figure 2.9
An adapted bathroom for aging in place. *(Designed by Cynthia Leibrock. Courtesy of Kohler Co.)*

veyed said they would like to remain in their current residences for as long as possible. The National Association of Home Builders (NAHB), in partnership with AARP, developed the **Certified Aging in Place Specialist (CAPS)** program, designed to teach professionals how to modify homes for aging in place.

Figure 2.9 features an attractive and adaptable bathroom that would suit physically able as well. And refer to *FYI . . . Tips for Designing for Aging in Place.*

The increasingly mature population also creates the need for a broad range of housing alternatives, from retirement villages to hospice care, with independent-living, assisted-living, and skilled nursing care facilities in between. A growing housing concept is that of Continuing Care Retirement Community, in which complexes are developed that provide varying levels of services and housing as needed. The elderly population, both the healthy and the frail, is a vital political and economic force for interior designers to consider.

Children Although not often viewed as a special user group, children pose unique design issues that require yet another area of expertise. As with aging, normal childhood development poses situational concerns that provide an opportunity for creative design solutions that enhance comfort and livability (Figure 2.10).

Figure 2.10
Special user group: Playroom for children with blocks in the corner. *(Courtesy of and designed by Sam Paxhia)*

FYI . . . Tips for Designing for Aging in Place

ASID created a set of guidelines for designers that includes the following tips for working with people who are planning to age in place:

- Gain knowledge of the aging process, life stage needs, and appropriate products.
- Help clients plan ahead.
- Understand the ergonomic needs of the frail and elderly.
- Locate master bedroom and bathroom on the ground floor.
- Create good traffic flow with few steps between rooms.
- Select furniture that is easy to move and to get in and out of, preferably with rounded edges.
- Reduce the amount of furniture to make it easier to get around.
- Use smaller kitchen appliances that are lighter in weight and easier to grip.

- Replace basement laundry rooms with smaller washers and dryers that fit in the bathroom or a utility closet.
- Employ color contrasts as an aid to visual acuity.
- Increase lighting, and use remote controls; avoid shadows.
- Create well-organized, easy-to-reach storage facilities.
- Consider smooth floor surfaces, and avoid thick carpet.
- Install a walk-in shower; build in a large, wide seat in the shower; or add a seat to the tub.
- Use slip-resistant floor tiles or smaller tiles with more grout lines.
- Install grab bars in the bath area and near the toilet; toilets should be adjustable in height.
- Use levers rather than knobs wherever possible on doors, cabinets, and sink fixtures.

Source: Aging in Place—Aging and the Impact of Interior Design. *(Washington, DC: ASID, 2001).*

The need for safety when children are involved is self-evident. The crawling and early walking stages pose a multitude of risks in the home. Various adjustments, or childproofing, must be made when a child is introduced into the family. Children do not naturally comprehend danger until about age six. Therefore, it is the adult's responsibility to ensure that hazards are eliminated wherever possible.

Perhaps less apparent are comfort issues for children. Child-sized beds, desks, chairs, and tables are commonplace. Adjustments in sink and toilet seat heights are now being produced with child anthropometric data in mind (Figure 2.11).

Choices designers make to furnish spaces for children affect their health, development, and safety. A growing concern is the rapid increase in asthma in children, with about 13 percent of American children

Figure 2.11
Furniture based on the anthropometrics of children. *(Iglooplay and Lisa Albin, designer. Photographer: Michael Crouser)*

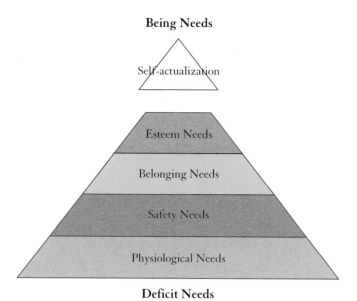

Figure 2.12
Hierarchy of human needs. *(Designing for Privacy and Related Needs by Julie Stewart-Pollack and Rosemary Menconi, Fairchild Books, © 2005, page 4)*

Figure 2.13
Clever use of storage room divider separates the territories for two siblings. *(Photo by Tim Ebert; interior designer credit: Esther Sadowsky, Allied Member ASID, Charm & Whimsy)*

diagnosed with this condition. (The relationships among allergens and specific products and finishes are discussed further in Chapters 8 through 10.)

Like the elderly, children have distinct needs relating to both color and light (see Chapters 4 and 7). Furthermore, with children using computer equipment at early ages, ergonomic data related to a child's physiology are being incorporated into the design of these products.

Behavioral Aspects of Spaces

According to the hierarchy of needs established by the sociologist Abraham Maslow, a human's most basic need, after nourishment and sleep, is to feel safe. It is difficult to satisfy higher-level needs, such as the need for self-esteem, if a person is starving, sleep deprived, and afraid of attack. Once people have a sense of safety, they go on to satisfy their other needs, including comfort, privacy, and individuality (Figure 2.12).

Territoriality This basic need for protection from harm and freedom from danger is expressed through a behavioral trait known as territoriality. A basic concept in the study of animal behavior, territoriality is usually defined as "behavior by which an organism characteristically lays claim to an area and defends it against members

of its own species."[25] This behavior, which is associated with nesting instincts, has also been documented in humans. Territoriality has often come to imply the need for self-identity and freedom of choice.[26] The adage "good fences make good neighbors" expresses the need for one's physical space to be delineated.

Similarly, the concept of privacy—the universal need to control how much and what types of interactions we have with others—is an essential ingredient in the quality of life.[27]

In interior design the boundaries of space may be defined very distinctly, for example, by using walls to create separate rooms or areas. Or, boundaries may be made subtler, for example, by using partitions or screens to define different spaces for different users or different activities (Figure 2.13).

Territoriality sometimes reflects status. In office environments, for instance, the boundaries for the executive areas may be set significantly differently from those for the clerical staff. Chapter 5 will provide additional considerations and solutions related to planning for various types of residential and contract spaces in relation to how people live, work, and communicate.

Proxemics Pioneered in the 1960s by Edward T. Hall, an American sociologist, **proxemics** is the study of

Table 2.2 Characteristics of Edward T. Hall's Four Distance Zones
Zone: Intimate distance Close Phase: 0'–6"; Used in lovemaking, wrestling, comforting, and protecting Far Phase: 6"–18"; In public, being this close may make people uncomfortable; they compensate by avoiding eye contact
Zone: Personal distance Close Phase: 18"–30"; Most Americans become uncomfortable when strangers are this close; expressed colloquially as being "in my face" Far Phase: 30"–4'; The distance at which someone is kept "at arm's length"
Zone: Social distance Close Phase: 4'–7'; Used by people who work together or those who gather in casual social situations Far Phase: 7'–12'; Used in formal business and social discourse; large desks in offices of important people hold visitors at this distance
Zone: Public distance Close Phase: 12'–24'; A formal style of distancing Far Phase: More than 25'; Used by public figures and actors; beyond 30', people must exaggerate or amplify their gestures and voice to be perceived

Figure 2.14
Crowded market in Macau. *(Getty Images)*

the nature of spatial distances maintained by people under different circumstances. In his book *The Hidden Dimension*, Hall describes the challenges involved in generalizing these zones of personal distances among people, recognizing many cultural differences. Based on observation and interviews with individuals whom he describes as a sample of healthy adult business and professional men and women, primarily from the northeastern United States (and notwithstanding acknowledged cultural differences), Hall identifies four distinct distance zones: **intimate distance, personal distance, social distance,** and **public distance.** Characteristics of these zones are summarized in Table 2.2.

Each of us, regardless of our personal or cultural experiences, can relate to how often we experience dis-

comfort related to these zones in a variety of different contexts (Figures 2.14).

The way in which people interact under different circumstances is the basis for space planning and furniture layout. In fact, the concept of space between people is at the very core of furniture design. Specific features of furniture design, especially relating to seating, can provide very strong direction in how people are expected to interact (Figure 2.15a–c).

The concept of **behavioral setting**, or **behavioral mapping**, addresses the desire to distinguish spaces according to activity. It is predictable that people sleep in bedrooms and, therefore, need beds or some reasonable facsimile in the way of furnishings. It is generally not considered good design to have a home office in the same area as the bedroom. In densely populated areas, where space is at a premium, interior designers face some extra challenges. Delineation of boundaries and objects according to prescribed, predictable patterns of behavior is critical to space planning (discussed further in Chapter 5).

Personalization When the basic needs for safety and comfort are satisfied, humans strive for their environments to reflect individuality. The designer Clodagh expresses it this way: "A home cannot be truly beautiful unless it functions in harmony with who we are . . . it's about pleasure: discovering what pleases us and creating an environment that will celebrate those qualities and sustain us."[28]

Numerous examples can be given of how **personalization** is effected in interior design. At one time, the cubicle, a compartmentalized, impersonal, boundary-oriented approach, was typical of office design. Although workers may still have their territory carved out for them according to their status and job functions, today's office workstations are designed to allow for greater individual personal expression. The employee may be offered a choice in selecting the color of office partitions, type of chair used, or computer monitor screen saver. The concept of open-office space planning has been the backbone of many of the products developed by companies such as Steelcase and Herman Miller, as well as smaller producers. The collaborative, team approach to work, especially in a design environment, has significantly impacted space-planning decisions as well as the selection of furnishings.

Adolescents, commonly known for their need to express their differences from adults and children, may be at odds with their parents about how to design their private spaces (Figure 2.16). Such human factors may become part of a designer's problem-solving efforts in trying to satisfy all his or her clients.

Figure 2.15

Furniture design and placement often dictates proxemic relationships. a. Companion (or confidante) chair, 1851; b. Personal and social space is provided; c. Public space from the seats to the stage is typical in a theater. *(a: DeAgostini Picture Library/C. Postel; b: Cliff House Hotel; Designer: Garry Cohn; Design Company: Douglas Wallace. Photographer: Andrew Bradley; c: The Performing and Visual Arts Theater, Cairo, by Shahira H. Fahmy Architects. WAN, http://www.worldarchitecturenews.com)*

Figure 2.16

This room, designed for an adolescent, features elements that reflect the personality of the child. *(GuglielmoGalvinRedovern. Designed by Marlene McKibbon)*

CULTURAL CONSIDERATIONS

As part of social groups, individuals want their spaces to promote positive and effective communications and associations among people. People have varying needs for privacy, interaction, and socialization. As a part of cultural groups, people need to feel that their spaces promote a sense of familiarity and common ground, demonstrating shared values, norms, and attitudes. When we speak of culture, we may be referring to the geographic, regional, or ethnic identity of a people; an individual's religious or spiritual association; a people's objects or traditions; even a particular lifestyle.

In an increasingly connected global business environment, cultural sensitivity becomes an important trait for interior designers. This sensitivity involves being aware that a client's inclination toward certain design decisions may be influenced by his or her cultural identification or experience. This applies to both residential and contract projects.

When designers are involved in developing a prototype for a business with multiple branches, such as a retail store, hotel, or restaurant franchise, one of their tasks is to enhance that business's brand identity. Respecting cultural differences while maintaining a company's look and personality is another of the challenges facing a designer, who may be working on projects for outlets in such disparate locations as Chicago and Saudi Arabia.

The global marketplace provides opportunities for interior designers to select products made by artisans and craftspeople from around the world who use indigenous materials and traditional methods. These handmade items offer a special touch. Nonprofit organizations, such as Aid to Artisans and Good-Weave, promote the needs of artisans and workers in developing countries. Aid to Artisans, an international nonprofit organization, provides assistance in the promotion of these handcrafted goods to a broad market base, whereas GoodWeave, an internationally recognized nonprofit group, sets standards to eliminate unfair child labor practices and provides educational opportunities for children in Nepal, India, and Pakistan. There are many profit-making companies that have developed "more than fair trade practices" in working with artisan groups, providing opportunities for better wages while creating marketable products (Figure 2.17a–c).

ENVIRONMENTAL FACTORS

The discussion of human factors concentrates on only one of the world's resources. The relationship of the population to environmental resources, such as matter and energy, is the focus of environmental science. The design community has increasingly become involved in the effort to sustain Earth's resources for future generations.

Sustainable Design

The term *sustainable design*, introduced in Chapter 1, conveys an approach to design that focuses on preserving the natural environment and its resources for the future. The sustainable movement derives from a paper titled "Our Common Future" (also known as the Brundtland Report), which identifies worldwide concerns that threaten the future. "Humanity has the ability to make development sustainable to ensure that it meets the needs of the present without compromising the ability of future generations to meet their own needs."[29] Energy conservation and the use of sustainable resources (often referred to as green products) are primary considerations, as summarized in the 3Rs: *reduce*, *reuse*, and *recycle*. Additional Rs now include *renew*, *reclaim*, *repurpose*, *restore*, *reinvent*, etc.

A limited interpretation of sustainable design focuses on the greenness of a product's ingredients, such as choosing cork over mahogany for its renewability. Consideration of manufacturing techniques and transportation to the end user, especially in relation to energy conservation and waste management, adds a more complete picture. An increasing world challenge is water conservation. "Blue is the new green" is a phrase used to emphasize the importance of water conservation, especially in developing nations, where the potable water supply may be endangered. In a recent article for *Interiors and Sources*, Keri Luly, a sustainability programs manager, states, "Currently, 2.8 billion people live in places with some degree of water scarcity, and it predicted that 75 percent of the world's population will be by 2025."[30] One aspect to the challenge of sustainability is **environmental stewardship**, the responsibility of global citizens to manage and preserve our natural resources.

Recently, attention has been paid to the science of **biomimicry** to help solve these problems. The concept, established by the biologist Janine Benyus, uses

Figure 2.17

Cultural diversity in products is featured in the array of global furnishings available for interiors. While many furnishings are fabricated using Old World techniques, others are inspired by traditional designs adapted to modern tastes. a. Antique and contemporary textiles from Central Asia; b. African products featured at ICFF 2010 by Amaridian; c. The Design Collaborative, a nonprofit arm of the 3form company, works with African women using traditional techniques and natural products in the production of innovative partitions. *(a: Photo by Megan Thompson for Tessera b: Photo provided by the Author. c: Courtesy 3form)*

nature as a model to inspire designs and processes that solve human problems. At biomimicry's base is the belief that studying nature will uncover effective and sustainable solutions to issues such as thermal comfort, indoor air quality, and acoustical privacy.[31] Another idea being put forth is that of **cradle to cradle**, described by William McDonough and Michael Braungart in their 2002 book of the same name. *Cradle*

Figure 2.18
Interior designer Cynthia Urbanik designed this retail environment for Dress for Success, a charitable organization, Charlotte, North Carolina. In addition to providing her services pro bono, the project demonstrates adaptive reuse of a former warehouse. *(http://www. LassiterPhotography.com)*

to cradle expresses the notion that products be developed with the potential for continuous renewability, that is, so as to live on forever in some form, without doing harm. This is in direct opposition to a cradle-to-grave approach, in which goods are made with obsolescence in mind, thereby creating the need for more consumption.

Another view of sustainability encompasses the ethics of environmental justice, a principle or system of beliefs aimed at ensuring that all people in our global community have healthy and aesthetically pleasing environments. Design that is in the public interest and that is cost-effective is part of this equation. Many designers and design firms are donating their time and services on a pro bono basis on projects for charitable organizations (Figure 2.18).

Design with a conscience looks to measure progress by social, ecological, and economic benchmarks.[32] A study of design firms found that more than one-third of the design firms that had diversified their practice added *Sustainability Analysis* as a department within their organization.[33]

Environmental Law and Issues

Environmental law strives to provide a bridge between the human factors discussed in the first part of this chapter and environmental factors. As in the passage of the ADA, legislation that aims to prevent negative situations is often a reactive response to actions. The area of environmental law has rapidly expanded, in part because of a series of lawsuits resulting from unsafe conditions, defective or unsafe products, and negligence. According to C. Jaye Berger, an attorney specializing in building construction, real estate, and environmental law, this is the most likely area in which lawsuits might affect design professions.[34]

Laws, so commonplace now that they are almost taken for granted, significantly affect the design of restaurants, clubs, and corporate spaces. These include laws against public smoking and distribution of hazardous substances, such as poison or flammable materials, as well as laws related to recycling.

Sick office, or **sick building syndrome,** is a term that was created in the 1980s to reflect a high level of worker absenteeism or a lack of productivity attributed to vague, hard-to-diagnose complaints, such as dizziness, faintness, and fatigue. These maladies were discovered to be caused, in most cases, by exacerbation of the negative effects of pollutants, such as paints, stains, synthetic chemicals, and adhesives, from inadequate air circulation. **Volatile organic compounds (VOCs),** which are found in many products, such as solvents and adhesives, produce toxic fumes and gases that dissipate with time. However, this process, known as **off-gassing,** has proven to be unhealthy to individuals and to the ozone level of the atmosphere. A more recent term to describe illnesses that result from deficiencies in the design of the built environment with respect to **heating, ventilation,** and **air-conditioning (HVAC)** (discussed in Chapter 8) is **BRI (building-related illnesses).**

It is likely that regulations concerned with the environment and human safety will continue to proliferate as more and more risks are identified and linked to unsafe conditions.

Not all design improvements in these matters are mandated by legislation; many are based on voluntary efforts, sometimes as a reaction to consumer demand or business competition. One of the more significant movements has been the development of the guidelines issued by LEED, introduced in Chapter 1. LEED (Leadership in Energy and Environmental Design) is an internationally recognized green building certification system providing third-party verification that a building, residential or commercial, was designed and built using strategies aimed at improving performance in energy savings, water efficiency, air quality, and stewardship of resources and sensitivity to their impacts throughout the building life cycle. LEED for Neighborhood Development extends the benefits of LEED beyond the building footprint, into the neighborhood the building serves. There are also several types of LEED accreditation for individual practitioners involved in designing and constructing buildings under the category "LEED AP" (LEED accredited professionals).

As more and more projects and professionals achieve higher levels of accreditation, it becomes essential for businesses and professionals to aspire to meet the standards and reach the ever-rising bar.

Terms such as *global warming, carbon footprint,* and *greenhouse gasses* are increasingly part of today's vocabulary. Energy use falls within a designer's control. As described in later chapters, interior designers can specify the installation of energy-efficient solutions.

Related to conservation of resources (land, energy, and money) is a growing push for compact design. This means more efficient space planning and product design, reduced square footage, and an overall reduction in consumption of energy and goods. It has now become both smart and fashionable to design small (Figure 2.19).

Over time, buildings, interiors, and products become obsolete. A goal not only for historic preservationists but also for architects and designers is **adaptive reuse,** converting obsolescence into relevance by designing through change, not demolition. Thankfully, many buildings of historical significance are being identified as viable projects for new uses. For example, the Limelight Marketplace, in New York City's Chelsea district, is a 19th-century-Gothic-revival-church-turned-nightclub-turned-dilapidated-vacant-structure that was converted into an upscale shopping emporium (Figure 2.20a and b).

Design in the Public Interest

Design as activism supports the notion that professionals such as interior designers and architects have a role in efforts to improve civic and community well-being. Many initiatives begin with engagement of neighborhood residents and organizations in the planning stages of even small projects.

The majority of the world's designers focus all their efforts on developing products and services exclusively for the richest 10 percent of the world's customers. Nothing less than a revolution in design is needed to reach the other 90 percent.[35]

An early attempt to create functional and affordable designs for buildings, spaces, and furnishings is not

Figure 2.19
Small (actually called a "Tiny" award winner) design is reflected in this studio apartment in Houston, Texas, measuring 450 square feet. Apartment Therapy blog 2010 "Small Cool 2010: Chris' Furniture Testris Tiny Division #1. *(©2011 Chris Nguyen | AnalogDialog)*

new. For instance, Swedish modern design in the early 20th century, known as **functionalism**, sought to create designs appropriate for modern industrial society. Its proponents believed that good design should be readily available to all classes and would improve the standard of living. Manufacturers engaged skilled artists to create high-quality, attractive, inexpensive, utilitarian furnishings that fostered democratic, or egalitarian, design. However, the Utopian notions of the early functionalists were based on the personal experiences of elite, educated architects, not on carefully planned and executed studies of human needs. Studies that take into consideration user surveys and interviews and that rely on user participation often produce more meaningful long-term recommendations.

Possibly no other area relies more on the collaboration of disciplines to develop solutions and design "for the other 90 percent," a design-for-all philosophy. It is estimated by organizations such as UNICEF that

most of the world's population does not have regular access to food, clean water, or shelter. Organizations such as Habitat for Humanity look to bring low-cost housing to those in need. Catastrophes such as Hurricane Katrina, in 2005, which devastated much of New Orleans and other Gulf areas; the Deepwater Horizon oil spill in the same area five years later; and the 2010 earthquake in Haiti spurred the development of collaborative design and economic ventures to rebuild those communities (Figure 2.21). Indeed, most would agree that more far-reaching, preventive measures to protect ecosystems are in order.

THE ROLE OF EDUCATION

The increasing number of courses aimed at human factors and the environment in interior design programs demonstrates the unique role interior designers can play in these vital areas. These courses include building

Figure 2.20
Adaptive reuse of a church is now known as the Limelight Marketplace in the Chelsea area, New York City. a. The exterior of the Gothic Revival style church and the stained glass windows were preserved; b. Interior view. *(a: Photo provided by the Author; b: "The Limelight Nightclub Becomes a Marketplace" by Florence Fabricant, published May 4, 2010,* New York Times, *photo by Hirosku Musuiki for the* New York Times/Redux)

Figure 2.21

Katrina Cottage, a prefabricated, small, and affordable home created by Marianne Cusato and Eric Moser following Hurricane Katrina in the Gulf of Mexico area, United States. Plans were then sold at Lowe's retail stores in various configurations. *("Small and Fabulous: Modular Living as It Should Be," by Rob Beschizza, w.red.com January 7, 2008)*

Senior Thesis Project on Sustainability: Part 1: An Education in "Green"

Green Museum of Natural Sciences & Sustainable Technologies

There is no Planet B. Today the world is more conscious about decisions concerning the environment. With changes to our climate and endangered species becoming increasingly more threatened, the time for action is yesterday. Earth is our only home, and we need to invest in its protection for future generations.

Energy conservation and environmental preservation are at the forefront in architecture and design. More new construction is considering the implementation of sustainable practices than ever before. Research in alternative energy, including wind, solar, and water power, and sustainable practices are providing interior designers with environmentally responsible solutions to spaces. It is imperative that the general public understand its effect on the environment and begin to change its lifestyle to become more sustainable. Through education and awareness, living "green" will become second nature to our children. By providing educational areas in which children can interact and play, sustainability will carry through to daily life and change how children see the world and their part in it. They have the opportunity to be part of the new wave, to save the planet.

This facility will provide a fresh and cutting-edge museum experience. The museum will offer visitors the chance to interact with living exhibitions of indigenous plant and animal life in the simulated natural habitats.

Figure a
Aqua tunnel and rainforest exhibit, part of the sustainable museum designed by Jessica Yahn Quezada for her senior thesis project. *(Peter Johnston, instructor; Takashi Kamiya, Chair, Interior Design Department, F.I.T. 2010 senior thesis)*

Source: Adapted from Jessica Yahn Quezada, "Green Museum of Natural Sciences and Sustainable Technologies," F.I.T., BFA thesis, 2010.

regulations, human factors and interior ergonomics, environmental systems, ecology and the built environment, green design, environmental psychology, and historic preservation. Senior theses of undergraduate interior design programs place great emphasis on sustainability in projects. The increasing number of programs, including master's degrees in sustainability and related fields, indicates the level of concern about these subjects.

Large-scale institutions are partnering and collaborating with each other and with educational

programs to problem solve, using innovative, multidisciplinary approaches.

Trade conferences provide opportunities for students and designers to further their education in the areas of socially responsible design. Trade conferences also provide the opportunity for manufacturers and suppliers to introduce new products, many of which relate directly to these issues.

Museums as educational institutions continue to curate exhibitions that promote the understand-

Design School Competition Sponsored by Trade Show

The International Contemporary Furniture Fair (ICFF), held annually in New York City, sponsors a design school competition. In 2010 Maryland Institute College of Art (MICA), in Baltimore, Maryland, won the honor of the best design school exhibit. For the winning project, a group of environmental design students transformed age-old materials into environmentally friendly furniture and other products.[a] "Materials that have been around for a long time have been able to evolve and prove themselves to be safe, sustainable, and pleasant to use and work with," said MICA instructor Inna Alesina. "Humans have slowly perfected craft techniques for using traditional materials in smart, minimal and safe ways."[b]

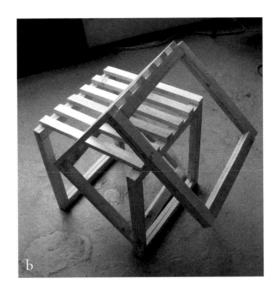

Figures a–c
Student entries for the ICFF 2010 Design School Competition: a. SpoolSeat, Jute Chair; b and c. Stool that doubles as a bench. *(Design by MICA students: John McGlew for Double Stool; Karine Sarkissian for Spool Seat; Project director and photography: Inna Alesina faculty at Environmental Design at MICA (Maryland Institute College of Art)*

Sources: [a] *(ICFF International Contemporary Furniture Fair) 2010, Javits Convention Center, New York City, May 15–18, 2010.*
[b] *"Environmental Design Exhibition Wins Best Design School Category at ICFF; NY Times Highlights MICA's Involvement," MICA, May 17, 2010, www.mica.edu/news/environmental_design_exhibition_wins_best_design_school_category_at_icff.html.*

ing of these crucial topics as well. One example is the Triennial Why Design Now? series, sponsored by The Smithsonian Cooper-Hewitt National Design Museum. The installation in 2010 featured innovative sustainable projects from 45 nations to address the social and environmental issues of sustainability. Its purpose was to raise crucial questions, such as, how can we discover beauty and wisdom in simple forms that use minimal resources and enhance human health, prosperity, and comfort while diminishing the conflicts between people and the global ecosystems we inhabit?[36]

Summary

In addition to creating aesthetically pleasing interiors, interior designers are increasingly expected to design spaces that provide for the health, safety, and welfare of others. Whether working in the world of contract or residential interiors, designers must be informed about the needs of those they serve. Interior design education today includes a strong focus on both human and environmental factors that affect current and future needs. We call this approach socially responsible design. It is a set of values that directs a designer's decision-making process.

Knowledge of how we experience space through our senses is an essential component in understanding how form and function work together. The designer's aim is to create a space that offers an enhanced sensory experience.

The field of interior design has benefited greatly from many branches of scientific research in fields such as psychology, sociology, and physiology. Anthropometrics is the study of human dimensions. Standard furniture and clearances are based on categories of norms that represent typically 90 percent of any particular group, such as the average adult male or female. This information is used, along with an understanding of biomechanics and physiology, to foster a better fit between humans and the built environment—the focus of the field of ergonomics.

The Americans with Disabilities Act (ADA) prohibits discrimination in public spaces and has paved the way for accessible, or barrier-free, design. Designing for special populations requires a sensitivity and understanding of particular needs that may require specific solutions. All people at one time have been or may be part of any of the following groups of special users: the physically, visually, hearing, neurologically, cognitively, or mentally impaired; the aging, both healthy and frail elderly; and children. Universal design aims to provide access to good design for as many people as possible (inclusivity) and includes improvements in private as well as public spaces.

The basic instinct to lay claim to one's space is called territoriality. It is closely linked to the human need for safety. Once the need to feel secure is met, people strive toward individualizing that space, a behavior referred to as personalization. Sociologist Edward T. Hall conducted studies that examined the spatial distances between people that are comfortable under different circumstances. He coined the term *proxemics* in describing zones of physical distances between people, ranging from intimate to public. Although culturally influenced, these concepts help designers with interior space planning.

Another element of socially responsible design involves respect for cultural diversity in designing spaces on a global level and involving oneself in a global dialogue concerning design ideas, indigenous resources, and artisanal techniques.

Designers are concerned not only with the current needs of their clients, but also with their future needs and the needs of future generations. The concept of sustainable design reflects the attitude that natural resources—human, in fact, all life, land, water, and energy—need to be preserved for the future. An exciting outgrowth of this field is the explosion of products and technologies that preserve rather than destroy our resources. Smaller, more efficient, affordable built environments are another result of growth in this field.

Sustainable design takes a long, comprehensive view based on the belief in the power of design to improve lives. Increasingly, the interior design profession has broadened its scope to participate in local, regional, and global solutions in the public interest.

Vocabulary

accessible (barrier-free) design

acoustics

adaptive reuse

aging in place

Americans with Disabilities Act
(ADA)

anthropometrics

aromatherapy

auditory

autism spectrum disorder (ASD)

behavioral setting (behavioral
mapping)

biomimicry

BRI (building-related illness)

Certified Aging in Place
Specialist (CAPS)

cradle to cradle

environmental stewardship

ergonomics

functionalism

heating, ventilation, air-
conditioning (HVAC)

homeostasis

human engineering

intimate distance

off-gassing

olfactory

personal distance

personalization

phototherapy

proxemics

public distance

seasonal affective disorder
(SAD)

sick office (sick building)
syndrome

social distance

socially responsible design

tactile

territoriality

thermal

volatile organic compound
(VOC)

white noise

work-related musculoskeletal
disorder (WMSD)

Exercise: Survey Your Space

Now that you are more aware of human and environmental factors, tour your living space to see how well it holds up to the levels of health, safety, and welfare discussed in this chapter. You may want to limit this survey to one or two main living areas. Use this checklist for guidance on how to rate your space.

	Good	Bad	Neutral
Provides sensory experience	_____	_____	_____
Expresses individuality	_____	_____	_____
Fosters privacy	_____	_____	_____
Fosters socialization	_____	_____	_____
Provides comfortable fit	_____	_____	_____
Promotes safety and health	_____	_____	_____
Is suitable for activities	_____	_____	_____
Is adaptable, flexible for change	_____	_____	_____
Conserves energy	_____	_____	_____
Demonstrates compact use of space	_____	_____	_____

Exercise: Exploring the CD-ROM

Take advantage of the contents of the CD-ROM to increase your understanding of proxemics. Follow the instructions for Starting the CD-ROM on pages xix–xx and click on Chapter Two: Socially Responsible Design.

Proxemics: Keep a journal for two consecutive days on your personal experience of "spatial distances." For example: "In a coffee shop on a counter stool, elbow-to-elbow (intimate space = 2″), not too pleasant." Or, "In the school elevator between classes, elbow-to-elbow (and back-to-back) (intimate space = 1″), uncomfortable and stressful."

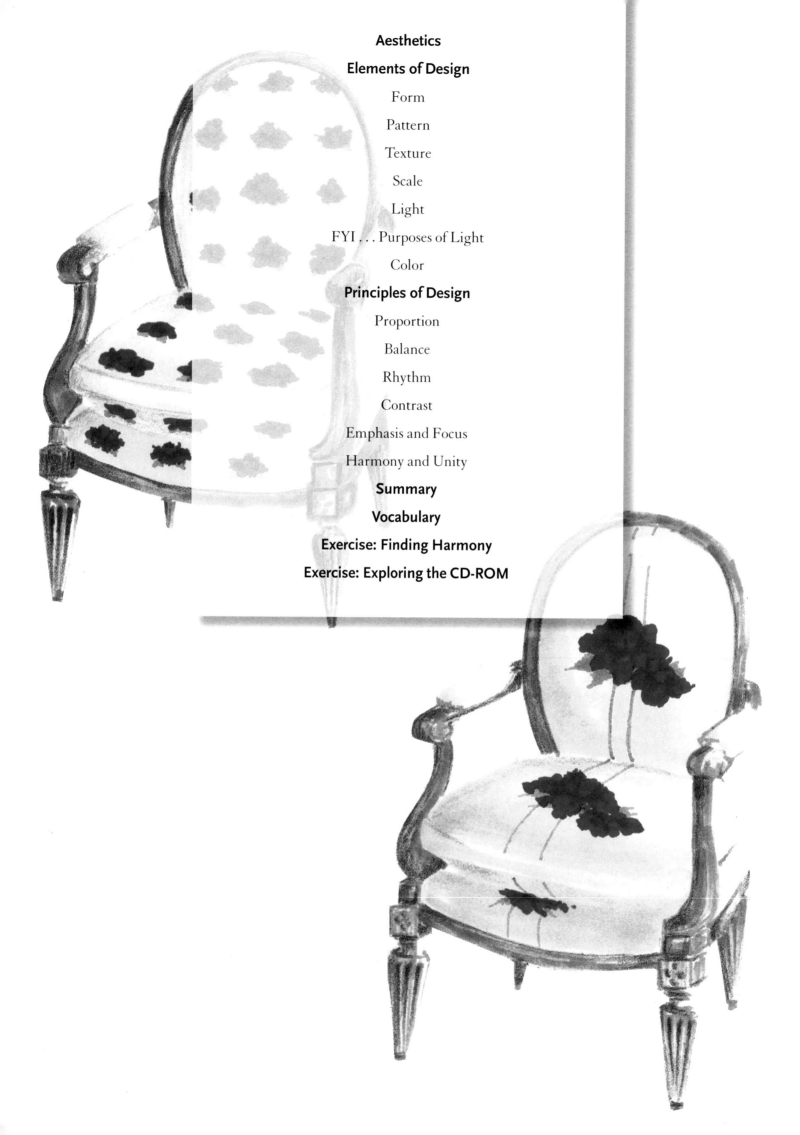

3

Design Theory: Aesthetics, Elements, and Principles of Design

Design—whether for interiors, graphics, fine arts, textiles, or industrial products, to name just a few applications—has several key features. Among them are an intended purpose, original ideas, skillful planning of the arrangement of parts, and culmination in a complete artistic unit. **Design theory** is a way to direct design based on a system of beliefs or philosophy. It is not a style.[1] This chapter addresses the building blocks that produce good design, that is, design that is successful in meeting its intended artistic and functional goals.

AESTHETICS

Aesthetics, derived from the Greek word relating to perception, may be defined as the study or theory of beauty and our responses to it. Aesthetics is the branch of philosophy that deals with art: its creation, its forms, and its effects.[2] When something is said to be beautiful, the description denotes a pleasing appearance. If the standards by which we judge beauty are objective and therefore reasonably universal, is that in conflict with the notion that beauty is in the eye of the beholder? How do we factor in taste? Does form follow function? These questions are perpetually discussed and debated by designers in all disciplines.

In the dictum "form follows function," aesthetics drives the "form," or the *visual aspect*. Interior designers also need to determine whether a design is successful in a particular context, place, and time. The design should serve its intended purpose, that is, the "function" part of the dictum. Although we all have individual tastes and preferences, depending on our experiences and exposure, there is general consensus regarding what is pleasing to the senses and what is a positive experience. Fashion may come and go, but the essence of what makes for good design remains.

Examining the bones, not merely the skin, of a composition helps a designer determine what is valid or convincing. Although we might not favor the fashion of the day during Queen Victoria's reign, an experienced, attuned, and trained eye will be able to discern the good Victorian from the bad, and what lies in between. Hindsight is helpful for detecting whether we have been influenced by current trends. The universal standards for good design tend to transcend culture, geography, and time. Understanding the rules of aesthetics, through knowledge, observation, and research, gives the designer the confidence to break the rules *intentionally*, not by happenstance. Innovators in art and design have an understanding of how the general population will react to their work. For example, the 20th-century artist Pablo Picasso aimed to upset the status quo and generate a variety of responses, even negative ones, to his creations. A good design is understandable on some level; however, it makes sense even if the meaning is esoteric and not considered the preferred solution by many observers.

To create or synthesize a composition, whether it is an interior, a building, a sculpture, or a painting, it is helpful first to analyze. What are the most basic building blocks of the composition? What are the existing components? What problems or solutions do they pose? What may be developed, added, changed, or eliminated? How does a designer group these elements? The purpose of any design is to organize its various parts into an integral whole. How are the components in the composition combined to create harmony? These are some of the questions explored in this chapter.

Design theory is influenced by many factors, such as historical precedent, environmental design research, and technology. Designing may be thought of as using skills designers have learned to match human needs with available technical resources within the practical constraints of business. Design thinking relies on intuition—ideas that have emotional meaning—and functionality. It is the integration of inspiration and rationality[3] with art and science.

History provides a valuable contribution to design theory by suggesting how past designs solved problems or represented particular ideals.[4] The design process is holistic and contextual. We are affected by our environment as our environment, in turn, impacts us. Throughout this text, research is noted to validate the relationship between humankind and its environment. Another critical influence on design is the understanding of how perception influences our sense of space. **Gestalt psychology**, the study of perception and behavior based on responses to integrated wholes, purports that humans naturally perceive things as a whole so that they are complete and therefore comprehensible. To begin to synthesize the units that make up the whole (or the perception of the whole), we analyze the tools designers use to create.[5] As a student progresses in his or her design education and participates in a studio project, a *design concept* will be developed, a conceptual framework from which to apply the theories learned here.

ELEMENTS OF DESIGN

The following are basic building blocks of design that we call **elements**:

- Form
- Pattern
- Texture
- Scale
- Light
- Color

Form

The architect David Kent Ballast defines form as "the basic shape and configuration of an object or space. It is often the way we first distinguish one thing as being different from another."[6] It makes sense to backtrack to see how a three-dimensional form is established by looking at line and shape (one- and two-dimensional concepts). Actually, before a line exists as a single dimension, it exists as a point. A point is actually an abstract notion, and unless combined with another point, suggesting a beginning and an end, it is not

Figure 3.1
Fallingwater, a residence in Pennsylvania built by American architect Frank Lloyd Wright between 1936 and 1939, demonstrates the tranquility provided by use of the horizontal plane. *(Courtesy Western Pennsylvania Conservancy)*

Figure 3.2
The use of a horizontal dado or chair rail is a traditional architectural feature in formal dining rooms, such as the one at Monticello by Thomas Jefferson. *(Thomas Jefferson Foundation, Inc., at Monticello; photograph by Philip Beaurline)*

discernible. Seen in relation to each other, two points become a line. A **line** indicates either length or width. As a line shifts direction, developing both length and width, it defines a **shape**, a two-dimensional unit. The addition of the third dimension, depth or volume, produces the boundaries of a solid or of a void.

A line is a one-dimensional unit that gives direction to a space. It may be straight or curvilinear. Straight lines may be horizontal, vertical, or diagonal.

A **horizontal line** is one that is parallel to the plane of the earth, its horizon. This type of line denotes stability, ever-present nature, rest, and repose—qualities that represent our perception of the earth's horizon. The American architect Frank Lloyd Wright (1867–1959) championed the use of horizontal lines in many of his buildings. Fallingwater, a residence he built between 1936 and 1939 for Edgar Kaufmann Sr., near Mill Run, Pennsylvania, exemplifies the strong use of the horizontal plane (Figure 3.1). The feeling created is one of connectedness to the earth because the structure is grounded in its natural environs.

Interior designers use horizontal lines in many different ways. One of the more common ways is to alter the viewer's perception of the size of a space. Traditionally, walls may be divided horizontally with the use of a dado, or chair rail that approximates the height of the top of a typical chair (Figure 3.2), or with a picture rail, placed higher, to showcase artwork. This division alters the viewer's perception of the room because the viewer tends to focus on the lower portion of the room, closest to eye level. This change in focus creates a feeling that the space is smaller and, therefore, more cozy and personal.

Vertical lines are perpendicular (at a right angle) to the horizon. They denote resistance to the force of gravity. A skyscraper exemplifies the effect of the vertical line in its strength and upward movement.

Opened in 2010 during a deep world recession, the Burj Khalifa, in Dubai, United Arab Emirates, boasts the title of tallest tower in the world, at a staggering height of one-half mile (Figure 3.3a). The Empire State Building was completed in 1931 in New York City during the Great Depression. Now dwarfed at a mere 1,453 feet, the building is still considered an American icon, one of the wonders of the modern world, a symbol of ascendency and optimism (Figure 3.3b).

A **diagonal line** is one that is at an angle. It denotes an even more pronounced dynamic motion than a horizontal or a vertical line. A diagonal line may create tension. If not used carefully in a space, or if overused, the sharp angle of a diagonal line can produce a feeling of

Figure 3.3
Relative verticality. a. Burj Khalifa b. Empire State Building *(a: Dmitry Erokhin / Alamy; b: © imagebroker / Alamy)*

instability and threat. The architect Daniel Libeskind favors this line, using it in many of his projects, as seen in his installation for the Denver Art Museum (Figure 3.4).

A **curvilinear** line is a bent line—one that deviates without a sharp angle. In contrast to straight lines, which may be thought of as representing the male human body, curvilinear lines evoke the gentler and softer outlines of the female body. Another way to envision the different sensations that are evoked is that straight lines, particularly those that are vertical or diagonal, suggest a direction or force that moves outwardly or externally, whereas an attribute of the curvilinear line is a more inward or enveloping direction. The spiral structure of the Guggenheim Museum, in New York City, demonstrates a shift for Wright two decades after Fallingwater (Figure 3.5).

Shape is a two-dimensional unit that describes the contours of lines. Another way to discuss shape is to speak of its relationship to a **plane**, or *flat surface*. Interior designers and architects are often concerned with rectilinear shapes, as they form planes, such as those of floors, walls, and ceilings.

Two broad categories of shape are geometric and organic. **Geometric shapes**, whether straight or curvilinear, are regular. Examples include the square, rectangle, triangle, and circle. With knowledge of one dimension, a mathematical formula can be used to calculate other dimensions. For instance, if you know the diameter of a circle, and the appropriate formula, you can calculate its circumference.

Considered an introverted shape, the circle is often associated symbolically with a feminine sensibility, in contrast to shapes composed of straight lines, which are thought of as having a more masculine identity. The square, with its equilateral sides (lines of the same dimension), denotes regularity and tranquility. The rectangle, with less equality between length and height, is the most commonly used shape in architecture. The triangle's dynamic use of three lines has been associated with energetic stability.

Figure 3.4
Daniel Libeskind utilizes a series of sharp angles in the Denver Art Museum. *(Frederic C. Hamilton Building at the Denver Art Museum, 2006, © Denver Art Museum; Photographer Jeff Wells. All Rights Reserved)*

Figure 3.5
Solomon R. Guggenheim Museum, New York City, completed in 1959: Built by Frank Lloyd Wright in the latter part of his career, the organic, circular structure is an evolution from previous styles that were more linear. *(© Solomon R. Guggenheim Museum)*

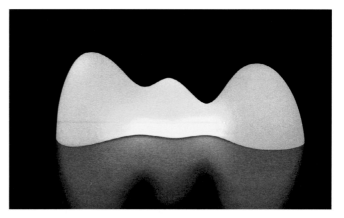

Figure 3.6
Industrial designer Karim Rashid's "blobjects" represents amorphic forms. *(Fairchild Books)*

Organic shapes are based on nature and living objects, whether in the animal (and human) or plant kingdom. One type sometimes used by designers may be described as amorphous or amorphic, that is, without a definitive shape. A good example of an amorphous shape is the amoeba, a primitive organism. The designer Karim Rashid utilizes this blob-like shape in the furniture and products he designs (Figure 3.6). An irregular shape may also be said to be biomorphic or zoomorphic, that is, representing human or animal components. Yet another type of organic shape

Figure 3.7
Line, shape, and form: As straight and curved lines move in more than one dimension, they take shape, forming the square, rectangle, triangle, and circles. As they take on the third dimension of depth, they are called forms. *(Christopher Barrett/ Hedrich Blessing. Designed by Gensler)*

is *botanical*, representing the plant world, including vines, leaves, flowers, and fruits.

Organic shapes may be naturalistic (that is, realistic), stylized (meaning representational, denoting the basic or essential components of the shape of an object), or abstract (nonrepresentational, in that they are not easily recognizable as given objects in the real world).

Form, as a three-dimensional unit, is made up of shapes on different planes. The regular, geometric forms are the cube, sphere, cone, cylinder, and pyramid. The terms **volume** and **mass** are also used to describe these complete, encased spatial dimensions. As with line and shape, interior designs are often enhanced by a pleasing mix of varied forms. Successful designs often incorporate a mixture of straight and curvilinear forms (Figure 3.7).

Forms may be composed of **solid**, or *positive*, areas and **void**, or *negative*, areas (hollow spaces). Sculptural objects, whether designed for fine art or the built environment, often play on the use of positive and negative spaces (Figure 3.8a). In some instances, equal importance may be given to solid and void design elements in a single form, such as a piece of furniture or a structure. The interior environment may also be designed to demonstrate the effect of the combination of both positive and negative elements (Figure 3.8b).

Figure 3.8
a. An intriguing yet relaxing use of solid and void in this children's space; b. Interior with solids and voids designed by Karim Rashid. *(a: Design © Rosan Bosch Ltd., photographer, Anders Sune Berg; b: © Frank Ouderman. Designed by Karim Rashid)*

Pattern

The repetition of a specific motif is known as **pattern**. A **motif** may be thought of as a shape, theme, or figure. The individual motif of a pattern is discernible as a distinct entity, whereas texture, discussed later in this chapter, appears as an overall tone.

Patterns may be either **applied** or **structural**. An example of an applied pattern is the design repeated by printing a fabric; the design achieved in a fabric through weaving is a structural pattern (Figure 3.9a).

On a larger, architectural scale, the way in which the rectangular shapes of bricks are arranged produces a structural pattern (Figure 3.9b).

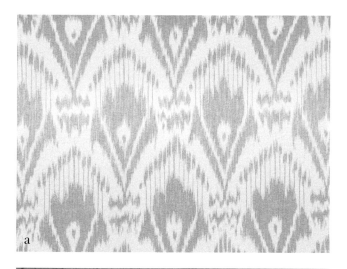

Figure 3.9
The similar pattern is applied in a. the fabric print and b. typical Islamic architecture, featured here in Barcelona, Spain. *(a: Threads available through Lee Jofa; b: Provided by the Author)*

Designers use pattern to enhance visual interest and project distinct moods. Motifs, like shapes, may be geometric or organic and expressed in naturalistic, stylized, or abstract ways. Within each of these categories are innumerable motifs identified by specific, commonly accepted traits. For example, geometric patterns common to surface materials, such as fabric and carpet, include stripes, a series of horizontal or straight lines; checks, a series of repeated squares; or plaids, a less regular arrangement of boxes and rectangles. Diagonal lines form various patterns, such as the chevron and flame stitch. A common pattern based on the circle is the polka dot.

Some of the earliest patterns are based on representations of nature. These types of designs have appeared in the works of cultures around the world from ancient times to the present and are universally popular. They may express the natural as well as supernatural world, through geometric or organic designs that are representational, stylized, or abstract.

Organic motifs (Figure 3.10a) include botanical images, such as plants, leaves, and flowers, whereas figural motifs feature humans or animals. For example, paisley, a stylized botanical motif originating in India, is derived from a reference to plant forms. French-inspired toile is an example of a figural pattern that depicts a pastoral scene of people, animals, or plants (Figure 3.10b). Common zoomorphic prints are representative of the markings of the hides of exotic animals, such as the leopard (Figure 3.10c).

A pattern may convey a theme, such as traditional, primitive, country, contemporary, casual, or sophisticated. The patterned textile in Figure 3.11 appears to be contemporary but was woven more than 2,000 years ago, in pre-Columbian Peru, reflecting the enduring appeal of the primitive theme.

A pattern may also be described in terms of its scale (see Figure 3.15). It is important for designers to keep in mind that when the individual components of a pattern are very small in scale, or viewed at a distance, the pattern will appear as a texture.

Patterns and combinations of patterns in both residential and contract interior design can produce a variety of physiological and emotional responses, reflecting their symbolic and cultural meanings.[7] People perceive patterns differently, depending on their demographic characteristics (including gender,

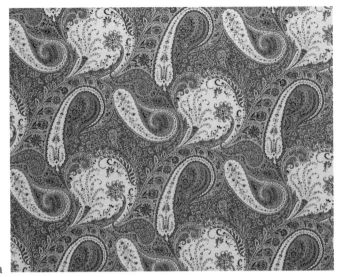

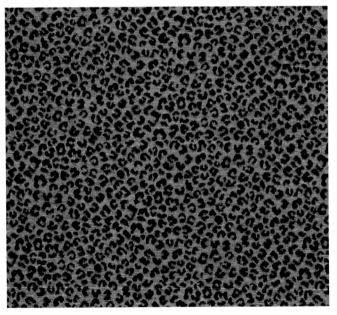

Figure 3.10
Examples of a stylized botanical motif in a. a paisley; b. a pastoral scene in the toile; and c. a zoomorphic print in the leopard pattern. *(a and c: Threads available through Lee Jofa; b © Condé Nast)*

Figure 3.11
Peruvian textile showing traditional patterns. Fragment, 600–300 B.C. Part of the border of a mantle. Made in Peru. Cotton, wool. Technique: stem stitch on plain weave, 50 × 23 cm (19 11/16 × 9 1/16 in.). *(Photo: Matt Flynn. Cooper-Hewitt, National Design Museum, New York City. Photo credit: © Cooper-Hewitt, National Design Museum, Smithsonian Institution / Art Resource, NY)*

regional, and age differences) and personal and cultural experiences. Pattern is significantly influenced by the setting in which it is applied. The extent to which mixed patterns are perceived as pleasing is also a matter of cultural preferences and personal taste.

Ornament is visual detail that is not functional, but rather purely decorative. The degree of ornamentation favored in a design varies with time and context (see Chapters 11, 12, and 13). The decades of Queen Victoria's reign were characterized by use of ornamentation, often to the point of excess, but some who thought of themselves as reformers during that time considered ornament a crime, laying the foundation for modernism.

Texture

The features of a surface, both its construction and its finish, are its **texture**. Texture is a sensory experience that may be **tactile**, meaning that it can be felt by touch, in addition to being visual.

Certain visual textures merely appear to possess a three-dimensional structure that could be felt. For example, with a simple faux (meaning "fake") painting technique called sponging, colors are layered so that the surface appears to have a structural texture. Although the sponged surface is flat to the touch, visual interest is enhanced by this illusion of tactile texture, as if it had depth (Figure 3.12a and b). **Trompe l'oeil** is another artistic technique that tricks the eye, causing the viewer to imagine a structure having significant three-dimensionality rather than being flat.

Texture becomes even more significant when the colors used in a space are muted or uniform. In these instances, a variety in textures serves to prevent monotony. A mix of coarse and smooth, large- and small-scale textures maintains greater visual interest than surfaces that have uniform textures (Figure 3.13).

Light plays a significant role in how texture is perceived. Shiny surfaces, such as a highly polished metal, reflect light. Matte surfaces, such as cork, absorb light. Again, designers need to consider the desired effect. Paint sheens, for example, vary from highly reflective, or gloss, to flat, or matte. The glossier the sheen level selected, the more visible imperfections will appear. The angle of light across a surface projects shadows that change the way texture is seen and may even create patterns.

Distance also affects the way we perceive texture. As with pattern, for texture to be perceived from a distance the detail must be of sufficient size for the dimensional quality of the surface to be discerned. When designers are selecting finishes, the samples they evaluate need to be large enough, and viewed at varying distances and under varying lighting conditions, to enable a determination of how they will actually present themselves in the space.

Scale

The size of an object can be measured by the length, width, and depth of its surfaces. When comparing the relative size of two or more objects, we speak of **scale**.

Often, we speak of comparing something to the **human scale**. Despite idiosyncratic differences among people, there is consensus about a recognizable, constant range of what we expect human size to be.

Figure 3.12
Textures such as those found in nature may be enhanced by age, or simulated with faux painting techniques such as Venetian plaster. *(a: © Decorfin; b: Photo by Warren Appel © 2005 The Shanti Shop www.shantishop.com)*

Figure 3.13
Interior designer Tony Chi mixes a variety of textures to enhance the visual interest in his design for the Intercontinental Hotel in Geneva, Switzerland. *(Tony Chi, designer for Intercontinental Hotel, Geneva)*

We may describe an interior space that has a high-pitched ceiling as having a cathedral ceiling, evoking a sense of space and grandeur that is not on a human scale (Figure 3.14a). Artists find the juxtaposition of various scales an intriguing metaphor, as demonstrated by the Crown Fountain, a contemporary art installa-

Figure 3.14
Scale: using the size of a human as a known and recognizable standard of measurement. a. Grand Central Terminal, New York City; b. Crown Fountain, a public art installation designed by Jaume Plensa, Chicago. *(a: © Alan Schein Photography/CORBIS; b: Provided by the Author)*

tion in Chicago (Figure 3.14b). Alternatively, we may describe an interior that uses a low ceiling plane as conveying a feeling of comfort for humans occupying that space. The scale of furnishings, doorways, and windows may also be used to alter a viewer's perception of a space. A designer's strategic use of scale in the architectural elements and interior details may evoke different sensations, ranging from intimate to impersonal.

Scale often compares an object with the space it inhabits. When furnishings seem to fit appropriately in the volume of a space, we may not even be aware of scale as an issue. When the fit is poor, however, we may become unsettled by the disproportion in scale between a form and its enclosure.

Scale may be judged by eye or instinct based on our common expectations. If we are accustomed to sofas ranging in size from 54 inches to 84 inches, for example, a sofa outside that frame of reference in either direction may be described as small or large in scale. Patterns in fabrics may also be described as small or large scale, for instance, a floral pattern with a repeat of 2 inches versus one of 8 inches. Consider the example of a chair upholstered in a rose-patterned fabric that permitted only one rose to fit on the back of the chair; we would describe that pattern as large scale. Even a rose pattern with a repeat of 3 inches (similar in size to a real, fully opened rose) would seem relatively large for use on a chair, especially a small-scale chair (Figure 3.15).

Light

Without light there would be no visible form, color, or texture. Comprehending the power of light gives a designer an enormous repertoire of ways to influence a space.

Any discussion of light as a design element includes both quantitative and qualitative descriptions. People perceive light in terms of the level of illumination, or brightness, as well as its comfort and relation to a sense of well-being. Lighting design combines science and art. As with other areas of knowledge that depend heavily on advances in technology, lighting design is a specialty requiring ongoing learning. Consider how information about computer technology becomes outdated on a continuous basis; this applies to lighting information as well. One of the best lessons an interior design student can learn is to appreciate the

Figure 3.15
The same floral patterns used to upholster the same chair demonstrate significantly different scale. *(Fairchild Books)*

complexities of lighting design and know when to call upon expert collaboration.

Three different layers of lighting—ambient, task, and accent—are used to achieve the following varied purposes:

- **Ambient** (meaning "to go around") **lighting** is diffuse, uniform illumination that provides for safe movement. It is also referred to as *general lighting.*
- **Task lighting** illuminates certain areas of a space to facilitate specific activities, such as reading. It can serve to define functional areas of a room, such as the entertainment area of a hotel guest room. It is also referred to as *local lighting.*
- **Accent**, or, **key**, **lighting** creates an emphasis or focus, such as to highlight a painting, an objet d'art, or a sculpture.

By using more than one layer to illuminate a space, the interior designer can add interest and versatility while fulfilling basic lighting needs. See *FYI . . . Pur-*

Figure 3.16
The three layers of light: ambient, task, and accent. *(Courtesy of GE Lighting)*

poses of Light. This applies to both residential and contract design (Figure 3.16).

Categories of Light The two basic categories of light are natural and electric. **Natural light** includes daylight, flame, candle, and skylight. **Electric** or **artificial light** includes incandescent, fluorescent, neon, high-intensity discharge, and LED (light-emitting diode). Chapter 7 further explores shapes of light, distribution of light, types of lamps (bulbs) and their housing, luminaires (fixtures), temperatures and colors of light, and the application of light for residential and contract spaces.

Color

Considered by many to be the most recognizable design element, color is a powerful tool that projects a space's personality. Children generally learn to name colors before they can identify shapes. Chapter 4 further discusses the meaning of color to the interior designer in terms of its physical properties, its impact on perception and mood, and the effects it can have on other colors and other components of a space.

Without light, there is no color. The science of physics deals with color as a physical property of light. Each color is differentiated from the others by its wavelength. When light passes through a glass prism, it refracts, or breaks, into wavelengths. The spectrum of light that humans are able to see is known as the **visible spectrum**. It ranges from red to violet (or purple). Red has the longest wavelength, violet the shortest. Red is the warmest color, violet the coolest. In between are orange, yellow, green, blue, and indigo, a blue-violet. White light is composed of the three **primaries of light**: red, green, and blue.

When we speak of color as *substance,* we are referring to pigmentation, such as dyes (natural and synthetic) and paints. The three **primaries of color** as pigment are red, yellow, and blue. When these primary colors are mixed together, the result is black.

There are many commercial ways to name colors, but a more scientific and universal language of color is based on three distinct attributes: hue, value, and chroma (Figure 3.17).

- **Hue** is the family of a color, or the way we distinguish one color, such as red, from another, such as yellow. In everyday conversation, people use the words *color* and *hue* interchangeably, but hue is a more precise term for a color's family.
- **Value** is the degree of lightness or darkness of a color. When white is added to a hue, the value is heightened, creating a **tint**. Conversely, when black is added to a color, the value is lowered, creating a **shade**.
- **Chroma** is the purity, saturation, or intensity of a color. Adding gray to a color lowers its

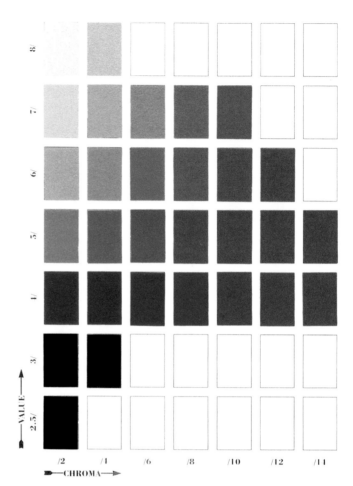

Figure 3.17
Color's three attributes: Munsell's theory describes hue, the family of color; value, the lightness or darkness of color; and chroma, the brightness of color. *(Fairchild Books)*

chroma. This type of color is also called a **tone**, a muted version of a hue. (Other ways of changing chroma are discussed in Chapter 4.)

If you were limited as an artist or designer to only a few jars of paints, you could attain a virtually infinite combination of colors with red, blue, yellow, white, and black.

PRINCIPLES OF DESIGN

The second most fundamental way to analyze a design composition is to consider how the principles of design are applied. Design principles are thought of as more complex than elements. Whereas elements are singular components of a design composition, **principles** are the rules or guidelines that govern the use of these elements within the composition. Thus, the aspects I have previously identified as elements may be thought of as components of the principles.

The discussion that follows focuses on six design principles:

- Proportion
- Balance
- Rhythm
- Contrast
- Emphasis and focus
- Harmony and unity

Proportion

In contrast to scale, which describes the relative size of an object to one or more objects *outside* itself, proportion is concerned with the relationships of parts within a whole. In other words, scale involves external relationships, and proportion involves internal relationships. Proportion may encompass the relationship of parts to a whole object, or the relationship of parts to other parts within a composition that is seen as a whole entity.

This concept is not limited to the study of interior design. In our day-to-day lives, we use proportion in a variety of situations. For example, in describing a woman as "short," we compare her overall stature with a known size, perhaps an average height for an adult woman of 5 feet, 5 inches. This is an example of scale, that is, a comparison of something with an external object. Alternatively, a description of a man as "stocky" denotes proportion: an internal comparison of parts and of width in comparison to height (his width is wider than expected in comparison to his height, or vice versa). Similarly, "squat" and "elongated" denote proportion; they address the ratio of certain dimensions (in this case, width and length) within the whole, compared with each other and with our expectations for that particular form (Figure 3.18).

Another everyday example that can help explain this principle is a cooking recipe. One person's apple pie might be "sweeter" than another's because the ratio of sugar to the other ingredients in the recipe is greater in the former than in the latter. It is not the absolute quantity of sugar that makes for the sweeter taste, but its quantity relative to the amounts of each of the other ingredients and the total ingredients of the whole.

Much of our perception of proportionate or disproportionate relationships occurs instinctively. In

Figures 3.18
Andree Putnam's elongated sofa. (*Andree Putnam's Crescent Sofa, available exclusively through Ralph Pucci International; photo by Antoine Bootz*)

fact, we are more likely to perceive "out of proportion" than we are to perceive "in proportion," which we consider the given, or expected. In examining the terms *well-proportioned* and *ill-proportioned*, the architect Arrol Gellner concludes that sometimes we just need to let our rational minds step back and let our instincts tell us what looks right.[8] Nonetheless, over the years numerous mathematical formulations have been devised as a means of understanding and quantifying these ratios. One such formula, known as the **golden section**, or **golden mean**, was utilized by the ancient Greeks. It was thought to approximate the best proportions, producing the most universally appealing relationship among parts. Figure 3.19a illustrates the formula believed to produce a rectangle that has the most pleasing proportions.

This geometric approach was used by the ancient Romans and later by Renaissance architects. The architect Andrea Palladio's *Four Books of Architecture*,

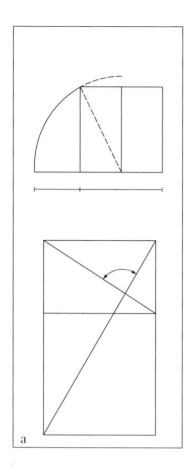

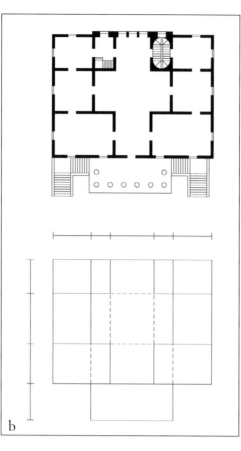

Figure 3.19
a. Golden mean; b. Palladian structure;
c. Le Corbusier's modular grid based
on the proportions of the human body.
(Fairchild Books)

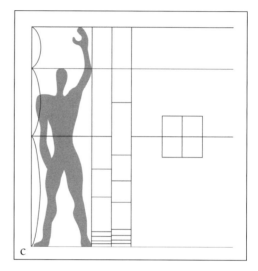

c

published in 1570, describes this sense of proportion (Figure 3.19b).

In the 13th century, Fibonacci, an Italian mathematician, devised another mathematical way of describing proper proportions. His numerical calculation is presented as a series of consecutive numbers. Each number is the sum of the two preceding numbers: 0, 1, 1, 2, 3, 5, 8, 13, 21, 34, and so on. In other words, 3 is to 5 as 5 is to 8.

Consider the proportions we are accustomed to. Most rooms are rectangular, for instance, 8 feet by 13 feet, or 13 feet by 21 feet. Standard sizes of carpets come close to the 5-by-8-foot proportion that can be derived from Fibonacci's calculation. Pictures and picture frames also use similar proportions, such as 5 inches by 7 inches and 8 inches by 10 inches.

In the 20th century the Swiss architect and designer Le Corbusier used a formula for proportion that relied on the examination of human dimensions (Figure 3.19c).

Knowing these expectations, designers may wish to play with proportions to create the unexpected. Phillipe Starck is a contemporary designer known for his dramatic play with proportion in the hotel spaces he designs (Figure 3.20). Another approach for mod-

Figure 3.20
Phillipe Starck uses unexpected proportions in his hotel design.
(Courtesy of and designed by Philippe Starck; photo by Richard Davies)

ern interiors is to apply more classical rules of proportion as they are more expected and therefore more readily considered acceptable.

Balance

Balance is the state of equilibrium. In design, balance is the arrangement of parts in a composition to achieve equality. Equality in design is achieved when features have the same **visual weight**. It is not necessary for the components on either side of a room actually to weigh the same; the visual weight of objects may be influenced by their size, shape, texture, color, complexity, placement, or position. The arrangement around a real or imagined *centerline*, the **axis**, will define the degree of balance. To have balance, the elements must have equality in effect, force, or importance. And that can be accomplished in a variety of ways.

A typical axis is the vertical line from ceiling to floor through the midsection of a room. A less often utilized, but still significant, axis is the horizontal line at the midpoint of a room that separates the top half of the room from the bottom half. A design that considers both axes gives a more complex balance to a space.

Three types of balance may be used in design: symmetrical, asymmetrical, and radial (Figure 3.21a–c). **Symmetrical balance** is a formal, static, and traditional type of balance achieved through the arrangement of identical elements around a common axis. This is also known as a *mirror image*. When a design relies on symmetrical balance, both the designer and the client need to recognize that a change in one item will necessitate a change in its identical counterpart on the other side of the axis.

Asymmetrical balance is defined as the achievement of equilibrium through equal visual weight of

Figure 3.21

Equilibrium: symmetrical, asymmetrical, and radial balance. a. This space, designed by Darren Henault, demonstrates the formal, mirror-image approach of symmetrical balance, in which elements are identical on either side of the vertical axis and also here on the horizontal axis; b. A design by Jason Claire features a skilled use of visual weight to achieve asymmetrical balance; c. Radial balance is applied in the dining room by designer Paula Grace. *(a: Designed by Darren Henault; b: design by Jason Claire/Vastu. Both photos by Timothy Bell; c: Photoshot/Red Cover/Ken Hayden)* non-identical elements around an axis. The result is a composition that is flexible, dynamic, and informal. Although asymmetrical balance may be more difficult to achieve than symmetrical balance, its advantage is that it is a more fluid approach to design. Conditions that create greater visual weight include large size, highly textured or detailed objects, complex or unusual shapes, and dark elements.

Asymmetrical balance should not be confused with a lack of balance, in which elements of the composition do not demonstrate equal visual weight. Lack of balance may be perceived as disconcerting and unstable.

Radial balance is an equilibrium that relies on a center point, which serves as the axis around which elements of equal visual weight are arranged. Although less commonly employed than either symmetrical or asymmetrical balance, radial balance is often used for ceremonial spaces.

Rhythm

Rhythm is characterized by a recurrence of successive elements in a periodic pattern of repetition. As with musical notes, the spacing may be regular or irregular. The intervals between notes in a waltz, which is regular, may be contrasted to those in a jazz interpretation, with its stops and starts, representing less regularly spaced intervals. The cadence of the waltz is more orderly and stable than that of the jazz piece, although the rhythm of the jazz piece may be more exciting.

Rhythm in design may be created through the use of linear components, such as a series of architectural columns or windows. Other rhythmic elements can be achieved through the use of colors or shapes positioned thoughtfully around a space or in sequence. A progression of lighting elements may also provide a rhythmic sensation. It is important to recognize that repetition alone does not convey rhythm. The concept of movement as one perceptually travels through the design is essential. A particular motif or color dispersed throughout a space may move us visually through the space without our even being conscious of it (Figure 3.22a and b).

Contrast

Contrast is the way we perceive the differences between things. Although sameness, or unity, is an important desire in human nature, contrast is equally

Figure 3.22
a. Rhythm in architectural elements is seen in this colonnade of columns and arches in Guatemala; b. Colorful stripes in this exterior in Guatemala create a rhythmic pattern. *(Provided by the Author)*

Figure 3.23
Contrast is achieved through lightness and darkness, straight lines and curves. Here a metal sculpture by Pablo Picasso is silhouetted in the Chicago Institute New Wing through the contrast against filtered light. *(Provided by the Author)*

Figure 3.24
The degree of contrast may be subtle or dramatic, or perceived even as chaotic, in this Dorothy Draper design for the Greenbrier Hotel. *(Beall Gordon/Condé Nast)*

important. People thrive on variety, change, even opposition, but to varying degrees and under different circumstances. Any two or more features placed in opposition may achieve contrast. It may be expressed in the difference between light and dark, curvilinear and straight, near and far, old and new, smooth and rough, plain and ornate, small and large, and so on (Figure 3.23). The differences may be striking or subtle. As with any other element or principle, there is no magic formula for how much is warranted for a particular client or application. For some people and in certain situations, a high degree of contrast may induce tension or stimulation overload (Figure 3.24). For others, or under different circumstances, the same degree of contrast may be experienced as a pleasing level of stimulation or arousal.

Emphasis and Focus

When a designer employs the principle of emphasis, the result is a composition in which one feature demands attention. That feature is also known as a focus, or focal point. The concept of emphasis requires that something hold a dominant status compared with other components in the space, which are then considered subordinate.

Dominance, or importance, may be assigned by virtue of any of a number of factors. A feature may command attention because of its large size in relation to the space or other objects within the space. Or, a focal point may be established by the interest of detailing, texture, architectural or historical factors, color, and so on (Figure 3.25). The tools available to a designer to create a focal point are numerous. However, using too many focal points in a space may become distracting and may defeat the purpose of the design. Conversely, a composition with no focus may be perceived as monotonous and bland.

There can be no emphasis without contrast. However, the converse is not true. A design can have contrast

Figure 3.25
Emphasis: Dale Chihuly's glass sculptures demand attention, as in this installation for the Columbus Museum of Art, attracting attention as a focal point. *(Dale Chihuly. Rio delle Torreselle Chandelier, 1998. Columbus Museum of Art, Columbus, Ohio. Photo by Richard K. Loesch)*

and not achieve emphasis if all the dissimilar elements are equated visually. For example, a room painted with black walls, white ceiling, and an equal distribution of dark and light furniture will be high in contrast but may not create any focus.

Harmony and Unity

Harmony is the culmination of a designer's attempt to combine various parts into a pleasing whole. It represents the sum total of all the concepts discussed thus far.

The components of a harmonious composition are considered congruous; they belong together. Any feature removed or changed will affect the totality or the integrity of the composition. Harmony exists in the difficult to attain, delicate balance between unity

and oneness on the one hand and contrast and variety on the other. Harmony presumes a common thread among components to reinforce an overall design theme, so that the whole is greater than the sum of its parts, similar to Gestalt theory, mentioned earlier. Perhaps the designer Tony Chi alludes to this elusive quality in what he terms invisible design, "what touches you rather than what you see."[9] Although unity is essential to achieving harmony, a certain proportion of components in a composition should be varied to avoid monotony.

Unifying threads may be achieved in a variety of ways. There may be a similarity of shape throughout the space, such as the repetition of circular forms. There may be harmony in the application of a unified color scheme (Figure 3.26a). (Color theory will

Figure 3.26

Three faces of harmony. a. A refined harmony in this interior demonstrates a subtle variety of traditional and modern elements with unified colors and balanced visual weight; b. In a different manner, the bedroom designed in Istanbul, Turkey, is also harmonious. It relies on the repetition of rectilinear elements, simple vertical and horizontal lines and forms. Variety in texture and proportion brings contrast to offset potential monotony; c. Amy Lau has achieved a very active sense of harmony in her colorful, retro-inspired installation for the Kips Bay Showcase. *(a: © Martin Harvey/Corbis; b: © Thomas Loof. Designed by Baris Kansu; c: Design © Amy Lau/photography Kris Tamburello)* be discussed further in Chapter 4). Or, a particular motif or pattern, such as a floral theme, may be interspersed throughout the space to create a harmonious feeling.

Harmony is difficult to master, but it is ultimately the standard by which design is judged. Harmony may be quiet and soothing (Figure 3.26b), or it may excite, challenge, and foster change (Figure 3.26c).

Summary

Interior designers learn to analyze a composition in order to create a composition. Although good design is expected to be aesthetic, it needs to serve a purpose such as functionality and comfort for the user. This is the balance between form and function. There are many influences on design theory, including historical precedent and environmental and technological considerations. Design considerations are best made within a holistic and contextual framework combining emotional, creative, ethical, and rational processes.

The most basic of the building blocks of design are called elements. They are form, pattern, texture, scale, light, and color.

Form that is three-dimensional is derived first from a point, next from a line that is one-dimensional, then from a shape that is two-dimensional. Patterns, either structural or applied, are a repetition of a motif. Motifs are often based on features in the natural world and may be imbued with much symbolism and feeling. Patterns are described as being either geometric or organic and are expressed in naturalistic, stylized, or abstract ways. Texture may be visual or tactile, or both. Texture is a tool that interior designers use to create interest, especially when the color scheme is muted. Scale is the relative size of one object compared with an external object of known size. Designers often rely on comparisons with human dimensions when demonstrating scale. A pattern made up of very small-scale motifs takes on the appearance of a texture.

Without light, there would be no visible form, color, or texture. Lighting, a powerful tool for the designer, serves many purposes, among them providing visibility and establishing a mood. Lighting solutions, whether natural or electric, may rely on one or a combination of the following layers: ambient, task, and accent lighting.

The human eye can perceive a wide range of color, known as the visible spectrum, from red, the warmest hue, to violet, the coolest. Color conveys feelings and mood.

Principles of design include proportion, balance, rhythm, contrast, emphasis and focus, and harmony and unity.

Although many mathematical formulas, such as the golden section, or golden mean, can be used to judge proportion, it is often perceived instinctively, based on our experiences. Whereas scale speaks to external relationships, proportion deals with internal relationships: the comparison of parts within a whole to one another or to the whole. Balance, or a state of equilibrium, is achieved through a system of visual weight. This can be accomplished symmetrically, asymmetrically, or in a radial way around an axis point. The repetition of features, like the notes of a musical composition, produces a rhythm that takes the eye through a space. Differences create contrast, a vital part of an interesting composition. Designers may contrast a variety of elements, such as shapes, colors, scale, or pattern. Juxtaposing features with contrasting importance creates emphasis or a focal point. Factors affecting the degree of importance a feature holds may be its size, intricacy, lighting, color, or location, among others.

A composition is considered to be successful, good, and whole if it has achieved harmony. Harmony presumes a pleasing balance between unity and variety.

Vocabulary

accent (key) lighting	horizontal line	shape
aesthetics	hue	solid
ambient lighting	human scale	structural pattern
applied pattern	line	symmetrical balance
artificial light	mass	tactile
asymmetrical balance	motif	task lighting
axis	natural light	texture
chroma	organic shape	tint
curvilinear line	ornament	tone
design theory	pattern	trompe l'oeil
diagonal line	plane	value
element	primaries of color	vertical line
electric light	primaries of light	visible spectrum
form	principles of design	visual weight
geometric shape	radial balance	void
Gestalt psychology	scale	volume
golden section (golden mean)	shade	

Exercise: Finding Harmony

Select two full-page color images from any magazine or designer's website. These images may show either residential or contract spaces. Choose one space you feel reflects the design principle of harmony and another that does not reflect that principle.

Using your knowledge of the elements and principles discussed in this chapter, prepare a written justification of your choices. Present your observations of what makes one space harmonious and what makes the other less so. Describe the features you consider to be successful and those you consider less successful. Use the concepts and vocabulary terms associated with elements and principles of design to express your assessment.

Exercise: Exploring the CD-ROM

Take advantage of the contents of the CD-ROM to increase your understanding of the elements and principles of design. Follow the instructions for Starting the CD-ROM on pages xix–xx and click on Chapter Three: Design Theory: Aesthetics, Elements, and Principles of Design.

Elements and Principles of Design: Choose any two of the elements and two principles of design. For each element and principle selected, photograph or sketch examples in "the built environment" such as furniture, buildings, or a space where the specific element or principle is the focus of the design.

CHAPTER

4

Color Theory and Application

Color is one of the most basic, yet most powerful, design tools. Throughout the ages, people have expressed themselves through the use of color. Natural pigments have been applied to skin as adornment and tribal identification, painted on walls for decoration and as a means of communication, and used to dye clothing (animal skins and textiles) and embellish cookware (Figure 4.1).

Even today, if one were on a limited budget, it would be possible to transform one's space dramatically through a change in paint color. Yet, as basic as this tool may appear, it is extremely complex. Color may be studied from several vantage points and is analyzed by diverse bodies of scientific and technical knowledge. Although it may be true that some people intuitively have what may be called a good color sense or a way with color, most individuals are able to hone their skills through a better understanding of the effects of color and its meanings.

No color is inherently wrong, although its particular amount, intensity, or depth may indeed be wrong for the light of a particular space. By manipulating the variables that create color, any number of combinations can be achieved that will bring life and, literally, light to the architectural space.[1]

Figure 4.1
African face painting as captured by photographer Hans Silvester is rich in color, decoration, and symbolism.

In Chapter 3 the three basic attributes of color as substance, or physical matter, were discussed: hue, the family name of a color, such as red; value, the degree of lightness or darkness of a hue (achieved through the addition of white or black); and chroma, the degree of brightness of a hue. Color depends not only on these inherent qualities, but also on the circumstance in which it is viewed, for example, at daylight or at dusk, at a distance or up close, and by different individuals. Consequently, color's nature is ever changing.

Observing natural objects under different conditions allows us to see the range and subtleties of color. Consider the pigeon, often maligned as a dirty nuisance. Observation reveals the shimmering, rainbow-like array of blues and purples encircling the neck of this otherwise gray bird. Or, look closely at rusted iron; the rust's texture can be intriguing, and its color range of warm hues is a palette unto itself. Similarly, stones exhibit variations that upon closer inspection feature a variety of colors (Figure 4.2 a–c.).

This chapter expands the discussion of color theory, begun in Chapter 3, beyond the role of color as one of the six elements, or building blocks, of design. Here, the focus is on color analysis from several scientific standpoints, the relationships of colors to one another, and the interplay of color with other design elements and principles and with human factors. How color theory is applied to interior design is also explored (see *FYI . . . The Role of Color within a Space*).

Figure 4.2
Nature provides us with color, often unexpectedly. a. Pigeon; b. Rust; c. Stones.

THE SCIENCE OF COLOR

Many branches of science are concerned with theories that systematize color. Theories abound that address how color affects the human mind, body, and spirit. Among the traditional branches of Western science that theorize about color are physics, chemistry, physiology, psychology, and sociology. Additionally, the Eastern world has provided us with a system of associations for color, such as those practiced in Feng Shui. Metaphysical studies that rely more on the understanding of transcendent, or supernatural, reality offer us systems that associate colors with their counterparts on the human body. Various pop culture specialists and merchandisers have conceived a plethora of color names made up of catchy phrases to depict different personalities, lifestyles, moods, and trendy applications of color. For example Pantone's annual color pick (Tangerine Tango for 2012) or one of Benjamin Moore's color story of Earth and Sky.

Applying the more traditional and scientific theories to the practice of interior design is the focus of this chapter. As with any other artistic endeavor, a successful design might arise from breaking or bending the rules. However, it is usually by understanding the rules and making a deliberate choice to improvise that a successful "accident" occurs. Design is a product of just that: intent and planning.

Physics

One of the natural sciences, physics deals with the individual components and interactions of matter and energy,[2] not living organisms. For our purposes, it explores how *color is a product of light*. In physics, color is discussed as originating from light and is called **additive color**. Additive color is distinguished from **subtractive color**, which is reflected from a surface or object colored by dyes, pigments, or other substances. The latter is more appropriately the subject of chemistry and physiology, discussed later.

Sir Isaac Newton (1642–1727), an English mathematician and physicist, is credited with developing the **spectral theory of color** (Figure 4.3a and b). In the late 1660s, Newton demonstrated that when a beam of daylight is passed first through a window and then through a triangular glass prism onto a wall, the light **refracted**, or *bent*, at different angles to the wall, into bands of light pulsations (electromagnetic energy)

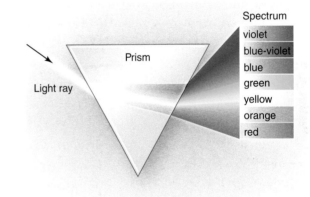

a

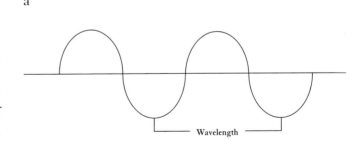

b

Figure 4.3
Spectral theory of color includes the a. prism, visible spectrum, and; b. wavelength. Infrared and ultraviolet are not part of the visible spectrum.

commonly called **wavelength**. The shortest wavelength bends the most, and the longest bends the least. Wavelengths that are not absorbed into the wall's surface or transmitted through it are **reflected**, or *bounced back*, carrying information about the color. A visible spectrum, or rainbow of colors, is thereby projected onto the wall. The range that is visible to the human eye goes from red to violet.

The **visible spectrum** is a continuum, with no finite, or fixed, separation between zones. Different wavelengths are described within ranges, commonly measured in **nanometers (nm)**. The longest wavelength range, between 650 nm and 700 nm, is known as red. Violet, the shortest, is in the range of 390 nm to 430 nm. *Orange, yellow, green,* and *blue* are the names typically given to the hues in succession within this spectrum. The decision about the exact point at which each of these six hues begins and ends is somewhat arbitrary. However, there is general agreement about the meaning of the names *red, orange, yellow, green, blue,* and *violet.* Some color specialists include indigo as a blue-violet at a range in between the range of blue and violet.

Colors in the spectrum are also described by temperature, ranging from warm to cool, with red being the warmest and violet the coolest. Red or yellow content in a hue makes it seem warmer, and blue content causes a hue to seem cooler.[3]

At either end of the spectrum are colors that are invisible to the human eye, such as infrared (used in microwave ovens), which are longer in wavelength (approximately 780 nm to 5,000 nm) and warmer, and ultraviolet (used in X-ray machines), which are shorter (ranging from 100 nm to 380 nm) and cooler. The visible spectrum is generally considered to be the range from approximately 400 nm to 700 nm.

As discussed in Chapter 3, the three primary colors of light are red, blue, and green (Figure 4.4). Mixing various combinations of these three can produce any other color, and, combined in equal strengths, they add up to white, or colorless, light. This property of the colors of light is called the **additive theory of color**. No other color beams of light can be combined to create red, blue, or green. When white light falls on an opaque object, the surface of the object, such as Newton's wall, absorbs certain wavelengths of the light and reflects others. This property is called **selective absorption**. Blue is perceived when red and green

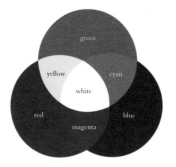

Additive color process

Figure 4.4
The three primaries of light: the additive theory of color. Red, blue, and green produce white.

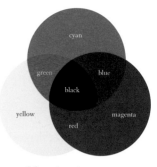

Subtractive color process

Figure 4.5
The three primaries of pigment: the subtractive theory of color. Red, yellow, and blue produce black.

are absorbed; green is perceived when red and blue are absorbed; and so on. Knowledge of how colors are influenced by light is useful for the interior designer, who must understand the effects of natural and electric lighting on the perception of color.

Chemistry

Like physics, chemistry is a natural science. It deals with the composition, structure, and properties of substances as well as their transformations.[4] For the interior designer, the chemist's focus on color as substance may be of more importance than the physicist's focus on color as light. The designer most often deals with color as substance, or matter—in other words, with how color is produced as a reflection of a colored object or surface. Tangible substances significant to the realm of the designer include both natural and artificial dyes, colorants, pigments, stains, and paints. As discussed in Chapter 3, the primary colors of substance are red, yellow, and blue. When they are combined in equal amounts, black, or the lack of color for substance, is created, although the actual result may appear to be a muddy brown or gray, depending on the impurities in the substance. The way colors of substances are produced from the primaries red, yellow, and blue is called the **subtractive theory of color** (Figure 4.5).

The reshaping of the rainbow of colors into a circular pattern, a **color wheel**, provides a useful tool for organizing color. These color wheel systems, discussed in greater detail later in this chapter, generally depict 12 principal hues. Combinations of the three primaries

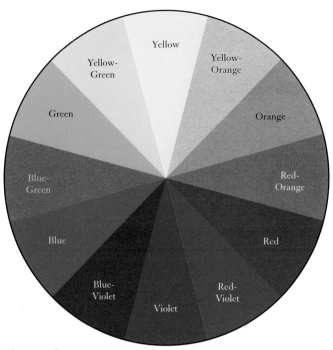

Figure 4.6
The 12-hue color wheel, showing primary, secondary, and tertiary colors.

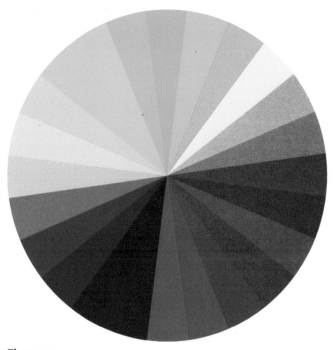

Figure 4.7
The extended, or 24-color, wheel.

(red, yellow, and blue) produce the three secondary hues: orange, green, and violet. When a primary and secondary color are mixed, six tertiary hues are created: yellow-orange, yellow-green, blue-green, blue-violet, red-violet, and red-orange (Figure 4.6).

The warm colors are yellow-green, yellow, yellow-orange, orange, orange-red, and red. The cool colors are red-violet, violet, violet-blue, blue, blue-green, and green. Because hues exist on a continuum, with no distinct lines of separation, artists and designers often find themselves disagreeing on the point at which yellow-green, or even green, starts to become cool or red-violet starts to appear warm.[5]

The mixing of a tertiary hue with a secondary or a primary one produces another extension. For example, yellow-orange mixed with orange produces yellow-orange-orange; yellow with yellow-orange produces yellow-yellow-orange. When all the combinations of a tertiary with a primary or secondary are mixed in this way, the number of hues expands to 24. This extended level is referred to as the **quaternary** level of colors (Figure 4.7). Beyond that, the distinctions become too subtle to describe by using the names of the hues.

These hues may be varied with the addition of black or white, resulting in a wider range of color. Adding white results in a higher value, producing a tint, whereas adding black results in a lower value, producing a shade.

In the mixing of color, the addition of gray alters chroma (see Chapter 3). Another way to lower chroma in a hue is by adding its complement, that is, the hue opposite it on the color wheel. The result is a tone of the hue. Thus, by mixing any of the various complements on the color wheel (Figure 4.8a–c), for example, red and green, a tone can be produced. The result will range from grayish to muddy brown or black, depending on the particular hues and their ratios. Another way to describe this process is **neutralization**. The colors that result are muted because the combination of opposites functions in the same manner as adding gray to a hue.

The subject of color includes the opposite concept of achromatic, or "no-color," hues. *Neutrals* is the common name for this group. Strictly speaking, the true definition of *neutral* is black, white, and the range of grays that officially are not hues. The grays are mixtures of black and white in varying ratios and are called **neutral grays**. The value of the gray may change, but the saturation is always the same. They include no colorant.

The various color systems discussed later in this chapter, including the Munsell system,[6] provide a

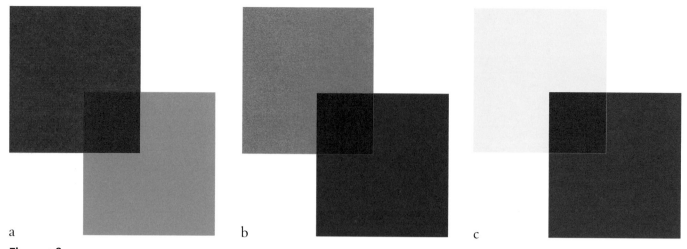

Figure 4.8
Pairs of complements mixed to neutralize a hue, creating a tone. a. Red and green; b. Orange and blue; c. Yellow and violet.

range of neutrals on a scale generally between 0 and 10 to illustrate the intervals of value. (White is 10, and black is 0, with the range of neutral grays in between.) Experimenting with white and black paint to create your own gray scale provides a valuable lesson in appreciating the subtleties involved with gray. For instance, it takes many drops of white to make black appear lighter, whereas only a small amount of black needs to be added to white to greatly lower its value.[7] Additionally, because paints are not pure black or white, some variation will exist between the gray scale produced with this exercise and those of other systems, including Munsell (Figure 4.9).

The neutral gray scale is used as a point of reference to judge the equivalent values of hues. Compare a colored fabric or commercial paint chip with a neutral gray scale. Slide the color swatch alongside the gray scale until you find a value that is equivalent to one of the gray values; when the edges appear to blur the most, you are at the appropriate point. Once mastered, this technique can be a tool for matching tones to create a certain type of color scheme. It takes practice to train your eye; usually, it is easier to determine the values of dull colors than those of bright hues.

In contrast to neutral gray, the term **warm gray** denotes the mixture of gray with some yellow or red. A **cool gray** has some blue or violet.

Neutrals also generally include ranges of brown. Labels such as *off-white*, *tan*, *cream*, and *beige* loosely identify versions of brown. **Brown** is defined as "any of a group of colors between red and yellow in hue, of

medium to low lightness, and of moderate to low saturation."[8] Brown, therefore, is a term that is an amalgam of various hues in different ranges of values and chromas (Figure 4.10). There are also mixtures of the ranges of brown with gray, sometimes referred to as **taupe** or **greige**, with the former having a lower value and the latter a higher value.

Physiology

The branch of science called physiology is concerned with the human perception of matter. For humans to recognize color, three components are necessary: light, vision, and perception. The human eye is the sensory receptor by which information about light is collected. Like a camera lens, the lens of the eye focuses light on the retina. One layer of the retina is made up of light-sensitive receptor cells, known as cones and rods, which receive the image formed by the lens. The cones receive light for daytime vision; and the rods, for night vision. They then translate the light into signals that travel by way of optic nerves to the part of the brain that handles vision. The brain then processes the information about light into visual sensation (vision), or sight. Although not trained as a physiologist, the interior designer needs to become sensitive to physiological differences among people and to how these differences can influence their appreciation of design, including color (see Chapter 2).

The importance of color to the interior designer relates more to how a color is perceived than to its intrinsic physical properties. It is thought that people

Figure 4.9
Munsell neutral
gray scale.

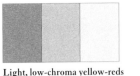

Light, low-chroma yellow-reds

Dark, low-chroma yellows

Dark yellow-reds

Figure 4.10
The various hues in different ranges of values and chroma levels
of brown.

are able to distinguish millions of hues in their various values and chromas. However, it is more practical to work from the basis that we perceptually combine these millions into a more manageable quantity. Perception is developmental and changes through the normal aging process. For instance, at birth, babies are not able to perceive hues, only black, white, and gray. This limitation results from the underdeveloped configuration of their rods and cones. Within a week's time, a baby sees his or her first hue: red. The color red, perhaps because it is the first hue seen, has significant physiological (and psychological) effects. Most people, when exposed to bright red, react physically with a measurably faster pulse and heartbeat and may even visibly turn red as their blood vessels expand. The psychological associations of red are explored later in this chapter.

The physiological changes in the eyes of elderly people also alter the perception of color. An older person may not be able to distinguish among hues that are dull. Incapacitation owing to injury or disease, such as cataracts or macular degeneration, which afflicts many elderly people, may alter color perception. There is also evidence that the eye's lens thickens and yellows, even in "normal" aging, so that it is less able to absorb the blue and violet portions of the spectrum. These are not simply aesthetic challenges for a designer. The use of low-contrast color schemes (discussed in more detail later in this chapter) or a reliance on tones may actually pose safety challenges. If a person is not able to distinguish between objects or planes, such as those of a floor, stair, or curb, safe walking is compromised.[9]

Sensitivity to the needs of a person with an emotional or mental illness includes an understanding of how color (and pattern) may help or hinder that person's response to the environment. For some, an environment of subdued colors, with few patterns, may provide a more calming experience than one that is overly active, with many contrasts of bright colors and patterns. For others, however, interiors that are subdued may further depress mood.

Color blindness, or **color deficiency**, is a genetic condition in which the cone receptors are diminished. It is more common among men than women. To varying degrees, a person with this condition has difficulty distinguishing the values of certain pairs of colors, generally red and green, both of which appear to resemble tones of gray. Recognizing this situation, an interior designer may need to accommodate the discrepancy, perhaps by limiting the use of these two hues for the client.

Related to perception of color is the role played by positioning of colors. **Simultaneous contrast** is one of many observations noted by the chemist Michel-Eugène Chevreul (1786–1889) in his position as the director of dyes at the Gobelins tapestry factory, near Paris. His understanding of the perceptions of color greatly influenced the Impressionist artists. Chevreul's findings demonstrate that to change the perception of a color, it is enough to change the color of its surroundings. Josef Albers, who headed the Department of Design at Yale University, later elaborated on the concept of simultaneous contrast, publishing the *Interaction of Color* in 1963.

There are three different ways in which colors influence each other when placed next to each other, or are simultaneously viewed. They do so by the three attributes of hue, value, and chroma (Figure 4.11).

- *Simultaneous contrast of hue*. Placing two colors next to each other causes the perception of differences in those colors that are not perceived when we look at them separately. For example, if violet is placed next to blue-green, it will appear more reddish than if it were placed next to red-violet, which will cause it to appear more bluish.
- *Simultaneous contrast of value*. A tint appears even lighter when placed next to a shade that is lower in value. Conversely, a shade will appear darker when placed next to a tint.

- *Simultaneous contrast of chroma*. Placing complements on the color wheel next to each other, for example, red and green, causes the intensity of each hue to intensify in saturation. However, when red is placed next to yellow, a hue that is closer to red on the color wheel, the red will lose some of its intensity, as will the yellow. Another way to manipulate the perception of a color's saturation would be to place the color against a gray background, which would result in a brighter appearance.

Other concepts that deal with the interactions between colors include afterimage, or successive contrast; optical mixing; vibrating color; and advancing and receding color.

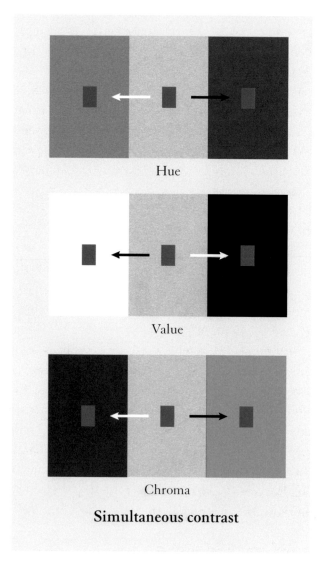

Hue

Value

Chroma

Simultaneous contrast

Figure 4.11
Simultaneous contrast of hue, value, and chroma.

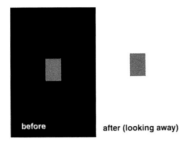

Figure 4.12
Successive contrast (afterimage): red and green.

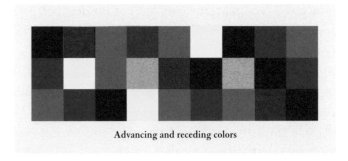

Advancing and receding colors

Figure 4.13
Advancing and receding hues.

Afterimage, or **successive contrast**: the perception of color is altered when colors are viewed in sequence (that is, successively), rather than simultaneously, or side by side. If we stare at an area of red, for example, and then focus on a white area, or merely close our eyes, a faint image (or afterimage) of green, its complement, will appear (Figure 4.12). It is as if the brain is seeking sensory equilibrium by balancing the intensity of one color with its opposite. This is one reason why surgical scrubs are green or blue-green: to neutralize the effect of red blood.

Optical mixing: when two contrasting colors in small quantities are placed side by side, because they cannot be perceived separately as two distinct hues they appear to mix and therefore neutralize. This phenomenon becomes important to the interior designer in selecting textiles.

Vibrating color: when strong contrasts of color with high saturation are juxtaposed, the eye does not adequately focus on the two, causing the edges of each hue to blur and shift. This phenomenon is most apparent in bold striped patterns, particularly in small spaces, where the stripes appear to move—an effect that can be very unsettling.

Advancing and receding colors: warm hues appear to advance, or move closer to the viewer, and cool colors seem to recede, or move farther away (Figure 4.13). Additionally, shades tend to recede, whereas tints tend to advance. An intense color advances, but a tone of that same hue will recede. Understanding the nature of color in this way affords the designer another tool for manipulating features of a space (in this case, its perceived volume) with choices for wall, ceiling, and floor finishes.

Psychology and Sociology

The branch of science that studies the mind and behavior is psychology.[10] Psychology includes specific fields of study relating to people both as individuals and as social beings (because we are part of cultures and other groups). An area that psychology examines is the emotional significance that different events, objects, or people hold for an individual. Emotional responses may be triggered by memories or perceptions surrounding occurrences experienced by an individual. These responses may be influenced by expectations and values that are held by an individual or that have symbolic associations.

It is the *meaning* of color for an individual that is important when we consider the psychology of color. We speak of someone as having "an emotional reaction" to a color. The preferences expressed by people concerning color in its myriad varieties may be categorized by expressions of love or hate more often than by those who say, "Don't care." As one color specialist has noted, "Colors are the catalyst for feelings, molding moods, and enhancing our lives."[11] Studies that concentrate on the emotional impact of color are used to market various products, forecast future trends, and help us better understand consumer reaction to a color.

Understanding the psychological meaning of color includes awareness that color is experienced within context and circumstance. For example, a person's reaction to red while in a hospital setting may be vastly different from his or her reaction to red when visiting a child in a kindergarten setting. Experiencing the color yellow-green for a short period while waiting for someone in a hotel lobby may be a positive or neutral experience, but a negative experience when one eats three meals a day in a room painted that color.

There are many contextual factors directing a person's response to color, including religious and generational differences. In Asia, white is the color of mourning, but it is the typical bridal color in the West, where black is worn for funerals. Many individuals of European ancestry consider it bad luck for a child or young adult to wear black; it has held connotations relating to death. Yet, with our world becoming smaller through technology, some of these traditions and taboos are fading.

The cultural or societal context of a color (which is more the subject of sociology) is of great significance because of symbolic references. Red, our most primary color, generates perhaps the greatest reaction. In earlier times, red dyes were expensive to produce and, therefore, a symbol of power and wealth. Today, red remains a symbol of good luck in China and India, to be worn at weddings to promote a couple's good fortune, including fertility. The power of red within a Western framework is more likely to be associated with seduction and sexuality.

Although some symbolism is universal such as blue signifying the color of the sky and/or water, the existence of cultural differences needs to be recognized. Table 4.1 summarizes symbolic associations of common hues in Western and Eastern cultures.

Moreover, practitioners of the Chinese art of Feng Shui base their ideas about color on the **bagua**, an ancient tool for understanding how the environment relates to life (see Figure 4.14):

- Red is the color of luck or good fortune.
- Yellow stands for self and health.
- Green represents exuberant growth and family.
- Brown is a color of contemplation and meditation.
- Pink connotes love, joy, happiness, and romance.
- Blue is associated with sky and water and symbolizes spirituality, understanding, tranquility, and composure.[12]

There are also psychological associations widely attributed to neutrals. Pure white is thought to represent purity, innocence, and cleanliness. Black denotes drama, depression, and death. Dark grays may convey a sense of authority or be foreboding. Light grays may be viewed as bland. Brown is associated with earthiness.

	West	**East**
Red	Danger Passion Love	Good luck Happiness Celebration Fertility
Orange	Healthy Warning Active	Healthy Happiness Cheerful
Yellow	Expansive Sunny Optimistic	Wealth Power Masculinity
Green	Nature Serenity Soothing	Youthful Prosperity Infidelity
Blue	Traditional Soothing	Immortality
Violet	Spiritual Creative Royalty	Inner peace Wealth
Black	Death and mourning	Water
White	Purity Innocence	Death Mourning

Table 4.1
Color Associations in Western and Eastern Cultures

Fig. 4.14
Bagua color wheel as used by Feng Shui practitioners. (© *Anton Zimarev | Dreamstime.com*)

Additional Theories

There is growing interest in an approach to the meaning of color that attributes colors to corresponding body organs and functions as well as studying the healing properties of color.

Drawing on the findings of Semyon Kirlian, a Russian electronics technician in the 1950s, the child development specialist and interior designer Antonio Torrice described these associations. Torrice found that children spontaneously pick color preferences that correspond to a physical part of their anatomy that is either still developing or deficient[13] (Figure 4.15).

Chakra, from the Sanskrit word meaning "wheel," is a system that considers seven zones of spiritual energy that begin with the base of the spine or groin and that conclude at the head or crown. These zones correspond to auras—spiritual energies in various wavelengths that surround a person, similar to a faint halo. The auras, in turn, correspond to the colors ROYGBIV (red, orange, yellow, green, blue, indigo, and violet). In other words, like Newton's prism, the body is believed to refract energies. Each of the auras and zones also corresponds to specific bodily functions, thought processes, and psychological traits. For example, violet, located at the highest point of the body, the crown, is the most spiritual of auras. The base of the spine and the groin are the least spiritual. Their auras are red.

Chromatherapy is a method of alternative medicine in which healing is achieved through color and is related to a holistic approach to design. For interior designers it is important to be thoughtful regarding the amount of color, its saturation and value, as well as the balance of contrast, including both cool and warm tones.[14]

COLOR SYSTEMS

Many different color systems are used by designers and artists as tools for organizing color theory into practical applications. Many systems used today help artists and designers communicate generally accepted understandings about color—its sequence from cool to warm, the principal hues, and the relationships of hues to one another—that can be used to create harmonious schemes.

An example is the color wheel developed by David Brewster (1781–1868), a Scottish physicist, which was later modified by Louis Prang, an American printer, lithographer, and publisher. Various manufacturers produce several color wheels commercially, but most are based on the 12-hue wheel of the Brewster-Prang system. Albert Munsell (1858–1918), an American artist and educator, developed a comprehensive system to understand color (Figure 4.16). However, because

Figure 4.15
Antonio Torrice's "body" colors.

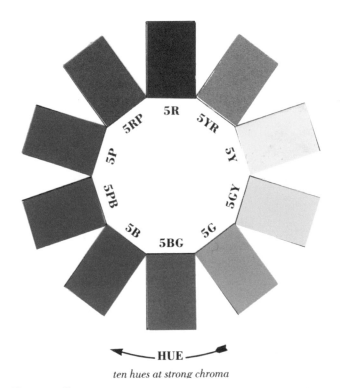

HUE

ten hues at strong chroma

Figure 4.16
Munsell color wheel.

Munsell used a system based on only 10 hues, there are some confusing discrepancies when the Munsell system is compared with the standard 12-hue color wheels based on the Brewster-Prang system.

Other color systems serve as tools for interior designers as well as designers in other specialties, particularly graphics and fashion. Among these systems are the Color-Aid and the Pantone systems.

Color's Relationship to Other Design Elements and Principles

Light and texture significantly interact with and affect color, both as independent agents and as partners. For example, a color may be selected based on a matte surface, such as a chip of flat paint with no sheen. When one is viewing a chip that has the same hue, but a glossy surface, the color will appear markedly different. The way in which light reflects off both surfaces will differ, creating significant changes in the hue.

A deeply textured object (highly dimensional) will absorb more light than a faintly textured object. The shadows created by the light influence the characteristic of the hue (Figure 4.17). The angle and quality of light also have a significant impact on the way a color reads, or is perceived.

Iridescence is a lustrous effect of light and color mixing, resulting in a rainbowlike array of colors (Figure 4.18). This effect may be created when light, natural or artificial, refracts off a surface that is slick, either as a natural condition or in a manufactured product designed to cast that effect. Colorants mixed with metal components create yet another special effect because the play of light with that surface will change both components.

The amount of light that is transmitted through a material will influence its character, as will adding a colorant to a translucent, or transparent, object. Tinting window glass with a color, which may be done to reduce glare or heat, will give a slightly different cast to the hues in a room.

Designers often choose which of the two elements, texture or color, will be dominant. If a space is designed with little color or with a very subtle range of values and chromas, greater interest may be provided through use of varied textures. Or, conversely, color may be played up while the texture is played down.

Daylight

Cool white fluorescent

Incandescent

Figure 4.17
The effect of various types of light on color.

Figure 4.18
Iridescent glass mosaic tile.
*(Photographer: Marci Brandt
Portland, Oregon)*

As with any other element, viewing color from a distance reduces its apparent scale; **fusion**, or optical mixing, occurs. For example, a carpet that appears to be made up of small green and red fibers when viewed up close will read as muddy brown when experienced from a realistic distance and installed in the actual space.

The principles of design may be influenced by color choices as well[15] (see Chapter 3). Perception of visual weight is critical to balance, and color may be influential in this equation. For example, cool colors appear to be heavier (that is, less luminous) than warm colors, which are perceived as lighter (that is, more luminous). According to Ron Reed in *Color + Design,* "Interior spaces are generally more accepted and pleasing to the user when small amounts of intense color are balanced by larger amounts of duller color."[16] In other words, proportion, or the relationship of parts to a whole (in this case, color as part of a space), is a factor in color selection, type, and quantity.

Recalling the quality of movement in the principle of rhythm, color alternations and progressions visually direct us through a space. Similarly, a focal point may be derived by color choice; even a small, dark object placed in a contrasting, stark white space will command attention. Finally, a discussion on the relationship of color to harmony, the culmination of our understanding of design elements and principles, follows.

COLOR HARMONY SCHEMES

A designer's experience and confidence will be enhanced by a knowledge of color theory and the guidelines that follow. Color systems provide both a starting point and a framework in which to operate. Differences in a designer's (and client's) temperament, talents, and comfort level concerning color will determine how strictly principles of design are applied in the use of color.

For many interior designers, color theory and application become a career specialty. Some serve other designers as consultants or collaborators. Many artists and designers from different fields become involved with associations and organizations that are concerned with color as an impetus for marketing and trend forecasting. (Chapter 13 discusses color in relation to trends and the forecasting associations that predict palettes.)

The design principle of harmony is nature's way of saying that something makes sense (see Chapter 3). The natural environment provides a timeless guide and a source of inspiration for color schemes. One approach might be to devise a harmonious palette by

Figure 4.19
Nature inspires color palettes. a. An autumn scene demonstrates a warm analogous scheme; b. The Scarlet Macaw, a primary triadic scheme. *(a: Photographer: Ian Britton/freefoto.com; b: Provided by the Author)*

replicating the array of colors in autumn leaves (Figure 4.19a) or the primary color scheme of a beautiful bird (Figure 4.19b). Could we then say that any combination of color has potential? Yes. However, having a framework for narrowing the choices from infinity to an exciting but manageable array of options makes sense.

A first step in organizing this approach to color schemes is to distinguish between those that use colors that are related and those that use contrasting colors. Simply put, **related color schemes** are derived by focusing on unifying, or similar, attributes of the selections, whereas **contrasting color schemes** depend on the differences among the choices. Generally speaking, the related schemes are considered more calming and stable, whereas contrasting schemes are more dynamic and active. Given all the possible variations within these two broad categories, there is plenty of room for choices within both. In fact, the two main distinctions are best viewed as representing a continuum between unity and variety.

Both related and contrasting color schemes may be executed in a choice of hues in the high-value range, called **high key**, or in the low-value range, called **low key**. Hues that fall in between may be referred to as a **mid-value scheme**. Achromatic schemes and accent schemes may fall into either category of related or contrasting schemes.

Related Schemes

Two commonly used related schemes are monochromatic and analogous schemes. Achromatic and accent color schemes may also be related.

Monochromatic Color Schemes Schemes derived from the use of only one hue are called **monochromatic color schemes**. In the context of hue, the word *monochromatic* is somewhat misleading. The prefix *mono* means "one"; however, the values and chromas of the one hue may be multiple. It may help you to think of this category as a "monohuematic" scheme. A monochromatic color scheme may be devised of hue variations of many different values and chroma levels to avoid monotony. Any of the hues may serve as the basis for this type of related color harmony scheme. With only a single color making a statement, the physiological and psychological associations of that hue must be considered before it is selected.

The temperature of a color may serve as a criterion for selection. The choice of a hue on the warm side of the color wheel will have different effects from a choice among the cooler hues. Figure 4.20 demonstrates the division of the 12-color wheel into six warm

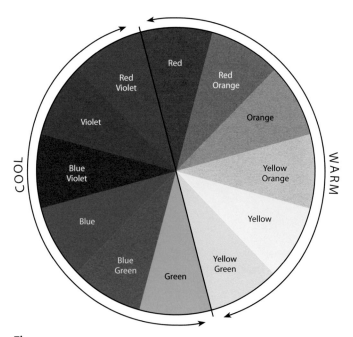

Figure 4.20
Cool and warm hues on a 12-color wheel.

Figure 4.21
Monochromatic color schemes. a. Warm; b. Cool. *(Interior design by Author)*

and six cool hues. Figure 4.21a and b shows interiors in each temperature zone.

Analogous Color Schemes The approach to harmony derived from combining hues adjacent to each other on the color wheel is called an **analogous color scheme**. Because several different color wheels are available, with differing numbers of hues,[17] it makes more sense to describe an analogous scheme as a range of adjacent hues that remain in one temperature zone, rather than solely by the number of adjacent hues. In this way, an analogous scheme would be further described as warm or cool, not both.

Hues exist on a continuum, and those close to a change in temperature usually read as either warm or cool. It is therefore recommended that an analogous scheme contain no more than five hues, even though

each temperature zone technically includes six. For example, a range from red to yellow would clearly read warm; a range from green to violet would clearly read cool. If a sixth hue were added to each range—yellow-green to the warm and red-violet to the cool—the schemes based on these ranges might seem to be contrasting, not analogous.

A cool analogous scheme may be chosen to offset the effects of a space in a very hot climate or an interior with a southern exposure. Conversely, a warm analogous scheme may be devised to offset the coldness of a climate or of a northern exposure (Figure 4.22a and b).

Analogous color schemes tend to evoke a sense of permanence, calm, and stability. They are often used for spaces that provide for extended occupancy rather than for occasional use.

Figure 4.22
Analogous color schemes. a. Warm; b. Cool. *(Interior design by Author)*

Contrasting Schemes

The types of color schemes that employ contrast include complementary, triadic, achromatic, and accent schemes. Contrasting color schemes will, by their very nature, include both warm and cool temperature zones, some with more extreme contrasts than others.

Complementary Color Schemes One type of contrasting harmony that provides a sense of activity and motion is produced by **complementary color schemes**. Within this category are actually three subsets of schemes.

Direct complementary color schemes use two hues that appear in direct opposition on the 12-hue color wheel. The most commonly used are a combination of a primary and a secondary color; but the possibilities also include two opposite tertiary hues, such as red-violet and yellow-green.

Which pair of complements is selected will make a difference in the level of contrast. Colors differ as to when they reach their strongest **luminosity**. In other words, hues reach their strongest chroma, or trueness, at different value levels. At one extreme, yellow reaches its truest, or most yellow, state at a high value. Its opposite, violet, reaches its most violet state at a lower value. When we look at the color wheel, we may perceive the yellow as lighter, as if it has some white tinting it, whereas violet may appear to have some black added. Therefore, when pairing true yellow and true violet, the designer is establishing a highly contrasted direct complementary scheme. This combination is dramatic. Another way to grasp this concept is to visualize mixing paint. Adding one drop of violet to a tablespoon of yellow paint causes a dramatic change, whereas the converse hardly matters. Juxtaposing blue and orange produces less contrast than juxtaposing

Figure 4.23
Direct complementary color scheme. *(Interior design by Author)*

Figure 4.24
Split complementary color scheme. *(Interior design by Author)*

yellow and violet. Green and red as a pair provides even less contrast (Figure 4.23).

Reducing the tonal intensity of one or two of the hues or providing shifts in value will lessen the contrast in the scheme. In other words, reduced chroma levels and closer values are more restful and calming in their effects.

Split complementary color schemes downplay the effect of contrasting complementary colors. Rather than using two hues that are directly opposite each other on the color wheel, as in a direct complementary scheme, three hues are chosen. The combination of three hues softens the blow, so to speak. After one hue is selected, rather than heading directly across the color wheel, the designer chooses the two hues on either side of the opposite point. For example, if green were to be selected, instead of using red, its direct complement, the two hues adjacent to red—red-orange and violet-red—would be

selected. Geometrically, the choices form a triangle in which two of the sides are equal in length, and the third is shorter; an isosceles triangle (Figure 4.24).

As with all the schemes depicted so far, the degree of contrast is also affected by the variations in value and chroma.

Double complementary color schemes use two pairs of complementary colors, for example, red and green combined with violet and yellow.

Tetrad color schemes are a variation of the double complementary scheme. They also use four hues, but the hues are equidistant from one another on the color wheel, geometrically forming a square on the color wheel. An example would be a scheme of violet, yellow, blue-green, and red-orange.

Double complementary and tetrad schemes must be controlled carefully. If the chroma and values differ too much, the scheme might appear too random.

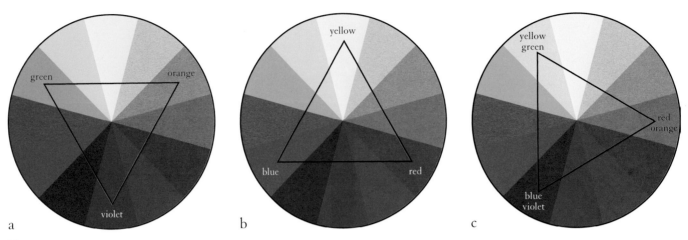

Figure 4.25

Triadic color schemes. a. Orange, green, violet; b. Red, yellow, blue; c. Red-orange, yellow-green, blue-violet.

Triadic Color Schemes Hues that are combined to create **triadic color schemes** form an equilateral triangle on the color wheel, in which all three sides are equal. The three hues are equidistant from one another. Typical schemes include the three primary colors, red, yellow, and blue. More subtle variations include the three secondary colors or tertiary colors (Figure 4.25a–c).

When accomplished through pure chroma, triadic schemes are very active, playful, and cheerful. The use of the primary triadic scheme for children's activity rooms reflects this concept. Creativity is stimulated in the presence of bold primaries. Some people may consider unadulterated colors brash and primitive; others enjoy the original and basic qualities of the primary colors from which all others emanate. Even a triadic scheme made up of red, yellow, and blue can be tamed by altering tones and values, creating a complex and sophisticated palette perhaps more widely accepted by adults. While maintaining some level of contrast and motion, the pace is slowed down (Figure 4.26a and b).

Achromatic Schemes Strictly speaking, **achromatic color schemes** are composed of white, black, and gray, with no hue. An achromatic scene that is related includes a series of grays that are close in value. When a scheme is composed of only black and white or grays of very different values, this combination creates a contrasting scheme. Because black represents the lowest value and white the highest, the contrast is extreme. Additionally, because low values recede, and high values advance, the result is a very active and dramatic composition (Figure 4.27).

An achromatic scheme that uses gray, alone or in combination with black, white, or both, may produce a calm effect. However, in taking this approach one risks designing a static and cold space. But a wide range of neutral grays may provide interest when there are other contrasting elements, such as style, texture, and form (Figure 4.28a).

An achromatic scheme may be devised that includes neutralized versions of any hues in the warm or cool spectrum. The first impression may be that an achromatic scheme is relatively easy to accomplish. However, given the subtleties involved with gray, and its values and undertones, it is actually difficult to arrive at a harmonious combination. Although similar, warm and cool grays often do not work well together.

When successfully implemented, achromatic color schemes provide a wonderful backdrop for certain applications. When the merchandise in a store is to be accented and considered the main color for the space, an achromatic interior puts the emphasis on the merchandise. Likewise, an interior that features colorful artwork will be well served with this type of color scheme.

Materials that may inspire the black, white, and grays for achromatic schemes include metals, such as steel, chrome, and iron, and stone, such as concrete, granite, cement, and marble.

Although generally listed among the achromatic schemes, harmonies produced with brown, tan, and beige are not, strictly speaking, achromatic. Similar to the neutralized hues mentioned earlier, this group is actually made up of various hues. These hues usually fall into the warm side of the color wheel. This color harmony scheme is often called a **neutral color scheme**.

a

b

Figure 4.26
Triadic color schemes. a. Saturated; b. Toned. *(Interior design by Author)*

Figure 4.27
Dramatic (high-key) achromatic color scheme for an interior. *(Interiors by KAA Design; Photographer: Erhard Pfeiffer)*

Figure 4.28
a. Achromatic scheme in neutral grays of varied values; b. Warm neutral color scheme for a contract space. *(a: © Arcaid Images / Alamy; b: Tony Chi, designer for Intercontinental Hotel, Geneva)*

Considering nature as an inspiration for color schemes, it is easy to see the appeal of this combination. Earth, with its variety of warm hues, is identified psychologically with nurturance, solidity, and centeredness. As with schemes that use mainly gray, one risks the possibility of monotony and stagnation. However, if one considers the full range available in the various hues of beige and brown, this color scheme need not be boring. A subtly executed neutral color scheme can be sophisticated rather than static. Materials that suggest this scheme include terra-cotta, brick, wood, cork, and grasses such as bamboo, as well as metals, such as copper and bronze. The addition of varied forms and textures will enhance the vitality of a neutral scheme (Figure 4.28b).

Accent Schemes One way to alter any of the aforementioned schemes is to create an **accent color scheme**. This may be built upon a related, contrasting, or achromatic scheme. An accent color or a neutral may be introduced to offset an established scheme to make it less predictable. One approach is to introduce a second hue in a monochromatic scheme to relieve the sense of oneness that some viewers may find boring. Another approach is to introduce a hue into an achromatic scheme. Or, alternatively, a small amount of a complement may be added to an analogous or a monochromatic scheme. For instance, a room that is primarily based on various shades, tints, and tones of green may have red as an accent color. In a space that relies on saturated or deep colors, white woodwork provides relief to the visual intensity. Applying paint or stain to woodwork serves to accent, or make the details of a space's architecture stand out. An accent scheme may introduce a cool spot into a very warm room, or a ray of warmth into a cool room (Figure 4.29). (See *FYI . . . Choosing Color* for more suggestions and the role of color in design and *In the Spotlight: Color Confidence* for examples of designers, use of color.)

Figure 4.29
An accent scheme for an interior space in traditional blue and white is executed with a contemporary country twist by William Diamond and Anthony Baratta. *(Design by Diamond & Barratta; Photo: Michael Mundy)*

FYI . . . Choosing Color

Color selection overlays many other design decisions, several of which are suggested throughout this text. Some general considerations regarding color choice follow.

- *The occupants' associations with colors (perceived and actual, cultural and personal).* What are the psychological attributes they ascribe to color? Obtain an understanding of the clients' feelings associated with color.
- *Special considerations regarding the occupants.* As a result of the normal aging process, differences in perception are inevitable. The designer needs to be aware of genetic deficiencies as well as physical and mental conditions that could cause significant perceptual differences.
- *The purpose of the space and the activities to be carried out.* If the space is expected to host a high degree of activity and stimulation, consider more contrast. If the space is to accommodate rest, an approach that relies on relatedness, utilizing tones rather than high saturation, is advisable.
- *The amount of time to be spent in a space.* Is the intent of an eating area to encourage occupants to linger over a meal or to eat quickly? Is the interior of a bedroom designed for a one- or two-night hotel stay or for daily use?
- *The importance of the effect of color (and light) on skin tone.* In high-end clothing sales and the healing environments of health-care facilities, this sensitivity to color is crucial.
- *An appreciation for how flexible the space needs to be.* The degree of flexibility will depend on seasonal changes, transience in occupancy, and the clients' need for variety, growth, or other changes.
- *The character of a space, or its personality.* This is largely made or undermined by decisions about color.
- *Historical references to be reinforced through a particular color palette.* Designers and clients may want to make a statement about a particular period; similarly, they might choose to emphasize an idea of reform or forward thinking.
- *Decisions do not exist in a vacuum.* They are part and parcel of other decisions made concerning the elements and principles of designs.

In the Spotlight

Color Confidence

Some designers exude confidence and fearlessness in their color choices. Among them are Jamie Drake, Karim Rashid, and Eileen Kathryn Boyd.

Jamie Drake: "I love what I do. I love style in every form. There is nothing more exciting than incorporating bold, vibrant colors with a striking mix of genres and periods to create lively, magical spaces that inhabit memories and enrich lives.[a]

Figure a
Jamie Drake's design for a high-rise apartment above New York uses a palette of orange, pinks, blues, and blue-violets. (© *William Waldron*)

(continued)

Color Confidence, *continued*

Figure b
Karim Rashid's unabashed use of color in a contract space is seen here in the World Lounge, Istanbul, Turkey. *(Design: Karim Rashid; Photo: Cemal Emden)*

Karim Rashid: "I'm a big believer in strong color, because it heightens human emotion when you walk in."[b]

Eileen Kathryn Boyd: Color is not merely an outlet of personal expression, but rather a state of mind which infiltrates all that we are and do. Color and composition are inseparable; each client has a unique color story just waiting to be expressed.[d]

Sources:
[a] *"DesignTies Welcomes 'The King of Colour,' Jamie Drake."* DesignTies, *June 4, 2009, http://design-ties.blogspot.com/2009/06/designties-welcomes-king-of-colour.html,*
[b] *Craig Kellogg, "Walkthrough Healthcare,"* Interior Design, *February 2010.*
[c] *Adapted from Eileen Kathryn Boyd's website, www.ekbinteriors.com/.*

Figure c
Eileen K. Boyd's space for the Kips Bay Showhouse successfully combines saturated versions of secondary and tertiary hues. *(Courtesy of Eileen Kathryn Boyd Interiors)*

COLOR LANGUAGE

Throughout this chapter, color has been referred to in technical terms. This is to enable designers and students to communicate using a universally understood vocabulary. Painters working with oils as their medium develop a common language using the names of pigments relating to that medium. An interior designer who is also a painter may have to toggle between the two dialects. For instance, viridian is blue-green, alizarin is red-violet, and yellow ochre is a tone of yellow.

Producers and consumers of textiles, cosmetics, cars, personal products, and furnishings may use a different vernacular to identify colors. Some terms, including names of colors, are more readily acknowledged among a large number of people; others are more esoteric. For example, many people could agree on what is meant by *pastel pink, navy blue,* or *emerald green.* However, in today's global society, it can be difficult to determine which terms will be readily understood by your audience. What will *kelly green* mean to people from Eastern lands? One important reason to learn the technical attributes of color is to enhance clear communication.

As consumers and sellers of products and ideas review your designs, you will enliven the discussion by using more *colorful* names. Merchandisers and manufacturers are able to choose from or invent a seemingly limitless variety of names. Some names evoke an understanding based on the similarity of a color to a reference in nature; examples are jade, rust, spruce, straw, burgundy, and lavender. Others may be more regional or industry specific. Revlon's Fifth Avenue Red was a particular shade of nail polish and lipstick that was popular among the fashion-minded in the 1950s. Similarly, the homemaker shopping for a new refrigerator in the 1960s commonly understood the meaning of Harvest Gold.

HISTORICAL PALETTES

The study of color throughout history is limited by our knowledge of what existed in very early times. Our understanding of historical color schemes is a product of knowledge that has been preserved in one way or another. Modern technology used to analyze paints used in historic interiors and exteriors has helped further our knowledge of the true historical color palettes. It has furthered our understanding not only of *what* was used in a geographic region and *when,* but also of a color's meaning. Chapters 11 and 12 review the historical references to color as part of the history of style and furnishings. Chapter 13 explores the future trends of color.

Summary

Color is one of the most basic, yet most powerful, tools available to an interior designer. Throughout the ages, people have expressed themselves through the use of color. Color plays a major role in influencing a space such as establishing mood and altering the perception of a space's volume.

Color may be studied from many vantage points, including the various sciences of physics, chemistry, physiology, psychology, and sociology. A basic understanding of these viewpoints helps the interior designer to plan environments that enhance rather than hinder the experience of a space. There are many questions to be raised by the interior designer in choosing color, such as the lighting conditions under which color will be viewed, including the time of day, and the specifics of the existing conditions, such as northern or southern exposure.

Color has complex physical properties of both light and substance, and these properties influence the ways in which colors interact with one another and with other design elements. Emotional responses greatly affect the way in which color is experienced. These responses are influenced by personal, group, and cultural experiences, such as the differences between Eastern and Western cultures. Many systems have been developed to organize how we view colors. These systems provide a tool that designers can use when combining colors to create harmony. The resulting color schemes may be categorized as related, contrasting, achromatic, and accent schemes.

Manufacturers and marketers regularly assign their own commercial names to color. While not necessarily scientific, they add a distinct flavor to the conversation, such as Pantone 2012 color of the year *Tangerine Tango.* Colors used throughout history and future directions (trends) in color are the subjects of Chapters 11, 12, and 13.

Vocabulary

accent color scheme

achromatic color scheme

additive color

additive theory of color

advancing colors

afterimage (successive contrast)

analogous color scheme

bagua

brown

chromatherapy

color blindness (color deficiency)

color wheel

complementary color scheme

contrasting color scheme

cool gray

direct complementary color
   scheme

double complementary color
   scheme

fusion (optical mixing)

greige

high key (color range)

iridescence

low key (color range)

luminosity

mid-value scheme

monochromatic color scheme

nanometer (nm)

neutral color scheme

neutral gray

neutralization

optical mixing

quaternary level

receding colors

reflect

refract

related color scheme

selective absorption

simultaneous contrast

spectral theory of color

split complementary color
   scheme

subtractive color

subtractive theory of color

taupe

tetrad color scheme

triadic color scheme

vibrating color

visible spectrum

warm gray

wavelength

Exercise: A Color Scheme for a Celebrity's Bedroom

You may choose any of the following as your hypothetical client: the president of the United States; the governor of your state; your favorite designer, artist, or performer; or another person approved by your instructor. Conduct research to determine what your client's needs might be, based on his or her lifestyle and preferences. Consider the basic applications of color theory.

Write a brief description of your client (approximately 250 words), including the basics of the bedroom space, such as location and size; the desired mood and effect; and your approach to color in your design. Indicate whether you have chosen a related or contrasting color scheme and why. Describe the basic hues, values, and saturation. Use paint chips or color chips to signify your choices for the major components of the space, such as walls, ceilings, floors, fabrics, and furniture finish.

Exercise: Exploring the CD-ROM

Take advantage of the contents of the CD-ROM to increase your understanding of color schemes. Follow the instructions for Starting the CD-ROM on pages xix–xx and click on Chapter Four: Color Theory and Application.

Color Schemes in Nature: Select an image featuring a scene from nature that you find appealing, from any source (for example, a magazine or catalog). Visit a hardware or paint store and select paint chips representing the main hues in the image. Arrange the chips into a color harmony scheme and mount along with the image on a suitable size illustration board. For example, an autumnal scene might translate into a warm analogous scheme featuring a variety of tones, tints, and shades of yellow, yellow-orange, and orange.

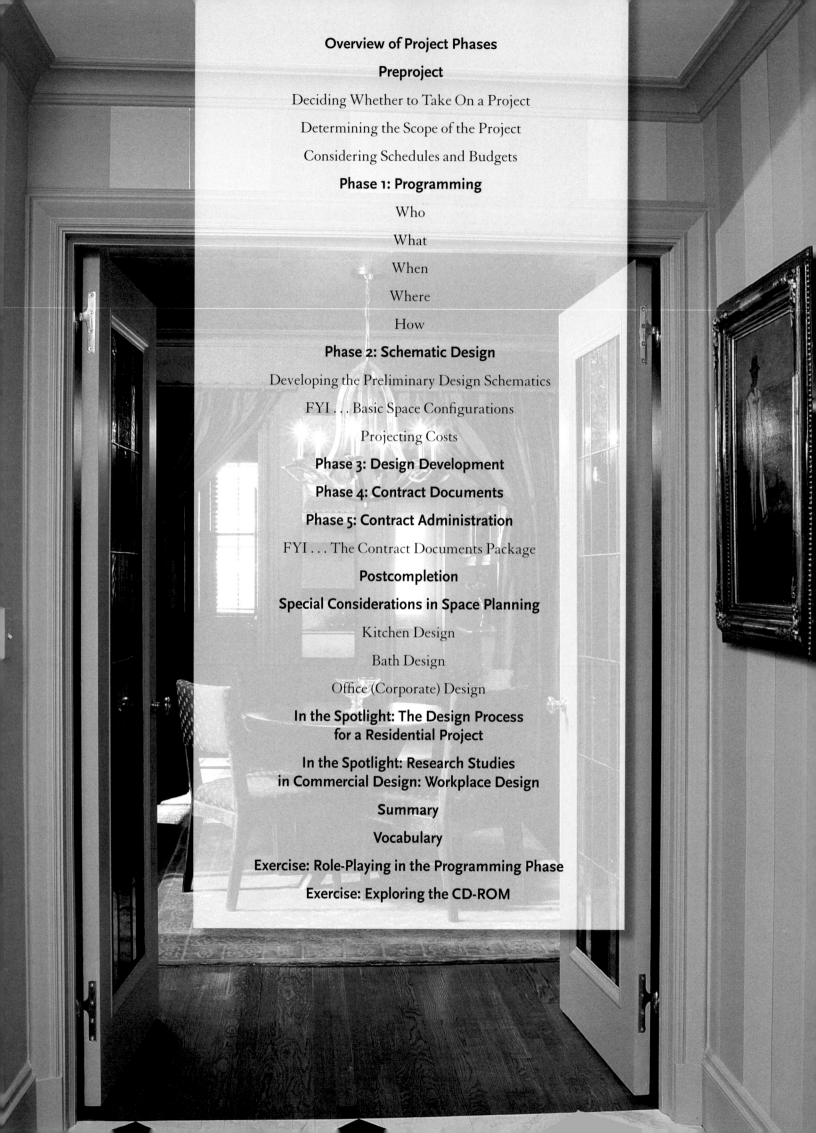

CHAPTER 5

The Design Process

Rome wasn't built in a day, nor are most interior design projects. Each project is taken through a series of steps. Many projects flow in a logical sequence, whereas at other times steps occur concurrently. Some projects go through a full series of stages, from project engagement to post-completion. Others go through only some of the steps. The scope or size of a project, the degree of design involvement (e.g., from demolition through furnishings), or the level of complexity (e.g., single use or multipurpose) may determine the number of steps, requiring only limited involvement or a full range of services on the part of an interior designer.

In Figure 5.1a the fitness facility demonstrates collaboration between architect and interior designer. In contrast, the furnishing of the bedroom in Figure 5.1b was a project undertaken by a sole interior designer.

In a small firm or a firm with only one interior designer, the lead designer is in charge of project management. In larger firms a separate **project manager** may be assigned to manage the phases of a project to ensure not only that a prescribed work plan is developed, but also that the project is executed according to that plan and in a timely manner. The project manager also makes certain that all **deliverables** are completed. Examples of deliverables are floor plans and other drawings. Another responsibility of the project manager is to see that the project stays within budget.

This chapter presents a breakdown of the various phases of a design project. The creative process may seem to unfold instinctively (as it does on so

Figure 5.1
a. An example of a large design project, Deloitte's corporate fitness center located in downtown Manhattan; b. Master bedroom for a residential interior design project. *(a: Walter Dufresne. Photographer/Designed by Lothrop Associates LLP; b: Interior design by Author; photo by Peter Dressel)*

many so-called reality television shows); however, most projects evolve through thoughtful planning, collaboration, and execution.

OVERVIEW OF PROJECT PHASES

Interior designers, whether working independently or as part of a larger team, delineate the various phases of a project in commonly accepted ways, although some variations exist among professionals and for different types of projects. A system of outlining the various phases helps communicate common expectations for clients, interior designers, and other interested parties—milestones for completion of design profes-

sionals' responsibilities on the project and measures of project completion for billing purposes.

Here, I present one commonly used approach to organizing the interior design process, spelling out the tasks involved under each of the five essential phases described. This approach serves as a foundation for a contract or agreement between a client and an interior designer (see Chapter 14). The following list summarizes the key tasks in each phase:

1. *Programming phase.* Through data gathering and analysis, a designer determines the requirements that need to be met, culminating in a design concept that expresses the proposed character of the space. A written program or plan of action is developed as well as preliminary budget estimates and projected time schedules.
2. *Schematic design phase.* Drawings and other documents are prepared to depict the design concept and solutions, including the formulation of ideas for space allocation, layouts for furniture and equipment, and types of finishes to be used.
3. *Design development phase.* Drawings and other documents are refined and executed to scale, with greater detail for client approval. Preliminary budget estimates may be revised at this time.
4. *Contract documents phase.* The requirements for both interior construction and furnishings are documented for the client's written approval. When necessary, the designer assists the client with the bidding, procurement, and selection process for contracted goods and services.
5. *Contract administration phase.* This phase involves the execution of the design plans, including oversight of work performed by tradespeople, to see that they are consistent with the design concept. The purchase, delivery, and installation of goods—which may be a significant part of this phase for the interior designer—are discussed more fully in Chapter 14.

This chapter adds two steps, one before the project begins (**preproject**) and one following project completion (**postcompletion**). Unless a student is involved in an internship program or has had on-the-job experience, he or she will not experience the final stage of the contract administration phase, which includes purchasing and installation, or the postcompletion step.

PREPROJECT

Because the many hours spent before a project actually begins are, indeed, part of the project, I include an additional step. This preproject step may be thought of as similar to the prologue of a play. It is the step at which the relationship between a prospective client and an interior designer is established.

Projects and clients may come to a designer or a design firm in any number of ways, such as a referral from a previous client or as the result of advertising. Sometimes, a prospective job turns into a project rather easily and quickly; other times, the process may be more complicated. Networking and marketing techniques are explored in Chapter 14.

Deciding Whether to Take On a Project

Many leads do not turn into jobs for a variety of reasons. For instance, a prospective client may have preconceptions about what is involved in an interior design project, but, after initial discussions with an interior designer, may not feel ready to proceed. Or, a prospective client may not realize the time and money involved in a particular renovation or refurbishing.

Whether or not an interior designer has the same taste or style as a prospective client, a rapport between the two should be established for the process to flow. Some clients look to a designer to make most or all the decisions; others bring their own definite preferences. A designer may turn down a job if it involves potentially litigious or unethical situations. For example, someone might ask a designer to sidestep the process of seeking any necessary building permits or ask that the designer not bill sales tax when it is required.

Determining the Scope of the Project

During the first meeting with a prospective client, the designer attempts to determine the scope of the project, recognizing that it may evolve along the way. For example, is the project to include demolition and construction or space planning and furnishings? Which rooms or areas of the space are within the scope of the project? Are there areas of priority that should be considered first? It is also at this early stage that the client and designer discuss the scope of the designer's role.

The designer may determine that other consultants, such as architects, engineers, or contractors, need to be retained, or the client may already have contracted for these services. Specialists, such as lighting designers and acoustical experts, may also need to be part of the project.

Considering Schedules and Budgets

Although many factors, such as manufacturing delays, may take scheduling out of the control of an interior designer, the subject of time frame needs to be addressed during this preliminary stage. Many projects are time sensitive; they must be completed in time to meet occupancy needs. For example, company executives responsible for the relocation of their staff need to feel confident that the project will be managed in a way that ensures the target move-in date will be met—or, that, worst-case scenario, the design team will come up with satisfactory alternative solutions. The scheduling requirements of specific clients, such as health-care facilities, become paramount because any inconvenience to the users of the facility may be unacceptable. For residential clients who are selling one home and moving into another, a target completion date is also essential.

One cannot predict the future or happenstance; however, a competent interior designer, as a project manager, must assess whether and how he or she can meet the prospective client's needs. One must consider the number of staff or freelance assistants needed for the project and take into account work already underway for other clients.

At this preproject stage, while budget parameters and completion target dates are discussed, it is wise to treat these factors as merely broad stroke estimates and goals. Throughout the process, revisions to both may be made as client and designer agree on adjustments.

There are several ways in which designers charge for their services (see Chapter 14). The scope of services, responsibilities of designer and client, and many other factors become part of the contract or letter of agreement drawn up and signed by both the client and the interior designer. Once the scope of the project is determined, along with the method of compensation and other major areas previously mentioned, a contract is written to document these and other items and signed by all relevant parties. Generally, the client pays the designer a **retainer**, or deposit for services to be rendered, and this payment is included with the signed contract. It is then that the design process officially begins.

PHASE 1: PROGRAMMING

Programming means the scope of work, which includes conducting research; identifying and analyzing the needs and goals of the client or occupant(s) of the space, or both; evaluating existing documentation and conditions; assessing project resources and limitations; identifying life, safety, and code requirements; and developing project schedules and budgets.[1]

The key components of this initial phase are to:

- Ascertain, review, and document the applicable requirements of the project, including: personnel, space, furniture, furnishings, and equipment needs
- Prepare a budget and schedule
- Provide a written program of the requirements

This first official phase of a project may take different forms, depending on the nature of the project, but it will always be a critical step. It includes examining and documenting the existing conditions about the site and space; the client profile; and the occupant or user requirements, such as the functions to be accommodated in the space. For commercial, or contract, spaces, interviews with several people may be conducted as well as **desk audits** (review of a company's organizational chart, policies, practices, and procedures). Budget and time constraints and planning for sustainability should also be part of this initial analysis.

Existing conditions is a term used to describe the architectural features of the site. **Field measurements**, or *field survey*—measurements of the space conducted on-site, including ceiling height, doors, and windows—may be done, with special note taken of electrical outlets, heating and ventilation features, wall and floor finishes, architectural features, environmental concerns, natural lighting conditions, and so on

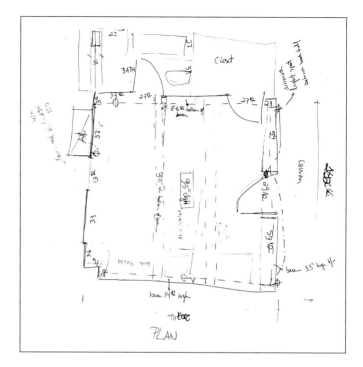

Figure 5.2
On-site (field) measurements and notes. *(Courtesy of Freya Block)*

(Figure 5.2). Survey of the existing furniture and equipment that may remain in the space may also be done. Techniques for recording this information will be explored in Chapter 6.

For medium- to large-size contract projects it is generally advisable at this point to have consultation from other disciplines, including architecture; engineering; and other specialties, such as acoustics, fire and safety, building code compliance, and so forth.[2]

An interior designer may be involved in a project at a time when a client is first making the decisions to have the space built. In that case, the existing conditions may include how the property is **sited** (that is, located or positioned, such as northern or southern exposure), and the designer may make suggestions regarding placement of entrances and windows and other structural decisions.

Local ordinances, such as those relating to barrier-free access, may influence interior design planning. A review of applicable laws should occur as part of the assessment of existing conditions.

It is useful to take photographs during this phase, to serve both as documentation for marketing purposes, such as "before" and "after" comparisons (Figure 5.3a and b), and as a reminder of features of the

Figure 5.3
Before and after photos taken show a hallway renovated into a dining room. *(a and b: Designer John A. Buscarello, ASID. Photographer: Atusushi Tomioka)*

space, to enhance note taking that will be used in design development. Inherent in this phase is the concept of planning. This is the stage of research, data collection, and analysis.

Think of the word *program* as a script for a performance. A program begins with the **design concept**. This is a generalized idea, or vision, not only of how the interior will look, but also of how it will serve the users. The program then outlines the order to be followed (just as Act I, Scene 1, does for a play), the features to be presented (the set, the dialogue), and the people participating (the cast of characters). It is a **plan**, or system by which action may be taken toward a goal. One might say this is the *who, what, when, where,* and *how* of the design project.

Who

Who are the parties involved? There are times when a designer may have a contract to perform interior design services with a party other than the user of the

space. Consider the following example. The party to whom the designer is responsible is the owner of a restaurant. The designer must have an understanding of the needs and desires of not only the owner and the staff to be employed, but also the restaurant patrons, or the targeted market the owner would like to attract: the **end users**.

What are the characteristics of the occupants? Researchers use the term *demographics* to characterize individuals or groups of individuals. Such traits as age, sex, marital status, occupation, and income level are considered. One restaurant owner might describe his or her clientele as "young, upscale urban professionals, mainly singles in their 20s and 30s." Another restaurateur might cater to a distinctly different group of users, such as "suburban, blue-collar families in the moderate income level, with preschool and school-age children." The target market of a fast-food restaurant will have requirements different from those of customers seeking to linger over a leisurely late-evening meal.

Figure 5.4
Restaurant interiors. a. McDonald's restaurant in Serbia is an example of a fast-food restaurant; b. Casual fine dining at Proof restaurant at 21C Hotel, Louisville, Kentucky. *(a: White Packert/ GettyImages; b: © 2011 Kenneth Hayden, Louisville, Kentucky)*

The dining environment needs to be very different for these user groups (Figure 5.4a and b).

The human factors described in Chapter 2 are vitally important in programming. Physical requirements based on anthropometric, ergonomic, and proxemic factors; sensory experience; territoriality; and personalization will come into play in data gathering and analysis.

Furthermore, details that speak to the culture of the users may be important. As we saw in Chapter 2, many influences need to be considered in space planning and layout, among them cultural background. The particular style of a space may also be influenced by cultural background. Issues of personal style and lifestyle cut across the categories of "who" and "what" as we look at the how the occupants live and function in a space. Individual lifestyle preferences; interpersonal interactions; and corporate culture, including issues of status (think "corner office"), may all be additional ingredients in programming as well as needs for public versus private and enclosed versus open. The use of traditional Japanese shoji screens, featured in Figure 5.5, allows for flexibility in the alteration of space configurations as changes in use occur.

What

Data must be collected to understand the functions of a space. For a typical residential project, this information includes the types of rooms, areas, or zones that either have been constructed or need to be established and that will serve the basic universal functions: eating, sleeping, playing, and working.

Figure 5.5
Japanese-style space features movable shoji screens. *(© Roslyn Banish. All rights reserved)*

How discrete do the areas need to be? What areas might serve multiple functions? Considering the space limitations and lifestyle of many contemporary households, design solutions often must allow for multitasking. Does a room need to provide accommodations for overnight guests as well as a home office? Does a basement need to allow for a media area as well as a gymnasium? Does a garage need to offer additional storage?

Within each of the functional areas, additional questions may need to be asked. For example, consider the various ways in which the everyday function of eating is accomplished. Does the family cook meals or order takeout? When the family entertains, how many guests might be invited to dine? Will these meals be primarily sit-down dinners or buffet-style parties?

For an office situation, how does a manager plan to meet with his or her employees? Does he or she require a private area for conferencing or a space for team meetings? Are there issues of hierarchy or status? What provisions are required for amenities, such as lounge areas, cafeteria, and so on? Are support staff centrally located or assigned to specific units?

Are transitional spaces, such as entries, foyers, or lobbies, needed? How are people expected to experience a space upon entering and exiting?

Circulation patterns—that is, how people move around the space, including inside to outside; the direction of door swings; and the widths of corridors, hallways, and stairs—are also analyzed in this phase (Figure 5.6).

Many beginning steps in the allocation of space are directed by existing conditions, such as entries and exits and access to windows and light. The desire to have a space appear larger or the need for areas devoted to special interests, such as music or art, may be important considerations. The degree to which space must be conserved and storage requirements are other aspects to be considered in the allocation of space. An example of a design that maximizes storage and conserves space is the use of the area below a stairwell to create a home office/study. In Figure 5.7 a niche is devised out of a stairwell to create an office area that is located within the family's hub of activity.

Space allocation decisions must take into account the dimensions of furniture and equipment. Adaptability, flexibility, and preparedness for changing needs are also looked at in this phase (see Chapter 2).

When

There are at least two ways in which considerations of *when* influence a design project. The first is in relation to functions the user undertakes in certain interior

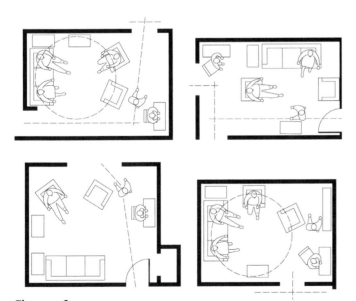

Figure 5.6
Circulation patterns to enable conversational behavior.

Figure 5.7
Home office in stairwell niche. (*Photograph by Phillip Ennis. Designed by Andrew Chary*)

areas. The designer's consideration of a specific area may center on the time of day at which activities usually occur. For instance, decisions about the lighting of an interior space are linked to the time of day when the area may be used. Use of a living room area primarily during the evening hours necessitates planning for sufficient artificial light. Similarly, the lighting plan for a restaurant and lounge needs to accommodate both daytime and late-night use.

The frequency of user activities may also be vital in determining space allotment. For instance, if overnight guests will be accommodated infrequently, it may not be appropriate, when overall interior space is limited, to allocate a substantial and separate guest room area. A more practical and appropriate plan may be to furnish a study area with a sofa bed. Figure 5.8 illustrates how an interior designer carves out areas in a loft to create an efficient multipurpose use of the space.

The second way in which time is considered throughout a project involves the necessity of keeping the various steps within the estimated time frame. As project management experience increases, the designer will be able to predict more easily and more accurately the time it will take for the steps to be completed. As with any phase of the process, schedules may need to be revisited throughout.

Where

Some decisions regarding where functions take place seem quite obvious, such as placement of the kitchen near the dining room or positioning of a bathroom door so that it does not open into the living area. However, other decisions about placement may be subtler. Understanding a client's lifestyle may help direct these relationships by establishing zones for the interior space and areas that define specific functions.

One main distinction is between open (free) and closed (discrete) planning. Modern open planning associated with early Western 20th-century notions may be seen as a breaking away from being "boxed in" by the constraints of the conventional enclosures of the discrete rooms typical of 19th-century Victorian houses (to be discussed further in Chapter 12).

Some contemporary houses are built on a grand scale, with open planning for an ample living area, referred to as a **great room**. Formerly called the Great Hall in medieval days (see Chapter 11), this space often combines the functions of socializing, entertainment, and dining and perhaps even includes study or work. Figure 5.9 illustrates one example of a residential floor plan for a great room.

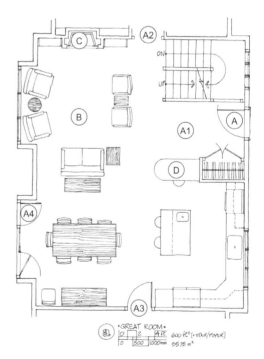

Figure 5.9
An example of a floor plan showing furniture placement for a residential great room. (Residential Interior Design: A Guide to Planning Spaces *by Maureen Mitton and Courtney Nysteun,* © *2011. Reproduced with permission of John Wiley & Sons)*

Figure 5.8
Combination office, den, and guest room. (© *Tim Lee Photography. Designed by Barbara Bell)*

Similar to the open plan of the great room is loft living. An early form of adaptive reuse, the loft was often an industrial space left basically intact that served as a reasonably priced alternative to more conventional apartments or studios. Today, loft living is considered a fashionable housing or work environment option and is in high demand (Figure 5.10a and b). Like the modern great room, lofts usually have high ceilings, and their large open areas encourage an approach to space planning that is less distinct (e.g., without walls), incorporating other techniques, such as varied floor levels or color, to designate different zones (Figure 5.11a and b).

This is in sharp contrast to the lifestyle represented by many types of houses, including town houses, in which smaller, discrete rooms dictate a very different approach to furniture layouts with spaces that are more private and intimate and that are dedicated to single functions, such as sleeping, reading, cooking, and dining.

Figure 5.10
a. A spacious residential loft with kitchen, dining, and living areas; b. Loft space converted for corporate use. *(a: Interior design by Meichi Peng. Photography: John Horner; b: Interior design by Meichi Peng. Photography: John Homer; b: Courtesy of OZ Architecture)*

Figure 5.11
Residential master bedroom suite. *(a and b: Photos by David Duncan Livingston, designed by Benning and Associates)*

Yet another housing trend is the allocation of space into **suites**, or adjoining rooms with related functions, which again implies multifunctional planning. The most common of these is the master bedroom suite, which generally includes a bedroom, dressing room, walk-in closet, bath, perhaps sauna or spa, and sitting area (Figure 5.12a). An adjacency of bath to sleeping area is often the configuration in hotel design, as in Figure 5.12b.

Another demonstration of multifunctionality is in the planning of retail spaces. No longer just environments to sell a company's products, retail spaces often provide entertainment serving as art galleries, event venues, and café/lounge areas. Another retail trend is the **pop-up retail** store. Big-box retailers such as Target (Figure 5.13) have been using this approach to supplement their ongoing retail establishments for some time to test out the viability of selected locations, to test-market new products, or for seasonal merchandising. Other companies have taken advantage of low overhead costs and favorable leasing rates to occupy vacant space temporarily. This phenomenon of temporary retailing demands special design skills and may be considered a cross between retailing and exhibit and display design.

How

The preceding considerations are part of the data collection stage. While this is happening, the designer will be processing much of the information and thinking about solutions. In fact, the designer may be sketching, taking notes, and even making suggestions to clients. However, this time is all part of the preplanning. The actual planning does not truly begin until all the preliminary data are gathered, organized, and documented in writing. It is *then* that the designer analyzes the information and synthesizes the information gathered. The end result of this phase is the compilation of a program similar to a script that, in turn, will direct the actual design. A project statement, or design concept, is a summary that delineates the objective to be achieved at the end of the design process.

There is a fine line between where analysis ends and synthesis and interpretation begins. However, when we design interior spaces, the design process is not linear or

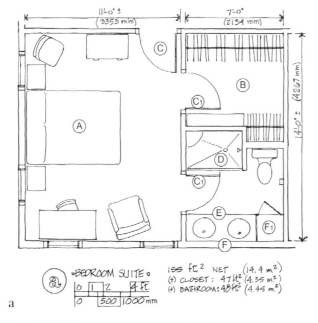

Figure 5.12
a. Example of a floor plan for residential master bedroom suite;
b. An elaborate hotel bedroom/bath suite in the Leela Palace, Kempinski Udaipur, India. *(a:* Residential Interior Design: A Guide to Planning Spaces *by Maureen Mitton and Courtney Nysteun, © 2011. Reproduced with permission of John Wiley & Sons; b: The Leela Palaces, Hotels and Resorts)*

Figure 5.13
Target's Bullseye Bodega, New York City. *(© Richard Levine / Alamy)*

necessarily only step-oriented. We do a number of different tasks, some in sequence and some simultaneously.

Most real-life projects require an ongoing cyclical process of testing followed by evaluation and adjustment. With every step the designer aims for a higher level of problem resolution.

PHASE 2: SCHEMATIC DESIGN

This phase, which begins once the client approves the preliminary program (including the design concept), encompasses the graphic representation of the design plans. The essential steps during the **schematic design phase** are to:

- Draw preliminary diagrams showing the functional relationships for personnel and operations
- Create space allocation and preliminary furniture and equipment layouts
- Prepare design studies indicating the types of fixtures, furnishings, and equipment (often shortened to **FF&E**) as well as finishes and materials

Developing the Preliminary Design Schematics

The term **schematic** denotes a diagrammatic representation of the framework for a plan. However, there are many ways in which designers visually represent their ideas to clients. We may think of the schematic design phase as the preliminary design development stage, during which ideas are worked out. The designer's concept and scheme for the space, and the overall plan for how these will be accomplished, may be presented to the client in a variety of ways, depending on the nature of the project and the designer's style.

The analysis and interpretation of the functional relationships among the *who*, *what*, and *where* discussed in the programming phase are documented in the schematic design phase.

Further refinement of depicting the relationships between spaces is the goal of studying adjacencies: "There are three basic types of adjacency needs: people, products, and information."[3] *FYI . . . Basic Space Configurations* summarizes the types of configurations suggested by David Kent Ballast.

For residential projects and less complex contract projects, this documentation may take the form of

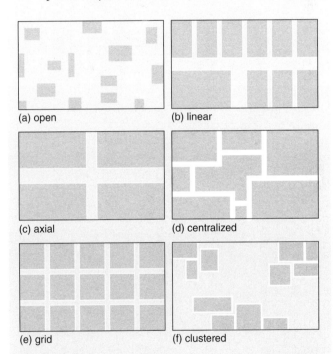

bubble diagrams. These diagrams may be very general, depicting overall zones, or areas of space by type of activity, or they may be detailed, indicating the location and proportional sizes of the areas shown (Figure 5.14).

For larger contract projects, these relationship studies are generally more complicated. Referred to as adjacency studies, they result in the decisions about what should be happening near what. Adjacency studies depict organizational and hierarchical corporate structure, space requirements, operational flow, and circulation patterns in order to develop a plan that will accommodate the functions users must carry out and indicate where these are to be accomplished. A criteria matrix is one technique for condensing and formatting many of the programming requirements, including square footage needs and adjacencies (Figure 5.15). When multistory spaces are involved, a stacking diagram may be used to represent the locations of major components within the space.

This preliminary schematic phase includes the development of a plan for how the furniture and equipment should be laid out—that is, a preliminary floor plan, or furniture layout plan (Figure 5.16a). A floor plan may be either sketched or done to scale, with each dimension measured and replicated on paper in relative terms. For example, one foot of actual floor space is usually represented on paper as one-fourth of an inch, or 1/4″ scale. A floor plan is, in essence, a horizontal cut of the space as viewed from above.

Furnishings can be of unique dimensions if they are customized. However, there are many standards that help designers plan how to allocate space and arrange furnishings in the space. Templates of typical furniture styles and sizes, such as the one featured here, are helpful at this stage. Sketches to illustrate the concept statement may also be done at this phase.

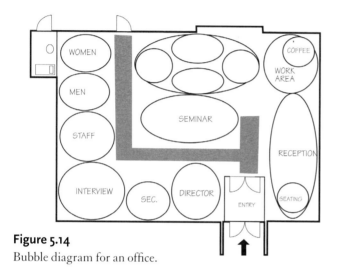

Figure 5.14
Bubble diagram for an office.

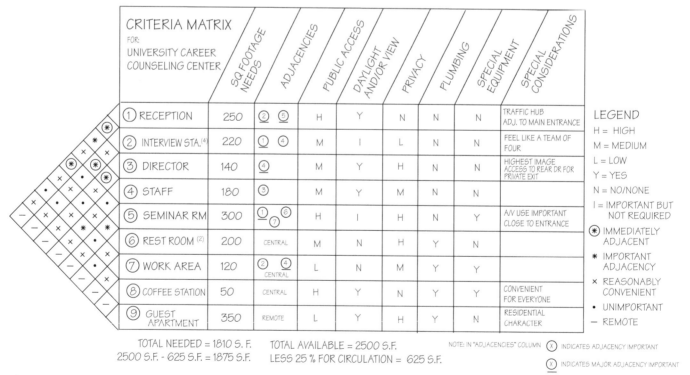

CRITERIA MATRIX
FOR:
UNIVERSITY CAREER COUNSELING CENTER

	SQ FOOTAGE NEEDS	ADJACENCIES	PUBLIC ACCESS	DAYLIGHT AND/OR VIEW	PRIVACY	PLUMBING	SPECIAL EQUIPMENT	SPECIAL CONSIDERATIONS
① RECEPTION	250	② ⑤	H	Y	N	N	N	TRAFFIC HUB ADJ. TO MAIN ENTRANCE
② INTERVIEW STA.(4)	220	① ④	M	I	L	N	N	FEEL LIKE A TEAM OF FOUR
③ DIRECTOR	140	④	M	Y	H	N	N	HIGHEST IMAGE ACCESS TO REAR DR FOR PRIVATE EXIT
④ STAFF	180	③	M	Y	M	N	N	
⑤ SEMINAR RM	300	① ⑥ ⑦	H	I	H	N	Y	A/V USE IMPORTANT CLOSE TO ENTRANCE
⑥ REST ROOM (2)	200	CENTRAL	M	N	H	Y	N	
⑦ WORK AREA	120	② ④ CENTRAL	L	N	M	Y	Y	
⑧ COFFEE STATION	50	CENTRAL	H	Y	N	Y	Y	CONVENIENT FOR EVERYONE
⑨ GUEST APARTMENT	350	REMOTE	L	Y	H	Y	N	RESIDENTIAL CHARACTER

LEGEND
H = HIGH
M = MEDIUM
L = LOW
Y = YES
N = NO/NONE
I = IMPORTANT BUT NOT REQUIRED
⊛ IMMEDIATELY ADJACENT
✳ IMPORTANT ADJACENCY
× REASONABLY CONVENIENT
• UNIMPORTANT
– REMOTE

TOTAL NEEDED = 1810 S. F.
2500 S.F. - 625 S.F. = 1875 S.F.
TOTAL AVAILABLE = 2500 S.F.
LESS 25 % FOR CIRCULATION = 625 S.F.

NOTE: IN "ADJACENCIES" COLUMN ⓧ INDICATES ADJACENCY IMPORTANT
ⓧ INDICATES MAJOR ADJACENCY IMPORTANT

Figure 5.15
Criteria matrix with adjacencies.

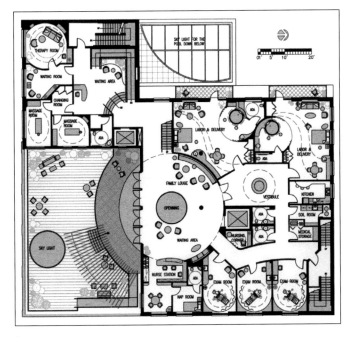

a

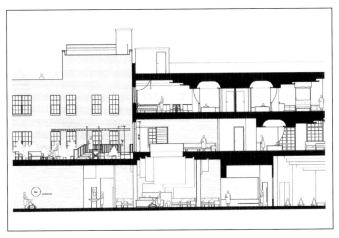

b

c

Figure 5.16
a. Floor plan; b. Section; c. Perspective. *(a, b, and c: Courtesy of and designed by Mika Fukuyoshi)*

Additional drawings may include **elevations** or **sections** (Figure 5.16b), which provide a vertical slice of the picture. The designer may also create sketches that illustrate **details** to help define the design concept. An example of a detail for a residential project may be a sketch of an idea for the style of window coverings to be used throughout. A detail sketch for a contract project may depict the designer's ideas for the type of hardware to be used for the doors and windows. **Perspective drawings** (Figure 5.16c) add volume, or three-dimensionality, to the concept for the design of the interior space. (The techniques involved in preparing drawings for the client, both manually and using the computer, are covered in Chapter 6.)

Sample boards, also called **material boards**, may be prepared by an interior designer at this phase to illustrate the types of materials and furnishings being considered to carry out the design concept, or a less structured type of presentation may be made to show the client examples of paint chips, fabrics, and photos of furniture in addition to roughly executed sketches. Similarly, other types of boards, sometimes referred to as mood, inspiration, or concept boards, give the client a sense of the style of furnishings and details. Color schemes may be shown on these boards or presented as separate studies, called color story boards, especially when the development of a palette is a critical aspect of the design scheme (Figure 5.17).

Figure 5.17
Example of presentation board showing color story for a residential bedroom project. *(Designer/ Design Company Garry Cohn. Client Nick and Kate O'Neill Residence. Location: Gray Stones, Ireland)*

Projecting Costs

It is during the schematic design phase that costs are projected, based on costs incurred for comparable projects. This estimate establishes a sense of what the job will cost in labor and materials, design services, and the services of other professionals and tradespeople. By the end of the programming phase, a designer preparing the schematics may be in a relatively good position, using information gathered to that point, to project a cost based on previous similar projects. Most trade suppliers of products and services will provide the designer with an estimate of costs. As these are obtained, the designer can develop the preliminary budget to be presented to the client, based on the initial design concept.

PHASE 3: DESIGN DEVELOPMENT

The essential steps during this phase are to:

- Prepare refined drawings and other documents for client approval that characterize the interior construction of the project, including any aspects not previously specified, such as colors, materials, furnishings, and equipment
- Adjust preliminary costs as needed

The key to the **design development phase** is the preparation of more refined drawings than were prepared for the schematic design phase. It is at this point that the designer receives written approval from the client concerning the plans. This approval may be contingent on refinements and greater detail in many drawings. Clients should not be expected to comprehend or interpret all the information presented in technical drawings. Explanatory sessions are usually necessary to help orient the client with the proposals and to enhance the client's understanding of the visuals. It is beneficial for the designer to provide the client with more detailed perspectives and sample boards than were presented in the schematic phase, so that the choices may be more easily understood and visualized.

It is during this phase, as well, that a more complete and detailed budget is prepared and presented to the client.

PHASE 4: CONTRACT DOCUMENTS

The essential tasks in this phase are to:

- Prepare for client approval drawings, specifications, and other documents, such as purchase orders, setting forth in detail the requirements for the interior construction, fabrications, and installation
- Assist the client in the preparation of requests for proposals to do the work, as well as the selection of people to perform the work

One way to think about the contract documents phase is as the point in the design process during which the drawings presented could serve as the basis for actual construction and installation. The term *contract* in this case does not indicate that the project under development is a commercial, or contract, design project; rather, it signifies that the documents prepared serve as legally binding agreements, ensuring that the plans will be executed as expected.[4]

- **Contract documents** are the set of documents that are part of the legal contract for services between two or more parties. These typically include detailed instructions to the contractor, construction documents, and specifications.[5]
- **Working drawings** is a term often used for those detailed drawings that define the work to be constructed. This may include title sheet, partition plans, power and communications plans, reflected ceiling plans, material and finish plans, and furniture layout plans as well as elevations, sections, and details along with the drawings of associated consultants.

The term *contract* also applies to documents other than drawings that serve as contracts between parties, such as those used to purchase products or services from a supplier. These documents serve as the basis for cost estimates from general contractors or building tradespeople who may provide bids to complete the job.

Once these documents are agreed to, the interested parties must authorize any changes. Those authorized changes are referred to as **change orders**.

A change order is just one example of the correspondence, or transmittal that goes back and forth between a designer and a client as well as other participants.

The phrase *For Design Intent Only* may be added to documents that are prepared to signify those that are not meant to qualify as documents authorized for construction purposes.

The term plan, in this context, refers to any of several types of drawings depicting proposed layouts on a particular plane, such as the floor or ceiling. A **schedule** provides supplementary notes, such as a recommended type of fixture and its location. **Specifications** are clarifying information that further details specific recommendations, such a manufacturer's brand and model number for a product. **Performance specifications** are expectations for products, such as how well they will perform (or last) under specific conditions (e.g., heavy-duty traffic).

Qualified architects contracted by the owner may perform the services relating to preparation of the construction documents, or an interior designer qualified by state regulations may prepare these drawings. Many interior designers prepare working drawings from which built-in furniture, cabinetry, and other details are constructed. **Shop drawings** are "drawings, diagrams, illustrations, schedules, performance charts, brochures, and any other data prepared by the contractor or any subcontractor, manufacturer, supplier or distributor, which illustrate how specific portions of the work shall be fabricated and/or installed."[6] *FYI . . . The Contract Documents Package* lists the key components for Phase 4 of the design process.

Some large-scale projects, such as government or public institutions, require that any work be performed by qualified tradespeople selected through a **competitive bid process**. Even if not required, whenever construction or demolition is part of a project, it is advisable that the client go through this process as well. A critical role for the designer during this phase is to assist the client in the bidding and selection process.

The rule of thumb is that any **bid procurement**, or *request for proposals*, should be sent to at least three firms (usually three general contracting firms). In an ideal world the contract documents would clearly depict and state, according to standardized conventions, the proposed work to be done. Descriptions of specific materials, such as the type, size, and characteristics of these materials, would be definitive and clear. The graphic and written language would be uniform so that any three firms would have the same understanding of what they were being asked to respond to. The three firms would then submit their proposals for how the work would be done, by whom, and at what cost. In other words, the person reviewing the proposals would be comparing apples with apples.

However, we don't live in a perfect world, and often the three responses will look very different and have widely varying costs attached to the work and materials. It is then necessary to sift through the responses, comparing them with the bid documents and requesting clarification of specific costs as necessary. The designer can serve as a facilitator for the client during these discussions.

The interior designer should be familiar with the bid documents, even when he or she did not actually prepare them, to assure that the concept the designer has developed, and that has the approval of the client, is portrayed accurately in the contract documents package.

PHASE 5: CONTRACT ADMINISTRATION

The National Council for Interior Design Qualification offers us this definition of **contract administration**:

> the set of services which may include developing and monitoring schedules and construction costs; ensuring construction is completed in conformance with contracts and design intent; liaison with contractors and consultants throughout the course of construction; reviewing shop drawings and submissions from the contractor; observing and commenting on construction progress; monitoring move-in and furniture installation; and conducting required post-occupancy evaluations.[7]

FYI . . . The Contract Documents Package

The following list summarizes the key components of the **contract documents package:**

- The **title sheet,** essentially a cover sheet, includes the name and location of the project, a list of all drawings and documents included in the package, the title block (i.e., the letterhead and logo of the person or firm preparing the documents, including license, registration, or certificate number and stamp mark, if appropriate), and lines on which the client will indicate his or her approval with signature and date.

- General notes for construction are aimed at the general contractor. These may be part of the title page; alternately, when several tradespeople, such as electricians, painters, and plumbers, are involved in a project, specific notes may be made on each of the various plans described below.

- The **demolition plan** outlines existing conditions to be eliminated prior to renovations that involve construction of structural components.

- The **furniture and equipment plan** is one or a series of floor plans that identify all "movable" furnishings as well as built-in cabinetwork, fixtures, and appliances, such as for kitchens and bathrooms. These plans may be accompanied by elevations and details to depict customized units, such as a reception desk, store display fixtures, or a home entertainment unit.

- The **construction plan** shows walls, partitions, columns, doors, and windows. Rooms are identified for reference, such as "master bedroom" or "media room." Accompanying elevations and details provide additional information to depict dimensions and materials, especially for features that are key to the overall design concept.

- The **reflected ceiling plan** includes all architectural elements that interface with the ceiling. It may detail the types and locations of lighting and ceiling fan fixtures; ceiling materials; sprinkler, smoke detector, and air temperature control systems; and partitions that touch the ceiling.

- The **lighting plan** may be combined with a reflected ceiling plan or a separate plan. It includes all fixtures, such as portable table and floor lamps, wall sconces, and dimmer and switching controls.

- The **power and communications plan** includes telephone and electrical wiring information for computers, acoustical equipment, security, intercom systems, and so on.

- The **finish plan** notes the surface coverings. Again, depending on the complexity of the project, there may be one or several schedules, such as a plan for all wood finishes and another for paint finishes.

- The **door and window schedules** typically are presented in a format that includes the number, size, material, and hardware for interior doors and windows. Elevations that depict special details, such as paneling or etching, as well as the mechanisms, give further information.

- The **ADA building code compliance plan** demonstrates barrier-free requirements according to the Americans with Disabilities Act (ADA) as part of, or in addition to, the construction plan.

The laws and regulations governing the project and the specific services spelled out in the contract will determine an interior designer's activities during the contract administration phase. The following tasks may be involved during this phase:

- Ordering merchandise and ensuring proper delivery and placement
- Obtaining permits
- Coordinating purchase of FF&E and supervising installation
- Supervising installation or construction work of subcontractors
- Conducting site inspections
- Issuing documents relating to project completion

Purchasing is often a very complex task, and the designer's role in this activity is a complicated one. As noted earlier, responsibilities involved in purchasing FF&E are included in both the contract documents phase *and* the contract administration phase. If the owner and designer agree that the designer will purchase FF&E on behalf of the owner, with the owner's money, those duties should be outlined in a separate statement. (Several documents that relate specifically to purchasing are recommended.) Because of their complexity, the documents or contracts relating to purchasing are reviewed in detail in Chapter 14, along with discussion of delivery, installation, and inspection of goods.

The direct role of the interior designer regarding contract administration may vary from overseeing the construction (remodeling, renovation, or new construction) to client hand-holding. The terms *oversight*, *supervision*, *inspection*, and *administration* are at times used interchangeably and perhaps too loosely. Because an interior designer is not truly in charge of building tradespeople, he or she does not wish to be held responsible for any consequences of construction. These responsibilities are assigned to the general contractor involved with the work. It is unwise for the designer to present him- or herself as a general contractor. In fact, home improvement contractor licensing laws in many jurisdictions prohibit individuals from performing home improvement services without the proper license.[8]

Even when interior designers may have been actively involved in the preparation of the documents discussed in Phase 4, their supervision of the installation of the project may be limited, with the general contractor, engineer, or architect assuming a more extensive role.

In any event, *the interior designer remains responsible to the client for assuring that the design concept is carried out.* And this is often no easy task. It may require regularly scheduled or more informal conferences with all interested parties, and routine on-site (field) visits to observe the progress and quality of the work being done. The interior designer may be instrumental in coordinating the schedule of contracted work and may prepare a **punch list**, a list that outlines outstanding or deficient items at the final stages of installation, to be reviewed with the client.

All these services are part of the crucial role the designer plays—that of alleviating as much anxiety as possible for the client. Many projects require the client to move for a period of time during demolition, renovation, or construction. Services to help clients, both residential and commercial, may include arranging and scheduling the client's move and facilitating temporary relocation.

POSTCOMPLETION

The final step in the design process is postcompletion, or *postoccupancy evaluation (POE)*. Although this phase may be incorporated as part of Phase 5, above, it may be prudent to give this topic its due as a complete phase of its own. Using the earlier analogy of the process's being like a play, this would be the epilogue. In actuality, there is often no one cutoff date when the designer's responsibility for a project ends, especially for residential projects.

It is helpful to both client and interior designer to evaluate the end results. This evaluation may be a formalized walk-through of the space to compare the results with the previously prepared documents. A standardized form or protocol for this survey may be used, particularly for complex or large projects, as illustrated in Figure 5.18. This not only aids in assessing the current project, but also provides information

A. General Questions:

What is your connection with the project?
☐ Principal ☐ Other

Were you involved in the planning / Design Task Force?
☐ Yes ☐ No

How satisfied were you with the planning process?
☐ Very Satisfied ☐ Somewhat ☐ Not Satisfied

At what point did you participate in the process?
☐ At the start ☐ In the middle ☐ Toward the end

How much of your time was spent on this project as a percentage of your work week?

How satisfied are you with the overall project?
☐ Excellent ☐ Good ☐ Reasonable ☐ Poor

With whom did you spend the most time?
☐ Project Manager ☐ Construction Manager ☐ Other

What were the best things about the project?

What were the worst things about the project?

Did the completed project meet the "Design Task Force" objectives?
☐ Yes ☐ No ☐ No Opinion

How satisfied were you with the planning process? It was...
☐ Excellent ☐ Good ☐ Reasonable ☐ Poor

Did you participate in partnering?
☐ Yes ☐ No

If you participated in partnering, was it...
☐ very beneficial ☐ somewhat beneficial ☐ not beneficial

Were the partnering principles carried out during the project?
☐ Always ☐ Most of the time ☐ Sometimes ☐ Not at all

What were the benefits of partnering and what recommendations would you make to improve partnering:

Did you ask the contractor to make adjustments that changed the duration?
☐ Yes ☐ No ☐ No Opinion

Did the project meet the time requirements?
☐ Yes ☐ No ☐ No Opinion

Did the project meet the quality requirements?
☐ Yes ☐ No ☐ No Opinion

Have all the minor "Punch List" items been completed?
☐ Yes ☐ No ☐ No Opinion

Were the Prop. MM "Voter Guide" requirements essentially completed?
☐ Yes ☐ No ☐ No Opinion

If you could influence the District to strengthen, change, or modify the existing process, what would you propose?

C. Facility Questions:

How do you rate the lighting?
☐ Excellent ☐ Good ☐ Reasonable ☐ Poor

How do you rate the ventilation?
☐ Excellent ☐ Good ☐ Reasonable ☐ Poor

How do you rate the appropriateness of the materials used?
☐ Excellent ☐ Good ☐ Reasonable ☐ Poor

How do you rate the maintainability of the new facility?
☐ Excellent ☐ Good ☐ Reasonable ☐ Poor

How do you rate the overall design?
☐ Excellent ☐ Good ☐ Reasonable ☐ Poor

How do you rate the overall functionality of the completed project?
☐ Excellent ☐ Good ☐ Reasonable ☐ Poor

What recommendations would you make to improve the design of the facility?

* = Input is required

B. Process Questions:

How satisfied were you with the;

Project Management?:	☐ Excel
Construction Management?:	☐ Excel
Inspection?:	☐ Excel
Architect?:	☐ Excel
Contractor?:	☐ Excel

Figure 5.18

An extract from a postoccupancy evaluation (POE) form for a contract project.

valuable to the interior design firm in managing future projects.

The postcompletion step may entail several meetings with all interested parties, such as the client and employees, general contractor, and architect. Alternatively, it may involve a few follow-up phone calls to the client, asking how things are going and whether any additional services are required. Usually, a satisfied client and designer will remain in touch for some time, often resulting in subsequent projects or referrals.

In the Spotlight: The Design Process for a Residential Project illustrates each phase of the design process for a residential project.

SPECIAL CONSIDERATIONS FOR SPACE PLANNING

With the growing complexity of the activities and projects assumed by interior designers, a discussion of special considerations has the potential to be virtually endless. A few areas are introduced here that are often presented as components of assignments given to design students within their first year of study: kitchen, bath, and office (or corporate) design.

Planning for kitchens and baths has become a growing specialty area in both new construction and renovation. Many interior designers become **certified kitchen designers** and **certified bath designers**. The appellations for these specialty credentials are **CKD** and **CBD**, respectively.[9]

Kitchen Design

Even for residential kitchens many factors must be considered in planning. Among them are accessibility and adaptability issues, functionality for efficient work activities, and various social and cultural approaches to the most basic human need: sustenance.

Although there are many ways to approach kitchen planning, the **triangle kitchen design** method, which considers the three primary elements—water, cooling, and heating—or the workstations—sink, refrigerator, and cooktop—is still popular. Figure 5.19 illustrates design concepts based on the work triangle for the residential kitchen.

Kitchen design trends include an increase in the number of cooks in a household, the popularity of commercial grade and size appliances, and the prepon-

derance of gadgets. Kitchen islands have become an integral part of residential kitchens. They may serve a variety of functions or simply provide additional food preparation surface (Figure 5.20a and b).

Moreover, the advent of the outdoor kitchen has not quelled the interest in full-service indoor residential kitchens; rather, it has provided an additional opportunity for the designer's input.

Efficiency in kitchen space planning is not a new notion. Perhaps one of the more significant innovations in modern kitchen design occurred decades ago, after World War I. In an effort to create affordable housing for working class families, small rental apartments were built as public housing. Ten thousand units were built in the 1920s for a housing project in Germany that featured what was to become known as the Frankfurt Kitchen. Along with the architect Ernst May, Margarete Schütte-Lihotzky, an Austrian architect and social activist, created a compact kitchen complete with furniture and major appliances—the first fitted kitchen (Figure 5.21). Inspired by the narrow ship galleys in which sailors were required to cook, this kitchen led to the more contemporary versions of it referred to as **galley kitchens**, as shown in Figure 5.22.

Bath Design

A full bathroom has three basic activity areas: sink/grooming; toileting; and bathing/showering. Generally, sinks are placed closest to the door, and bath or shower, near the rear.[10] A **powder room**, or *half-bath*, contains toilet and sink areas, with no bathing facilities. Baths for multiple, simultaneous users, including in hotel situations, often provide additional partitions to separate the various activities performed in the bath areas, enhancing privacy (Figure 5.23).

Planning for public restroom spaces is very much dictated by ADA compliance (see Chapter 2). Today, more and more residential designs are adapting the features of commercial designs for the benefit of occupants with varied needs. Height-adjustable toilets, roll-in showers, temperature controls, and vanity designs with wheelchair clearances are just a few of these improvements in bathroom planning. The interior designer and advocate for universal design Cynthia Leibrock featured Kohler products for her home in Colorado, which serves as a model for aging in place (Figure 5.24).

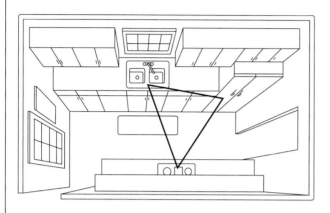

Corridor or galley kitchen

Ideal for small spaces. Parallel walls allow the cook to move easily from one workstation to another. Allow at least 4 feet of space between the counters. To maximize efficiency, consider teaming the sink and refrigerator on one wall, with the cooktop centered on the other wall.

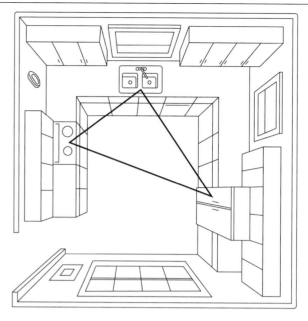

U-Shape kitchen

An efficient, versatile plan with one workstation on each of three walls. An 8x8-foot space is the minimum needed for a U-shape kitchen; this provides at least 4 feet of work space in the center of the room. To maximize efficiency in a larger kitchen, consider placing one of the workstations in a freestanding island.

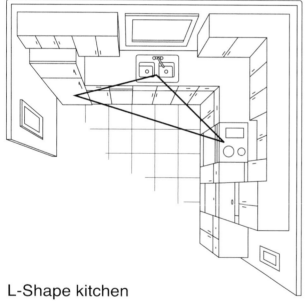

L-Shape kitchen

More efficient than a U-shape plan, this arrangement places two workstations on one wall and the third on an adjacent wall. The placement of the workstations is critical; work should flow from the refrigerator to the sink and then to the cooktop and serving area.

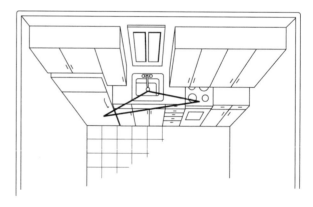

Single-wall kitchen

The most space-saving plan, often seen in vacation homes or studio apartments. The one-wall plan works best when the sink is centered on the wall and flanked on one side with the refrigerator and on the other with the cooktop. If possible, allow 4 feet of counter on both sides of the sink.

Figure 5.19
Basic kitchen configurations.

a

b

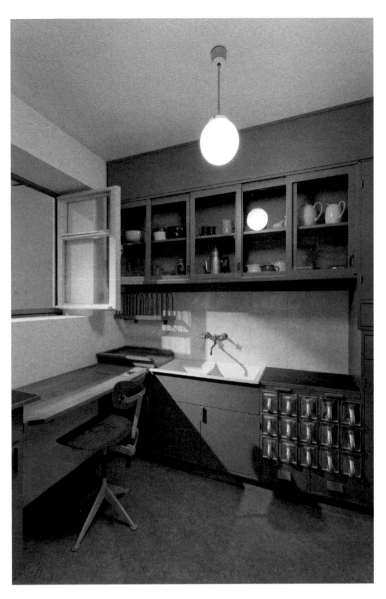

Figure 5.21
Frankfurt Kitchen from the Ginnheim-Höhenblick Housing
Estate, Germany. 1926–1927. *(Schütte-Lihotzky, Margarete
[1897–2000]) (© Frankfurt Kitchen Location: The Museum of
Modern Art, New York City. Photo credit: Digital Image Photo
credit: The Museum of Modern Art/Licensed by SCALA / Art
Resource, NY)*

Figure 5.20
a. Kitchen islands may be small and simple to provide additional
food preparation areas b. or as opportunities for additional sink,
cooktop, or serving areas. *(a: Photo by Simon Upton Photography
from his website. Interior design by Darryl Carter; b: General
Electric Co.)*

Figure 5.22
Galley-style kitchen. (© *Andreas von Einsiedel / Alamy*)

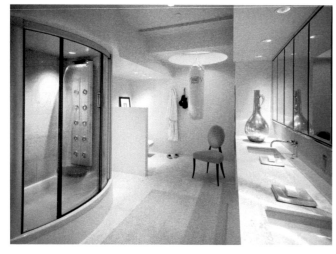

Figure 5.23
A privacy partition separates the toilet from the otherwise spacious bathroom. (*Courtesy of Kohler*)

Figure 5.24
ADA-compliant master bathroom for Ft. Collins, Colorado, Idea House for Aging in Place. (*Courtesy of Kohler Co., designed by Cynthia Leibrock*)

The Design Process for a Residential Project

The following narrative and illustrations highlight key aspects of the stages for one interior design project that involved steps in the design process.

Prologue: The Preproject Step

The prospective client had been a client of this interior designer on two previous occasions. They first met through a mutual friend at a tennis match. This time, the services of the interior designer are being explored for the first space the client owned, rather than rented.

Act I: The Programming Phase

Scene 1: Presenting the Nature of the Project

The prospective client recently purchased an apartment. Although the client is prepared to expend monies for some renovations and furnishings, she hopes to keep many of her furnishings from previous apartments. She would also like to retain many existing features of the site.

Scene 2: Introducing the Principal Players

Cast of Characters: Client Profile

The client is a single, professional woman in her thirties who enjoys respite from her stressful and challenging position in the financial industry. She lives alone with one cat. Her lifestyle at home is rather quiet and casual, although she occasionally entertains friends. She hosts weekend guests at times, but no more than two at a time. Although she does not often prepare elaborate meals for herself or company, it is important that she have an efficient and low-maintenance kitchen.

The client is 6 feet tall and requires furnishings and storage to accommodate her proportions comfortably. She wants a secure environment that is energy efficient and flexible in lighting.

Her sense of style is traditional and romantic, and she is eager to learn more about architecture, furnishings, and decorative arts. Although fiscally prudent, she is prepared to spend what is necessary to achieve her goals for the space, that is, to create a comfortable, spacious, and gracious respite from a busy work and travel schedule.

The household cat plays a key role in this space. She requires a litter box, food area, and scratching posts. Furnishings and finishes must be of high durability and low maintenance.

In an apartment, noise is a consideration for this client as well as her neighbors. This means that carpet must be considered for a substantial part of the flooring, and any demolition and construction must be done with consideration of the existing bylaws of the building's board of directors and of local ordinances.

Stage Set: The Physical Site

The apartment is a 1,500-square-foot, two-bedroom apartment in a 1930s high-rise building located in an elegant urban neighborhood. It is on the 12th floor and has expansive views of a park and museum. The large living room has a fireplace and two windows with northern and western exposures, providing a significant amount of daylight. The fireplace is original to the structure. The dining room is small, but two additional spaces that separate the dining room from the entry to the apartment offer the potential for a more creative use of this transitional area than is provided by the current layout.

The kitchen is a galley configuration, long and narrow, with a mixture of older and newer fixtures. Although it has two windows, it is dimly lit.

A long hallway joins the public spaces to the more private living quarters. This area of the apartment has two bedrooms and two bathrooms. The two bathrooms were renovated recently by the former owner but are not to the current owner's taste. They were done in a contemporary style that is not consistent with the character of the apartment, the building, or its neighborhood. Furthermore, the

(continued)

The Design Process for a Residential Project, *continued*

bathroom off the hallway has a floor that is raised several inches above the floor of the rest of the apartment. This makes it inaccessible for anyone with ambulatory issues who would visit as well as awkward and inconvenient.

Set Design: The User Requirement

1. **Private Zone**
   Sleeping area
   Queen-size bed
   Television and VCR
   Reading area
   Book storage
   Adequate clothing storage: suits, long
       gowns, off-season
   Adequate linens storage
   Dressing
   Bath with shower, low maintenance
       and sanitary
   Display of art and personal photographs
2. **Semiprivate Zones**
   Accessible guest bath with shower area
   Sleeping for guests (one or two)
   Minimal entertainment (music, television)
   Reading area
   Minimum storage needs
   Low maintenance
3. **Work Zones**
   Desktop computer, monitor, printer
   Storage for books, files, magazines
   Meal preparation
   Storage for household and cleaning
       supplies
4. **Social Zone**
   Entertaining
   Relaxation, music
   Display of art and accessories

Scene 3: The Design Concept Is Developed
The style will be Art Deco (see Chapter 12), in harmony with the building's style, although not slav-

ishly defined. It will emphasize the feminine spirit of the period, using a variety of textures and finishes suitable for owner and pet.

It is decided that consultation and collaboration with an architect and a general contractor are necessary, because of the significant demolition and construction needed to achieve the project goals. Interior design services will provide assistance to the client with these contracted services.

Both bathrooms and the kitchen will be demolished and reconstructed with new configurations and FF&E. The central corridor of rooms from the entrance through the dining room will be altered to provide for a more effective transition and more cohesive look.

Act II: Schematic Design through Contract Administration
Scene 1: Schematic Development
A revised floor plan and sample boards are developed for the project and presented to the client for approval.

Scene 2: Contract Documents
Time passes. Backstage discussions can be heard. The client has approved the plans. The play continues with the collaboration of the expanded ensemble: client, cat, interior designer, architect, general contractor, tradespeople, suppliers, and neighbors.

Scene 3: Contract Administration
Demolition and construction proceed, and the client's space begins to take on features of the new design.

Epilogue: The Postcompletion Step
Despite the inconvenience of demolition, some unexpected twists and turns, and some punch list items that remain to be completed, the client and her cat are enjoying their new home.

The Design Process for a Residential Project, *continued*

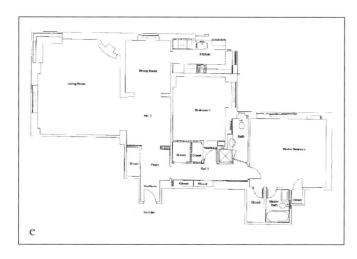

Figures a–f
Before pictures.
a. View from entry;
b. Kitchen;
c. Guest bath;
d. Floor plan;
e. Revised floor plan;
f. Demolition.

(continued)

The Design Process for a Residential Project, *continued*

Figures g–i

After pictures.

g. View from entrance;

h. Kitchen;

i. Guest bath.

(Interior design and photos provided by the Author)

Research Studies in Commercial Design: Workplace Design

Steelcase, Inc.

Generation Y is the name used for the demographic group of people born between 1980 and 2000, numbering 32 million in the U.S. workforce. Characteristic work style includes the ability to multitask and focus; ignore surrounding stimuli; and shift easily between focused work, socializing, and collaboration. According to a study led by the Steelcase Research Group in 2010, this group's attitudes and behaviors about work are changing the nature of workplace design for all ages.

Major findings:

- *Work needs to be meaningful and purposeful.* It must make an impact through personal and collective success.
- *The workplace is wherever I am.* The office is about connecting with others and solving problems.
- *Trust is developed both offline (face-to-face) and online (virtually).* Includes videoconferencing.
- *Work and life are one without clear separation.* Flexible schedules and telecommuting are common.

(continued)

Research Studies in Commercial Design: Workplace Design, *continued*

Mega multitasking – Multitasking is no big deal. Gen Y workers expect to juggle multiple tasks simultaneously.

Extreme focus – Gen Y workers are comfortable working with and among others.

High-intensity work – Using multiple monitors and keyboards is the norm. So is shifting easily between focused work, socializing, and collaboration.

Peer-to-peer networking – The chat line is always open. Workers check with peers constantly since social networking is part of life.

Figure a
Generation Y work spaces.

- *Continuous connection and collaboration is critical.* The workplace must be saturated with, and support, social networks. Kitchen-like collaboration spaces where workers can plug in computers and have meetings, relax, work, or both, is one solution.[a]

Gensler, Inc.

Gensler, one of the world's largest architecture and design firms, commissioned an online survey in 2009 regarding the changing nature of the workplace in both the United States and the United Kingdom. There were 900 participants in the United States and 300 in the United Kingdom. All staff levels were represented and as well as nine industries, with equal geographic distribution. Four work modes were identified: focus, collaboration, learning, and socializing. In companies in which the workplace design supported these work modes, there was a significant rise in not only worker satisfaction, retention, and productivity, but also profits. More effective space planning, rather than additional square footage, made the difference.[b]

Sources:
[a]*Adapted from Chris Congdon, "Generation Y Gets to Work and the Workplace Will Never Be the Same,"* ASID Icon, *March/April 2010.*
[b]*Adapted from Janet Pogue, "The Office Evolution,"* Contract, *May 2009.*

As noted earlier, water conservation is a priority in public and private "wet" areas, such as bath, kitchen, and laundry (see Chapter 2). For that reason, the installation of "smart" appliances and fixtures that conserve both quantity and temperature of water will direct many design decisions. Examples of these products are shown in Chapter 10.

Office (Corporate) Design

The concepts of collaboration, team building, and open planning are changing the nature of office design. Shifts in approaches to contract design are generally based on research on productivity, worker satisfaction, customer satisfaction, sales, sustainability benchmarks, and other measurable outcomes.

In a 2010 profile in *Contract* magazine, Bill Bouchey, the design director for M Moser, a multinational architectural firm, discussed the challenge and satisfaction of today's corporate design: "Having to provide effective solutions that combine workflow/patterns, human nature, and branding, and are also visually beautiful, demands a rigor and passion that is exciting and ultimately satisfying."[11] Bouchey stressed the benefit to corporations that have the courage to overcome hierarchy and remain flexible and the importance of sustainability and global awareness. He also addressed the future of corporate design: "A continued and growing emphasis on collaboration, branding, and choice of settings in the workplace in order to be competitive and grow—all while reducing overhead costs—lies ahead. . . . The feeling of connectivity (getting work done with others) will always take precedence over all virtual tools."[12] *In the Spotlight: Research Studies in Commercial Design* focuses on two research studies on workplace design conducted by Steelcase, Inc. and Gensler, Inc.

Summary

A design project may pass through many stages, depending on the scope and complexity of the project, the agreement between interior designer and client, and local regulations governing specific services. The five basic phases are (1) programming, (2) schematic design, (3) design development, (4) contract documents, and (5) contract administration.

The preproject step is the period leading up to when a prospective job becomes a project; it is the period during which the client–designer relationship is established. Postcompletion, or postoccupancy evaluation, is the time when the designer follows up with the client to evaluate the results of the project and any other carryover needs.

Throughout the process, there is an ongoing communication among all interested parties. Documents are prepared as preliminary design concepts and solutions and then refined for client approval and implementation. Many of these documents, among them working drawings and perspectives, are discussed in more detail in Chapter 7.

Space planning is a major component of the interior design process. Human and cultural factors as well as environmental issues are accounted for in the process. Trends in home construction and research into how people live and work influence the design process and its solutions. Special considerations in areas such as kitchen and bath require additional specific expertise. Significant shifts in office design are influenced by an increased global perspective, emphasis on collaboration, and technological advances.

Vocabulary

ADA building code compliance plan	certified bath designer (CBD)	competitive bid process
adjacency study	certified kitchen designer (CKD)	construction plan
bid procurement	change order	contract administration phase
bubble diagram	circulation pattern	contract documents package
		contract documents phase

(continued)

Vocabulary *(continued)*

criteria matrix	furniture and equipment plan	punch list
deliverables	galley kitchen	reflected ceiling plan
demolition plan	great room	retainer
design concept	lighting plan	sample board (material board)
design development phase	performance specifications	schedule
desk audit	perspective drawing	schematic
detail	plan	schematic design phase
door and window schedule	pop-up retail	section
elevation	postcompletion step	shop drawing
end user	(postoccupancy evaluation	sited
existing conditions	[POE])	specifications
FF&E (fixtures, furnishings,	powder room	stacking diagram
and equipment)	power and communications	suite
field measurement (field survey)	plan	title sheet
finish plan	preproject step	triangle kitchen design
floor plan (furniture layout	programming phase	working drawing
plan)	project manager	zone

Exercise: Role-Playing in the Programming Phase

The goal of this exercise is to become familiar with the basics of the preliminary steps in the programming phase. To do that, you will conduct research about your client, his or her needs and desires, and the space through observation of the existing space and key features and through asking the right questions about the *who*, *what*, *when*, and *where* of information gathering.

Select a classmate to work with whose living space is accessible and convenient to you. Each of you will have the opportunity to role-play the client and interior designer. At your site, you will be the client; at your classmate's site, you will be the interior designer.

Complete the following steps in your role of the interior designer:

1. Prepare a list of questions beforehand.
2. Interview the client, and take notes.
3. Tour the site with the client, and take notes.
4. Prepare a brief summary (which may be in "bullet" format) describing the *who*, *what*, *when*, and *where*. Include a list of next steps you would need to take to develop a design concept.

Exercise: Exploring the CD-ROM

Take advantage of the contents of the CD-ROM to increase your understanding of designing efficient kitchens. Follow the instructions for Starting the CD-ROM on pages xix–xx and click on Chapter Five: The Design Process.

Kitchen Efficiency: There are many ways kitchen appliances and work spaces are laid out. Sketch or photograph a kitchen space that you use, or another cooking area in which you can prepare a meal or snack for yourself. Document your movements and note how the layout helps and/or hinders your activities. Consider, for example, if cabinets are difficult to reach, or if some movements are wasteful. Prepare an analysis discussing how efficient the layout is. How would you change the layout to make it more efficient?

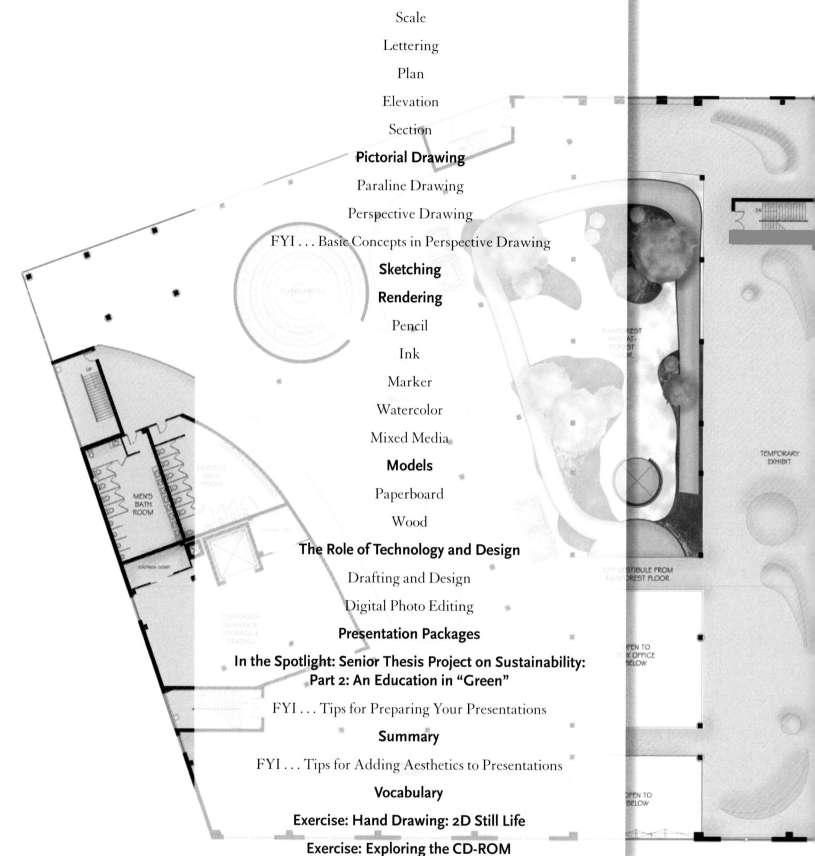

6

Communicating the Vision

Designers communicate their ideas and solutions in many ways. The main ways can be thought of as visually, verbally, and through writing. This chapter concentrates on the way designers present their work visually.

The general term *visual presentation* encompasses several different techniques for communicating ideas. The issue of visual representation produced by hand versus computer is commonly discussed among students, educators, and professionals. Both have their place, although it is generally recognized that students should first be introduced to the requirements of hand drawing and drafting before the computer counterparts to those processes. Professionals view hand drawing as an important skill, particularly during the early phases of a project, referred to as ideation, the process of generating and developing ideas and design concepts. Hand drawing encourages this process of generating design ideas as well as their evaluation.[1] "Throughout the design process, we use drawings to guide the development of an idea from concept to proposal to constructed reality."[2] Each of the following categories of drawings will be explored first as done by hand. Adaptations to computerization follow later in the chapter.

Sketching is a rough, loose way of drawing, in which the key features of an object, space, or concept are outlined. Sketches often serve as a quick way to communicate ideas to others and are based on approximations rather than exact measurements. Sketching, like brainstorming, a technique used in other industries to stimulate ideation, allows the designer to test ideas and solutions in a less restricted way. Sketching is typically thought of as done by hand, but it may be done via computer programs as well. Again, while convenient, many believe that during the initial design phases the hand expression is of greater value to the process.

Drafting applies to technical drawings based on measurements, whether they are done manually or are computer generated. Some drafted drawings are two-dimensional, depicting only the vertical and horizontal planes; others, such as perspectives, are three-dimensional, incorporating the additional dimension of depth.

Rendering is the term applied to the various techniques used to flesh out designs so that they ring more true to life. Rendering, which may be done at any stage of the design process, translates the interior finishes to be used—the textures, patterns, and colors—as well as the effects of light in the space and on objects in the space. The addition of **entourage**, or scaled elements within a space, such as people and plants, is a form of rendering. The techniques and styles of rendering range from a simple insertion of shadows on a floor plan to detailed watercolor drawings showing art and accessories.

Model construction and the materials used to create models are introduced in this chapter. The chapter discusses the use of **computer-aided drafting and design**, known as **CAD, CADD,** or **CAD/D,** to produce various types of drawings, sometimes referred to as digital drawings. Other software programs, such as those used to animate, model, collaborate, or add text and photos, are also introduced.

Visual communication serves several purposes, and an understanding of these different purposes helps the designer and student select an appropriate type and style of visual for each need. These purposes are as follows:

- Conceptualize
- Present and share ideas with clients
- Communicate with contractors, tradespeople, and suppliers
- Market or promote the designer (discussed in Chapter 14)

DRAWING EQUIPMENT AND SUPPLIES

All types of presentations require a basic set of equipment, tools, and supplies.

The most critical investment is the purchase of an appropriate drawing surface. Drafting tables are available in many sizes and price points, with a variety of features and options. A minimum of 38 inches wide and 26 inches deep is recommended to accommodate large studio projects. A table with a self-healing (scratch-resistant) vinyl cover is best. An adjustable lighting fixture with both incandescent and fluorescent lamps that can be screwed onto the table is recommended. A 23-inch by 31-inch drafting board with a vinyl cover may serve as a portable option.

A **parallel rule**, or *straightedge*, is a helpful tool. Some surfaces include this feature, or it may be purchased separately. It consists of a bar the same width as the table, attached with screws, that slides up and down by a pulley. Used in conjunction with triangles, the parallel rule replaces the T square.

Another useful item is a light box, which allows one drawing to be easily traced from another drawing. A light box is convenient when multiple versions of a drawing need to be produced or when inking a drawing based on a pencil rendering. A glass-top table with a small portable lamp placed underneath it can serve as a substitute.

Portfolios used to carry drawings are available in a range of sizes. Because many projects require large-scale drawings, a portfolio may be as big as 23 inches by 31 inches. Quality and cost of portfolios also vary widely, from paper, at the low end, to leather, at the high end. Toolboxes, available in different sizes and shapes, may be used to organize many of the supplies listed in Tables 6.1 and 6.2.

Table 6.1 is an inventory of recommended basic supplies for interior design students. Additional supplies, geared more specifically to rendering and presentations, are listed in Table 6.2.

ORTHOGRAPHIC DRAWING

Interior designers use **orthographic drawing** to communicate their ideas and designs to target audiences. An orthographic drawing is a two-dimensional projection of a plane, like a slice through a space, and can

Table 6.1
Drawing Supplies and Their Use

Item	Description and Use
Architectural scale	12″ triangular plastic ruler with various scales, preferably with color-coded sides. Flat, pocket-sized version is helpful for reading scaled drawings on-site.
Bond paper	High-quality, bright white paper for all-purpose drawing.
Compass	6″ with beam and inking attachment. Used for lines not found on predefined templates, large circles, and other geometric shapes.
Disposable pen	This is a low-cost, low-maintenance substitute for technical pens, which are costly and often require maintenance.
Drafting brush	Useful for removing dust from lead erasures.
Drafting tape roll, $\frac{1}{4}$″ wide	For holding down drawings on a board. Drafting dots are a convenient alternative.
Dry powder pad	Also called pounce powder, used to absorb unwanted dirt and dust.
Erasers	White plastic or vinyl, kneaded, and ink erasers. Electric erasers are useful for eliminating ink lines.
Erasing shield	This is used to isolate small areas for erasing.
Felt-tip or rolling ball pen	Available in black and numerous colors, with different types of points, from very fine to broad.
Flexible curve	This is used to draw rounded or curved spaces.
French curves	Set of templates used to guide drawing of curvilinear objects.
Leads	Graphite (commonly called lead) pencils with different lead weights, used for measured and freehand drawing. Lumograph is high-quality graphite. Ordinary wooden pencils, mechanical (automatic) refillable pencils, and lead holders to use with a variety of lead weights. Leads are labeled by standardized weights ranging from hard (H), to medium (F), to soft (B); the harder the lead, the lighter and finer the line. Additional numbers further add to the range (e.g., 2H is not as hard as 4H, and 6B is softer than 4B). B leads are softest and are used for sketching, not drafting. F, H, 2H, 3H, 4H, 5H, and 6H are generally used for drafting. HB leads are relatively soft leads for dark, thicker line work and for hand lettering. Nonphoto blue leads are useful for drawing guidelines and will not show when drawings are photocopied or reproduced in blueprinting. Experiment and practice before determining which leads work best for your hand and technique; F, H, 2H, 3H, and 4H are good for beginners.
Lead holder	Leads sold separately fit into the holder for drafting; some are self-sharpening. The holder provides for flexibility.
Lead pointer	This serves as a lead point sharpener when using a lead holder.
Sharpener	Use a battery-operated, electrical, or standard sharpener or sandpaper block to sharpen points of wooden pencils.

(continued)

Table 6.1
Drawing Supplies and Their Use, *continued*

Item	Description and Use
Sketch pad	No larger than 9″ × 12″ so that is can be carried easily for impromptu use.
Technical pen	This is used for precisely inked drawings. It is costly and requires great care with cleaning.
Templates	Plastic, stencil-like tools that use standardized dimensions for furniture and equipment; generally at $\frac{1}{4}$″ scale. Select an all-purpose template with furniture, door swings, and toilets, another with plumbing fixtures, and one with shapes such as circles and ellipses.
Tracing paper roll	18″ or 24″ wide, white or yellow, preferred by some for preliminary or rough drawings with soft leads or markers. Often referred to as trace.
Triangles	45/45 and 30/60 degrees used in combination with straightedge to draft vertical and angled lines.
	Generally made of clear plastic in sizes ranging from 12″ to 16″, with inking edge; a 3″ triangle is useful to guide hand lettering. Adjustable version can be set to any angle.
T square	Wooden, with clear plastic edges, is preferred to metal; 36″ is long enough for most projects.
Vellum	Translucent, durable paper for finished technical drawings, ink, and CAD drawings.

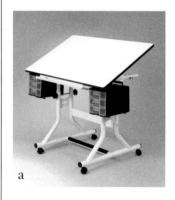

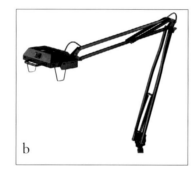

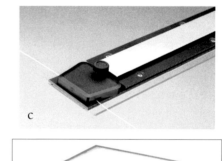

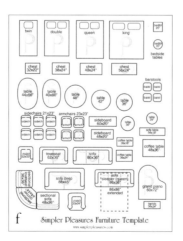

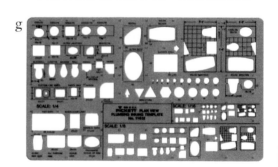

Figures a–g
Drawing equipment. a. Drafting table. b. Desk light. c. Parallel rule. d. Light box. e. Drawing supplies. f. Furniture template. g. Plumbing fixtures. *(d: Courtesy Blink Art supplies; f: Courtesy of Simple Pleasures)*

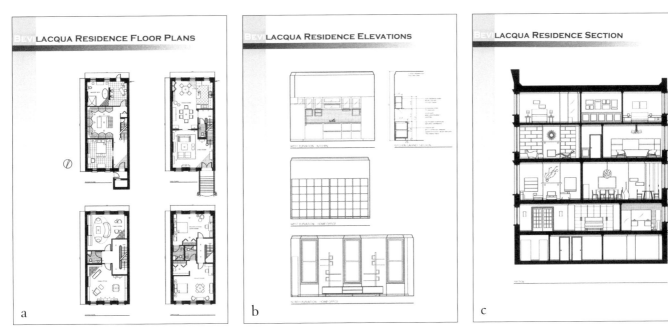

Figure 6.1
Cuts through a space for a student project. a. Floor plan; b. Elevation; c. Section. *(a, b, and c: © Cristina Rosadia-Bondoc)*

be vertical or horizontal. This type of graphic representation, either manual or computer generated, is a measured, or technical, drawing. Generally following bubble diagrams and matrices discussed in Chapter 5, the orthographic drawings that interior designers most often use are plans (including floor plans and reflected ceiling plans), elevations, and sections (Figure 6.1a–c). These drawings are usually created during the schematic, design development, and contract documents phases of a project (see Chapter 5).

Generally, more than one type of orthographic drawing is needed to understand a space. For example, a table denoted on a plan as a 24-inch circle does not communicate the table's height in relation to the other furniture, such as a nearby sofa. An elevation of that area of the space would provide this information.

Scale

The concept of scale (see Chapter 2) is essential for orthographic drawing because it allows the designer to draw actual spaces and objects at greatly reduced sizes so that their relationships may be represented on paper. Scale is the ratio of a measuring unit to the full size it represents. For example, stating that something is drawn at $^1/_{12}$-inch scale, or 1 inch = 1 foot, 0 inches means that $^1/_4$ of an inch on paper represents exactly 1 foot of actual size.[3] As noted earlier, when a scale changes, the *proportion* does not.

Many different scales are used in the architecture and design fields. The triangular **architectural scale**, with a total of four architectural scales per side and a total of 12 architectural scales on a triangular scale (Figure 6.2), is most often used for interior design. The scales range from the largest, in which 3 inches

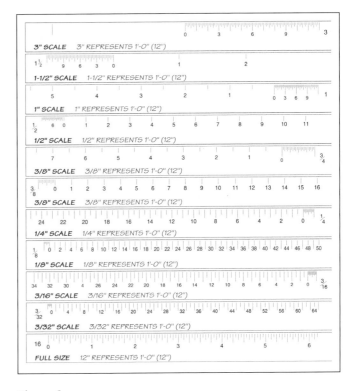

Figure 6.2
Architectural scales.

represents 1 foot, 0 inches, to the smallest, in which $\frac{1}{8}$ inch represents 1 foot, 0 inches. The most frequently used scales for orthographic drawings are the $\frac{1}{4}$-inch and $\frac{1}{8}$-inch scales. The $\frac{1}{4}$-inch scale is often used for residential projects, whereas the $\frac{1}{8}$-inch is usually used to depict large contract spaces, such as office complexes, airports, and hotels. As a general rule, the larger the scale chosen, the more detailed the information will be. Larger scales, such as $\frac{1}{2}$ inch, are frequently used to depict details in elevations and sections. The scale must be indicated on the drawings, for example, "scale $\frac{1}{2}'' = 1'-0''$." These architectural scales are also available using the metric system. Alternatively, a metric conversion chart or tool may be used in conjunction with the conventional U.S. scale (see Figure 6.2 and Basic Metric Conversion Table, page 496).

Lettering

Many practitioners believe that hand drawings look best with hand lettering, although computer-generated lettering has become popular. Written information is needed not only on orthographic drawings, but also on other visual presentation boards. Printing should look professional and be executed confidently and with consistency.

The smaller the scale used for hand lettering, the easier it is to control. The larger the scale, the heavier the line weight should be (see later discussion). The size and, to some degree, the style of the lettering depend on the purpose of the text; on who will view it, and how; and on the proportion of text to the presentation as a whole.

Typically, there should be no slant to the vertical lines. A small lettering guide may be used to assist in drawing vertical lines. Very light pencil lines should be made to control spacing, height, and width of letters. A commonly used lettering is the **block style**, which is wide and square in shape and usually done in upper-case (capital) letters (Figure 6.3).

Even the most standard software programs provide numerous lettering options. Computer software programs have made lettering convenient and flexible, offering a vast array of typefaces, colors, font sizes, and styles to choose from. (Chapter 14 further explores the relationship of lettering styles to presentation packages.)

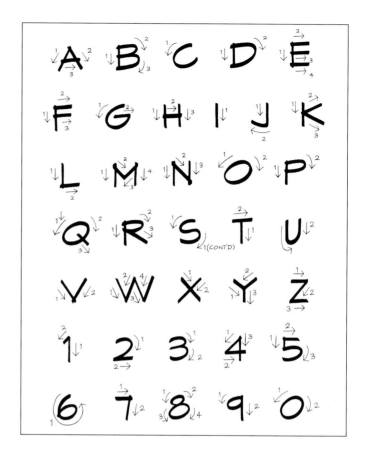

Figure 6.3
Block-style lettering.

Plan

Plan is used as a general term to denote any drawing in which two dimensions (the length and width of the space and its contents) are projected in scale onto a flat surface (i.e., the paper). More precisely, the floor plan is a specific view, sometimes referred to as a bird's-eye view, of a space. It is as though an observer were sitting on a glass ceiling and looking down into the space. This is the plan most commonly used by designers. When complete with furnishings, it may be referred to as a furniture plan. In contrast, the reflected ceiling plan, although also a horizontal slice across a space, is from an opposite viewpoint. Here, it is as if a mirror on the floor plane were reflecting the objects located on the ceiling, such as light fixtures. (The reflected ceiling plan will be explained further in Chapter 7.)

Because height is not drawn on a plan, a **cut line** is decided upon. This line can be thought of as a horizontal slice taken through the plan at a specific height, usually 4 feet up from the floor, for a floor plan. Elements positioned higher than the cut line are drawn differently from elements that appear below this point. For example, a dashed line indicates cabinets that are above the cut line. Multiple plans thus help clarify the intended design. Elevations and sections for key components may also be necessary to provide a more complete picture of the space.

Other types of plans were identified in Chapter 5 as part of the contract documents package. These plans, which are highly technical and specific, include demolition, construction, and power and communication plans.

Certain conventions are used in orthographic drawings to communicate specific pieces of information, such as windows, walls, partitions, doors, and stairs. Some conventions relate to line weights and types of lines; others relate to graphic symbols and placement.

Line Weight The general rule of thumb for all drawings is that the boldest line weight (darkest or thickest) is used to signify the components closest to the viewer, such as walls; a medium line weight is used for fixtures and furniture; and the finest line weight (lightest or thinnest) is used for surface details. These different line weights are achieved by using a range of different lead (graphite) types for different components in the plan.

A number and lettering system is used to designate lead types from soft to hard. B (often used for sketching) is the softest and H the hardest. The softest lead produces the darkest line. Leads typically used for interior design purposes are F, H, 2H, 3H, and 4H. F or H, the softer of these leads, would be used for walls, to produce the darkest lines. (With a technique known as **poché**, from the French for "pocket," the designer fills in the two lines of the wall to create its thickness.) The slightly harder and lighter 2H would be used for furniture and stairs, and, in broken or dashed lines, to indicate cabinets and archways. The hardest and lightest of the leads, 3H or 4H, would be used for floor surfacing or details, such as rendering marble. Each line drawn must maintain the same weight from beginning to end (Figure 6.4). It is advisable to practice drawing both vertical and horizontal lines and their intersections.

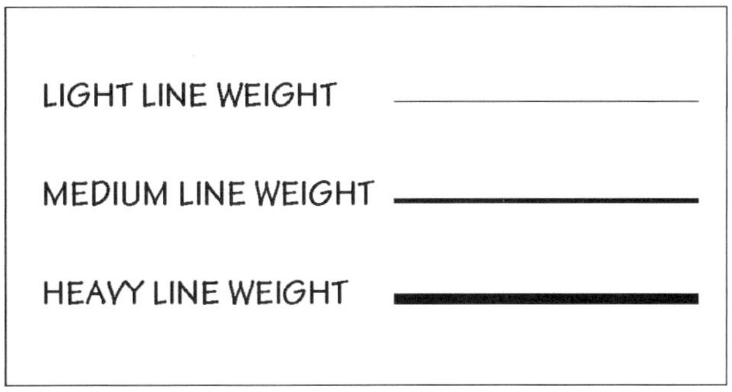

Symbols All plans should indicate the orientation of the site. A north-facing arrow, or the letter *N*, is the standard convention for orienting the plan. When a plan is supplemented with accompanying drawings,

Figure 6.4
Strokes created with several different lead weights.

such as an elevation or a section, cross-referencing is needed (Figure 6.5a–c). A typical method of linking a plan to a corresponding elevation or section is to place an arrow pointing toward a detail to be shown in the elevation or a component to be drawn in the section. This detail or component is then assigned a numerical designation, enclosed in a circle.

As discussed in Chapter 5, different types of plans require different types of symbols. On reflected ceiling plans, for example, specific symbols are used to designate the types of lighting fixtures, such as chandeliers. Plans generally include a **legend**, a list of symbols and their explanations.

Title Block As mentioned in Chapter 5, the title block contains the client's name and address, the name of the interior design firm and designer, registration information, and the number of pages (Figure 6.6a and b). Designers may have a supply printed for their firm as clear, adhesive-backed labels. Templates are also available with CAD programs.

Elevation

Whereas floor plans show placement and the tops of furnishings, elevations show the heights and details of architectural features, such as moldings, and furnishings, such as built-in cabinets, window treatments, and art.

Elevations are derived from the floor plan, as if you were in the room, facing a wall head-on. Rather than a horizontal slice of a space, as is represented in a plan, an elevation is a vertical slice through the space. The selection of the wall(s) to be shown in an elevation may be based on several decisions. The goal may be to highlight interior features that are not seen on a floor plan because of their relationship to the cut line, such

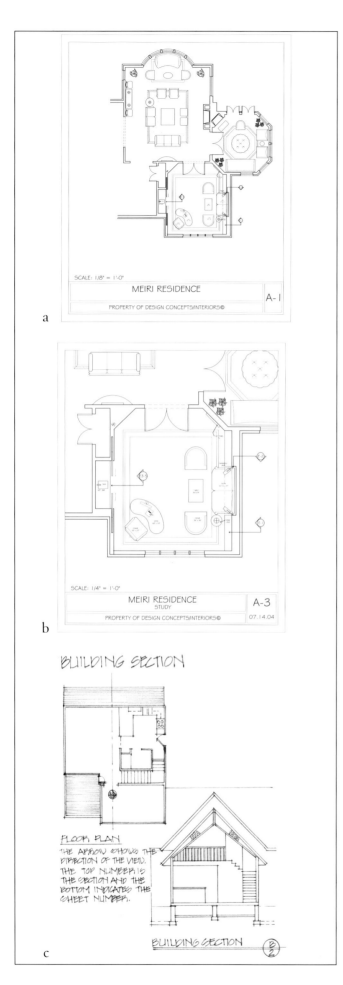

a

b

c

Figure 6.5

a. Main floor plan; b. Close-up of portion of the main floor plan with symbols cross-referenced; c. Floor plan cross-referenced to corresponding building section cross-referenced. *(a and b: Courtesy of Phyllis Harbinger/ DCISTUDIO; c: Illustrations by Diana Bennett Wirtz from* Hand Drafting for Interior Design *by Diana Bennett Wirtz, Fairchild Books, © 2010)*

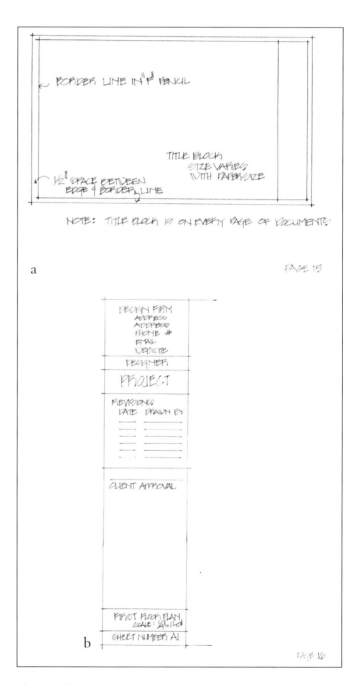

a

b

Figure 6.6

a and b. Title blocks for hand drawings. *(a and b: Illustrations by Diana Bennett Wirtz from* Hand Drafting for Interior Design *by Diana Bennett Wirtz, Fairchild Books, © 2010)*

a

FRAGRANCE WALL ELEVATION
SCALE: 1/4" = 1'-0"

KITCHEN ELEVATIONS

KITCHEN ELEVATIONS ARE USED TO SHOW DESIGN
DETAILS, THE CABINET STYLE AND DESIGN STYLE
OF THE AREA

KITCHEN ELEVATIONS ARE GENERALLY IN HALF
INCH SCALE IN ORDER TO SHOW MORE DETAIL

YOU CAN SHOW DETAILS OF THE FOLLOWING:
    WINDOWS
    WINDOW COVERINGS
    CABINET STYLE
    BACK SPLASH DESIGN
    MOLDING
b   SPECIAL EFFECTS

Figure 6.7
Detailed elevations. a. Display fixtures for a student's retail project; b. Elevation of a residential kitchen wall showing cabinetry, appliances, and decorative finishes. *(a: © Cristina Rosadia-Bondoc; b: Illustrations by Diana Bennett Wirtz from* Hand Drafting for Interior Design *by Diana Bennett Wirtz, Fairchild Books, © 2010)*

as crown molding, which is more than 4 feet above the floor, or a wall may be selected because it highlights an architectural feature, such as a fireplace, or unique or custom-designed furnishings, or wall and window treatments (Figure 6.7a and b).

Elevations are two-dimensional; therefore, there is no perspective. Only a line indicates the ceiling and floor planes. In a corresponding plan, the line weight communicates important information about the elevation. Any portion of a wall that is closer to the viewer is drawn in a bolder line. The standard convention is for the line representing the floor to be bolder than the ceiling, to "ground" the drawing. Details should be drawn using a lighter line weight than is used for furniture.

When created for presentations, rather than as contract documents upon which construction is based, elevations do not contain written information, such as dimensions and other technical data. Like plans and sections, however, they are based on scale and include titles, symbols, and scale notation. Elevations are typically better understood by a client than are floor plans. Like plans, elevations may be embellished through rendering techniques (see later discussion).

Section

Sections are slices through the structure of a building or interior that show greater detail. For an interior section the scale is usually $\frac{1}{2}'' = 1''{-}0''$ or $1'' = 1''{-}0''$. Fireplaces, kitchen cabinets, and other custom-designed furniture are examples of objects that a designer might wish to select for a section drawing (Figure 6.8). The term **detail** may be used to describe a section that depicts the design of an object, such as the lamp in Figure 6.9a and b. Different line weights are used to differentiate exterior, or outer, limits (darkest lines) and interior details (lighter lines). Like elevations, sections must be cross-referenced to the floor plan. When sections are used as contract documents, specifications concerning construction and materials are also noted.

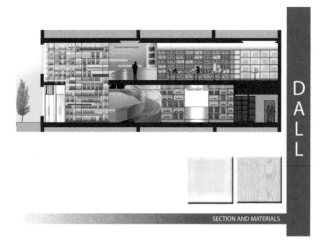

Figure 6.8
Section of a two-story building for a student's retail project.
(© Olesya Lyusaya LEED AP)

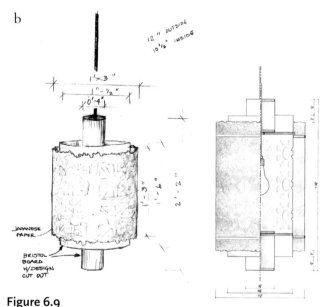

Figure 6.9
a. Elevation by student for Furniture and Studio Detailing Project; b. Detail of lamp fixture. *(a and b: Courtesy of Tamison Rose, New England School of Art and Design at Suffolk University)*

PICTORIAL DRAWING

Unlike orthographic drawing, which generally requires multiple drawings, **pictorial drawing** provides a more realistic view of a space through the use of a singular graphic. Pictorial drawings are categorized as either paraline or perspective drawings.

Paraline Drawing

A **paraline drawing** is regarded as the simplest, easiest, and most accurate of the three-dimensional drawings. Certain principles apply to the different types of paraline drawings: Vertical lines are drawn parallel to one another. The scale that was used to draw the plan is used. The width and length measurements of the furnishings used on the floor plan remain the same. However, height is added, not just for walls, but also for each piece of furniture and architectural element, such as windows and doors.

Plan Oblique A type of paraline drawing that is a projection from an existing plan rotated to the angle the designer selects is termed **plan oblique** or **axonometric**. The most common choices are 30/60 degrees and 45/45 degrees. The total degrees of each choice always add up to 90. As shown in Figure 6.10, the 30/60-degree angle is a more natural or realistic view; the 45/45, a steeper view.

Isometric Projection Isometric projection drawings also rely on the use of angles. In this instance, there are a total of three axes, each at 30 degrees (Figure 6.11). These drawings tend to be more time-consuming to produce than plan oblique drawings. Circles are drawn as ellipses or by using templates as a guide. These drawings are generally used to communicate form and spatial relationships as well as for technical and construction documents.

Perspective Drawing

The three types of **perspective drawing**—one-point, two-point, and three-point—are all three-dimensional representations. Because three-point perspective is not a commonly used technique for interiors, it is not explored in this text. Perspective drawings are particularly useful for client presentations because the view is more natural than an orthographic representation of space.

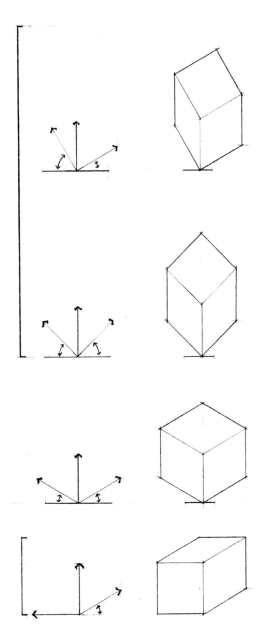

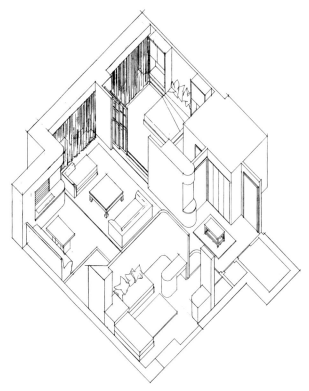

Figure 6.11

Isometric drawing. *(Courtesy of Nicholas Politis, Fashion Institute of Technology)*

Figure 6.10

Paraline drawing. *(Illustration from* Hand Drawing for Designers *by Douglas R. Seidler and Amy Korté, Fairchild Books, © 2009)*

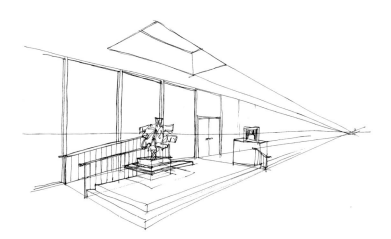

Figure 6.12

One-point perspective with a right vanishing point.

Different methods for producing perspective drawings can be used to create appearances ranging from simple concepts and ideas to more complex technical information. All types of perspective drawings share certain basic characteristics, summarized in *FYI . . . Basic Concepts in Perspective Drawing.*

One-Point Perspective One-point perspective is so named because it has one vanishing point, which sits on the horizon line. Parallel lines of the same size form the ceiling and floor and the two side walls. The three major choices for selecting a station point depend on what you want to capture in the drawing. If all three walls have equal importance, you will want to view the space as if facing the middle of the back wall. This way, both the left and right walls will be the same size and of equal importance.

A drawing with the vanishing point on the right (Figure 6.12) tells us that the right wall has little significance for the design. Perhaps it contains only a door or an archway that is to remain as is, without renovation.

FYI . . . Basic Concepts in Perspective Drawing

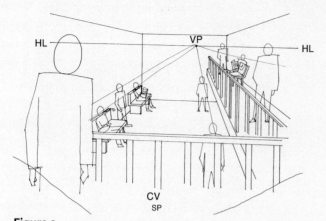

Figure a
Sample of a perspective drawing.

- The **picture plane (PP)** is an imaginary transparent plane, like glass, through which the area to be drawn is viewed. The surface of the drawing paper becomes the picture plane. The relationship of an object to the picture plane (whether its front plane is parallel to this plane or angled) determines the type of perspective.

- The **horizon line (HL)** represents the viewer's eye level. The standard convention is for this to be approximately 5"–0". As an object is moved below the viewer's eye level, the top of the object is seen, not the bottom. Conversely, an object above the horizon line has its bottom surface viewed.

- Lines in perspective converge toward one or more **vanishing points (VPs)**. Parallel lines appear to converge as they move toward the same, or a shared, vanishing point on the horizon line. Picture yourself driving down a road and looking at the telephone poles on the side of the road. They are the same distance from, and parallel to, one another, yet they seem to come together as they move away from you, meeting on the horizon line at the vanishing point.

- The **station point (SP)** is the location from which the space is viewed.

- The **cone of vision (CV)** is an angle of view that represents the range of sight of the viewer. If the angle chosen is very wide, elements on the perimeter may appear to be distorted, especially with digitally produced perspectives.

- Near objects overlap objects that are farther from the viewer. In perspective the objects do not stand alone, like soldiers standing at attention.

- As objects move closer to the viewer, they appear to become larger. Conversely, as they move farther away, they seem to become smaller. This is called **diminution in size**.

- Selection of view—that is, deciding what should be captured in the drawing—is a crucial step in the process.

The back wall and left wall in this case are of more importance, showing the planned design changes. The selection of the vanishing point on the left conveys the opposite importance.

Two-Point Perspective Like one-point perspective, two-point perspective has a horizon line positioned at eye level, but this time there are *two* vanishing points sitting on the horizon line. The one on the right is called the right vanishing point (RVP), and the one on the left is called the left vanishing point (LVP) (Figure 6.13).

Figure 6.13
Two-point perspective with both a left and right vanishing point.

Figure 6.14
Forms and shapes redrawn into furnishings.

sphere, cone, and cylinder, either separately or in some combination (Figure 6.14). With the exception of the cube, the other forms will appear the same in both types of perspectives.

- *Cubes* can be turned into chairs or tables in either one- or two-point perspective, depending on the view.
- *Spheres* can be turned into cups, vases, or lighting fixtures with the addition or subtraction of a few lines.
- *Cones* can be transformed into home accessories, such as lamp shades.
- *Cylinders* can be made into columns and home furnishings.

Plan Projection Method This method, sometimes referred to as a refined linear perspective, is a drawing based on a completed floor plan and elevation done to scale. With plan projection an attempt is made to present the best view of the space, and so a decision must be made regarding the view to be selected; therefore, the location of the station point and the cone of vision are important considerations.

Prepared Grid Method Another method for drawing one- or two-point perspectives is using a prepared grid (Figure 6.15a–e). You may create a grid and use it

As in one-point perspective, changing the station point can change the view.

Basic Geometric Forms Almost all one- or two-point perspective drawings can be created using four of the basic three-dimensional geometric forms: cube,

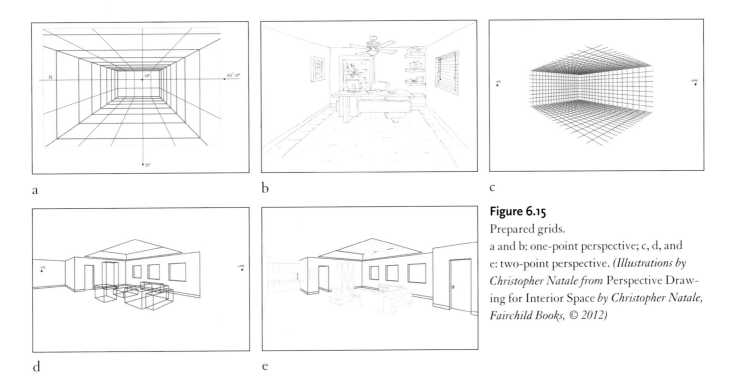

a   b   c

d   e

Figure 6.15
Prepared grids.
a and b: one-point perspective; c, d, and e: two-point perspective. *(Illustrations by Christopher Natale from* Perspective Drawing for Interior Space *by Christopher Natale, Fairchild Books, © 2012)*

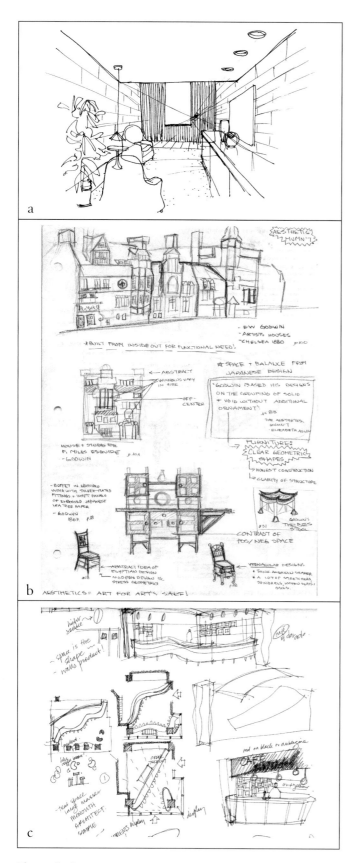

Figure 6.16

Sketching styles. a. One-point perspective in ink; b. Ink and pencil sketch; c. Concept sketches in planning stages. (*b: © Kate M. Narwani of Kate Marie, Inc.; c: Illustrations by Tiiu Poldma from* Taking Up Space: Exploring the Design Process *by Tiiu Poldma, Fairchild Books, © 2009*)

as a guide, using a second sheet of paper as an overlay, and avoid having to erase the grid. Grids may also be purchased in a variety of formats that feature different views with varying vanishing points, station points, and cones of vision. It should be noted that the use of a prepared grid requires manipulation to adapt to each individual situation. A series of drawings is usually required to provide a fully executed perspective using this method.

SKETCHING

When first meeting with a client, a designer may make quick sketches to convey an idea, whether about a room arrangement, a customized piece of furniture, or a design detail. The practice of hand sketching, using a variety of media, provides a designer with an expanded repertoire for communication. As mentioned earlier, this skill also aids in ideation, or idea development, including design problem solving. The sketching of bubble diagrams is one such application. A variety of individualized sketching styles, purposes, and media are illustrated in Figure 6.16 a–c. Sketching is a method of capturing, processing, validating, and perhaps interpreting observations in a direct and personal way. The term *thumbnail* is used to describe a small and concise drawing (Figure 6.17). As a preliminary drawing it may serve as a reference from which to work before embarking on a large-scale version of a drawing.

Many of the materials referred to in Tables 6.1 and 6.2 are used for sketching, among them soft leads, ink, and markers.

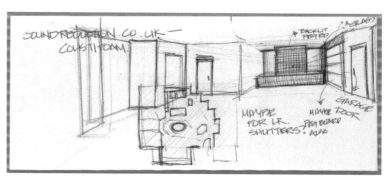

Figure 6.17

A thumbnail sketch serves as the basis for a larger drawing. (*Courtesy of Jennifer Angulo*)

RENDERING

It is important for the designer to make the entire design process easy and understandable for the client, and renderings are one way to achieve this. Renderings change line drawings into presentations of depth that clearly communicate the concept, showing how suggested selections will look when pulled together. The extent to which drawings are rendered, to bring them as close as possible to the real thing, depends on several factors, among them time and money. Drawings can be rendered simply or elaborately, at little expense of time and money, or very expensively.

Rendering may enhance any drawing, ranging from quick sketches to more complicated drawings. Rendering is not limited to perspective drawings. Floor plans and elevations may also be rendered to add more information as well as visual interest. In talking about the physical layout during meetings with clients, for example, the proposed color schemes, pattern, and materials work hand-in-hand with the layout.

Color can be dropped into quick sketches using either colored pencil or markers, which are easy to apply and require no time to dry. The addition of textural renderings in pencil or ink in a floor plan enhances the understanding of the materials being used (Figure 6.18a–c).

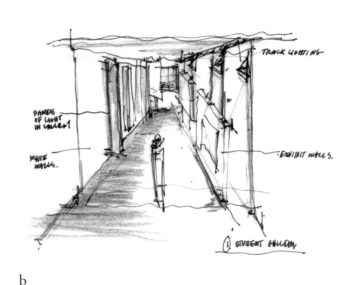

a

b

c

Figure 6.18

a. Finished hand-drawn pencil furniture plan with shading and textures rendered in pencil; b. Student's detailed sketch in ink and colored pencil drawing with notes; c. Elevation drawn in ink and rendered with a loose style. *(a: Illustrations by Diana Bennett Wirtz from* Hand Drafting for Interior Design *by Diana Bennett Wirtz, Fairchild Books, © 2010; b: Illustration from* Hand Drawing for Designers *by Douglas R. Seidler and Amy Korté, Fairchild Books, © 2009; c: Courtesy of Drew McGukin)*

The adage *Time is money* holds true here. When opting to create a rendering, a designer should know what media to use, and when, to achieve the best results in the least amount of time. The supplies listed in Table 6.2 and described below include a wide selection of media for use either alone or in combination. Although suggestions and techniques are provided in this text, you should always try other methods and experiment with these and other supplies.

The major media are pencil, ink, marker, and watercolor. Charcoal, chalk, pastel, or gouache is sometimes employed. Media are used either alone or in combination, referred to as mixed media.

Pencil

Pencil is a relatively inexpensive, yet convenient, rendering method. **Graphite** ("lead") pencil is an effective way to render shadows and textures and add depth to floor plans and elevations. Figure 6.19a–g illustrates a variety of techniques, such as shading, hatching, crosshatching, stippling, and scribbling, that may be used. Colored pencil works well on many types of paper; the smoother the paper, the less grainy and more uniform the result. Pencil may be successfully used for preliminary sketches or finished presentation drawings.

Ink

Renderings in ink are usually done in waterproof black or sepia (a variation of brown) to create graded tonal values. By narrowing the spaces between stroke marks, a tonal progression from light to dark is created. The use of different strokes and placement of different amounts of pressure on the pen result in varied line weights. Other techniques, such as cross-hatching,

Table 6.2
Rendering and Presentation Supplies and Their Use

Item	Description and Use
Black watercolor pencil	For rendering marble and other details.
Cement pickup	Rubber square useful for lifting paper and other materials off the board when using cement.
Cutting board	Cut-resistant surface with grid patterns. Used for convenience when cutting boards, materials, and so on.
Disposable black ink pens, fine to micropoint	For outlining and adding definition to drawings.
Double-faced tape	Used to mount heavy samples, such as wood, tile, and stone.
Illustration board	All-purpose backing for all media.
Knives	Snap-off cutter, utility knife, and X-Acto knife with #1 blades for cuts into various thicknesses of paper and boards. Blades should be changed frequently between cuts.
Marker pad	Paper that is less translucent than vellum, used for markers to lessen bleeding of the pigment.
Markers	Warm gray for shading, shadow, and color changes. Cool gray for glossy surfaces, such as metal. Other colors for a variety of finishes. Colorless blender to soften edges.

Sample drawing supplies.   *(continued)*

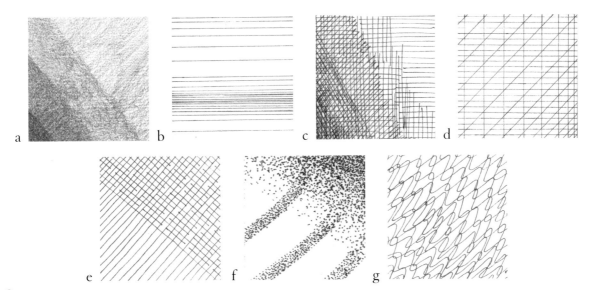

Figure 6.19

a. shading; b. hatching; c. cross-hatching; d. cross-hatching; e. cross-hatching; f. stippling; g. scribbling (*Illustrations from* Hand Drawing for Designers *by Douglas R. Seidler and Amy Korte, Fairchild Books, © 2009*)

Table 6.2 Rendering and Presentation Supplies and Their Use, *continued*	
Item	**Description and Use**
Metal ruler with cork back	Used as a stable measuring and cutting edge.
Paper (rubber) cement	All-purpose adhesive for mounting drawings. Used on both surfaces to be adhered.
Paper cement thinner	Used to thin cement, for easier application.
Paper cutter	Vary in size to accommodate image sizes. Useful tool for trimming. Grid surface helpful for alignment.
Removable (painter's) tape	For preliminary layouts.
Scissors	General utility type for cutting. Pinking shears may be used for fabrics to avoid frayed edges; it is preferable to tape fabric edges around a board surface.
Watercolor block, cold press 140 lbs., 10″– 14″	For general watercolor rendering use.
Watercolor paint set, transparent, in pans; set of 24	For general watercolor rendering use.
Watercolor brushes	Sizes 1, 5, 8, 12; size 1 made of ox hair for watercolor rendering of foliage. Various sizes for general watercolor rendering use.
White glue	All-purpose adhesive.
Wax-based colored pencils, box of 24 or more	For rendering pattern, marble, wood grain, etc.
White charcoal pencil	For highlights, reflections, and correcting mistakes in watercolor renderings.

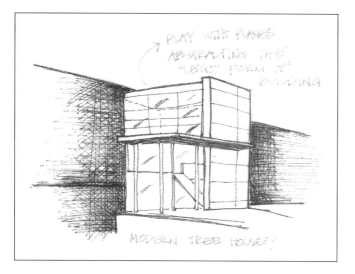

Figure 6.20
Cross-hatching in ink conveys the designer's "Play with Planes."
(*© Cristina Rosadia-Bondoc*)

a

which is used in pencil drawings, may be used for ink drawings as well (Figure 6.20).

Marker

Because marker can be applied quickly and dries almost immediately, it is called a fast medium. Markers are also referred to as studio, or art, markers. Marker is a versatile and expedient medium, adaptable to both preliminary and finished drawings (Figure 6.21a–c).

Many markers come with two different nibs (ends): one broad (blunt), which can be turned in three positions to give three different widths, the other with a finer point. Ultrafine markers may be used similarly to ink pens for drawing lines. Markers are available in many colors and can provide several more color combinations by layering one color on top of another. Using a gray marker under a color will alter the intensity and value of that color. Markers that are colorless, referred to as blenders, are also available to soften edges between colors. Creating a marker color chart for reference is useful.

Use of either warm or cool grays alone is effective for showing depth. This rendering technique is used

b

Figure 6.21
Examples of marker renderings of interior spaces. (*a: Courtesy of Drew McGukin; b: Courtesy of and rendered by Constance Johannsen; c: Illustrations from* Hand Drawing for Designers *by Douglas R. Seidler and Amy Korté, Fairchild Books, © 2009*)

c

widely for magazine and brochure layouts because it prints well.

When marker is used on paper that is highly absorbent, such as bond and Bristol, the color blends less easily and is more saturated and deeper. Conversely, when it is used on less absorbent paper, such as vellum and trace, the colors are more muted and lighter. Layout bond paper treated for marker is a sensible choice. When it is applied to the back of trace paper, a lighter tone is produced. Pencils are often used to highlight marker renderings, including white pencil.

Watercolor

The most painterly medium to use is watercolor. Welldone watercolor renderings are beautiful paintings. They require not only great skill, but also time and expense. For these reasons, they are more likely to serve as finished presentation drawings for large-scale projects, rather than as process tools. (See Figure 6.22a and b)

Many people regard a watercolor rendering as a softer expression of a space than can be produced by a computer. Although watercolors are less likely to be used for contract projects, some interior design firms continue to use them despite the advent of computer-generated renderings.

Watercolor paints may be transparent or opaque. The transparent form is available in pans, for convenience, and is more widely used for rendering interior spaces. Opaque watercolors may be used to cover a mistake in the initial rendering.

Watercolors are applied in layers. Because the paint is water based, it takes time to dry. When you render in this medium, color matching is an important factor. You can use a white charcoal pencil to correct mistakes.

The use of black-and-white paints creates an effective tonal rendition of a space and is an appropriate alternative to full-color rendering, especially when the drawing will be reproduced in gray values for a publication.

Figure 6.22
a. Flat wash watercolor drawings of an entry hall and b. Robert Martin's gouache rendering of a living room designed in 1970 by Yale R. Burge. *(a: Illustration from* Hand Drawing for Designers *by Douglas R. Seidler and Amy Korté, Fairchild Books, © 2009; b: Robert Martin. Courtesy of Yale R. Burge Antiques)*

The effect achieved with watercolor rendering is highly dependent on the type and quality of brush used as well as the technique. Sable brushes are considerably more expensive than synthetic-fiber brushes. To apply a wash (thin layer of color) over large areas, use an angled, $1/2$-inch thick brush, which is easier to use than a straight-edged brush. The wash can be applied to paper that is wet or dry, called a wet wash or dry wash, respectively. The color goes on quickly and smoothly. A fan-shaped brush with hard bristles can also be used to apply watercolor to either a wet or a dry surface; a wet surface produces a more muted, impressionistic look.

Paper selection is an important ingredient affecting the appearance of the finished watercolor. Highly absorbent paper is used with wet or water-soluble media, such as watercolor. Watercolor paper comes in various weights and finishes, sold as sheets or as a block. The three finishes are hot press (smooth finish); cold press (having a slight tooth, or texture); and rough (high texture), which is used less often for watercolor renderings of interiors. When sheets are used, they should be those designated as 140 pounds or heavier; otherwise, the paper will ripple. Paper designated as 140 pounds or lighter should be in block form. Illustration board cold press #80 is excellent for watercolor. The number 80 refers to the weight of the paper. Although cold press is only slightly absorbent, it holds watercolor because it has tooth.

Gouache (and tempera) paints are more opaque than marker and watercolor and are capable of creating both softness and hardness. They are generally more time-consuming to execute but have been a traditional medium for capturing interior renderings.

Effective use of pastel chalk or pencil creates highly textured and detailed drawings. Oil painting, an expensive and time-consuming rendering technique, is not typically used for commercial purposes, but rather, to create a pure artistic expression of a space. (Figure 6.23a and b)

Mixed Media

The previously mentioned methods can be mixed in many ways in one drawing. For example, marker with pencil is effective in rendering wood.

Illustration board cold press #80 and bond paper are suitable choices for mixed media presentations.

a

b

Figure 6.23
Mixed Media. a. marker and colored pencil and b. watercolor, gouache, and colored pencil. *(a: © Cristina Rosadia-Bondoc; b: Illustration by Christina M. Scalise from* Interior Design Illustrated: Marker and Watercolor Techniques *by Christina M. Scalise, Fairchild Books, © 2008)*

Kraft paper, a coarse brown paper, yields a more informal appearance. All allow for use of a combination of markers and pencils.

MODELS

A three-dimensional model done to scale is an effective way to show the volume of an interior space. Such a model simulates the experience of walking in the space.

Models used by the designer to explore design ideas are referred to as **study**, or **sketch**, **models**. At this stage, model making generally serves as an exploration of the form and relationships of the space rather than providing the details of its furnishing and finishes. Entourage, either ready-made or individually constructed, may be dropped in. The addition of a person assists in the perception of scale. The materials chosen for a study model may be inexpensive (Figure 6.24a). More finished models, called **presentation models**, are typically prepared for large-scale commercial projects. The expense in both time and materials usually increases as one proceeds from a study to a presentation model. The latter may use materials such as textiles, plastic, metals, mesh, and wire. People who specialize in model construction may be hired by firms to produce presentation models for a project.

As with rendering and, to some degree, all types of visual presentation, the purpose of the model should be clear before embarking on it. Time, effort, and money expended for a presentation that are not commensurate with its purpose is wasteful for both students and professional designers.

Models may be made of various materials, among them paperboard and wood. Several types of adhesives are available to hold the model components together. Choices depend on the type of materials used to construct the model, ease of application, drying time, and expense. Additionally, some noxious adhesives may pose health concerns and raise issues of safety and possible negative effects on the environment.

White glue is often used for paperboard. When it is used for wood models, the items may need to be clamped to hold them together while the glue dries. Paper (rubber) cement can be used for gluing lightweight materials, such as paper and fabric. An alternative is the use of pins to allow for easy modification of the model if paperboard or foam core board is used.

Figure 6.24

Models. a. Student's study model to explore space and scale done with inexpensive materials; b. Presentation model in inexpensive wood; c. Presentation model in costly hardwood. (*a: © Corbis Super RF / Alamy; b: Courtesy Brooks + Scarpa Architects; c: Model and photo provided by Midwest Studios*)

Paperboard

Paperboard tends to be lightweight, inexpensive, and easy to cut. Foam board, also called foam core, consists of a polystyrene core sandwiched between two sheets of paper. It comes in various thicknesses and a range of colors, although white is most often used for models. Corrugated board, a rippled version of cardboard that is typically brown in color, is inexpensive and can be cut easily. It is also attractive as an environmentally friendly alternative, as are chipboard, a rigid material made from recycled waste paper, and illustration board with high rag content (closer to that of cotton).

Wood

More expensive and time-consuming to work with than paperboard, wood is used less often for preliminary studies than for final presentations (Figure 6.24b). Balsa is light and porous and can be cut with a simple hand tool, such as a blade or knife. Balsa is easy to carve and is available in blocks, strips, sheets, and veneers. Basswood, also a light-colored wood, sands better than balsa; it has a slight grain and is available in a variety of forms, including those used as ornamental moldings. Other, more expensive hardwoods with more distinctive graining and coloration, such as cherry and mahogany, may also be used (Figure 6.24c). Working with such woods may require the use of power tools.

THE ROLE OF TECHNOLOGY AND DESIGN

Dependence on computer technology is a feature of virtually all industries today, not just those involving design. CAD is only one aspect of computerization, which has had an impact on the way business is conducted. Other types of computer software, especially those that relate to business practices, are discussed in Chapter 14. Additionally, many interior design students and professionals supplement their digital drawings through the use of CAD software such as Adobe Photoshop (as discussed below).

Drafting and Design

Many professionals use both hand and computer to generate drawings, with varying degrees of reliance on one or the other, and at different stages of the design process. Sometimes, they toggle between the two; other times, they combine both practices for one project, even for one drawing.

The student of design needs to understand the essential principles and conventions of manual drawing before being introduced to the world of CAD. CAD is based on the same fundamentals discussed earlier in this chapter. Computer software programs have the capacity, sometimes referred to as functionality, to produce images, ranging from simple sketches; to two-dimensional line drawings; to plans and elevations; to panoramic, animated, rendered perspectives with complete entourage that "walks" the viewer through the space. However, even with such complex and "intelligent" software, the user must input the data (at least most of the time, as of this writing).

Many different software programs are available for both two- and three-dimensional drawings, with tremendous variation in price, user-friendliness, and capability. Most also include three-dimensional modeling (simulation) and rendering capabilities of varying degrees of complexity. Although there may be a significant learning curve, once mastered, CAD can provide accuracy, speed, and convenience. The ability to generate drawings, even relatively simple floor plans, using a CAD program is a valuable skill for a prospective employee.

CAD is widely used in firms that prepare orthographic documents. In addition to creating precise, detailed drawings, the software offers a much more convenient way of storing changes made, including change order requests; organizing pagination and page replacements; and preparing legends and specifications. With manual drafting, in comparison, organization is often a challenge; it can be difficult, for example, keeping track of the multiple drawings (layers) produced for one space, such as the floor plan, the reflected ceiling plan, and so on (Figure 6.25).

Some firms outsource their CAD work (i.e., hire on a freelance basis) when required to show intricate detailing in renderings and for final presentations. The work of one such firm is shown in the advertisement in Figure 6.26.

The ability to render perspective drawings with relative ease and flexibility is another reason that CAD has become so popular. Many software programs con-

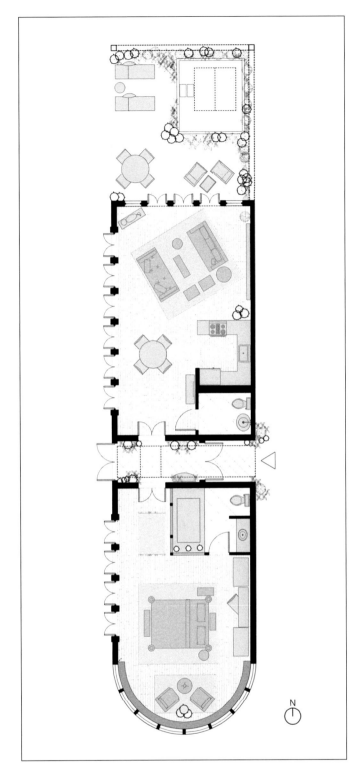

Figure 6.25
Computer-generated floor plan. *(Provided by Francine Smith)*

tain rich libraries of template symbols, shapes, forms, furniture, and textures that may be used as is or customized. The ability to render building materials becomes rather easy using these tools. Changes in choice of color, pattern, materials, or lighting conditions can be accom-

Figure 6.26
Computer graphics outsourced: Drafting Design Services, New York City. *(Courtesy of Drafting Design Services, Inc.)*

plished with a few commands, in contrast to the time spent producing several hand renderings.

Rather than relying solely on the template of furniture styles in the library of a particular software program, many designers create their own library of furnishings or combine the template styles with other computer template versions individualized to a particular project. When a rendered drawing is created by a user who is skilled in both freehand and computer-generated drawing, it is often difficult to discern whether the drawing is manual or computer generated. Throughout this text, computer-generated drawings and hand drawings are commingled, perhaps providing testimony that this is the way of the future. This trend gives new meaning to the term *mixed media*.

Building information modeling (BIM) refers to advancement in recent years over more traditional digital drawing in the architecture and design industry.

BIM is an emerging approach to the design, analysis, and documentation of buildings.[4] This software application integrates design documents in order to present the full picture of a building. The program, with its emphasis on collaboration, has the capacity to serve the many disciplines involved with a project over the course of time. BIM addresses spatial relationships; light analysis; geographic information; and quantities and properties of building components, including the processes of construction, facility operation, and maintenance. Although its utility reaches well beyond the needs of the design student, BIM is becoming increasingly popular for complex studio projects.

Following is a partial listing of software applications used for drafting and design:

AutoCAD and AutoCAD LT

AutoCAD, by Autodesk, and its more premier version, AutoCAD LT (which has rendering features), are the leaders in the CAD market for the architectural and design community. AutoCAD programs and suites of programs offer two-dimensional drafting and three-dimensional modeling with different levels of complexity and a range of prices. Benefits include the ability to change a drawing easily and quickly; produce more precise and clear drawings; save or store drawings on CDs or post on the Web; exchange and share drawings with other professionals and consultants quickly and effectively; and use other programs in combination, such as Excel and Photoshop.[5]

Revit Architecture

This BIM tool, another Autodesk product, is used in the architecture, design, engineering, mechanical, and construction industries. A single database file may be represented in various ways, such as plans, sections, elevations, legends, and schedules. Because changes to each representation of the database model are made to one central model, changes made to one representation of the model (e.g., a plan) are easily applied to other representations of the model (e.g., an elevation). Revit drawings and schedules are always fully coordinated in terms of the building objects shown in drawings. An extensive library of materials, textures, and accurate artificial and natural lighting effects allows for creation of realistic, lifelike renderings.

3ds Max Design

3ds Max Design is an animation and visual effects package also from Autodesk. One can generate, explore, and evaluate a concept's impact early in the design process. Animated walk-throughs of the space and accurate daylight analyses aid in the understanding of how the design functions.

SketchUp and SketchUp Pro

Google SketchUp is considered an easy and intuitive program for accurate three-dimensional modeling. The program is based largely on two concepts: edges (straight lines) and faces (two-dimensional shapes). Two-dimensional drawings are easily extruded into three dimensions with a "Push/Pull" command, as in making a square into a cube. The Pro version has additional features, among them the ability to export easily into AutoCAD and 3ds Max. Image files, such as JPEG, TIFF, and PDF, are easily imported. As part of the Google family, SketchUp works well with Google Earth, which enhances design work involving aerial views, siting, landscape, and terrain.

Form·Z

Manufactured by AutoDesSys, this program offers an integrated animation environment, in which objects, lights, cameras, and colors can be animated and manipulated over time. Form·Z is an example of a general purpose, three-dimensional modeling program that combines two-dimensional drafting and rendering with three-dimensional sculpting. Enhancements to the basic software package include greater rendering capabilities and methods for simulating the lighting of interior spaces. Like other CAD programs, this type of software can aid in the design process as well as create final presentations.

Figure 6.27a–c shows examples of student work using computer software.

Figure 6.27

Student computer-generated drawings. a. Perspective incorporates photographic entourage; b. Concept sketches digitally drawn for thesis project; c. Section digitally drawn and rendered in gray scale, with text and images embedded. *(a: © Cristina Rosadia-Bondoc; b: Courtesy of Jessica Yahn Quezada; c: Laura Robertson)*

a

Lobby & Piazza Sketches

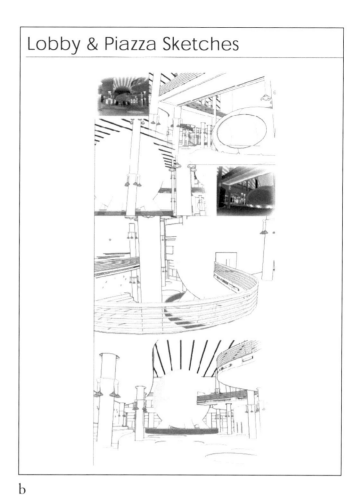

b

c

Digital Photo Editing

Other computer applications are manufactured for designers in several fields, including **digital photo editing**, the manipulation of photographic images. These programs are often used to supplement the drafting and modeling applications for digital drawings of interiors, exteriors, and buildings. In addition to the software (and a PC-compatible or Macintosh computer), a scanner and printer are needed. It is also helpful for students to build their own entourage libraries by downloading images and photographs of people and objects in plan, elevation, and perspective to serve as a ready reference when needed.

In the hands of a savvy user, photo editing can alter a designed space significantly. As with all photographic techniques, lighting can be manipulated or compensated for. Images can be cropped, enlarged, distorted, superimposed, or layered. Colors can be toned or made more saturated. Levels of opacity can be manipulated. The miracles of digital photo editing can be used by interior designers to help conceptualize their designs in much the same way that sketching and modeling can.

A significant share of this market is held by Adobe, which manufactures several programs, including Photoshop, Illustrator, and InDesign, that can further enhance images prepared by hand, generated by computer, or photographed.

Photoshop

Photoshop is primarily geared toward digital photo manipulation and photo-realistic styles of computer illustration. Adobe Illustrator as well as Adobe InDesign are companion products of Adobe Photoshop. These programs are useful for developing typesetting (creating unique and distinctive lettering) and logo graphics, making them desirable for branding and marketing.

3DViz

This is a software program developed and used by engineers to create photo-realistic imagery of products and spaces (Figure 6.28).

Figure 6.28
Photo-realistic perspectives: a student working with *3DViz*. (© *Danielle Vacca, Cazenovia College*)

AccuRender

McNeel AccuRender, created by architects, is used to develop photo-realistic renderings from AutoCAD drawings.

PRESENTATION PACKAGES

The visuals discussed thus far are pulled together into an organized composition, or package, for presentation purposes in many different ways. Interior design students generally compile multiple orthographic and pictorial drawings, often combined with sample boards, concept sketches, and models, for final presentation in a studio class or thesis project (Figure 6.29 a–d).

Although each presentation package differs in terms of overall appearance, style, size, materials, media, and even organization, there are general considerations that guide all design compositions—and all presentation packages *are* design compositions. Attractive and effective presentations, regardless of their style, are derived from the foundation of design elements and principles explored in Chapter 3. You will be reminded of much of the vocabulary used in that chapter in *FYI . . . Tips for Preparing Your Presentations* and *FYI . . . Tips for Adding Aesthetics to Presentations.* (Also see Chapter 14 for more information on creating portfolios.)

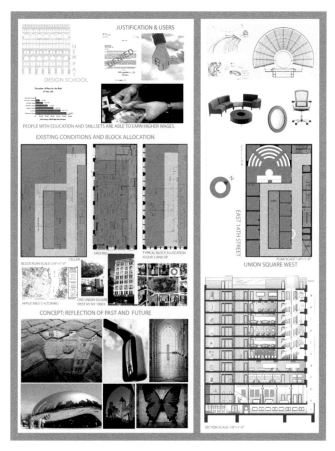

a

b

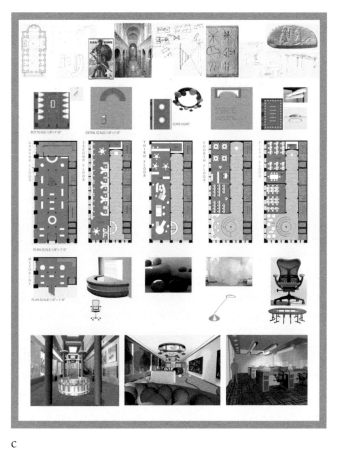

c

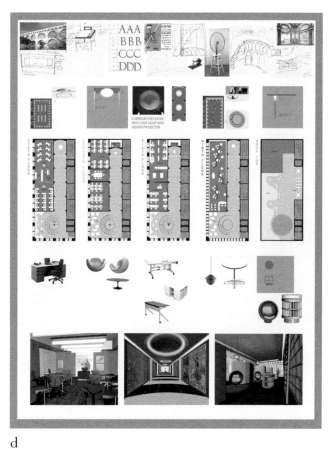

d

Figure 6.29
Boards prepared for a senior thesis project presentation demonstrate how various types of drawings and techniques successfully integrated into one harmonious package. *(a–d: © Olesya Lyusaya LEED AP)*

Senior Thesis Project on Sustainability: Part 2: An Education in "Green"

Jessica Yahn Quezada, "Green Museum of Natural Sciences and Sustainable Technologies," FIT, BFA thesis, 2010

Jessica's project, for her BFA thesis in Interior Design, is a multistory adaptive reuse of a building to house the Green Museum, an institution dedicated to sustainability, located in New York City.

Adapted from Jessica's accounting of the process of communicating her vision:

In the first 2 weeks of thesis class, we were encouraged to hand sketch. This included drawing conceptualization of the use of space through block drawings, circulation, hierarchy, and matrix diagrams. After that, I began to work in AutoCAD to develop two-dimensional plans and sections. As I worked on my plans, I began to draw elevations in AutoCAD of built-in furniture (later developed in three-dimensional models in AutoCAD). At the same time, I also began to sketch perspectives in AutoCAD.

Early on, plans for the final presentation boards were considered. Layouts were created in Adobe InDesign to show scale and proportion.

Rendering of finished plans was done in AccuRender. Editing of images; intial rendering; and the addition of figures, lighting, and other details were done with both AccuRender and Adobe Photoshop.

The oral presentation of my thesis project included a movie I made in Apple, through iMovie; GarageBand was the program used for sound editing. A Web site for the thesis program was also developed and showcased at the school's Conference on Sustainability in March 2010.

Three of the many boards displayed for Jessica's thesis presentation are featured in Figures a, b, and c.

Rainforest & Aqua Tunnel Sketches

Second Floor Plan

Rainforest & Aqua Tunnel

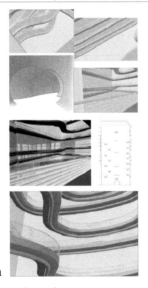

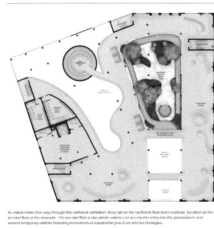

a

b

c

Figures a, b, and c

a. Concept perspective sketches done in AutoCAD; b. A 2D floor plan developed in AutoCAD, rendered in Adobe Photoshop and AccuRender; c. 3D perspectives rendered in AccuRender and Adobe Photoshop. *(a, b, and c: Courtesy of Jessica Yahn Quezada)*

FYI . . . Tips for Preparing Your Presentations

- Consider the purpose of the presentation before deciding on size and style.
- Determine how much time and money you can expect to spend on the package.
- Review the physical setup of the room where the presentation is to take place. How will boards be mounted or rested? What is the viewing distance? What are the lighting conditions? Consider the human factors, such as hearing when giving oral presentations and visual perception when deciding on size and position of boards and text.
- Decide whether any written and oral communications are needed to supplement the visuals, and prepare these in advance.
- Plan for how the package will be protected and transported.
- Find out whether any specific protocols or instructions need to be adhered to, such as size, number, or color of boards; type and placement of text; or scale of drawings. Are there guidelines indicating which components may be hand drawn or computer generated or whether templates, stencils, or machines for lettering, printing, or drawing may be used? Schools and firms may have specific standards. These may also extend to safety precautions regarding the use, storage, and disposal of specific materials.
- Prepare concept sketches, then thumbnail versions to judge layout, before embarking on final presentations.
- Experiment with various types of adhesives for mounting heavy samples, such as marble, to ensure they hold. Position heavier samples toward the bottoms of boards.
- Neatness counts.

Summary

Interior designers communicate their ideas and solutions visually, orally, and through writing. The many tools and techniques available today offer an array of options for preparing visual presentations. Despite the popularity of computer-generated drawing, the importance of learning the fundamentals of manual drawing cannot be overstated. The main purpose of all these graphic expressions—whether quickly executed, simple black-line sketches or carefully done, expensive color renderings—is to communicate effectively.

Students need to acquire a basic set of supplies and equipment for drawing (both freehand sketching and technical, measured renderings), creating models, and putting together presentation packages. Many of these supplies can serve several purposes.

Interior designers rely on two types of drawings—orthographic and pictorial. Orthographic drawings include the different types of plans, elevations, and sections used to convey the proposed design. Certain conventions regarding scale, lettering, line weight, symbols, and title block are followed when producing these drawings. Pictorial drawings, which are categorized as either paraline or perspective drawings, project a realistic view of a space. These drawings can be produced using estimated, plan projection, and prepared grid methods.

Sketches and rendered drawings provide an opportunity for the designer to emphasize his or her personal expression and style. A variety of methods and tools may be used, such as pencil, ink, marker, watercolor, and mixed media. Rendered drawings contribute additional information and an expressive quality to freehand sketch and technical drawings as well as those generated by a computer. All of these visuals, as well as three-dimensional models, whether for study or for final presentations, may be produced by use of computer-aided drafting and design (CAD programs)

Creating a presentation package—whether for a studio class or thesis project—relies on the practiced techniques and application of the design elements and principles.

FYI . . . Tips for Adding Aesthetics to Presentations

- Maintain a consistent orientation for all boards—either all vertical or all horizontal.
- Borders of some sort tend to unify the various components on each board. Text and lines help stabilize or ground oddly shaped drawings.
- Decisions about the size and placement of the various components on a board, as well as the boards themselves, involve consideration of proportion and emphasis. For example, leaving too much empty space between or around components may make individual components look insignificant, instead of emphasizing their importance. Alternatively, a composition that is too dense may create an uncomfortable grouping with the sense that the components are in competition with one another and cannot breathe.
- Consider the relative size of components, especially on sample boards. Although exact scaling is not used for materials, avoid using disproportionate sizes to represent the role played in the space. An obvious example would be the use of a large paint chip to represent a trim color and a smaller sample for walls and ceiling.
- To the degree feasible, try to place samples according to their location in the space, such as floor surfaces on the bottom of the board and windows and ceiling surfaces toward the top.
- Be mindful of axes, distribution of visual weight, and symmetry for placement of graphics and text. Aim to have each board for a project attain similar visual weight and impact.
- Choose borders, lettering, and colors and textures of mounting surfaces that reinforce and enhance the design concept, rather than fight it. An inappropriate example might be the choice of a typeface with flourishes in the presentation of a conference room design for a conservative banking firm. Similarly, a stark contrast between drawings and background, such as a soft watercolor rendering placed on a black surface, may be inappropriate for presentation of a master bedroom design.
- Avoid lettering that overpowers images or is too skimpy (faint, thin, or small) for the overall visual weight and style of the presentation.

Vocabulary

architectural scale

block style

Building Information Modeling (BIM)

computer-aided drafting and design (CAD, CADD, or CAD/D)

cone of vision

cut line

detail

digital photo editing

diminution in size

drafting

entourage

graphite

horizon line

isometric projection

legend

orthographic drawing

paraline drawing

parallel rule

perspective drawing

pictorial drawing

picture plane

plan oblique (axonometric)

poché

presentation model

rendering

sketching

station point

study (sketch) model

vanishing point

Exercise: Hand Drawing: 2D Still Life

The objective of this exercise is to explore and practice your hand-drawing skills in two-dimensional sketching and rendering based on observation. You will be composing a still life to serve as your model.

Select a flat surface, such as a desk or table (kitchen, dining, end, coffee, and so on). Arrange at least three objects on the surface, such as a book, drafting/drawing supplies, a vase with flowers, a bowl with fruit, sculpture, or a lamp. Have available a supply of drawing tools to experiment with, such as graphite and colored pencils, ink pen, straightedge, markers, or watercolors.

First, sketch the composition in plan, then in elevation, using either graphite, ink, or ultrafine marker. Then render details such as color, shadows, and textures in any media you choose. Select the appropriate paper for your media and a size that's useful for a portfolio of your work (for example, 9 inches by 12 inches to 14 inches by 17 inches).

Exercise: Exploring the CD-ROM

Take advantage of the contents of the CD-ROM to increase your understanding of selecting the appropriate software for your projects. Follow the instructions for Starting the CD-ROM on pages xix–xx and click on Chapter Six: Communicating the Vision.

Choices in Computer-Aided Design: Numerous software programs are available to substitute for, or enhance, interior design students' hand drawings. Research five programs from among those noted in the text or others you may be familiar with. Prepare a comparative summary of each, including key features, advantages or disadvantages, time required to learn, ease of use, and price. Consider how you would use these programs in current or future school projects. Are some programs more appropriate for some aspect of the process than others?

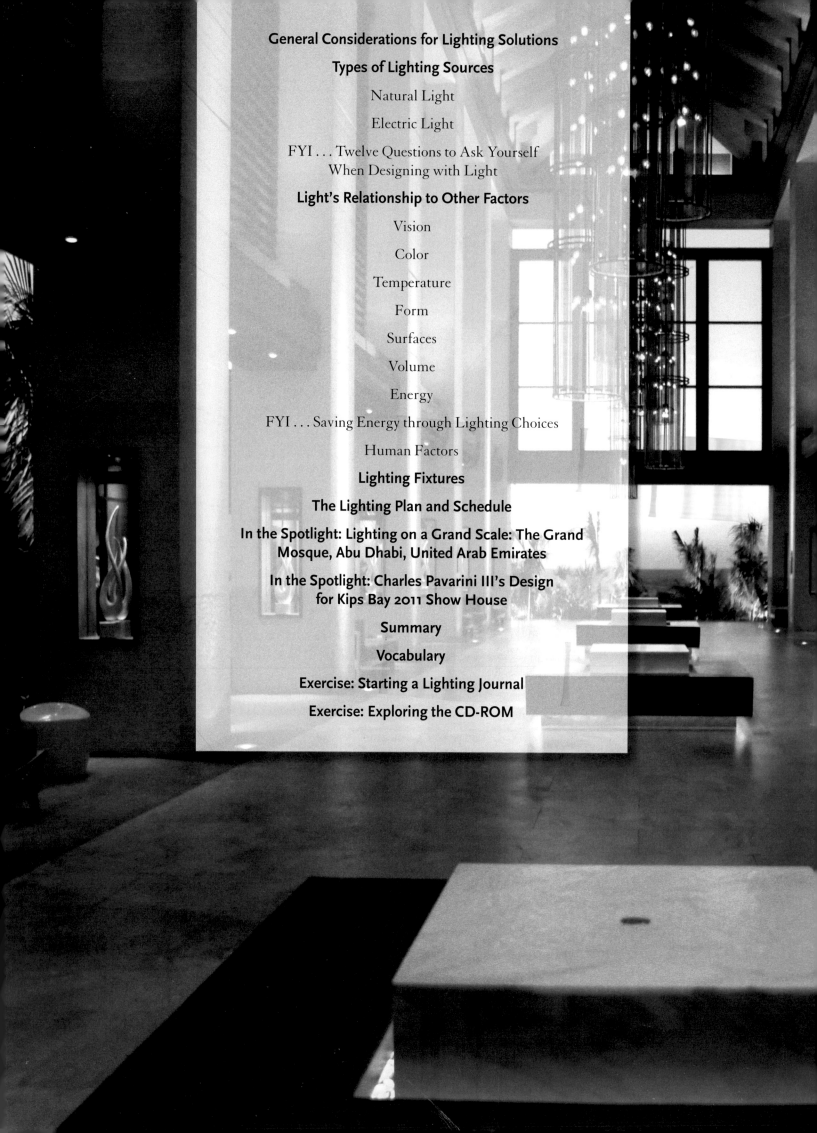

CHAPTER 7

Light and Lighting Systems

L ighting design is introduced in this chapter to familiarize the beginning student with the terminology employed in, and the scope of, this design specialty. Light, as mentioned in Chapter 3, is an important element for interior designers. Without light there is no color, an equally powerful tool. An introduction to theory and practical applications for both residential and contract spaces is presented.

The two basic categories of light sources are natural and electric, each of which may be used to provide any of three basic purposes: ambient, or general, lighting; task, or local, lighting; and accent, or key, lighting (Figure 7.1a and b). These methods may also be referred to as the "layers" of lighting. At times, only one method is used. More complex—and usually more versatile—lighting solutions involve more than one method, or layer.

Light provides visibility in which to move about, can create dramatic or theatrical effects, conveys mood and feeling, and even enhances well-being. Interior designers use light as a tool for manipulating the perception of space and other elements within the space, such as color and texture.

This chapter describes the shapes and distribution of light; the types of **lamps** (*bulbs*, in layperson's terms) and fixtures available; lighting applications; and the relationship of light to other elements, human factors, and the environment. Both the quantity and quality of light are of importance to design solutions; these issues will also be discussed in this chapter.

Figure 7.1
Purposes of light: ambient, task, accent. a. Consumer sites such as this GE page features how residential spaces may be enhanced by the three layers of light; b. Designer Jeffrey Beers' hospitality space effectively incorporates a sophisticated use of complex lighting layers. *(a: Courtesy of GE Lighting; b: © Sharon Lowe / Alamy)*

GENERAL CONSIDERATIONS FOR LIGHTING SOLUTIONS

Most of what we see of light is what is reflected from a surface, not the light itself. Therefore, the surface characteristics of the space and the objects within that space must be considered. A lighting solution is application specific, meaning its success can be truly evaluated only within the context of the requirements of a specific client or user group for a particular function.

The thought process of designing with light should start early on (see *FYI . . . Twelve Questions to Ask Yourself When Designing with Light*). Having an appreciation for the power of light fosters good design habits, which include considering light at the inception of a project, rather than as an add-on.

TYPES OF LIGHTING SOURCES

Sources of lighting are categorized as being either natural or artificial in origin. Natural sources of light include daylight and flame. Artificial sources are mainly electric in origin.

Natural Light

Daylight is actually a combination of the light from the sun, the sky, and the atmosphere. The direction and quality of the natural light, in particular, from daylight, is often considered during the architectural planning stage, when decisions are made about the location and orientation of buildings on a site or of spaces within a structure. The placement and type of windows and doors are discussed in Chapters 8 and 9. How windows are treated, such as the choice of shades, blinds, solar films, shutters, or draperies, is also reviewed in those chapters and in Chapter 10.

Daylight is actually not synonymous with *sunlight*, but rather *skylight*. Whereas direct sunlight can produce glare and excessive heat, daylight is the desirable harvesting of sunlight into optimal conditions.[1]

Daylight, which is even in its distribution, is generally considered the standard for determining true color. Daylight enhances visual acuity for reading and writing. Integration, or daylight harvesting, of daylight into interiors plays a significant role in energy conservation and improved well-being.

Certainly, interior designers must also be aware of the different temperatures of light. Is the natural light source considered to be in the warm or cool range? Additionally, it is important to have an appreciation of the effects of natural light on both mood and the various surfaces within the space (e.g., the interplay with texture and colors and the effects of changing conditions, such as fading).

Electric Light

The practical application of electric light that began more than a century ago laid the foundation on which an extensive repertoire for the design of interiors has been built. Interior designers rely heavily on the manipulation of electric light to control the desired effects for a project. The technology of lighting changes at a dramatically fast pace.

FYI . . . Twelve Questions to Ask Yourself When Designing with Light

The following questions begin the thought process of designing with light:

1. What is the task to be performed in the space, and for how long? Offices, residences, stores, and theaters require very different solutions, as do kitchens, bedrooms, and bathrooms.
2. Are multiple tasks or activities planned for? How versatile, flexible, and portable must the lighting systems be? Where do the activities occur within the space, and at what time of day?
3. How is the space configured, including transitional areas, such as entrances and foyers? The lighting in these areas may need to accommodate activities for both day and night.
4. Who are the occupants? Determine their characteristics such as age, disability, style preference, skin tone, and so on. For example, a person aged 55 or older requires twice the light level of a 20-year-old.
5. What are the existing conditions of the interior, its orientation, and its environment? What are the nature and extent of the natural light available, and at what exposure? What is the effect of the climate on the interior?

6. How big is the volume of the space, including the height of the ceiling? Are there any architectural features, such as high windows or skylights, which will affect the available natural lighting or effectiveness of electric lighting, or both?
7. What finishes or textures exist in, or are planned for, the space? How will they absorb the light or reflect it into the space? For example, are the walls glossy or matte?
8. Are there special elements or objects that need to be highlighted?
9. What is the desired mood or ambience? Is color selection or color matching, or rendition, a major point of the overall design solution? For example, color is a major consideration in a sales environment. It may be less important for an airport terminal.
10. How critical are energy-conservation issues? Electric lighting consumes more than 19 percent of the world's energy.
11. What is the budget for lighting at the outset, for installation, and for ongoing maintenance?
12. Are there special codes, laws, standards, and regulations governing the lighting systems and applicable labor laws, such as the use of licensed electricians?

Sources: Adapted from Susan M. Winchip, Fundamentals of Lighting, *2nd Edition (New York: Fairchild, 2011), 172–173. Adapted from WorldWatch Institute, www.worldwatch.org.*

Incandescent lighting was the first type of electric lighting to be used. Thomas A. Edison (1847–1931) invented the first type of incandescent lighting in 1879. This is the form of electric light that is produced by the application of electric energy to a thin wire filament until it reaches the point of **incandescence**, a temperature that causes the filament to glow. In contrast to natural daylight, which appears white under ideal conditions, incandescent light is warmer. Incandescent light has fewer blue and green wavelengths and more wavelengths in the red range. Therefore, incandescent light is perceived as more yellow, creating a cozy feeling or mood.

Incandescent lighting generates more heat than other types of electric lighting. Because so much of its energy is consumed as heat, which is not the principal function of a lamp, incandescent lighting is less energy efficient as a source of light than these other sources. Its initial cost is low. However, **luminance**, its level of brightness, is not sustained throughout its life, especially when compared with other lamps. (The terms *luminance* and *brightness* are often used interchangeably, although there is a subtle distinction. The quantity of light that reaches the eye is its level of *luminance*, whereas the perception of the amount of lightness seen is its *brightness*.)

That incandescent lighting may create shadows provides for dramatic or romantic effects. On the negative side, this can cause eyestrain or hide elements that may need to be seen or emphasized. The effects can be controlled to varying degrees with lenses, filters, and reflectors.

There are many types of incandescent lamps, among them the standard A, halogen, and reflector, which come in various shapes, sizes, and wattages. A **watt**, symbolized by the letter W, is the unit of measurement of the power consumed.

The standard, or **A** (for **arbitrary**), **lamp** is commonly used in residential settings. Typical household wattages are 25 W, 40 W, 60 W, 75 W, 100 W, and 150 W. The nature of the light provided by A lamps may differ according to whether the glass encasement is clear, frosted, tinted, or silvered. The screw-in base may be either standard or a larger base, called a mogul base, seen more often in older, vintage floor lamps.

Halogen is a subcategory of incandescent lighting that was introduced in 1959. It is more accurately called **tungsten-halogen** or **quartz-halogen**, depending on its casing. Halogen lamps come in a variety of shapes, sizes, and wattages. They have several advantages over the A lamp; among them is that more hues are perceived in their true state, as if under white light. In other words, halogen renders color better (see later discussion). Another advantage of halogen is that it burns at a continuous rate, or level, of brightness, whereas standard bulbs fade out during their lifetime. Halogen is, therefore, more predictable in its effect. (See Figure 7.2a and b).

Compared with the standard A lamp, halogen has a higher rate of **efficacy**. This is the criterion that is used to evaluate the amount of brightness a lamp

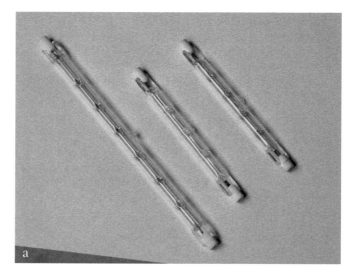

Figure 7.2
Various halogen lamps. (© *Changzhou Gaorui Electric Co., Ltd*)

source provides in comparison with the energy used. Halogen releases more light for the amount of energy input than the A lamp.

Over the decades, the use of halogen systems has spread from mainly display for commercial applications to a wide variety in both commercial and residential applications for ambient, task, and accent lighting. Although more costly at the outset than A lamps, halogen lamps have developed into cost-efficient solutions for lighting, even for those with moderate budgets. The halogen lamps used for ambient and task lighting come in a variety of shapes.

The numbering system for wattages in halogen lamps differs from that for standard lamps. Manufacturer labels often compare the two; for instance, a label may note that a 150 W halogen is equivalent in brightness to a 75 W standard lamp. Many people think that because halogen is hotter, it is generating more heat. This is a misconception. The housing is more concentrated, and therefore the lamp itself is actually much hotter to the touch, but it is not producing more heat. However, the lamp should not be touched directly, nor should it be exposed to flammable materials.

Reflector lamp is the term used for several types of incandescent lighting sources that direct how the light is reflected, causing a manipulation of its shape and focus. A reflector is a surface of mirrored glass or polished metal shaped to project the beam from a light source in a particular direction. Reflectors may be part of the lamp itself or part of the housing of the fixture. They are available in various beam spreads and are especially useful for accent lighting. The **beam spread**, or distribution of the light, is determined by the shape and faceting of the reflective surface.

One type of reflector lamp that is widely used in outdoor applications is the **PAR (parabolic aluminized reflector)** (Figure 7.3). Essentially, PAR lamps are made of two pieces of glass fused together; one is the reflector, and the other the lens. The surface of the lens determines the beam spread. These lamps are categorized by size, and dividing this number by eight yields an approximate diameter of the lamp in inches. PAR lamps may be operated on **low voltage**. Voltage (V) is a measurement of electric potential. In the

United States and Canada, *standard voltage*, also called **line voltage**, is generally 120 V. This higher voltage must be stepped down (usually to 12 V) using a transformer before individual residential and commercial customers can use it.

Another commonly used reflector lamp in residential and commercial settings, such as restaurants and stores, is the **mirror reflector (MR) halogen** (Figure 7.4). Like the PAR, this variety is described by size, in particular by diameter (again approximated by dividing the size by eight). An MR 11, a common type, is $1\frac{3}{8}$ inches in diameter; an MR 16 has a 2-inch diameter. MRs operate on low voltage. With improved technology, small transformers are available that are actually part of the fixture. MR systems are often part of a track or cable system suspended from the ceiling (see later discussion).

Fluorescent lighting was first introduced for use at the 1939 World's Fair (in New York City). In this type of lighting, a glass tube is filled with a low-pressure mercury vapor, producing an invisible ultraviolet radiation that activates white phosphorous crystals inside the lamp. The phosphorus glows, or fluoresces, converting the ultraviolet energy into visible light energy. A general characteristic of fluorescent lighting is that it is diffuse and, unlike incandescent lighting, casts few shadows. It is therefore used for general lighting but may also serve for task lighting. Fluorescent lighting

Figure 7.3
PAR (parabolic aluminized reflector) lamp. *(© Paul Kevin Picone/P.I. Corp.)*

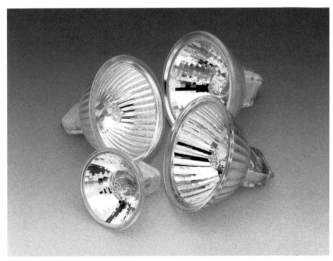

Figure 7.4
Various MR (mirror reflector) lamps. *(© Fubar24x7 /Dreamstime .com)*

Figure 7.5
A contract interior with fluorescent lighting. *(Mark Dell'Aquila Eagle-Eye-Images)*

gained popularity for use in offices because of its efficiency (Figure 7.5). It lasts longer, uses less energy, and is less costly to maintain than incandescent lighting, and it does not generate unwanted heat.

The early drawbacks of fluorescent lighting—eye discomfort; poor ability to depict colors accurately; cold, gray appearance; noisiness; and flickering—have been reduced through technological advances. As energy conservation becomes more important, the efficiency of the newer fluorescent lamps has increased the popularity of this lighting choice.

Fluorescent lamps are manufactured in linear tubes of different widths and lengths, as well as circular tubes. A significant advance in fluorescent light-

ing was the development of the **compact fluorescent lamp (CFL)**. It consumes less power, lasts longer, and renders colors better than other fluorescent lamps. According to recent studies, replacing incandescent lamps with CFLs could reduce lighting energy demand by nearly 40 percent, increasing its popularity.[2] CFLs are retrofitted to replace standard incandescent lamps in existing fixtures, including those used in residences. Another improvement has been the design of fluorescent lighting to provide accent lighting, useful in product display. The ability to control the level of illumination of fluorescents individually, with a dimmer, allows for more flexible application as well as greater energy conservation (Figure 7.6).

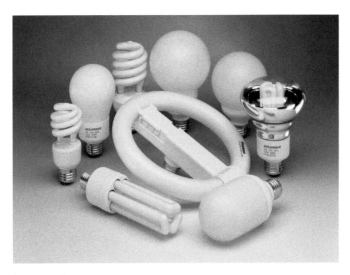

Figure 7.6
Various fluorescent lamps. (© *Paul Kevin Picone/P.I. Corp.*)

Neon lighting is colored light that is produced as a result of different gases, or vapors. Neon has less applicability to residential design than to contract design. Its most common use is to provide high visual impact in commercial signs and billboards (Figure 7.7). Because neon lamps are long lasting and bend easily, they can be installed in rather inaccessible places.

High-intensity discharge (HID) lamps were developed in the early 1930s, and considerable improvement has been made since then. Passage of an electric current through a gas under high pressure produces light in HID lamps. HIDs come in a variety of sizes and shapes (Figure 7.8). There are three basic categories of this lamp: mercury vapor, high-pressure sodium, and metal halide. A significant difference among these types is the way in which colors are depicted. Metal halide, especially when combined with ceramic, provides the most accurate color of the three types of HID.

HID lamps are extremely efficient and are used for large-scale commercial applications. Typical uses of HID lighting—in particular, the more efficient high-pressure sodium types—are for streetlamps, highway lighting, airport runways, stadiums, and parking lots.

Figure 7.7
Neon lighting creates an exciting environment in a Beijing market. (© *Panorama Media [Beijing] Ltd. / Alamy*)

Figure 7.8
Various HID (high-intensity discharge) lamps. (© *Paul Kevin Picone/P.I. Corp.*)

HIDs are used when lighting must remain on for long periods and where maintenance (e.g., changing lamps) would be inconvenient. HIDs take a long time to start up. Their main drawback has been the limited color-rendering abilities of these lamps. However, with improvements in this area, a wider range of applications is expected.

Fiber optic lighting uses a remote source for illumination. The light source is housed in a box, and the directional lamp is usually metal halide or tungsten-halogen. Advantages include safety, ease of maintenance, low transmission of heat, and small amounts of infrared and ultraviolet wavelengths. They may be placed in wet spaces, such as pools and showers, as the illuminating box is installed remotely, in a dry location.

Solid-state lighting (SSL) is a relatively new technology in lighting that uses semiconducting materials to convert electricity into light. *Solid-state lighting* is an umbrella term encompassing light-emitting diodes (LEDs) and organic light-emitting diodes (OLEDs). **Light-emitting diodes (LEDs)**, developed in the 1960s, are based on inorganic (non-carbon-based) materials. **Organic light-emitting diodes (OLEDs)** are extremely thin sheets of carbon-based compounds that illuminate when their electrodes are stimulated by an electrical charge[3] (Figure 7.9). This paper-thin

Figure 7.9
A huge, complex hospitality LED project. (© *Yas Hotel in Dubai*)

technology can be envisioned for wall coverings and window shades. Additionally, LEDs are considered a low-maintenance installation. That there are no damaging heat emissions or ultraviolet emissions is yet another advantage.

Since their introduction, the technology has improved dramatically, such that their use is no longer limited to exterior lighting and digital displays. Digitally controlled LEDs provide flexibility in color, brightness, and special effects, deeming them effective for both interiors and exteriors of commercial buildings such as hospitality and retail.[4] The Yas Viceroy, a luxury hotel in Abu Dubai, features a state of the art LED canopy that creates a symphony of color and shade cause guests to marvel.

LIGHT'S RELATIONSHIP TO OTHER FACTORS

Light is a basic tool of an interior designer. It affects the ability to see and to perceive the colors, color temperatures, shapes, forms, surface textures, and volumes of objects in a space.

Vision

Perception of light is controlled by the physiology of the eye, in conjunction with the brain and optic nerve impulses. Incoming light enters the cornea, a transparent covering in front of the eye, and passes through the pupil, the opening in the center of the eye. The amount of light admitted through the pupil is governed by a group of muscles known as the iris. In response to bright light, the iris narrows, and in response to low levels of light, it widens.

The light continues to the lens, which modifies its curvature to focus the light, producing an image on the retina. The retina contains two types of cells, called rods and cones (see Chapter 4). In dim light the rods react to brightness, but not to color. The cones operate in brighter light and give us our color perception. The rods and cones then relay their visual information through the optic nerve to the brain, which interprets the information into vision. Any obstacle to the process in this complex network will affect the perception of either light or color, or both.

The ability of the eye to focus at different distances (near and far vision) under normal conditions is called **accommodation**. **Adaptation** is the normal process of the eye's adjusting to changes in the brightness of light. Brightness that is more than the eye can naturally adapt to is called **glare**. Glare may be produced directly, by the angle of the light, or indirectly, by light bouncing off a reflective surface. The latter is called **veiling reflection**. The proper positioning of light sources to avoid glare is of major concern to an interior designer. In the work environment, for instance, improper light placement can have serious consequences for workers who use computers.

Color

White light is often equated with daylight. However, daylight varies with the season, latitude of the location, time of day, and environmental or weather conditions. At varying times of day, or on cloudy days, the wavelengths are not always balanced, creating faint tints of color. It is important to recognize that colors may be influenced by the direction, or orientation, of the natural light. For example, northern light is generally cooler, or bluish, whereas light from the south is warmer, or yellowish.

Electric light is considered whitest when it approaches the equivalence of daylight. Therefore, when we speak of white light or **full-spectrum light**, we are assuming that conditions are as close as possible to a clear day at high noon. The term **metamerism** describes the phenomenon in which colors under different lighting situations do not appear the same. The eye adapts to these varying conditions, correcting the differences, so that red is still perceived as red, green as green, and so on. This latter phenomenon is called **color constancy**.

You can observe the different capabilities of various lighting sources to render colors accurately under different conditions in your own environment. Although improvements in color-rendering ability have been achieved, certain categories still do better than others. An international system for comparison was developed to rank light sources with respect to color rendering. This system is known as the **color rendering index (CRI)**. With 0 as the lowest rating and 100 as the highest, a standard rating system is applied to various types of lamps, styles, and manufacturers. This is an invaluable tool for an interior designer. Table 7.1 compares the CRI ratings of various electric light sources and includes suggested applications.

An essential step in the interior design process is to evaluate colors of finishes and fabrics under the lighting conditions for which they are planned. The effect of light on the color of skin tones is another important consideration. The many differences in skin color among people can be further distinguished by blue (cool) or yellow (warm) undertones. Incandescent (and natural) sources are considered more flattering for people with warm undertones than cool fluorescent and HID, which may cause their skin to appear gray or dull.

Temperature

One way to describe the appearance of light is to categorize it by its apparent temperature (warmth or coolness), known as **chromaticity**, and the colors that are associated

Table 7.1
Lamp Specifications and Suggested Applications

Lamps	CRI Rating (approx.)	Suggested Applications
Incandescent	97–100	Residential special applications such as niches, sconces, nightlights, pendants
Halogen	97–100	Residential, hospitality, gallery, high-end retail
Fluorescent	80s	Color-critical areas such as galleries, jewelry displays, medical examinations, offices, retail, libraries, hospitality, classrooms, conference rooms
Fluorescent	70s	Galleries, healthcare facilities, offices, retail, classroom, hospitality, residential
Ceramic Metal Halide	60s–90s	Offices, retail, hospitality, healthcare

Source: Winchip, *Fundamentals of Lighting,* 2nd Edition, © 2011 Fairchild Books, page 38.

with it. Color temperature is measured in degrees on a **Kelvin scale**, named after the scientist who discovered the phenomenon. The Kelvin scale is a shorthand way of referring to how warm or cool the light is, or, in other words, the ratio of red to blue. Lower Kelvin values represent warmer temperatures, and higher values represent cooler ones. Manufacturing specifications are available that delineate Kelvin ratings.

Form

Light is intangible until it strikes an object or surface. **Throw distance** is a term used to describe how far and at what intensity the illumination will go. As the throw distance becomes greater, the pool of light increases, causing the intensity of the light to diminish.

There are two basic ways to categorize the direction of illumination. **Diffuse** lighting, such as fluorescent, does not illuminate any specific object, but rather, provides an overall uniform illumination to a space. In contrast, **directional** lighting travels in a single direction, illuminating specific objects and surfaces.

As mentioned earlier, beam spread is the path that light takes when it is directional (Figure 7.10). This terminology is used by lighting manufacturers and is especially helpful to designers when making choices for display or accent lighting. Beam spread can be illustrated graphically using different shapes of triangles. Generally speaking, a beam spread angle of less than 25 degrees is considered a **spot**, whereas one of more than 25 degrees is termed a **flood**.

The line of light is characterized in ways other than beam spread. Light lines are described as either direct or indirect and up or down. The form of distribution depends on the design of a fixture, its placement, and its orientation. Light that strikes its primary target first is considered **direct**. When light is first directed toward a secondary object before striking its

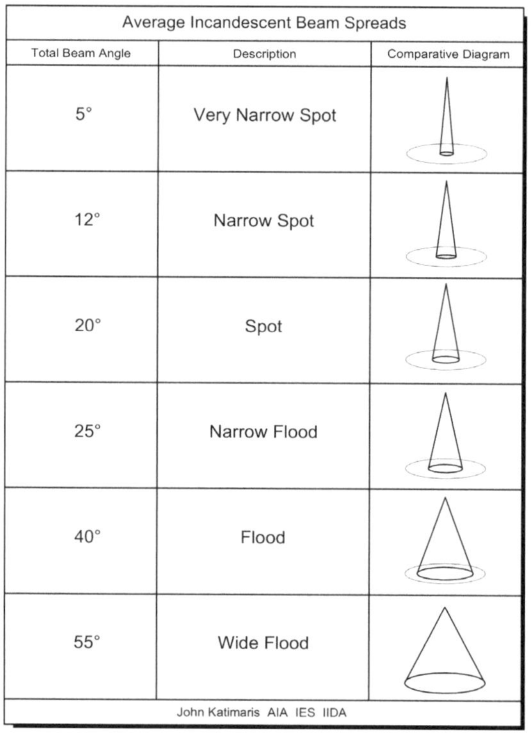

Average Incandescent Beam Spreads		
Total Beam Angle	Description	Comparative Diagram
5°	Very Narrow Spot	
12°	Narrow Spot	
20°	Spot	
25°	Narrow Flood	
40°	Flood	
55°	Wide Flood	

John Katimaris AIA IES IIDA

Figure 7.10

Beam spreads. *(Created and provided by John Katimaris/K + A Associates)*

primary target, it is **indirect**. Both direct and indirect light can happen by way of an upward or downward path, hence the terms **up lighting** and **down lighting**. When an object is lighted from behind, through **backlighting**, a silhouette is produced; the object is blackened while the background is illuminated. This technique is generally used for accent.

Surfaces

A key concept for an interior designer to appreciate is how differently light may be absorbed or reflected, depending on the surface it is directed upon. Visualize the effect of light bouncing off a ceiling that is painted matte black compared with the same amount and type of light bouncing off a ceiling that is glossy white. Relying on our personal observational experiences, without using any scientific calculations, we understand that in the former case little light would be reflected into the space and that in the latter much light would be available to illuminate the space.

Although particularly important when selecting paint finishes for walls and ceilings, this concept also influences the selection of materials used throughout a space. A texture that is smooth and metallic will reflect the light off the surface, whereas a dull, coarse texture will absorb the light into its pores or crevices.

A measurement called **light reflectance value (LRV)** is another design tool. LRV is measured on a scale from 0 to 100 percent. At 0 percent no light is reflected; at 100 percent all light is reflected. To illustrate, cement typically reflects 25 percent of light, whereas brick typically reflects only 13 percent. Paint manufacturers provide LRV information, on either the sample included in decks, or color charts, or on request from a company representative. In general, it is expected that the ceilings and walls will have a high LRV; the floor can be at a lower level. However, this approach may vary, depending on the specific use of the space. For example, if a designer's goal is to provide a high level of illumination that does not overextend the energy resources for electric light, he or she would be wise to check the LRV level of all major surfaces for that space, especially in choosing finishes for walls and ceilings. Table 7.2 shows the LRV for different materials.

Another significant relationship between light and surface involves how planes are illuminated.

Table 7.2
Light Reflectance Value (LRV) of Materials

Material	LRV (Reflectance)
Mirrored and optical coated glass	80–99
Metalized and optical coated plastic	75–97
Processes anodized and optical coated aluminum	75–95
Polished aluminum	60–70
Chromium	60–65
Stainless steel	55–65
Black structural glass	5
Plaster	90–92
White paint	75–90
Porcelain enamel	65–90

Source: Winchip, *Fundamentals of Lighting,* 2nd Edition, © 2012, Fairchild Books, page 48.

Architectural features and surfaces—in particular, walls—may be altered with lighting techniques. There are essentially three different ways to illuminate wall surfaces: washing, grazing, and scalloping (Figure 7.11a–c).

Wall washing is a technique used to provide a smooth distribution, or wash, of light over a vertical surface or plane, usually an entire wall. This minimizes the texture of the surface. The placement and spacing of fixtures to achieve this effect are based on calculations that consider the dimensions of the wall (height and length). Most lighting manufacturers publish recommended spacing for fixtures they consider to be suitable for wall washing.

If the texture of the wall is such that a higher level of illumination is desired for emphasis, **wall grazing** is the technique employed. In general terms, the spacing between lighting fixtures is reduced so that the angle of the light directed at the surface is sharper. In wall grazing the fixtures on the ceiling are located approximately 12 inches from the wall.

Scalloping is a particular type of grazing that calculates spacing in such a way as to create overlapping pools of light shaped like a scallop. This wall lighting technique is essentially a form of accent lighting.

Figure 7.11

Lighting techniques: a. wall washing; b. wall grazing; c. scalloping. *(a: Adrian Wilson/ Redcover.com; b: Courtesy of and designed by Philippe Starck; c: © United States Holocaust Memorial Museum)*

Volume

The quantity of light needed for a space is dependent on both the volume and the function of the space and must be determined in relation to occupant characteristics.

Consider a typical 20-year-old college student reading in a dormitory or in the school library. The level of illumination required in both spaces is the same; however, the volume, sometimes referred to as the cavity, of the room will have a crucial impact on what lighting choices are required to reach that level of illumination. The height of the space, not merely the length and width, should be considered. Cubic space (i.e., length multiplied by width, multiplied by height), rather than square footage, is the proper way to consider the volume of a space. Thus, the lighting solution for the college library might be very different from that for the dormitory.

Measurement of luminance is a complex process. Essentially, existing levels of light delivered to a surface are measured in **foot-candles (fc)**, usually with a light meter. The metric equivalent is called **lux**. One fc equals 10 lux. Computer software programs are available to assist with these calculations. Professional lighting associations, such as the Illuminating Engineering Society of North America (IESNA), publish guidelines for recommended levels of luminance, such as that needed for reading. To illustrate the range of foot-candles needed for different activities, watching a movie in a theater requires only 1 fc, and general office work requires between 30 fc and 100 fc; however, 2,000 fc are needed to perform surgery.

Energy

The illumination of a space results in a significant consumption of energy. The U.S. Energy Policy Act passed by the U.S. Congress in 1992 (EPAct92) and EPAct 2005 set forth requirements for lamp labeling and energy efficiency. Today, attention is increasingly being paid to providing lighting solutions that do not waste energy. The U.S. Environmental Protection Agency (EPA) has determined that lighting consumes approximately 23 percent of the electricity used in buildings. Additionally, approximately 20 percent of the electricity used for air-conditioning is required as a result of heat generated by lamps.[5]

FYI ... Saving Energy through Lighting Choices

- Make use of natural **daylighting** by arranging furniture to maximize daylight useful for reading, cooking, and so on.
- Concentrate light where it's needed by using track lighting or table or floor lamps where appropriate.
- Suggest compact fluorescent lamps in place of standard A lamps.
- Use automation technology, such as motion detectors and occupancy (and vacancy) sensors as well as other control options, such as light

sensors for outdoor fixtures, timers, and dimmers.
- Specify HID lamps for outdoor applications, such as backyards and driveways.
- Specify lamps with **Energy Star ratings**.
- Consider LEDs, especially for outdoor applications, such as task lighting), including under cabinet fixtures in the kitchen.
- Balance aesthetic considerations with LRV considerations to allow for maximum illumination possible.

Sources: Adapted from American Council for an Energy-Efficient Economy, http://www.aceee.org/; Lighting Research Center, http://www.lrc.rpi.edu/; American Lighting Association, http://www.americanlightingassoc.com/; and Residential Lighting, 2nd Edition, by Randall Whitehead © 2009, John Wiley & Sons.

Each lamp product manufactured is identified by **lamp life**, a term that denotes the average rated life span of a lamp (i.e., how long before it is expected to burn out). For example, 750 hours of light might be expected from a standard A lamp designed for household use, whereas a more costly extended-service lamp may last 2,500 hours.

Efficacy is the criterion used to rank sources of light in terms of their energy. Halogen is more efficacious than a standard incandescent lamp because less heat is thrown off, wasting less energy—energy that may be used for the purpose of generating light. Generally, only 10 to 15 percent of the energy consumed to illuminate an incandescent lamp produces light, whereas 85 to 90 percent of the energy consumed produces heat.[6] **Lumen** is the international unit used to measure the quantity of light, sometimes referred to as **luminous flux**. A typical 20 W fluorescent lamp produces 1,200 lumens. A 75 W standard lamp produces 1,190 lumens. The two lamps produce almost the same amount of light, but the fluorescent uses 25 percent of the energy the incandescent lamp uses. The

relative efficacy of lamps is measured in **lumens per watt (lpW)**.[7] Efficacy is an important consideration in green design: Sustainable design requires the use of lamps that conserve energy and have a high efficacy rating, excellent light output, long life, high lumen maintenance, high color rendering, color stability, low mercury levels, and flexible disposal options.[8]

Human Factors

Increasingly, studies have concluded that quantity and quality of both daylight and artificial light may significantly affect our health, safety, and welfare. As noted in previous chapters, design decisions are based not merely on aesthetic choices, but also on a deeper level of the human experience. A designer may create a mood or ambience for a space that offers a particular sensory experience for the moment, as in a romantic interlude over dinner. The potential, however, for more long-lasting reactions, both positive and negative, may be influenced by the interaction of light and our experience with those lighting choices. **Photobiology** examines this interaction. **Phototherapy** is an application of this knowledge to enhance both psychological and physiological healing, discussed later.

Light can create contrast. If there is a high degree of contrast, most people will be stimulated into a higher degree of activity; conversely, they will be more sedentary with a lower level of lighting contrast. A high degree of activity may be called for in some situations, for example, in a classroom; however, in other situations the same high degree of contrast may prove ineffective, causing overstimulation or distraction. The converse is also true, for example, when occupants of a room with lighting that is too low key become drowsy rather than calm.

Seasonal affective disorder (SAD) is a psychological condition in which depression, often accompanied by sleeplessness, occurs as daylight decreases during the fall and winter seasons. This may also result from an individual's inadequate exposure to sunlight owing to a work or living environment. SAD goes beyond the commonly expressed feeling of being "down" when deprived of seasonal variations or sunshine. Various therapies, often using full-spectrum lighting, are employed to alleviate the symptoms.

The effect of lighting in health care has been a major focus for evidenced-based design. Simply put, "change the lighting; improve your health."[9] Phototherapy has been successful in helping regulate the biological clock regarding sleep–wake patterns, known as **circadian rhythm**. Imbalances in circadian rhythm may occur as a result of SAD, transitory jet lag, or serious conditions, such as Alzheimer's and other forms of dementia, or during periods of hospitalization or long-term institutional care. Numerous studies under controlled conditions have demonstrated that through introducing artificial lighting that is closer to natural daylight (i.e., full spectrum, white, or blue-white light), improvements in behavior and health occur.

Lighting solutions for health-care facilities are complex, as the needs of patients and staff members differ. Ideal lighting conditions will vary for different types of spaces as well, for example, a surgical theater versus a waiting area. Color rendition plays a significant role, in addition to the direction and amount of illumination. Patients need light that makes their skin tone look healthy; doctors need accurate lighting for assessment of patient health.[10]

LIGHTING FIXTURES

Lamp is the technical term for what is commonly referred to as a bulb, and **luminaire** is the proper term for the complete lighting unit or fixture. The luminaire consists of the lamp(s) and the parts designed to distribute the light, including lenses, reflectors, baffles, diffusers, louvers, and shades; to protect and position the lamp(s); and to connect the lamp(s) to the power supply, including ballasts and transformers. Power supply elements include wiring, dimmer controls, and switches.

Luminaire systems may be thought of as either architectural or structural (i.e., fixed or portable) systems.[11] The architectural systems are planned for at the inception of the project, installed before occupancy, and are essentially permanent (they can require costly renovation to change). Portable lighting may also serve to provide the three layers of lighting, but it is a system that is more readily altered or substituted and that may be influenced by style or decorative appeal. Both systems accommodate a variety of lighting sources, such as incandescent, fluorescent, HID, and LED.

Fixtures that are basically hidden in the architecture, often the ceiling, are called **recessed** (Figure 7.12a). **Cove lighting** is an architectural lighting system that is used to distribute light across a ceiling (see *In the Spotlight: Charles Pavarini III's Design for the Kips Bay 2011 Show House*). A cove is a channel that may be constructed from many different types of materials, such as wood molding at the juncture between a wall and ceiling. Incandescent lamps, in particular, halogen, are often the light source used, especially when a romantic or traditional feeling is desired. However, fluorescent tubing may be used as the lamp source to provide illumination when uniform and energy-efficient lighting is desired.[12] Other special effects may be achieved by employing other types of lamps, such as LED and neon.

Lamps that are affixed to a ceiling or wall so that the lamp and its housing are revealed are called **surface-mounted**, or **flush-mounted**, **fixtures**. A wall-mounted fixture is called a **wall bracket**[13] or **sconce** (Figure 7.12b).

If the fixture is **suspended**, the terms vary to describe the suspension mechanism. If the fixture is suspended only slightly, it may be referred to as **semirecessed** or **semiflush**. It is called a **pendant** when

Figure 7.12
Lighting fixtures. a. Recessed lighting; b. Sconces; c. Track and cable lighting. *(a: Bob Schimer/ Hedrich Blessing; b: Photograph by Phillip Ennis; c: Christopher Barrett/ Hedrich Blessing. Designed by Tigerman McCurry)*

Lighting on a Grand Scale: The Grand Mosque, Abu Dhabi, United Arab Emirates

One of the largest mosques in the world, the Sheikh Zayed bin Sultan Al Nahyan is designed to accommodate more than 40,000 worshippers. The lighting scheme needed to relate to the complex architecture and interior design while being sensitive to the materials used. It was necessary that the light sources be discreetly placed and give the requisite levels of illumination for functionality, while highlighting various intricate architectural features.

Light sources were integrated into coves, niches, and ledges and behind carved latticework, all providing indirect wall washing. The use of blue (a spiritual color) and white lighting linked the interior light to the exterior lighting of the mosque, which changes daily.

The Qibla wall, the wall that worshippers face, is a unique, luminous art piece incorporating fiber optic lighting.

Source: Adapted from specification sheet from Speirs and Major, www.samassociates.com.

Figure a

IESNA Illumination Award winner for lighting design. Grand Mosque, Abu Dhabi, UAE. Lighting design by Speaks and Major Associates features 19,000 metal halide luminaires. (© *Dominic Byrne / Alamy*)

---

suspended from the ceiling on a longer stem or chain (what is commonly known as a chandelier).

Fixtures may be suspended from a **track,** or **cable system** (Figure 7.12c). The tracks and cables may be flush mounted, or they may be suspended from the ceiling. The fixtures are often movable on the system, allowing for flexibility in creating different lighting conditions. The cable system provides even greater flexibility in that it may be curved on-site, creating a sculptural effect.

Portable luminaires are usually placed either on the floor or on a table (or desk, shelf, and so on). Floor lamps may be at a standard height for task lighting (generally reading) or for more general ambient lighting. Other floor lamps are height adjustable. Another

name for a standing floor lamp used for overall lighting is a **torchiere.**

The type of shade or globe selected for a portable fixture will significantly influence the direction and amount of illumination. For example, an opaque black shade will throw less light than one made of translucent rice paper.

THE LIGHTING PLAN AND SCHEDULE

Depending on the nature of the project, the lighting plan (a set of technical drawings) developed may be composed of various parts. Typical components are the reflected ceiling plan, fixture schedule, power and

Charles Pavarini III's Design for the Kips Bay 2011 Show House

Charles Pavarini III Design Associates, Inc., designed *The Lounge* for the 2011 Kips Bay Show House in New York City. The project dramatically demonstrates Pavarini's signature style for architectural effects and lighting ingenuity. The use of light as a design tool reflects Pavarini's philosophy on lighting influenced by his experience in the theater industry as a performer, set designer, costume designer, and producer.

The ceiling finished in hand-cast architectural plasterwork gives reference to the building's history coupled with high technology. Custom pierced molding in the cove designed by Pavarini allowed for an intricate colored LED cove lighting system within a layered soft neutral setting to highlight the architectural focal points and custom furnishings designed by Pavarini.

Figure a
Cove lighting used by Charles Pavarini III in his design for Kips Bay 2011 Show House. *(Photo by Dan Eifert. Design by Charles Pavarini III Design Associates, Inc.)*

signal plan, wiring plan, communication plan, and legends (see Chapters 5 and 6).

Certain symbols are universally accepted and serve as parts of the legend to stand for the different elements involved in the lighting plan. The symbols on the reflected ceiling plan (a drawing made from the view of the ceiling) denote not only the placement of fixtures, but also other characteristics, such as whether they are surface mounted or suspended (Figure 7.13a and b). Plans that show the information for

electrical outlets, switches, controls, and wiring may be developed to assist the contractors and electricians involved with complex installations. A communication plan would include intercommunication signals, sensor devices, and security systems. Schedules include the specifics needed for purchasing, such as the quantity, style number and name, manufacturer, and characteristics of the lamp and fixtures. A lighting specialist or consultant should be contacted when necessary.

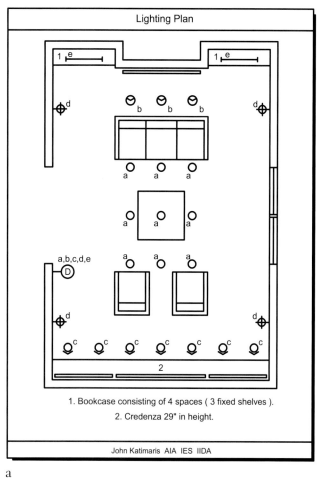

		Luminaire Symbols
⊙		Chandelier
⊗		Table or Floor Lamp
⊢⊕		Wall Sconce
○		Recessed Circular Aperture Downlight
⌢○		Recessed Circular Aperture Wallwasher
⊖		Recessed Circular Aperture Adjustable Accent Light
□		1'x 1' Recessed Fluorescent Troffer
▭		1'x 4' Recessed Fluorescent Troffer
□		2'x 2' Recessed Fluorescent Troffer
▭		2'x 4' Recessed Fluorescent Troffer
⌢○—⌢○		Track Light
⊢——⊣		Strip Light
▭○ ○▭		Suspended Linear Fluorescent
⊢Ⓔ		Wall Mounted Illuminated Exit Sign
Ⓔ→		Ceiling Mounted Illuminated Exit Sign with Directional Arrows

1. Bookcase consisting of 4 spaces (3 fixed shelves).
2. Credenza 29" in height.

John Katimaris AIA IES IIDA

John Katimaris AIA IES IIDA

a   b

Figure 7.13
a. Lighting plan; b. Lighting symbols. *(a and b: Created and provided by John Katimaris/K + A Associates)*

Summary

Lighting is a complex design element that is evaluated by both quantitative and qualitative measurements. It can be measured in terms of its apparent temperature, color, reflectance value, and level of brightness, or luminance. Light serves several purposes: ambient, task, and accent. General considerations for lighting decisions are based on an assessment of the nature of the project and its occupants.

Lighting design incorporates an understanding of both natural and electric light sources. The technology to improve lighting quality, energy conservation, and applicability to a variety of situations advances quickly. The development of fluorescent and high-intensity discharge lamps with better color-rendering capability is just one of these advancements.

Light for the interior designer is considered in relation to other factors, such as form, surface, texture, temperature, and color. Like color, light may be used to manipulate the appearance and volume of a space as well as to create contrast, emphasis, and mood. Energy conservation is critical to the designer's decision-making process.

Increasingly, the relationship between light and human factors has received much attention. The effects of light on perception, mood, and health have been proven through scientific research.

Luminaires may be architectural, such as cove lighting, or portable, such as torchieres. Light may be positioned to create up, down, or backlighting conditions.

A series of drawings is developed to describe the lighting plan. Among them are the reflected ceiling plan and the fixture schedule. A lighting consultant or specialist is used when necessary.

Vocabulary

A (arbitrary) lamp
accommodation
adaptation
backlighting
beam spread
cable system
chromaticity
circadian rhythm
color constancy
color rendering index (CRI)
compact fluorescent (CFL)
cove lighting
daylighting
diffuse lighting
direct lighting
directional lighting
down lighting
efficacy
Energy Star ratings
fiber optic lighting
flood beam spread
fluorescent lighting
flush-mounted fixture
foot-candle (fc)

full-spectrum light
glare
halogen
high-intensity discharge (HID) lamp
incandescence
incandescent lighting
indirect lighting
Kelvin scale
lamp (bulb)
lamp life
light-emitting diode (LED)
light reflectance value (LRV)
line (standard) voltage
low voltage
lumen
lumen per watt (lpW)
luminaire
luminance
luminous flux
lux
metamerism
mirror reflector (MR) halogen lamp
neon lighting
organic light-emitting diode (OLED)

PAR (parabolic aluminized reflector) lamp
pendant
photobiology
phototherapy
quartz-halogen
recessed fixture
scalloping
seasonal affective disorder (SAD)
semiflush
semi-recessed fixture
solid-state lighting (SSL)
spot beam spread
surface-mounted fixture
suspended fixture
throw distance of light
torchiere
track system
tungsten-halogen
up lighting
veiling reflection
wall bracket fixture (sconce)
wall grazing
wall washing
watt

Exercise: Starting a Lighting Journal

Sketch three settings that demonstrate at least one type of lighting (ambient, task, or accent lighting). These settings might be a museum, gallery, bedroom, café, classroom, library, etc. Draw in whatever medium you are comfortable, such as pen, pencil, or marker. Sketch the parts of the room, the planes, and finishes that appear to be affected by the light source. Use a yellow highlighter to show the direction, shape, and spread of the light beams. Note on your sketch the type of room, such as café or museum; the function of the light, such as ambient, task, or accent; and the type of light sources, such as incandescent, fluorescent, or daylight. Record any other observations. These may include glare; quantity and quality of light; relationship of the light to other elements, such as texture, color, or mood or other human factors; and energy efficiency or waste.

Exercise: Exploring the CD-ROM

Take advantage of the contents of the CD-ROM to increase your understanding of the quality of light and its affect on color. Follow the instructions for Starting the CD-ROM on pages xix–xx and click on Chapter Seven: Light and Lighting Systems.

Quality of Light: Colors appear differently under different lighting conditions, artificial and natural. Select a rendered project you've done for class, such as a colored pencil sketch, or a perspective rendered in color markers. View under several lighting conditions, such as daylight, fluorescent, and halogen lamps. Note any changes, such as white becomes more warm (or yellow); gray appears bluish (or cool); or hues become brighter or more dull under different conditions.

8

Architectural Design Elements: The Shell

The relationships among the earth, builders, structures, and inhabitants have been observed, discussed, debated, and written about for as long as they have coexisted. The dialogue continues, whether it is to understand the roles of the architect and the interior designer, the exterior and the interior, or the makers and the users. Often, the discussion is more about hierarchy and degrees of importance of these counterpoints, rather than their collaboration.

In his *Four Books of Architecture*, the 16th-century Italian Renaissance architect Andrea Palladio (see Chapters 1 and 3) discusses what he believes should be the architect's main concerns when planning a building:

> Great care ought to be taken, before a building is begun, of the several parts of the plan and elevation of the whole edifice intended to be raised: For three things, according to Vitruvius, ought to be considered in every fabrick[1] for without which no edifice will deserve to be commended; and these are utility or convenience, duration and beauty. That work therefore cannot be called perfect, which should not be useful and not durable, or durable and not useful, or having both these should be without beauty.[2]

It is often the architect's domain to be concerned with the exterior, and the interior designer the interior. Stanley Abercrombie, while chief editor of *Interior Design* magazine, proposed that although many historical surveys of architecture illustrate building exteriors, it would be shortsighted to assume that great buildings of the past lacked great interiors. He further declared that interiors have perhaps a greater power, as they surround us. When we enter a building, we cease being merely an observer, but become its content as well.[3]

This chapter and the two that follow present information in a sequence from *the outside in*. The steps take us from the contextual relationship between a space and its environment to the details that individualize the space for its occupants.

Although the interior designer may not have responsibility for many of the structural, or load-bearing, elements of the building referred to in Chapter 1, it is important to have an understanding and appreciation of the materials and techniques used and the impact on the design of the interior space. The framework for building the structure, and the mechanical systems that are put into place during construction, make up the shell of the space. The term *mechanical system* is often used interchangeably with *environmental control systems* to refer to systems relating to heating, ventilation, and air-conditioning; water supply and waste disposal, or plumbing; acoustics; and power and communication.

Many of the materials used during the shell construction may also be used in nonstructural, or non-load-bearing, ways to enhance the interior space such as a concrete floor. Although far from the final step in the interior design process, the application of these materials is referred to as the finishes. We may think of this next layer as the lining of the structure; this is the subject of Chapter 9. It is in the lining that design elements are integrated with the architecture of the space, and decisions concerning space planning and layout come into play. For example, partitions may be added to define zones or behavioral settings, as discussed in Chapter 5. The interior designer's expertise in the many material finishes available—their specifications, where to find them, and their application—helps define the character or mood of the space as well as how it functions for its occupants. The beginnings of surface design address this perimeter layer. The articulation of walls to floors and ceilings, often referred to as woodwork or millwork, is covered in Chapter 9.

Chapter 10 considers the furniture and equipment, fixed and portable; the floor and window treatments;

and the finishing touches, often termed accessories. This is the step in which personalization (see Chapter 2) can most effectively be achieved.

SITE, ORIENTATION, AND CLIMATE

Like the nesting instincts of birds, the human nesting instinct is expressed in different styles. The impact of the site, the orientation of the structure, and the climate in which the nest is placed all play major roles.

"Location, location, location." This expression is often used to predict the future success of a business venture. The thinking behind this motto is that the success or good fortune of an individual, family, community, or organization is based to a large degree on the environment of which it is a part, that is, its context. Location obviously becomes an important consideration when deciding where to situate one's space. Thoughts about where to build and with what materials fuel the many lively and necessary dialogues that include the interior designer. Informed interior designers need to be aware of not only how an environment and its resources can affect current and future occupants of a space, but also of the impact the occupants and space will have on the environment. The resurgence of interest in the lessons of our ancestors is at the heart of the specialties related to sustainable green design, adaptive reuse, and energy conservation (see Chapter 2).

As hunters and gatherers, our ancestors survived by having expert knowledge about their surroundings. For much of humankind's existence, this understanding of nature and respect for its power enabled people to predict the weather, find water, and survive in a sometimes-hostile environment. To a degree, owners and builders in today's industrialized societies have neglected the worldview that we are one with nature. However, there are many lessons to be learned from less-industrialized societies, including indigenous Native American populations. The link between one's life and one's natural environment is mirrored in the roots of the entire world's cultures; one can see many similarities among Asian and African groups in terms of how the interdependency of humanity and nature is defined.

Feng Shui practitioners express the importance of this connection through an emphasis on placement, specifically, the art and science of the proper connections among humans, their living and work spaces, and their environments. The American architect Frank Lloyd Wright, who was strongly influenced by Japanese art and philosophy, also engaged the role of nature in his work. His theory was that the core of a home should extend outward into the landscape. He termed this **organic architecture**. Much of his work in the American Midwest in the early 20th century (known as prairie style) featured horizontal planes reflecting the prairie landscape. His structures reach out, using the environment, its site, and its space (Figure 8.1).

Taking responsibility for the interiors of his buildings, Wright used similar materials for both the exterior and the interior to further this sense of oneness. He essentially redefined the concept of rooms by eliminating walls between living spaces. His early version of the **open plan**, or *open floor plan*, had the fireplace, or hearth, as the core of the home. It was reflective of the spirit of American freedom. This resonates with current attitudes for both residential and contract projects as illustrated in a residential plan by Vicente Wolf (Figure 8.2).

Figure 8.1
Frank Lloyd Wright's Taliesen West. *(Photo by Kate Chesley. Copyright © Frank Lloyd Wright Foundation, Scottsdale, Arizona)*

Figure 8.2
A spacious residential open plan designed by Vicente Wolf. *(Vicente Wolf Designer; Vicente Wolf Photographer)*

However, Edith Wharton, Wright's contemporary, warned in 1902 of the serious indifference to privacy of modern times.[4]

The geographic location of a structure also plays a major role in how it is built. One can easily imagine the very different approaches that would be used when designing a residence in the African desert, for example, compared with a mountainside home in the Canadian Rockies or a beach house in the Caribbean. And not all housing is permanent. Nomadic cultures remain in parts of the world. In some instances, the housing moves with the dwellers as they migrate. This is the case in the mountain steppes of central Mongolia, where the **yurt,** or *ger,* serves as a portable dwelling. Its construction is a wood lattice-framed structure covered with felt made from sheep's hair. The yurt is considered more homelike than a tent and has thicker walls. The notion of the yurt structure has become popular in other parts of the world, including North America, and many types are being manufactured for temporary or semi-permanent primary or secondary housing (Figure 8.3a and b). Later in this chapter other examples of housing and building styles are featured. They demonstrate an array of different materials based on different climates, circumstances, and cultures, with a peek into the spaces and the experience within.

Other characteristics of the site are also analyzed. For example, the properties of the soil on which a building will be built need to be considered when determining the foundation to see if the soil will support the foundation.

Once the location of the site is determined, the orientation of the building (i.e., the direction it faces) is a major factor to be considered. A good first step is to determine where exposure to outside factors takes place. In which direction do the **fenestrations** (doors and window openings) face: north, south, east, or west? Are there ways in which the fenestrations can be relocated or adapted? The relationship of these decisions to energy conservation is significant. Daylighting, introduced in Chapter 2, is a major factor. In most geographic locations, daylighting is best maximized from the south side of the building; the next best would be from the north. The services of a landscape architect or designer may be useful in planning for shading techniques to control the sun's lighting effects, especially during summer months.[5] When furnishing

Figure 8.3

a. Woman dressed in traditional clothing at a traditional yurt in Central Asia; b. Contemporary housing based on the yurt system. *(a: Sergei Mikhailovich Prokudin-Gorskii Collection [Library of Congress]; b: © COMPAGNON Bruno/SAGAPHOTO.COM / Alamy)*

interiors and choosing materials, such as textiles, the designer needs to consider whether fading will occur from strong daylight streaming in. Color schemes should be developed based on the intensity and quality of natural light. For example, in cool, temperate zones, a warm color palette for the interior may be in order, whereas a cool palette may work best in warm climates. Orientation has an effect on the choice of exterior and interior building materials as well.

As discussed in Chapter 2, a person's sensory experience is determined by many factors that are influenced by orientation and climate; among these is thermal sensation. The inherent temperature of a region and its changes throughout the day affect many

Figure 8.4
Post-Katrina single home with hurricane-protection features
built by Make It Right Foundation, New Orleans, Louisiana.
*(Homeowner with new home by Concordia Architects. Photo credit:
Virginia Miller)*

structural and interior design choices. For instance, a structure located in an area with strong wind or heavy precipitation, such as in hurricane zones, needs to be designed differently from one in an arid region (Figure 8.4). Seasonal affective disorder, a condition in which people become depressed when deprived of natural lighting (see Chapters 2 and 7) , is another example of how siting may influence design decisions.

The orientation of fenestrations will affect how windows and doors are treated (i.e., dealt with) in terms of issues such as temperature and privacy. The way in which a structure is oriented and designed will direct many interior design decisions affecting how and when privacy is maintained.

Collaboration among architect, interior designer, engineer, and landscape designer may facilitate solutions to address many of these and other climatic concerns. Careful selection and placement of trees, for example, can define vistas and views as well as provide shade that reduces overexposure to sunlight, secures privacy, and reduces some sounds and vibrations.[6] Also see *In the Spotlight: Incorporating Culture, Location, Materials, and Innovation in the Built Environment.*

BASIC BUILDING COMPONENTS

The components discussed next are those about which perhaps the greatest and most effective communication and collaboration take place among building design and trade professionals; it is at this stage that the essential structure of the nest is defined. This is also the stage at which both an interior designer and a client place the most faith in the competencies of the other professionals working on the project.

As noted in Chapter 2, the expression of personalization in a space cannot occur until basic needs (many of them physical) are met. The components chosen at this stage form the shell of the physical structure—a structure that must meet its occupants' needs for physical safety and comfort. The structural components that are essential for the shell include the foundation, floors, walls, roof and ceilings, fenestrations, vertical transit systems (stairs, ramps, elevators, lifts, and escalators), and environmental control systems.

Foundation

The foundation of a building is the substructure that is intertwined with the ground, including the soil on which it is placed. Both the ground and the foundation must be able to support the structure being built. Once again, we see that decisions about housing are contextual with nature. Expectations for the location regarding rainfall, frost, and snow conditions will be taken into account. It is the foundation that must withstand and support the loads—essentially, the weight that is imposed upon it. A structure must be able to bear several different types of loads. Among them are the **dead load**, the relatively fixed weight of the building's structure and permanent equipment, and the **live load**, the occupants and furnishings, including movable equipment. The term **gravity load** may be used to describe both dead and live loads. **Lateral loads** include wind loads and earthquake loads, planned for in the original design of the building. They are referred to as **dynamic loads** when they occur suddenly, with great impact or in seismic proportions.[7]

In Chapter 1 I noted the distinction between load-bearing and non-load-bearing structures as a key factor in differentiating the responsibilities of interior designers and architects. Load-bearing structures include those on vertical planes, such as walls and columns, and horizontal planes, such as ceilings, beams, and floors. The loads may come from inside or outside the structure. Several materials and methods may be used in developing the foundation. Among the materials used are wood and concrete, a mixture of Portland cement (a blend of minerals ground into a powder and hardened

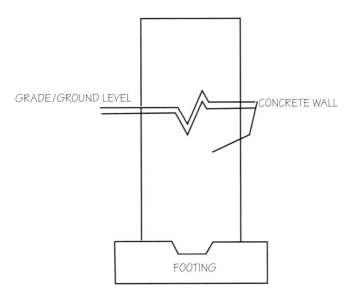

Figure 8.5
Components of a foundation.

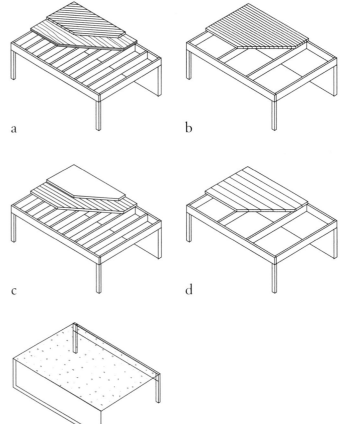

Figure 8.6
Flooring systems. a. Wood joist; b. Wood plank and beam; c. Steel joist; d. Steel beam and docking; e. Concrete.

with the addition of water) and aggregates, such as sand or gravel. Concrete foundations may be reinforced with steel rods, known as **rebar**, for "reinforced bar."

The term **footing** describes that part of the foundation that extends below the soil to provide stability by distributing the load. In this context the term *grade* is used to refer to the ground level, and footings are said to be below grade (Figure 8.5). A thorough knowledge of the characteristics of the ground, including soil studies, and the climactic concerns will help in determining the choices for the foundation.

Floors

Subfloor is the term used to refer to the structural floor, which often is not the finished floor surface. Using the earlier analogy, the subfloor is part of the shell, whereas the finished floor is part of the lining. Although not exposed to the impact of climate, as is the foundation, the subfloor system must support live loads safely. It is connected to both the foundation and the wall systems. The flooring system may be constructed at, below, or above grade.

One typical system, especially for single family homes, is made of wood. In the **joist system**, wood or concrete beams (joists) are spaced close together, horizontally, to support load-bearing walls. Then a deck (platform) made of either wood or concrete is applied over the joist system (Figure 8.6a). In the **plank-and-**

beam system the joists are spaced farther apart (Figure 8.6b). Similar techniques are employed when steel is used; however, its strength allows for a greater span, or distance, between supports (Figure 8.6c and d). Skyscrapers are constructed with steel floor systems. The floor is then decked, often with concrete.

Buildings with multiple floor levels are often constructed with **concrete slab systems,** in which concrete is reinforced with rebar (Figure 8.6e). The concrete is either poured or prefabricated (i.e., prepared off-site) in slabs of various configurations. The inherent fire-resistant properties of concrete and its low cost make it a commonly used building material, especially for public spaces.

Glued laminated timber, also called **glulam**, is a type of structural timber product composed of several layers of smaller pieces of timber laminated together to form vertical columns or horizontal beams as well as curved, arched shapes. Connections are usually made with bolts or plain steel dowels and steel plates. Glulam is stronger than similar-sized members made of solid wood and suffers less from movement caused by moisture changes because the individual laminations are dried to a close tolerance during manufacture. Glulam is proving to be a sustainable alternative to concrete and steel, with the ability to be used for heavier loads and for much longer spans. It can also be manufactured in straight and curved shapes, providing aesthetics without forfeiting structural requirements.

Increasingly, an additional layer of flooring is added to buildings above the subfloor to allow for wiring. This approach is useful in spaces that will contain many computers. The raised flooring may be installed as a modular system to allow for easier access. A raised floor may also provide space for heating systems (see later discussion).

Walls

Like structural floor systems, exterior walls may be constructed to include the finished surface, or a separate layer may be applied for the finish. Interior walls may or may not be load bearing. They serve to define space and direct circulation or traffic and may also house the electrical wiring.

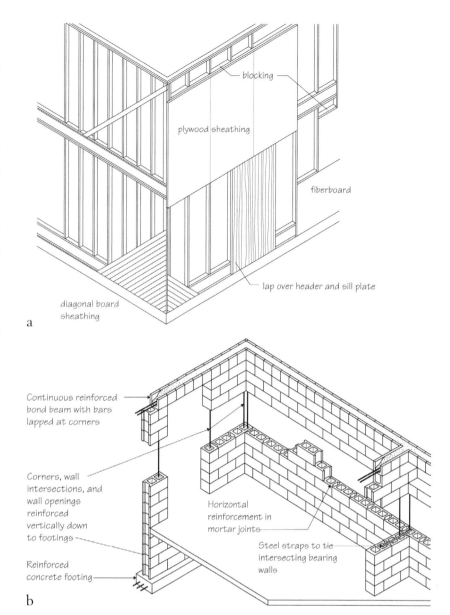

Figure 8.7
Wall framing systems. a. Wood stud wall sheathing. b. Reinforced concrete block walls.

Wall systems may be constructed of wood, steel, or masonry. **Masonry** is the term used to describe certain building materials, including concrete, brick (kiln-fired clay), and stone (various types of rocks). These materials are generally bonded together with **mortar**, a mixture of water and cement. Factors to be considered in wall construction include the loads from above; ability to connect to the foundation, floor, and roof; window and door openings; fire resistance and weather controls; and compatibility with the finished surface desired.

The **stud wall** is a typical flexible system that may be constructed in either wood or metal (Figure 8.7a and b). A stud is a small, upright element (member),

often referred to as a **two-by-four (2 × 4)**, although available in larger sizes. In actuality, a wooden two-by-four measures $1\frac{1}{2}$ inches by $3\frac{1}{2}$ inches. Studs that are 6 inches wide, called a **two-by-six (2 × 6)**, are used more often today to accommodate wiring and plumbing devices. These systems may be prefabricated in panels that are brought to the construction site.

Framing wall systems are similar to stud construction, but fewer vertical posts (vertical beams) are attached to a top plane and a bottom runner. The wall must then be **sheathed**, or wrapped with a layer, often of **plywood** (thin sheets of wood glued together) or **fiberboard** (compressed fibers of wood bonded together, also

Figure 8.8
Lath and plaster interior wall. (© *Manor Photography / Alamy*)

in sheets). In older buildings these frames were sur-
faced with **lath**, or wood strips, or were attached to the
beams. Then wet plaster was applied (Figure 8.8). In
more recent years, **drywall construction** has become the
norm. Here, the building walls are framed with panels made of the mineral gypsum, a calcium sulfate, over
metal lath. These panels are commonly called wallboard, Sheetrock, plasterboard, **GWB (gypsum wallboard)**, or **GWP (gypsum wall partition)**. A **partition**,
as it relates to an interior wall, may be floor-to-ceiling
height or a partial height. It may be fixed or movable;
the latter may be used when flexibility is needed, especially to divide office spaces or for multipurpose areas.
The standard sizes for these sheets are 4 feet by 8 feet,
to accommodate average ceiling height. Sheets are
available in different thicknesses, with $^5/_8$ inch and $^1/_2$
inch being the most common dimensions.

Wall systems may also be constructed of masonry.
Standard-sized bricks used for exterior walls typically
measure 8 inches long by 4 inches wide by 3 inches
thick. Many people find that exposed, unfinished brick
provides a particularly appealing aesthetic for an interior wall (Figure 8.9a).

Not only does masonry (including brick) come in
different colors and textures, but also various installation techniques allow for a myriad of structural patterns. For some applications an interior wall of stone
or concrete might satisfy the intended aesthetic.

Concrete may be formed into bricks, either as solid
blocks or as hollow, more lightweight blocks (Figure
8.9b). Used also for furnishings, concrete and concrete composites are now offered in a variety of colors
and finishes. Because concrete is porous, it should be
treated or sealed to prevent water damage. Innovations in waterproofing as well as other surface coatings
include plant-based oils, a more sustainable application than petroleum-based oils.

Stone used for exterior walls may be rough or finished (Figure 8.9c). Rough stone, called **rubble**, may
be arranged in either a random or a more consistent
coursed pattern on a regular horizontal plane. Finished, or hewn, stone is called **ashlar** (Figure 8.10a–d).

Masonry walls provide an efficient way to withstand compression, the load from above. The downside, however, is that they are not good at withstanding
tension, or lateral stress. A period of settling occurs
during which masonry walls may crack from expansion and contraction owing to changes in the temperature or humidity level before achieving stability.

Masonry walls may be reinforced for strength
with steel rods or metal ties to increase their ability
to withstand tension. Exterior masonry walls may be
constructed as a solid material or in layers, with a thin
surface, called a veneer, on top. Composed of a quality
material facing a less expensive substructure, a veneer
is an economically efficient way to provide a refined
surface finish. Interior brick wall surfaces may be constructed using a veneer attached to the stud frame.

Roofs

The tilt, or slope, of the roof needs to take into account
climatic concerns, such as drainage of precipitation,
deflection of solar energy, and ventilation. A **gable** is
the triangular shape achieved when a roof structure is
not a horizontal plane. It may be at a high pitch (i.e.,
steep) or a low pitch, depending on the angle of the
rafters, the beams used to support the roof. The closer
the rafters are to vertical, the steeper the roof.

A triangular bracing configuration in either wood
or metal, called a **truss**, serves to distribute the load
evenly. This type of configuration is used as a frame-

Figure 8.9

a. An interior wall constructed of bricks; b. An interior partition constructed of concrete; c. An interior rubble stone wall. *(a: Colin Sharp/Redcover.com; c: ©Tim Lee Photography)*

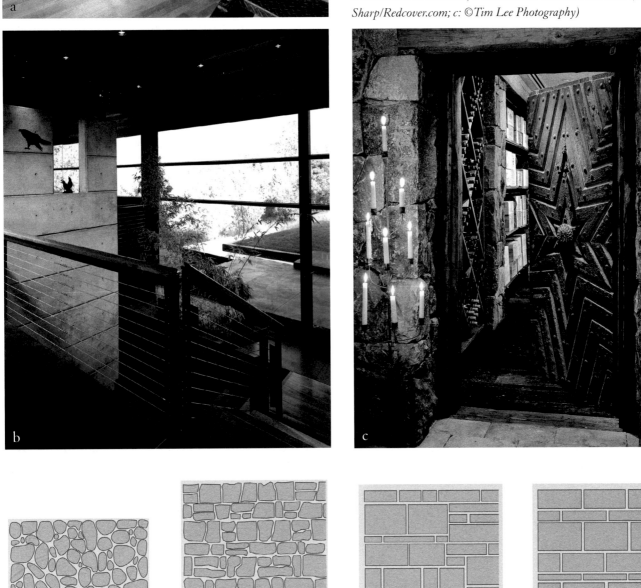

Figure 8.10

Line drawings of stone. a. Random rubble; b. Coursed rubble; c. Random ashlar; d. Coursed ashlar.

work for supporting a roof. It can be sheathed with a finished surface, as are floors, walls, and other structural surfaces, or enhanced with a decking format, often of plywood, gypsum, or fiberboard. Trussed supports may also serve as the finished ceiling, providing a decorative element in addition to their structural value (Figure 8.11a and b).

Roof design and construction must also withstand loads from below, such as the ceiling and suspended lighting fixtures. As with subflooring, the roofing system may support mechanical or electrical lines. The shape of the roof and the ceiling imposed will determine how well these other systems are accommodated. Sloping roofs may allow for storage, such as crawl spaces, or even provide additional habitable space.

The roof shape will also influence the choice of roofing finish material, the ceilings, the layout of the interior spaces, and the exterior's aesthetic. Different feelings may be evoked, depending on the slope, pitch, and orientation of the roof. Consider the roof design in Figure 8.12a and b, shown from the outside as well as the interior space

Ceilings

For a one-level structure the ceiling can be considered the lining of the roof and therefore less a structural element than a finish. For multilevel structures the ceiling is actually a floor system from above that serves as the ceiling of the space below. Once again, the material chosen may provide a finished plane or merely the structural system. A popular type of structural ceiling is the **cathedral ceiling**, an expansive triangular shape that evokes the grand scale of religious edifices.

Often, the appearance of a ceiling is based on surface finishing that simulates architectural, or structural, elements. For example, exposed truss or beamed-ceiling configurations may truly be the unfinished roof structure or merely a surface or finishing detail added to evoke an architectural vocabulary. Wood beams that do not serve as support are added to an interior space to create a rustic feeling. Figure 8.13 shows a ceiling in which recycled wood beams were installed to provide character to the space.

Domed, vaulted, and arched ceilings were employed historically as structural systems, particularly in churches. In modern projects they may be used

Figure 8.11

a. Metal (steel frame) truss system; b. Wood truss system. *(a: Photograph by Sharon Risedorph. Design by Bohlin Cywinski Jackson; b: James Mitchell/Redcover.com. Designed by Charlie Anderson)*

Figure 8.12
High-pitched roof from both the outside and inside. *(a: Ken Hayden/Redcover.com; b: James Mitchell/Redcover.com. Designed by Charlie Anderson)*

Figure 8.13
Reclaimed wood beams added to the ceiling creates character to the space. *(Photograph by Phillip Ennis. Designed by Andrew Chary)*

Figure 8.14
Styles of ceilings. a. Domed; b. Vaulted; c. Cathedral. *(a: Bob Harr/Hedrich Blessing. Designed by Skidmore, Owings & Merrill LLP; b: ©Eric Taylor Photography; c: Courtesy of and designed by Sam Paxhia)*

more for the aesthetic drama they provide than for structural considerations. Like cathedral ceilings, these types of ceilings infuse a space with an aura of importance (Figure 8.14a–c). However, shifting attitudes regarding aesthetics, comfort, and energy usage have resulted in criticism of this design choice in certain contexts, particularly residential. Heating and cooling these rooms can be expensive, and they are often drafty and noisy from echoes. Moreover, a growing numbers of home buyers find that this design wastes space that could be used instead for additional rooms.[8] Trends in ceiling design are discussed further in Chapter 13.

Ceilings may be attached to, or flush with, the roof or suspended, or dropped, to accommodate heating, ventilation, electrical, lighting, and acoustical systems. Suspended ceiling system applications are discussed in Chapter 9.

Fenestrations

The importance of openings for windows and doors, or fenestrations, can hardly be overstated. Our first encounter of any interior, and therefore our primary appreciation of that space, is the entry into it. Entrance is not merely a physical movement, but also a psychological one. A well-thought-out concept for the whole interior (a role of the interior designer) is necessary for a well-designed entrance.[9]

Again, Edith Wharton, who was perhaps both proponent and critic of the early modern styles, had something to say about her contemporaries' lack of attention to the basics of fenestrations:

> Not only do they [the openings in a house] represent the three chief essentials of its [a building's] comfort—light, heat, and means of access—but they are the leading features in that combination of voids and masses that forms the basis of architectural harmony. In fact, it is chiefly because the decorative value of openings has ceased to be recognized that modern rooms so seldom produce a satisfactory and harmonious impression. It used to be thought that the effect of a room depended on the treatment of its wall-spaces and openings; now it is supposed to depend on its curtains and furniture.[10]

Doors and windows serve the exterior as well as the interior of a space. Among the functions of exterior doors and windows are direct entry, exit, and passage; provision of privacy and security; insulation of the interior from exterior climatic and environmental forces, including sound and vibrations; and provision of additional light, ventilation, and vista to the interior. Interior doors serve to define zones, behavioral settings, or rooms, and to direct traffic. They also provide for privacy and sound absorption.

Many choices are available today in both standard and customized doors and windows. However, the old lessons of Palladio still apply concerning the need for planning so that the door and window openings will be compatible to each other and with other structural elements, such as the frame, walls, and ceiling.

This chapter explores choices involved in the structural aspects of doors and windows; the treatment of windows and doors is covered in Chapter 9. However, there are areas in which it can be hard to distinguish between the two. An example is energy conservation. An example might be the use of a particular drapery treatment to save energy as well as add character to the space.

Many of the factors discussed in Chapter 5 are critical considerations when choosing windows and doors as exterior and interior components. The initial, programming phase of a project includes research aimed at assessing factors relating to climate, site orientation, style, and occupant requirements for sensory satisfaction, psychological and physiological comfort, safety, and well-being. The requirements for adequate light,

ventilation, fire safety, and privacy are among many needs identified during this stage.

You should become familiar with the terms used to describe windows and doors, as relates to their construction (including hardware, such as hinges, knobs, levers, latches, and locks), type of operation, and style. The extensive vocabulary relating to windows and doors is essential to maintain accurate communication with suppliers, installers, and clients.

Doors Of doors, Palladio writes, "The place to be chosen for principal [exterior] doors, is where a free access may be had to it from all parts of the house."[11] Doors serve to articulate, or resonate, decorative presence and meaning. For Palladio the principal door spoke to the quality of the master of the house. As can be seen in Figure 8.15a–c, decorative door styles abound.

Used alone or in combination, wood, metal, glass (and, to a lesser degree, plastic) make up the main materials used for doors. The woods used may be hardwood, such as oak, or softwood, such as pine, in solid construction or veneered, with thin slices of wood laminated together. The metal used is generally steel, stainless steel, or aluminum. Metal doors are

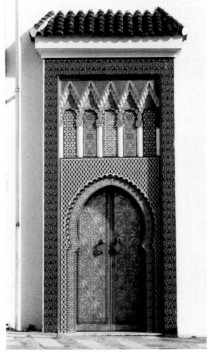

a   b   c

Figure 8.15
Styles of exterior doors. a. Palatial-style door for hotel in India, Leela Palace Kempinki; b. King's Palace, Morocco, made of carved brass; c. Gothic-style oak door, Barcelona, Spain. *(a: © Rudolf Tepfenhart | Dreamstime.com; b and c: Provided by the Author)*

more typically used for commercial construction, with wood being more common for residences.

Doors may be constructed as solid or hollow core or with laminated surfaces. They are typically set within a frame or **jamb**. A **threshold** is customarily placed under the door and may be built from any of several materials, among them wood, metal, and stone. A **mullion** is a thin vertical member that divides the components of a door or window. Tables 8.1 and 8.2 describe typical doors by type of operation, use, and style.

Table 8.1
Types of Doors by Operation

Revolving door. (© *Image Source / Alamy*)

Type	Description	Considerations for Use
Overhead	Runs on a track system that opens vertically. May be operated manually or remotely, generally with the mechanism for opening at the top.	For exterior use, residentially, for garages, and commercially, for loading docks.
Revolving	Panels, usually of glass, rotate around a center axis, either at a constant speed or as determined by people entering through the door.	For exterior use, generally in commercial applications. Doors in which the edges of the rotating door panels provide a closed seal with the edges of the door frame offer better thermal insulation than swinging, sliding, or overhead doors.
Sliding	Bypass doors allow for only 50% opening or one door width, as one door slides past another from an overhead track. Surface doors sliding from an overhead track provide for 100% opening. Pocket doors allow for 100% door opening and are constructed to slide into the width of the wall. Shoji are sliding doors (or screens) of Japanese origin made of translucent materials, such as rice paper, within a wood frame.	For both interior and exterior use. Sacrifice acoustical and thermal insulation for space saving.
Swinging	Typically side-hinged. May swing inward, outward, or in both directions.	Used for both interior and exterior. Provide several advantages, such as acoustical and thermal insulation, but the need for sufficient clearance must be considered.

Table 8.2
Architectural Styles of Doors

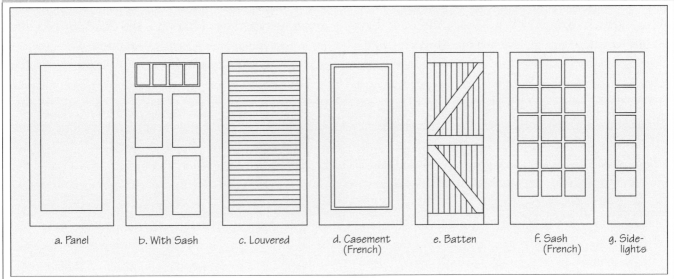

a. Panel b. With Sash c. Louvered d. Casement (French) e. Batten f. Sash (French) g. Side-lights

Figures a–g

Types of doors by style.

Style	Description
Batten	A rustic style, in which wood slats, or strips, serve to reinforce the door. May be used for barns, attics, or basement entries.
Dutch	Side-hinged door divided horizontally so that the top and bottom can be opened separately.
Folding	Interior door type. May be constructed with side hinging or a top or bottom tracking mechanism. May have many configurations, ranging from bifold (two panels that open to one side), typically used for closets, to accordion (multiple panels), typically used to divide large spaces, particularly multifunction areas.
Flush	Has a contemporary, or modern, appearance. Surface is an unbroken, continuous plane.
French	Most often these are double doors with a pattern of rectangular glass panels from top to bottom. Used as interior doors or exterior doors leading to a balcony or porch.
Louvered, or Jalousie	Constructed of glass horizontal slats that can be tilted up or down to control light and ventilation.
Panel	Surface has a broken plane, which may be either raised or recessed. Often called a rail and stile, with rail being the horizontal and stile being the vertical member; originally a structural component only, but now may serve a more purely decorative function. Adds dimensional interest and appears more traditional in style than a flush door.
Sash	Comprises several types of doors (and windows), including: Sidelight: A narrow vertical pane of glass, generally installed in pairs, that flanks a doorway. Transom: A horizontal, or transverse, pane of glass that is generally installed above a door to provide ventilation but maintain privacy. Fanlight: A semicircular windowpane, often with radiating mullions, like the ribs of a fan, that is placed over a door or window.
Screen	A metal wire mesh encased in either a wood or metal frame. Generally used to keep out insects.

Windows

Of windows, Palladio notes the importance of correct number and size:

> It is to be observed in making the windows, they should not take in more or less light, or be fewer or more in number, than what necessity requires: therefore great regard ought to be had to the largeness of the rooms which are to receive the light from them; because it is manifest, that a great room requires much more light to make it lucid and clear, than a small one: and if the windows are made either less or fewer than that which is convenient, they will make the places obscure, and if too large, they will scarce be habitable, because they will let in so much hot and cold air, that the places, according to the season of the year, will either be exceeding hot or very cold, in case the part of the heavens which they face, does not in some manner prevent it.[12]

If the eyes are the windows of the soul, then windows are the eyes to the world. Centuries ago, before glass was a readily available and fabricated material, windows were literally exterior wall openings—small cutouts in the structure of the building. They provided the necessities of ventilation, access to daylight, and the opportunity to look out at times to ensure protection from unwanted intruders and perhaps, to a lesser degree, to enjoy a connection with the environment via vista and view. They may have been covered with fabric or shutters. There is some evidence that there was a scant use of glass for windows by the ancient Romans. The orientation as well as the size and shape of windows also gave character to a space. When providing for a spectacular view, the size and position of a window may direct the design for both floor and furniture plans.

Windows still serve the same purposes, although the options for how they are designed, constructed, and used are enormously greater now. Decisions about where to place windows and how they should be treated are based on many factors, among them the site's orientation and climate and concerns for energy conservation. Two categories of windows that are specifically defined by their placement within a structure are the **clerestory**, a row of windows along the top of the wall, and the **skylight**, a window placed in a roof or ceiling. Both are designed to maximize daylighting with an economy of wall space. The clerestory, placed high on the wall, may also project onto the roof line, whereas the skylight always does. Table 8.3 highlights factors to be considered when choosing windows.

Although glass (including stained glass for churches) was available in Europe during the Middle Ages, it was not until the Industrial Revolution in the late 19th century that glass was mass-produced for everyday use. The hallmark of the use of glass as a construction material, that is, **glazing**, was the Crystal Palace, built in London in 1851 (Figure 8.16a). Further advances in technology allowed for the development of another fixed glass structure, the **curtain wall**, a wood or metal frame sheathed with glass, epitomized

Table 8.3 Considerations in Choosing Windows	
Factor	**Solution**
Architectural style	Research authenticity of existing windows or create reasonable contemporary facsimiles.
Cold weather	Use wood-framed windows sheathed with enameled metal or vinyl. Use insulating treatments.
Safety	Research security systems and applicable local fire regulations. Place decals to identify expanses of clear glass.
Temperature extremes	Use double, triple, thermal, or storm windowpanes. Use few windows.
Ventilation	Consider placement to allow for cross ventilation.
Warm weather and extreme sunlight	Use awnings or overhangs. Tint glass with a solar screen to prevent glare and fading and to provide insulation.

Figure 8.16

Styles of windows. a. Crystal Palace; b. Curtain-wall construction by Le Corbusier; c. Contemporary residential picture window.
(a: Great Exhibition of 1851. Decoration of the transept, Jones, Owen [1809–74] / Victoria & Albert Museum, London, UK / The Bridge-man Art Library International; b: © o2 Architectural Photography / Alamy Villa Savoye "Les heures claires" 82, Rue de Villiers 70300 Poissy (France) Arch. Le Corbusier, Pierre Jeanneret (1929–1931); c: Courtesy of and designed by Sam Paxhia)

by the 20th-century modern architect Le Corbusier (Figure 8.16b). Contemporary residential architecture often makes use of **picture windows,** large expanses of glass, which are generally fixed (Figure 8.16c).

Although today's windows are most often made of glass, some transparent or translucent synthetic materials are also available. Acrylic, a type of plastic, is used in certain applications. These materials are more resistant to cracking and breaking, but they are much more susceptible to scratching than is glass. Glass is a mineral in the silicate family. Fusing silica sand at very high temperatures with some additives, including liquid, produces the glass in use today. Techniques such as laser etching may be used to embellish glass for decorative features; other techniques are available to improve its strength, durability, and utility.

Tempered glass is glass that has been strengthened by a special heat treatment to prevent breakage. **Safety glass,** similar to tempered glass in its resistance to impact, is produced by laminating a sheet of transparent plastic between sheets of clear glass. When safety glass does break, it falls into very small pieces rather than one dangerous piece. **Wire glass** is a form of glass in which a metal mesh system is infused into the glass to resist shattering. It is applicable for windows requiring fire resistance, such as in exit stairwells. Another fire-rated glazing material is **electrochromic,** glass treated with a ceramic coating that darkens when an electric current passes through it. This glazing is considered energy conserving, as it controls the emission of light, ultraviolet energy, and solar heat.[13]

Improved processing has led to the development of **float glass,** which has generally replaced plate and sheet glass for use in windows. In this process, the molten glass moves out of the furnace along a flat, molten metal, producing a glass that is freer from distortion, with better heat insulation properties than its predecessors. It can be produced in virtually any thickness.

Windows, whether fixed or operable, are typically made up of a frame (composed of a head, jamb, and sill) and a sash (Figure 8.17). Window frames may be constructed of any of the following materials, alone or in combination: wood, metal, and plastic. **Muntins**, or mullions, may be used to separate the panes of glass. **Casing**, or trim, may be placed to line the interior head or side or used as an exterior. A **shim space** helps stabilize the window unit.

Table 8.4 describes several standard types of windows by operation. These types of windows are used in both residential and commercial applications, and many are used for both exterior and interior structures. Table 8.5 describes windows by their architectural style.

Vertical Systems

The manner in which people (and furnishings and equipment) move up or down inside or outside a space is the subject of vertical transit, or transportation, systems. These systems include stairs, ramps, elevators (or lifts as referred to in the United Kingdom), and escalators. They may serve both functional and aesthetic purposes, as noted by Palladio in his discussion of the importance of staircases.

> The stair-cases will be commendable if they are clear, ample, and commodious to ascent, inviting, as it were, people to go up: They will be clear, if they have a bright light, and if . . . the light is diffused equally every where alike: They will be sufficiently ample, if they do not seem scanty and narrow to the largeness and quality of the fabric; but they are never to be made less wide than four foot, that if two persons meet, they may conveniently give one another room . . . The steps ought not to be made higher than six inches of a foot; and if they are made lower, particularly in long and continued stairs, it will make them the more easy, because if rising one's self the foot will be less tired; but they must never be made lower than four inches: the breadth of the steps ought not to be made less than one foot, nor more than one and a half.[14]

Although some of the dimensions and ratios have changed over the centuries (partly because of changing anthropometric data), more recent practice and legislation have reinforced Palladio's concepts concerning the strong tie between stair construction and human physiology and movement. Essentially, his dictums factor into many of today's ergonomic considerations relating to treads, risers, pitch, headroom, and handrails for vertical transit.

The structural standards and decorative styles for stairs differ based on their use as interior versus exterior elements, in residential versus commercial applications, and because of different user needs. However, certain principles apply. Stairs must be able to carry load safely and provide for passage.

The **tread** is the depth of the stair, and the **riser** is the height. A tread of 10 inches and a riser of 7 to $7 \frac{1}{2}$ inches are considered average. Building codes for residential stairways are generally less stringent than for public use. Treads and risers should be proportioned so that the sum of the two risers and one tread is not less than 24 inches or more than 26 inches. For most stairs, a 7-inch riser and an 11-inch tread is a comfortable combination. The angle of the stairs may also be referred to as its slope or pitch.[15] Commonly, this is described in terms of steepness. Walking on too steep a path makes ascent and descent difficult and dangerous. The width, or breadth, of a stair is also a factor in safety and influences the usage of handrails to stabilize gait. Generally, a staircase that is more than 5 feet wide requires a center rail to divide the space and allow for two-person passage, in addition to side handrails. Long runs, typically continuations of stairways that exceed 24 stairs, should have **landings**, or resting areas.

Although not adhering exactly to the calculations proposed by Palladio, the idea that one is not comfortable or safe under certain conditions remains the same. Walking on steep stairs on which one's foot cannot securely make contact, one feels the need to make contact with the handrail for additional stability. Similarly, poor lighting conditions or slippery surfaces can make even the most able-bodied individual feel vulnerable. In addition to standards detailed by the Americans with Disabilities Act (ADA), local ordinances and codes impose requirements on the design and construction of stairways regarding enclosures for

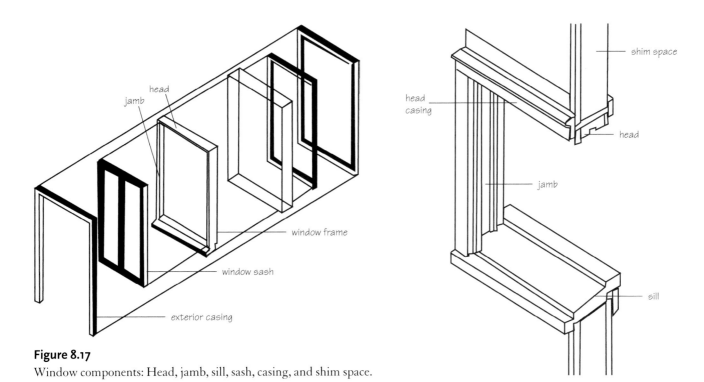

Figure 8.17
Window components: Head, jamb, sill, sash, casing, and shim space.

	Table 8.4	
	Types of Windows by Operation	
Type	**Description**	
Awning	Hinged at the top, they can swing inward or outward.	
Fixed, or stationary	Cannot be opened; alternative ventilation and fire safety measure must be in place. May be used in combination with operable windows.	
Hopper	Hinged at the bottom, they swing inward.	
Louvered, or jalousie	Glass horizontal slats can be tilted up or down to control for light and ventilation.	
Operable casement	Like doors, the panes are hinged on the side to allow for inward or outward swinging.	
Pivot	Hinged at the center of both the top and bottom, they can be pivoted on a vertical plane.	
Sash	Featuring a vertical sliding movement in either single- or double-hung sash windows. The most common type is the double-hung sash, in which two glass areas slide vertically, allowing for 50% ventilation.	
Sliding	Featuring horizontal sliding movements, they are typically composed of two to three sashes.	

Figure a
Types of windows by operation.

Table 8.5
Architectural Styles of Windows

Figures a and b

a. Featured in this photo are a roundel (center) and an arched window; b. Skylight for the Chicago Institute New Wing.
(a and b: Provided by the Author)

Style	Description
Arched	Generally provided to replicate a building's architectural vocabulary. May be shaped in various manners or styles, including Roman, Gothic, and Palladian (see Chapter 12).
Bay or bow	Window structures that project outward, rather than being flush on the same plane as the walls of a building.
Cathedral	Like the roof line of the same name, applies a triangular shape to the top of a window, often one of a grand scale.
Clerestory	Narrow window openings that are placed high on a wall, generally lined up in a string to provide ventilation, access to daylight, and privacy.
Dormer	Similar to the bay or bow, this window also projects outward, specifically at attic level, and may be constructed in many shapes and configurations.
Skylight	Installed in the ceiling or roof, or both, and used to provide additional daylight. May be made of either glass or acrylic. May be operable, often by remote control, or fixed.
Special shapes	Include round (or roundel), portholes, and hexagonal shapes. May be installed, generally as fixed windows, for decorative impact.

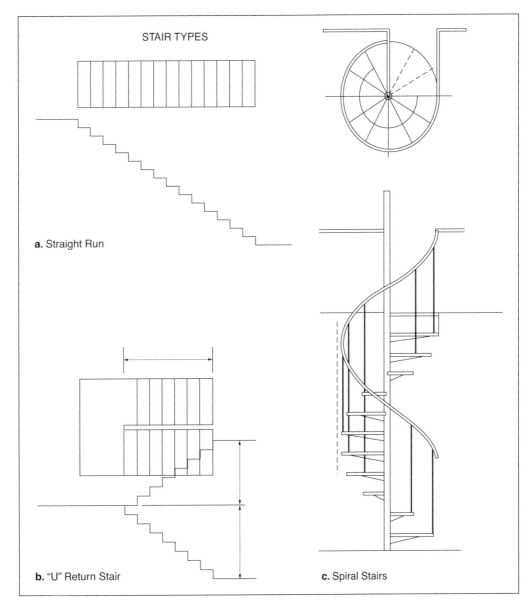

STAIR TYPES

a. Straight Run

b. "U" Return Stair

c. Spiral Stairs

Figure 8.18

Types of staircases. a. A straight run staircase may be either continuous or with a landing; b. A return staircase may be either U- or L-shaped; c. A spiral staircase is a fully circular, oval, or curving structure with or without a landing.

fire safety exits. Best practice generally entails exceeding those minimums.

The basic types of stairway systems are the straight run, return, and spiral. These are described and illustrated in Figure 8.18a–c. Stairs are constructed from many materials, among them wood, steel, and concrete. As with doors, metal is more commonly used for commercial construction, and wood for residences. The designer can choose from many styles of construction with many possible decorative additions. As with the other building elements discussed in this chapter, structural factors must be taken into consideration, along with aesthetic elements. Figure 8.19a and b illus-

trates the differences in impact achieved through use of a classic spiral staircase and one that is more contemporary in style.

Ramps Like stairs, ramps provide a transition from one level to another, serving both exterior and interior needs. They are often associated with ease of mobility for those with ambulation challenges. They also facilitate vertical transit of freight, furnishings, and equipment.

As with stairs, the dimensions, slope, surface, and additional supports for ramps need to be considered. The standard for the slope of a ramp is 1:12. This

Figure 8.19
a. Spiral staircase in a contemporary home; b. The central circular stairwell of City Hall, New York City. *(a: © Tim Street-Porter/Beateworks/Corbis Outline; b: Photograph by Eric Laignel)*

means that for every 12 feet of run, there should be an increase of 1 foot in rise, or level (Figure 8.20). To achieve this gradual slope, much linear space is consumed. Although ramps are required for public spaces to meet standards of barrier-free design, some experts believe their use should be kept to a minimum, with more building construction done at grade level. Cynthia Leibrock, an interior designer, and James Terry, an architect, for instance, point out that ramps segregate disabled people by creating separate entrances. Often, these structures are architectural add-ons rather than conceived of as integral to the architecture (Figure 8.21). Of further note, more than 20 percent of wheelchair users cannot use a 1:12 ramp.[16]

Elevators, Lifts, and Escalators
Elevators, lifts, and escalators are other structural components that are within the purview of the architect or engineer. These vertical transit devices are most often

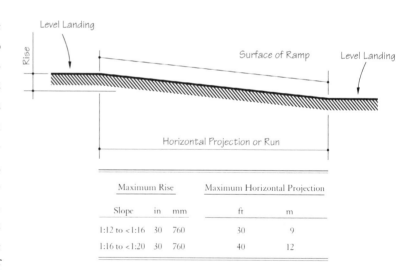

	Maximum Rise			Maximum Horizontal Projection	
Slope	in	mm		ft	m
1:12 to <1:16	30	760		30	9
1:16 to <1:20	30	760		40	12

Figure 8.20
The recommended rise for a ramp should not exceed a 1:12 ratio.

Figure 8.21
A ramp can be a creative architectural feature. *(Architect: RTKL Associates Inc. Photography: Anice Hoachlander)*

used in commercial settings and apartment buildings. They serve to transport freight, occupants, or equipment. Because they often provide an alternative to stairs for people with ambulation or visual difficulties, special attention must be made to incorporate barrier-free features. Call buttons in elevators must include raised (Braille) designations placed no higher than 3 feet above the finished floor level (Figure 8.22). This height also helps children use the buttons. Audible announcements are desirable as well. Other features, such as emergency two-way communication inside the car, should include both tactile and visual instructions.

Escalators, or moving stairs, like ramps, require ample space (Figure 8.23). A landing space is also required at arrival and departure points. Escalators are usually installed at a 30-degree angle. Lifts,

Figure 8.22
The interior panel of an elevator, showing Braille call buttons. *(© Royalty-Free/Corbis)*

Figure 8.23
Escalators are effective methods for transporting people in public spaces such as department stores, subways, and airports. *(AP Photo/Al Behrman)*

Figure 8.24

A wheelchair lift. *(Courtesy of RAM Manufacturing Ltd.)*

particularly for wheelchair use, are a space-saving alternative to ramps (Figure 8.24).

ENVIRONMENTAL CONTROL SYSTEMS

The heating, ventilation, air-conditioning, water supply, waste disposal, acoustical, and power and communication systems that are germane to a building's functioning are all environmental control systems. The term *mechanical systems* is often used to incorporate heating and cooling, plumbing, and fire protection, whereas *electrical systems* includes power, lighting, and communications.[17] These structural components, relevant to the realm of FF&E, can also affect sensory experiences, particularly those relating to acoustics. To a greater extent, these mechanical systems are becoming computerized. Concerns about energy conservation play a dominant role in the criteria for selection, installation, and use of these systems. As a result, energy conservation issues are increasingly important considerations in the interior designer's education, training, and practice.

HVAC

The acronym **HVAC** stands for *heating, ventilation, and air-conditioning systems.* These systems rely on natural and mechanical operations to varying degrees. Several factors, in addition to the control of temperature, need to be considered when choosing these systems, including air quality and circulation and moisture level, or humidity.

Heat sources include solar energy, which is generated by the sun's radiation; heat that is created as a by-product of the operation of equipment; and body heat, which is generated from human metabolic activity. Heat is only one of the by-products of energy used by people; transportation and electricity are two others.

The choice of lighting fixtures, whether fixed or portable, is often an interior designer's responsibility (also see Chapter 7). The generation of heat by these fixtures, in comparison with the main objective of providing illumination, is just one way in which the interior designer's decision making affects the structural aspects of a building. For example, the average incandescent light bulb uses 95 percent of its energy input generating heat, which is usually unwanted. Use of these bulbs in many fixtures throughout a building thus has ramifications for the amount of energy (and money) expended to cool the surrounding air.

The interior designer can save energy and money by specifying energy-efficient heating and cooling systems, fixtures, and appliances. Although the initial cost may be higher, products and services that have a higher efficiency rating will have a lower **life-cycle cost** (a calculation of cost relative to the product's life expectancy).

Heating An interior space may be heated in many ways: naturally, mechanically, conservatively, or wastefully.

Solar energy, broadly defined, is the energy radiating from the sun, or radiant energy. **Passive solar energy** systems capture and store direct solar energy to heat buildings and water without the use of mechanical devices. An example is a well-insulated, airtight house with large insulating windows that face the sun, known as **direct solar gain**. **Active solar energy** systems harness energy from the sun mechanically. Rooftop devices, greenhouses on urban rooftops, solaria, wind turbines, and hydroelectric devices are some of the ways that solar energy is harnessed and converted into electricity (Figure 8.25a and b).

Sunlight may also be turned into energy through the **photovoltaic effect**, the basic physical process through which a photovoltaic (PV) cell converts sunlight into electricity (Figure 8.25c). Sunlight is composed of photons, that is, packets of solar energy. These photons contain different amounts of energy that correspond to the different wavelengths of the solar spectrum. When photons strike a PV cell, they may be reflected or absorbed, or they may pass right through. The absorbed photons generate electricity. An individual PV cell is usually quite small, typically producing about 1 or 2 watts of power. To boost the power output of PV cells, they are connected together to form larger units, called modules. Modules, in turn, can be connected to form even larger units, called arrays, which can be interconnected to produce more power, and so on.

The oldest source of renewable energy known to humans, used since our ancestors learned the secret of fire, is fuel from **biomass energy**, or energy from plant and animal wastes. Wood remains the most widely used source of biomass energy. For roughly one-half of the world's population, wood is the main source of energy for heating and cooking. In more developed, or industrialized, countries, such as the United States, the use of wood as the principal source of heat for the interior climate and for cooking has become virtually obsolete.

It is recognized, however, that there is a wide variety of biomass energy resources, including wood by-products that are sustainable, such as paper mill residue, lumber mill scrap, and municipal waste. Other plants that may be used for biomass fuels are corn grain, soybeans, and wheat straw. Efforts are being made to grow crops specifically dedicated to use as fuel resources, such as fast-growing trees and grasses as well as algae.[18]

Traditional fireplaces may be wasteful of energy, as they use wood as fuel (Figure 8.26a). Wood-burning stoves are more efficient and emit less air pollution than open hearths. In recent years, a substitute for the architectural hearth has been found in the manufacture of freestanding fireplaces that use ethanol (also called ethyl alcohol or grain alcohol), a plant derivative, generally made from sugar or corn. Ethanol is considered clean burning and smokeless and does not require venting (Figure 8.26b).

Fossil fuel is made from buried deposits of decayed plants and animals that have been exposed to heat and pressure in the Earth's crust over hundreds of millions of years, before the dinosaurs, hence the name *fossil fuel*. There are three major types of fossil fuel: coal, oil, and natural gas. Coal is the world's most abundant fossil fuel. For heating it has been largely replaced by oil, a fossil fuel that is less damaging to the environment. The burning of coal emits toxic pollutants into the air and is also believed to be responsible for much of the increase in the Earth's temperature seen in recent decades. This global warming is thought to occur through the **greenhouse effect**, the trapping and buildup of heat in the atmosphere. In addition, coal mining disrupts the land's surface, and runoff from surface mining operations can pollute rivers and streams. Although efforts have been made to convert solid coal to a synthetic natural gas, it is an expensive proposition.

Oil is a refined version of a flammable liquid extracted from Earth's upper strata and is the main source of energy for heating (and fueling automobiles) in the United States. This heavy reliance on oil has many implications, ranging from economic and political consequences to issues of sustainability of Earth's

Figure 8.25

a. An urban rooftop garden at Chicago's City Hall; b. Wind turbine system; c. A photovoltaic solar panel system. *(a: Image by City of Chicago. All rights reserved; b: © Tebnad \ Dreamstime.com; c: © Jaromír Ondra \ Dreamstime.com)*

Figure 8.26
a. This fireplace in a family room features the traditional materials of stone and brick with a wood mantel; b. Ethanol-fueled, free-standing fireplace. *(a: Photograph by Phillip Ennis. Designed by Denise Balassi; b: © mediacolor's / Alamy)*

resources. Oil consumption by Americans is high, but the United States has only a very small reserve of the world's oil, and it is expensive to tap. Using alternatives to oil in heating systems is a key goal of designers sensitive to the codependency of humans and the environment.

Natural gas burns hotter and produces less air pollution than any other fossil fuel. However, it must be converted to liquid natural gas before it can be shipped from one country to another, which is expensive and dangerous, owing to the potential for explosions.

Heat stored in, or generated by, water is the basis for hot water and steam heating systems. In a hot water system, water heated by a furnace is circulated through pipes housed in baseboard units. With steam heat, water is heated until it produces steam, which is then piped through a radiator system. This type of heating system is generally found in older homes.

Forced hot air is a heating system that relies on a furnace to warm the air, which is then circulated through ducts to outlet openings in the interior, known as **grilles**, or *registers*. Suspended ceilings can generally accommodate these ducts in the space that is called a **plenum**.

At one time a feature primarily of new commercial buildings, heating with hot air is being accommodated today within residences as well, generally within a raised structural floor. This is called **radiant air heating**. While generally installed within floors, the system may be accommodated in walls and ceilings. Another heating system that has become popular is **hydronic**, a cost-effective, energy-efficient radiant heating system. A liquid system, hydronic radiant floor systems pump heated water from a boiler through tubing laid in a pattern underneath the floor. In some systems, the temperature in each room is controlled by regulating the flow of hot water through each tubing loop. This is done by a system of zoning valves or pumps and thermostats (Figure 8.27).

Ceramic tile is the most common and effective floor covering for radiant floor heating, as it conducts heat well from the floor and adds thermal storage because of its high heat capacity.

Another form of heating is electric. Electric heating converts electric power into heat and delivers it through either baseboard units that warm the air or direct radiation from panels in ceilings or walls.

Figure 8.27
Hydronic radiant heating system for flooring. (© *Alamy*)

Although it is considered clean and nonpolluting, electric heat is expensive.

Ventilation Clean air is essential to well-being, whether provided by cross ventilation of breezes from windows or by motorized fans circulating the air. Either excess humidity or lack of moisture in the air can cause physical discomfort and exacerbate allergic conditions and skin irritations. Systems that either humidify or evaporate excess moisture from an interior may be a concern for interior designers during construction or post-construction as a way to alleviate the effects of structural deficiencies.

Air-Conditioning The *AC* part of HVAC essentially refers to air-cooling systems but may also include control of moisture level, or humidity. Air-conditioning may be centralized throughout the interior, or it may be provided through distinct components that affect a smaller area, usually a defined room. Generally, centralized air-cooling systems should be planned during a building's construction. Not considered to be aesthetically satisfying, these systems are hidden whenever feasible.

Water Supply and Waste Disposal

Plumbing systems are a major aspect of the mechanical layer of a building's structure. They provide the water supply needed in bathrooms and kitchens for drinking, washing activities, and eliminating waste products (drainage) from those areas. The **rough plumbing** stage is the time when the planned placement of pipes and drains is crucial (Figure 8.28). It is often at this stage that the designer needs to obtain information from the engineer or architect to plan properly for the functional layout of spaces.

Relocation of kitchen and bath areas is dependent on the functions of water supply and waste disposal.

Figure 8.28
Rough plumbing for shower between studs of new framing at home construction site. (© *David Young-Wolff / Alamy*)

Such plans should not be made without serious consideration of these issues. Renovation projects that require major relocation of rough plumbing systems are likely to be expensive.

Poorly designed plumbing systems can be a maintenance nightmare for the owner, wasteful of energy resources, and a safety hazard. Safety measures that restrict the temperature of hot water coming out of bath and kitchen faucets can be implemented at the rough plumbing stage or through the selection of fixtures that provide protective features. Control of water temperature is an important consideration when children and frail individuals will use a space.

Water use is a key issue in resource conservation, as noted in Chapter 2. The Energy Policy Act (EPAct) of 1992 developed minimum standards for water consumption, including toilets, showerheads, and faucets. Designers are often in the position of specifying fixtures and appliances that control the flow of water or provide for recycling of the water supply. This is yet another key area in which a designer's knowledge of new and improved resources can play a pivotal role not only in consumer satisfaction, but also in conservation of natural resources. Chapter 9 describes new product designs and improvements in these areas.

Another water conservation approach is to reclaim water from domestic wastewater, industrial process waters, or agricultural irrigation systems. **Graywater** is domestic (nontoilet) wastewater that can be treated for nonpotable (nondrinkable) use, such as landscaping.

National policy, in part directed by the Department of Energy, National Renewable Energy Labs (NREL), defines the type of future sought for the built environment, that of zero energy buildings. A **zero energy building (ZEB)** is a residential or commercial building in which energy needs have been greatly reduced through efficiency gains, such that the balance of energy needs can be supplied with renewable technologies. The designation **Zero Energy Home (ZEH)** is given to single, private homes. This type of building uses efficient construction and appliances with commercially available renewable energy systems (often photovoltaic), such as solar water heating and solar electricity. *In the Spotlight: Zero Energy Building* outlines the development of one such ZEB, in San Jose, California, a contract space. However, in striving to reduce our energy addiction (as it is sometimes called), each one of us, design students included, can make strides by following or facilitating energy-saving practices (*In the Spotlight: Zero Energy Building* Figure a). Also see *FYI . . . Tips for Saving Energy*.

ACOUSTICAL SYSTEMS

The choice of materials and finishes used in building components has a direct impact on the ability to control the transmission of sound. Materials and finishes capable of controlling the transmission of sound are described as having good acoustical value. The shape of an interior space also influences the direction and impact of sound waves. Sound transmission may be controlled in part by the position, angle, shape, and dimension of partitions, walls, and ceilings. During construction, noise control can be addressed through installation of heavy floor and ceiling structures. Additional layers of glazing for windows and use of double doors help ensure appropriate acoustical values.

Acoustical decision making must consider the uses to which a proposed space will be put, as well as the users. Structural ceiling height, for instance, is a key factor in the design of dining spaces. To attract a lively Generation Y clientele, a restaurant may favor a high, unfinished ceiling surface that creates an ambience enabling patrons to be seen and heard. The low acoustical value is appropriate for this market, which enjoys the effect of bouncing sound waves. The same noise level would be considered unbearable in the common dining area of an independent or assisted-living housing unit designed for seniors.

Acoustical considerations are important to the interior designer when planning for communication and security systems. A growing number of residential and contract projects require expertise in acoustics for media centers. These facilities may take the form of an entertainment theater, conference center, or space for telecommuting tasks. Additional acoustical controls are discussed in Chapter 9.

POWER AND COMMUNICATION SYSTEMS

Other building tradespeople are usually responsible for power and communication systems, but interior designers can play a pivotal role in the way these systems support and enhance occupant activity and lifestyle. Electrical systems comprise the power or energy

Incorporating Culture, Location, Materials, and Innovation into the Built Environment

The Rural Studio: Alabama, United States

The Rural Studio was founded in 1993 by two Auburn University architecture professors, Dennis K. Ruth and the late Samuel Mockbee, to give architecture students hands-on experience and to improve the living conditions in rural Alabama. Students are given the opportunity to expand their knowledge through building their own designs, but they also put their skills to use in one of the poorest areas of the United States. In context-based design learning, rather than designing from the outside, students are encouraged to understand and experience the particular needs of their clients for themselves.

One such project is the Lucy House, Mason's Bend, Hale County, Alabama (2001–2002), for the Harris family. Not only did it draw on traditional vernacular forms, but it also incorporated a very sustainable building shell structure: carpet. With the help of a corporate sponsor, Interface, the world's largest manufacturer of carpet tiles as well as a supporter and practitioner of sustainability, the students were challenged to use non-recyclable carpet scraps in the building's construction. Interface donated 72,000 tiles of carpet which were stacked and compressed with reinforced metal rods to form a solid mass. They were then held in place by a wooded ring beam.[1]

The Gando Primary School: Burkina Faso, Africa

Dié´be´do Francis Ke´re´, a local of this village of 3,000, was the first person from his community to study abroad. Trained as an architect, he combined his European education with his dedication to design using traditional methods to build the Gando Primary School. The villagers were involved in every aspect of the school's construction with the government providing training in brick-making. The building is a model of passive solar design. A double roof structure overhangs the building, creating shaded areas, and protects the classrooms underneath from heat gain. Each classroom has its own mud-brick

Figure a

The Lucy House, constructed of recycled carpet tiles donated by Interface Carpet. (*The Lucy House © Timothy Hursley*)

ceiling that insulates it from hot air circulating above. Local craftsmen cut an ordinary indigenous wood with a handsaw and welded the pieces together to form lightweight roof trusses. Two neighboring villages built their own schools following the cooperative approach used for the Gando School.[2]

Figure b

The Gando School features passive solar heating. (*Location: Burkina Faso; Country: West Africa; Client: Gando Community; Architect: Kere Architecture; photo by Siméon Douchoud*)

(continued)

Incorporating Culture, Location, Materials, and Innovation into the Built Environment, *cont.*

Disaster Relief: Hurricane Katrina, New Orleans, United States

In 2005 Hurricane Katrina flooded 80 percent of the City of New Orleans and killed 1,577 people. Hardest hit was the Lower 9th Ward where more than 4,000 homes were destroyed by the storm and the surge of water caused by the breach of the Industrial Canal levee. Two years later, frustrated by the lack of progress in rebuilding, and after meeting with community groups and families, actor Brad Pitt established the Make It Right Foundation. Its goal was to build 150 green, affordable, high-quality design homes in that hard hit area by December 2010.

Many architectural and design firms contributed to the development of single family home designs using the traditional New Orleans **shotgun house**. The format is a simple and narrow home to fit the lots in the Lower 9th Ward, narrow face to the street with great depth to the back of the lot. They also all include porches, a feature highly valued in the neighborhood that places a premium on sociability and connectedness to the community. All of the homes built to date have been certified as LEED platinum for their energy efficiency and sustainability.

Storm-resistant features include: houses are raised between five and eight feet above grade, beyond minimum federal requirements; special impact-resistant fabric is fitted to the window frames to be fastened when needed; escape is available from the attic to access the roof during storms; and wall sections are built to withstand 160 miles per hour winds.[3]

Housing for Haiti: Response to 2010 Earthquake: Clemson University SEED-Haiti

In January 2010 a 7.0 magnitude earthquake struck near the Haitian capital of Port-au-Prince, leaving almost one-quarter of a million dead. The damage to buildings was severe, leaving almost 200,000 houses destroyed or badly damaged. One and a half million people were left to live in shelter camps; over one half million left the area.[4]

One solution posed for housing was recycled shipping containers. Recycling old shipping containers

Figure c
Single family shotgun home post-Katrina style. *(Home by Graft Architects. Photo credit: Alexei Lebedev, Make It Right)*

is both a sustainable and economical solution to the growing worldwide need for additional housing. Shipping containers, essentially structural shells, would prove to be an excellent solution in seismic areas.

SEED-Haiti is an environmental and humanitarian solution for providing relief housing with the adaptive reuse of surplus shipping containers which in time may also provide for more permanent housing solutions. This solution uses the many shipping containers that are already in Haiti and the large number of shipping containers that are being sent to Haiti with relief supplies. The containers are not only hurricane and earthquake proof but are also fire, mold, and vandalism proof. The SEED design transforms a 40′ shipping container into a home for six to ten people with a minimum amount of effort. The container is cut with readily available equipment and utilizes low-impact foundation technology to lift the home off the ground for ventilation and protect from flood. It is also covered with a secondary roof to keep the home cool. It is a low-cost emergency solution. The SEED home is equipped with two low-cost pallet-sized "pods" (water pod and energy pod) that meet the basic needs of access to drinking water, human sanitation, and food preparation. The emergency garden proposed for the roof also serves as insulation. The container's simple cuts in the horizontal planes provide natural cross ventilation.

(continued)

Incorporating Culture, Location, Materials, and Innovation into the Built Environment, *cont.*

It is believed that this solution not only meant to serve as emergency housing has potential for the Caribbean and similar areas for long-term, permanent housing.[5]

Sources:
[1]*Adapted from* Design Like You Give a Damn: Architectural Responses to Humanitarian Crises, *edited by Architecture*

for Humanity, Metropolis Books, page 147, and Rural Studio website.
[2]*Adapted from* Design Like You Give a Damn: Architectural Responses to Humanitarian Crises, *edited by Architecture for Humanity, Metropolis Books, pages 251–255.*
[3]*Adapted from the Make It Right website.*
[4]*UN Office for the Co-ordination of Humanitarian Affairs.*
[5]*Adapted from www.cusa-dds.net/seed, Clemson University, Clemson, South Carolina, SEED-Haiti website.*

Zero Energy Building: IDeAs Z2 Design Facility, San Jose, California

Integrated Design Associates, Inc., is a California and Colorado–based consultancy that provides electrical engineering and lighting design solutions for buildings. Its headquarters in San Jose, California, is called a Z2 Design Facility; "Z2" signifies both net zero energy and zero carbon emissions. The intent of the design was to demonstrate that thoughtful design and sustainable techniques can simultaneously achieve high energy efficiency with high comfort for its occupants, at an affordable price. It was developed to create a net zero energy, zero carbon emissions, allowing it to make zero contributions to global warming.

Formerly a bank branch, the 1960 building is 6,500 square feet in an urban setting on a 34,000 square foot site. The original building was windowless.

The building harvests daylight and uses automatic lighting controls to reduce electric lighting energy consumption; it also provides outside views, occupancy sensors, and radiant heating and cooling in the floor. A rooftop photovoltaic system supplies 100 percent of the electricity needed.

Electrochromic glass on the windows automatically reduces solar gain when there is direct sunlight, reducing transmission and glare. Sliding glass doors on the façade are constructed from laminated glass with photovoltaic cells.

Wall and roof insulation was upgraded. Water conservation was incorporated with the installation of waterless urinals, low-flow, dual-flush toilets, and high-efficiency faucets.

The parking lot area was almost totally demolished and its materials recycled. Much of the area was replaced with landscaping, including a rock garden and low water use plants. Sidewalks were widened to provide safer access for cyclists and pedestrians, as well as access to public transportation.

The company's motto is "At IDeAs we believe that we change the world through our sustainable design . . . one building at a time."

Figure a
Exterior of Z2 facility. *(Courtesy of IDeAs)*

Source: www.ideasi.com/home.html.

produced, the wiring and controls to direct it, and the devices that harness and process this power for utilitarian and aesthetic purposes. Electricity is used to run everyday household equipment, lighting, and HVAC systems. Its role in communication is critical. Consider the equipment that relies on electricity: telephones, computers, facsimile machines and copiers/scanners, entertainment media, and security and intercom systems.

Choices made or influenced by the interior designer affect not only aspects of physical safety, but also energy conservation, aesthetic integrity, ease of operation, and lifestyle enhancements. Because of their technical nature, electrical systems and the equipment they support are fields of ever-changing products and new inventions. To meet the fast-forward challenges of electrical systems, a designer needs to stay informed about new technical information and applications. Topical literature, including manufacturer and supplier information, and talking with expert tradespeople are ways to keep one's knowledge base up to date.

Electrical, power, signal, and communication systems may be treated separately if there are many specialized components for each or if the project as a whole is large or complex. As discussed in Chapter 6, a series of working drawings and specifications may be prepared for each of these structural systems. For example, the electrical components for lighting may be handled as part of a reflected ceiling plan.

The need to feel safe and secure was identified by psychologist Abraham Maslow decades ago as crucial, even primal, to the human experience (see Chapter 2). Certainly, post 9/11, this need is consciously evident all too often. Sophisticated security systems may be desirable for residential as well as contract projects, necessitating a separate set of working drawings or as part of the electrical plan. Systems to detect intrusion and provide warning against property tampering may be sufficiently complex to require the consultation of a security expert. The interior designer will play a critical role in coordination and in making sure that this is accomplished with the overall design concept and client needs in mind.

Additional plans may be required for fire safety. These may include fire prevention; limiting the extent and spread of fire or smoke, known as compartmentation; and detection and warning systems. Again, although the interior designer does not design or install these systems, he or she needs to be sufficiently aware so that design considerations do not cause interference with fire safety measures.[19]

Summary

Many of the structural components (the shell and lining) of an interior are the responsibility of architects, engineers, and building tradespeople. However, the role of an interior designer is crucial, both as collaborator and to ensure that what is constructed is what was designed in the earlier project phases. Familiarity with the basic building materials and construction systems, and the vocabulary used to describe them, enables a designer to facilitate the process.

The contextual framework for any interior involves choices about siting and orientation. An understanding of climatic aspects of a particular environment is needed to plan appropriately for the foundation, floor and wall systems, roof, ceilings, and fenestrations. Many of the structural building materials used for the shell of the building are also used for the lining, or finishes, of the interior. These materials include wood, concrete, metal, and stone.

Many different types of doors and windows are available, with differing modes of operation. There are also many styles from which to choose when designing residential and contract projects. These styles and details influence the character of a space.

The vertical transit system comprises stairs, ramps, lifts, and elevators used to move from one level to another. In addition to being functional components, these choices may suggest a particular aesthetic for a space.

Environmental control systems include the heating, ventilation, and air-conditioning systems. These structural or mechanical systems, as well as water, waste disposal, and acoustical systems, significantly affect the sensory experience of a space. Energy conservation increasingly influences the choice of electricity and power systems. Communication technology and applications can be used for interior spaces to enhance the physical safety and sense of well-being of their occupants.

Vocabulary

active solar energy
ashlar
biomass energy
casing
cathedral ceiling
clerestory
concrete slab system
curtain wall
dead load
direct solar gain
drywall construction
dynamic load
electrochromatic
fenestration
fiberboard
float glass
footing
fossil fuel
framing wall system
gable
glazing
glulam (glued laminated timber)
gravity load
graywater

greenhouse effect
grille (register)
GWB (gypsum wallboard)
GWP (gypsum wall partition)
HVAC (heating, ventilation, and air-conditioning systems)
hydronic
jamb
joist system
landing
lateral load
lath
life-cycle cost
live load
masonry
mortar
mullion
muntin
open (floor) plan
organic architecture
partition
passive solar energy
photovoltaic effect
picture window
plank-and-beam system

plenum
plywood
radiant air heating
rafter
rebar (reinforced bar)
riser
rough plumbing
rubble
safety glass
sheathed
shim space
shotgun house
skylight
stud wall
subfloor
tempered glass
threshold
tread
truss
two-by-four (2×4)
wire glass
yurt
ZEB (Zero Energy Building)
ZEH (Zero Energy Home)

Exercise: LEED Locally

Research a local LEED-approved residential project in either your hometown or the area where your college is located. The project may be a single home or a multi-housing complex. Prepare a summary of the key features behind the qualification level it received. Include information related to the following:

- Energy efficiency
  - Lighting
  - Heating and cooling
  - Daylighting
- Indoor air quality and ventilation
- Reducing toxic substances
- Sustainable materials
- Water conservation

Exercise: Exploring the CD-ROM

Take advantage of the contents of the CD-ROM to increase your understanding of a designed interior space and acoustics. Follow the instructions for Starting the CD-ROM on pages xix–xx and click on Chapter Eight: Architectural Design Elements: The Shell.

Acoustical Experiences: For three different interior spaces (for example, your dorm room or apartment, a classroom, library, retail store, and/or a movie theater), take notes about the acoustical experience. Note in writing highlights of the space, its volume, materials such as stone floor, heavy draperies on windows, high ceiling, etc. Also take note of the audio experience for you in the space, such as noise, vibration, difficulty or ease in hearing others (up close and at a distance), clarity of voices or music, and the presence or absence of audio equipment such as speakers or microphones. Write down any suggestions for improving the acoustical experience of that built environment.

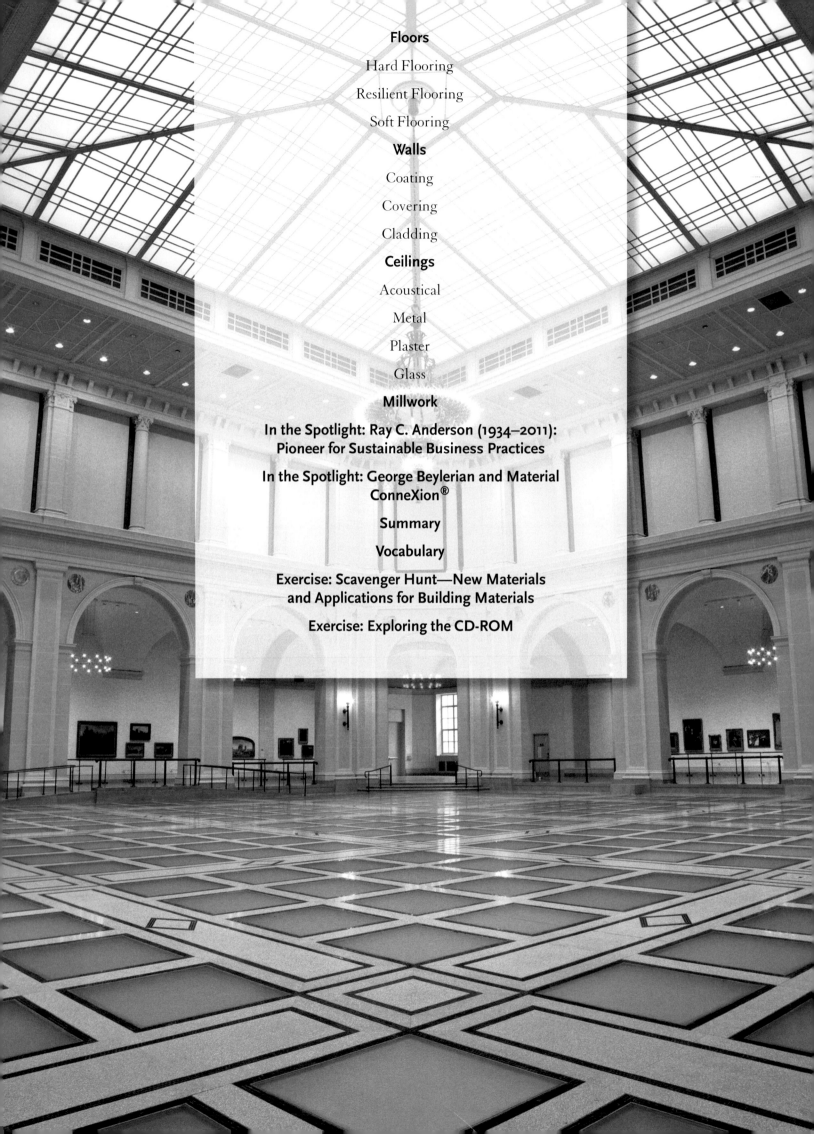

9

Finishing the Interior:
The Lining

An array of materials and technology is available to the interior designer who is converting raw spaces or adapting existing spaces into finished interiors. The choices made by the interior designer influence not only the aesthetic appearance of the space, but also its functionality. Supported by well-thought-out and executed design concepts and space planning, proper material specification should satisfy both the physical and psychological needs of the space's occupants.

Designs must adhere to code and regulatory requirements and should also encourage environmental sustainability. Selection of materials and finishes to convey the design concept should also meet sociological and psychological, functional, maintenance, life-cycle performance, environmental, and safety requirements.[1]

Designers need to stay informed about the constantly changing material world, while being mindful of safety, comfort, and the considerations of socially responsible design, including energy and resource conservation. Traditional materials and methods are combined with innovations in manufacturing, application, and finishing, thus capturing a vast selection of natural and synthetic resources and processes. The industries that produce these material goods are increasingly sensitive to the private and public watchdogs that enforce regulations and evaluate the performance of companies in terms of environmental impact. Among these organizations is the U.S. Green Building Council (USGBC), which developed the rating system LEED (Leadership in Energy and Environmental Design), which considers a building from the perspective of green design (see Chapters 2 and 8). When specifying products, interior designers can request information about environmental friendliness as well as technical information from the companies whose products are being considered.

The cross-fertilization of ideas and materials between the worlds of fashion and interiors has been recognized for centuries, with fashion usually taking the lead. This is particularly true of textiles and will be explored further in Chapter 13. In our modern technological age, however, a number of industries are involved in idea generation and solutions. Sources for inspiration to expand the capabilities of materials may come from fields as diverse as computer technology, aerospace design, medical research, and printing.

Several materials have already been introduced in Chapter 8 as components in constructing the building, that is, the shell. They include concrete, stone, brick, metal, wood, and glass. In some cases, there is little distinction between the materiality of the exterior and the interior of a space. Following in the footsteps of Frank Lloyd Wright, who advocated the practice of organic architecture (see Chapter 8), architectural student interns at Taliesin West explore the use of materials that serve both the outside and the inside of a building's design. This approach to the concept of total design is illustrated in the student housing at Taliesin West and in a space designed by Clodagh, also a proponent of total design (Figure 9.1a and b).

This chapter explores the use of these building materials, plus many others, for the lining of the interior space, which includes floors, walls, ceilings, and millwork. Several of these materials are used not only for the interior lining, but also for "feathering the nest" (adding the interior furnishings and finishing touches), the subject of Chapter 10.

FLOORS

Floor coverings are typically classified as hard, resilient, or soft. The choice of flooring is dependent on the appearance and comfort sought, as well as on the ability of the subfloor beneath it to provide support. Before selecting a material, the designer must consider several factors, among them resistance to wear and tear, susceptibility to disease and environmental conditions, initial

Figure 9.1
Total design concept is illustrated by these designs. a. Student housing in Taliesin West. b. Interior by designer Clodagh.
(a: Photo © Aris Georges, Taliesin; b: © Ken Hayden Photography)

cost, ease of installation and maintenance, and life-cycle cost. A major consideration is the many issues centering on safety, including fire-retardant properties. Other important considerations include the relationship to allergens, physical comfort for the user, and noise and heat insulation properties. The type of user and the activities projected in the space are critical pieces of information. Sustainability issues related to flooring are significant. The choice of floor coverings and the way in which they are installed can also help define behavioral settings and zones, such as in establishing conversation areas and aid in way-finding (Figure 9.2a and b).

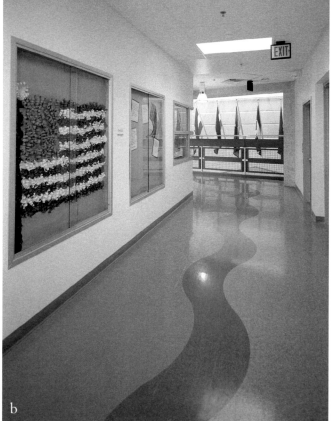

Figure 9.2

a. An area rug is used to define a conversation area; b. Here a pattern in flooring assists in way-finding. *(a: Courtesy of Malene b; b: Courtesy of Armstrong World Industries, Inc.)*

Hard Flooring

The **hard flooring** group includes wood, bamboo, stone, ceramic, and glass. All of these materials are used for both residential and commercial projects. Hard surfaces may be slippery, especially when wet, and to varying degrees can cause stress on users' joints.

Figure 9.3

Hardwoods used in flooring. a. Red oak; b. Mahogany. *(a: © Weaber Hardwood Flooring and American Hardwood Information Center at www.HardwoodInfo.com; b: © Thomas Spier/Artur)*

Wood

Wood floors are generally made from **hardwood**, or *deciduous*, trees, trees that bear broad leaves in an annual cycle of growth and decay. The volume of hardwoods in American forests today is 90 percent greater than it was in 1960. The U.S. Forest Service forecasts indicate that further increases of 15 to 20 percent are expected through 2030.[2] North American species that are used for flooring include oak, poplar, ash, cherry, maple, and alder. Oak, particularly red oak, remains the most commonly used hardwood for flooring (Figure 9.3a). Oak is known for its striking grain and color range. Some less commonly used woods for flooring are imported woods, such as teak from Brazil and Asia and mahogany from South America (Figure 9.3b).

Softwoods in the *coniferous* species, such as pine and fir, are also used for flooring but are less durable than hardwoods and more susceptible to decay. These species are commonly known as evergreens, and the trees bear needle-like leaves.

Hardwoods feature high shock resistance in comparison with other hard surfaces, offering some resistance to pressure upon contact. For flooring, this means less risk of damage and, for the user, less stress on the musculoskeletal system. Hardwoods are also more durable than other hard surfaces. They may be prefinished or finished on-site.

On-site installation allows the wood to adjust to its environment before the appropriate finish is applied. Because wood is susceptible to changes in moisture and temperature that can make it swell or shrink, it is generally treated. Finishing helps maintain consistent coloration and texture, protect the wood from moisture and stains, and preserve the overall uniformity of the wood. Prefinished floors are often surface treated with polyurethane, a synthetic material made with resins that forms a protective shield on the surface of the floor. On-site finishing may use deeper-penetrating sealants that are absorbed into the wood fibers. These are usually natural waxes and oils or acrylics. Any of these finishes may vary from matte to glossy, depending on the desired look. The addition of stains to alter the natural color of the wood is essentially an aesthetic decision.

Additional finishing techniques may be applied to change the character of the wood, such as bleaching, pickling, distressing, painting, or stenciling (Figure 9.4). However, some of these techniques, especially bleaching, may weaken the wood and may create a toxic environment during installation. **Acrylic impregnation**, a technique used to add strength to wood floors, involves the injection of acrylic into the wood itself. It is used for high-traffic commercial projects.

Wood flooring may be applied in several ways, including strip, plank, and **parquet**, sometimes referred to as *block*. All three types may be installed by **tongue-and-groove** construction (Figure 9.5a). In this method a joint is formed by fitting a projection cut along the edge of one board, the tongue, into a recess carved along the edge of another, the groove. Other methods of joining include glue and **spline**, in which

Figure 9.4
Stenciled wood floor. *(Design: Nancy Boszhardt; Photography: George Ross)*

TYPICAL JOINTS

Tongue and Groove	Spline
a.	**b.**

Figure 9.5
Standard joinery. a. Tongue-and-groove method; b. Spline method. *(a and b: Fairchild Books)*

a thin strip forms a key between two boards to lock them together (Figure 9.5b).

Strip is the typical way that hardwood flooring is installed. The strips are usually $2\frac{1}{4}$ inches wide and are attached with nails to the subfloor. Plank, used more typically for outdoor installations, such as decks and patios, is similarly installed. Planks vary in width but are generally between 3 inches and 8 inches wide; planking wider than 8 inches is generally more costly. Although strip and plank flooring are often used to evoke a rustic feeling, they serve modern interiors well (Figure 9.6a).

Parquet flooring consists of blocks of hardwood, generally formed as squares that may be applied in various patterns. The squares, composed of smaller pieces of wood, typically range in size from 6 inches to 27 inches. The herringbone parquet pattern featured in Figure 9.6b is based on rectangular blocks. Parquet flooring may be bordered with strip flooring and gen-

erally is considered more formal in appearance than strip or plank flooring.

A distinction is made between solid hardwood and **all-wood construction**. *Solid construction* implies that each exposed part is made of hardwood lumber; *all wood* denotes the use of veneer, or thin layers of wood bonded together with the grains running in different directions. This may also be called **engineered**, or *laminated*, flooring. Engineered flooring is considered more dimensionally stable than solid hardwood and more resistant to the effects of moisture. Another

Figure 9.6

a. Wide plank flooring; b. Herringbone-style parquet floor; c. Engineered teak; d. Wood floor from recycled oak wine barrels. *(a, b, and c: Courtesy of Armstrong World Industries, Inc.; d: Cheryll Larson – Gaeteno, Inc.)*

advantage is that rare or expensive woods, such as teak from Asia, cherry from Brazil, and wenge from Africa, can be used in smaller quantities for the top surface, with hardwood plywood making up the other layers (Figure 9.6c). This approach helps minimize the harvesting pressures on rare wood species.

A growing number of companies are specializing in the reuse of woods for flooring as well as for ceiling beams. The use of vintage wood (also called salvaged, remilled, rescued, reclaimed, or recycled wood) serves as a conservation measure and provides appealing character, with its lived-in look. The wood may be from a demolished building or even from old wine barrels, as shown in Figure 9.6d.

Several manufacturers produce high-pressure laminate flooring that simulates the look of wood as well as other materials. This flooring is a combination of paper and synthetic materials and is created using sophisticated printing techniques.

Bamboo Bamboo is increasingly becoming an alternative to wood flooring. This species of grass is considered very environmentally friendly because it is a renewable and sustainable natural resource that grows very quickly and is harvested in three to five years. More than 1,000 species are harvested throughout the world. In the United States, bamboo flooring is imported mainly from Asia, from countries such as Vietnam and China. It can be manufactured in solid or engineered construction, finished or unfinished, and installed by the strip or plank methods. It can be left natural or carbonized, a process that darkens the bamboo. It is considered to be harder than oak and more dimensionally stable as well as environmentally safe. Bamboo can also be used for other surfaces, such as walls and ceilings and for furniture (Figure 9.7).

An innovation in bamboo flooring has been the introduction of a hybrid of cork and bamboo, in which strands of shredded bamboo are woven and infused with seams of cork, which has increased acoustical properties. Although cork is considered resilient rather than hard (see later discussion), this type of flooring may be specified for a commercial project because of its density and dimensional stability.

Figure 9.7
Bamboo interior. *(Photography by David Joseph; designed by Matsuyama International)*

The hard floorings discussed so far may be finished in a variety of ways. Often, a natural or pigmented oil finish is applied, sometimes by hand, rather than harsher topical chemicals.

Stone As discussed in Chapter 8, stone is a form of masonry building material. Within this category are many types of rocks that may be used for flooring as well as for other interior building components and decorative accents. Stones are quarried, or excavated, from areas in many different countries. Among the types of stone used for flooring are marble, travertine, granite, slate, and limestone. These organic materials also may be manufactured in combination with other substances, such as resin and epoxy; they are then termed aggregate. Examples are terrazzo and concrete. Concrete has gained in popularity beyond its capabilities for the building shell. For interior surfaces, such as finished flooring, additional minerals, such as silicates, are added to the traditional ingredients of cement and water, to produce a harder surface that is also more abrasion resistant and polished in appearance. Conventional concrete made of Portland cement (see Chapter 8) may be substituted with fly ash concrete. Fly ash is a waste product of coal power plants and has less of an environmental impact than cement. Additives, including coloring pigments, staining, glazing, and waxing, are used to change the appearance of concrete when used as a finishing treatment. Concrete is often applied in a poured slab, but it can also be manufactured into tiles. No longer relegated only to industrial spaces, concrete has earned a place in high-end residential and hospitality design.

The term *tile* is often used, loosely, to refer to any number of materials, such as ceramic, carpet, glass, or stone. More accurately, however, *tile* speaks to the shape and type of installation of a material, rather than the material itself. In this usage, *tile* refers to the unit of a material as differentiated from other applications, such as slab (which may cover an entire surface) or poured (as in aggregates of materials). Similarly, the term *mosaic* denotes smaller units of tiles that may be composed of various materials, including ceramic and glass, as shown in Figure 9.8.

Stone floorings for interiors are usually installed as tiles, available in various sizes and thicknesses. Tiles and mosaics may be individually hand set; more often, however, they are premounted in groups on mesh to allow for easier and more precise installation.

Technological advances have increased the options available for designing and installing many types of floors. In particular, water jet laser cutting has enabled manufacturers to create intricate patterns, including curvilinear designs, with relative ease and exactness. There is virtually no limit to pattern design, which ranges from traditional geometric grids to random patterns to precise, computerized designs.

Additionally, the spacing and color of the **grout**, the filler used between the tiles (generally a mortar or cement mixture), can affect the character of the floor. For example, large-scale tiles will appear to be uniform, larger, and more formal when surrounded by small grout outlines than when a thicker application of grout is used. The latter produces a checkerboard pattern that is more casual in appearance (Figure 9.9).

As a natural product, stone is subject to variations in shading, veining, coloration, and texture. Different finishing techniques create different appearances

Figure 9.8
Glass mosaic "rug." *(Courtesy of ANN SACKS)*

Figure 9.9
Tile and grout patterns. *(Jake Fitzjones/Redcover.com)*

and also influence safety and maintenance. Common finishes include tumbled, honed, and polished. A tumbled finish retains the natural rough surface of the stone, giving a rustic or antique look (Figure 9.10a). A honed finish provides a smoother surface. A polished finish is a smoother and slicker surface that gives a more formal appearance (Figure 9.10b). The more highly polished the stone, the less slip-resistant it is. For this reason, in certain applications, marble may be grooved as a safety measure against slipping, especially where water may be present, such as in bath areas or on stairs. Stone may be sealed for protection against staining.

Although different properties are inherent in the various stones available for flooring, the choice of a particular material is often based on its appearance and texture, either natural or treated, and the application pattern used, rather than the precise category of rock. Several popular types of stone flooring materials are shown in Figure 9.11a–d.

- *Marble*. Long identified with luxury and classic beauty, especially when polished, marble is available in a wide range of colors and degrees of veining. The colors range from the traditional whites to black, green, blue, brownish-yellow, and red. The most commonly used marble for flooring, however, is the white and cream variation referred to as *bianco carrara*. Italy remains a significant producer and exporter of marble. Spain and China are also large exporters of marble to the United States. Marble is used for both residential and commercial applications. It is versatile enough to create an aesthetic that is either Old World or modern. Marble is durable (although the lighter colors stain easily) and has an initial high cost. Its disadvantages are its slippery surface when polished and wet and its lack of shock absorption, which can cause muscular fatigue for the user. Because it is cold to the touch, the climate of the installation also needs to be considered.

- *Slate*. The textured surface of slate is the result of hundreds of millions of years of sedimentation of Earth's particles. The deposits consolidate into shale, a soft, layered rock, which is transformed by heat and pressure into slate. The split-layered texture and clefts in the surface can be left natural or honed smooth. Slate ranges in color from black to gray, purple, and green, reflecting the trace metals in the sedimentary stone. It is quarried mostly from the Appalachian Mountains of the United States. Softer slates are imported from Africa and Asia. Brazilian slate is also available; it has a less pronounced cleft surface. Because slate is susceptible to staining and scratching, it is generally treated with a protective finish, either a surface sealant or an impregnating treatment that penetrates into the slate itself. Slate has a moderate-to-high initial cost, and because of its uneven surface, it may be hazardous as flooring, particularly when wet.

- *Granite*. This hard, crystalline rock contains traces of minerals, such as quartz crystal. The

Figure 9.10

Marble finishes. a. tumbled; b. polished. *(a: © Nsmphoto | Dreamstime.com; b: © Gianni Muratore | Alamy)*

Figure 9.11

Stone floor materials. a. travertine (a type of limestone); b. slate; c. granite; d. terrazzo (a type of aggregate). *(a: © Luigi Roscia | Dreamstime.com; b: © Avital Aronowitz)*

typical color is a cool gray, but other colors, such as light and dark brown, are available. Because of its durability, granite is recommended for high-traffic areas; however, it is costly. In addition, like marble and slate, granite is very hard and slippery when polished and has a cold surface. Italy is the principal exporter to the United States, but Brazil, India, and China now export a significant amount of granite as well.

- *Limestone.* This is a form of calcium carbonate that characteristically has a light gray appearance, with little variation. Travertine is a form of limestone known for its pitted look. Its coloration is usually a yellow-beige. When used for flooring, the surface holes may be filled with epoxy for easier maintenance and safer footing. Travertine is not as hard as granite. It is exported to the United States from Turkey, Italy, and Mexico.

- *Aggregate.* This generic term includes ground-up stones, particles, or chips combined with liquid additives and other admixtures. Terrazzo is a form of aggregate material that is created when marble or other stones, such as granite, are crushed into chips, congealed with a liquid epoxy or mortar mixture, dried to a hard surface, and then polished. Terrazzo can be manufactured in premade casts or poured in slabs, like concrete. Used frequently in the mid-20th century, particularly in high-traffic commercial application, terrazzo is enjoying a revival in popularity, especially as a sustainable alternative. The waste produced when fabricating stone panels, for example, is used along with other fillers, such as glass shards, for aggregate materials.

Ceramic A general term, *ceramic*, refers to products used for flooring and other structures, as well as ornamentation, made of clay (fine particles of earth or soil) that is fired at a high temperature to produce earthenware. Ceramic building materials are generally manufactured in brick, tile, or mosaic form. Two commonly used ceramics for flooring are terracotta and porcelain. The quality of ceramic tile varies greatly, which significantly affects its durability and resistance to water damage, temperature changes, and chemical abrasion. The types of finishes are typically glazed, a highly polished surface; unglazed, a natural surface; and painted. Ceramic tiles are manufactured in many countries, among them Portugal, Italy, Mexico, France, Spain, and the United States.

Terra-cotta, meaning "baked earth," is often reddish-brown in color (Figure 9.12). It generally requires a penetrating sealer and topcoat sealer to protect its surface from moisture. A high-quality ceramic tile used for flooring is **porcelain**. This type of ceramic tile is considered highly resistant to water and stains in both glazed and unglazed varieties. Porcelain tiles may be manufactured to simulate more costly resources, such as marble, granite, and slate, while providing properties of durability and relatively low maintenance. Porcelain is suitable for indoor and outdoor applications, such as patios and pool surrounds.

Ceramic tiles may be produced with traces of minerals, which provide iridescence to their appearance. They may also be combined at installation with tiles made of metals, for accent. Similarly, inserts made of other materials, including metal; semiprecious gems, such as lapis and tiger's eye; and shells, such as mother-of-pearl, are suitable as accents when combined with other materials for flooring.

Glass Although not often used for flooring, glass is increasing in popularity for dramatic applications. When used for stairs or flooring, it should feature a nonslip texture. The translucent quality of glass can be used to enhance the effects of light, creating an airy, spacious feeling. Glass is also available in tile form. Glass may be used as an accent with other products, in particular, ceramic tiles, to provide an interesting textural contrast (Figure 9.13).

Figure 9.13
Glass tile floor in the Brooklyn Museum. (*View of the third floor, Beaux-Art Court, at the Brooklyn Museum, post-2008 renovation. Project architects: Polshek Partnership. Photograph courtesy of the Brooklyn Museum*)

Figure 9.12
Ceramic flooring: rustic terra-cotta. (*© Dutourdumonde / Alamy*)

Resilient Flooring

Resilient flooring materials provide greater shock absorption than hard surfaces, offering advantages to the user. Resilient surfaces have more give and bounce and, therefore, more forgiveness on impact, which means that neither the surface nor the object it collides with incurs as high a level of damage as is usually the case with harder flooring surfaces. This type of flooring has a lower impact on the musculoskeletal systems of people walking on it; it is more ergonomically satisfying in that way. It is also more slip-resistant. For these reasons, it is often used for high-traffic areas, including school and play spaces, kitchens, laundry rooms, basements, and bathrooms.

This group of flooring is used for a significant portion of contract and residential projects. Once relegated to institutional settings and utility rooms, resilient flooring can now be seen in luxury stores, hospitality areas, and homes because of innovations in technology that have improved its performance and appeal. Resilient flooring is often less costly than many of the hard surfaces and is available in a wide range of products and installation patterns.

Resilient flooring includes the various categories of both natural and synthetic surfaces, including vinyl, rubber, linoleum, cork, and laminates. Applied with adhesive, it is available in tile form, typically as squares ranging from 9 inches to 18 inches, and as sheets in 6- and 12-foot rolls. It is hygienic, and many varieties conceal stains and scuff marks.

Vinyl Manufactured products in the family of chemicals known as polymers, specifically PVC (polyvinyl chloride), make up the category of **vinyl**. It is classified into two groups: solid vinyl and vinyl composite. Solid vinyl is more resilient (and more expensive) because it typically contains 90 percent vinyl, compared with vinyl composite, which may contain only 20 percent vinyl and 80 percent limestone.

Thanks to exceptional photo imaging capabilities, vinyl products can simulate the look of other surfaces and patinas, surfaces that appear to have been changed by aging or weather conditions. Although simulated marble was once the standard choice, especially in residential projects, many products now feature various textures of wood, metal, granite, concrete, and textiles

Figure 9.14

Installing vinyl strip flooring. (© *Caro / Alamy*)

(Figure 9.14). Many of these simulations are meant to be whimsical and fun rather than serious imitations. Vinyl products may be treated to provide antistatic properties, especially for medical operating rooms, to prevent sparks. In addition to a variety of commercial applications, these products are often used residentially in kitchens, utility rooms, and playrooms.

Rubber True rubber is a material made from a natural elastic, viscous substance tapped from tropical rubber trees. A synthetically produced polymer is also called rubber.

Rubber flooring may be initially costly, but its life-cycle cost is relatively low. It is used in high-traffic, commercial applications, including gymnasiums, health clubs, health-care facilities, senior centers, schools, transportation terminals, and shopping centers. Rubber is also used for ramps, stair treads, and landings. It requires little maintenance and withstands daily wear and tear well. It provides good traction and a comfortable walking surface. It is not only resilient and quiet, but also virtually slip-proof and can tolerate damp conditions. Rubber flooring is coordinated with rubber wall bases and other accessories for consistent transitioning. Most rubber products have raised profile patterns. Many companies engaged in green design use recycled rubber from tires to produce flooring, including tiles that resemble terrazzo, as well as for other products. Rubber is also used in combination with cork. Recycled rubber is used in a

Figure 9.15

A recycled rubber floor for a children's hospital. *(St. Vincent's Hospital, Indianapolis, Indiana, courtesy ECOsurfaces)*

a

colorful and playful design for a children's hospital in Figure 9.15.

Linoleum A processed mixture of natural substances, **linoleum** contains solidified linseed oil from the flax plant, cork and wood flour (pulverized wood that resembles sand), limestone, and pigments. Linoleum is backed with jute and installed in sheets or tiles, and it has a long life cycle. Introduced in the late 1800s, it became popular in the 1930s and 1940s and then fell out of favor (Figure 9.16a). Today, linoleum is experiencing resurgence in popularity because it is a green product. Most often used in commercial applications, it is beginning to attract attention in the high-end residential area because of its low impact on the environment and natural resources. Linoleum is very durable and is available in many colors and patterns (Figure 9.16b).

Cork Cork is material that is extracted from the bark of the cork oak tree. Cork is a replenishable material because it is extracted without felling the tree. The largest sources of cork are Spain and Portugal.

Cork absorbs sound and is fire-retardant and buoyant. It is used for flooring in both residential and commercial applications, typically in tile form (Figure 9.17). Cork can be installed by gluing the tiles down or by using the floating floor plank method of installation. In this method a combination of materials wrapped around a core of high-density fiberboard

b

Figure 9.16

Linoleum, *Then and Now.* a. Ad from the 1930s showing installation of linoleum wall material; b. Contemporary linoleum floor. *(a: © M&N / Alamy; b: Courtesy of Armstrong World Industries, Inc.)*

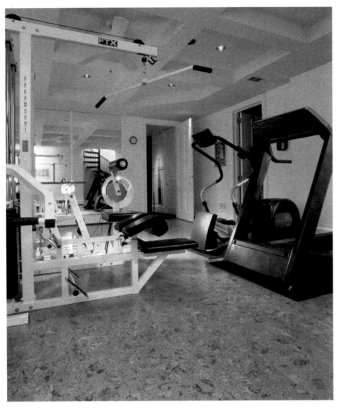

Figure 9.17
Cork floor used in a high-traffic installation. *(Courtesy of Cork Direct)*

(HDF) and cork is coated with water-based polyurethane and installed using tongue-and-groove joinery. An advantage of cork beyond its acoustical value is that it is a flexible material that can conform to the shape of the subfloor, which may not always be level. The range of color is warm, from yellow to brown.

Laminate Laminate is a generic term used to describe several products, including flooring, doors, and furniture created by high-pressure lamination techniques; it implies a multilayered product. Laminate flooring is a combination of materials around a core of HDF (Figure 9.18). It may simulate the look of wood, stone, or ceramic. This type of flooring is considered dimensionally stable, low maintenance, and low in allergens. It is not waterproof but is more resistant to water than natural wood floors. Although sometimes installed with adhesive, it is more commonly layered over the existing floor in a floating installation, which minimizes concerns related to type and condition of the subflooring. Laminate flooring is available in planks or tiles in a variety of patterns and colors.

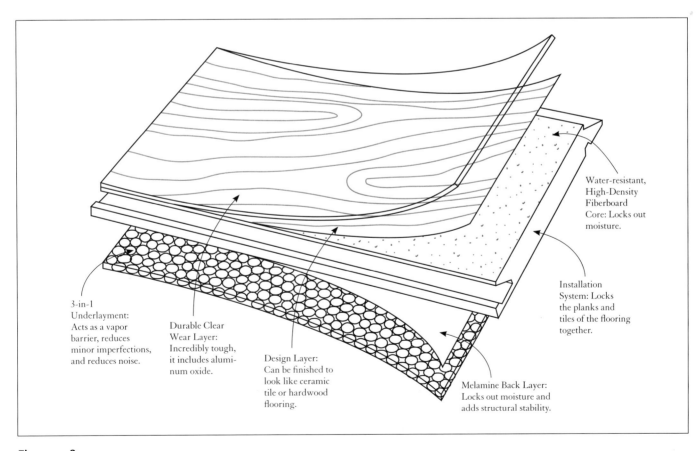

Figure 9.18
The various layers of laminated flooring systems.

Soft Flooring

The majority of soft flooring is composed of **fiber**, a natural or synthetic thread or filament that is capable of being sewn, woven, or spun into yarn. Fibers are made into **carpets**, which completely cover an area and are anchored securely, or **rugs**, movable units covering a portion of a space. The use of various natural and manufactured fibers for textiles is discussed in Chapter 10. The fibers commonly used for both carpets and rugs are listed in Table 9.1.

From a design perspective, a carpet, installed wall-to-wall, tends to unify the elements of a space. Rugs may be selected for decorative accent (discussed further in Chapter 10) or to define zones, such as establishing a conversation area (Figure 9.2a) or separating a dining area from a living area in a great room. There are many types of rugs, which can vary in size or style, or both, among them area rugs; scatter, or throw, rugs; and runners.

The several different ways in which soft flooring may be produced—by hand or by machine, dyed or printed—result in a number of different surface characteristics. A choice of fibers is available, which may be used alone or in combination. The manufacture, installation, disposal, and reuse of soft flooring are significant issues in terms of sustainability. Carpet is used in very large quantities and represents the major use of synthetic fibers, such as nylon, as delineated in Table 9.1. The manufacture of synthetic fibers has been criticized for its energy-wasting and polluting process, and

Table 9.1 Commonly Used Fibers for Soft Floor Covering		
Type	**Origin**	**Characteristics**
Wool	Animal	Expensive, resilient, and long-lasting. Soft, luxurious hand. Inherently soil- and fire-resistant. Dyes well. Wool from the Himalayan region is rich in lanolin, which gives it luster. Many Tibetan-type and Chinese rugs incorporate silk, which creates a mixture of luster levels in pattern.
Cotton	Plant	Casual appearance. Stains easily. Is not durable when pile is high; flat-woven cotton wears well.
Sisal (coir, hemp, cocoa, sea grass, jute)	Plant	Casual appearance. Relatively inexpensive but not durable. Highly susceptible to staining, and difficult to clean with a vacuum. Formerly used primarily in tropical climates, it has become a modern design statement in residential interiors in all climates.
Nylon	Synthetic	Inexpensive, strong, and very long-lasting. Dominates soft floor covering market. Newer varieties have built-in soil and stain resistance and static protection. May be treated with antimicrobial finish when used in health-care facilities. Requires regular cleaning.
Polyester	Synthetic	Excellent color clarity and retention. Resistant to water stains. Pile height will not be adequately restored after bearing weight because it lacks resiliency to bounce back.
Acrylic	Synthetic	Similar to wool in appearance, it is moisture- and mildew-resistant. Has low static level.
Olefin	Synthetic	Strong, colorfast, with low static properties. Low pile and tight construction are required for long wear.
Blends	Combination	Most common is wool in combination with synthetic, which reduces cost of all-wool construction and adds durability to positive qualities of wool, especially in combination with nylon. Wool in combination with sisal or other grass fibers adds luxurious texture to otherwise scratchy fiber.

the synthetic-fiber industry is making efforts to reduce the negative impact of this process. One significant contribution has been in reclamation, the practice of recycling carpet materials for the production of new goods. Another advance in sustainability has been the use of adhesives made from plant proteins and soybean oil in the manufacture of carpet backing.

Originally woven on narrow looms, carpet today is manufactured as rolled goods, typically 12 feet wide. Wider rolls are also available; these allow for more continuous, seamless installations in large spaces. The term **broadloom** is sometimes used to describe both 12-foot and wider rolled goods. Carpet is also manufactured in tiles, which allows for easier (and less costly) replacement of damaged areas. This is an advantage not only in commercial applications (Figure 9.19a), but also for high-traffic residential areas, such as playrooms (Figure 9.19b). It is sometimes referred to as modular carpeting.

As with hard and resilient flooring, several factors must be considered before specifying the use of carpet in residential or contract applications. From a safety perspective, rugs—especially fringed or smaller, scatter rugs—can be hazardous, causing trips and falls. Similarly, carpets or rugs in which the height of the pile (the fiber) is high, although soft to the touch, may pose ambulation problems for those using wheelchairs, canes, or walkers. It is also important to look at how soft flooring, and its installation methods, will affect the air quality, including allergen levels. Other considerations involve transitions between areas, level changes, and the components needed between walls and floors. For example, a high-pile carpet may require a higher threshold to an adjoining wood floor than would be necessary when transitioning from marble to wood.

The choice of **underlayment**, that is, the backing and padding to be used, will influence not only the comfort of the floor covering, but also its longevity. Materials used for padding and backing include jute and latex in various thicknesses.

The majority of carpets are constructed using a tufting technique rather than weaving, which is more often

Figure 9.19
Modular carpet tiles used in a. commercial design and; b. children's room. *(a: InterfaceFLOR™ Commercial 'Vermont' Collection; b: © Sangria carpet tile, FLOR)*

used in making rugs. Weaving techniques, and methods for producing nonwoven goods, are described in more detail in Chapter 10. Several casual, country-style rugs are produced for residential use, including braided, corded, and rag. These rugs, which are not woven on looms, were originally made by hand from fabric scraps.

Tufted Carpet or rugs, whether **tufted** by machine or hand, are composed of a variety of layers. The **pile**, or *face yarn*, is thrust through a primary backing. An adhesive is then applied, and a secondary backing is bonded to the pile. The greater the density of the pile (i.e., the more yarns per inch), the longer the goods will last.

The yarn loops may be cut (**cut pile**) or left uncut (**loop pile**), producing distinctly different textures that also affect the appearance of the goods. A carpet may also consist of both, known as cut and loop pile (Figure 9.20f). Sculptured carpets have a mixture of cut and uncut yarns at different levels, creating a greater textural quality.

An example of the cut style is **plush**, or *velvet*, in which the pile is deep (Figure 9.20c). **Saxony**, another

type of cut pile, has more twist to the yarn than plush and is considered less formal than the plush style (Figure 9.20d). Another less formal type is **frieze**, in which the yarns are twisted, forming a curly, textured surface (Figure 9.20e). Deeper-cut piles have a luxurious look and are not suitable for high-traffic areas; they are more appropriate for bedrooms. High-density, lower-cut piles are manufactured to stand up to heavier traffic in both residential and commercial applications.

Uncut, or loop pile, carpets withstand traffic better than cut piles and are generally the carpet of choice for commercial projects when soft floor covering is desired. Examples include one-level loop pile and multilevel loop pile (Figure 9.20a and b).

Woven Carpets and rugs, whether **woven** by machine or by hand, are produced by interlacing yarns or strands of fiber in a pattern that combines **warp** (lengthwise) and **weft** (width-wise, crosswise, filling) yarns. They may be constructed with or without the use of knots (Figure 9.21).

Wilton is a wool carpet woven on a specific type of loom, called a Jacquard loom (Figure 9.22a). Wilton carpet is limited in color because the Jacquard loom typically can accommodate only three to six colors in a pattern. Jacquard weaving is a costly procedure that is used to produce high-end goods.

In the past, France was noted for its production of finely woven tapestries and rugs, such as **Savonnerie** and **Aubusson** (Figure 9.22b). Scandinavia's version of the woven rug is called a **rya**. A Greek woven, long-pile wool rug popular in the 1960s, the **flokati**,

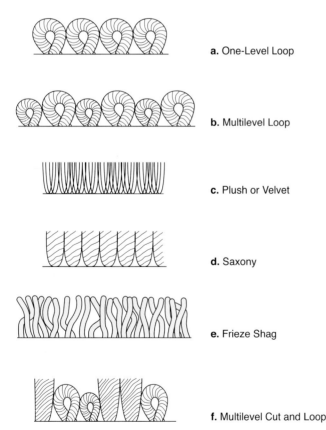

a. One-Level Loop

b. Multilevel Loop

c. Plush or Velvet

d. Saxony

e. Frieze Shag

f. Multilevel Cut and Loop

Figure 9.20
Tufted carpets. a. One-Level Loop; b. Multilevel Loop; c. Plush or Velvet; d. Saxony; e. Frieze Shag; f. Multilevel Cut and Loop.

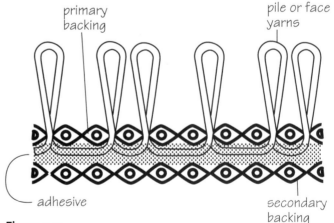

primary backing

pile or face yarns

adhesive

secondary backing

Figure 9.21
Material is woven by interlacing warp (lengthwise) and weft (crosswise) yarns in a pattern.

a

b

d

c

Figure 9.22

Woven carpets. a. Wilton custom designed for England's Earl of Pembroke; b. Antique Aubusson; c. Flokati rug in a 1970s interior; d. Flokati rug used in 2011. *(a: © RON BLUNT / ronbluntphoto.com; b: Aubusson carpet, last quarter of the 19th century (textile) by French School (19th century). Private Collection/ Photo © Christie's Images/ The Bridgeman Art Library; c: John Fowler, architect. Photo credit: Norman McGrath; d: MELANIE ACEVEDO / Condé Nast)*

Figure 9.23a and b
Oriental rugs, *Then and Now.* a. Isfahan carpet, Central Persia, first quarter of the 17th century; b. Contemporary rug inspired by ancient tradition of mehndi in India, handmade in Nepal. *(a: Isfahan carpet, Central Persia, first quarter of the 17th century [textile], Persian School [17th century] / Private Collection / Photo © Christie's Images / The Bridgeman Art Library International; b: Courtesy Malene b)*

has regained popularity (Figure 9.22c and d). It is considered a natural version of a shag rug. **Kilim** is a category of woven rug attributed to eastern European countries; it is flat and similar to the rugs produced by Native Americans, referred to as Navajo (or Navaho), and to **dhurrie** rugs made in India.

Because of the labor-intensive nature of production, handwoven rugs are more likely to be produced overseas, especially in Asia, or imitated using domestic manufacturing methods. When genuine, they are highly prized, particularly when authenticated by government standards.

For the contemporary interior designer the term *Oriental rug* may mean several things. Technically, it refers to a handwoven rug made in Asia, whether antique or contemporary. However, it has also come to denote the styles and motifs associated with designs from areas in the Middle East, including those designs that are now machine made. These rugs come from a vast and diverse region that includes China, Persia (now Iran), Central Asia, North Africa, Turkey, Afghanistan, India, Pakistan, Kashmir, Tibet, and Nepal. Therefore, the weaving techniques, natural dyes, and motifs used vary considerably. Typical motifs include geometric patterns, stylized animals, flames, trees, and garden symbols. Conversely, rugs made in parts of Asia, particularly in Nepal, also now represent motifs from all over the world, including contemporary, Western-inspired designs or modernized versions of African or Indian motifs (Figure 9.23a and b).

Especially when choosing antique (those produced before the mid-1800s) and semiantique (late 19th-century) Oriental rugs, a designer should have a reliable supplier or have developed specialized expertise in this area. Antique rugs were made using natural dyes, whereas newer rugs may also contain synthetic dyestuffs. Additionally, antique rugs have a higher knot-per-square-inch count than newer versions.

In the Spotlight: Ray C. Anderson (1934–2011) focuses on the late Ray C. Anderson, the worldwide leader in the design, production, and sales of environmentally responsible modular carpet.

WALLS

The surface and finishing materials applied to interior walls vary in both type and cost. Moreover, the partial walls, partitions, and panels used in many contract applications may be treated in various ways. The selection depends largely on the function of the space, soundproofing and fireproofing needs, budget considerations, durability requirements, energy conservation, and the aesthetic desired.

The demand for panels and panel systems, which are not only aesthetically pleasing, but also efficient, has grown, in part owing to the increase in open planning. This is also true for residential spaces, where panels, screens, and partitions are often replacing traditional full walls to divide space. The term *space articulators* is also used for elements that define, reconfigure, or showcase interior space. These may be freestanding (and used for ceilings as well) and are composed primarily of tensile recycled polyester content (Figure 9.24).

Walls and partitions are typically finished in one of three ways: paint and paint product coating; wall covering of paper, vinyl, or textiles; or cladding, such as with masonry materials. Panels are usually covered in vinyl or textiles.

Walls may be left unfinished, as is often the case when brick is used, or clad with masonry and other materials as a finishing treatment (see Chapter 8). Ceramic tiles are frequently used to finish walls in areas where moisture is present, such as baths, restrooms, kitchens, pools, and fountains.

Walls may also be embellished with wood detailing, most often as trim for doors and windows. This enhancement to the lining of the interior is known as **millwork**. When designed and executed with a high level of artistry and skill, millwork provides a significant textural layer to an interior space. Wood as a wall treatment is discussed later in this chapter. Most often, interior walls are painted or covered with paper, vinyl, or textiles.

Figure 9.24
Space articulators help to define space and acoustical value and also provide decorative impact in this office space. *(Juxtaform, LLC, creators of Juxtaform Space Articulators. Design by Helen Logan, SNS Architects & Engineers, PC Installation site at Russell Research)*

Coating
Painting and decorative painting are two types of finishes used in residential and contract projects.

Paint Paint and paint products are the most widely used finishes for interior walls because of their infinite range of color, textural variety, and adaptability to alteration. Various techniques, many used for centuries, may be employed to enhance the visual interest of paint. Paint as a surface coating is used for protection against weather corrosion, fire, and germs, as well as for decoration. For some projects it is a principal consideration, as in the residential project illustrated in Figure 9.25.

Paint is essentially a mixture of **pigment**, that is, natural or synthetic coloring matter, suspended in a liquid vehicle, or **solvent**, with a **binder** to harden the liquid. Additional ingredients, known as extenders or additives, provide different sheen levels and other

Figure 9.25
Interior designer Jamie Drake illustrates the creative use of color in his projects. *(Photoshot/Redcover/Henry Wilson)*

characteristics, such as washability, mildew prevention, and fire-retardant qualities.

Paints are divided into two categories, based on the type of binder used: **latex**, or water based, and **alkyd**, or oil based. Instead of natural oil, alkyd paints today use as a binder **resin**, a natural, yellowish, translucent substance usually formed from plant secretions. Resins also come in synthetic varieties with similar properties.

The quality of latex paint, and therefore its cost, reflects the proportion of pigment—especially, titanium dioxide, the main white pigment—to binder, and water. The higher the percentage of titanium dioxide, the better the coverage. These higher-quality paints may not require that a primer be used to prepare for the finish coat. Latex paints with a binder that is 100 percent acrylic are the highest quality, known

for their stain resistance and durability. **Enamel** is a high-gloss paint coating.

Until fairly recently, oil-based paint was favored by professional housepainters for its coverage and richness. However, oil-based paint takes a long time to dry, has a strong odor, yellows, and discharges damaging gases, known volatile organic compounds (VOCs), into Earth's ozone layer. Ever-increasing health, safety, and environmental concerns, coupled with improvements in the manufacture of water-based latex paints, have led to a decline in the use of oil-based paint. However, some professional painters still prefer to use oil-based paints, particularly in kitchens and bathrooms and on wood molding and other wood or metal substrate. Oil-based paints are often used for exterior surfaces.

Paints are further classified by **sheen level**, the degree of a surface texture's reflectance of light. Although there are differences among paint manufacturers, typical sheen levels used for interiors, from the least amount of sheen to the highest, are as follows: flat, eggshell, semigloss, and gloss. As a general rule of thumb, flat paint is the most forgiving, meaning that it is better at hiding imperfections in wall surfaces, and gloss is the least. Conversely, the higher the sheen level of the paint, the easier it is to clean and the more resistant to moisture. For these reasons, semigloss and gloss are often used in kitchens and bathrooms and on molding. However, the higher sheen does not provide a higher resistance to fungus or mildew buildup. Eggshell finish (sometimes referred to as satin), not to be confused with the off-white color, is popular for residential interiors because it strikes a balance between flat and gloss that is feasible for most wall surfaces. Eggshell provides for relative ease in cleaning and also camouflages minor wall imperfections. Many manufacturers have recently developed flat finishes that are similar in properties to higher-sheen finishes. Washable matte or flat finishes are available through most paint companies in an array of colors.

The preparation and priming of the wall are the most significant parts of the painting process. A **primer** is the first coat applied to the substrate to prepare it for subsequent finishing coats. The choice of primer is more dependent on the surface it will cover than on the type of subsequent coating. Primers may have an oil or a latex base. Many paint companies have succeeded in producing a combination of finish and primer paint coating in one. Primers may also serve as sealers on porous substrates, such as wood and gypsum wallboard (GWB). **Skim coat** is the term used for an extensive preparation of walls that are in poor condition. First, the entire wall is covered with sheetrock. Then canvas is applied with a sizing compound, usually a wallboard composition or lime plaster. Only then does the actual task of paint covering begin. Extensive wall preparation is very labor intensive and costly.

Decorative Painting *Decorative painting* is a term that covers a wide variety of ancient and modern techniques that extend the versatility of paint products to create a multitude of subtle or dramatic effects. Artisans who specialize in one or more techniques may be employed to provide these services in either commercial or residential applications. Muralists are fine artists who create paintings directly on walls (or ceilings). They often employ trompe l'oeil techniques, which fool the eye by creating an illusion of relief on a flat surface (Figure 9.26a). **Faux finishing** refers to fake renderings of various natural materials or patinas, such as old painted plaster or distressed finishes; *faux bois* mimics wood, and *faux marbre* mimics marble (Figure 9.26b and c). Faux finishes may also simulate other stones and gems, such as tiger's eye, tortoiseshell, and malachite.

Many other painting techniques can be applied to add texture and dimension to a space. These techniques rely on the selection of more than one color to provide a range of contrast, from subtle to dramatic.

Figure 9.26
Decorative paint finishes. a. Trompe l'oeil; b. Faux bois; c. Faux marbre. *(a: © Angelo Hornak / Alamy; b: Design Red Studio, www .designredstudio.com; c: Courtesy of Evergreene Painting Studios Inc.)*

Figure 9.27
Broken color technique in this green color wash. (*Design Red Studio, www.designredstudio.com*)

Figure 9.28
Metal effects shown here in silver. (*Design Red Studio, www.designredstudio.com*)

They are sometimes referred to as broken color techniques.

- *Glazing*. A transparent film of color is suspended in oil- or a water-based medium and vehicle and applied over a base coat to achieve depth of color.
- *Color washing*. A coat of thinned, translucent paint is applied over a white or colored ground (Figure 9.27). This technique can provide a distressed or aged effect that simulates textures, such as leather.
- *Sponging*. A base coat of paint is applied by brush or roller. Additional layers of other colors are applied by dabbing a natural sea sponge lightly dipped in paint in a random movement, beginning with the darkest colors to add depth.
- *Rag-rolling*. This encompasses various techniques of adding and then removing layers of pigment, usually tinted hues, to create the look of marble, plaster, or stone. Typically, a glaze is applied with a soft brush and then lifted off with a rolled cloth.
- *Dragging and combing*. This technique, the coasting of a dry brush or comb over a wet glaze, is often used to represent broadly wood grain or a weave.

Many of these techniques originated in ancient times but today use modern and less toxic materials, for example, water-based instead of oil-based paints. Entire wall surfaces or trims may be decorated with these finishes, and they can simulate the appearance of wood accents and paneled wall divisions, which would otherwise be achieved with millwork.

Other decorative finishes include stenciling and gilding.

- *Stenciling*. Traditionally a substitute for costly wall coverings, stenciling can be used to create artistic styles ranging from quaint and folksy to dramatic. A design, or motif, is cut, or scored, into a piece of acetate, and paint is then applied very lightly or pounced over the stencil. This step is repeated as the stencil is moved from place to place, creating a pattern. Special brushes and paint are used, and the stencils may be store bought or custom designed.
- *Gilding and other metal effects*. These are very labor-intensive and delicate techniques used to apply accents of gold, silver, or less expensive composite, or alloy, metals. These effects are most often used on ceilings but may also be applied to walls, as in Figure 9.28.

Another way besides decorative painting to simulate the look of older plaster walls is the use of a recently developed technique consisting of a trowel application of a mixture of plaster; sand; cellulose; and ochre, a yellow-colored mineral used as natural pigment. This mixture mimics the look of plaster.

Covering

Full or partial walls can be covered with many different surfacing materials, among them paper, vinyl, and textiles; an array of other natural products, such as leather, grass, and cork; and mixtures of fibers with sand, glass, metal, or other mineral particles.

Paper Wallpaper, with its rich history in the decorative arts, has seen a resurgence of interest as a wall treatment. The popularity of wallpaper, in particular those finished by hand, for example, painted, screened, or printed, has blossomed in the 21st century. In addition to contemporary designs, there are many that remain traditional, such as Oriental style (Figure 9.29).

Wallpaper is generally used for residential areas with light traffic, where ease of cleaning is not a major consideration. The paper can be affixed to the wall using a wheat or cellulous paste applied to the back; alternatively, the paper may come prepasted from the manufacturer. A wide range of patterns and textures is available. Many patterns simulate natural looks, such as wood and stone. Besides the standard selections available, a limitless range may be customized for color and pattern. Both standard and customized papers may be obtained from a variety of domestic and foreign resources.

Patterns may be applied to wallpaper using various methods, among them block printing, roller printing, and screen printing (see Chapter 10). Wallpaper may also be hand painted and customized. Hand-painted paper that simulates the surfaces of metal, leather, or wood may be torn and applied for a seamless look. Nonwoven varieties that are fire rated and easy to repair may be suitable for certain commercial applications.

Paper is sold either by the yard or in rolls. Standard wallpaper rolls manufactured in the United States measure 27 inches wide and contain 4 to 5 yards on a single roll. They are generally sold in double-sized rolls. European rolls are usually 11 yards long by 21 inches wide, a total of 55 square feet per single roll. When exploring the global marketplace designers should keep in mind that measurements may vary from country to country.

Figure 9.29
Hand-painted wall covering. (*De Gournay's Askew hand-painted wallpaper in Special colourway on Blue Grey Dyed Silk. Interior design by Kelly Wearstler/KWID design. © Annie Schlechter/Art Rep*)

Vinyl Initially developed for use as a wall covering in commercial settings, vinyl is now also produced for residences, particularly in high-use areas, such as bathrooms, laundry rooms, kitchens, children's rooms, and playrooms. Vinyl has a waterproof surface and is tougher than ordinary papers; it stands up well to grease, steam, and fingerprints. Because it is easy to clean, vinyl is favored in health-care settings. Vinyl-coated papers fall between the two categories of vinyl and paper coverings and provide a good balance of properties in more formal residential areas, such as hallways and bedrooms.

Contract-grade vinyl wall coverings are classified by type (I, II, or III), according to federal criteria. The type number refers to the weight of the product, which determines the appropriate use. For a light-use area, including ceilings, type I (7 ounces to 13 ounces per square yard) is sufficient. Type II (generally 21 ounces per square yard) is more suitable for general-use areas, such as hallways and lobbies. Type III (more than 22 ounces per square yard) is needed for heavy-use areas, such as elevators.

Figure 9.30
Vinyl wall covering. *(Photograph by George Lambros, courtesy of Maya Romanoff)*

Figure 9.31
Upholstered wall covering in a restaurant setting. *(Courtesy of and designed by Studio Gaia)*

Vinyl wall coverings are backed with a woven cloth or nonwoven fabric of varying weights (Figure 9.30). The heavier the face, the heavier the backing required. Like wallpaper, these coverings come in an array of colors, patterns, and styles.

Although vinyl has many advantages, it is not considered a green product and therefore has been subject to criticism. Efforts have been made to reduce some of the damaging aspects of the manufacturing process, by using a percentage of recycled vinyl, substituting water-based inks and coatings, and eliminating ozone-depleting chemicals.

Textiles As wall coverings, textiles include both natural and synthetic fabrics. Natural textiles used for wall covering include cotton, linen, silk, and wool, in particular felt. Rayon is also now being used for wall coverings. Synthetic fibers include nylon, olefin, polyester, and Xorel, a synthetic woven fabric trademarked by Carnegie Fabrics as an alternative to vinyl. Xorel is durable, easy to clean, and inherently flame retardant, and it has a long life cycle. Synthetic fibers may be used alone or in combination with the paper and vinyl products previously mentioned. The characteristics

of natural and synthetic textiles are discussed in more detail in Chapter 10.

In earlier times, tapestries and carpets were used as wall hangings to provide both insulation and decoration. Installation of textiles directly onto walls is a more recent practice. Fabric wall covering, especially when installed with a layer of padding, provides good acoustical value. However, thermal and acoustical advantages must be weighed against other considerations, such as staining and mildew resistance. Because textile wall covering does not withstand moisture and soiling as well as vinyl or masonry walls, it is not suitable for high-use areas, such as bathrooms, laundry rooms, kitchens, and children's rooms. Therefore, a current common use is for conference rooms or boardrooms.

Fabric marketed for wall covering is typically backed with paper to provide stability. Fabric may be panel wrapped, that is, wrapped around a wood or fiberboard panel and then attached to the wall. Fabric may also be upholstered to the wall (Figure 9.31), that is, attached to the wall by a series of clips or tacks that hold the fabric taut.

As discussed earlier, in addition to fixed walls, panels and partitions play an increasing role for the lining

Figure 9.32
Felt furnishings by Anne Kyyro Quinn: wall covering, ottoman, and throw pillow. *(Provided by the Author)*

Figure 9.33
Printed wood veneer wall covering by Trove. *(Alcyone 202, printed on White Birch Veneer by TROVE, www.troveline.com)*

of interiors. Polyester, olefin, and fiberglass are used in panel systems because they are resistant to flame and have good **dimensional stability**, a reference to the material's ability to hold its shape. Less toxic solutions are being explored, among them the substitution of nontoxic materials, such as recycled wool, cotton, and hemp fibers and the use of foam made from gypsum, which has acoustical properties. Panels clad with recycled cotton denim have been produced that are considered comparable in quality to particle board; small pieces of postconsumer recycled fabric are mixed with a nonformaldehyde adhesive, pressed at high temperature, trimmed, and finished.

One significant natural and sustainable alternative to the potentially harmful synthetics used is felted wool, known as felt, a building material developed thousands of years ago in Central Asia. The versatility of this material in the hands of contemporary artists crafting walls and partitions is shown in Figure 9.32. As it is valued for its acoustical and inherently flame-resistant properties, many companies are producing both custom and standard partitions and panels in this material.

Other Coverings Perhaps in response to the heavy reliance on vinyl, natural products have been gaining in popularity for wall coverings. Among these products are leather, grass cloth, cork, and wood veneer. A natural wood veneer covering developed by the design house Trove is backed with a Forest Stewardship Council (FSC) cloth material, making it a green alternative. Trove's digital imagery wallpapers are recyclable and use nontoxic inks and a wax-based coating that is washable and durable (Figure 9.33).

Concrete, invented by the Romans thousands of years ago, has now been transformed into a cloth to create safe, durable, noncombustible structures.[3]

Leather tile is an expensive wall treatment but provides a naturally evolving patina that some consider luxurious and elegant.

Grass cloth was quite popular as a wall covering for many years but fell out of favor with the advent of synthetics, which offered many practical advantages. It has recently regained popularity. One of the disadvantages of grass cloth in comparison with other alternatives is that the seams show after application. However, in the current climate, which favors sustainable materials, these products are now being manufactured and marketed to a broad audience (Figure 9.34a and b). Raffia, jute fiber, and reeds are included in this category as well.

Figure 9.34

Grass cloth. a. *Then* and b. *Now*. *(a: Design: Jeffrey P. Elliott; Photo: Jason Jung/Estetico; b: Custom designed for the Metropolitan Home Showtime house 2008, New York City, by White Webb)*

The use of cork and cork composites has also increased with the interest in cork's environmental value.

Cladding

Cladding is the use of masonry, such as metal, stone, ceramic, glass, wood, solid-surfacing, and laminate materials, as a wall finish.

Masonry Masonry materials can provide a decorative statement as well as bring to interiors the same properties they bring to the construction of a space, such as acoustical or thermal properties. Some of these materials are applied to both vertical surfaces and finished flooring. Marble or travertine is costly but has a dramatic impact when used for vertical installations and walls. They are most likely to be used for expansive areas and are installed in sheets. Figure 9.35a–f features an array of masonry cladding applications.

Metal Metal sheets can give a dramatic and rather industrial look to an interior. Highly valued in Japan, tin is a metal used for interior wall cladding in both residential and contract projects. It is lightweight and nontoxic and has a lustrous texture.

More often, a metal wall treatment also involves the use of a laminated product to reduce the cost of the metal while adding durability.

Ceramic Ceramic, in tile form, now makes up a significant share of the wall surfacing market. Many

Figure 9.35
a. Marble: Lobby wall in Blanca Carerra marble; b. Metal: Elevator cab in mixed metals including stainless steel and aluminum; c. Ceramic: Simple and elegant Italian white ceramic tile accented with 24K gold inserts; d. Glass block provides borrowed light for this interior; e. Mirror: Antiqued mirror tiles serves as a romantic backdrop in this living room area; f. Laminate: Decorative wood veneer laminate for a retail space. *(a: © Tim Street-Porter/Beateworks/Corbis; b: © Image Source / Alamy: c: Artemide Oro Giallo 10, Bisazza glass mosaic border, Vetricolor and Oro Bis collections. Bisazza Design Studio, www.bisazza.com; d: Ken Hayden/Redcover.com. Designed by Andrew Peck.; e: © Pieter Estersohn; f: Treefrog veneer, of Chemetal, Inc. Photo by Eric Laignel, Zooey Showroom, New York City, designed by Stefan Beckman)*

ceramic tiles that are suitable for floors are also suitable for walls and backsplashes, vertical surfaces designed to protect the wall behind a sink, stove, or countertop. (However, tiles that are suitable for walls, backsplashes, and countertops may not always hold up as flooring.) Ceramic tile is used for full walls or to provide decorative accents and borders for other wall surfacing materials. Ceramic tile is available in a wide variety of sizes, shapes, thicknesses, glazes (including metallic), patterns, and colors. It may be arranged in mosaic form; on a diagonal; or in other formations, such as pictorial panels.

Glass Glass may be applied in tile or block form as a wall cladding treatment. Glass block is a transparent or translucent glass that is usually made by fusing two pieces of glass together to allow for light diffusion. Glass may also be used in a mosaic tile treatment or as an aggregate of recycled glass from beverage bottles and stemware.

Although relatively expensive, glass is useful for letting in natural light or borrowed light from adjacent spaces. It is used in residences, restaurants, and other spaces, often as partial walls, for a decorative effect. In addition to its importance as an architectural feature, glass is an art medium. Layers of glass, both float and safety, embedded with a variety of perforated metals can be backlit and used in place of conventional glass for shower enclosures, doors, stairs, room dividers, and so on.

One such expression is influenced by *washi,* a traditional Japanese technique for paper and parchment making. This has inspired new techniques of fusing organic materials, such as thin layers of bark, between glass layers. Other materials, such as metals and textiles, are treated in a similar fashion.

As a mirror, glass can enhance the dimensions of a space. Antique mirror finishes have a mottled appearance. This effect can be produced in new mirrors by adding the chemical mercury to clear glass to create a distressed, silvered appearance that evokes a romantic mood.

Solid Surface Solid surface is a category of synthetic material (a polymer) used to simulate marble, granite, stone, and other natural materials. It is considered an elegant alternative to natural stone. The advantage of solid surface over laminated synthetics is that the color and

pattern run through the entire product, in contrast to the seam of core material visible on the edges of laminate.

Most often used for countertops in residential settings, solid surface can also be used for interior walls in residential or contract spaces. This product is also commonly used for signage. It is produced in sheets and is durable and damage-resistant. Some products are enhanced with natural particles, such as quartz or shell, to add luster.

Laminates Various types of laminated surfaces may be employed as wall cladding. The use of metal laminate as a wall surface treatment has become increasingly popular, particularly in commercial projects. This product consists of a thin metal foil applied by high pressure to a backing. Popular metals used in this way include stainless steel, aluminum, tin, brass, copper, and alloys, or combinations of metals. The finishes may be brushed, matte, or polished in natural or patina states. Metal laminates may be embossed, etched, or perforated, creating additional dimension, texture, and pattern. They are available as sheets or tiles. This type of wall treatment is most suitable for light-duty vertical interior surfaces that may be exposed to moisture.

Other general-purpose laminates, commonly used for retail display, toilet and dressing room privacy partitions, and workstations, are made from synthetic materials, such as plastic, in finishes that are either solid colors or simulations of natural materials. This type of surfacing is also available in 100 percent recycled goods. Engineered wood panels (see Chapter 8) also may be used to clad walls. Wood veneer, in a multitude of choices, is also used for laminated panels.

Resin, mentioned earlier as a binding substance in paint, is also a material used for walls, panels, and partitions. When natural resin is used, the color is in the yellow-brown range. Essentially a composite of molten acrylics or polyesters formed into sheets, synthetic resin material may be manufactured in a variety of colors. Resin also serves as a medium in which to embed natural objects, such as grasses, leaves, pebbles, and so on. It is common for a substantial portion of the resin base to be made of recycled material.

Often retaining a translucent quality, resin products allow for light transmission while providing privacy and are particularly dramatic when backlit.

CEILINGS

Sometimes referred to as the forgotten plane, a space's ceiling is an opportunity for decorative and functional impact. Figure 9.36 shows how a ceiling was customized to reflect the context of a restaurant.

The most common type of ceiling is one made of painted GWB, the same material used for walls. Ceilings may be painted with any of the decorative finishes already described or with a mural (Figure 9.37).

An additional layer is often added to the structural ceiling for acoustical value. Some ceiling treatments,

Figure 9.36
A highly dimensional ceiling was designed for the Rosso Restaurant in Ramat Ishay, Israel, by SO Architecture, to reflect the contours of the desert topography of the region. *(Rosso Restaurant–Team: Shachar Lulav, Oded Rozenkier in cooperation with architect Eran Mebel; Photo by Asaf Oren)*

Figure 9.37
This unique, elaborate ceiling, part of the Museum of Fine Arts Boston, was painted by John Singer Sargent in 1921. *(Ceiling Mural, Museum of Fine Arts Boston, John Singer Sargent, 1921)*

in addition to being decorative, provide fire-retardant features, humidity and mildew resistance, and insulation properties. Another consideration is the light reflectance value (LRV) (see Chapter 7) of finished ceilings. One principal reason to finish a ceiling, particularly for commercial applications, is to provide a space for mechanical and electrical ducts, plumbing, and recessed lighting. This space, the plenum, is provided by way of a suspended ceiling (see Chapter 8).

Acoustical

Acoustical ceilings are typically manufactured as tiles or panels of various sizes and textures. Installation is often in the form of a suspended ceiling grid system, with aluminum separating the tiles or panels (Figure 9.38). Most acoustical ceiling material is made of mineral fiber. Some panels are made of glass-reinforced gypsum, fiberglass, or vinyl-gypsum combinations.

This type of ceiling is principally used in open-office plans, schools, hospitals, and other contract situations in which noise distraction must be minimized.

A system with an LRV of 80 percent or more reduces glare and provides greater energy efficiency. Some acoustical ceiling materials have high recycled-product content and properties, and are treated to inhibit mold and mildew.

In contrast to the rather plain-looking standard acoustical tiles used in many commercial settings, newer styles feature dimensional, sculptural looks that are more appropriate to high-end commercial projects.

Metal

Originally, metal was used on ceilings as an inexpensive way to hide damaged plaster. Ceiling tiles or panels (and moldings) were made of tin, which was stamped or embossed to provide architectural and visual interest.

In modern construction, which does not typically use plaster, metal ceilings are most often installed for decorative purposes, to resemble 19th-century homes and commercial interiors. Today, these panels are manufactured from steel and then protected with a poly-

Figure 9.38
Acoustical ceiling in the offices of the CNN building in New York City. *(Adrian Wilson/Beateworks.com. Designed by Mustafa Kemal Abadan of Skidmore Owings & Merrill)*

Figure 9.39
Tin metal ceilings in various finishes. (© *Chicago Metallic Corporation*)

urethane finish or, alternatively, plated with chrome, copper, or brass or even painted (Figure 9.39). Other metal ceiling treatments have a more modern, sleek look and may be used in large-scale commercial projects.

Plaster

Products made of gypsum and reinforced with other materials, such as glass, have generally replaced plaster as a building material for new construction. However, several companies continue to offer ornamental plasterwork that relies on traditional designs and techniques. These services may be part of a historic preservation project or a customized high-end interior project (Figure 9.40).

As with tin ceiling tiles, look-alike products made of polyurethane provide a significantly lower-cost alternative to plaster ornamentation, particularly for ceiling treatments. These look-alike products usually are not used in high-end residential design, but rather in do-it-yourself projects.

Glass

A "glass ceiling" is most often thought of as a barrier in employment opportunity, but real glass ceilings are starting to gain popularity in the world of interiors. Contemporary designers are exploring the use of translucent materials, including tempered glass, fiberglass, mica, resins, and other glass and glasslike products, which allow artificial and natural light to be maximized (Figure 9.41).

Figure 9.40
Use of plaster as ornamentation on ceiling and walls applied in a traditional manner. (*Brian Harrison/Redcover.com*)

Figure 9.41
Glass provides unusual, translucent ceilings. (*Interior at FCNL* © *2011 Jim Morris*)

MILLWORK

Millwork is woodwork, such as wall and ceiling panels, molding, door finishes, window trim, cabinetry, mantels, and built-in furniture. This includes products ready made at mills as well as customized, architectural millwork. Millwork may be applied sparingly, as in the iconic modern interior shown in Figure 9.42a, or more elaborately, as in the traditional-style contemporary interior featuring raised paneling and molding in Figure 9.42b. Millwork tends to shape the character of a space; therefore it is not readily removed and replaced. Also, it can be a costly investment. For this reason, millwork selection is a significant and rather permanent step in the process of lining the interior, applicable to any room. This is an area in which the designer plays a key role in shaping the interior architecture for the client.

Whether prepared by the interior designer; architect; or tradesperson, such as a carpenter, the contract or working documents for millwork require extensive, detailed information. Customized cabinetry in today's homes may be confined to bathrooms and kitchens or extend to entertainment centers, storage areas, libraries, and bars. In commercial projects, customized cabinetry and other types of woodwork may be applied to a variety of spaces, from elevator banks to hotel lobbies, conference rooms, boardrooms, and corporate hospitality spaces.

The materials used for millwork vary in type and grade. They may include solid wood, but more frequently millwork relies on composite materials, veneers, and reconstituted woods, such as fiberboard and plywood.

Extensive use of wood for walls, ceilings, and built-in cabinets, bookcases, or furniture evokes a warm feeling. Depending on the choice and treatment of the wood itself, and the application selected, the effect can be luxurious or rustic. Because the choice of wood as a material is often based largely on its inherent beauty, designers may opt to have the wood finished with clear treatments to protect rather than disguise it. Finishing with a transparent lacquer provides more protection than oil- or wax-rubbed treatments; however, the latter may be favored for their authenticity.

Wood installed flush on walls, ceilings, and doors in simple vertical boards, planks, or strips provides a casual appearance, whereas raised paneling is more formal. **Wainscot**, a treatment used on interior walls, generally consists of wood panels that cover the lower part of the wall and run to a point approximately 4 feet

Figure 9.42

Millwork in different styles. a. Modern, streamlined millwork is featured in this iconic residence designed by Mies van der Rohe, 1951; b. The millwork for this contemporary space by interior designer Marshall Watson is elaborately detailed with paneling, molding, window frames, and bookcases. *(a: Photography: Jon Miller, Hedrich Blessing; Image courtesy of Carol Highsmith; b: Designer: Marshall Watson. Photo: Mick Hales/Greenworld)*

Ray C. Anderson (1934–2011): Pioneer for Sustainable Business Practices

Ray C. Anderson was the founder and chairman of Interface, Inc., a company he began in 1973, in Atlanta, Georgia. Starting with only 15 employees, his global firm is now a billion-dollar enterprise, and the worldwide leader in the design, production, and sales of environmentally responsible modular carpet manufactured for the commercial and institutional markets under the InterfaceFLOR brand, and for residential markets under FLOR. The company is also a leading designer and manufacturer of commercial broadloom under the Bentley Prince Street brand.

Anderson was a visionary, known for his advanced and progressive stance on industrial ecology and sustainability. In 1997, after being influenced by a series of writings, including Paul Hawken's *The Ecology of Commerce,* Anderson set forth a new vision for his company to "do well by doing good."

At age 64 Anderson led the company on a new initiative known as Mission Zero, with a promise to eliminate all negative environmental impact by the year 2020 through the redesign of processes and products. Pioneering new technologies geared to reduce or eliminate waste and harmful emissions are coupled with increased use of renewable materials and energy sources. From 1996 to 2010, through process improvements and energy efficiencies, the company reduced the energy used to manufacture its carpet by 43 percent and greenhouse gas emissions by 44 percent, in absolute terms (94 percent when factoring in offsets). During the same period the company grew its net sales by 27 percent.[a]

Anderson authored two books on his philosophy and strategies: *Mid-Course Correction: Toward a Sustainable Enterprise: The Interface Model* and *Confessions of a Radical Industrialist: Profits, People, Purpose—Doing Business by Respecting the Earth.*

In 2010, in recognition of his role in transforming the flooring industry, Anderson received the American Society of Interior Designers' Design for Humanity Award, an honor reserved for a humanitarian who has made significant contributions to the Society. At that time he was applauded for the forward-looking sustainable manufacturing practices implemented at Interface, Inc., which set a new standard for the industry and as a trusted source in the field continuing to shape industry practices through speeches that were both relatable and compelling.[b]

The following year he passed away after a long battle with cancer, only days after receiving an honorary doctorate from his alma mater, Georgia Tech, at the age of 77.[c]

Sources:
[a]*Adapted from Erin Meezan, Interface press release, April 10, 2010.*
[b]*Adapted from ASID National Conference 2009 Awards Ceremony, introduction of Ray Anderson, "ASID Announces ASID Award Winners," www.asid.org.*
[c]*Adapted from* Interiors & Sources, *August 9, 2011, Stamata Business Media.*

George Beylerian and Material ConneXion®

The first edition of this text (2006) spotlighted George Beylerian's vision to provide a resource for the exploration and promotion of innovations in materials and applications for manufacturers and designers. Today Material ConneXion is in six countries (on three continents) with plans to open 10 additional libraries throughout China by 2017. Every month, an international panel of experts reviews 50 to 60 new materials sourced from around the world for inclusion in the materials library. Only a few are selected. The jury of experts and subscribers to Materials ConneXion come from diverse industries, among them architecture, product design, interior design, fashion, packaging, defense, transportation, and medicine. Several of the selections related to the built environment are featured in this chapter and in Chapter 10.

Material ConneXion has enhanced its relationship to education since 2006. More than 100,000 students currently have access to the firm's materials online database through university subscriptions. As educators seek to better prepare students for life after graduation, materials libraries have become an important teaching method for design schools looking to inspire creativity while giving students hands-on experience with the cutting-edge tools of their trade.

One of the first institutions to recognize the importance of materials libraries was the School of Architecture at the University of Texas at Austin. Kendall College of Art and Design in Grand Rapids, Michigan, boasts a materials library designed by Material ConneXion that is the largest of its kind in any school or university,

"Access to materials stimulates creativity and innovative thinking," said Dr. Oliver Evans, Kendall's Vice President and Chancellor.

In today's digital age, when so many aspects of education are moving out of the classroom and onto the web, educators are realizing that even the most sophisticated online programs still cannot replace hands-on learning. On-site materials libraries help schools bring a sense of discovery and serendipity back into the design process. They supplement the studio environment with a rich palette of resources and promote interdisciplinary interaction and an awareness of the trends and developments that are shaping our world.

Source: Adapted from "Innovation in the Classroom: Design Schools Embrace the Materials Library," Matter 7.3, The Education Issue, Material ConneXion®, by Alison Zingaro.

George Beylerian and Material ConneXion®, *continued*

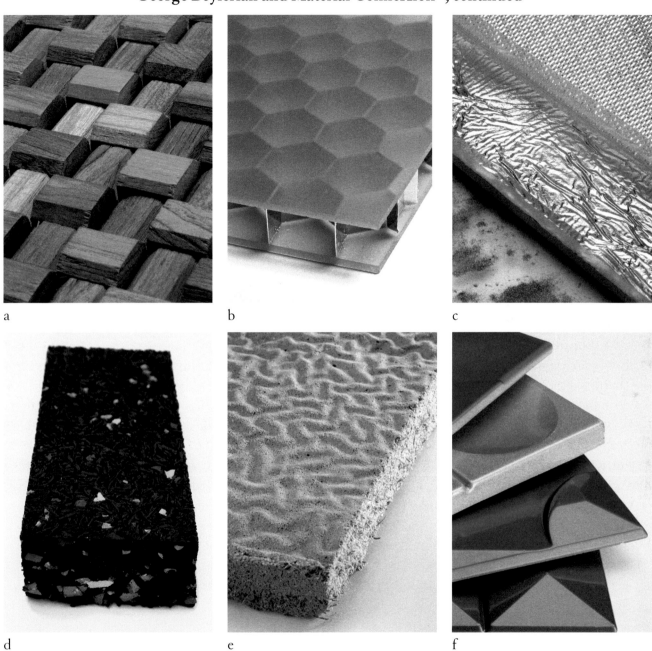

Figures a–f

a. Small teak pieces adhered to a plywood back create a sculptural effect; for wall coverings or room dividers; b. Ultra-light honey-comb aluminum core bonded to acrylic is available in a wide range of colors and finishes; for interior architectural design and furniture applications; c. Decorative glass panels are laminated with layers of laser-cut metals and foils; customizable in different textures and finishes; d. Anti-slip, flexible floor covering is composed of 100 percent pre-consumer shoe rubber waste; e. Wall and ceiling panels are composed of 80 percent clay and 20 percent natural fiber; they are odor absorbent, temperature regulating, and recyclable; f. Tiles composed of 80 percent cement and 20 percent natural fiber are spray coated with iridescent or metallic paint; for interior wall decoration. *(All figures courtesy of Material ConneXion)* above floor level. *Dado* is another term used for wainscoting. The term **chair rail** refers to a strip of wood placed about 4 feet above the floor on an interior wall.

A ceiling that is **coffered** is made up of sections of recessed panels As a category of millwork, coffered ceilings may be used to evoke a traditional and grand interior space. These typically are made of wood, but less expensive imitations of this elegant treatment, formed of plastic, are also available.

The technique of connecting wood members together, called **joinery**, is a specialized skill. A fundamental understanding of the basic types of joinery used for both millwork and furniture is helpful to the interior designer to understand the qualityof construction. The tongue-and-groove and spline methods used in flooring also apply here. Other methods, such as dado, rabbet, and miter, are illustrated in Figure 9.43a–c.

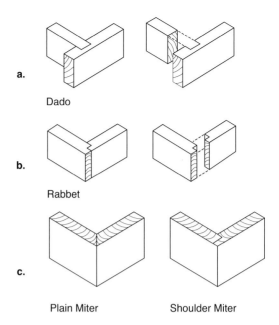

Figure 9.43

Typical joinery. a. Dado; b. Rabbet; c. Miter.

Summary

The interior designer and client face many decisions when finishing the interior lining of a space. Successful choices are ones that are informed and that consider many factors, including budget, function, user requirements, style, and eco-friendliness. A fundamental knowledge of the physical properties and aesthetic characteristics of materials used in lining the interior will assist the designer during the decision-making process.

In addition to the building materials reviewed in Chapter 8, a vast array of products and technology is available to treat surfaces of floors, walls, and ceilings. Not simply decorative, the finishing of interior surfaces may offer advantages such as protection against wear and tear, fire and moisture resistance, and acoustical improvements.

Flooring surfaces are divided into three categories: hard, resilient, and soft. An advantage of resilient flooring over hard flooring is its low-impact surface. Among the hard surfaces are wood (both soft- and hardwoods), bamboo, stone, ceramic, and glass. Vinyl is a commonly used material for resilient flooring, in either solid or less expensive composite forms. Another popular flooring choice in this category is laminate. Rubber, linoleum, and cork products are environmentally supportive natural alternatives in the category of resilient flooring.

Carpets and rugs make up the soft flooring category. These soft floor coverings are made of many different natural and synthetic fibers, using a variety of hand and machine techniques.

Coating, covering, and cladding are the three basic methods used to finish walls and partitions. Painting is the method most commonly used to coat walls. Paper, vinyl, textile, and other materials are options for covering a wall surface. Masonry, metal, laminates, ceramic, glass, and solid surface are options for cladding walls.

Acoustical tiles and panels absorb noise and are used for ceilings in many commercial projects. More costly materials that are applied less commonly to ceilings include metal, plaster ornamentation, and glass.

Woodworking techniques are used in the production of millwork, which can embellish the architectural features of an interior space. Millwork is often used as trim on windows, doors, and ceilings. Wainscoting and chair rails are other common applications. High-end paneling and custom cabinetry are more luxurious options.

Many new products and applications of materials are continually being introduced to the architectural and design communities. The trend is to seek innovation in the development of products that are attractive and functional yet environmentally friendly.

Vocabulary

acrylic impregnation	fly ash	rug
aggregate	frieze	rya
alkyd paint	grout	Savonnerie
all-wood construction	hard flooring	Saxony
Aubusson	hardwood (deciduous) tree	sheen level
binder	joinery	skim coat
broadloom	kilim	softwood (coniferous) tree
carpet	laminate	solid surface
chair rail	latex paint	solvent
cladding	linoleum	spline
coffered ceiling	loop pile	terra-cotta
cork	millwork	tongue and groove
cut pile	parquet (block) flooring	tufted
dhurrie	pigment	underlayment
dimensional stability	pile (face yarn)	vinyl
enamel	plush (velvet) pile	wainscot
engineered (laminated)	porcelain ceramic	warp
faux finishing	primer	weft
fiber	resilient flooring	Wilton
flokati	resin	woven

Exercise: Scavenger Hunt—New Materials and Applications for Building Materials

The goal of this exercise is to find new products, manufacturing techniques, or applications for lining interior spaces. Your list should feature products or uses of products that are not described in this text—those that are truly "hot off the press."

Various research methods may be used, such as visits to showrooms, manufacturing sites, project sites, or trade shows. You may also review catalogs, trade and shelter publications, articles, news briefs, and books. Websites, in particular those maintained by government or public agencies, educational sources, or professional associations, may provide you with a substantial amount of information.

Aim to include at least one new product or application that is suitable for finishing each of the following surfaces: floor, wall, and ceiling. Summarize each product, and include an illustration. In your summary, consider the relationship of the product to such factors as aesthetics, sustainability, universal design, ergonomics, and life-cycle cost.

Exercise: Exploring the CD-ROM

Take advantage of the contents of the CD-ROM to increase your understanding of how the carpet industry has addressed sustainability. Follow the instructions for Starting the CD-ROM on pages xix–xx and click on Chapter Nine: Finishing the Interior: The Lining.

Sustainability and the Carpet Industry: Many carpet manufacturers have been improving their sustainability practices and are accomplishing this in various ways. Examples include the use of renewable, recyclable material, reuse, and reclamation of materials. Production and installation of alternatives in carpet backing include the use of plant-based adhesives. Research three companies and prepare a comparative summary of their claims of sustainability in the production and installation of carpeting for either residential or contract applications.

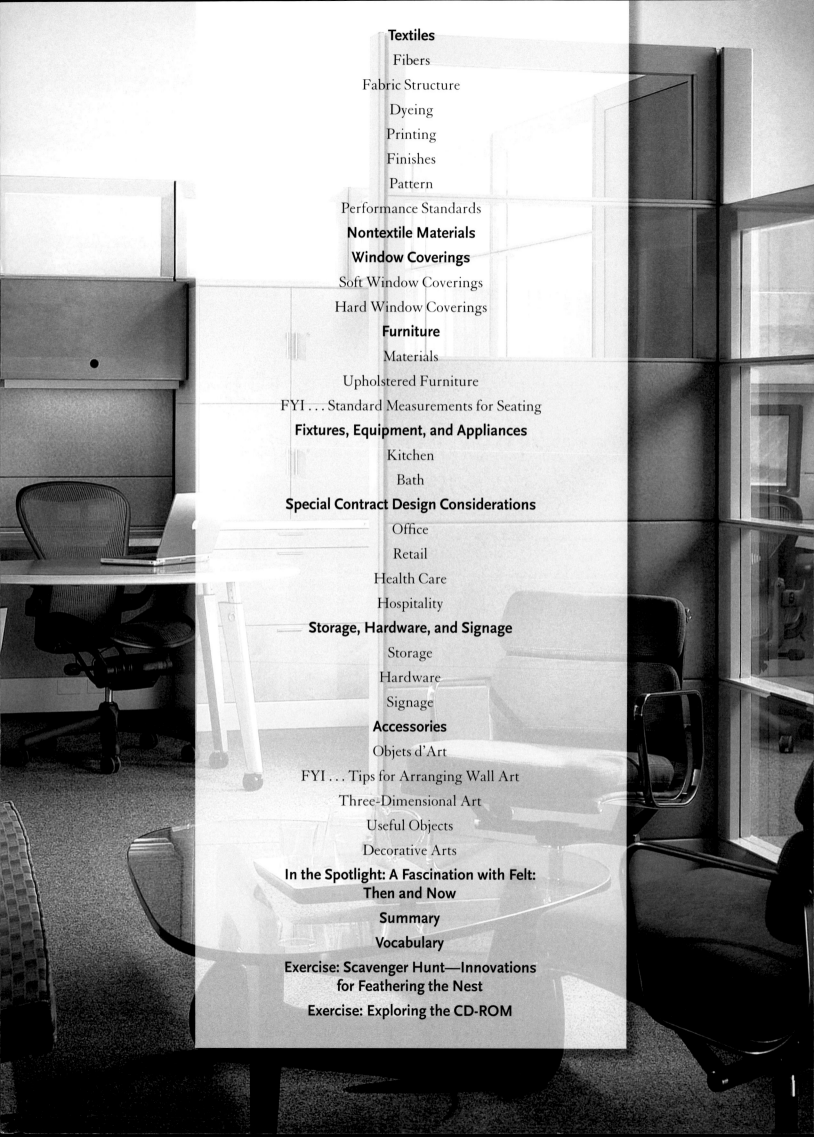

Furnishing the Interior: Feathering the Nest

Having moved from the structure of the space, the shell, to the interior architecture, the lining, in this chapter I cover the balance of fixtures, furnishings, and equipment (FF&E). With the nest built, the interior designer continues to furnish it—to *feather* it. This is the step during which the interior is personalized. Once again, the designer considers form, function, safety, and environmental standards.

Many of the materials discussed in earlier chapters are used at this stage, but for different applications. This chapter explores these materials further and introduces FF&E, appliances, and accessories.

TEXTILES

Chapter 9 introduced the use of textiles to treat walls, floors, and ceilings. This chapter further describes the characteristics of various textiles and their use in the treatment of windows; as upholstery for furniture; for accessories, such as bed, bath, and table linens; and as wall art (Figure 10.1).

Formerly used to denote only woven fabrics, the term **textile** today refers to any cloth or fabric, manufactured in a variety of ways. Nonetheless, most of the textiles used for interiors are woven. In addition to being categorized as woven or nonwoven, a textile may be classified by its structural components (i.e., its fiber, either natural or synthetic), color (natural or dyed), construction (yarn: thread, strand, or filament; fabric: cloth, or other material made by natural or synthetic manufacturing), finish, performance, and end-use application.

Figure 10.1
An assortment of contract and residential textiles. *(Courtesy of Fairchild Books)*

The vocabulary for the world of textiles is extensive, and terms commonly used are often commonly misused. For example, although frequently used to refer to a large-scale flower pattern, **chintz** is a finishing treatment, not a specific pattern. Similarly, **damask** is not a pattern, but rather a particular type of weave; nonetheless, a two-tone floral, no matter how it is manufactured, may be called damask (Figure 10.2a and b). **Jacquard** is the name for a specific loom invented in 18th-century France that assists in the production of weaving large, complex patterns, rather than one particular print pattern. Many technical and scientific words are used on fabric labels, and organizations exist whose purpose is to establish standards for textile properties and performance.

Figure 10.2
a. Chintz as a floral pattern fabric used by interior designer Mario Buatta, known as the Prince of Chintz; b. Nonwoven damask pattern on fabric for bed linens and as vinyl wall stickers.
(a: Interior design by Mario Buatta®. Photography by Scott Frances; b: © Ctsoukas_Dreamstime.com Composite and wall art by www.vinylattraction.com)

Figure 10.3
Spun silk fiber. (*Cheryl Kolander, www.aurorasilk.com*)

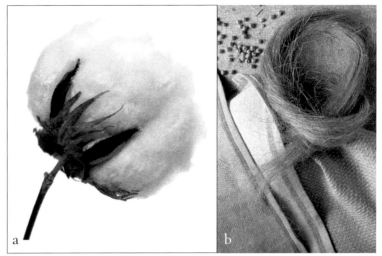

Figure 10.4
Natural cellulosic fibers. a. Cotton ready to be picked; b. Linen fiber and fabric. *(a: © Istockphoto; b: Jacqui Hurst/CORBIS)*

Although the interior designer's first thoughts in selecting a fabric may concern color, texture, and pattern, these choices should be informed by the other considerations described in this section.

Fibers

Textiles may be classified as being composed of either natural or manufactured fibers or, as is often the case, a combination of several fibers from different categories.

Natural Fibers Natural fibers are classified as protein (animal), cellulosic (plant), or mineral (rock).

Protein Fibers Wool is supplied for interiors primarily from the fleece of various breeds of sheep. Although relatively expensive, wool inherently provides excellent qualities for use in the built environment: resiliency, elasticity, flame resistance, and stain repellence. It has a smooth **hand**, or feel to the touch. Mohair, the fleece of the Angora goat, is a lustrous and expensive protein fiber that may be used for plush upholstery fabric. Increasingly, attention is being given to the production of organic wool, which entails adherence to procedures and certification of the federal government regarding the raising of livestock.[1] The natural dyeing of wool yarn is one of the requirements for organic certification. High-quality wool fabric is generally an expensive commodity.

Silk, harvested from the cocoons of moths, is prized for its rich luster (Figure 10.3). It is one of the strongest natural fibers but when in a fabric easily fades in sunlight and has only moderate resistance to abrasion. It is therefore not appropriate for heavily used furniture and should be lined when used for draperies. It can be blended with wool or linen. Silk comes in a variety of grades and is imported from many countries, but generally from Asia, at varying price points. Substituting soy products for silk fibers is a trend in the production of silklike alternatives. SOY-SILK brand fiber is made from the residue of soybeans produced during the manufacture of tofu. This process is 100 percent natural and free of petrochemicals, making it an extremely environmentally friendly product. Soy is a completely renewable resource.

Corn fiber, an annually renewable resource, is another environmentally friendly product. Like SOY-SILK brand fiber, corn fiber offers superior moisture absorption and ventilation properties, along with beautiful draping, softness, and warmth, and its color does not fade. Corn fiber is part of the new class of "green" textiles. These fibers provide the environment with a unique "cradle-to-cradle" approach, coming from the earth and being wholly biodegradable. Corn fiber contains no petroleum, and all products are manufactured to be eco-friendly and are being used in bed linen and other home fashion markets.

Cellulosic Fibers Cotton is obtained from the seed pod of the cotton plant, which is grown extensively in the southern and southwestern United States (Figure 10.4a). Fine-quality cotton is also imported into the United States from Egypt. The first use of cotton as a fabric is attributed to India, and the names of some cotton fabrics, including *calico* and *madras*, are derived from Indian (Sanskrit) words. Cotton is relatively strong and has a fine hand. It is not inherently fire-resistant but does release soil easily. It absorbs moisture and,

Figure 10.5
Jute carpet backing. *(Courtesy of Amy Willbanks, www.textile fabric.com)*

therefore, takes a long time to dry. As with wool, there has been an impetus toward organically raised cotton.

Linen, which comes from the stem of the flax plant, is used for upholstery, draperies, and wall coverings as well as tabletop accessories (Figure 10.4b). It has low abrasion resistance and low resiliency. Wrinkling can be reduced in the production of linen fabrics with the addition of resins or by combination with other fibers. Linen is considered a cool fabric, and it has a high luster.

Jute, derived from a grass and considered a green product, is used to create **burlap,** a material used in the construction of upholstered furniture and as the backing, or lining, for carpet and linoleum (Figure 10.5). Other fibers derived from plants or grasses include hemp sisal, coir (coconut), sea grass, ramie (China grass), and raffia. More recently, other natural cellulosic fibers can be found in the interiors market; among them are abaca (banana), pina (pineapple leaves), palm grass, and corn husks. Although often used for floor and wall coverings, these fibers are also being employed in the production of fabric. They are not recommended for wet areas due to risk of mildew and have only low to medium stain-resistance properties.

Mineral Fibers Asbestos, produced from the long fibers of certain minerals, was used extensively for insulation and as a fire-resistant material in the 20th century. However, the fibers were found to be carcinogenic and are no longer used.

Manufactured Fibers Manufactured fibers are classified as cellulosic, noncellulosic, or mineral. Many man-

ufactured fibers originate with a natural substance, generally a wood, plant, or oil that is chemically processed. Others that are synthesized exclusively from chemical polymers are referred to as synthetics.

Cellulosic Fibers The most commonly used fabrics in the cellulosic category are rayon and acetate. Although rayon was first patented in France in 1884, commercial use did not begin in the United States until the early 20th century. Acetate was first created in 1904, in the United States, and 20 years later was developed and manufactured as a textile. Both rayon and acetate consist of natural cellulosic fibers, primarily wood chips that are processed chemically. Another fiber, lyocell, was created in the 1990s and represents a breakthrough for sustainable practice, as the chemicals used in the production process are reclaimed and recycled. Tencel is lyocell's registered brand name.

Rayon, formerly called artificial silk, is frequently used for window treatments. It is generally less expensive than silk. Fabric made of rayon is soft and drapable, with a high luster (Figure 10.6). Rayon is often used

Figure 10.6
Rayon is a manufactured cellulosic fiber. *(© Bettmann/CORBIS)*

as a fill for other fibers when added sheen is desirable. Rayon is not dimensionally stable and stretches easily when wet. The most popular type of rayon is viscose. Rayon's performance is similar to that of cotton. Bamboo plants are replacing wood chips in the production of viscose rayon in order to create a greener product.

Acetate is inexpensive and dimensionally stable but wrinkles easily. It also burns and fades easily. Because it is not soft and drapable, it is more commonly used as a backing for draperies.

Noncellulosic Fibers Derived from natural gas, oil, coal, and water, these fibers are often referred to as synthetics even though they are produced from natural products.

Acrylic and modacrylic are frequently used as economical substitutes for wool because they have a similar appearance. They resist fading, drape well, and are resilient. Modacrylic is preferred for use in interiors because it is inherently more flame-resistant. It may be used for window coverings, especially for contract use, and for upholstery. Developed by Glen Raven in 1961 as a substitute for the cotton in awnings, Sunbrella is perhaps the most widely known brand of the category of solution-dyed acrylic. Once considered suitable only for outdoor use, these fabrics are now employed for interiors as well. Today, many fabric manufacturers have a line representing the indoor/outdoor fabrics in a variety of patterns and colors, beyond the original striped canvas awning associated with the category[2] (Figure 10.7a and b).

Nylon was the first truly synthetic fiber from the polymer group of chemicals (Figure 10.8). It is considered an extremely strong product, drapes well, and is used alone or in combination for upholstery and carpet. A typical use of nylon for interiors is in combination with wool, for floor coverings.

Figure 10.7
Outdoor fabrics. a. Traditional use for awnings; b. Outdoor fabrics come inside; an update of Old World, formal style. *(a: Photo supplied by Glen Raven, Inc. makers of Sunbrella® performance fabrics; b: Courtesy of Perennials® Fabrics)*

Figure 10.8
Nylon, shown here on spools, is a noncellulosic fiber. *(© Ted Horowitz/CORBIS)*

Polyester, originally trademarked as Dacron, is very strong and abrasion-resistant, dries quickly, and resists wrinkling and fading. A drawback is that it is prone to static. Like nylon, it can be used in combination with other fibers. It is commonly combined with cotton for vertical applications, such as drapery and partitions. Polyester is popular with the hospitality market because of its durability. As a green solution, recycled plastic bottles are now being used in its production.

Olefin is used for both indoor and outdoor carpet and upholstery. It is durable, quick drying, lightweight, and inexpensive—features that make it especially suitable for heavy-use upholstery and wall coverings.

Spandex, also referred to as elastene, was formerly limited to the apparel industry but is now being used in small quantities with other fibers for upholstery fabric. Its elasticity makes it useful when a fabric must cover a curvilinear form. Lycra is a trademark brand of spandex.

Mineral Fibers Glass and metallic fibers are increasingly being added in innovative ways to fabrics used for interiors. These fibers provide luster and textural interest.

Fabric Structure

Fabric structure is categorized as either woven or nonwoven, with the majority of fabrics being woven. Weaving is the process of interlacing two sets of yarns at right angles to form a fabric. As discussed in Chapter 9, the two sets of yarn are known as the warp and the weft. The warp is the yarn that runs lengthwise on a loom (the equipment used for weaving); the weft yarns are woven over and under the warp. When viewed up close, woven goods may be thought of as having a structural pattern, produced from one or a combination of weaving methods: **plain weave**, **twill weave**, and **satin weave** (Figure 10.9a–c).

Examples of fabrics produced with a plain weave are taffeta, ottoman, and gauze. Denim is in the twill weave family (Figure 10.10). Sateen falls into the satin category. Satin weaves are generally silky in texture.[3] These fabrics, as well as many others, are described in Table 10.1 (see p. 303).

Weaving first involves the production of yarns from fiber; nonwoven fabrics are produced with one

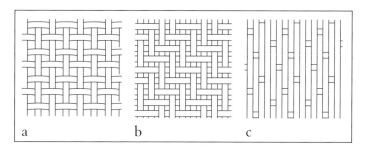

Figure 10.9
Weave structures: a. plain; b. twill; c. satin.

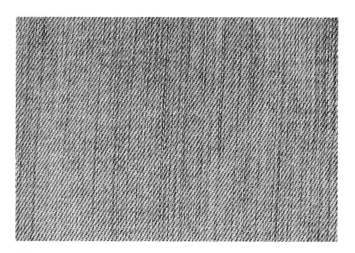

Figure 10.10
Denim is an example of a twill weave. (© *Veer*)

less step. Nonwoven goods are used less often than woven fabrics. They are expensive but are used for upholstery because of their combination of low maintenance and aesthetic qualities. Techniques for nonwoven textiles include needlework, such as knitting, crocheting, braiding, and tufting, as well as bonding and felting. Felting, a technique developed thousands of years ago, has been receiving much attention. Wool felt is a nonwoven fabric that is derived from a combination of wool, moisture, heat, and pressure. It has excellent shock and sound absorbency and is considered a green product. Examples from contemporary artists and designers are the focus of *In the Spotlight: A Fascination with Felt: Then and Now.*

Dyeing

Color may become part of a fabric at varying points in its production. Fabric that retains its natural color or, if synthetic, is left uncolored is called a **greige**, or **gray good**. Greige that is to be converted to a colored fabric can be done through a variety of dyeing processes. Following are the three most common methods of adding color to fabric:

1. *Yarn dyeing*. In this process individual strands in the fabric are separately colored. Stripes and plaid fabrics are generally produced this way.
2. *Solution dyeing*. This is a more economical process, whereby fibers, in an earlier form of production, are dipped into a dye solution. Standard, popular colors are used.
3. *Piece dyeing*. This is the process of dyeing whole pieces of fabric in a bolt. It is generally used for solid-colored fabric.

With the renewed interest in artisanal goods and techniques, there are currently many naturally dyed textiles available. A natural plant dye from the **indigo** plant, generally an inky blue color, is drawing much attention.

Printing

In contrast to structural pattern, which is produced during the weaving of a fabric, applied pattern results from the printing process (see Chapter 3). Most patterns and multicolored designs are created through a variety of printing methods in which color is applied after the cloth is manufactured. A few commonly used printing methods are described here. These methods relate not only to the treatment of fabrics for upholstery and window coverings, but also to wall coverings (see Chapter 9).

- *Block printing* of fabrics is a traditional hand operation in which separate wood blocks are carved for each color to be applied (Figure 10.11a).
- *Roller printing* (machine printing) is a form of direct printing that relies on metal rollers, or cylinders, engraved with a pattern for each color to be applied. This process is similar to newspaper and wallpaper printing (Figure 10.11b).
- *Photographic printing* is a process in which the fabric is treated with a light-reactive dye, and the negative of a photographic image is transferred onto the fabric.
- *Screen printing* is a method in which a fine mesh is mounted over a frame. Parts of the screen's surface are made opaque and therefore resistant to the color solution, similar to the way a stencil

is created. The color is then applied onto the frame with a squeegee. Because portions of the fabric are blocked, and only some receive the color, a pattern is created (Figure 10.11c). This may be done by hand or by a rotary mechanism.

- *Resist printing* includes several techniques, among them **batik** and **ikat**, which originated in Indonesia. Hot wax is applied to parts of the cloth. The wax prevents the dye from being absorbed and thus creates distinct patterns. Many contemporary fabrics simulate the look of batik and ikat without using this traditional printing method (Figure 10.11d and e).
- *Computer-aided design (CAD) printing* is increasingly being used. It may also be referred to as digital printing. Specialized programs and equipment discharge color patterns directly onto the unfinished greige goods (Figure 10.11f).

Finishes

After a fabric is produced, additional treatments may be used to improve its performance and aesthetic appeal.

A fabric's functional performance may be enhanced to increase resistance to wrinkles, water, soil, moths, and microbes and to reduce static and shrinking. Crypton, a trademarked brand, is a process that enhances a fabric's resistance to stains, moisture, and microbes, making it suitable for health-care applications, among others. Some fabrics are laminated with a clear vinyl film to make them durable and easy to clean. Teflon and Scotchgard are trade names for this type of protective covering. Fabrics may also be treated with resins to provide wrinkle resistance.

A heat-setting process may be used to pleat fabrics permanently. Purposeful shrinking of parts of the material to form puckering is another finishing technique that, like pleating, is an aesthetic choice. Another surface treatment used largely for aesthetic appeal is a wax finish that is applied by heat and pressure to create a glazed, or shiny, texture to the surface of a fabric, often cotton. The resulting textile may be referred to as **chintz** or polished cotton.

Adding a backing to a fabric increases its dimensional stability (the ability to hold its shape) and durability. Acrylic and latex are often used as backing for other fabrics to serve these purposes.

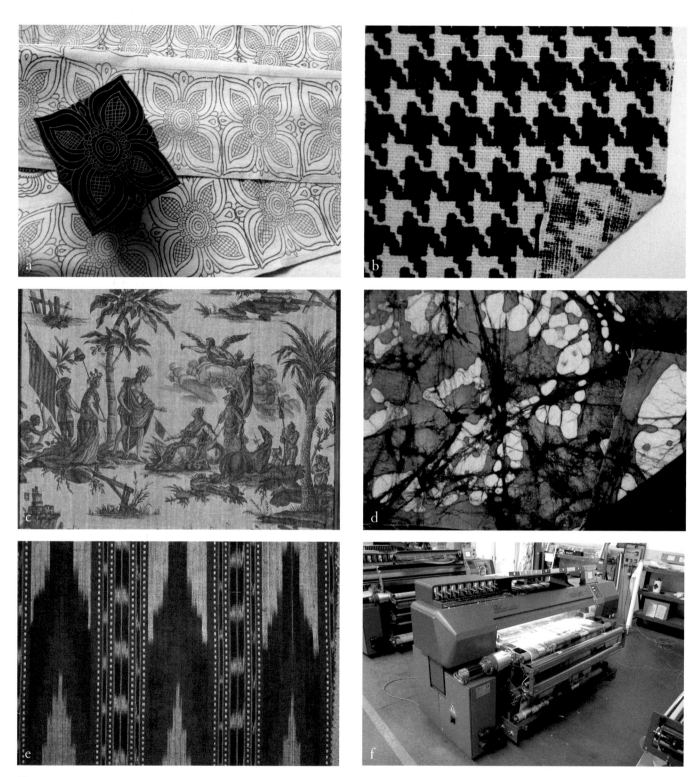

Figure 10.11

Printing techniques. a. Carved block and printed fabric; b. Roller print; c. Screen-printed toile; d. Resist printing: Batik; e. Resist printing: antique ikat; f. Digital printing equipment. *(a: Courtesy of Cheryl Kolander; b, d, and e: Courtesy of Amy Willbanks, www.textilefabric .com; c: Huet, Paul [1803–1869] [after] Toile de Jouy. Linen, manufactured by Jouy [1760–1842]. CFAC206. Photo: Christian Jean. Location: Musee de la cooperation franco-americaine, Blerancourt, France. Photo: Réunion des Musées Nationaux / Art Resource, New York; f: © Printer QualiJet HS made y La Meccanica, photo Federico Bonetti)*

Embellishing textiles is another way to add a finishing touch. Examples include needlework, such as the embroidery seen in the production of **Suzani** fabric, a traditional craft in Central Asia, particularly in Uzbekistan.

Pattern

The pattern or motif is an important consideration when choosing fabric for interiors. Two basic categories of patterns are geometric and organic (see Chapter 3). Within the category of organic patterns, different interpretative styles may be employed: naturalistic, stylized, or abstract. Furthermore, organic designs may be composed of either botanical (flowers, trees, plants) or figural (people, animals) representations. Many patterns and motifs are universally recognized; among these are **paisley**, a plantlike motif from India; harlequin, a geometric motif composed of diamonds in two tones or hues; and chevron, a geometric design prevalent in many places throughout the ages. Novelty, or conversational, prints are often used for children's spaces. Examples of pattern styles are shown in Figure 10.12a–f.

Patterns vary in both scale and direction. For the interior designer these are important concerns when

Figure 10.12

Patterns. a. Geometric (chevron); b. Flame stitch; c. Naturalistic floral; d. Stylized floral; e. Paisley; f. Figural conversational. *(a: © CN Digital Studio; b: © Zoffany 2007; c: © Athos Boncompagni _ Dreamstime.com; d: "Unikko" print by Maija Isola for Marimekko, 1965. © Marimekko Corporation; e: © Fairchild Books; f: CN Digital Studio)* fabric is used for window treatments or wall and furniture upholstery. The **repeat** of a pattern is the distance from the start of the pattern to the end of the pattern. This measurement needs to be considered for both horizontal and vertical directions (Figure 10.13). It is a critical element when estimating the amount of goods to be ordered for a particular installation (discussed further in Chapter 14).

Key in coordinating various fabrics into an aesthetically satisfying whole is an understanding of the elements and principles of design (see Chapter 3). In addition to the elements of color, texture, pattern, and scale, the principles of rhythm, contrast, balance, and harmony strongly influence how various materials work together in a space (Figure 10.14).

Performance Standards

Consumers expect the products they purchase to hold up to wear and tear, be comfortable to use, and not present a danger. For furnishing interiors, especially in public spaces, performance standards are important. Essentially, the performance of a textile is judged in five areas:

- *Flammability.* Its response to fire, either by extinguishing fire or reducing its spread.
- *Abrasion resistance (rubbing resistance).* Its ability to resist wear caused by contact with another fabric or rubbing.
- *Colorfastness.* Its ability to retain color properties under light and when wet.
- *Dry crocking.* Its ability to resist transfer of dye onto another surface when rubbed.
- *Physical properties.* Its ability to retain its original characteristics.

Several tests evaluate each of these properties. Perhaps the most critical test to pass is the one for flammability. Although local building code requirements vary, it is safe to say that most standards for commercial buildings are stricter than those for private residences. The **Tunnel test** is one test that rates a textile's response to heat and flame. The **Wyzenbeek test** method is commonly used to evaluate a fabric's ability to withstand abrasion. The results, noted in terms of **double rubs**, may be used as a guideline; the higher the number, the more abrasion-resistant the fabric. For example, a score of at least 15,000 double rubs should be achieved for contract upholstery; 30,000 double rubs is considered

A&B Cohen Fabrics

890 West 37th Street, New York, NY 10000
Tel: (212) 555-1800 Fax: (212) 555-1801

Exclusive
Width 54″ (137.2 cm)
Vert Rep 1″ Horz Rep 1/2″
Made in U.S.A.
38% Rayon 34% Polyester 28% cotton
Teflon

Figure 10.13
Pattern repeat information is provided on a tag attached to the fabric.

Figure 10.14
Coordination of various patterns in different scales, unified by a consistent color palette. (© melabee m. miller; interior design by Nancee Brown Interiors)

heavy duty. The **Xenon test** measures how well a fabric's color resists fading when exposed to light.

The **Association of Contract Textiles (ACT)** was founded in 1985 as a not-for-profit trade association to address issues related to contract fabrics. It provides uniform labeling of contract textiles, using graphic icons to represent each of the five performance standards (Figure 10.15).

NONTEXTILE MATERIALS

This category of materials, used for upholstery in both residential and contract interiors, includes genuine

Symbol	Function
🔥	flammability
✿	colorfastness to wet & dry crocking
✴	colorfastness to light
✷	physical properties
a	abrasion
A	abrasion

Figure 10.15
ACT product labeling icons.

leather converted from hides of animals, such as deer and cattle, and skins from smaller animals, such as lamb, goats, and calves. Color may be added as well as finishing treatments that provide luster, texture, embossing, or distressing, among other surface details. Leather that is woven or embossed may provide additional textural interest when upholstering furniture or walls. Suede, the flesh side of a hide or skin, is seldom used for upholstery because its color tends to rub off. Recent innovations have included the processing of salmon skins, a by-product of the food industry, as an alternative to animal leather. Although salmon skin was initially used for apparel and shoes, its application for home furnishings is underway.

Less costly simulated leather and suede coverings have been produced from synthetic materials in the polymer family. Among these are Naugahyde, a trade name for a material that resembles leather, and Ultrasuede, a trade name for one of several fabrics made of polyurethane but having the feel of natural suede. These simulated suede materials offer greater stain resistance and durability than their genuine counterparts. Another group that has soft, suedelike textures is known as microfiber, produced from fibers that are very lightweight.

Vinyl can also be used for upholstery. It may be manufactured to maintain the artificial look of shiny plastic, providing a more casual or retro style for an interior space (Figure 10.16).

Figure 10.16
Chrome and vinyl plastic bar stools. (© Owaki-Kulla/CORBIS)

WINDOW COVERINGS

Window coverings may be categorized as soft or hard, or a combination of the two. The treatment, or dressing, of windows may be chosen for purely functional reasons, purely decorative reasons, or both. Issues such as privacy, view, insulation, light and sound control, energy conservation, safety, cost, and appearance are considered in deciding how, when, and even whether a window is to be covered. Interior designers choose from a vast array of styles and materials, including trims and the hardware used for installation or decorative embellishment (Figure 10.17).

Although the appearance of the window treatment is a significant component of a design, questions regarding the need for privacy and control of light are paramount. The degree of light transmission (translucence, transparency, or opacity) is a critical consideration in the selection criteria for a material. The flexibility of a window treatment to accommodate changing lighting conditions during different times of the day and for different functions, such as dressing and sleeping, is another. Privacy concerns the visibility

Figure 10.17
Window dressing with exposed hardware. *(Courtesy of and designed by Jamie Gibbs)*

from the outside in. Also of importance is the degree of visibility from the inside out. Already noted in earlier chapters is the positive effect that vista and view, as well as a connection to nature, can have on well-being.

Energy conservation plays a key role in decision making about window coverings, such as the amount of heat lost or gained, particularly in public spaces.

The basic kinds of window treatments are drapery and curtain, blind and shade, shutter, and screen. The term *drapery* is more likely to be used for elaborate window fashions and *curtain* for those that are simpler and more informal. The length of the material (floor length for drapery and sill length for curtains) may also be used to distinguish these two soft window-covering treatments.

A blind consists of a series of slats that may be raised and lowered, opened and closed, and tilted. A shade operates up and down but, because it consists of a continuous piece of material, does not open, close, or tilt. Shutters, discussed in Chapter 8 as exterior window treatments, may also serve as hard treatments for the interiors of windows. Some treatments appear to

be soft yet are made from hard materials; these include coils made of woven wire mesh and glass beads.

Soft Window Coverings

Soft materials, such as fabric, are often used for draperies and curtains. Lengths vary, ranging from sill, to apron (below the sill), to floor length. The full range of fabrics and their properties are considered in the selection of soft window coverings. Fabrics noted to have drapability and dimensional stability are favored to create fluidity yet provide consistency in measurements once installed. A second layer of fabric may be added to the face fabric to serve as a lining, improving the blackout performance by preventing the transmission of light as well as preventing wrinkling and staining of fabric. Soft materials may also be used for shades and blinds.

Drapery Drapery may be installed as operable panels or fixed and stationary ones. Drapes may draw open to one side or to both sides (referred to as center draw) and may be pulled by a cord on a traverse rod or simply by hand when the fabric is hung from a pole. Some systems are motorized and operated remotely. Draperies may be composed of one layer or several layers, such as with an **underdrapery**, hung from a board, rod, or pole. Drapery styles are often defined by the type of header, as shown in Figure 10.18a–i.

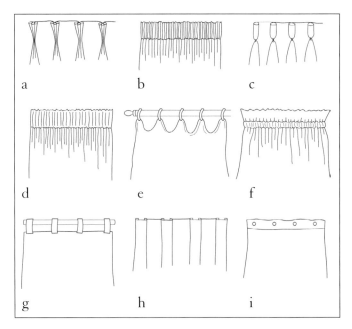

Figure 10.18
Types of drapery headings. a. French pleat; b. Shirred; c. Bell pleat; d. Pencil pleat; e. Scallop; f. Ruffle shirred; g. Tab; h. Box pleat; i. Grommet.

A **valance** is a stationary, soft top treatment, usually pleated or draped in some fashion that may or may not hide the hardware (Figure 10.19). Top treatments may also be constructed to serve as a frame behind which the fabric panels are hung. A **cornice** is one type of treatment made of wood. When upholstered with fabric, it is called a **pelmet**. Pelmets may also be fabricated without a wood frame if the fabric is sufficiently stiffened with buckram, a type of jute or cotton. A **lambrequin** frames the sides as well as the top of the window treatment (Figure 10.20a and b).

As with clothing fashion, hemlines vary. Panels that drop to the sill or to the apron are generally considered an informal window treatment. The traditional hemline for panels breaks from the floor to

Figure 10.19
Soft valance with pinch pleated header over drapery panels.
(© *melabee m. miller; interior design by Nancee Brown Interiors*)

Figure 10.20
Hard top treatments. a. Pelmet; b. Lambrequin. *(a and b:*
© *melabee m. miller; interior design by Nancee Brown Interiors)*

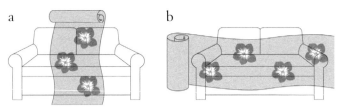

Figure 10.22
a. Fabric unrolled vertically; b. Fabric railroaded.

Figure 10.21
Puddled drapery. *(© melabee m. miller; interior design by Nancee Brown Interiors)*

about $1\frac{1}{2}$ inches above. **Puddling** is a formal, less practical installation in which excess fabric is draped on the floor (Figure 10.21).

The amount of yardage required for a window treatment depends on many factors, among them the measurements of the window, the width of the material, the vertical and horizontal repeat, the style selected, and the fullness desired.

Fabric used for interiors is typically 54 inches wide; however, drapery fabric, in particular sheer, translucent, or casement (open-weave) fabrics, are available in wider widths of 112 inches; this reduces the need for seaming. Another method that requires less seaming of fabric is known as railroading. This is a method of constructing fabric patterns so that they may be laid horizontally rather than vertically. This approach may also be used for upholstery, as illustrated in Figure 10.22a and b.

Fullness describes the ratio of fabric width to window width. For example, a very full, luxurious for-

Figure 10.23
An informal tailored window treatment. *(Courtesy of Restoration Hardware)*

mal drapery might be created with a triple fullness, in which three widths of fabric are used for every window width. Generally, a more tailored look is obtained by use of two to two-and-one-half widths' fullness. One factor to be considered when deciding on fullness is the weight of the material; for example, a velvet drapery might be too heavy if designed with triple fullness (Figure 10.23). Other factors that influence the calculation of fabric yardage include hems and **return** (the distance of the drapery from the wall).

Stackback is the amount of space taken up by the draperies when they are open. The width of the stackback is influenced by the fullness of the drapery. This,

Figure 10.24

a. In this elaborate window treatment, both swag and jabot are illustrated in the center and sides of the window, respectively. Also shown in this example is the stackback of the underdraperies; b. Traditional swag and jabot valances. *(a: James Kerr/Redcover.com; b: © melabee m. miller; interior design by Nancee Brown Interiors)*

in turn, affects the amount of light that passes through the exposed window as well as the view.

Drapery panels may be gathered in different styles, creating tailored or ornate looks. A **swag** (also called a **festoon**) is a semicircular-shaped fabric, whether fixed or draped loosely. It is often used in conjunction with a **jabot** (also called a **cascade**), which is a folded fabric that hangs down the sides of the window. These treatments, in addition to trimmings, expand the decorative possibilities of soft window coverings and are especially popular for more formal styles (Figure 10.24a and b).

Passementerie Passementerie, which derives from the French word *passement*, meaning "trimming," describes the array of ornamental trimmings used for soft window treatments (as well as for upholstered furniture and textiles for bed, bath, and tabletop). Examples of passementerie are shown in Figure 10.25a–n.

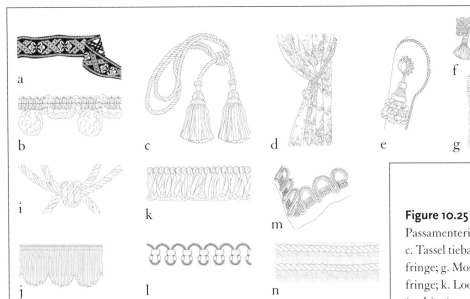

Figure 10.25
Passamenterie. a. Jacquard braid; b. Bobble fringe; c. Tassel tieback; d. Cord tieback; e. Rosette; f. Tassel fringe; g. Moss fringe; h. Key tassel; i. Cord; j. Bullion fringe; k. Loop fringe; l. Gimp; m. Braid; n. Piping (welting).

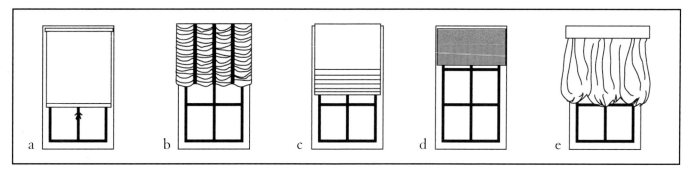

Figure 10.26
Soft shades and blinds. a. Rollup; b. Austrian; c. Balloon; d. Roman; e. Accordion pleat.

Blinds and Shades Blinds and shades as window treatments may fall into both soft and hard window covering categories and come in materials such as fabric, vinyl, metal, and wood. Both shades and blinds are generally installed inside the window frame and draw up, usually from the bottom, whereas draperies and curtains are installed outside the frame and draw to the sides.

Blinds and shades may be operated by hand or may be motorized. They may provide blackout and solar conservation features. Common categories of soft styles include roller (rollup), Austrian, balloon, Roman, and accordion pleat (Figure 10.26a–e).

Hard Window Coverings

Windows may be covered in part or exclusively with hard materials, such as wood, plastic, or metal. These materials may be used to make blinds, shades, screens, and shutters.

Roller, or Rollup, Shades These shades may be made of hard material, such as thin wood or bamboo slats, often in combination with textile yarns. Many roller shades produced today are solar shades made of a mesh fabric that filters light while allowing a view out. The degree of the mesh openings determines the amount of light filtration, calculated in percentages. The smaller the openings, the less light will enter, reducing the negative effects of exposure to ultraviolet rays.

Venetian Blinds A general category of horizontal slat window treatments, **venetian blinds** were made originally from wood. They are similar to a louver door that can be angled in different ways to control light and allow for privacy. For much of the 20th cen-

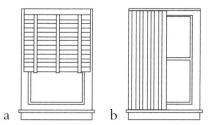

Figure 10.27
Hard shades and blinds. a. Venetian; b. Vertical.

tury, vinyl varieties were popular in both residential and commercial settings. The miniblind and microblind categories have slats that are 1 inch and $\frac{1}{2}$ inch wide, respectively. The late 20th and early 21st centuries have seen a return to wooden venetian blinds in both narrow and wide widths, in natural and stained woods. Simulated wood products, as well as aluminum, are also used (Figure 10.27a).

Vertical Blinds Vertical blinds are a similar concept, using vertical slats, or vanes, to control for light and privacy. Verticals are popular, particularly for expansive windows and patio doors. They are manufactured in standard sizes and lengths, in a variety of colors, as well as opacities, insulation levels, and flame-retardant features. They may be manufactured with fabric inserts and composed mainly of vinyl or metal. They can also be customized (Figure 10.27b).

Shutters Window shutters, like those used for doors, are another hard treatment that operates with a louver system to provide for flexible light control and insulation. They are manufactured in a variety of woods, vinyl-clad woods, and wood composites. The blades

Figure 10.28
Plantation shutters. *(Courtesy of Hunter Douglas Window Fashion)*

Figure 10.29
Screens: Wire mesh solar screens. *(Courtesy of Durasol Systems Inc.)*

may be narrow or wide; the latter are known as **plantation shutters** (Figure 10.28).

Awnings Generally for exterior use, awnings are usually rigid frames covered with fabric suitable for outdoor conditions. Awnings provide some protection from weather elements, including solar heat transmission, making them an eco-friendly addition.

Screens Screens as window treatments fall into two general categories: sliding and folding. Many are made of wood frames. Shoji, made of wood and translucent materials, such as rice paper, is a derivative of a Japanese style. Other types of screens include lattice, fretwork, and pierced, which allow for an artful diffusion of light.

Functional window screens made of metal mesh are designed to keep out insects. Other metal mesh screens manufactured today are created to reduce solar load, yet maintain privacy (Figure 10.29). More often for contract projects, windows may be retrofitted with security mesh systems to serve as a deterrent to intrusion or vandalism.

FURNITURE

The selection of furniture touches on virtually every aspect of the design process. An understanding of human factors—anthropometrics, ergonomics, and proxemics—guides the selection and placement of furniture (see Chapter 2) and has an influential role in space planning, layout, circulation patterns, and the creation of a period style or mood. Furniture style by period is discussed in Chapters 11 and 12.

Furniture as part of FF&E may be divided between upholstered goods and case goods. **Case goods** is the category of nonupholstered furniture, whether for residential or commercial use. Frequently, a case good, such as a bureau, bookcase, armoire, or wall system, is used for storage or display. This category includes entertainment, or media, systems; freestanding wardrobes; and modular workstations. The term may also be used to describe other large-scale furniture, such as pieces sold in sets for bedrooms and dining rooms. Case goods may be composed of wood or other materials, such as metal, grasses, and plastic, or combinations. Glass, mirror, and stone may also be used in furniture design, often as tabletops. The term **casework** usually refers to built-ins or furniture that is attached to walls, whether prefabricated or custom built. Casework may also be incorporated as part of millwork.

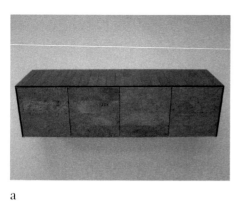
a

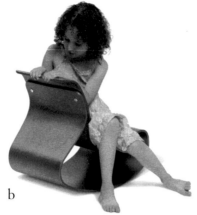
b

c

Figure 10.30

a. Cork and wood combination features cork from Portugal, birch plywood, maple, and wenge woods.; b. Bent Plywood Mod Rocker™ for children by iglooplay™ made of hardwood veneers; c. Plywood desk and chair for children by April Hannah, Brooklyn, New York (*a: © Joe Pipaz; b: Iglooplay and Lisa Albin, designer. Photographer: Michael Crouser; c: April Hannah © APRIL HANNAH LLC 2010–2011*)

Materials

Wood, metal, grasses, and plastic are commonly used for furniture. These materials may be used separately or in various combinations.

Wood The material for most furniture manufactured today, as in ages past, is wood. The properties of wood such as its natural beauty that make it suitable for exterior and interior construction are also appropriate for furniture construction. As with flooring, many types of wood construction are used in the production of furniture. In addition to solid wood production, furniture is made through lamination and veneering processes, such as particle board, pressed wood, plywood, and veneers, at varying price points. The common types of joinery, including mortise, tenon, miter, and dovetail, are used for furniture as well. The methods of providing additional protection to wood construction, such as staining, varnishing, and waxing, are also employed.

Cork, a type of bark harvested from a species of oak tree, is used not only for flooring (Chapter 9), but for furniture as well. No trees are cut down in the harvesting of cork; only the bark is extracted, and a new layer of cork grows, making cork a renewable resource for furniture manufacturing. The majority of commercial cork is currently grown in Spain and Portugal.

The advantages of using recycled wood and wood veneers (see Chapters 8 and 9) apply equally to furniture. Plywood furniture, such as that produced by Charles and Ray Eames in the 1940s (discussed in Chapter 12), may now be made from woods certified by the Forest Stewardship Council (FSC), using formaldehyde-free

Figure 10.31

Lounge chair made from reclaimed wood from the demolished Coney Island Boardwalk, Brooklyn, New York. (*The Cyclone Lounger by Uhuru, Brooklyn, New York, www.uhurudesign.com*)

adhesives (e.g., soy) and nontoxic finishes, making it a green alternative (Figures 10.30a–c and 10.31).

Metal Many varieties of metal (actually, alloys, or mixtures of metals), including aluminum, iron, steel, and chrome, are used for both contract and residential furniture. Metal furniture, like wood, usually has a finishing treatment that may be polished to a high gloss; brushed for a softer, satiny look; or treated for weather and scratch resistance. Different types of metals and combinations of materials are shown in Figure 10.32a–d.

- *Aluminum*. An abundant and lightweight material often used for outdoor furniture, tables, and chair frames because it does not rust. Although it traditionally has been used for

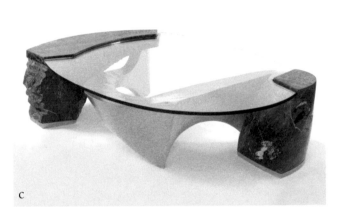

Figure 10.32

Metal furniture. a. Aluminum table and chairs; b. Copper bathtub; c. Mixed Media: Handmade table by Eric David Laxman of stainless steel, marble, and glass; d. Brass bed frame. *(a: Courtesy of Knoll, Inc.; b: © Herbeau Creations of America; c: Design and Fabrication: Eric David Laxman Title: Farella Cocktail Table; Photo credit: Sal Cordaro; d: © Spike Powell; Elizabeth Whiting & Associates/CORBIS)*

outdoor café and restaurant seating, its appeal has made it suitable for many other applications, including kitchen appliances (Figure 10.32a).

- *Copper*. Although costly, copper has resurfaced as a popular metal. It is largely imported from Turkey, in thin sheets, and is used for wrapping other materials, such as wood, to make tabletops as well as for other furniture, fixtures, and appliances (Figure 10.32b).
- *Iron*. An abundant material in many parts of the world. It is a heavy, strong metal that may be either cast (i.e., molded) into furniture or wrought (i.e., worked by hand) to create shapes and forms. Iron rusts when exposed to moisture, and the metal may be left in its natural state to develop an oxidized finish, baked with colored

enamel, or given an aged patina through any of several finishing treatments. It is often used as a table base to support a glass or stone top, for stair railings, or for other ornamental work as well as for bed frames.

- *Steel*. An alloy of iron and carbon that is characteristically hard and strong. When chromium is added, it becomes rustproof and is referred to as stainless steel. For many years, steel was used for office furniture, including file cabinets and desks, before being replaced by wood for high-end pieces. It has since regained popularity for both residential and contract use, especially in kitchens (Figure 10.32c).
- *Chrome*. Often combined in tubular form with leather upholstery to produce contemporary

furniture. Chrome is used primarily for the frames and legs of upholstered furniture.

- *Brass*. A zinc-and-copper alloy that produces a golden color. It is typically used for table bases and bed frames. Its finish may be polished (shiny) or antiqued (dulled or distressed) (Figure 10.32d).

Grasses Some of the grasses and other plant sources used in wall and floor coverings are also used to manufacture furniture. Much of this furniture is imported from Asian countries, where these materials (e.g., bamboo) grow plentifully. Many of these furniture types refer to the construction of the material rather than the specific botanical source. **Wicker** furniture, usually thought of as light and casual, is made by the weaving of twigs or vines. **Rattan**, a particular plant stem, is bent into shapes and used to construct furniture. **Cane** furniture is made from thin, woven strips of plant materials, typically used for seats in lieu of cushions. **Rush** is yet another weaving technique used for chair seats and other furniture. These materials may be left natural or painted. Manufacturers have also developed synthetic vinyl versions of this style of furniture.

Historically, furniture in the grass family was used in warmer climates, both indoors and outdoors, on porches. In recent decades, grass furniture has been designed for year-round use in many climates and regions and in many styles of residential and commercial products, ranging from casual to more formal settings. Grass furniture may be made more durable with a resin coating and used for hospitality installations (Figure 10.33).

Plastic As a group of synthetics, plastic is very versatile. It can be reinvented (and recycled) through experimentation and technology. Plastic may be molded, cast, or combined with other materials, such as resin and fiberglass. Plastic products are lightweight, inexpensive, durable, and easy to clean. Stacking plastic chairs are a space-saving solution used in contract settings. They are frequently used for multiple, or tandem, seating, such as in waiting areas (Figure 10.34a and b).

Furniture and accessories manufactured from a group of clear plastics trademarked as Lucite, among others, were popular in the 1930s, with plastic considered a glamorous modern material. This type of

Figure 10.33
Woven grass chair. *(Courtesy of Knoll, Inc.)*

a

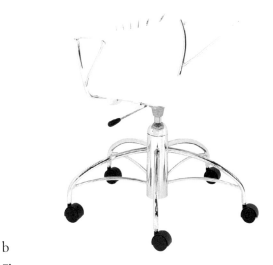

b

Figure 10.34
Plastic seating: a. Stacking chairs; b. Swivel chair. *(b: © Versteel® 2004)*

b

Figure 10.35
Lucite®, *Then and Now*. a. Early clear bed frame; b. Starck's Josephine chairs for Kartell. *(a: Photography by Phillip Ennis; b: Courtesy of Starck Network)*

a

b

Figure 10.36
Paper, *Then and Now*. a. Victorian chair made from papier maché, 1850; b. Contemporary seating of Kraft paper. *(a: Chair. Papier maché with pierced and painted back. England, c. 1850. Photo credit: Victoria & Albert Museum, London / Art Resource, New York) b: © molo)*

material is now manufactured in many colors. Philippe Starck, in his designs for Kartell, has been instrumental in popularizing the use of this material again (Figure 10.35a and b).

Plastic continues to be a commonly used product in many contract projects, including educational, institutional, health-care, and casual hospitality installations. The translucency that results when plastic is combined with resin makes for an interesting play of light, texture, and color. Another appealing feature of plastic is its ability to be produced in a wide range of colors, including metallic versions.

However, plastic presents a challenge to manufacturers, vendors, and designers because of its ecological costs. The chemical properties that make plastic appealing for many uses also pose environmental concerns. The recycling of plastics has increased, and these efforts have helped lessen somewhat plastic's reputation as an environmentally insensitive product.

Another disadvantage of plastic is that it scratches easily.

Other Materials Several manufacturers around the world are experimenting with combinations of natural and synthetic materials and processes in furniture. Solid surface, more commonly used for countertops (see Chapter 9), may also be fabricated into furniture. The use of other masonry materials (e.g., concrete) in the production of freestanding and fixed furniture is also being explored.

Paper, in the form of papier-mâché, was used during Victorian times as a material for furniture production (Figure 10.36a). Today, the use of Kraft paper is being explored by innovative companies, such as Molo, an award-winning collaborative studio in Vancouver that experiments with material and space. One of its lines is an adaptable, flexible seating system made from recyclable Kraft paper (Figure 10.36b).

Upholstered Furniture

The term **upholstery** has been used previously in this text to describe cladding of walls, partitions, and window-top treatments. Many of the principles that apply to upholstering of those components also apply to furniture. Upholstered furniture is made up of a frame, generally wood, surrounded by textile covering and fill. Several different materials and construction methods may be selected, and the role of the interior designer is critical to this process.

Although many upholstered pieces, such as chairs and sofas, may be purchased as standard, or stock, items, the interior designer may be involved in the selection of a customized piece, particularly for higher-end residential projects. This means that many more factors need to be considered, including human factors relating to comfort. An advantage of custom furniture is the capability to adjust the size of pieces and to alter measurements outside the standard range. These standard measurements, based on anthropometric data, are listed and illustrated in *FYI . . . Standard Measurements for Seating*.

The factory or work site where furniture is upholstered is called the **workroom**. The quality of

FYI . . . Standard Measurements for Seating

Sofa

- Back Height: 30 to 34 inches
- Pitch: 5 to 7 inches
- Overall Depth: 36 to 40 inches
- Inside Depth: 22 to 25 inches
- Seat Depth: 23 to 26 inches
- Deck (support) of Seat Cushion: 18 inches high
- Seat Height (top of cushion to floor): 18 to 20 inches

- Arm Height (from the floor): 23 to 25 inches
- Overall Lengths: 54 inches (love seat); 72, 84, and 90 inches (two to three seats)

Chair

- Seat Width (club): 30 to 34 inches
- Seat Width (dining or occasional, the term referring to lightweight, movable furniture): 18 to 24 inches

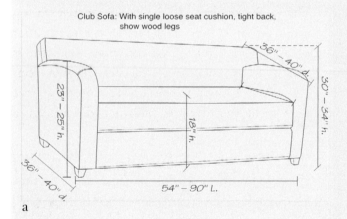

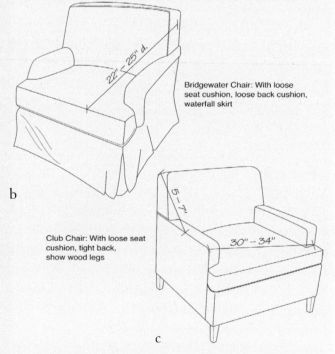

a

b

c

Figures a, b, and c
Standard dimensions of seating. a. Sofa with single loose seat cushion, tight back, and exposed wood legs; b. Chair with loose seat cushion, loose back cushion, and skirt; c. Chair with loose seat cushion, tight back, and exposed wood legs.

the workmanship and materials and the attention to numerous details determine the comfort and beauty of these generally high-priced goods. There is also a range in the amount of customization. Some workrooms use standardized frames constructed of one type of wood, in certain sizes, that may be finished with any number of stains or textures. However, there may be only a few choices for the fill (stuffing) of cushions, seat, back, arms, and headrests. Or, the customization may be virtually limitless, from frame to passementerie, meaning the designer will need to make many more choices. Figure 10.37a and b illustrates some of the materials and tools used to create a custom piece.

Process Especially for customized goods, the upholstering process may take more than three months because of the many stages involved in construction of the frame, fill, and cushion. Quality workrooms will invite the designer and client to sit in the upholstered chair, wrapped in muslin, prior to the application of the fabric. This allows for changes to be made in the shape and padding before the finished piece is delivered.

Frame The frame for high-end furniture is typically made of hardwood, such as ash or maple for durability. The wood is kiln dried to prevent warping and joined with dowels and glue (not stapled), using corner blocks, for solidly braced construction. The **deck** is the platform, steel springs, and padding structures that support the seat cushions. In **eight-way hand-tied coil spring construction**, considered the traditional

upholstery method, cords are intertwined or knotted to stabilize the construction (Figure 10.37c). Dining and occasional chairs do not generally use this type of construction; instead, elastic webbing strips are used over the fill.

The term **batting** refers to the filling material. In the past, horse or hog hairs were used, but today batting is typically a blend of polyester fibers. To prevent the springs from penetrating the batting, **webbing** made of burlap, in a basket-weave pattern, is laid over the springs.

Both seat and back cushions may be constructed as part of the frame, known as tight back, or they may be unattached and loose. Seating that is modern in style or used in contract spaces is more likely to have a tight back, because it requires less maintenance (such as fluffing, to retain the original cushion form, or profile).

The fiber content of the fill must be identified on a label provided by the manufacturer. The choice of cushion fill depends on the user's budget, proneness to allergies, and preference for resiliency and maintenance. Down is the fluffiest, softest, most expensive type of fill. It comes from the innermost feathers of waterfowl, generally geese. Down is often mixed with other feathers, both to lower the cost of the fill and to provide additional shape retention.

The back cushions of high-end quality seating commonly use a 50 percent down, 50 percent feather combination (50/50 ratio) that combines the softness of down and the resiliency of feathers. Combinations of 75/25 or 80/20, down to feather, are more expensive and require more fluffing of pillows and cushions to

a   b   c

Figure 10.37
a. Many materials such as horsehair, webbing, and twine are used in upholstering furniture; b. An upholsterer's specialized tools; c. The upholstery process. *(c: Courtesy of Gary Buxbaum)*

maintain shape. Many people are allergic to down and feathers; for these clients, cushions made of a foam rubber core are available. The cushion is wrapped with muslin or Dacron (polyester) and foam for further shape retention. For modern and sleek styles, and for contract use, standard seat cushions are composed of 50 percent foam and 50 percent down. As a guide, the more foam to down or feather, the firmer the cushions will be.

Categories and Styles Upholstered goods are often categorized as seating. Upholstered seating for both contract and residential use includes many styles and configurations. Some examples are two- and three-seat sofa, club chair, recliner, rocker, swivel chair (high and low back), sectional or modular sofa, love seat or settee, sleeper, chaise longue or daybed, ottoman or hassock, bench, occasional chairs (which may also be dining room or task chairs), stools, and banquettes (i.e., built-in dining seating). Upholstered seating includes styles with and without arms (Figure 10.38a–f).

Types of upholstered furniture may be given very specific names by manufacturers; however, some universally applied terms are also used. Three basic styles of seating are described by the following terms: **Lawson** has its arm height lower than the back height, whereas **tuxedo** has its arm height the same as the back height. A **Chesterfield** is a type of tuxedo, often upholstered in leather, with the back and inside of the arm rests **tufted**, that is, quilted and buttoned.

Upholstered seating may feature various treatments of the arms, legs, and frame. Rolled and flared arm seating adds to the overall dimension of the length of the piece without increasing the seating area. The amount of roll or flare may be minimal or exaggerated. Exposed frame or leg seating, or a combination, shows the nonupholstered portions of the piece. Typically, the metal or wood frame is finished in some way, such as by staining, painting, or gilding. Leg types include tapered, bun foot, and fabric covered.

Upholstery detailing is the phase that refines, or defines, the individualized character of the seating (as with window treatments). This detailing involves many design decisions and typically increases the cost of the goods considerably because of the labor involved and the materials selected. Some commonly used upholstery details are gimp, welt (including self-welt, contrasting welt, and double welt), quilting (including channel stitching and box stitching), nail heads, and skirting (including dressmaker and box pleat).

Figure 10.38
Upholstered seating styles and detailing. a. Recliner; b. Sectional sofa; c. Three-seat sofa; d. Love seat; e. Chaise lounge; f. Daybed.
(a–f: Courtesy of Restoration Hardware)

FIXTURES, EQUIPMENT, AND APPLIANCES

A substantial portion of these product categories also relate to kitchens, baths, and laundry rooms. Many artists and designers have partnered with manufacturers of bath and kitchen products to produce a wide variety of standard and customized products and systems that combine art and science. Many of these products are designed with energy efficiency in mind, as their use in both residential and contract projects accounts for a significant use of resources. A major governmental program in the United States that has proved useful in this regard has been the establishment of the Energy Star label on appliances (Figure 10.39). This is a joint venture of the Environmental Protection Agency (EPA) and the U.S. Department of Energy. The label allows the consumer to compare energy usage in conjunction with the associated costs. Since the inception of this program, greenhouse emissions have been substantially reduced and cost savings obtained, including tax credits for businesses and homeowners.

Kitchen

The basic functions to be accommodated in kitchen planning are food preparation, food and supply storage, cooking, refrigeration, washing and cleanup, garbage disposal, and ventilation (see Chapter 5). Additionally, many residential kitchens are large enough to accommodate serving and dining, household (or at least menu) management, audiovisual entertainment, and wine storage.

The essential fixtures and appliances required for a basic residential kitchen include sink, dishwasher, wall and base cabinets, counter surface, refrigerator, freezer, waste disposal, oven (conventional, convection, microwave), cooktop (electric or gas), and exhaust system. With recycling regulations in place in many communities, the design of recycling units in residential kitchens approaches a design sub-specialty. The placement and adequacy of electrical outlets for kitchen appliances are also important considerations.

A residential kitchen today may feature many of the accoutrements of the commercial or restaurant kitchen, such as multiple ovens and various foods preparation stations (Figure 10.40). Kitchen designs that offer ergonomic alternatives to the use of standard fixtures and layout are also available (Figure 10.41). Perhaps a countertrend to the expansive, commercial-like residential kitchen is the smaller, efficiency-style kitchen that maximizes space. Manufacturers of even luxury-level appliances are responding to the appeal of more efficient space planning by producing scaled-down versions of their high-quality lines (Figure 10.42).

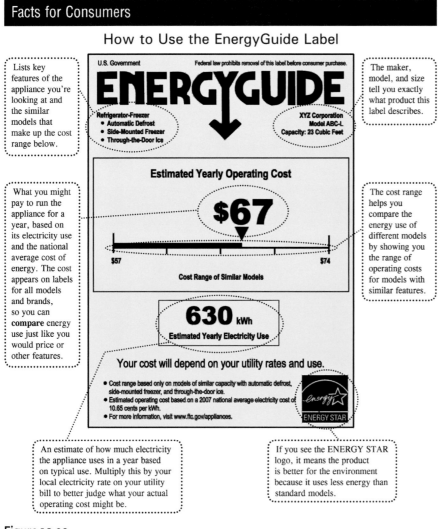

Figure 10.39
Energy Star label guidelines for appliances, for consumer use. (© *http://www.ftc.gov/bcp/edu/pubs/consumer/homes/rea14.shtm*)

Figure 10.40
Residential kitchen with several food preparation stations.
(Photography by Phillip Ennis)

Figure 10.41
Ergonomically designed kitchen. Snaidero's Acropolis, by
designer Paolo Pininfarina. This circular arrangement goes well
beyond the kitchen triangle concept to function as a command
center for the home. *(Pininfarina Design by Snaidero)*

Figure 10.42
Luxury style for an efficiency-sized galley kitchen. *(© General
Electric Co.)*

Appliances for the cooling and storing of wine are no
longer limited to the very grand-scale interiors and
may be found in these more modest-sized spaces.
Another growing trend is the outdoor kitchen. No longer just limited to a grill for barbeques, outdoor space
from large-scale to small patios may be used for cooking and entertainment areas (Figure 10.43).

In addition to residential and large-scale commercial kitchens for hospitality (see later discussion), interior designers may be responsible for small kitchens
and employee eating areas for more-modest-scale contract projects.

Bath

Some of the most basic human activities are carried out
in the bathroom. Bath areas, depending on one's lifestyle, may also include activities related to relaxation
and rejuvenation of the mind and spirit as well as the
body. The art of the bath is a tradition of Japanese culture that has had a significant influence on the modern
view of the bath as an oasis from stress (Figure 10.44).

The bath sink basin is an opportunity for the artisan
to make a statement of sculpture and art. The aesthetic

Figure 10.43
Outdoor kitchen. (© *General Electric Co.*)

a

Figure 10.44
Bathroom as oasis inspired by Japanese design. (*Photography by Daniel Aubry, designed by Clodagh*)

of the pedestal sink also serves as a decorative statement (Figure 10.45a and b). However, barrier-free design and sustainability play major roles in the designer's decision making for both residential and public bathrooms.

A well-designed bathroom incorporates ergonomic appliances, water-saving features for toilets and

b

Figure 10.45
Bath aesthetics. a. Detailed sink basin; b. Sculptural pedestal sink. (*a: © Sherle Wagner International; b: © BATi [PT Dharma Bati Bali, Indonesia], Product design: Marina Pandunata, Raja and BATi are registered of PT Dharma Bati Bali. www.batibali.com*)

Figure 10.46

A well-designed, accessible, bathroom can also be aesthetically designed. (© *Corbis Premium RF / Alamy*)

sinks, safety measures to control water temperature, and accessible bathing areas (Figure 10.46).

The importance of water conservation is being taken seriously by many manufacturers of bath fixtures. According to TOTO, a major global plumbing manufacturer, toilets consume more than 26 percent of a household's water resources; the average American family of four flushes more than 16 times per day.[4] Dual-flush systems allow for different waste disposal needs. Other high-tech toilets incorporate features such as heated seats and bidet attachments.

SPECIAL CONTRACT DESIGN CONSIDERATIONS

Office

Designing commercial office interiors poses complex challenges and is often thought of as an area of special expertise. This is due in part to the increase in regulatory controls involved with contract design and public spaces. Although many changes and trends that affect contract design also influence residential design,

including advances in computer technology, the complex organizational structure of companies may require specific knowledge in the areas of industrial psychology and group dynamics.

Contemporary companies usually organize their office spaces into open-plan landscapes. This calls for large areas to be zoned by using cubicles or workstations, rather than distinct rooms, for employees. Furnishings include panels, screens, partitions, shelving, storage, and accessories. Most cubicle systems are designed to provide flexibility in configuration, enabling them to accommodate many types of job functioning as well as the extensive wiring required for computer and communications equipment. Space planning in the work environment involves significant programming (see Chapter 5). It involves considerations of individual work, teamwork, conferencing, and training as well as corporate culture, hierarchy, and status, all of which influence the extent of open versus closed space (discussed in Chapter 13) (Figure 10.47a–d). Audiovisual equipment and the related support systems are yet another specialty in the design community.

Despite computerization, the "paperless office" is not yet a reality for most businesses. Therefore, filing and storage of hard copy remain crucial concerns for the interior designer. Standardized lateral and vertical filing cabinets continue to meet these storage needs.

Many offices still use distinct, enclosed spaces for certain activities, notably, executive offices, conferencing, reception, and support services (mail, maintenance, and so on). A special type of furniture used in office design is the **credenza**. Similar to the server or buffet used in residential dining spaces, the office credenza is used as a work surface and storage piece. Particularly when manufactured in wood, it may be part of an executive office suite of furniture. In addition to a sizable desk and ergonomically appropriate swivel chair, executive offices typically are furnished with tables and chairs for at least two visitors, or even a sofa. These items may be freestanding or combined in modular units (Figure 10.48).

Retail

Retailers require an array of equipment and furnishings, including fixtures for displaying merchandise and cash/wrap stations. The scope of the retail establishment, from small boutiques to immense shopping

Figure 10.47

Modular workstations. a–d. The Ethospace System, designed by Jack Kelley and Bill Stumpf for Herman Miller, features variety and control, including personalized screens. *(a–d: © Herman Miller, Inc.)*

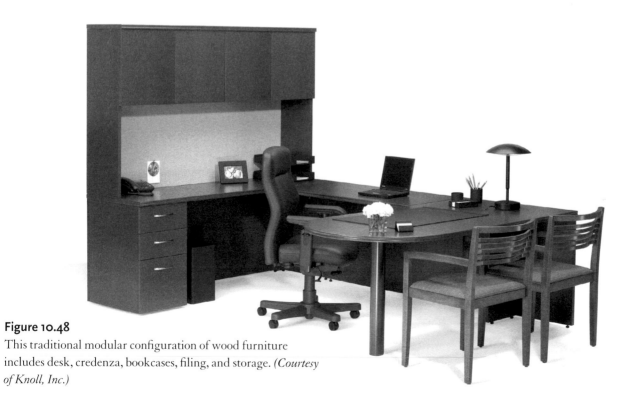

Figure 10.48

This traditional modular configuration of wood furniture includes desk, credenza, bookcases, filing, and storage. *(Courtesy of Knoll, Inc.)*

Figure 10.49
Retail Design. a. Fixtures and furnishings for a traditional men's clothing store; b. Contemporary retail design. (© *Callison Architecture, Inc.; b: Designer: Garry Cohn, Company: Garry Cohn for Douglas Wallace*)

malls, will influence many of the designer's decisions about furnishings. In addition to understanding the flow of customer traffic, inventory storage, lighting needs, and so on, the designer needs to consider the overall experience of the consumer in the space. Often, customized display fixtures are required to highlight product and increase brand awareness.

Retail pop-up stores (see Chapter 5) and trade show exhibits present challenges different from those of the permanent, brick-and-mortar store. Although these spaces may disappear within a matter of days, companies will invest in their design and installation to positively impact sales (Figure 10.49a and b).

Health Care

Health-care settings require textiles and other materials that provide safe and sanitary finishes; these facilities also require specialty furniture, appliances, and equipment. The needs may include equipment and furniture for nurse stations; medical, dental, surgical, and laboratory equipment; medical waste disposal; laundry and supply facilities; and storage facilities (Figure 10.50).

An important component for patient welfare and recovery is the attention given to the comfort and convenience of the person's visitors and care providers. Staff well-being is vital in the health-care industry. Caregiv-

Figure 10.50
Hospital command center. (© *Kumar Sriskandan / Alamy*)

ers, especially nurses, often experience high levels of work-related stress. Health-care systems arc recognizing that patient outcomes can be linked to the level of stress experienced by staff members. It is therefore important to provide health-care workers with opportunities for respite from their busy, physically and emotionally demanding routines. Through flexible options designed for differing work modes, the environment can improve both the staff's sense of well-being and their level of performance. Creating spaces with visual connectivity and opportunity for interaction promotes knowledge sharing, teamwork, and impromptu meetings. Transparent team rooms adjacent to nurses' stations encourage focused collaboration and provide a space for quiet, individual work (Figure 10.51a–c).

Hospitality

One of the essential design aspects of restaurants is the setup of a commercial kitchen. This requires very specialized knowledge because of the complexities of operation, statutory requirements relating to safety and health codes, and range of equipment available. The designer collaborates not only with the restaurant owners, but also with the chefs. The number of sections for specialized tasks depends on the nature of the restaurant or dining facility. Among the typical sections are hot food, salad and dessert, bakery, banquet, and short order. Within each of these sections are specialized stations, such as those for frying and broiling (Figure 10.52).

As with retail, the experience of the restaurant customer is very much influenced by the design of the space as well as the selection of furnishings, lighting, and acoustics. The mood for casual, informal dining will obviously be very different from the experience expected at an upscale, romantic restaurant.

The lodging industry is composed of many different types of accommodations, from facilities for extended stays that approach residential design, to destination resort spas. The selection and specifying of furnishings will be dependent on the nature of the lodging. For instance, an interior designer working on a resort spa project may be expected to furnish a beauty salon, massage therapy rooms, and a fitness center. A small, boutique hotel requires an approach different from that called for at a large-scale chain hotel. The capsule room, yet another lodging type in densely popular cities such as Tokyo, requires still other solutions (Figure 10.53a–c).

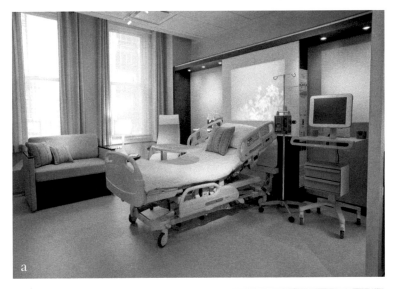

Figure 10.51

a: Inpatient hospital room; b. Caretaker lounge; c. Transparent team rooms adjacent to nurse workstations, Halifax Medical Center in Daytona Beach, Florida. *(a and b: Courtesy of Nurture by Steelcase; c: Courtesy of www.mcgowanofficeequipment.com)*

Figure 10.52
Commercial kitchen. *(© Roy Lawe / Alamy)*

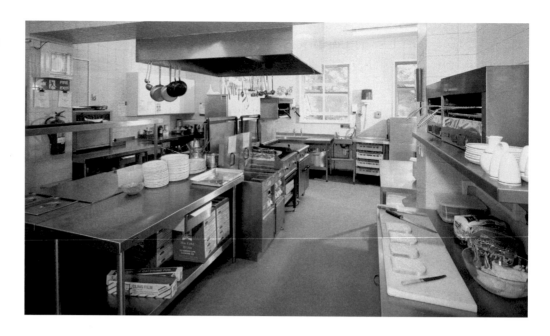

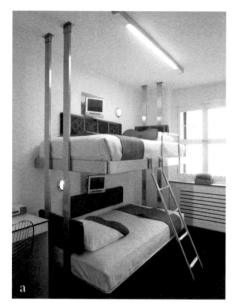

Figure 10.53
Types of hotel rooms. a. Boutique hotel for the thrifty traveler: Pod Hotel, New York City; b. Chairman's Suite, Ritz-Carlton Hotel, Shanghai, China; c. Capsule hotel, Tokyo, Japan. *(a: Courtesy The Pod Hotel; b: Courtesy of The Portman Ritz-Carlton, Shanghai, Photographer: Mr. Chris Cypert; c: © Chad Ehlers / Alamy)*

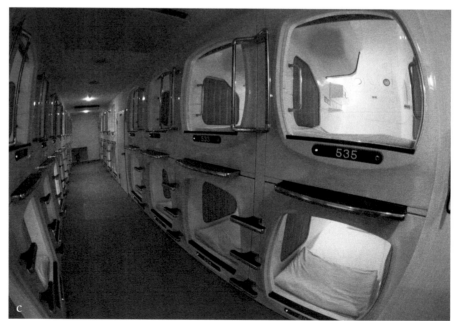

STORAGE, HARDWARE, AND SIGNAGE

Storage

Items such as books, audiovisual gear, computer equipment, office and desk supplies, toys, sports and hobby equipment, materials for art and music activities, toiletries, and table and bath linens may require storage. This may entail the use of stock items or customized pieces developed with input from the interior designer.

Storage and closet design is an industry related to interior design. It is not uncommon for students or graduates of interior design school to work in this field; they bring artistry and skill in addition to a keen sense of organization and knowledge of anthropometrics, ergonomics, and space planning. These are valuable assets for both the residential and the contract designer. Creative and innovative methods of storage are demonstrated in Figure 10.54a.

Designers may conceive of extensive millwork for closets or other items (Figure 10.54b). Designers of children's spaces often devise clever ways to store toys, craft supplies, books, and other treasures. Adaptability is also important when designing for children, as a child's needs may change before the child changes location. Accessibility to storage, its height for example, also needs to be considered for users with other special needs such as those in wheelchairs, or difficulty bending and reaching.

Hardware

Hardware is sometimes considered part of the architectural plan for a project (see Chapter 8). This industry continues to explore creative designs geared toward providing universal design solutions as well as a range of decorative styles and new materials. This category encompasses door, drawer, and cabinet pulls and handles; levers; locks; towel bars; grab bars; and coat hooks; among other items.

Manufacturers have been able to create products that, although functional in nature, are also artistic, even in the mass-produced categories. Other companies, considered semicustom and custom, produce hardware sometimes described as jewelry for the home, in

Figure 10.54
a. Customized closets as a design element in a contemporary space; b. Carefully designed millwork for a bedroom that stores and displays client's collection of antique quilts. *(a: Senzafine Walk-in Closet by Poliform Spa; b: © Interior Design by Barbara Sternau Interior Design)*

Figure 10.55
Hardware as jewelry by SA Baxter. *(Courtesy of SA Baxter)*

numerous finishes (Figure 10.55). Attention to engineering details and ergonomics creates user-friendly mechanisms, such as the accessible shelf of the kitchen cabinet in Figure 10.56.

Hardware for draperies (Figure 10.57) is another major sector of this product category, as are fireplace accoutrements.

Signage

Generally the purview of the contract interior designer rather than the residential designer, this category of accessory includes the array of signs used to identify spaces, exit plans, exits, location, directions, directories, and other instructions. Signage should be integrated into the concept and form of the architecture of the space. Compliance with ADA standards, addressing concerns such as raised text, Braille, and installation requirements, is also a consideration. Placement of signage is dependent on circulation patterns within the space as well as entry and exit. Fire safety regulations also play a role in the specifying of signage products to ensure efficient evacuation in case of emergency.

The importance of helping to direct inhabitant and occupant way-finding was discussed in Chapter 2. Pictograms (known as universal symbols) are included in this product category. Although pictograms are considered universal, geography and culture do influence how comprehensible these signs may truly be. Compare Figures 10.58 and 10.59.

In addition, the interior designer may be asked to collaborate with graphic designers to create a corporate identity or brand, which is then further conveyed through business brochures, stationery, logos, menus, or a combination of these.

Figure 10.56
Hardware designed with ergonomics in mind. *(Courtesy of Kohler)*

Figure 10.57
Drapery hardware. *(Courtesy of Continental Window Fashions)*

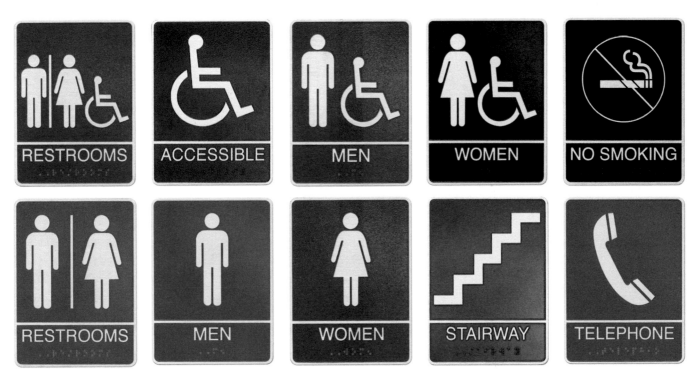

Figure 10.58
Universal signage: ADA signs (United States). *(Courtesy of SignWire Worldwide, Inc.)*

Figure 10.59
Universal signage: Tikal, Guatemala, Mayan ruins signage.
(Provided by the Author)

ACCESSORIES

Although often treated as an afterthought to projects, choosing accessories may be one of the more satisfying steps in the design process. This is true when clients incorporate their own personal collection, whether it is art of considerable financial or sentimental value, or photos, or other mementos. Design includes form and function, and although accessories may be subordinate to the essential functioning of the space, they fulfill other needs, notably, emotional nurturance and the longing to be surrounded by beauty and beloved objects.

Objects may be considered as solitary focal points of emphasis or unifying themes to harmonize a design concept. Often, items are part of a grouping or a collection. The design concepts learned by the interior designer (see Chapter 3) are translated into the ability to arrange the elements into a satisfying composition.

The role of the interior designer may be simply to arrange art and other accessories previously owned by the client. Or, the designer may be called on to consider a full range of accessories to carry out the overall design concept. Some projects, especially those involving corporate headquarters or the hospitality industry, may require the designer to collaborate with art consultants for the purchase, lease, design, or installation of original art. Many large corporations acquire art collections, and the interior designer may be involved in these decisions.

Accessories may be antique, antique reproductions, or contemporary objects, machine or handmade. Furnishings and finishes can also be thought of

Figure 10.60
Large-scale installation of customized mosaic tile for a restaurant, Bar Lodi, in Lodi, Italy. (© *Flo Smith / Alamy*)

as accessories. These include the lighting fixtures that serve largely for accent light; millwork, such as wall paneling; faux finishing techniques on walls and ceilings; mosaic tile work (Figure 10.60); and the passementerie used for upholstered furniture and draperies.

Some accessories, such as paintings and sculpture, may be purely decorative and aesthetic; other types of accessories also serve useful functions. In the final chapter of *The Decoration of Houses*, Edith Wharton discusses bric-a-brac as the nonessentials. She warns of the modern temptation to embellish interiors with trifles, knickknacks, and articles of small value, rather than true objets d'art. She divides accessories (bric-a-brac), or minor embellishments, into two main classifications: the object of art per se, such as the bust, the picture, or the vase, and those articles useful in themselves—lamps, clocks, fire screens, book bindings, and candelabra—which art has only to touch to make them the best ornaments any room can contain.[5]

Figure 10.61
Contemporary art used in a residential interior serves as a focal point. (*Photoshot/Redcover/Henry Wilson*)

Despite some arguable boundaries and the dual purposes (aesthetic and practical) served by many accessories, this remains a useful distinction.

Objets d'Art

Fine art may be two- or three-dimensional. Two-dimensional art includes a wide variety of media, notably paintings, drawings, prints, and photography, which are generally hung on walls (Figure 10.61). Although paintings and drawings are one-of-a-kind pieces, prints and photography, like reproductions of original art, are usually produced in multiples. Nonetheless, for the furnishing of an interior, the decorative value may be the determining factor for selection rather than the medium or the uniqueness of the piece (*FYI . . . Tips for Arranging Wall Art*).

- *Painting* (or "picture," as the term is used by Wharton) is the category of art that relies on the application of a pigment medium to a flat surface. The surface may be a stretched canvas, a wall (mural), fiberboard, wood, glass, or

FYI ... Tips for Arranging Wall Art

Figure a
Arrangement of art by interior designer Glenn Gissler. *(Design: Glenn Gissler; Photo: Gross & Daley)*

- The design principles of balance, proportion, contrast, rhythm, and harmony apply when arranging wall art.
- Lighting should be positioned in such a way as to avoid glare. Illumination should enhance the art. Plexiglass may be used instead of glass in framed art; although it is subject to possible scratching, it will not cause glare.
- Pictures should be arranged so that there is at least one relatively uniform horizontal and vertical plane.
- The amount of space should be in proportion to the composition. Too much space between pictures in a grouping will make it lack cohesiveness and harmony. Leave enough room—often two inches—for the pictures to visually breathe. On the other hand, too little space may create a dense, suffocating feeling.
- Use the heavy visual weight of deep or ornate frames, dark images, and dark mats with lighter elements to achieve equilibrium. Plan the arrangement using both the central vertical and horizontal axes to achieve balance.
- With formal, symmetrical groupings that have a theme or specific subject matter, plan for some variety or contrast. Mix the shape of the frames, or provide contrast between the images and the framing.
- Groupings reflect the architecture—the shape and dimension of the wall. A relationship should exist between art and architecture, regardless of whether a grouping or a single piece of art is used. The space dictates the size of the art. Similarly, the mat and frame are dictated by the art.
- A general rule is to hang wall art close to the standard horizon or viewing level, at approximately five feet. However, in areas where sitting is the principal activity (such as in a dining room), this may need to be altered. It is usually better to hang art lower than higher since diners' eye level at seating is lower.
- In groupings, the general rule is to hang larger pictures above smaller ones.
- To prevent the artwork from shifting, it is best to use at least two nails for each piece.
- Although interior designers may be comfortable doing the installation of the wall art, it may be advisable to secure the services of an art installer. Not only are they knowledgeable about wall construction and the appropriate hardware and tools to use, but they are also insured against damage to either the art or the walls.

textile. The choice of pigment and medium may be oil, water, acrylic, or gouache (a type of tempera that is a mixture of egg and water).

- *Drawings* may be divided by type based on the medium used, the surface chosen, and the application technique. Paper is the most common surface, and ink, pencil, and charcoal are common media. Drawings may be black and white or include color. Some are studies for paintings or sketches; others are intended to be finished pieces.
- *Printing* is the technique whereby an original image is replicated in multiples, or editions. The volume of multiples depends on the specific technique used. However, to have value as original fine art, prints are reproduced in a limited number, rather than by a photographic manufacturing process that can provide a virtually limitless number of copies.
- *Bas relief* is a form of sculpture in which forms or figures are projected from a flat background.
- Additional wall art categories include *fiber art* and *textile art*, such as tapestries, quilts, folded-and-cut paper, ceramic tile, and collage, a type of mixed media that uses paper as one medium.

Three-Dimensional Art

Sculpture is the most common three-dimensional art. As with two-dimensional art, the choice of material and technique is important in determining the style of the piece. Realistic (representational), stylized, or abstract forms may be rendered in metal, stone, glass, paper, plastic, resin, fiber, wood, or mixed media. Depending on the scale and application, sculpture may be placed on shelves, pedestals, or the floor or attached to walls or ceiling.

Found objects, generally architectural remains, may also serve as three-dimensional art. Furniture is often a way that an artist, designer, or architect communicates an idea or new direction for design (Figure 10.62). Sometimes, an artist's creation of furniture as art becomes the prototype for pieces to be manufactured.

Useful Objects

The designer can make a significant contribution to the appearance and function of a space by providing

Figure 10.62
Furniture as art. *(Photo by Margot Geist for © Mark Levin, Lewin Studio)*

input on the choice, placement, display, and storage of these objects, which are elements of most interiors.

Display An important consideration when accessories are to be taken seriously is how to display them. Among the many ways to display objects is in a piece of furniture termed a **curio cabinet**. The word *curio*, short for "curiosity," dates to mid-19th-century Victorian England (see Chapter 12), a period when travel to faraway places became more feasible for the middle and upper classes. People would bring back unusual or exotic objects as mementos of their trip, creating the need for furnishings to display these possessions.

Mirrors Originally called looking glasses, mirrors (in addition to being useful for personal reflection) are often used to enlarge interior spaces and expand the vista, as with the use of a mirror within a window frame. Varieties of mirrors include tile, framed, chevalier, beveled, antiqued (veined), and Venetian. Mirrors may enhance a sleek, modern interior or complement a traditional one (Figure 10.63).

Clocks In addition to telling time, clocks may become pieces of furniture, such as the case clock (sometimes sentimentally called a grandfather or grandmother clock, depending on the height). Others clocks, such as the mantel clock, are ornamental or, like the cuckoo clock, amusing.

Figure 10.63
Mirror-encrusted halls in home of the Maharaja of Jaipur, India.
(© Lebedinski / Dreamstime.com)

Screens Screens can be decorative as well as functional (Figure 10.64a and b). Their relationship to use as a division of space, and with window and door treatments, was discussed in Chapters 5 and 9. The shoji screen transmits light and has the added benefits of providing privacy and zoning. Another type of screen, the **Coromandel**, is named after a type of ebony from the coastal area of Mumbai, India, that is often used to construct it. This wooden screen is lacquered and decorated with Oriental motifs and scenes and serves not only as a space divider, but also as a sculptural accessory.

Decorative Arts

Decorative arts is a catchall term, similar to *applied art* or *craft*, often used in contrast to the *fine arts*. Throughout history, artisans, craftspeople, and designers have developed the skills to work with one or several materials to create objects that are both useful and decorative

a

b

Figure 10.64
Screens. a. Coromandel; b. Alvar Aalto screen. *(a: Provided by Lawerance & Scott Inc., Seattle, Washington; b: Screen 100 by Alvar Aalto. Courtesy of Artek oy ab)*

and that are generally intended for domestic use. What may be an everyday object when mass-produced by machine may be a luxury item when handcrafted.

The term *folk art* denotes the work of artists with less formal training. Arts and crafts techniques are passed down from generation to generation rather than studied in school. Similarly, the term *outsider art* denotes art that is produced by persons not generally associated with the artist communities in society, but rather, individuals with unique innate talents and expressions. Many of these untrained artists are discovered in prisons, mental institutions, and other non-mainstream situations. Appreciation of both folk and outsider art has increased, as have the prices paid for these works.

Among the major classifications of the decorative arts are objects made from ceramic, glass, metal, wood, and textiles.

Ceramics This is the general term used to describe items produced from potter's clay, whether purely decorative, functional, or both, such as table service and vases (Figure 10.65a–c). Ceramic ware may be constructed by hand techniques, such as pinch and coil, molded, or wheel thrown. Several types are differentiated, based on the firing method, clay body, and glazes used.

- *Art pottery* implies fine, highly ornamental wares decorated by hand.
- *Bisque* is an unglazed piece of pottery that has been fired once.
- *Porcelain*, also referred to as *hard-paste* or *true porcelain*, is translucent and glasslike and contains kaolin. Soft-paste porcelain contains powdered glass.
- *Bone china* is a type of porcelain made by mixing bone ash with clay.
- *Ironstone* is heavy white earthenware or clay that contains the mineral feldspar for strength.
- *Stoneware* is durable and waterproof and contains powdered rock. It is used for crocks and jugs. A typical example is salt-glazed, produced when handfuls of salt are tossed into the hot kiln.
- *Slip* is an opaque glaze made by thinning clay with water. It is then applied by hand dripping on the piece for decoration.

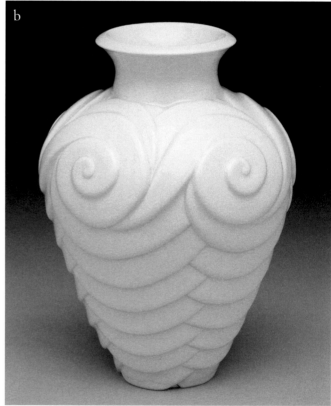

Figure 10.65
a, b, and c. Contemporary line of ceramic vessels by Lynne Meade. (*a, b, and c: Designs by Lynne Meade. Photos © George Post*)

Figure 10.66

Glass. a. Antique glass objects made from various techniques; b. A contemporary chandelier by Dale Chihuly; c. Leaded glass screen. *(a: © Exactostock / SuperStock; b: © Dale Chihuly; c: Dick Weiss, Rondels blown by Sonia Blomdahl)*

- *Majolica* wares are tin glazed and ornamented with colorful designs.
- *Faience* is earthenware glazed with a tin-based slip. It is often decorated with hand-painted motifs.

Glass The use of glass for decorative and functional purposes dates back thousands of years (Figure 10.66a–c). Various minerals may compose the glass body, such as silicate, flux (metal), potash, flint, and lead and tin oxides. Glass may be manufactured and finished or decorated in several ways. Two primary methods are free blown and mold blown (pressed). Among the types of glassware, both historic and contemporary, are the following:

- *Crystal* is a heavy, clear glass with a substantial lead content. It is usually cut, or faceted, called cut glass or lead crystal.
- *Etched* and *engraved glass* is decorated, like prints, with designs carved out of the glass using an instrument.
- *Leaded glass* is usually found in the form of windowpanes or decorative pieces made of glass parts fused together with lead. When stained with colors, like the windows of a church, it is often referred to as *stained glass*.
- *Pressed glass* refers to machine-manufactured glass as well as a style of old-fashioned glass in many patterns.
- *Art glass*, similar to art pottery, is a quality, handmade product of an artist or designer.
- *Murano* (*Venetian*) *glass* is named for the location in Italy that has continually produced quality blown glass for more than 1,000 years.

Metal More than any other metal, silver is used for fine, formal tableware; candlesticks; and serving pieces. Other metals, such as pewter, copper, chrome, aluminum, and brass, are worked for table, toiletry, and service objects. These, in addition to lead and iron, are used to create other household accessories, including fireplace equipment, such as andirons, tools, and screens. Metals are worked and finished in several ways to produce both decorative and functional objects. They may be hand wrought, cast, fused together through hot methods such as welding and soldering, or riveted.

As with printmaking and ceramic ware, metal objects may be finished with etching or engraving as decorative techniques. They may be polished, filed, carved, or oxidized to alter the patina. A base metal may be plated with another or combined with one that would create an alloy (Figure 10.67a and b). Some common terms associated with metal are defined below.

- *Sterling silver* is a fine-quality metal that combines a high ratio of pure silver to a small ratio of copper. The British system classifies sterling as 925 parts pure silver to 75 parts copper.
- *Silver plate* objects also combine pure silver with copper, but in a less costly manner. Generally, the copper and silver are fused together.
- *Hammered metal* is a decorative technique used on copper, brass, and aluminum that creates a dimpling effect by the use of a hammer.

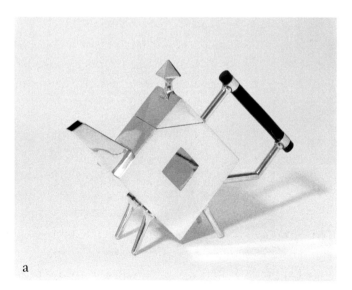

Figure 10.67

Metals, *Then and Now*. a. Electroplated silver teapot designed by Christopher Dresser, manufactured by Sheffield, 1880; b. Chrome teakettle by Michael Graves for Alessi, 1985. *(a: Dresser, Christopher [1834–1904]. Geometric teapot. Made by James Dixon & Sons, Electroplate. Sheffield, England, 1880. Photo credit: V & A Images, London / Art Resource, New York; b: "Whistling Bird Teakettle" courtesy Michael Graves Design Group)*

- *Chased metal* resembles engraved metal. One example, called repoussé, is an embossed relief.
- *Enameling* involves the application of a decorative finish of colored ground glass powders to a metal surface before firing. Cloisonné is one type of fine enamelware.
- *Graniteware (enamelware)* is produced by dipping iron or steel objects in a glaze made from quartz, borax, and feldspar and then firing them. This technique provided affordable substitutes for porcelain in the 19th and early 20th centuries.

Wood In addition to its importance as a material for building, millwork, and furniture, wood is used for many decorative objects, including candlesticks, vases, music boxes, and tableware. It may be carved, or whittled, into sculptures and tools or turned to create decorative and functional objects, such as bowls, which are then painted or stained. Some of the more collectible objets d'art and useful items are listed below.

- *Tramp art* is a woodcraft that dates back to 19th-century European immigrants to the United States and Canada. It is a form of folk art characterized by layered, chip-carved, notched decorations created with simple tools, such as pocketknives, and made from wood scraps and used wooden cigar boxes (Figure 10.68).
- *Marquetry* is a type of woodwork in which thin pieces of varied rare woods are applied as a veneer layer in a design motif on the surface of a wood piece. It has an appearance similar to that of parquet floors (see Chapter 9).
- *Burl* is a distorted grain in the surface of the wood that may be used as a veneer or solid wood for decorative objects. Its sinuous pattern is innately decorative.

Fibers Textiles are the mainstay of the bath and table linen industries. Antique and contemporary textiles may also serve as versatile vehicles for the expression of ideas. This category includes both fabrics and papers and combinations of the two, some of which are used as wall art. Woven fiber baskets, although functional, may also serve as a wall arrangement, as shown in the

Figure 10.68
A form of folk art, tramp art has transcended its original practical use and has become prized collectibles. *(Smithsonian American Art Museum, Washington, D.C., Hemphill/Art Resource, New York)*

hospitality installation in Figure 10.69a. Although tapestries and rugs traditionally have served to provide insulation and cushioning, they undoubtedly continue to serve as decorative art.

Techniques for production and application of textile and fiber decorative arts vary regionally and by style. Among the many significant decorative art techniques are needlework and quilting.

- *Needlework*, historically a skill learned by women, produces many types of decorated textiles for domestic use. Among them are embroidery, needlepoint, crewel, lace, cross-stitch, sampler, and beadwork.
- *Quilting* is an activity that is associated with American ingenuity, practicality, and social custom. It began as a craft whereby groups of women worked together to make bed linens out of scraps of printed cotton fabrics. Antique quilts featuring patterns passed down from generation to generation are now prized as

Figure 10.69

a. South African interior designer Stephen Falcke's installation of native baskets for the Saxon Hotel; b. Quilting represents not only a textile art but also a cultural expression, as in the work of the women from rural Gee's Bend, Selma, Alabama; c. Fiber art created from recycled fabric scraps in Cape Town, South Africa; d. Mielie Workshops, Cape Town, South Africa, founder Ardit Shutz.

(a: © National Geographic Image Collection / Alamy; b: Quilts of Fees Bend; c: © Edward Addeo. All rights reserved; d: Credit: Courtesy of Mielie)

a

b

c

d

wall art (Figure 10.69b). Similarly, women's groups have formed in various countries to create textile products that combine traditional methods with contemporary taste (Figure 10.69c–d).

Products for Bed, Bath, and Table A substantial component of the interiors market for both residential and commercial projects is the category of bed, bath, and table accessories. These items often play a major role in portraying a client's lifestyle.

Many of these products overlap with those in the areas of textiles and decorative arts. Institutional and hospitality sectors, in particular, require that

high-performance standards be maintained for these finished goods. Consideration of safety, comfort, laundering, and life-cycle costs is important when specifying these products. However, interior designers need to balance such considerations with aesthetic objectives; they need to weigh the items' decorative attributes. A wide range of products is available in both the trade and retail sectors. Fully customized items, particularly for textile products, are available to meet highly individualized requirements and tastes. The textile products for these categories are generally produced by the workrooms that make custom window treatments and upholstered furniture. Some manufacturers feature coordinated products (Figure 10.70). Or,

Figure 10.70
Coordinated bed linens in standard dimensions, including different types of pillow and bed coverings. *(Courtesy of Restoration Hardware)*

designers may be involved in creating custom coordinated goods, such as designs for beds.

Not all interior designers will be involved in the details of purchasing these accessories. However, given the extensive range of products marketed to clients as lifestyle essentials, residential designers can offer a useful service by helping edit these choices, even if they are not directly involved in purchasing them.

Flowers, Plants, and Other Natural Products The interior designer is often called on to furnish these items for both residential and contract clients during the design process, for special events, or even for regularly scheduled periods (e.g., specific holidays or other annual celebrations). Beyond the visual pleasures offered by nature, other sensory experiences can be enhanced, for example, through the pleasant smell of flowers, the relaxing sound of moving water, and the tactile quality of rock gardens.

The human connection to nature can also provide therapeutic benefits, as illustrated by the use of waterfalls in hotel lobbies, bird sanctuaries in nursing homes, fish tanks in executive offices, and gardens on rooftops and in kitchens. The benefits of aromatherapy, often used in the interior environment in the form of candles, were noted in Chapter 2. The experiential value of aesthetically appealing flower and candle arrangements enhances both residential and contract environments. Fresh-cut flowers in large-scale or intimate arrangements are used to greet retirement home residents, diners in restaurants, shoppers in stores, and visitors to museums or offices, among others. Additionally, being surrounded by live plants and flowers generally improves the air quality of an interior by bringing oxygen and moisture into the space. Examples of flower and candle arrangements in both residential and contract settings are shown in Figure 10.71a–c.

Figure 10.71
Floral arrangements and candles. a. Boutique hotel installation; b. Residential fireplace mantel arrangement; c. Retail arrangement.
(a, b, and c: Flowers and candle arrangements by Belle Fleur, New York)

A Fascination with Felt: Then and Now

Felt is considered man's first fabric. It is the material created by processing sheep's wool into a nonwoven textile that is traced back thousands of years. Nomadic tribes, particularly in Central Asia, made their tents, clothes, and floor coverings from the material. Today many of the same techniques remain in use in that part of the world and other regions. Contemporary artists are finding the medium of felt gratifying for its green attributes and versatility. It dyes easily, does not pill or unravel, and as a wool product inherently retards flame and repels water. Many artists and craftspeople rely on ancient methods of production, others have made modern adaptations, and many combine old and new techniques. The results are fascinating.

The main way felt is traditionally produced is known as a **wet process.** Felted fabric is produced using heat, moisture, and pressure to mat and interlock the fibers into a dense material. While this was originally all done by hand, machines are now often used to assist in the production of large quantities, especially of industrial felt sheets.

Figures a–e
a. A felt-making demonstration;
b. Janice Arnold's Yurt Palace interior view; c and d. Anne Kyyro Quinn's felt installations; e. Decorative felt sculpture by Ronel Jordaan featuring an array of succulents. *(a–e: Provided by the Author)*

(continued)

A Fascination with Felt: Then and Now, *continued*

Modern-day felt production includes use for:

- Apparel and fashion accessories
- Industrial insulation
- Musical instruments, toys, and billiard tables

Many of these products are no longer made of 100 percent natural wool but may combine synthetic fibers or other natural materials such as silk for added luster.

In 2009 the Smithsonian Institution's Cooper-Hewitt Museum in New York City presented an exhibition entitled *Fashioning Felt,* which explored the characteristics and evolution of making and using felt from its origins to contemporary uses. The educational and informative exhibition included hands-on demonstrations of the process of felt making.

A significant example relating to the built environment was the Yurt Palace designed by American Janice Arnold. The yurt, mentioned in Chapter 8, is a tent-like structure traditionally used as a portable home for nomadic people. The traditional yurt is a wood frame that is covered or wrapped in felt. Here, felt artist Arnold creates a decorated royal tent for the exhibit in the atrium space of the museum. Her work featured wool, Tencel, and silk.

Contemporary artists working in felt include Anne Kyyro Quinn, whose studio in London produce an array of handcrafted natural textiles for both residential and contract projects. Her installations include large-scale commercial spaces where acoustical value combines with artistic and sculptural features.

Ronel Jordaan, a textile designer based out of Johannesburg, South Africa, founded the enterprise Job Creation. Its objective is to train and employ women from the city township regions in her country. Her work is shown and purchased globally.

Summary

An ever-increasing range of materials and techniques is available for finishing and furnishing interior spaces, and the designer's involvement in this phase can be an enriching experience. Because the impact of these design choices on the space is significant, the designer is driven continually to pursue his or her education in this area.

The use of textiles at this phase of the design process requires not only an understanding of texture, color, and pattern, but also a familiarity with the properties of different fibers, including their structure and the steps involved in manufacturing and finishing. Performance standards for textiles are important considerations, particularly for contract projects, such as health-care facilities and the hospitality industry.

Windows may be treated in various ways and styles, usually differentiated as hard or soft coverings. Draperies, curtains, shades, blinds, screens, and shutters are included in these categories.

The upholstering of customized, high-quality goods, in particular, seating, is a complex, labor-intensive process performed largely by craftspeople in workrooms. Both the construction and finishing processes entail many design decisions, among them the type of fill, final fabric covering, and detailing, including the use of passementerie. Specialized types of furniture, equipment, and appliances are produced for kitchens and baths and various categories of commercial spaces. The product categories of hardware and signage represent a growing market segment for designer decisions.

For the residential and contract designer, the design concept may be personalized and made cohesive with successful selection and installation of accessories. In addition to providing enhanced decorative value, many accessories also serve useful functions.

Vocabulary

Association of Contract Textiles (ACT)	greige (gray) good	rush
batik	hand	satin weave
batting	ikat	stackback
burlap	indigo	Suzani
cane	jabot (cascade)	swag (festoon)
case good	Jacquard loom	textile
casework	jute	tufted
Chesterfield	lambrequin	Tunnel test
chintz	Lawson	tuxedo
cornice	paisley	twill weave
Coromandel	passementerie	underdrapery
credenza	pelmet	upholstery
curio cabinet	plain weave	valance
damask	plantation shutters	venetian blind
deck	puddling	webbing
double rubs	railroading	wicker
eight-way hand-tied coil spring construction	rattan	workroom
	repeat	Wyzenbeek test
fullness	return	Xenon test

Exercise: Scavenger Hunt: Innovations for Feathering the Nest

The goal of this exercise is to find new products, manufacturing techniques, or applications for furnishing interior spaces. Your list should feature products or uses of products that are not described in this text—those that truly are "hot off the press."

Various research methods may be used, such as visiting showrooms, manufacturing sites, project sites, or trade or craft shows. You may also review catalogs, trade and shelter publications, articles, news briefs, and books. Websites, in particular those of government or public agencies, educational sources, or professional associations, may provide you with a substantial amount of information. However, experiencing products, their texture and color, firsthand is significantly valuable.

Aim to include at least one new product or application that is suitable for finishing each of the following surfaces: floor, wall, and ceiling. Summarize each product and include a description and illustration. In your summary, consider the relationship of the product to factors such as aesthetics, sustainability, universal design, ergonomics, and life-cycle cost.

Exercise: Exploring the CD-ROM

Take advantage of the contents of the CD-ROM to increase your understanding of designing window treatments. Follow the instructions for Starting the CD-ROM on pages xix–xx and click on Chapter Ten: Furnishing the Interior: Feathering the Nest.

Window Treatments: Interior designers make a significant contribution in selecting window treatments in both residential and contract spaces. Considerations include type, operability, energy conservation, privacy, and acoustical value. Observe and sketch or photograph three different window treatments. Note on your drawing or photo the components of the treatment, such as whether it is backed, the type of top treatment, length (that is, sill height or floor length), and other details. Note how the treatment considers issues of privacy, light control, and energy conservation.

Table 10.1
Textiles for Interiors and Their Applications

Name	Description	Application
Alpaca	This fiber is obtained from the hair of a domesticated animal of the camel family. Alpacas are native to the Andes Mountains. The fibers are soft, fine, and lustrous. Alpaca fiber is softer than llama fiber.	Upholstery and rugs
Bark cloth	Authentic versions are cloth pounded from the bark of trees in areas such as Africa and Polynesia.	Contemporary definitions include rough woven fabric usually of cotton or cotton blends, printed with large patterns; decorative accents, draperies, upholstery; light use if authentic
Batik	Fabric that uses a method of resist dyeing that employs wax as the resist. The pattern is covered with wax, and the fabric is then dyed; the waxed patterns will not take the dye. The wax is then removed after dyeing by boiling the fabric, applying the solvent, or ironing over an absorbent substrate. This process can be repeated numerous times to obtain multicolored designs. Batik dyeing originated in Indonesia, where it was first employed on cotton.	Slipcovers and curtains
Batiste	Originally, a sheer linen fabric named for famous French weaver, Jean Baptiste, who produced delicate linen fabrics during the 13th century. Today, it may be made with a combination of cotton and such manufactured fibers as polyester. Normally solid colored.	Draperies and curtains
Bouclé	Derived from the French word meaning "curled." A woven or knit fabric made with all wool, rayon, cotton, or a combination of fibers. The surface of the fabric is looped or knotted. It has closed loops that vary in size and spacing.	
Brocade	Rich, heavy, jacquard woven fabric with raised floral or figured patterns emphasized by contrasting surfaces or colors. It is woven from more than one set of filling. Often it is made with gold or silver threads. The design appears on the face of the fabric, which is distinguished easily from the back. Brocade was originally produced in China or Japan. Currently, any of the major textile fibers may be used in a wide range of quality and price.	Draperies, upholstery, and decorative purposes
Brocatelle	Fabric similar to brocade but the pattern is raised and padded with stuffer yarns, made on a jacquard loom. The fabric usually has a firm texture and a high-yarn count, and may be made with a silk, rayon, cotton, or linen, or combinations. The appearance is blistered or puffed.	Draperies and upholstery

(continued)

Table 10.1
Textiles for Interiors and Their Applications, *continued*

Name	Description	Application
Buckram	Plain-weave, coarse, open fabric that is sized heavily and used as a stiffener between the lining and the surface cloth to give it shape or form. Made with cotton, linen, hemp, and other materials. Also made by gluing two open weave, sized cotton fabrics together. Usually white or plain colors.	Pelmets
Burn-out	Fabric made with two different yarns with a pattern effect produced by destroying one of the yarns in a printing process that employs chemicals such as acid instead of color.	
Canvas (see Duck)	General classification of strong, firm, closely woven fabrics usually made with cotton; originally made of hemp or unbleached flax. Produced in many grades and qualities and may be softly finished or highly sized.	Roman shades, exterior and interior awnings, and casual upholstery or slipcovers
Casement	Loosely constructed fabric that allows light transmission. May be white, printed, or colored.	Curtains and draperies
Cashmere (or Pashmina)	Fine, soft, downy wool produced by the cashmere goat, raised in the Kashmir region of South Asia and other areas, now including the United States. The hair is silky, soft, strong, and cylindrical. When used in combination with sheep's wool, the cloth has increased durability.	Fine bed throws, shawls, and blankets
Challis	Soft, drapable, plain-weave fabric made of wool, rayon, cotton, or manufactured fiber blends. Supple and lightweight, usually it is printed in small floral patterns. Originally, the fabric was manufactured in Norwich, England, in 1832, of silk and worsted wool.	Comforters and bedspreads
Chenille	Highly textured, yarn of cotton or manufactured fibers. After weaving, the fabric is cut lengthwise producing a continuous yarn that is then twisted.	Upholstery, trim, and bed and bath linens
Chevron (also called Herringbone)	Twill weave composed of vertical sections that are alternately right hand and left hand in direction, creating a continually reversed diagonal, zigzag pattern.	Curtains, slipcovers, and upholstery
Chintz (also called Glazed cotton)	Plain-weave cotton fabric, glazed, which was painted or block printed in India in brilliantly colored patterns of plants and animals. The term is now applied to any plain weave, printed or solid color, cotton or cotton blends that are glazed to a luster. The glazed surface is achieved by applying finishing materials such as wax or starch or a chemical resin, and then heat pressed.	Casual upholstery and slipcovers
Coir	Seed fibers that are obtained from fibrous mass between the outer shell and the actual nut of the coconut. The fibers are removed by soaking the husk in saline water for several months. Coir fibers are extremely stiff. They are resistant to abrasion, water, and most weather conditions. Sri Lanka is the major producer of coir fiber.	Outdoor mats, rugs, outdoor carpeting, and brushes

Table 10.1
Textiles for Interiors and Their Applications, *continued*

Name	Description	Application
Corduroy	Strong, durable fabric generally of cotton with vertical cut-pile stripes. The foundation of the fabric can be either a plain or twill weave. After the cloth is woven the floats of the pile are cut in their center; after cutting, the fibers tend to spring upward and later are brushed up to form the pile in ridges or cords. The stripes formed may be in any variety of widths, such as wide wale, narrow, or pinwale.	Curtains, draperies, slipcovers, and upholstery
Crewel	Embroidery made with yarn usually from fine worsted wool on some plain-weave, off-white colored fabric. Designs are generally inspired by East Indian or English foliage motifs.	Floor coverings
Crypton	Registered trademark process of Hi-Tex, Inc. Fabric offers many of the qualities of vinyl including resistance to stain, moisture, microbes; pliability; and durability.	Upholstery
Damask	Woven from one set of warp yarns and one set of filling yarns. Originally a rich silk fabric with woven floral designs made in China and introduced into Europe through Damascus, from which it derived its name. Now a broad group of jacquard woven fabrics with elaborate floral or geometric patterns made from many types of natural and manufactured fibers and combinations of fibers. The pattern is distinguished from the ground by contrasting luster and is reversible. In two-color damask, the colors reverse on either side. Damask is one of the oldest and most popular cloths.	Upholstery and draperies, table and bed products
Denim	Sturdy, heavy twill-woven cotton generally dyed blue. The term *denim* was derived from twilled fabric that was made in Nimes, France.	Casual upholstery or slipcovers
Dobby weave	General term for weaves made with several harnesses. Usually small, geometric patterns. Must have as many as 20 or 30 harnesses to produce the variety of shed required.	Upholstery and slipcovers
Duck (see Canvas)	Broad term for a wide range of strong, firm, plain-weave fabrics. Usually made of cotton, although sometimes linen or blends of cotton and manufactured fibers are used.	Tents, awnings, and casual slipcovers and upholstery
Dupioni (also called Shantung)	Plain-weave fabric made of uneven yarns to produce a textured effect. Originally made of wild silk yarns on handlooms in the Shandong province of China. Presently made of dupioni silk in which yarns retain all imperfections; rayon, cotton, or manufactured fiber.	Draperies and light-use upholstery

(continued)

Table 10.1
Textiles for Interiors and Their Applications, *continued*

Name	Description	Application
Felt	Made since ancient times, felt is a nonwoven sheet of matted material such as wood or certain manufactured fibers. True felting takes place by a combination of heat, moisture, and pressure where no bonding adhesive is used.	Floor and table covers, usually in green color; contemporary use includes throw pillows and upholstery and slipcovers, generally in a variety of colors and weights
Fiberglass	Generic fiber category defined by the Federal Trade Commission as "a manufactured fiber in which the fiber-forming substance is glass." Glass fiber is produced by combining glass-making ingredients, heating them in a high-temperature furnace, then extruding the molten glass in filament form. Glass fiber is strong but lacks abrasion resistance. It is nonflammable, does not conduct heat, and has good sunlight resistance.	Vertical blinds and panel partitions
Flamestitch	Similar to a chevron pattern but irregular, resembling a stylized flame.	Multipurpose
Flannel	Derived from the Welsh word which means "wool." A light- or medium-weight fabric of plain or twill weave with a slightly napped surface. Generally cotton or wool.	Upholstery and blankets
Fleece	Wool sheared from sheep or goats. The term is used especially for the entire coat of wool shorn from the sheep at one time in one piece then clipped. Or fleece can be a fabric with a thick, heavy, fleece-like surface; it may be a pile fabric or simply napped, sometimes of knit construction.	Blankets
Frieze	This fabric normally has a level, uncut pile surface made of multifilament yarns composed of stiff nylon fibers.	Draperies and upholstery
Gauze (also called Scrim)	Plain weave, generally of thin cotton yarns, loosely constructed, in solid colors. Originally produced for use in stage settings, may be dyed and used for stationary or traversing curtain panels in residential and commercial interiors	Draperies and bed canopies
Horsehair	Natural material used earlier as a filling in upholstered cushions.	Upholstery
Houndstooth	Pointed check effect produced by interlacing yarns of two contrasting colors.	Multipurpose
Ikat	Indonesian term for warp or weft resist-dyed fabric.	Multipurpose
Iridescent	Fabric with changeable color effects, especially due to reactions of light on the surface. May be the result of dye, finish, or weave.	Draperies

Table 10.1
Textiles for Interiors and Their Applications, *continued*

Name	Description	Application
Jacquard	System of weaving that permits the production of woven designs of considerable size and variety of colors; extremely complex interlacing patterns. The Jacquard loom was invented by Joseph Marie Jacquard in France during the early 19th century. The weave pattern is copied from the design paper by punching a series of cards. Depending on the design, the machine may carry a large number of cards.	Tapestry, brocade, damask, brocatelle, and floor covering
Lace	Openwork fabric produced by a network of threads, twisted together and sometimes knotted, to form patterns. It is made by hand or by machinery. Machine-made lace is used in window coverings, bed coverings, bed coverings, and tabletop accents. Hand-made lace, produced using small bobbin, is used as trimming for bedding products.	Curtains and trim
Lamé	Fabric woven with flat metallic yarns that form either the ground or the pattern. Derived from the French word *lamé,* which means "trimmed with leaves of gold or silver."	Draperies
Lampas	Similar to satin damask made of silk, rayon, wool, or cotton or combinations of these fibers. Made on a Jacquard loom with two sets of warp and one filling, usually in different colors. The fabric is characterized by elaborate designs typical of the 17th and 18th centuries. The detailed motifs are created by combining satin and sateen interlacings.	Draperies and upholstery
Leno weave	Variation of open, plain weaving process in which warp yarns are arranged in pairs.	Draperies and curtains
Lisere	Fabric that is woven from two sets of warp yarns and one set of filling yarns. In many lisere fabrics, the patterned bands are interspersed with satin-woven stripes.	Draperies and upholstery
Llama	Hair fiber retrieved from the South American llama, a domesticated animal of the camel family. Llama fibers are coarser and less strong than alpaca fibers.	Rugs
Macramé	A relatively heavy fabric constructed by knotting and twisting textile cords.	Decorative hangings
Marquisette	Group of lightweight, open-mesh, transparent fabrics made of cotton, silk, or manufactured fibers. Usually leno woven in a single color.	Curtains, mosquito nets, and bed canopies
Matelassé	Double cloth fabric. The quilted character and raised patterns are made on a Jacquard or dobby loom. Produced in a single color.	Bedspreads and upholstery
Microfiber	Used in the apparel industry for years and is quickly becoming a part of the home furnishing industry. Manufactured fibers with a denier of less than 1, which is the size of silk. Very fine filament or staple fiber, used to produce lightweight, drapable, soft fabrics.	Multipurpose

(continued)

Table 10.1
Textiles for Interiors and Their Applications, *continued*

Name	Description	Application
Mohair	Long, white, lustrous hair obtained from the Angora goat. It ranges from 4 to 12 inches in length growing in uniform locks, but it is comparatively coarse and lacks any natural crimp. Mohair is very resilient fiber, having fewer scales and less crimps than wool. The fibers are smoother, with fibers up to 12 inches in length, giving them a lustrous appearance. The goat is native to Turkey and derives its names from the province of Angora, where it has been raised for thousands of years; it is raised today in the United States and South Africa, as well as Turkey. The goats are sheared twice a year. Produced in solid colors.	Upholstery, floor coverings, draperies
Moiré	Finishing process that produces a wavy pattern resembling wood grain or watermark. Produced by engraved rollers that press the design into the fabric then heat set or chemically set. The difference in reflection of the rays of light from the uncrushed and crushed parts of the design results in the effect. Applied usually to ribbed fabrics of cotton, acetate, rayon, silk, and some manufactured fiber fabrics.	Multipurpose
Muslin	Group of firm, plain-weave cotton and cotton blend fabrics in a wide range of qualities and weights from lightweight sheers to heavyweight sheeting. May be finished in a variety of ways.	Sheets and pillowcases; used in its natural off-white color as the fabric between upholstery fill and finish fabric
Ninon	Smooth, crisp, lightweight silk or manufactured fiber fabric made in a plain weave with an open mesh. Heavier than chiffon. Used for sheer draw or stationary curtains, generally in combination with overdraperies.	Curtains
Nylon	A manufactured synthetic fiber with strength, elongation, abrasion resistance, and resiliency. Nylon is easily laundered and retains its dimensional stability and resiliency. The first synthesized manufactured fiber.	Carpet, rugs, curtains, bedspreads
Organdy	Lightweight, transparent fabric made in plain weave with a crisp hand that usually is made of very fine filament yarns. Most commonly used fibers are silk, nylon, polyester, or rayon. In silk, the stiffness is provided by natural gum that remains on the filament. In the manufactured fiber, a special finish is required.	Draperies
Ottoman	Firm, lustrous, plain-weave fabric with flat horizontal ribs and cords. Wool, silk, cotton, or manufactured fibers are used.	Upholstery
Piqué	Piques are mercerized, bleached, dyed, printed, often preshrunk, and sometimes slightly napped. A fiber obtained from the leaves of a pineapple plant grown mainly in the Philippines. It is used to produce very lightweight, sheer fabrics.	Curtains

Table 10.1
Textiles for Interiors and Their Applications, *continued*

Name	Description	Application
Plain weave (also called Tabby weave)	Double cloth generally of cotton but now made also with manufactured fibers. It is produced in narrow to wide wale. The plain weave is the simplest of the weaves, requiring only two harnesses to be produced.	Multipurpose
Plissé	Cotton fabric treated with a solution that shrinks part of the cloth to produce a puckered or crinkled effect. The finish is permanent if the fabric is not ironed when laundered.	Bedspreads
Plush	Warp-pile fabric with cut-pile surface longer than velvet and less closely woven. The weave is a variation of the plain weave. The ground generally is cotton, and the pile may be mohair, wool, cotton, or manufactured fiber. They may be made in plain or multicolored allover effects such as to imitate animal fur, or in a great number of jacquard patterns.	Carpets, draperies, and upholstery
Polyester	Polyester has been available in the domestic market since 1953. Like nylon, polyester gives the producer the ability to engineer fiber properties by controlling the shape and form of the fibers. With drawing and heat setting, the strength, elongation, abrasion resistance, resiliency, and dimensional stability of the fiber can also be controlled.	Floor coverings, curtain and drapery fabrics and linings, bedding, wall coverings, and table linens
Raffia	Fiber from various species of palm trees. Generally woven into basket weave.	Wall coverings and upholstery
Ramie	Cellulosic plant fiber similar to linen that is usually blended with other fibers. It is one of the strongest natural fibers.	Wall coverings and upholstery
Rayon	A manufactured fiber composed of regenerated cellulose, as well as manufactured fibers composed of regenerated cellulose in which substituents have replaced not more than 15% of hydroxyl groups.	Multipurpose
Repp (or Rep)	Fabric with closely spaced narrow ribs running in the direction of the filling. Can be made with any fiber or combination of fibers in several construction types.	Draperies and upholstery
Sateen	A filling-faced satin weave. Strong, lustrous cotton or cotton-blend fabric generally produced in colorful prints.	Curtains and slipcovers Lining
Satin	Smooth, generally lustrous fabric with a thick, close texture made of silk or manufactured fiber filament yarns in a satin weave. Generally, there are a higher number of yarns on the face than the back. The satin weave may be combined in a variety of ways with contrasting designs executed in taffeta, twill, pile, and other constructions, notably jacquard.	Bedspreads, linings, quilts Light-use upholstery Backing for heavier fabrics such as acetate

(continued)

Table 10.1
Textiles for Interiors and Their Applications, *continued*

Name	Description	Application
Sheer	Transparent or very lightweight fabric such a chiffon, crepe, georgette, or voile of various constructions and yarns, especially silk and manufactured fiber yarns. Sheers are made in both spun and filament yarn constructions.	Draperies, underdraperies, bed canopies
Silk	A natural protein fiber known for its softness, comfort, and luster. The leading producers of silk are China, Japan, and India.	Multipurpose
Spandex	These elastomeric fibers are widely appreciated for their high elongation, high elastic recovery, and high holding power.	Uphohlstry
Strié	Narrow streaked or striped effect almost the same shade as the ground. Can occur by design or as a result of defects in fabrics.	Multipurpose
Taffeta	Group of fabrics made with plain weave and possessing a fine, smooth, crisp, and generally lustrous face. Produced in many qualities, plain, printed, with changeable effects, such as moiré. Silk, cotton, and acetate are used now in the production of taffeta, though it was originally only made from silk. The term is derived from the Persian *taftah,* the term for a very fine, plain-weave, silk fabric, known during the 16th century as a luxurious fabric for women's wear.	Bedspreads, draperies, lamp shades, linings, and trimmings
Tapestry	Heavy, hand-woven or Jacquard loom fabric contrasting yarns with decorative designs usually depicting historical scenes. Construction types vary from region to region. Tapestry is of Oriental origin and initially was made either by embroidering a ground fabric or by weaving the pattern in the warp.	Wall hangings, floor coverings, upholstery, draperies, and throw pillows
Tartan	Originally a twilled woolen or worsted plaid worn in Scotland as shawls and/or kilts with different colors and patterns representing different clans and occasions. The term is also applied to any fabric with a similar pattern. Today, tartan plaids are made in many manufactured fibers as well as wool.	Multipurpose
Ticking	Term for strong durable, closely woven fabric in plain, twill, or satin weave, usually in blue and white stripes. Generally made from cotton or cotton blends. *Ticking* is a generic term for any fabric used to cover the exterior of mattresses, box springs, and pillows. Tickings may be plain or highly decorative.	Covering box springs, mattresses, and pillows Casual upholstery, slipcovers, or draperies
Toile de Jouy	Floral or scenic design, generally bucolic in style, on cotton, linen, or silk fabric usually printed with one color on a light ground, resembling fine engravings. Influenced by cotton prints from India popular in 18th-century France. A factory was established in France, at Jouy, near Versailles. The most famous prints from Jouy are in single colors printed from engraved copper plates. Modern versions are more varied in design motifs.	Multipurpose

Table 10.1
Textiles for Interiors and Their Applications, *continued*

Name	Description	Application
Trevira	Registered trademark by Hoeschst-Celanese for polyester fiber. Available in flame-resistant finish.	Multipurpose
Tweed	Rough wool fabrics with a wiry, somewhat hairy surface but soft, flexible texture. Made from wool and manufactured fiber blends in a variety of effects. The weave may be plain, twill, herringbone, or novelty, generally in two or more colors to produce heather effects. Originally handwoven near the Tweed River, which separates England from Scotland. Today most tweeds are spun and woven by machinery, although in the case of Harris and some other tweeds, they are handwoven of machine-spun yarn.	Multipurpose
Twill	A broad term for any fabric made with a twill weed.	Multipurpose
Ultrasuede	Registered trademark of Spring Mills for a nonwoven synthetic fabric impregnated with synthetic resins to produce a fabric made to resemble natural suede.	Draperies and upholstery
Velour	Heavy woven fabric finished with a close, dense pile that is laid in one direction. Most velour is composed of cotton fibers, which give the fabric a soft, warm hand. Originally made in wool, now also made in other fibers. Made to resemble velvet.	Draperies and upholstery
Velvet	Warp-pile fabric with short, closely woven cut pile that gives the fabric a rich, soft texture. Constructed of double cloth. Originally the pile was made of silk, but now also made of cotton, manufactured fibers, and various blends. May be given crush-resistant and water-repellent finishes, or embossed or patterned by the burn-out method.	Draperies and upholstery
Voile	Lightweight, sheer fabric with a crisp, wiry hand made of hard-twist yarns in a low-count, plain weave. Made of cotton, worsted, silk, rayon, or acetate. Made in solid colors, prints, and colored warp stripes. Novelty voiles are made with fancy yarns and flock dots.	Curtains
Wool	Comes from the follicles of sheep's skin. Wool fiber's combined properties cannot be duplicated by any other natural or manufactured fiber: flame resistance, thermal retention, felting ability, initial water repellency, and the ability to absorb water without feeling wet.	Multipurpose
Worsted	Term used to describe fine, long wool fibers and the fabric woven from yarn spun from combined wool. Worsted may be either piece or stock dyed; comes in a variety of weaves.	Upholstery
Xorel	Registered trademark of Carnegie Fabrics as an alternative to vinyl. Also a synthetic, it is less polluting than vinyl, flame-retardant, with a long life cycle.	Upholstery, wall covering, and panel systems
Yak	This fiber is produced from large oxen in Tibet. This soft, short fiber is hand plucked from the chest and belly.	Blankets

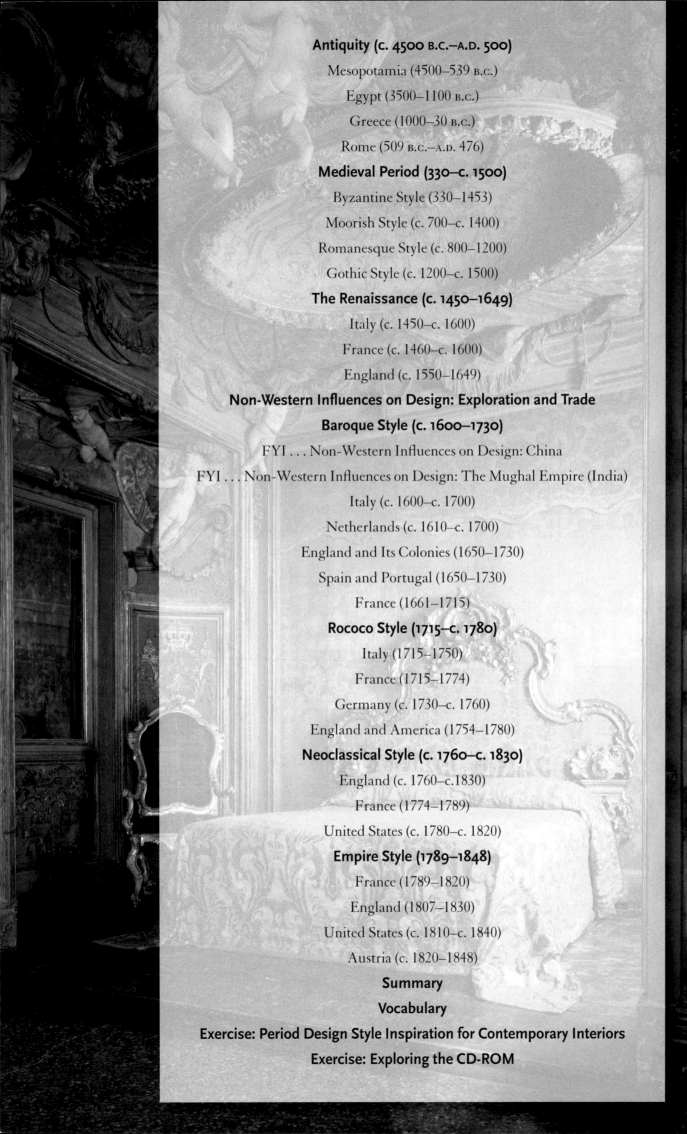

CHAPTER

11

Period Design Styles
Antiquity (c. 4500 B.C.–A.D. 500)–
Empire Style (1789–1848)

This chapter traces the design styles that significantly influenced the way in which people lived from ancient times to the premodern era. Although major architectural features are noted, the emphasis is on key aspects of the interior environment. The important features of residential spaces as well as public spaces, such as churches and temples, are pointed out. As style is a matter of context, examples of personal fashion and arts will also be illustrated to enhance the reader's understanding of the flavor of the period and how people lived in a particular place and time.

It is important to note that although the orientation is Western, recognition is given to the many influences and contributions of the non-Western world on Western design.

There is no single way to categorize period design style. The phrase has manifold meanings, one of which relates to time frame. Another meaning concerns how the events of a particular time period are expressed; in other words, the style of that period. For example, an element of the design style for residences during the Victorian period was the use of small, specialized rooms.

Periods in history are contextual by region, culture, and class. Historical periods are often categorized for convenience into fixed time frames, with a beginning and an end date. Although this approach provides neat parameters, this delineation has inherent limitations because it focuses on a given place at a given time, and different parts of the world have unique experiences.

However, some shared experiences and expressions may be identified that help define style, even when the exact time frames (beginning and end dates) do not coincide.

A style is the manner in which a tendency is expressed. It may evolve either from previous styles or as a reaction against them. Although styles may be discussed in chronological order, they often overlap, and more than one style exists at any given time. It is important to note that design change occurred much more slowly in periods covered by this chapter than in modern times because of geographical and technological constraints.

Styles are most likely to be associated first with a particular era, such as the medieval period, a time frame of hundreds of years in Europe that is also referred to as the Middle Ages. They may also be denoted by the ruling monarch of a particular country or region, such as "Georgian," after a series of British kings named George. An overall design style in certain regions may be named for the primary material used, for instance, the Age of Mahogany. And, finally, an influential architect, builder, or manufacturer may provide the nom de plume of a period, such as Chippendale style, named after Thomas Chippendale, a prolific 18th-century cabinetmaker in England.

In a survey of historical design styles, much of what is documented concerning the architecture and furnishings of the day refers to what was available to a distinctly elite or influential portion of the populace, consisting usually of royalty, wealthy landowners, and sometimes clergy. As with personal fashion, the styles of the moment may be adapted and modified for more common usage. These adaptations attempt to capture the essence of the style but, out of necessity, make use of available resources, in both materials and labor. In some instances, the result is a countrified version of a city style. At other times, it may be a modification of an expensively and finely crafted piece into a more crudely produced piece. The terms *provincial style*, *vernacular style* (design produced based on common practice and knowledge), and, in some cases, *colonial style* all denote such modified styles or adaptations.

Motifs are the symbols of a theme. Many motifs have existed throughout history and worldwide, and these have been transformed in countless ways. Although no one motif can totally convey a trend, a motif can symbolically represent certain aspects of a style. The cross, a symbol of Christianity, essentially relies on the intersection of a vertical and a horizontal line. However, it may be embellished with distinct variations over time and in the different regions of the world where Christianity is followed.

This chapter divides pre-20th-century design, particularly as it relates to the origins of European and Western design, into the following categories:

- Antiquity
- Medieval
- Renaissance
- Baroque
- Rococo
- Neoclassical
- Empire

Additional boxed features note highlights of contributions and influences of non-Western cultures. Several of the figures included in this and the following chapter illustrate historical influences on current style, presenting a look at then and now.

ANTIQUITY
(C. 4500 B.C.–A.D. 500)

To discuss the history of what may be referred to as Western society and design, we first must turn to other lands, including parts of Asia and Africa.

Mesopotamia (4500–539 B.C.)

What was known as Mesopotamia in ancient times is the area rich in complex civilizations now referred to as the Near East. Within that region were Sumer, Assyria, and Babylon (Figure 11.1).

During the last millennium before the Common, or Christian, Era (c. 900–c. 7 B.C.) the Assyrian and Persian civilizations contributed more directly than that of Egypt to Mediterranean (European) culture.

The people of this region relied heavily on the use of glazed tiles for friezes and wall treatments and polychrome (application of more than one pigment color) brickwork, such as on the Gates of Ishtar (Figure 11.2).

Buildings were constructed with large interior courtyards and slender columns holding up a wood-and-clay roof, a variation of the portico.

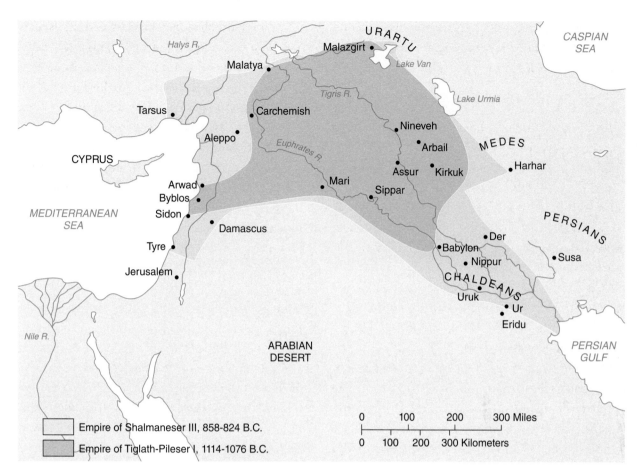

Figure 11.1

Map of Mesopotamia.

Figure 11.2

Polychrome glazed brickwork from Babylonia, Gates of Ishtar.
(© *Josep Renalias*)

The Sumerians were the first people to establish cities. The first empire was that of the Assyrians, a warlike people who were succeeded by the Babylonians, who in turn fell to the Persians in the 6th cen-

tury B.C. At its height, the ancient Persian Empire (now Iran) included areas in India and North Africa. These last Mesopotamian empires vanished under later conquests by the Greeks and Romans, from whom we most directly attribute the influences on Western—in particular, European—style.

Egypt (3500–1100 B.C.)

It is in two lands in northern Africa, Upper and Lower Egypt, later combined, that civilizations flourished, in the Nile Valley, leaving us with the most extensive remains from which Western civilization derives.

Several excavation sites have provided information that enables us to reconstruct the features of the domestic interiors of the ancient Egyptians. However, it is in the monumental architecture, the pyramids, the tombs for the ruling class, and other important public and sacred structures that significant traces survived. **Hieroglyphics**, a pictorial script painted or carved on the walls of these structures, offer details about Egyptian civilization, customs, religion, and technical skills.

Figure 11.3
Egyptian interior decoration as depicted on the back of King Tut's throne. (© *Richard Seaman, www.richard-seaman.com*)

Egyptian society was very hierarchical. The pharaoh, or king, was believed to be a god. The Egyptian belief in the afterlife spurred the development of sophisticated methods of preserving the body through mummification. Objects for use in the afterlife and status symbols were entombed with the body of the pharaoh and other members of the ruling class, providing additional information about this civilization.

Most Egyptian houses were constructed of mud bricks made from the earth of the Nile River. More monumental structures, such as temples and pyramids, were made of sandstone and limestone.

Domestic interior details, such as surface treatment and decoration, were dictated by social status. Nonetheless, there is evidence that the exterior and interior architecture of houses shared many common attributes regardless of their size or the social status of their occupants. The most significant architectural theme in defining space is the axial plan. Typical for Egyptian interiors is the **tripartite** layout, which divides the house into three main sections: a reception area, a columned central hall or living room, and private quarters.

The prevalent floor covering was whitewashed mud brick, with stone slabs in bathrooms. Glazed tile was sometimes used in palaces.

Walls were most often treated with plaster. A common decorative wall treatment involved a fresco-like process accomplished by applying pigment to wet gypsum plaster, which was then protected with either varnish or beeswax. Walls might be ornamented with paintings using geometric, plant, and animal designs; hung with rugs; or painted to imitate carpet patterns. Palace walls featured inlaid materials, such as faience (see Chapter 10). Walls were often divided by means of a dado (see Chapter 9) and ornamented with a cornice, molding, or a contrasting painted demarcation at the top of the wall; and a **frieze**, a decorated area between the cornice and dado. The lavishness of the Egyptian interior is seen on the throne chair featured in Figure 11.3.

Roofs were flat, and the few windows that existed were clerestories, a row of windows along the top of the wall. Some houses, especially those in urban areas and palaces, had more than one story. A **portico**, a roofed porch held up by columns, was widespread among the affluent. It provided shade, a windbreak, and outdoor living space. The use of a portico, or a similar structure, was an architectural feature that influenced many of the subsequent civilizations discussed later (Figure 11.4a and b).

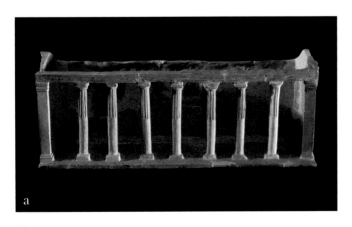

Figure 11.4
Then and Now. a. Model of an ancient portico; b. The White House, Washington, DC. (*a: © Gianni Dagli Orti/CORBIS; b: © VEER*)

Figure 11.5
Egyptian columns derived from lotus and papyrus plant features.
(© Elio Ciol/CORBIS)

Ceilings were painted to imitate fabric; later, ceiling decoration evolved to include stars, spirals, rosettes, and other plant forms. Before stone was introduced in the construction of structural, supportive columns, they were probably made from palm tree trunks and bundles of reeds. The capital, or top structure, of these columns was often carved with plant forms, in particular palm, papyrus, and lotus, which were indigenous to the region (Figure 11.5).

Wood was the main material used to construct furniture. Because native woods, such as sycamore and acacia, were of poor quality and in short supply, the Egyptians imported cedar from Syria and ebony from other parts of Africa. When native woods were used, a thin coat of plaster served as a cover to smooth the surface. Finer pieces of furniture and chests were adorned with ivory inlay or gilded.

Copper tools, such as chisels, awls, and axes, were used for woodworking. Veneer, plywood, and techniques for bending wood were also employed. The furniture that existed for the pharaohs was constructed with sophisticated joinery techniques, such as **mortise** and **tenon**, a system that combines a groove and projection to create a joint—a conventional method still used today.

The stool is one of the earliest types of seating, used by all levels of society. The Egyptians devised a folding stool using an X-configuration. Chairs at first were constructed as status symbols for nobility but later were used in ordinary houses. Beds could be simple or ornate, with frames supported by legs. The legs of both chairs and beds were often carved with animal features. Other furniture included small tables and chests for storing valuables (Figure 11.6a–c).

a   b   c

Figure 11.6
Egyptian furniture. a. Throne chair; b. Stool; c. Chest. *(a. Armchair of Saraton, daughter and wife of Amenophis III. c. 1370–1350 BCE. From the tomb of Iouya and Touyou. 18th dynasty. Location: Egyptian Museum, Cairo, Egypt. Photo credit: Bridgeman-Giraudon / Art Resource, New York; b: Chair, wood, stuccoed and painted linen seat. Egypt, New Kingdom. 1550–1069 BCE. From Thebes. Location: Museo Egizio, Turin, Italy. Photo credit: Erich Lessing / Art Resource, New York; c: Chest decorated with ivory. From the tomb of Pharaoh Tutankhamen. Egypt, 18th dynasty. Location: Egyptian Museum, Cairo, Egypt. Photo credit: Scala / Art Resource, New York)*

There is evidence of a high level of skill and artistry in working with metals, such as copper, bronze, gold, and silver, as well as semiprecious gems, such as amethyst, lapis lazuli, carnelian, rock crystal, and turquoise. Faience was used to decorate fine objects, such as jewelry. Glass was used in Egypt circa 1550 B.C. first for beads and inlays, then as vessels, such as for liquids.

The principal textile was linen cloth made by spinning and weaving fibers from the flax plant. Leather was used as a supplement and for the strapping in chairs.

The colors used in ancient Egypt were bold: red, blue, yellow, green, white, and black. Colors increased progressively in intensity from floor to ceiling, so that the most subdued hues were used at floor level, whereas the most brilliant were reserved for the ceiling.

Ornament was largely derived from symbolism (Figure 11.7). The sun represents royal dignity and the ankh life. The lotus and papyrus are the symbols of the two kingdoms of Upper and Lower Egypt, and the scarab, or dung beetle, is the symbol of resurrection.[1] Many motifs associated with this civilization served as inspiration in later periods, in particular for Empire style (see later discussion) and Art Deco (discussed in Chapter 12).

Greece (1000–30 B.C.)

Ancient Greek civilization may be divided into three broad periods: the pre-Hellenic, or archaic, period (c. 1000–480 B.C.); the Hellenic period, also referred to as the golden age (480–400 B.C.); and the Hellenistic period (400–30 B.C.), which elaborated on classical features of the 5th century B.C. During its history, Greece established cities in Asia Minor (also known as Anatolia, equating closely to the borders of modern-day Turkey), Egypt, Spain, France, and southern Italy and around the Black Sea.

It was during the Hellenic period that the independent Greek city-states banded together to defeat the invading Persians. Democracy was accomplished in Athens under the leadership of Pericles (443–429 B.C.). During this period, art and architecture achieved great stature. Under the reign of Alexander the Great (336–323 B.C.) in the Hellenistic period, the Persian Empire was conquered (Figure 11.8). This period pro-

Figure 11.7

Egypt motifs. *(Egyptian ornament from "Grammar of Ornament," 1868 [color litho] by Owen Jones [1809–1874]. Private Collection / The Bridgeman Art Library)*

vides the most archaeological evidence from which to draw conclusions about the buildings of ancient Greece. *De Architectura*, by the Roman architect Vitruvius, documented the architecture from this time. This voluminous work, written in the 1st century B.C., influenced architecture during the Renaissance and later in Colonial America.

As noted in Chapter 2, the aesthetics of design and principles of proportion, symmetry, and harmony ascribed to Western ideals of beauty are derived from the art and architecture of the golden age of Greece.

Most Greek houses were one- or two-story. **Post-and-lintel**, or **post-and-beam**, construction was used. This is a system of vertical and horizontal supports. Wooden stairs connected multiple floors. Stone was

Figure 11.8
Map of ancient Greece, c. 5th century B.C.

Figure 11.9
a. Greek order of columns: Corinthian, Ionic, and Doric; b. Polychrome ornamentation is featured in the restored News Building, Athens, Georgia. (*a: © Bettmann/CORBIS; b: Ionic Column Detail, Photo © Tim Buchanan Photography, © Allen Greenberg, architect*)

used for important public buildings, and temples were often constructed of marble. Because the mud brick used for houses did not survive, the archeological record has provided us with more information about the interiors of ancient Greek public buildings than of residences.

The role of the column in Greek architecture and interiors is significant. These columns are categorized into three major architectural orders—Doric, Ionic, and Corinthian—having a similar type of fluted shaft, or body, but a distinct capital. The **Doric** capital featured a simple horizontal plane at the top; volutes, or spirals, distinguished the **Ionic** capital; and the **Corinthian** capital, the most ornate, had carvings of the acanthus leaf, an indigenous plant (Figure 11.9a). Until the excavations in the late 18th and early 19th centuries, it was believed that most ancient Greek buildings were white. However, studies of excavated ruins showed that key structural elements of temples, such as the walls and columns, were accented by red, yellow, and blue paint. Green paint was used to a lesser degree. Color was highly saturated, with no tonal variety. Purple pigment, derived from a shellfish, was costly and considered regal.

Because we are accustomed to seeing the ruins of this ancient period with no visible evidence left of the saturated pigment of the polychrome, the colorful replicas in Figure 11.9b appear odd. However, the depiction of the décor in the News Building in Athens, Georgia, is based on history.

The **colonnade**, a series of regularly spaced columns, epitomized the notion of space in the Greek interior. The Greek residence was made up of a distribution of rooms—living room, kitchen, bathroom, and dining room—around a central courtyard. An emphasis was placed on privacy. Bedrooms, relegated more often to just the women of the household, were located on an upper floor.

Floors were made of earth, and those of the more affluent were treated with plaster or paint. The floors of important rooms were embellished with pebble or glass mosaics, some depicting mythological themes.

The walls of private residences were made of thick mud brick. In finer residences they were plastered or painted with decoration. Paint was applied in a solid color, such as red or ochre, a brownish-yellow, or in different colors or finishes to separate the field, dado, and cornice. In the Hellenistic period, stone finishes were painted.

Ceilings were mostly flat and painted or coffered (see Chapter 9) in cedar. Those of the first floor were quite high. Because the occupants reclined while dining, the ceiling was an important decorative, as well as functional, feature.

There were few window openings. They were placed high and framed simply in wood or stone. For public buildings, doors were sometimes paneled or covered with bronze sheeting, perhaps studded. Hanging fabrics were used to partition interiors.

Much of what is known about early Greek furniture comes from the study of details painted on ancient vases, a highly evolved decorative art form of the period (Figure 11.10). Some of the furniture that survived was made of metal and marble, although it is known that wood was used extensively, with dowel-and-tenon joinery and seats made of woven leather strips. Furniture was not fixed in place, but brought out and used as necessary, so most pieces were light in weight. The invention of the lathe, attributed to Assyria or Persia, had a major impact on Greece. The lathe was a tool used for wood turning, the process of fashioning wood pieces into various forms and shapes. It enabled users to round the legs of furniture and to produce more elaborate decorative carvings.

Three types of seats were used: stool, throne (Figure 11.11), and klismos. The stool was similar to those used by the Egyptians. The throne was made for gods,

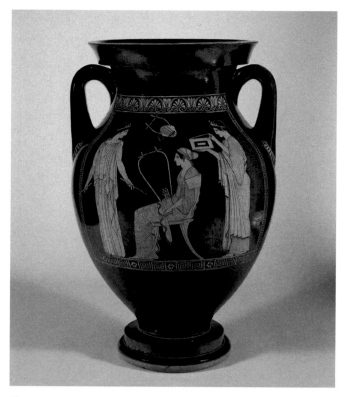

Figure 11.10
A klismos shown on a red and black clay vase. *(Courtesy of the Walters Art Museum)*

Figure 11.11
A throno (throne), c. 5th century B.C. *(Erich Lessing / Art Resource, New York)*

in several versions: with or without arms, with or without backs, and in varied heights. The iconic **klismos** is perhaps the most universally recognized of all the ancient Greek furniture. It was the typical seating in houses, most often wooden, with a woven leather-and-cord seat.

Modified and reproduced throughout history, the klismos has become a symbol of elegance and sophisti-cated construction. It features a curved back and legs that curve backward, later known as **saber legs**, and does not require stretchers for support. The klismos remains one of the most reproduced styles today (Figure 11.12a–d)

The **kline** was an elongated version of the throne. It served not only as a bed, but also as a couch for reclining at meals. Small, portable tables, often a tripod (three-legged), were used for dining purposes and

Figure 11.12

Klismos, *Then and Now*. a. CAD sketch of an original, 5th-century klismos; b. Robsjohn-Gibbings, c. 1937; c. Hollywood Regency style; d. Chair designed by John Hutton for Donghia. *(b: The Metropolitan Museum of Art, Purchase, Edward C. Moore Jr., 1924 [24.133] Photograph © 2001 The Metropolitan Museum of Art, Gift of Mr. and Mrs. Klaus G. Perls, 1997 [1997.145.1] Photography © 1997 The Metropolitan Museum of Art; c: Courtesy of Baker; d: Anziano [or Academy] Chair designed by John Hutton for Donghia)*

Figure 11.13
The tripod was a common furnishing in ancient Greece.
(© *The Metropolitan Museum of Art / Art Resource, New York*)

Figure 11.14
Variations on the Greek key and anthemion motifs.

stored under the bed when not in use (Figure 11.13). Chests for storage of clothing, jewelry, and household objects were paneled and lidded.

Women in Greek society spun and wove fabrics of wool and linen that were used as wall hangings, draperies for door passages and bed canopies, and seat covers. Designs were woven into the material, embroidered, or painted on.

The range of classical Greek motifs is extensive. Among the most common are the anthemion, or honeysuckle; key; laurel; egg and dart; zigzag; wave; scroll; and rosette[2] (Figure 11.14). As demonstrated later in this chapter and in Chapter 12, these motifs would reappear in their pure form and as derivatives in many later period design styles.

Rome (509 B.C.–A.D. 476)

The history of ancient Rome can be divided into two basic periods: the Republic (509–27 B.C.) and the Empire

(27 B.C.–A.D. 476). From 616 to 509 B.C., the Etruscans ruled the city of Rome. These kings from Etruria, in Asia Minor, brought the influence of the Orient, in particular the Near East, to Rome, including an extensive use of bronze. When the last Etruscan king was expelled in 509 B.C., the Republic was established. What followed was the acquisition of territory held by the Greeks. By 27 B.C., under Augustus, the boundaries of the Roman Empire extended from the Persian Gulf to North Africa and northern Europe (Figure 11.15). As the Roman Empire expanded, it was necessary to construct roads and bridges to maintain dependable communication. The Romans excelled in this area.

The first enclosed building designed specifically to serve as a permanent market was a Roman innovation.[3] In addition, the athletic stadium of modern times is directly derived from the Roman amphitheater.

Much of our information about Roman interiors comes from archaeological excavations at Pompeii and

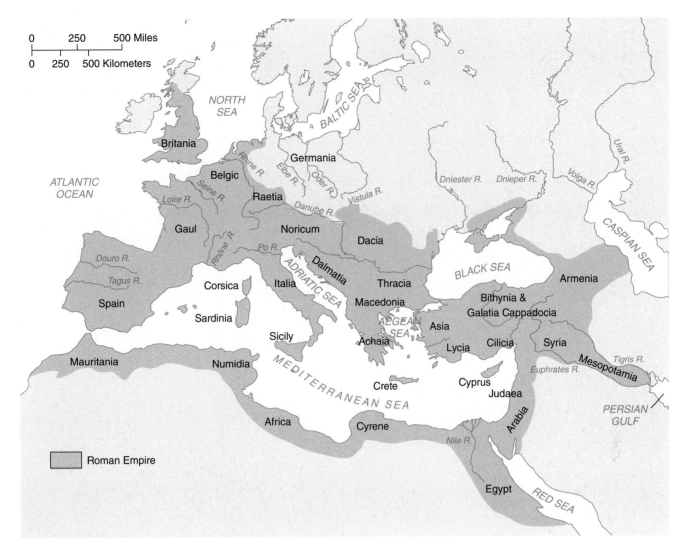

Figure 11.15
Map of the Roman Empire, c. 27 B.C.

Herculaneum, towns that included wealthy neighborhoods that were preserved under layers of ash and lava when Mount Vesuvius erupted in A.D. 79. Whereas the Greeks reserved their finest architecture for public buildings, such as temples and civic structures, the Romans elevated the stature of domestic buildings. Most Romans lived in multifamily, apartment-like dwellings with shared walls. Shops were often located on the first floor.[4]

Family life and the role of women were revered in Roman culture, and great attention was given to the interior space of houses. Although they drew heavily on Greek design, proportion was of less importance to the Romans, and they placed more emphasis on ornamentation. Also, for building construction, the Romans relied more on workers skilled in particular areas of expertise, the forerunners of the guild workers of the medieval period (see later discussion) and modern trade unions.[5]

A major contribution of the Romans to building construction was the development of concrete (see

Chapter 8), which was also used for interiors. Because it could be easily manipulated, concrete made it possible to shape everyday interiors in a variety of ways, such as with arches, domes, niches, stucco relief, and vaulted ceilings (Figure 11.16).

Other contributions were the highly sophisticated plumbing and heating systems. Bathhouses played a major role in the architecture and culture of ancient Rome. Most were large public facilities that housed a

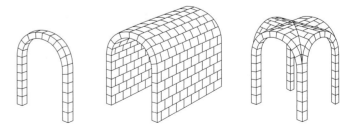

Figure 11.16
Roman contributions to architecture. a. Arch; b. Barrel vault; c. Cross vaults.

Figure 11.17
Ancient Roman bath. *(© The Granger Collection, New York City. All rights reserved)*

Figure 11.18
Couch (kline), fresco from Pompeii, and mosaic floor from Boscoreale, c. 50 B.C. *(© Werner Forman/CORBIS)*

pool, an exercise and sports area, and places to socialize, relax, read, and converse (Figure 11.17). Smaller baths in private homes also existed. The floors of Roman villas were often made of marble-and-glass mosaics. Although mosaics had been used in earlier civilizations, the Romans created elaborate designs, many of which depicted figures from myths and stories (Figure 11.18). Modern radiant heating systems derive from ancient Roman flooring raised to accommodate burning coal to warm the floors.

The use of concrete meant that walls could be expansive and uninterrupted, without need of support columns. Surfaces were painted in a variety of ways, with techniques that imitated the texture of stone, such as marble, or that gave an illusion of the presence of architectural features (trompe l'oeil; see Chapter 9), such as columns supporting the ceiling. Later, intricate ornamentation with Egyptian motifs and figurative themes flourished.

Another contribution of the Romans was the **fresco**, the technique of painting on wet plaster. This treatment often featured perspective drawing that extended the appearance of the space (see Figure 11.18).

Buildings were multilevel, and ceilings were flat or vaulted, coffered, or painted with designs of foliage, the zodiac, or animals. Cornices separated the walls from the ceiling. Since there were few interior doors used between rooms, more often draperies were used. When draperies were open, a rhythmic succession of rooms could be viewed, known as **enfilade**.

Roman architects used light as a prominent design element. Because privacy was important, there were few windows on the first floor. The tops of windows were generally semicircular. Doors were constructed of painted or paneled wood or bronze.

Most Roman furniture was derivative of Greek designs. However, the Romans were more concerned with opulence in material and ornamentation. Furniture was made of local wood, such as maple, as well as ebony and satinwood from Africa. Veneering and inlays of ivory, gold, and silver were popular. Metal, in particular bronze, was also used in furniture construction. Affluent citizens had furniture made with gold, silver, and bronze plating. Outdoor furniture was made of marble.

Popular furniture forms included stools, couches, and several styles of chairs and tables. The **cathedra** was a chair used primarily by women, resembling the Greek klismos, but heavier in proportion. Stools used a variation of the X-form called a **curule**, but were curved (Figure 11.19). Roman thrones were more imposing than those of the Greeks; tables served more purposes and took on different forms. In addition to the tripod, there were pedestal tables, anchored by a central support, and **trestles**, larger tables consisting of a wood or marble board atop lateral supports. Both Romans and Greeks added a back to their couches. When used for dining, three couches would be arranged in a U-shape. Like the Greeks, the Romans used couches for both dining and sleeping.

The Romans used the same color palette as the Greeks. Motifs borrowed from the Greeks included

Figure 11.19
Curule chair of ancient Rome.

astrological themes and plant forms, such as the acanthus leaf. Other motifs included animal forms, such as the lion and serpent as well as the griffin, a type of fantasy beast.

Arguably, there are many theories of what contributed to the end of the Roman Empire. Among them poor leadership, military blunders, even lead poisoning. However, among them were the excesses of the lifestyle and the bankrupting of financial resources that contributed to the fall of the Roman Empire. Although the tastes of the emperor Augustus were considered restrained, his successors became increasingly ostentatious. Nero (A.D. 37–68), the emperor who reputedly "fiddled while Rome burned," was notorious for his decadent and lavish lifestyle. His octagonal-shaped Golden House, in Rome, a setting of costly mosaics, marble interior walls, paintings, and mechanical devices, epitomized this lavishness.

MEDIEVAL PERIOD (330–c. 1500)

The period of approximately 1,000 years following the fall of the Roman Empire is known as the medieval period or the Middle Ages. During these years, wars and disease, including the plague, periodically ravaged western Europe, and for many people the focus of life narrowed to mere survival.

For much of the early medieval period, houses afforded little privacy. Houses of the wealthy landowners were built as walled-in castles that served as fortresses against invaders. Comfort, privacy, and sanitation were considered luxuries. Largely as a protection against attack, windows were small; walls, thick; and living arrangements, communal. Access to the living quarters, for security, was by way of a centrally located stairway.

The **great hall** provided space for the many serfs (peasants who worked the land) maintained by the

Figure 11.20
Great hall with dais along the back wall, trestle tables along the left wall, wood for fire in the center of photo, and a vaulted ceiling. *(By kind permission of Viscount De L'Isle from his private collection at Penshurst Place, Kent, England)*

landowner or lord. It was used for sleeping and dining as well as administrative functions, both religious and civic. The **dais**, a raised platform located at one end of a room, is attributed to this period. In medieval times the landowners dined on the dais while those of lower station sat below (Figure 11.20).

There were several styles during this period, some of them contemporaneous. Four subdivisions, each of which had a distinct impact on design style, are Byzantine, or early Christian (330–1453); Moorish (c. 700–c. 1400), Romanesque (c. 800–c. 1200), and Gothic (c. 1200–c. 1500).

Byzantine Style (330–1453)
The artistic productions of the Byzantine Empire are both European and Christian, but definitively characterized by non-Western influences. In 330, Emperor Constantine the Great, of Rome, created a seat of power for the Christian Church in Byzantium, in Asia Minor. His new capital, first called New Rome, then Constantinople (now Istanbul, Turkey), would become the largest city in the medieval world, with a racially and culturally diverse populace.

The Byzantine Empire flourished for more than 1,000 years (Figure 11.21). It signified the growth of Christianity, merging with an ancient Eastern culture.

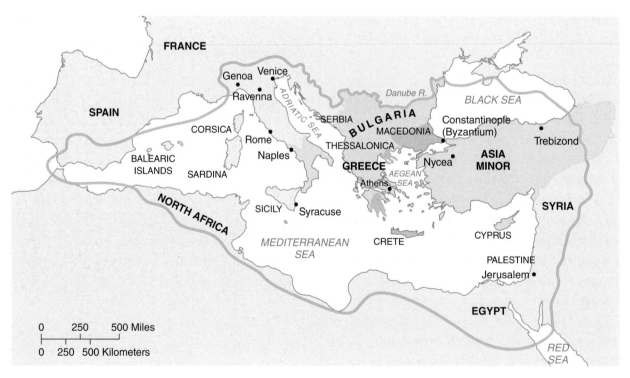

Figure 11.21
Map of the Byzantine Empire.

Many of the artisans were from the Orient, giving Byzantine style its mark of elaborate ornamentation in architecture, furniture, and the decorative arts. Artisans were trained in brilliantly colored **cloisonné** enamel work and illuminated manuscripts with gold. Silks were embroidered with gold threads. Mosaics decorated walls and ceilings.

Eventually, disagreements in the interpretations of Christianity by the Eastern and Western Churches led to the separation of the Roman Catholic Church and the Eastern Orthodox Church, which remains in effect today.

The Byzantine influence permeated much of Europe and North Africa and can still be seen in many parts of Europe, particularly in the cities of Ravenna and Venice, Italy, through which much of the trade from the Eastern Empire flowed into Western Europe.[6]

The dome, a traditional feature of the East, became a dominant element in Byzantine architecture, especially for churches. The most famous example of Byzantine architecture is the Hagia Sophia (Church of Holy Wisdom) in Istanbul, Turkey, shown in Figure 11.22a and b. (In the 15th century this church became an Islamic mosque.) St. Mark's Cathedral in Venice (Figure 11.23a), built in the 11th century, also illustrates the influence of Byzantium. Another particular Byzantine style of ecclesiastic architecture featuring bulbous domes shaped like onions developed in Russia. The slopes of the domes served to prevent build up of snow in the region's severe cold climate (Figure 11.23b).

Moorish Style (c. 700–c. 1400)

The term *Moorish* is derived from the name Morocco, a country in North Africa. The spread of the Islamic religion into the Mediterranean area of Europe by conquering Arabs and Berbers provided another non-Western influence during this period. Moorish architecture features brick as the major material for both structure and ornament, used in combination with stone and stucco. Religious buildings, known as mosques, featured columned halls arranged around an open, communal space containing a fountain or pool for ritual cleansing.

Evidence of Moorish style is largely found in Spain, Portugal, and Morocco. The Alhambra, in Granada, Spain, is a magnificent example of the Islamic presence in Spain (Figure 11.24a and b).

Intricate interlacing patterns combining straight and curved lines are prevalent, including geometric

Figure 11.22

Byzantine architecture. a. Hagia Sophia, Istanbul, 532–536; b. Interior detail of Hagia Sophia. *(a: Archimhb | Dreamstime.com; b: © Masterlu | Dreamstime.com)*

Figure 11.23

a. St. Mark's, Venice, 1042–1085; b. St. Sophia church in Kiev, Russia, built in the early 11th century, restored in the 12th century as shown, with onion bulb dome features. *(a: © Paul Hardy/CORBIS; b: © Dkorolov | Dreamstime.com)*

Figure 11.24

Moorish design. a. The Alhambra, Granada, 1354–1391, features carved stucco exterior and geometric tile detail; b. Interior detail in the Alhambra. *(a: © John Henshall / Alamy; b: © Derek White)* designs, five-pointed stars, and Arabic script. The effect is kaleidoscopic. As the Islamic world spread to South Asia (today's India and Pakistan) during the Renaissance, its influence on art and design also spread (see later discussion).

Romanesque Style (c. 800–1200)

Romanesque is a style of architecture and furniture that emerged from the mixture of invading Germanic tribes, including the Franks and Goths, Vikings (Norsemen or later Normans), Slavs, and Magyars.

The Romanesque style of architecture relies on heavy masonry construction, characterized by plain walls with little ornamentation. The greatest use of these architectural features in furniture occurred in Italy. Chests (called coffers or arks) were the most common types of furniture. At first they were simply hollowed-out tree trunks; later, hinged tops were added. A typical woodcarving design, **arcading**, reflected a succession of Roman arches (Figure 11.25).

Gothic Style (c. 1200–c. 1500)

By the 13th century, Europe had become somewhat more stabilized, as rivalries for land diminished. This relative peace gave rise to a new style of construction in which comfort and decoration were of greater significance. Interest in the arts and crafts reemerged.

Certain common characteristics distinguish the Gothic style, particularly as expressed in England and France. In comparison with the earlier, medieval period, more attention was given to domestic and secular architecture. Ecclesiastical design (i.e., design related to the church) did remain important. The cathedral of Notre Dame, in Paris, is perhaps one of the most widely recognized structures constructed in the Gothic style.

The development of craft guilds was another significant contribution. Monasteries had established strict standards, with supervision over workmanship. With renewed interest in secular construction, laymen were brought into the building trades to add to the complement of monks who had previously done most of this labor. These secular craft guilds grew quickly in England and France. The focus was a training system based on a level of competencies within ranks, ranging from apprentice, to journeyman, to master. Tradesmen were trained in specific areas, such as woodwork, metalwork, and stonework. This guild approach

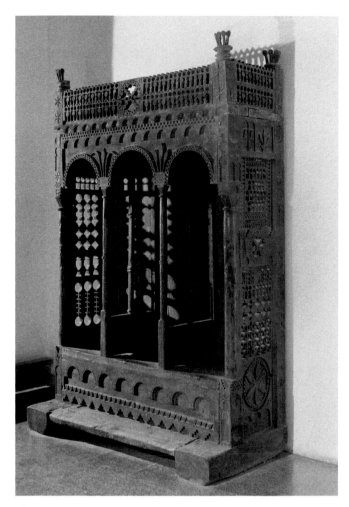

Figure 11.25

Romanesque arcading. *(Bench in presbytery of church of San Clemente de Tahull, Romanesque, 12th century. Photo credit: The Art Archive at Art Resource, New York)*

would be resurrected in modern times, during the arts and crafts movement (discussed in Chapter 12).

Most houses of the nobility included the **privy**: private quarters for the lord consisting primarily of a bed and sitting area, chapel, kitchen, and great hall. Secular and religious rituals occurred in the public areas.

Floors were covered with stone slabs, such as slate, granite, marble, and sandstone. Glazed tiles in a checkerboard pattern were used in later periods. Wide wood-plank floors were used in upper stories. Carpets were not typically used.

Wood and plaster were the essential interior wall surfaces. As the wealth of the lord increased, so too did the number of decorative elements. Carving and, to a lesser degree, paint enhanced the interiors. Oak was used amply in England, whereas walnut was more common in France. Wood paneling was often used on the lower part of a wall, typically with **linenfold**, a type of carving suggesting fabric folds. This ornamentation

Figure 11.26
Gothic chair featuring linenfold carving and storage seat, c. 1500 France. *(Collection Rijksmuseum Amsterdam)*

Figure 11.27
Vaulted ceiling and Gothic arches, Wells Cathedral, England, 1174–1425. *(Chris Hammond / Alamy)*

was used to adorn chests and chair backs as well (Figure 11.26).

Murals featuring religious themes or acts of chivalry (knightly activity) were also painted on walls. Wall painting was more prevalent for interiors in the Mediterranean region than in northern Europe at this time.

The vaulted ceiling (sometimes with flying buttresses) became a trademark of Gothic architecture, along with the pointed arch (Figure 11.27) (as differentiated from the rounded Roman arch). The great hall was generally two stories high and had the most impressive ceiling in the structure.

Because defense was a major issue in residential architecture, window openings were necessarily small. Wooden shutters placed on the inside protected occupants from the weather. Glass was a luxury, and when available, panes were small, diamond shaped, and set in lead. However, for important cathedrals, stained glass

became common, as exemplified by the **rose window** in the cathedral of Notre Dame (Figure 11.28). The tops of fenestrations could be either flat or shaped in a pointed arch. Carved openwork ornamentation, called **tracery**, often adorned the tops of windows. Door construction was usually of the board-and-batten type (see Table 8.2), with strap hinges. Like windows, doors were often arched, and paneling was used later in the period.

The life of the nobleman was nomadic because he often had to oversee far-flung properties. This meant that interior decoration and furniture were movable. Woven tapestries of wool not only served as portable decoration, but also helped prevent drafts and retain heat. They were often completed as a series of panels, reflecting a theme or story requested by the individual

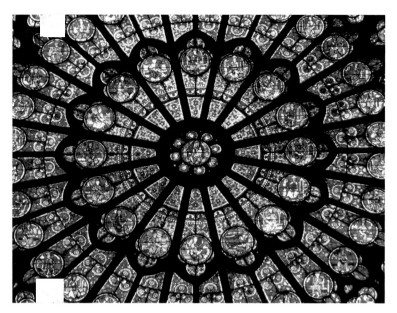

Figure 11.28
The stained glass rose window at Notre Dame Cathedral, Paris. *(Courtesy of Fairchild Publications, Inc.)*

Figure 11.29
High-back chair: The Coronation Chair in Westminster Abbey, made by Master Walter of Durham for Edward I in 1296, shows tracery and foil motifs. *(V & A Images / Victoria & Albert Museum)*

who commissioned them. Typical subjects were classical mythology; religious stories; and contemporary scenes, such as hunts. These tapestries became the prized furnishings of noble homes.

The chair was a status symbol (Figure 11.29). Only the lord of the manor or his designee sat on one; others were relegated to benches and stools. A table for dining was composed of a long board and trestle. The expression "chairman of the board" is derived from the fact that only the head of the household sat on a chair at the board, or table.

Typically, seating also provided storage space. Stools served as seating, tables, and sometimes storage. Chests remained the most common article of furniture, used to store and transport items. Other case pieces associated with this period are the credenza (credence), and **buffet**, which functioned as dining servers (Figure 11.30). In France the **armoire** held armorial equipment and clothing. Known as a **court cupboard** in England, it provided a place to display and store possessions, either the vestments, or ceremonial objects, of the church or the secular possessions of the wealthy.

Gradually, beds with feather mattresses replaced straw mats. Beds then became an expression of wealth and adornment. Textiles were used as curtains and canopies; and furs and tapestries, as bed coverings. The fabric damask (see Chapter 10), named after a

Figure 11.30
Gothic interiors: wall paneling, credence (or credenza), buffet, armoire (or court cupboard), and table. *(V & A Images / Victoria & Albert Museum)*

Figure 11.31

The Unicorn Tapestries, c. 1500, exemplify late Gothic achievements in wall hangings. *(The Unicorn Leaps across a Stream. The Hunt of the Unicorn. c. 1495–1505. Location photo credit: Image copyright. Photo credit: The Metropolitan Museum of Art / Art Resource, New York)*

floral pattern associated with the Near East, especially Damascus, was also employed to adorn beds. Textiles sometimes covered seating. The cradle, or crib, was developed during this period as a bed for a child.

The colors associated with this period were primarily red and green, drawing heavily from religious tapestries. The color red represented the wealth of the clergy and papacy. The series of seven wall hangings known as *The Unicorn Tapestries,* featured in Figure 11.31, demonstrates the use of these colors in harmony with the white of the unicorn.

THE RENAISSANCE (c. 1450–1649)

Originating in Italy, and spreading to France, Spain, and the Low Countries (modern Belgium, Luxembourg, and the Netherlands) before finally reaching England, the period of revitalization in Europe known as the Renaissance represented a return to the philosophy and ideals of classical Greece and Rome.

The Renaissance, which takes its name from the French word for "rebirth," was a period of increased stability, refinement, scholarly endeavors, and world travel. Many significant features relating to interiors developed during this period.

The need for a communal orientation to interior space became less important during this time of greater peace. The Renaissance interior displayed a disposition for privacy and was smaller in scale and proportion than the medieval interior. This change was partly inspired by the intellectual concept of humanism, which stressed an individual's dignity and worth on earth, thus reducing the influence of religion and heavenly aspirations. Rooms became smaller, more numerous, more private, and of singular purpose. Greater specialization was seen in the division of space and in the use of furniture.

Italy (c. 1450–c. 1600)

With the fall of Constantinople to Turkish invaders in 1453, Italy again took on a dominant role in the Western world, spurring a renewed interest in the arts, architecture, science, literacy, and culture. Although Rome was the seat of power for the Church, the stimulus for this rebirth of the arts came from Florence, Italy. It can be said that the 15th century was to Italy what the 5th century B.C. was to Greece. The Italian Renaissance was a period of fascination with antiquity and with the classical order established by the ancient Greeks and later adapted by the Romans.

The relative stability and peace among the Italian city-states allowed trade and commerce to flourish, bringing greater prosperity. Wealthy citizens turned their attention toward the building and decoration of secular buildings and houses. The concept of the apartment developed in Italy during this period.

Interest was renewed during the 15th century in the writing of Vitruvius, who in the 1st century had outlined the ideas of the ancient Greeks. Later, in the 16th century, the architect Andrea Palladio wrote the *Four Books of Architecture*, which laid out in great detail the classical proportions prescribed by the ancients (see Chapters 1, 3, and 8).

Lorenzo de' Medici (1449–1492) and his family, who ruled Florence during this period, made the city a center of learning, providing financial support to artists, architects, artisans, and scholars. Artistic advances included the use of oil painting, perspective drawing, sculpture, and gilding.

Italian floors were often made of colored ceramic tiles laid in a geometric pattern. Upper floors were constructed of wide-plank wood. The use of stone, especially marble and terrazzo, was generally reserved for public buildings.

Walls of the Renaissance period followed the tradition of compartmental division used in antiquity. The upper part of the wall was more highly decorated than the portion below the dado, and design motifs were placed symmetrically (Figure 11.32). Fresco painters used trompe l'oeil techniques with great virtuosity (Figure 11.33). The ability to portray perspective accurately was displayed on walls and ceilings in illustrations of landscapes and cities, which gave the illusion of depth and distance.

Ceilings were flat, vaulted, or covered in wood and then finished in stucco. Doors displayed extravagant detail and were often surrounded with carved wood and marble. Fireplaces, also a strong focal point, were highly decorated.

Figure 11.32
Renaissance wall decoration. (© Araldo de Luca/CORBIS)

Figure 11.33
Trompe l'oeil. Villa Barbaro c. 1550; architecture by Palladio, frescoes by Paolo Veronese. *(© Araldo de Luca/CORBIS)*

The primary wood for fine furniture during the 15th and 16th centuries was walnut. Many of the medieval construction techniques continued to be used. However, more elaborate decorative enhancement was employed. Additional categories of furniture developed to accommodate storage and display, including that of scholarly books, works of art, and collections of the master of the home. After the invention of the printing press, in the 15th century, lecterns and other furnishings related to reading and writing were needed.

A specific case piece that developed was the highly decorated **cassone**, a marriage chest in which a bride would hold her dowry (Figure 11.34a). The **cassapanca**, the forerunner of the modern sofa, was essen-

tially a cassone with arms and back added. Two chairs in the form of an X, the **Savonarola** and the **Dante** (Figure 11.34b and c), were status symbols. The **sgabello**, although not as comfortable, was typical seating (Figure 11.34d). The **sedia** (Figure 11.34e) was an armchair with a tall back and high, upholstered seat. The trestle table was still used for dining, and smaller tables now appeared for occasional use.

Textiles were significant elements in the treatment of beds. Silk, in large, colorful patterns, was frequently used. The harlequin pattern was based on the costume of the Italian comedy character, or jester, called *arlecchino*. Various needlepoint techniques were employed, among them the **bargello** and **flame stitch**. They regained popularity in the 1970s, and then fell

Figure 11.34

Furniture of the Italian Renaissance.
a. Cassone; b. Savonarola chair; c. Dante chair; d. Sgabello; e. the straight-back Sedia. *(a: Cassone chest, c. 1450. Depicts Solomon and the Queen of Sheba. Wood, painted and gilt. Location: Victoria & Albert Museum, London. Photo credit: V & A Images, London / Art Resource; b: Savonarola chair. Italian Renaissance. Location: Museo di S. Marco, Florence, Italy. Photo credit: Scala / Art Resource, New York; c: © Stockbyte Silver; d: Collection Rijksmuseum Amsterdam)*

out of favor. Now, these intricate, rhythmic patterns are often computer generated.

Accessories associated with Renaissance origin include the candelabra, small tables, mirrors, and majolica (see Chapter 10).

Colors such as red and green, used in earlier periods, remained important as well as gold (gilding). Blue became more prominent and was featured in many of the Oriental imports, such as carpets, ceramics, and tiles.

Ornamentation expressed the vocabulary of ancient Greece and Rome, with an emphasis on architectural features to define style. Among these were the **pilaster**, a column-like feature projecting slightly from a surface, such as a wall, and the **caryatid**, a sculptured female figure used in place of a column or support (Figure 11.35). The **arabesque**, an intricate pattern of interlacing plant tendrils, and the **grotesque**, monstrous and fantastical creatures, are typical Renaissance motifs, found in carved or painted versions, that were inspired by Eastern design.[7]

France (c. 1460–c. 1600)

Architects and artists who traveled to Italy in the 1400s brought back to their own countries a vision of the new style they found there. Because the French had been more entrenched in the Gothic style than the Italians, their interpretations were not always as true to the classical order. Nonetheless, Francis (François) I, the king of France from 1515 to 1547, combined Italian and French talents in the construction of the magnificent Fontainebleau Palace (Figure 11.36). Whereas Italian political power emanated from cities, with the establishment of Versailles the French nation increasingly looked to the countryside, outside of Paris.

Figure 11.35
Caryatids are a typical Renaissance architectural feature and motif adapted from classical Greek architecture. *(Caryatids, carrying a balcony for musicians. Marble, c. 1550. Location: Louvre, Paris, France. Photo credit: Erich Lessing / Art Resource, New York)*

Figure 11.36
The opulently decorated Francis (François) I gallery at Fontainebleau. *(© Sandro Vannini/CORBIS)*

In France, the concept of the apartment was taken further with the adoption of rooms in an enfilade arrangement, a succession of rooms through which one could pass directly. The idea of furniture **en suite**, in matching pieces for a particular area, began to spread throughout Europe.

The Italian influence on France flourished under King Henri II (1519–1559), whose spouse, Catherine de' Medici, of Florence, continued to hold sway over the social and political style of France even after his death. Under the reign of King Louis XIII (1610–1643), France was influenced also by Flemish and Spanish style.[8]

Ceramic floor tiles were used for floors; parquet wood floors were more often used in important spaces. The Fontainebleau Palace, for example, featured parquet floors in a herringbone pattern. Walnut paneling was used to cover entire walls, as were stone and plaster. Hangings, such as tapestries and painted canvases, also embellished walls.

Furniture in France, to an even greater degree than in Italy, combined Gothic features with Renaissance refinements and motifs, with an increased emphasis on comfort. Smaller tables for games and serving tea, brought back from the Far East, became fashionable. In early Renaissance France the diamond shape was a frequent decorative element, particularly for large case pieces. Most chairs remained rectilinear, with a high back and with or without a storage chest under the seat. These throne-type chairs eventually became lighter in weight and form. A type of chair associated with the French Renaissance is the **caquetoire** ("gossip chair"), intended to accommodate the width of a woman's skirt (Figure 11.37a). The signature storage pieces in France were the **armoire à deux corps**, a cupboard in two parts (Figure 11.37b), and the **lit de repos**, inspired by the ancient Greek couch. More complex techniques for upholstery were developed, such as attached upholstery, which replaced loose cushions.

Figure 11.37

a. French caquetoire (gossip chair); b. Armoire à deux corps, 16th century, Lyon, France. *(a: Caquetoire [Renaissance armchair with narrow back], walnut, 16th-century French. Credit: The Art Archive / Musée du Louvre Paris / Gianni Dagli Ort; b: Armoire à deux corps © Lyon MBA/Photo Alain Basset)*

England (c. 1550–1649)

Tardy in comparison with the revitalization occurring in Italy and, to a lesser degree, in France, England finally experienced a Renaissance of sorts. Stylistically, there is often a sharp division between Gothic and Renaissance on the European continent, yet in England sometimes the two blended in unexpected ways. Beginning with the reign of King Henry VII (1485–1509) and continuing through that of his granddaughter Queen Elizabeth I (1558–1603), England's sphere of influence expanded abroad. Building construction and décor began to incorporate designs from abroad, including those incorporating classical elements. Artistic endeavors focused on the literary and theatrical, with William Shakespeare (1564–1616) serving as a key figure. The predominant style during this period—Tudor (1485–1603), which includes Elizabethan (1558–1603) and Jaco-

bean (1603–1649)—represents the stages of Renaissance influence in England.

The first half of the 17th century was notable for a greater understanding of the classical vocabulary. Inigo Jones (1573–1652), an English architect, studied in Italy and was greatly influenced by Palladio. His work brought greater symmetry and refinement to English design at this time and had an impact on the American colonies as well. However, the English response to the Italian Renaissance was essentially indirect, influenced more strongly by France, Belgium, and Flanders than by Italy.

King Henry VIII's 1536 decree dissolving the monasteries diverted much of the riches of the English church into secular hands. This was a major force in the building of houses in the city and country for the middle class and aristocracy. Homes during this period often used a half-timbered type of construction

Figure 11.38
The Elizabethan Burton Constable Hall, England, was built in the 16th century. By the 17th century, the Long Gallery (as shown) featured elaborate furnishings and collections for display. *(Marquess of Salisbury and Jarrold Publishing)*

featuring an oak frame darkly stained by tar and a filling of branches and plaster. Roofs were thatched. The medieval great hall remained. The parlor was used for family dining and as an informal sitting room. On the upper story a **long gallery** that extended along the building's façade became a characteristic feature. This gallery typically was used for exercise, games, and social events and to display collections, such as Chinese porcelains (Figure 11.38).

Furniture remained sparse, and the methods of construction were not significantly different from those of the Middle Ages. Oak was used during much of this period, with walnut becoming more prevalent in the later part. Trestle tables remained, although more permanent table varieties, such as the refectory table, were also used. Like the caquetoire, the English **farthingale** chair was made to accommodate

the hoop skirts worn by women during this time (Figure 11.39a). **Turkey work**, a heavy fabric that imitated Eastern carpet design, was used to cover seating.

Paneled chests became more prevalent, such as the **nonesuch (nonsuch)** (Figure 11.39b). Varieties of the cupboard were used for both storage and display. The court cupboard contained open spaces, whereas the **press cupboard** had more closed space for storage. Tables with expandable tops were used, such as draw-leaf, drop-leaf, and gate-leg. The **melon** and **cup and cover** are the names given to table legs with bulbous turnings. This type of carving reflected the influence of craftsmen from Flanders (today mostly in Belgium).

Features of the English bed used by nobility during this time included a freestanding front post. The Great Bed of Ware (Figure 11.40) represents a new-found extravagance in its architectural features.

a

b

Figure 11.39
Oak furniture of the English Renaissance, 16th to 17th centuries. a. Farthingale chair with turkey work; b. Nonesuch chest. *(a: Turkey-work upholstery chair. Inv.: 428–1896. Photo credit: Victoria & Albert Museum, London / Art Resource, New York; b: V & A Images/ Victoria & Albert Museum)*

Figure 11.40
The Great Bed of Ware, England, c. 1590. *(V & A Images/ Victoria & Albert Museum)*

NON-WESTERN INFLUENCES ON DESIGN: EXPLORATION AND TRADE

Trading ships to the Orient brought back many of the textiles and accessories used by the English during this time. Among the goods imported were Chinese porcelains, Turkish rugs, and hand-painted cottons from India. The influence of the non-Western extended beyond England as travel to and trade with exotic lands became more common.

The 16th century was an important time around the world. The Renaissance was flowering in Italy, the Ming dynasty in China, and the Mughals in India. It was also the time of the voyages of discovery by European mariners, among them Columbus and Magellan, to places such as Africa, India, the West Indies, the Orient, and the Americas.

Also see *FYI . . . Non-Western Influences on Design: China* and *FYI . . . Non-Western Influences on Design: The Mughal Empire (India).*

BAROQUE STYLE (c. 1600–1730)

The term *Baroque* derives from the Portuguese word *barroco*, meaning "irregularly shaped pearl." The seashell motif became a symbol of this period. It began as an architectural movement, but as it took hold, it became associated with many other arts, in particular those relating to furniture and accessories. The Baroque style originated in Rome under the auspices of ecclesiastical leaders, primarily in the area of fine art. It became more pervasive in France under the monarchy of Louis XIV (1643–1715), known as the Sun King, the builder of Versailles. As it took hold, it became associated with many other arts, in particular those relating to furniture and accessories. The style had a strong influence in many parts of the Western world, including England and its colonies, the Low Countries, and Spain and Portugal and their colonies. Baroque style was also evident in other parts of Europe, including Germany, Austria, and Scandinavia, but for a shorter period.

The style is characterized by flamboyance, complexity, contrast of light and dark, and bold ornamentation. Other words used to describe this style are *muscular*, *explosive*, *theatrical*, *emotional*, and *exagger-*ated. Baroque style relied more heavily on the individual talents of its creators than on formal rules of design.

For much of Europe this period began as the Age of Walnut. Trade with the East fostered new domestic activities, necessitating new furnishings relating to tea and chocolate indulgences.

The Baroque interior provided a backdrop for social events, both secular and ecclesiastical, and was designed in grand proportions. It may be said that this period gave birth to the modern concepts of interior decoration and furnishing. Furniture was arranged en suite. Upholstery, especially textiles for the bed, took on even greater importance (Figure 11.41). Damask, brocade, velvet, brocatelle, needlepoint, chintz, and crewel embroidery were important components of interiors. The scale of patterns on textiles was as grandiose as befitting the furniture and architecture.

Figure 11.41
Italian Baroque bedroom, Sagreda Palace, Venice, Italy, with damask upholstery and bed linens. *(Stuccowork, probably by Abbondio Stazio of Massagno [1675–1745]. Location photo credit: Image copyright. Photo credit: The Metropolitan Museum of Art / Art Resource, New York)*

FYI . . . Non-Western Influences on Design: China

In contrast to countries such as Holland and Portugal, which pursued and established global connections, China was introspective regarding its economy and politics. Walled towns surrounded by cultivated lands were unified during the Ch'in dynasty (255–206 B.C.), which some believe gave rise to the country's English name.

Reverence of the **qi** (**chi**), thought to be the breath that created the universe, dates back to ancient times. The flow of qi, or energy, forms the basis of the art of Feng Shui, in which alignment and contrast (the forces of yin and yang) largely determine how a structure is sited and the construction of exterior and interior spaces, even in modern times.

Parallel to the rise of Christianity in Europe as a reaction against paganism was the rise of Buddhism in ancient India as a reaction against that country's religious teachings. Buddhism was introduced to China c. A.D. 65. The **pagoda**, a multilevel structure whose stories are separated by upward-curving roofs, was first built in China as a Buddhist temple and was believed to ward off flood, deter winds, and improve the prosperity of the people (Figure a).

Although furniture was used sparingly in China, it was crafted with skill in carving and joinery. Lacquering developed early to protect wood from damage by insects. Made from the sap of the lac tree indigenous to China, lacquer forms a resistant surface. A specific lacquering technique that included paintings of landscapes and birds was used often to decorate screens. These objects and the technique became known as Coromandel (named for a coast of India). Lacquered items became valued exports to Europe, as did pieces featuring other Chinese techniques for ornamentation.

The early Chinese sat on the ground or floor, but by A.D. 200 both stools and chairs had been developed. It is significant that taller chairs are considered as originating from outside of China. Armchairs with

cushions of silk, brocade, or fur were suitable for important persons. Folding chairs were used by travelers (Figure b), including warriors.

a

b

Figures a and b
a. Pagoda of Songyue Monastery, Mount Song, Henan, China, A.D. 523; b. Chinese folding chair. *(a: China Images/Alamy; b: Courtesy of Fairchild Books)*

FYI . . . Non-Western Influences on Design: The Mughal Empire (India)

The Mughal rule in India and its art flourished in the 17th century. The Taj Mahal was built by the emperor Shāh Jāhan as a tomb for his late wife. It is made of sandstone and marble decorated with semiprecious stones (Figures a and b). During the Mughal Empire many pavilions were constructed for both residential and administrative use, featuring seating of pillows and carpets. Many features that originated during the Mughal period have been adapted for contemporary use as well such as low seating (Figure c).

Figures a–c
View of Taj Majal Palace, India. a. Exterior vista; b. Detail of an interior space; c. Low seating in a contemporary Indian pavilion. *(a: © VEER; b: © Angelo Hornak / Alamy; c: Courtesy of the Indianapolis Museum of Art)*

Italy (c. 1600–c. 1700)

The furniture of 17th-century Italy, in particular the port city of Venice, was theatrical, magical, and seductive. Venice had a long history of trade with the Byzantine Empire, the Islamic world, and the Far East. The Venetians melded their roots in Western and Eastern cultures with an especially individualistic regional Baroque style. Much of the furniture was walnut, but painted surfaces and Chinese lacquering were also popular.

The artist Gian Lorenzo Bernini (1598–1680), a prominent architect, was a major influence during this

Figure 11.42
St. Peter's Basilica, Vatican City, Rome. (© *Michele Falzone / Alamy*)

period. St. Peter's Basilica (Figure 11.42) in Vatican City demonstrates the enormity of the scale and grandiosity of the Baroque style. Italian artisans skilled in painting, stucco, marble, and woodworking were in great demand and were also commissioned to work on projects elsewhere in Europe, particularly Germany, Austria, and Russia.

The use of horizontal wooden slats as window coverings appeared in the early 17th century in Venice, giving rise to the term *venetian blinds*. The technique **pietre dura**, a patterned mosaic of colored stones, was also an Italian Baroque innovation.

Netherlands (c. 1610–c. 1700)

The Baroque style flourished in the Netherlands during the prosperous times of the early 17th century. Imports, such as ivory, ebony, and porcelains, available through the trade activities of the Dutch East India Company, played a key role in the style.

Ebony furniture imported from Ceylon (now Sri Lanka) was constructed of solid wood, with turned legs, carvings, and woven cane seats, the first to appear in Europe. The use of woven cane, which allowed for air circulation, was an important feature of furniture for the indigenous populations in the tropical colonies of many European countries. This cross-fertilization of design style between mother country and colonies is an example of colonial style.

In the latter part of the 17th century, the French influence on the Netherlands became stronger, in part because of the return of the Huguenots. The Huguenots were a group of Protestants, many of Dutch origin, who had been living in France, when Louis XIV, in 1685, revoked the Edict of Nantes, an act assuring the religious freedom of Protestants. Many of these refugees returned to Holland and later traveled to England and the American colonies. They brought with them a long tradition as skilled craftsmen, cabinetmakers, weavers, glassworkers, and silversmiths as well as the influence of French taste. Among them was Daniel Marot (1661–1752), an architect-designer whose engravings served as templates for a whole sphere of decorative details, from candlesticks to elaborate bedchambers (Figure 11.43).

Marquetry in floral design was a feature of much of the Dutch furniture of this time. An exceptionally finely detailed type of marquetry, known as seaweed, was used to adorn furniture and accessories. A recognizable furniture form was the **chest-on-stand** (Figure 11.44).

In addition to importing Chinese porcelains, the Dutch produced **Delftware**, a ceramic that was often decorated with Asian motifs. A notable feature of Dutch interiors was the use of oil paintings, which were hung wherever possible, including above doors and windows.

England and Its Colonies (1650–1730)

Although the Baroque style began during the Carolean, or Restoration, period in England and continued under the reign of James II, the subsequent reign of William and Mary (1689–1702) was most clearly associated with the height of the style. When William III, Prince of Orange (in the Netherlands), married Mary Stuart, the daughter of James II, the influence of the Dutch on English style became even more pronounced.

The Great Fire of London in 1666 destroyed much of the classical architecture of earlier movements, including that of Inigo Jones. The architect Sir Christopher Wren (1632–1723) is credited with the major reconstruction of London. This reconstruc-

Figure 11.43
Marot design for a state bedchamber. *(V & A Images/ Victoria & Albert Museum)*

Figure 11.44
Dutch Baroque chest-on-stand with floral marquetry by Jan van Mekeren of Amsterdam. *(Courtesy of the Rijksmuseum)*

Figure 11.45
Woodcarving by Grinling Gibbons. *(© Adam Woolfitt/CORBIS)*

tion was more theatrical and less restrained than the classical vision of Jones. Wren traveled to Versailles and Fontainebleau in France and brought back the Baroque influence to England.

The intricate, naturalistic woodcarvings of Grinling Gibbons (1648–1721) marked the height of the Baroque style in England. Gibbons, who became Master Carver to the Crown, was famous for his elegant yet large-scale sculptural carvings of vegetables, fruits, flowers, and birds (Figure 11.45). These carvings often served as overmantels, panels placed above fireplaces.

Although most European design moved from the Baroque to a lighter style known as the Rococo (see later discussion), English design did not follow suit. Instead, during the early to mid-18th century, it retained much of the muscular Baroque flavor in a rather unique style known as **English Palladian** or **Anglo-Palladian** (c. 1715– c. 1760).

William Kent (1685–1748), who began as a painter, was heavily influenced by the architectural styles of Palladio and Inigo Jones after studying in Italy. As an architect, as well as a landscape and interior designer, he developed an all-encompassing approach to design. His furniture was called architect's furniture. The **console**, a table similar in appearance to a large wall bracket, with a mirror above, became the hallmark of his design. It was generally gilded and elaborately carved, with a marble top (Figure 11.46). The shell was a favorite motif of Kent.

Known first as early colonial style, American taste was soon dictated primarily by the William and Mary

Figure 11.46
Architect's furniture by William Kent: Gilded mahogany table with a marble top, c. 1730s. *(Kent, William [1685–1748] [design]. Console Table. Probably made by John Boson [fl. 1720–43] for Richard Boyle, earl of Burlington, for Chiswick House. Photo credit: V & A Images, London / Art Resource, New York)*

Figure 11.47
American William and Mary highboy. *(Courtesy of Bridgeman Art Library)*

style, which lasted beyond the monarchs' reign (Figure 11.47). This is a term we use now, but not how people referred to the style in Colonial America. The two key areas of early settlement in the United States were Virginia and New England. The homes of Colonial Williamsburg, in Virginia, including plantations, tended to have more opulent furnishings and a stronger color palette than their counterparts in New England, which was populated by descendants of the Puritans. Painted oak chests from Massachusetts and Connecticut were popular during this period.

Spain and Portugal (1650–1730)

Perhaps the most exuberant of the Baroque styles can be ascribed to the Iberian countries of Spain and Portugal. Widespread colonization of areas now comprising Mexico, the southwestern United States, Brazil, the Philippines, India, and Macao (an island off the coast of China) spurred mixtures of European and indigenous styles. The **vargueño**, a writing cabinet, is a significant piece from Spain (Figure 11.48). The Portuguese **contador** is a version of the chest-on-stand.

The Spanish Baroque style was most evident in the Catholic churches that combined European taste with the native cultures of the Americas. *Pre-Columbian* is the name for the period and styles of the indigenous, or native, Indian populations of the Americas. One example is seen in a former convent for Dominican nuns, now a hotel in Oaxaca, Mexico (Figure 11.49a). The Portuguese Baroque style is evident in the architecture of Ouro Perto, Brazil (Figure 11.49b), as well as a church in Antigua, Guatemala, that remains in operation today (Figure 11.49c).

Figure 11.48
Spanish vargueño in Baroque style. *(© Christie's Images)*

Figure 11.49

Iberian Colonial Baroque style. a. Santa Catalina, Oaxaca, Mexico; b. Brazilian church in Ouro Petro, Brazil; c. Baroque church today in Antigua, Guatemala. *(a: © Bob Krist/CORBIS; b: © Peter M. Wilson/CORBIS; c: Provided by the Author)*

France (1661–1715)

During the reign of Louis XIII, early signs of change began in France with the rise of the middle class, or nouveau riche.

The French Baroque style achieved a more unified approach in 1661, when King Louis XIV appointed Jean-Baptiste Colbert (1619–1683) as minister to preside over the arts and buildings for the Crown.

Baroque became a national style under Louis XIV with the building of the Palace of Versailles, outside Paris. Thousands of members of the court lived there, observing an intricate system of rituals to highlight the king's supremacy. Magnificence, majesty, and ritual were the prevailing ideals during this monarch's rule; Louis XIV was a monarch who represented himself often in the guise of Apollo, and referred to himself as the Sun King.

Significant artists working during his reign included François Mansart (1598–1666) and Louis Le Vau (1612–1670), who organized the talents of others. In 1663 the painter Charles Le Brun (1619–1690) was put in charge of the Gobelins, the factory responsible for the decoration and furnishing of royal residences, marking an unprecedented position of power in interior design history.

The craftsmanship of furniture making had become so exacting that specialists emerged. Among them were the **menuisier**, a joiner who worked in solid wood and carving, and the **ebeniste**, who specialized in veneers and marquetry. André Charles Boulle (1642–1732) perfected another marquetry technique, which would become known as **boullework** (Figure 11.50). This type of elaborate and exquisite furniture featured brass-and-tortoiseshell inlay. A variety of case pieces were developed during this period, among them the **bureau plat**, or *writing table*, and the **commode**, or *chest of drawers*.

Although Venice had dominated the market for plate glass, in 1665 a factory opened in Paris that provided vast quantities of mirrors for Versailles. Mirrors became a significant feature of interiors throughout Europe following the construction of the Hall of Mirrors at Versailles (Figure 11.51).

ROCOCO STYLE (1715–c. 1780)

Like the Baroque style that preceded it, the Rococo made its first appearance in Italian painting. But it was

Figure 11.50
Wardrobe (armoire) designed by André Charles Boulle for King Louis XIV. *(Boulle, André Charles [1642–1732]. Wardrobe, oakwood, covered with ebony and mother-of-pearl inlay. Lead, tin, horn and colored woods, gilt bronze. Paris, early 18th CE. Location: Louvre, Paris, France. Photo credit: Erich Lessing / Art Resource, New York)*

in France that it became an influential style of interior design, before spreading throughout Europe. The style was associated with the young king of France, Louis XV (1710–1774), and his mistress, Madame de Pompadour (1721–1764).

The term *Rococo* derives from the French word *rocaille*, meaning "rock," which denoted shell-covered rockwork used to decorate artificial grottoes. The shell was also a motif of the Baroque style; however, the Rococo version was lighter and more often applied, whereas the Baroque was sculptural and more often carved. This distinction between carved and applied surface decoration is a key difference between the Baroque and Rococo styles.

There was essentially no equivalent Rococo style in architecture, because Rococo was primarily a style

Figure 11.51
Versailles Hall of Mirrors, by Le Vau and Mansart, 1678–1686. (*Bernard Dupont / Alamy*)

of interiors. In contrast to the muscular style of the Baroque, the Rococo focused on delicacy. Characteristics included fanciful and lighthearted ornamentation, asymmetry, and comfort. Rococo represented youth, romance, informality, freshness, and charm. The style was a reflection of the times, which were associated with pleasurable diversions, such as love, music, and the countryside, as depicted by the artist Jean-Honoré Fragonard (1732–1806) in his painting *The Swing* (1767) (Figure 11.52).

The curvilinear carvings of the Baroque style became more swirling, airy, delicate, and asymmetrical in the Rococo. These elements are sometimes referred to as **C** and **S curves** because of the forms they took. Elaborate stuccowork was a feature of this period. There was less of a reliance on classical architecture, and less regard for geometry. In 2008 the Cooper-Hewitt National Design Museum, in New York City, mounted the exhibition *Rococo: The Continuing Curve, 1730–2008*, a testament to the enduring influence of the Rococo through the centuries. The 19th-century Art Nouveau movement in France, in many aspects, grew out of the artistic tradition established during the Rococo period (also see Chapter 12).

Figure 11.52
The Swing, painted by Fragonard. (© *The Swing [oil on canvas] by Jean-Honoré [1732-1806]. Photo © Christie's Images*)

Because intimacy was one of the characteristics of the Rococo period, apartments were smaller in size. Before this time, most furniture was made to be movable and suitable in any location. In a typical Rococo-style town house a suite of rooms would be designed entirely for entertaining and reception, with furniture specifically created for those rooms and activities. Life for the upper middle class (known in France as the bourgeoisie) became more leisurely, with family life idyllically featured in portrait paintings, such as those by François Boucher (1703–1770), as shown in Figure 11.53.

Italy (1715–1750)
Italy's commerce declined during this period, which caused many local craftsmen to find work in other countries. Venice, however, maintained much of its wealth and was a leader in the production of furniture. A significant characteristic of the Venetian Rococo style is fanciful painted scenes used to disguise poor-quality wood and workmanship.

France (1715–1774)
The Rococo period marks the beginning of an important role for merchants in relation to interior design. Influential clients, such as King Louis XV, commissioned Parisian dealers, highly regarded for their taste, to supply them with furniture. Some of the artisans during the reign of Louis XV worked first in the Baroque style, under the reign of Louis XIV, in a transitional style known as regence, and later in the Rococo style. Among them were Jean Bérain (1637–1711), Juste-Aurèle Meissonier (1693–1750), and André Charles Boulle, mentioned earlier.

Carpets began to be more expansive, covering much of the parquet wood flooring. Two royal factories that produced fine carpets in Oriental and classical patterns were Savonnerie and Aubusson (see Chapter 9).

Walls were decorated with **boiserie**, raised, carved panels in themes that represented specific functions such as harp motifs for a music room, such as in Figure 11.54. The **trumeau**, consisting of a mirror and painting, was a decorative feature used over a door, mantel, or cabinet.

As mentioned previously, a major characteristic of the Rococo interior was furniture that was designed for a specific room. Given the influence on style of Madame Pompadour, the needs and comforts of

Figure 11.53
Portraiture of a family in a Rococo interior by Boucher. (*The Afternoon Meal, 1739 [oil on canvas] by François Boucher [1703–70] Louvre, Paris, France/ The Bridgeman Art Library*)

Figure 11.54
Boiserie details for interior walls in Marie Antoinette's boudouir in the Fontainebleau Chateau. (*Rousseau, Pierre [1750–1810] [attributed to]: The Queen's Apartments: boudoir of Marie Antoinette. Reign of Louis XVI [1774–1792]. Photo: Georges Fessy. Location: Chateau, Fontainebleau, France Photo credit: Réunion des Musées Nationaux / Art Resource, New York*)

women dictated much of the furniture developed during this period. Furniture became lighter and easier to move in response to the needs of holding conversations and entertaining. An additional distinguishing feature of the Rococo style is the dominance of the **cabriole leg**, a curved furniture leg modeled on that of an animal.

Many styles of seating were used (Figure 11.55a–d), ranging from two upholstered armchairs, the **bergère** and the **fauteuil** (a version with open sides), to the sofa, which provided seating for two or more. Sofa types included the **settee**, **canapé**, lit de repos, **duchese**, and **marquise**, as well as the **tête-à-tête**, a seat made for

Figure 11.55
Rococo seating. a. Bergère; b. Fauteil; c. Marquise chair; d. Canapé. *(a: Louis XV Wing chair (one of a pair). Wood base painted green decorated with flowers, leaves, and rosettes. Covered in silver and gold brocade decorated with palms, leaves, and multi-colored floral bouquets. 99.2cm × 81.3cm × 67.5cm. Photo: Jean Schormans. Location: Chateaux de Versailles et de Trianon, Versailles, France. Photo credit: Réunion des Musées Nationaux / Art Resource, New York; b: Louis XV queen's armchair, one from a set of four, c. 1755. 97.5 × 62 × 60cm. OA10595. Photo: Daniel Arnaudet. Location: Louvre, Paris, France. Photo credit: Réunion des Musées Nationaux / Art Resource, New York; c: Delanois, Louis [1731–1792] Wingchair or Bergere en cabriolet [from a pair]. c. 1765. Stamped L. Delanois. OA6548. Location: Louvre, Paris, France. Photo credit: Réunion des Musées Nationaux / Art Resource, New York; d: Réunion des Musées Nationaux / Art Resource, New York)*

two, for courting. The **tabouret**, a type of stool, was the seating used by ladies in the king's presence.

Significant to the Rococo period was advancement in upholstery techniques. Alterations in the way the frame was constructed allowed the upholstery to be changed seasonally.

Several case pieces typical of this period were used for writing, such as the **bureau plat,** a substantial writ-ing table for the gentleman, and the **bonheur-du-jour,** or ladies' desk (Figure 11.56a and b). **Ormolu** mounts (carved brass on furniture edges) were especially favored. The **bombé** chest, often with a curvaceous serpentine front, was also popular (Figure 11.56c). The **gueridon** was a stand to hold candelabra (Figure 11.56d).

The French employed techniques that simulated Oriental lacquering. Among them was a varnish

Figure 11.56

French Rococo furniture. a. Bureau plat featuring ormolu mounts on cabriole legs; b. Bonheur-du-jour (ladies' writing table); c. Bombé commode by Charles Cressent, c. 1745; d. Gueridon. (*a. Desk of Louis XV at Versailles, c. 1740. Photo: Daniel Arnaudet. Location: Chateaux de Versailles et de Trianon, Versailles, France. Photo credit: Réunion des Musées Nationaux / Art Resource, New York; b: Risen Burgh, Bernard II van [BVRB] [after 1696–1766]. Writing desk. Location: Chateaux de Versailles et de Trianon, Versailles, France. Photo credit: Réunion des Musées Nationaux / Art Resource, New York; c: Cressent, Charles [1685–1768]. Commode with monkey, c. 1745. OA 6868. Photo: Chuzeville. Location: Louvre, Paris, France, Photo credit: Réunion des Musées Nationaux / Art Resource, New York; d Pedestal candelabrum from the salon of Apollo. Pedestal "aux enfants" by Babel and Foliot. Reign of Louis XVI [1774–1792]. Photo: Daniel Arnaudet. Location: Hall of Mirrors, Chateaux de Versailles et de Trianon, Versailles, France. Photo credit: Réunion des Musées Nationaux / Art Resource, New York*) developed by the Martin brothers that was a rich green in color. It became known as **vernis martin**.

A particular style of cotton print, **toile de Jouy** (named for the French factory outside Versailles, at Jouy) achieved popularity. This is a fine cotton fabric, generally white, printed with a scene in one color. In line with Louis XV's and Madame de Pompadour's love of country life, pastoral images became typical patterns for this textile. The scenes were copied from engravings, such as the one shown in Figure 11.57. Toile de Jouy has seen a revival in the 21st century.

French Rococo style was also greatly influenced by Chinese motifs. The French interpretations were called **chinoiserie** (Figure 11.58a). **Singerie** was a specific, related motif that featured humorous depictions of monkeys (Figure 11.58b).

Color palettes were light. Often, soft, pale pinks, yellows, and blues were used against a cream-colored

Figure 11.58

a. Chinoiserie; b. Singerie. *(a: Carel, Jacques-Philippe [18th century CE] Chest of drawers with chinoiserie design in coromandel lacquer and bronze. French, from the reign of Louis XV [1723–1774]. Photo: Daniel Arnaudet. Location: Louvre, Paris, France. Photo credit: Réunion des Musées Nationaux / Art Resource, New York; b: Huet, Christophe [1700–1759] Chimney screen:* The Monkeys' Reading Lesson. *From the "Grande Singerie" [Monkey Room]. 72 × 58cm. Photo: Harry Bréjat. Location: Musée Condé, Chantilly, France. Photo credit: Réunion des Musées Nationaux / Art Resource, New York)*

Figure 11.57

Toile de Jouy, Rococo print from 1784. *(Cooper-Hewitt National Design Museum, Smithsonian Institution)*

Figure 11.59
Portrait of Madame de Pompadour by François Boucher, 1756. *(Marquise de Pompadour [1721–1764]. Nee Jeanne-Antoinette Poisson. Mistress of Louis XV of France. Oil on canvas by François Boucher)*

background. The scale of patterns was small and featured flowers, bows, and ribbons. The style of Madame de Pompadour's fashions (Figure 11.59) had a very direct influence on the decorative elements and fabrics for interiors as well.

The Rococo styles of the provinces emulated the essence of the royal style but were produced more conservatively. Provincial styles flourished during the 18th century. A 20th-century American version, known as French provincial style, was based on the countrified versions of French Rococo (Figure 11.60).

Germany (c. 1730–c. 1760)

Most palaces in Germany retained much of the earlier Baroque flavor during this period. Perhaps the most significant contribution to the Rococo style to come from Germany was the discovery of **kaolin**, white clay, the long-held secret of the Chinese recipe for hard-paste porcelain. The plasticity of this type of porcelain allowed the artists of the Meissen factory to create ceramic masterpieces not previously possible in Europe (Figure 11.61).

Another German expression of Rococo style was the intricate carvings in the furniture produced by the craftsmen of the Black Forest region. These carvings often portrayed hunting scenes.

Figure 11.60
Contemporary American French provincial style. *(Designed by Michelle Allman. Photo by Nathan Schroder)*

Figure 11.61
Meissen porcelain. *(© Wolfgang Kaehler/CORBIS)*

England and America (1754–1780)

Although the term *Rococo* is not often used to describe English or American interiors of the period, some similarities can be observed in what are called the Queen Anne, early Georgian, and Chippendale styles. In England and, by derivation, America, these styles are also lumped together in a period that is variously called the Age of the Cabinetmaker or the Age of Mahogany.

The floors of this period were primarily wood. Stone, such as marble, was used only in the grandest homes. Walls and ceilings were often highly decorated by painting directly on the plaster. Alternatively, large painted canvases surrounded by frames of elaborately worked stucco were hung on walls. Mythological themes were often the subject of these paintings. Wallpaper, hand painted, hand blocked, or machine printed, gained importance.

Although the work of William Kent, discussed earlier, was concurrent with the Rococo style in Europe, it did not possess many of the features associated with Rococo themes, such as comfort and the leisure-time activities that were part of the middle-class lifestyle. Another cabinetmaker better understood the needs of the middle class. He was Thomas Chippendale (1718–1779), whose influential book, *The Gentle-Man and Cabinet-Maker's Director,* was first published in 1754. Although he himself executed few of these designs, craftsmen in Britain and America copied them extensively.

Many of Chippendale's designs were created in mahogany and adorned with Rococo features, such as the cabriole leg, asymmetry, rounded forms, ribbons, and shell decoration. Accents on furniture during this period also included broken pediment (Figure 11.64a), claw feet (Figure 11.62a), brass batwing drawer pulls (Figure 11.62b), and fretwork. Chippendale's designs,

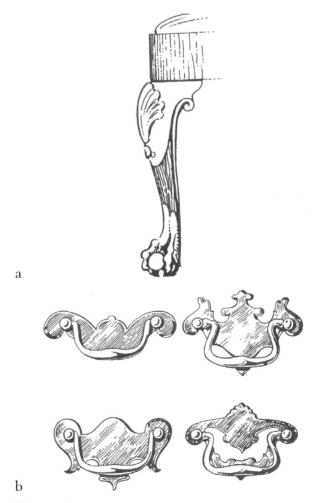

a

b

Figure 11.62
a. Chippendale leg with shell decoration and ball and claw foot;
b. Batwing drawer pulls.

like those of the French Rococo designers, often reflected Chinese motifs, but unlike the French, his work also included a revival of Gothic style (Figure 11.63a–c). After his death, his son and partner continued to run the factory until 1822, adapting to what would become the Neoclassical style.

The shortage of walnut prompted craftsmen to turn to mahogany imported from Cuba, Santo Domingo, and Puerto Rico as their primary wood. The characteristics of mahogany allowed it to be carved with crisp details. Specialized tables, often multifunctional, included card and tea tables. The **bachelor chest** was a small chest used at the bedside. The chest-on-chest was produced in both the **highboy**, or **tallboy**, and **lowboy** varieties (Figure 11.64a).

For much of the 18th century, England dictated design in its colonies. However, the pollination of ideas extended in both directions.

Although the reign of Queen Anne of England lasted from only 1702 to 1714, the style given her name persisted and was adapted in America for some time thereafter. Distinctly regional adaptations developed, partly as a result of differences in the native woods in the regions settled by colonists. The style of French-influenced regions, in particular, such as Charleston and New Orleans, differed greatly from that of its northern counterparts (Figure 11.64b). The **splat back**, or **vase back**, is the chair associated with the Queen Anne style in America, and much like the klismos of ancient Greece, this style of chair has been reproduced in many varieties throughout the centuries (Figure 11.64c).

Another significant style of furniture, of Dutch origin, was the **kast (kas)**, similar to an armoire, but wider, at times measuring 8 feet high and 8 feet wide. Often, provincial varieties of lesser-quality wood were painted, using techniques such as **grisaille**, which was developed during the Renaissance for painting in gray scale. The kast was generally used to store household lines and other valuables that were part of a bride's dowry (Figure 11.64d).

NEOCLASSICAL STYLE
(c. 1760–c. 1830)

The Neoclassical style began as a reaction to the excessive flourishes of the Baroque and Rococo styles. It was also an expression of enthusiasm for the new details about classical style uncovered during the excavations of Pompeii and Herculaneum, in Italy, beginning in 1763. Ironically, the Neoclassical style was less prevalent in Italy than it was in France, England, and other

Figure 11.63
Chippendale chairs. a. Rococo; b. Gothic; c. Chinese. *(a: Courtesy of The DeWitt Wallace Museum. © The Colonial Williamsburg Foundation; b: Chippendale, Thomas [c. 1709–1779]. Gothic armchair. Photo: A. C. Cooper. Photo credit: © DeA Picture Library / Art Resource, New York; c: Chippendale, Thomas [c. 1709–1779]. Gothic armchair. Photo: A. C. Cooper Photo credit: © DeA Picture Library / Art Resource, New York)*

Figure 11.64

American Queen Anne–style furniture. a. Chippendale carved and figured mahogany block front chest-on-chest with broken pediment, Massachusetts; b. French-inspired vignette; c. Queen Anne carved and figured walnut side chair, Maryland, c. 1750; d. Dutch colonial kas (kast) painted in grisaille. *(a: The Hawley-Clarke-Lyman family Queen Anne carved high chest of drawers, Hadley or Springfield area, Massachusetts, c. 1750–70 [cherrywood] by Eliakim Smith [1735–75] [school of] Private Collection/ Photo © Christie's Images/ The Bridgeman Art Library; b: Courtesy of* Antiques and The Arts Weekly, *David S. Smith photos.* Pine Trees at Varengeville *by Claude Monet was displayed above a marble top commode by François Garnier, c. 1720, at M.S. Rau Antiques, New Orleans, Louisiana ; c: Courtesy of The DeWitt Wallace Museum. © The Colonial Williamsburg Foundation; d. Provided by the Author)* countries, including Germany, Russia, and Scandinavia. The refinement and restraint of Neoclassicism stemmed from the 18th-century philosophical and political movement, the Age of Enlightenment, whose main tenet was faith in the power of human reason. The movement caused much social and political foment and stirred movements for political independence in many regions, including the American colonies and France.

Two influential proponents of Neoclassical style were France's King Louis XVI (1754–1793) and Britain's Robert Adam (1728–1792), an architect. The Neoclassical style also had a major influence on the history of interior design in America. Very rich Americans admired the French taste, epitomized by the young Queen Marie Antoinette (1755–1793), whereas the middle class looked more to the English for style.

The interpretations of Neoclassicism by 18th-century designers stressed a return to the rectilinear form, replacing the C and S curves of the Baroque and Rococo styles. Although many of the same materials were used during this period, shape and ornamentation changed.

Much of the informality of the Rococo period remained. Furnishings for middle-class leisure activities, such as card playing and tea parties, continued to develop, with more emphasis on multiple-purpose pieces. One significant change to the interior space was the popularity of the formal dining room, which included an extension-type table with several leaves that was matched to a set of chairs, commodes, and servers.

England (c. 1760–c. 1830)

Robert Adam returned to England from a trip to Italy with a renewed interest in ancient Roman civilization, largely inspired by the etchings of Roman buildings by Giovanni Battista Piranesi (1720–1778). Equipped with an extensive knowledge of antiquities, Robert, along with his brother James, also an architect, began to accept commissions from the wealthy and fashionable gentry of London. Robert Adam, and perhaps to a lesser degree James, became successful as a designer of interior space. All furnishings were designed by them to coordinate with the interior architecture.

The Adams' treatment of surfaces, floors, walls, and ceilings became unified and symmetrical. Attention to these details was their signature. Their interpretations of the styles of antiquity revolved more around ornamentation than structure. Emphasis was placed on a concept of interior design that included complete design from ceiling to carpets. For example, a pattern on the floor would be repeated in the ceiling design.

The essential classical division of walls into field, dado, and cornice was employed. Surfaces were relatively flat, with lightly raised and delicate ornamentation, such as grotesques and arabesques. The dusty caves uncovered during the early excavations of Pompeii influenced the Adams' color palette. Pale and muted colors, as well as white and gray, were used for walls (Figure 11.65). Much of the boiserie and furniture to coordinate with the walls and ceilings was gilded.

Although most people could not afford the services of the Adam firm, others were able to translate the brothers' style into middle-class terms. Among them was George Hepplewhite. His book *The Cabinet-Maker and Upholsterer's Guide*, published posthumously in 1786, disseminated this knowledge widely. Much of Hepplewhite's furniture was made of mahogany, constructed rather simply, with an emphasis on function. However, his designs are considered to be very well proportioned and elegant, with finely crafted (although sparingly used) veneering and accessories (Figure 11.66).

Another influential figure of the time was Thomas Sheraton, considered to be more a designer than a

Figure 11.65

Robert Adam interior: Etruscan Room at Osterley Park, Middlesex, England, 1761–1780. (© *The National Trust*)

Figure 11.66
Hepplewhite sideboard.
(© Peter Harholdt/CORBIS)

a　　　　　　　　　　b　　　　　　　　　　c

Figure 11.67
Sheraton drawings. a. Sideboard; b. Sofa table; c. Dumbwaiter table.

cabinetmaker. His chief work, *Cabinet-Maker and Upholsterer's Drawing Book*, was issued in four parts between 1791 and 1794. Although his drawings often served as inspiration rather than as prototypes for manufacturing, Sheraton's influence was great, spanning not only Neoclassical style, but also later styles, including those of the Victorian period (Figure 11.67a–c).

Accessories of this period reflected activities of the leisure class. Among them were boxes and small tables for needlework, small nesting tables for refreshments, tea caddies, and tables for cards lined with baize, a type of wool felt. Josiah Wedgwood (1730–1795), a ceramicist, was commissioned by Adam (later also by King Louis XIV of France) to execute classical themes for interior architecture, such as wall and ceilings, as well as for dinnerware and other accessories. **Jasperware**, a type of porcelain object known for its matte glaze, remains popular as traditional tableware today (Figure 11.68).

Figure 11.68
Jasperware by Wedgwood. (© *Andreas von Einsiedel / Alamy*)

Figure 11.69
French Neoclassical style: Petit Trianon at Versailles. *(Gabriel, Ange-Jacques [1698–1782]. South Facade with the flowerbeds of the French Garden. 1762. Photo: Gérard Blot. Location: Petit Trianon, Chateaux de Versailles et de Trianon, Versailles, France, Photo credit: Réunion des Musées Nationaux / Art Resource, New York)*

France (1774–1789)

Distinguishing features of the French revival of classicism were an emphasis on informal landscape and the integration of architecture with the environment (Figure 11.69). Although small in scale, both the interiors and the exterior of Petit Trianon at Versailles (commissioned by Louis XV for Madame de Pompadour and later given to Marie Antoinette by Louis XVI) are examples of this harmony.

Floors were treated in much the same way as during the Rococo period, including wood parquet, marble in formal rooms, and Oriental-style rugs from the Savonnerie and Aubusson factories.

The furniture styles of France, like those of England and other European countries, became more restrained (Figure 11.70a and b). Rounded chair backs and cabriole legs were generally replaced with straight lines. Chairs legs were often fashioned after fluted columns, with a rosette block. Boulle marquetry, which had been popular during the reign of Louis XIV, enjoyed renewed popularity. Simpler mahogany

Figure 11.70
French Neoclassical furniture. a. Secretaire-à-abattant; b. Chiffonier. *(a: Drop-leaf secretary of mahogany and gilt bronze. From the office of Mme. Adelaide at the chateau de Bellvue. OA9532. Photo: Daniel Arnaudet. Location: Louvre, Paris, France. Photo credit: Réunion des Musées Nationaux / Art Resource, New York; b: Chiffonier. Mahogony, copper, gilding, and St. Anne marble. 148cm × 96.5cm × 40cm. Photo: Gerard Blot. Location: Chateau, Fontainebleau, France. Photo credit: Réunion des Musées Nationaux / Art Resource, New York)*

furniture was sometimes adorned with porcelain. The **secretaire-à-abattant**, a type of fall-front desk that combined writing surface with drawers, gained in popularity. Smaller pieces included the **chiffonier**, a chest of drawers, and a **semainier**, a tall, narrow chest of seven drawers, one for each day of the week.

As in England, the motifs were derivatives of those used in antiquity, executed in soft and muted colors.

United States (c. 1780–c. 1820)

The equivalent of the Neoclassical style in the United States is the early Federal style, named for the federation of states that followed the independence of the colonies in 1776. Philadelphia became the seat of the government in 1787 and had a great influence on the style of interiors as well as the manufacturing of fine mahogany furniture. Thomas Jefferson, who signed the Declaration of Independence, had already executed classical, symmetrical structures in Virginia.

Other influential centers of manufacturing during this period were Boston and Salem, Massachusetts; Newport, Rhode Island; and Baltimore, Maryland. Regions developed their own specialties. For example, Connecticut manufacturers were producing a great variety of chests of drawers. Furniture styles were derived from the drawings of Hepplewhite and Sheraton. Mahogany was used predominately, but painted furniture was also popular, especially outside the major cities.

Typical motifs in the American version of Neoclassical style were the eagle, (the emblem of the federation) and classical motifs such as griffins and acanthus leaves.

EMPIRE STYLE (1789–1848)

The French Revolution and the execution of King Louis XVI marked the beginning of a period that produced the Empire style. This style was yet another revival of the Greco-Roman classical style, but with an emphasis on military and Egyptian themes. The Empire style was most decidedly associated with the rise of Napoleon Bonaparte (1769–1821) and his self-proclamation as the emperor of France in 1804. His military campaigns, especially those in Egypt, set the tone for what would be a heavy, masculine style of décor, often referred to as Napoleonic style. This was a more elaborate and theatrical expression of Neoclassical design, one that detractors have described as grandiose and pretentious.

a

b

Figure 11.71
French Empire style. a. Josephine's bedroom at Malmaison; b. Napoleon's council room. *(a: © Massimo Listri/CORBIS; b: Interior view: Salle du Conseil [Council Room], on the ground floor. Photo: Arnaudet; Schormans. Location: Chateaux de Malmaison et Bois-Preau, Rueil-Malmaison, France. Photo credit: Réunion des Musées Nationaux / Art Resource, New York)*

France (1789–1820)

The political instability that had begun during the reign of Louis XV escalated to the point of revolution in 1789, followed by the execution of Louis XVI and Marie Antoinette in 1793. Over the course of two succeeding governments, known as the Directoire and the Consulate, Napoleon rose from common status to power through his military might, and he won the hand of a sophisticated young widow named Josephine, who became his wife and, later, empress. The architects Pierre-François-Leonard Fontaine (1762–1853) and Charles Percier (1764–1838), who had studied together in Paris and Rome, were commissioned to redesign the Château de Malmaison to reflect the increased interest in archaeology. Etruscan and Egyptian motifs were used to ornament this interior, which was styled as an elaborate tent, representing Napoleon's military campaigns (Figure 11.71a and b).

Many historians subsume Empire style within the broader classification of Neoclassical. However, there are reasons to deem Empire a distinct style. Distinct differences exist between the two in terms of style of fashion and color palettes. Also, the significance of exotic themes and materials is more prevalent in the Empire style. Ironically, although the Napoleonic style of furniture was more grandiose than that of the Neoclassical style, women's fashion, as reflected in their dress and hair styles, reflected the simplicity of the antiquities. Note in the portrait of Empress Josephine echoes of the draped, unstructured, close-fit style of the fashionable ladies of the ancient Greco-Roman periods (Figure 11.72).

Several types of seating, beds, and mirrors were popular in this period (Figure 11.73a–c). Among them was the **lit bateau**, a boat-shaped bed draped with fabric that was placed with one side against the wall. Versions of the resting, or day, bed from ancient civilizations included the **recamier** and the **chaise longue**. The **gondola chair** was shaped to follow the contours of the body. Typical case pieces that continued to be popular were the console and the commode.

Fabric was used extensively in tent-like fashion, extending from ceilings to walls. Lustrous fabric, such

Figure 11.72
Portrait of Empress Josephine by Gérard in Greco-Roman-inspired fashion. *(Portrait of Empress Joséphine of France, François Pascal Simon Gérard [1770–1837]*

Figure 11.73
Empire-style furnishings. a. Lit bateau; b. Recamier; c. Cheval mirror. *(a: Berthault, Louis-Martin [1770–1823]. The bed of Mme. Recamier. Mahogny, bronze, gilt, ebony. 1795–1799. From the Chamber of Mme. Recamier. Photo: Daniel Arnaudet. Location: Louvre, Paris, France. Photo credit: Réunion des Musées Nationaux / Art Resource, New York; b: La Vallee aux Loups, house in which writer and statesman François-Rene Vicomte de Chateaubriand lived from 1807 to 1818. Mme. de Recamier was a frequent visitor. The "Recamiere," divan on which J.-J. David painted Mme. Recamier. Empire, 19th CE. Location: La Vallee aux Loups, Chatenay-Malabry, France. Photo credit: Erich Lessing / Art Resource, New York; c: Swing mirror from the bathroom of the empress's small apartments. Mahogany, bronze, and gilt, from First Empire [1804–1814]. Photo: Gerard Blot. Location: Chateau, Fontainebleau, France. Photo credit: Réunion des Musées Nationaux / Art Resource, New York)*

as silk, was used for bed canopies. Draperies were often hung asymmetrically, over sword-style rods, in the swag, or festoon, style (see Chapter 10).

Rich jewel tones characterize the Empire style. In addition to gold and black, sapphire blue, ruby red, and emerald green were popular in France. Motifs included the bee, Napoleon's symbol, and the swan, that of Josephine. Both true and fantastical references, such as the griffin, dolphin, lion, sphinx, and eagle, were used as well as the laurel wreath, stars, arrows, swords, and bold stripes.

England (1807–1830)

The Regency style in England is not related to *régence* in France. However, it corresponds to the Empire style in France (Figure 11.74). It took its name from the prince regent, the future King George IV, who, along with the royal ministers, governed for his father, King George III, during the king's periodic bouts of mental illness. A key proponent of the style was Thomas Hope, a collector whose *Household Furniture and Decoration,* published in 1807, combined his background as a furniture maker and his archaeological knowledge of Egypt, Turkey, Syria, and Greece (Figure 11.75).

Much of furniture in the Regency style was painted black and red or cream, in reference to the color schemes of the antiquities. In addition to Greco-Roman and Etruscan influences, Gothic motifs were also employed. There was a strong Asian presence, notably in decorative techniques, such as pen painting, faux bamboo, and lacquering. This style was a precursor to the eclectic revival style (discussed in Chapter 12). The Royal Pavilion at Brighton, by the architect John Nash (1752–1835), set the stage for the next period in England and America (Figure 11.76), especially in its flair of exoticism.

United States (c. 1810–c. 1840)

The later years of the Federal style were marked by the development of American Empire style. This style combined features of the English Regency and French Empire styles of the same period (Figure 11.77).

Duncan Phyfe (1768–1854) was a cabinetmaker born in Scotland who settled in Albany, New York.

Figure 11.74
The Regency Room at the Geffrye Museum, London, c. 1815. *(Courtesy of the Geffrye Museum)*

Figure 11.75
British Regency furniture: Side table made of gilded pine, black marble, mirror glass, and bronze mounts, designed by Thomas Hope, 1800. *(V & A Images/ Victoria & Albert Museum / Art Resource, New York)*

Figure 11.76
The Brighton Pavilion music room, by John Nash, 1815–1821.
(© Massimo Listri/CORBIS)

Figure 11.78
Duncan Phyfe chairs with lyre. (*Side chairs from the Duncan Phyfe Workshop, 1810–20 [mahogany] by Scottish School [19th century] © Collection of the New York Historical Society, United States/ The Bridgeman Art Library*)

Figure 11.77
Empire Parlor at Winterthur, Delaware. (© *Winterthur Museum & Country Estate*)

The war between England and the United States in 1812 led to a stronger French influence in America. However, Phyfe and many of his contemporaries continued to be influenced by the English designs of Chippendale, Hepplewhite, and Sheraton. Phyfe's designs featured the lyre, a classical Greek harp, as structural support for furniture (Figure 11.78). Dining room furniture, including mahogany sideboards and extension tables, are closely associated with this style. The eagle, the symbol of the new republic, was used extensively to embellish furniture and could frequently be found at the top of a mirror frame.

As with English Regency style, American Empire style mixed characteristics from many cultures and served as a transition to Revival style.

Austria (c. 1820–1848)

A regional variation of Empire style developed in central Europe from the needs of a prosperous and growing middle class and its emphasis on domesticity. The Austrian Empire at the time included present-day Austria, Hungary, Germany, Poland, and the Czech Republic as well as north-central and eastern Italy (Figure 11.79). Its influence also spread to parts of Scandinavia.

Overall, the Austrian style represented a lighter and simpler expression of Empire than the French style. The designs were originated by cabinetmakers rather than designers. To accommodate urban residents, many of the pieces were smaller in scale, relatively lightweight, and less formal than their French equivalents. The popular fall-front secretary was a response to this clientele's need to save space.

The name given this style was *Biedermeier,* after Gottlieb Biedermeier, a fictional character in a German magazine. It represented the kind of furniture that

Figure 11.79
Map of the Austrian Empire.

would be suitable for the common man. Biedermeier is more narrowly a style of furniture than a comprehensive style of design. The furniture was characterized by light-colored fruitwoods, such as pear, with strong grain patterns, sometimes sparingly ornamented with inlay or ebonizing (Figure 11.80). It retained Neoclassical features in the use of columns, pediments, and lyres that were integral to the structure of the piece. Although Biedermeier furniture was meant to fulfill the needs of the middle class, it remained a relatively precious commodity because of its cost.

The fabrics used often featured a striped pattern. However, the size of the stripes, as well as the colors, was generally more restrained than those of the Napoleonic style.

Figure 11.80
Biedermeier sofa, Vienna, Austria, c. 1830. *(Courtesy Ritter Antik, www.ritterantik.com)*

Summary

Recognizable period design styles tell us much about the lifestyles of the rich and, to a lesser degree, about the common folk. For each of the styles examined in this chapter, there were transitions, adaptations, and regional distinctions. For each style there were also subsets of styles, for example, the Gothic style as part of the medieval period.

The design of interior spaces, furnishings, and ornamentation in the western hemisphere has been influenced most directly by the ancient Greek and Roman civilizations. However, the influence of non-Western cultures, in particular those of Egypt, China, and the Near East, has been an almost continuous thread throughout Western history.

For each period, one region has taken the lead in style because of a strong penchant for design on the part of a ruler, the power or influence of individuals, or the ability to spread ideas. In antiquity we look first to Greece; in the medieval period, to the Byzantine Empire; in the Renaissance, to Italy; for the Baroque style, to Florence, Versailles, and Holland; for the Rococo style, to France; for the Neoclassical style, to England and Paris; and for the Empire style, to France.

Over the course of history, categories of furniture developed in response to changing needs. Pieces considered commonplace today, such as the bed and chair, were status symbols in the past. The availability of fabric and the comfort of upholstery are other examples of how interiors have changed over many centuries.

Different times called for different spatial compositions. The communal great room served a purpose in much of Europe during the Middle Ages but became outmoded during the Renaissance, when smaller, private quarters were more appropriate. The need for movable furniture as opposed to rigid room arrangements; changing preferences for formality versus informality; and the availability of resources, both natural and human, have all had a major impact on the design of interiors.

Vocabulary

arabesque	cassone	enfilade
arcading	cathedra	English Palladian
armoire	chaise longue	(Anglo-Palladian)
armoire à deux corps	chest-on-stand	en suite
bachelor chest	chiffonier	farthingale
baize	chinoiserie	fauteuil
bargello	cloisonné	flame stitch
bergère	colonnade	fresco
boiserie	commode	frieze
bombé	console	gondola chair
bonheur-du-jour	contador	great hall
boullework	Corinthian	grisaille
buffet	court cupboard	grotesque
bureau plat	curule	gueridon
C and S curve	dais	highboy (tallboy)
cabriole leg	Dante chair	hieroglyphics
canapé	Delftware	Ionic
caquetoire	Doric	Jasperware
caryatid	duchese	kaolin
cassapanca	ebeniste	kast (or kas)

(continued)

Vocabulary, *continued*

kline

klismos

linenfold

lit bateau

lit de repos

long gallery

lowboy

marquise

melon (cup and cover)

menuisier

mortise and tenon

nonesuch (nonsuch)

ormolu

pagoda

pietre dura

pilaster

portico

post-and-lintel (post-and-beam)
  system

press cupboard

privy

qi (chi)

recamier

rose window

saber leg

Savonarola chair

secretaire-à-abattant

sedia

semainier

settee

sgabello

singerie

splat back (vase back) chair

tabouret

tête-à-tête

toile de Jouy

tracery

trestle

tripartite

turkey work

trumeau

vargueño

vernis martin

Exercise: Period Design Style Inspiration for Contemporary Interiors

Interior designers often incorporate period design style into contemporary interiors. For each of the seven periods described in this chapter, select one example from magazines or books of a residential or a contract interior that you feel demonstrates effective incorporation of period style. Look for a variety of inspirations, including treatments of walls, windows, ceilings, and floors, in addition to furniture, color, and accessories.

Use labels, such as sticky notes, to write down key terms.

Exercise: Exploring the CD-ROM

Take advantage of the contents of the CD-ROM to increase your understanding of the variations of styles associated with Louis XIV, Louis XV, and Louis XVI. Follow the instructions for Starting the CD-ROM on pages xix–xx and click on Chapter Eleven: Period Design Styles: Antiquity (c. 4500 B.C.–A.D. 500)–Empire Style (1789–1848).

Furniture Styles and Leg Shapes: Furniture styles through the ages evolve in many ways. Among them is the shape of the legs of both chairs and tables. This variation in style may be demonstrated by examining key differences among the furniture styles associated with the reigns of Louis XIV, Louis XV, and Louis XVI. Either sketch or find images from museum websites, magazines, or auction catalogs that demonstrate typical legs of chairs or tables from each of the three King Louis periods mentioned in this chapter. Label each sketch or image accordingly. Note the similarities and differences.

CHAPTER 12

Period Design Styles:
Revival Styles (c. 1830–c. 1880) to Contemporary Style (1960–Present)

Chapter 11 concluded with the first quarter of the 19th century. Among the significant events of this period were two notable occurrences in England. One was the opening of the Royal Pavilion at Brighton, built during the years 1815 to 1821 by John Nash. This individualistic design displayed an extravagant mixture of Oriental styles and was a precursor to the eclectic movement. The other was the Industrial Revolution. Key inventions that made industrialization possible would influence the architecture, design, and tastes of future generations.

Cast iron and plate glass played major roles in engineering, manufacturing, transportation, building, and ornamentation. The manufacturing of large plates of glass after 1840 and the removal of taxes on glass and windows changed the appearance of buildings, both inside and outside. The Crystal Palace, built by Sir Joseph Paxton (1801–1865) for the Great Exhibition of 1851, was based on a conservatory, but its prefabricated iron-and-glass structure makes it perhaps the first modern building (Figure 12.1). It was also at the Great Exhibition that Michael Thonet (1796–1871) showed his laminated bentwood furniture, produced by a technique that transformed the mechanization of furnishings.

The first half of the 20th century saw an explosion in the growth of the middle classes and, in turn, their demand for housing. This period saw an increase in city and suburban populations. No longer was the ownership of

Figure 12.1
The Crystal Palace, designed by Sir Joseph Paxton for the Great Exhibition in London, 1851. (© *Historical Picture Archive/CORBIS*)

expansive land for farming the only symbol of wealth. Conspicuous consumption, the philosophy that more is more, led to the acquisition and accumulation of furnishings and collections from around the world to embellish interiors. Taking its cue from England, which had achieved prosperity through the success of railways, banks, and industries, the United States looked to the future with great optimism. This modern world was capable of mechanized production—fast, plentiful, elaborate, and available to the masses.

The ideals of comfort and convenience dictated many features of the housing built during the late 19th century. Many homes in England, and later in the United States, were built as row houses or town houses in or near the emerging business centers and rail stations. Although many of these attached and semi-attached structures were similar in their use of building materials and layouts, they achieved unique

traits through embellished architectural details. Often, this meant elaborate façades with references to classical architectural details in brick, stone, and iron. Among the exterior ornaments were cast-iron columns fashioned after classical marble ones (Figure 12.2).

Elaborate millwork, brackets, and friezes framed the drawing rooms in the interiors of these houses. These rooms served as transition spaces for guests, giving a first impression of the affluence they would witness in the great Victorian mansions (Figure 12.3).

One of the notable features of interiors during this period was the increased separation of rooms assigned for specific purposes and activities. Children had nurseries, servants, their own rooms. The drawing room and dining room were for company and to display family treasures. Especially in the United States, with improvements in plumbing, defined bathrooms became more common.

Figure 12.2
This cast-iron façade, in lower Manhattan, exemplifies the merging of art and commerce during the Industrial Revolution. *(Photographer: David Wasserman/Brand X Pictures)*

Figure 12.3
The Victoria Mansion in Portland, Maine, features extensive millwork by Herter Brothers, c. 1858–1860. *(Courtesy of the Victoria Mansion)*

The period associated with the reign of Queen Victoria is marked by an elaborate use of accessories. The style that would come to be called Revival style was a cluttered one, overcrowded, abundant with items, and overstuffed with fabric. Fabrics, objets d'art, porcelains, and carpets were shipped or brought back from voyages around the world, especially to the East. Styles, as well as goods, were imported from abroad.

The mid-19th-century approach to **revivalism** was to bring back aspects of previous period styles in an eclectic way. This was different from the **historicism** employed in earlier styles, such as Neoclassical, in which stricter, studied references to a period style were replicated. During the Victorian era, different period styles were revived, at times loosely interpreted, for different types of rooms. A Rococo-inspired room, with its fluid lines, might be suitable for the boudoir, whereas the Gothic style was considered better suited for the library. Specialty rooms, such as the smoking room, the billiard room, or the bathroom, might be decorated with more exotic elements based on Moorish, Turkish, or Hindu (Indian) styles.

The fervor of nostalgia that characterized much of the period, combined with an eclectic adaptation and revival of period styles, often without a purist's attention to accuracy, resulted in some misguided interpretations. The end result provoked a reform movement by the end of the 19th century. For some idealists, the free-flowing approach to historical reference was vulgar and debased. For others, the fruits of industrialization turned sour when the classical rules of proportion and harmony were abandoned by the advent of mass production and lower standards of quality. **Eclecticism**, as the style is sometimes called, combining a little of this, a little of that, led some critics to conclude that this design style had no language of its own.

In the latter half of the century, the aesthetic of Japan, a more restrained approach to design, captivated some designers, who would steer their course in a different direction. After many twists and turns, a myriad of strains of modernism would emerge in Europe, Britain, and the United States. The seeds of the modern movement were thus planted, ironically, in the historical revivals of the 19th century.

REVIVAL STYLE (c. 1830–c. 1880)

Different regions demonstrated variations in the application of period styles to interiors; however, a few common themes can be identified, notably the impact of industrialization, the growth of the middle class, and an emphasis on comfort.

England (c. 1830–c. 1880)

Queen Victoria reigned over the British Empire from 1837 to 1901. During her reign the Empire expanded across the continents of the world, which led to the saying "The sun never sets on the British Empire" (Figure 12.4). (Also see *FYI . . . Non-Western Influences on Design: Colonialism.*)

The term **Victorian** is often applied not just to the period of her reign, but also to the eclectic and revivalist styles that were common, especially in England and the United States, during this period. It is useful to segment this long period by predominant styles, influences, and movements. Often referred to as early Victorian (1837–1860), mid-Victorian (1860–1880), and late Victorian (1880–1901), the first two periods can be categorized as Revival styles and the latter period as a time of rapid and significant change encompassing several reformist movements. Whereas the Revival styles would remain popular in England and the United States, the reform movements would take hold among avant-garde circles internationally.

The Great Exhibition of 1851, in London, marked the height of mass production during Queen Victoria's reign and served as a benchmark for the Revival style. The Medieval Court, constructed for the Great Exhibition by Augustus W. N. Pugin (1812–1852), inspired

Figure 12.4

Map of the British Empire during the reign of Queen Victoria.

FYI . . . Non-Western Influences on Design: Colonialism

During her reign, Queen Victoria colonized parts of every existing continent in the East and West. Two of these areas included South Asia and islands in the Caribbean.

India, the largest country (actually, a subcontinent) in South Asia, came under the rule of the British Empire in 1858 and remained as such until 1947, when the nation regained its independence. In 1876 Queen Victoria was proclaimed Empress of India, creating a more personal link to the region that most Britons were familiar with only as a trading center for Western interests. India has for thousands of years had a culture rich in architecture, design, and textiles. Although British custom, such as "high tea," and fashion influenced the indigenous population, colonial influences cross-pollinated to enrich the West with new and unique styles (Figure a). The ancient paisley motif and its use in textiles for both interiors and apparel is one design influence that has already been mentioned.

Furniture styles included ornately carved and pierced pieces made from local woods often from Bombay (now Mumbai) (Figure b). Other typical Indian characteristics for furniture were inlaid ivory and mirrors. Contemporary versions of this blended style are referred to as **British Raj**, **Anglo-Raj**, or **Anglo-Indian**.

The British West Indies, a large group of islands in the Caribbean that were under British control during the 19th century, demonstrate another mixture of indigenous and colonial style. This area represents a significant region of the African Diaspora, largely resulting from the centuries of slave trade. Islands (now independent) that were part of this group include Barbados, Jamaica, and Antigua.

Plantation owners used local labor and materials to build their plantation houses, also known as the great houses. To furnish these houses, Victorian style designed for often-chilly England was adapted to tropical climates. The style that developed was inspired not only by elements found in the local environment, such as the pineapple and palm leaves, but also by the heritage of its African population. Typical were the planter, or plantation, chair, generally with a cane seat to allow for air circulation, campaign furniture that made transporting easier, and poster beds with mosquito netting.

Figures a and b

a. Indian interior blends local and British style; b. Intricately carved, pierced chairs, Bombay, India, c. 1870. *(a. © Dhruv Singh for Alsisar Hotels; Chairs, c. 1870. Bombay Presidency. Carved and pierced blackwood with later upholstery. ©V & A Images, Victoria & Albert Museum / Art Resource, New York. Photo credit: V & A Images, London / Art Resource, New York).*

Figure 12.5
Pugin's Medieval Court, c. 1837, epitomizes the early Gothic Revival style. (© *Adam Woolfitt/CORBIS*)

Figure 12.6
A Belter laminated rosewood sofa, 1856, features tufted uphol-stery. (*Belter, John H. [1804–1863] Rococo revival sofa, New York, c. 1856. Laminated rosewood and silk damask upholstery. Photo credit: V & A Images, London / Art Resource, New York*)

the Gothic Revival style (Figure 12.5). Following his conversion to Catholicism, Pugin meticulously re-created the ecclesiastical architecture and furnishings of the medieval period. He is most famous for assist-ing architect Charles Barry (1795–1860) in the recon-struction of the Palace of Westminster, for which he also designed most of the furniture. Pugin was a pure and passionate historicist. In contrast, many revivalists who achieved success during this period were not as exacting in their interpretations.

Although Gothic style influenced the exterior of structures during this time, the interiors were more heavily influenced by French taste, especially that of King Louis XV. As described in Chapter 11, the Rococo style associated with Louis XV's reign was noted for its emphasis on comfort as well as form. During the late 19th century this style was adapted for the English middle class in the furniture that most strongly reflected women's taste, such as seating

for the drawing room. In addition to seating, console tables and mirrors were created in the Rococo style. This version of the Rococo, the Rococo Revival style, was treated with deeper carving and more padding in the upholstery than the original Rococo style. **Tuft-ing**, the buttoning of upholstered fabric, was typical of Revival furniture of this time (Figure 12.6). Another popular Revival was the Renaissance Revival style. Because it was fashionable to mix styles *within* an inte-rior, the Elizabethan style, considered gender neutral, was appropriate for dining rooms.

Technological advances and new materials added to the repertoire of furnishings during this period. For example, papier-mâché, a material made from pressed paper pulp, began to be used commercially for furni-ture making beginning in the 1830s. The nature of the medium enabled it to be poured into molds marked with sinuous curves. The finished pieces were often **japanned** black, then inlaid with mother-of-pearl, gilded, or painted, creating delicate yet functional pieces.

Michael Thonet, who was Austrian, is mentioned here because his work was shown at the Great Exhi-bition of 1851. In the factory he opened in 1849 in Vienna, he was able to manufacture bentwood furni-ture, creating inexpensive and light, yet strong, forms. He developed a method of construction (through the new use of steam) that was well suited for mass pro-duction (Figure 12.7).

In addition to its use in the manufacture of ele-ments of building façades, and outdoor garden furni-

Figure 12.7
Thonet bentwood rocker. *(© Gebrüder Thonet GmbH, Franken-berg, Germany)*

ture, cast iron became commonplace for indoor use, in particular in public spaces, such as restaurants and bars, because of its durability.

Metal beds with head- and footboards of cast iron or brass gained popularity, often replacing the four-poster wooden bed. Also seen in this period was an explosion in mechanical furniture, including the revolving bookcase and swivel and rocking chairs. The combination of functions within one piece is sometimes considered bizarre by today's standards.

The East, notably Turkey, inspired many new pieces of furniture. Among them was the **ottoman** (called **pouf** in France), a type of low, upholstered seat-ing that became popular in several variations and that remains popular today. Other examples are the **cozy (cosy) corner**, a type of banquette resembling a railway compartment, and the **companion chair**, which was displayed at the Great Exhibition.

Hall trees (also known as hall stands, and which were used to hold coats, hats, and umbrellas), plant stands, tea tables, and worktables were typically used. With the expansion of the British Empire into tropical climates, lightweight materials became fashionable. Wicker furniture and summer-weight materials, such as sisal, for floor coverings, became popular in some regions year-round or were used seasonally in colder climates.

The treatment of walls changed with the invention of **lincrusta** in 1877. This commercially produced paper was long lasting and could be scrubbed clean. It was designed in a variety of bas-relief patterns that could be painted or varnished to resemble leather, wood, or plaster. They were often applied for the dado. **Anaglypta** was a lighter-weight version used to provide textural variation for ceiling and walls. Both are still manufactured today.

Taller windows, made possible because of advanced manufacturing techniques, meant that more fabric was needed for window coverings. Drapery treatments were often multilayered and abundant or fussy by modern standards (Figure 12.8). Many interior windows

Figure 12.8
Elaborate drapery treatments in Queen Victoria's railway carriage, 1869, England. *(© NRM/SSPL/ The Image Works)*

were dressed with sheer lace panels, velvet panels, or elaborately carved valances and many intricate tassels, fringes, and other passementerie. It was common to change fabrics for both windows and furniture seasonally. Thus, slipcovers of lighter-weight muslin or cotton would be used over heavy velvet sofas as a cooler alternative during warm seasons.

Floors were generally of wood parquet. Linoleum, first manufactured during this period (see Chapter 9), was used in the latter part of the 19th century. Small scatter rugs in a variety of patterns, some actually prayer rugs from the East or shawls from India, would be strewn across the wood floors as well as over furniture. One such pattern type, paisley (see Chapter 10), became a favorite of Queen Victoria's. Originally a pattern inspired by plant forms for a woolen textile made in India (part of the queen's empire), paisley took its name from the town in Scotland where this woolen fabric was first manufactured in the British Empire.

Another trademark of this style was the elaborate use of accessories. As middle-class Britons returned from their now-affordable trips abroad, many began the hobby of collecting. Curiosities, later called curios, bric-a-brac, or knickknacks, were at first interesting scientific and natural discoveries, such as rocks, shells, and fossils from the far corners of the globe. Keeping scrapbooks, pressing flowers, and collecting specimens of nature were activities that inspired many new accoutrements. This leisure pastime of the middle class expanded to include a passion for collecting porcelain and other so-called whatnots (Figure 12.9). Shelved units, also called **whatnots** (some with glass, others open), were produced to display these curios (see Chapter 10).

The colors associated with the Revival style include red and green, inspired by the revival of Gothic schemes. It was during this period in England that the color purple was first synthetically produced (Figure 12.10). The term **mauve** was coined in 1859 to

Figure 12.9
The Victorian whatnot shelf was used to display curios. *(Whatnot, attributed to either Jenners and Bettridge or McCallum and Hodson of Birmingham, c.1851 [wood and papier maché] by English School [19th century]. © Leeds Museums and Galleries [Lotherton Hall] U.K./ The Bridgeman Art Library)*

Figure 12.10
Victorian dress in mauve fashion, c. 1862: This silk dress is dyed with Sir William Henry Perkin's (1838–1907) original mauve aniline dye. The purple, even though it has faded, has a richness unachievable by natural dyes. The introduction of synthetic dyes had a huge impact on both the textile industry and fashion. *(Photo credit: SSPL/Science Museum / Art Resource, New York)*

describe the color resulting from this new dye matter. Before this development, purple had been used sparingly because the natural sources used to produce this dye were so costly. With the advent of mass production, however, varieties of purple became available, significantly altering the color palette of both this period and later times.

United States (c. 1830–c. 1880)

American style in the mid- to late 19th century, particularly that of interiors, was largely influenced by English taste. The love of invention and experimentation with new materials and the ability to mass-produce products were equally as important for the growing American middle class as they were for the British.

The Gothic Revival style in America was more often reserved for the architecture of public build-

ings and churches. American architecture at this time also reflected the influences of France and Italy, notably in the use of Renaissance Revival style, sometimes referred to as Italianate style.

Furniture in America at this time was most often created in the Rococo Revival (Louis XV) style. By the mid- to late 1880s, New York had become home to several new German immigrants, many with cabinetmaking backgrounds, including John Henry Belter (1804–1863), who opened a factory in New York City in 1858. Belter had patented a laminating process using several thin layers of rosewood, glued together in a cross-grained fashion to provide tensile strength. After being pressed and steamed, the laminate was carved by machine in the Rococo style. This furniture, popular in parlor suites or ensembles, became a typical feature of the American home (Figure 12.11).

Figure 12.11
Belter suite of furniture from a parlor in Astoria, New York, c. 1852, installed in the Metropolitan Museum of Art, New York City. *(The Rococo Revival Parlor, c. 1852. Architectural elements from the La Roque Mansion. Location: The Metropolitan Museum of Art, New York City. Photo credit: The Metropolitan Museum of Art / Art Resource, New York)*

Figure 12.12
Boudoir in Turkish Revival style in the Hotel de Beauharnais,
Paris, France. *(Photo credit: Erich Lessing / Art Resource, New York)*

Figure 12.13
The Eiffel Tower. *(Provided by the Author)*

A generation after the Crystal Palace, in England, the Turkish Bazaar at the 1876 Centennial Exhibition, in Philadelphia, inspired many American and French interiors to emulate the exotic flavor of the East (Figure 12.12).

France (c. 1830–1871)

The comparable age of revivals for France corresponded to the reigns of King Louis Philippe (1830–1848) and Emperor Napoleon III (1852–1870), the latter period being known as the Second Empire. The Eiffel Tower (Figure 12.13), constructed for the Paris World Exposition of 1889, is the outgrowth of the industrialization that characterized France during this period.

As in England and America, apartment complexes emerged to house the growing middle classes. Often, the first floor was designated for commercial enterprise, with balconied floors above.

Empress Eugénie, the wife of Napoleon III, had a great interest in Marie Antoinette, and the Neoclas-sical Revival style, also known as Louis XVI Revival style, was popular for important public and private French interiors. Furniture was upholstered and tufted to meet the desire for comfort. This mixture of restrained historical forms with overstuffed upholstery produced somewhat discordant pieces.

Rococo style was also evident during the Second Empire. New materials, such as papier-mâché, were used here as well. Pieces were often decorated with inlaid porcelain plaques from the Sèvres factory. Ormolu mounts were thinner, and less expensive materials were used for boullework. Empire-style motifs, such as dolphins and lyres, were sometimes used for furniture arm supports. The **indiscret,** or *conversation sofa*, originated during the reign of Napoleon III (Figure 12.14).

The work of Jean Zuber (1773–1853) was an important French contribution to interiors during this period. Continuous rolls of wallpaper enabled his firm to screen print panoramic scenic designs featuring landscapes and seaports seamlessly (Figure 12.15).

Figure 12.14
Indiscret sofas featured in Napoleon III's apartments. (© *Actinic-Blue / Alamy*)

Figure 12.15
Zuber panoramic wall panel. (© *INTERFOTO / Alamy*)

Many of these panels featured thousands of hand-carved blocks and hundreds of colors.

AESTHETIC MOVEMENT (1868–c. 1900)

The Aesthetic movement has been viewed at times as a reform movement directed against the height (or depths, depending on one's point of view) of the style prevalent during the later years of Queen Victoria. At other times, this movement has been considered an extension of Revival style. Nonetheless, the Aesthetic movement represents the first of several reform movements, including its close relative, the Arts and Crafts movement, which served as the bedrock for modernism.

England (1868–c. 1900)

In his book *Hints on Household Taste* (first published in 1868), Charles Locke Eastlake reacted against the commercialism of home decoration, emphasizing the more personal tradition of the handicraft. In the text, Eastlake uses the term *aesthetic* to refer to a style of furnishings lighter in color, form, and carving. Because of the influence of his publication, including several editions published in the United States, the term *Eastlake style* is sometimes used to refer to the British and American furniture produced in this genre.

More rectilinear in form than its Revival counterparts, Eastlake-style furniture features shallow carving or inlay (Figure 12.16). Eastlake proposed that construction be "honest," with no pretense of imitating antique pieces.

The opening of Japan to trade by Admiral William Perry in 1854 greatly contributed to the influence

Figure 12.16
Eastlake-style furniture. (*Desk, c. 1877. Kimbel & Cabus [New York City, active 1863–1882]. Oak, nickel-plated brass and iron hardware/ Art Resource, New York*)

of Japanese design on the taste of the British reformers. Japanese art and design were favored for their identification with nature, simplicity, and clean lines. Aficionados of this style included the designer E. W. Godwin (1833–1886), the architect Thomas Jeckyll (1827–1881), and the writer Oscar Wilde (1854–1900) as well as the artist James Whistler (1834–1903), who were Irish and American, respectively, but who lived in London.

Godwin was a colorist and designer of furniture, wall coverings, and textiles. An aesthetic ideal, inspired by Eastlake, was that furniture be built as a form of art, hence, **art furniture**, a term coined by Godwin. The Aesthetic reformers proposed that every aspect of daily life should be glorified through art. In 1884 Godwin designed a white room for the flamboyant Oscar Wilde, which later influenced the decorator Syrie Maugham (see Chapter 1). For Whistler, Godwin designed interiors in soft, quiet color schemes, favoring yellow. His furniture design was inspired by Japanese influences. An ebonized mahogany-and-brass sideboard, circa 1877, is shown in Figure 12.17.

The Peacock Room, also designed in 1877, was a collaborative effort between the architect Jeckyll, who, like Godwin, worked with Japanese-inspired interiors, and Whistler, who assumed the role of decorator.

The room is now housed in the Freer Gallery in Washington, D.C. In addition to the peacocks (symbolizing beauty) for which it was named, the room features gilded leather and walnut latticework panels, which display Oriental porcelains (Figure 12.18).

The peacock motif was also used for a fabric designed by Arthur Silver in 1888 for the Liberty Shop in London, which featured Japanese objects among the Aesthetic movement pieces. The design was recently adopted for the Target Store's Liberty line for home décor and fashion.

Mixing the notion of medieval craft guilds with an interest in Japanese design, the Aesthetic movement is sometimes referred to as **Anglo-Japanese** style. The impact of the Japanese culture and aesthetic on Western modernism is explored further in this chapter and *In the Spotlight: The Influence of Japan on Western Modernism.*

The term **Japonism**, the influence of the arts of Japan, was first used by Jules Claretie in his book *L'art français en 1872*, published in that year. Japanese art was thought of as being less symmetrical, and in direct contrast to Greco-Roman art, notions that appealed to the early modern reformers' desire to be free of Western artistic conventions. Japanese printmaking techniques and styles greatly influenced the Impressionist artists in Europe and America and would later influence the works of Frank Lloyd Wright and Charles Rennie Mackintosh.

United States (1868–c. 1900)

Following the distribution of Eastlake's text, Oscar Wilde further expounded on the merits of the Aesthetic movement through his lectures while on tour in the United States in 1882. The Herter brothers, of New York, opened their factory, which produced high-quality furniture in this style, as did Daniel Pabst, in Philadelphia. Like Godwin, the Herters also designed works in the Anglo-Japanese style (Figure 12.19).

An important attendee at the Philadelphia Centennial Exposition in 1876 was the progressive English designer Christopher Dresser (1834–1904). His reduction of form to its structural necessity was influenced by the Japanese aesthetic. His designs and manufacturing of silverware placed him among the first of the independent designers to combine art with industry (Figure 12.20). He, too, influenced the Aesthetic movement in America.

Figure 12.17

Godwin sideboard, c. 1877, made by William Watt, features ebonized mahogany with brass pulls and hinges and glass panels. *(V & A Images/ Victoria & Albert Museum / Art Resource, New York)*

Figure 12.18
The Peacock Room epitomizes the spirit of the Aesthetic movement. *(Harmony in Blue and Gold: The Peacock Room, designed by James McNeill Whistler [1834–1903] 1876–77. Freer Gallery of Art, Smithsonian Institution/ Gift of Charles Lang Freer/ The Bridgeman Art Library)*

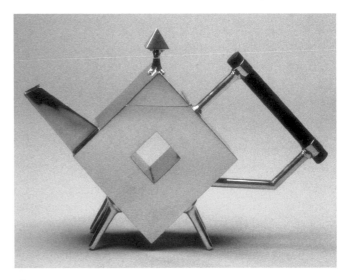

Figure 12.20
This Christopher Dresser teapot is an iconic example of the early modern design movement. *(Cooper-Hewitt National Design Museum, Smithsonian Institution / Art Resource, New York)*

Figure 12.19
Anglo-Japanese table by Herter Brothers, New York, 1877–1878. *(Herter Brothers [fl. 1865–1880s] Center Table, c. 1874. Rosewood, ebonized cherry, maple, satinwood, stained woods, and brass. Location: Wadsworth Atheneum Museum of Art, Hartford, Connecticut. Photo credit: Wadsworth Atheneum Museum of Art / Art Resource, New York)*

ARTS AND CRAFTS MOVEMENT
(c. 1880–c. 1915)

The reformers associated with the Arts and Crafts movement, like those of the Aesthetic movement, appreciated the honesty of craft characteristics of the medieval period. One aspect that distinguished the proponents of Arts and Crafts style from their contemporaries, however, was their zeal in rejecting the machine.

The utopian vision of this movement—that well-designed products should be available to a broad base—was seldom realized. Because fine craftsmanship remained an expensive way to create quality products, the style could not successfully be employed on a massive scale without the use of machinery. Nevertheless, this ideal continued to strike a respondent note in people who longed for the simpler life, a more egalitarian society in which manual labor and craft, as well as mechanized inventions, were held in high esteem.

England (c. 1880–c. 1910)

Not just a design movement, Arts and Crafts in England also proposed a moral code and vision. The movement's initial proponent was the professor and philosopher John Ruskin (1819–1900). As a standard-bearer for England's native style, as expressed through the medieval guild system, Ruskin believed that the evils of industrialization could be eradicated with a commitment to the handmade.

His disciple, William Morris (1834–1896), struck a balance to make Ruskin's ideals more palatable, realistic, and, therefore, broader in their appeal. Morris was a factory owner from an educated and successful family. In addition to being a poet and writer, Morris pursued perfection in craft. He became adept at many artistic endeavors, among them textiles, wall covering, and book design.

Handloom weaving became popular because the homespun art was considered a respectable endeavor. Textiles and wallpaper associated with this style were designed with stylized natural motifs, generally flat, two-dimensional depictions of flowers and leaves, similar to those of medieval tapestries (Figure 12.21).

Furniture was generally constructed of oak, with minimal carving. Joinery, such as dovetail, peg, and mortise-and-tenon methods of construction, was proudly exposed. Ornamentation was limited largely

Figure 12.21
William Morris textile design. *(V & A Images/ Victoria & Albert Museum / Art Resource, New York)*

to metal hinges, drawer and door handles, and upholstery tacks. Chair seats were of rush or covered simply in leather. Upholstery was kept to a minimum. Two styles of furniture of medieval origin, the sideboard, or serving table, and the settle, a wood bench with back and arms, were typical case pieces of this period.

United States (c. 1890–c. 1915)

By 1890 the Arts and Crafts movement had spread to the United States, where various craft communities were created, based on the ideals of Morris. The Roycroft community, in East Aurora, New York, was one. The most successful workshop was that of Gustav Stickley (1858–1942), who, having traveled abroad, had become a disciple of Morris and Ruskin. In 1901 Stickley created the magazine *The Craftsman* in order to spread the word about the movement to smaller communities. It was in this publication that his oak furniture designs were featured. His reclining armchair, known as the Morris chair, paid homage to William Morris (Figure 12.22).

Other prominent Americans identified with the Arts and Crafts movement included Charles and Henry Greene, of California. Their architectural design of both exteriors and interiors, known as shingle, or bungalow, style, blended Japanese aesthetics and American practicality (Figure 12.23). Furniture produced during this time was also known as mission style, after the Franciscan mission churches in San Francisco, where the Greene brothers opened their shop.

A similar aesthetic was incorporated in the early work of Frank Lloyd Wright (1867–1959). His early commissions, such as the Winslow House in Oak Park, Illinois, outside Chicago, represented what became known as Prairie Style. Following the dictum of his first employer, Louis Sullivan (1856–1924), Wright believed in the concept of total environmental design. This later became known as organic architecture (see Chapter 8). Although Chicago was associated with the technology of the skyscraper boom, it also had strong links to the tenets of the Arts and Crafts movement. In contrast to the dictates of the zealot Ruskin, there machines served a purpose, in bringing the finest in design to the average person in the United States.

Figure 12.22
Gustav Stickley's William Morris chair. *(Courtesy of Fairchild Publications, Inc.)*

Figure 12.23
The Gamble House in Pasadena, California, by Greene and Greene, is an example of shingle or bungalow style. *(© Douglas Keister, www.keister photo.com)*

Figure 12.24
Dining room of Robie House, designed by Frank Lloyd Wright, 1908–1910. (© *Farrell Grehan/CORBIS*)

Wright's Usonian houses of the early 1900s, although never constructed, represented a blueprint for the middle class—inexpensive construction, use of machine technology, and an appreciation for aesthetics. Like many others during this period, Wright was greatly influenced by Japanese design after studying art there in 1905, as seen in the interior of the Robie House (Figure 12.24). He employed a mix of traditional materials and techniques, in particular related to joinery, yet his use of space was adventurous. His approach to design was to break down the barriers of tradition, expressing the freedom of America.

Many decorative art forms are associated with this period, among them ceramics. The glazes used for both tiles and vessels were similar to those dating back to the medieval guilds. A popular glaze was a dull matte green. Simple plantlike forms, like those of Japanese ceramics, were executed. Work in copper and leaded stained glass, reminiscent of medieval craft, was also part of this style (Figure 12.25). The colors of

Figure 12.25
Copper lamp made by Dirk Van Erp. (*Copper lamp by Dirk Van Erp*)

the accessories, notably soft, earthy reds and greens, were also the predominant colors for the interiors.

Although not truly a part of the Arts and Crafts movement, a similar sensibility was evidenced in a unique segment of the U.S. population, a religious community known as the Shakers. They were an ascetic, spiritually disciplined, group of worshippers, originally from England, who settled in parts of the Northeast. The Shakers relinquished worldly goods and took part in a communal lifestyle that included strict rules to maintain honesty and restraint in the manufacture and decoration of furniture. A collection of furniture was developed, made from maple and pine, in basic, clean lines, to complement their simple interiors. Because they did not procreate, the Shaker communities died out, leaving a limited, yet highly prized, supply of original Shaker furniture.

The Shakers stressed cleanliness and humility. Pegboards affixed to walls to hold chairs during floor cleaning and as cupboards for storage are hallmarks of the Shaker style. Modern reproductions, although machine made, pay homage to the simple, rectilinear form; order; and regularity, as well as the lack of surface decoration, of the original Shaker furniture (Figure 12.26).

Other uniquely American regional, or provincial, styles from this period include the folk designs of emi-grants from countries other than England, notably Dutch and German settlers in the East and Scandina-vians in the Midwest. The makers of rural furniture often imitated the decorative details and styles of the 18th century, using *faux bois* techniques (see Chapter 9) or colorful floral and symbolic motifs to enhance simple goods (Figure 12.27). Stencils were used instead of expensive imported wallpapers to adorn windows and walls. One craft that developed during the 19th

Figure 12.27
Colorful painted chest is a typical example of Pennsylvania Dutch and Scandinavian folk furniture. *(The Metropolitan Museum of Art, Rogers Fund, 1923. [23.16] Photograph © 1981 Metropolitan Museum of Art)*

century among these emigrant groups was tramp art (see Chapter 10), named after the itinerant German and Scandinavian laborers who settled primarily in New York and Pennsylvania.

Another American regional style, with characteristics similar to the Arts and Crafts movement, was the rustic Adirondack style. Although many residences built during the turn of the century, such as the cottages of Newport, Rhode Island, retained the style of continental European revivals, a regional expression evolved elsewhere. Many upper-middle-class and wealthy families from New York City could afford to retreat to cooler regions during the summer months. A popular destination was Saratoga, located in the Adirondack Mountains of upstate New York. Lodges, seemingly quaint, yet quite substantial, were built as retreats from the industrial city life. They were furnished with furniture pieces made of branches, called **twig furniture**, as well as furniture of horn (Figure 12.28).

ART NOUVEAU (C. 1880–C. 1910)

Corresponding to the height of the English and American Arts and Crafts movements (and in conjunction with the continuing influence of Revival styles) is a style that became known as Art Nouveau, or the new art. Its intent was to break away from references to previous styles. However, rather than breaking from *all* tradition, the new art movement departed more specifically from the very academic representation of classical style and focused instead on the imitation of nature.

Although often mentioned alongside Arts and Crafts, Art Nouveau is unique in its wide international appeal. As in the Arts and Crafts movement, artists and designers created interpretations of Japanese symbols and styles. However, an essential difference between the two styles is noteworthy. Whereas Arts and Crafts relied on the use of *native*, common materials, such as oak, objects in the Art Nouveau style featured exotic, expensive materials, such as mother-of-pearl from shells, enamel, and gold. In a word, Arts and Crafts was homey; Art Nouveau, elegant, and its references to exoticism and eroticism were new. It was also compatible with modern technology. Although it spanned only a brief period, Art Nouveau was very influential, especially in the decorative arts.

Several significant divergent, yet related, strains of Art Nouveau emerged in France and Belgium, Scotland, Austria and Germany, and the United States. The French and Belgians developed a curvilinear style of Art Nouveau. Another significant version, more restrained and rectilinear, emanated from Glasgow, Scotland, and was known as the Glasgow style. A similar style was seen in Vienna as part of the Vienna Secession, and, later, the Wiener Werkstätte; a comparable style in Germany was called the Jugendstil. Art Nouveau in the United States was expressed on a more limited scale, largely through the glass and jewelry work produced by Louis Comfort Tiffany (1848–1933).

France and Belgium (c. 1880–c. 1905)

The emerging Art Nouveau in France and Belgium relied almost exclusively on references to nature in its curvilinear, sensuous, flowing, organic forms. Characterized by **whiplash curves**, sinuous, thin lines, the style's range of decorative motifs included dragonflies and other insects, and plant tendrils. In many respects, its form was closer to the Rococo style than to the styles of the reform movements occurring elsewhere in Europe. The artist Alphonse Mucha (1860–1939) was born in Moravia (now part of the Czech Republic) and lived in Vienna, but he eventually settled in Paris in

Figure 12.28
Horn table, San Antonio, Texas, c. 1880–1890. *(Courtesy the Witte Museum)*

1887. He is best known for his advertising and theater posters, featuring feminine subjects, emphasizing the movement of whiplash curves (Figure 12.29).

Art Nouveau was a style of elegance within a sociopolitical context. This dichotomy was embodied in the work of the Belgian architect and designer Victor Horta (1861–1947). Because the link between Art Nouveau and socialist politics was strong in Belgium, the movement was thought of as the art of the people. Horta, considered a revolutionary architect at the time, was commissioned to build an important work in the Art Nouveau genre. His Maison du Peuple (House of the People), built between 1895 and 1899 but later destroyed by fire, was a monument to the democratization of the Belgian applied and decorative arts.

The new style took its name from a shop that was opened in Paris in 1895 by Siegfried Bing (1838–1905), a German entrepreneur with an admiration for the Far East. The shop, Maison de l'Art Nouveau, served as a gallery from which Bing promoted interesting pieces in the new style alongside Japanese furnishings. He sponsored the work of several artists, among them Eugène Gaillard (1862–1933), to create a suite of rooms for his pavilion space at the Paris World Exposition of 1900. It was there that Gaillard achieved his success.

A legacy of this period in France is the work of architect-designer Hector Guimard (1867–1942), whose complex ironwork designs in the sinuous vegetal style adorned the entrances to the Métro, the Paris underground rail system, several of which remain today (Figure 12.30). These designs were shown at the Paris Exposition.

Guimard's significance to this period also stems from his approach to interiors. The shapes of the rooms he designed were as free-flowing as the wayward growth patterns of plants. He was also associated with the concept of total design; that is, designing all the details of an interior, from stained glass to lock plates, thus emphasizing a sense of unity. Like the

Figure 12.29
Lithograph advertisement for the Job cigarette company by Mucha, 1898. *(Mucha, Alphonse [1860–1939]. Advertisement for the cigarette papers 'Job.' 20th CE. Location: Musée des Arts Décoratifs, Paris, France. Photo credit: Scala/White Images / Art Resource, New York)*

Figure 12.30
The Porte Dauphine entrance to the Paris Métro underground rail system, designed by Hector Guimard, c. 1900. *(© Paul Almasy/CORBIS)*

artist-designers of the Aesthetic and Arts and Crafts movements, Art Nouveau designers produced interiors as ensembles.

As in France, the Belgian designers, such as Henri van de Velde (1863–1957), were concerned with the total interior environment. Van de Velde was commissioned by Bing to create four room settings for his shop. He also served as a link between the movement in Belgium and France and the versions taking place in the German-speaking countries, such as the Vienna Secession movement.

The advent of the motion picture and the new style came together at the Paris World Exposition of 1900, reinforcing the sense of movement. As had happened before, the connection between art and machine shaped the discussion and destiny of popular taste. The sense of movement and freedom is also evident in the drastic changes that clothing styles would take for the modern woman of this day as evidenced with unconstructed and loose garments.

In addition to the Parisian movement, the French province of Nancy was significant to the flourishing of the new style. Émile Gallé (1846–1904) founded L'École de Nancy, an industrial arts alliance, in 1901. Under his direction the lavish craft of marquetry was revitalized, using a variety of fruitwoods and other exotic woods. Plants and animals were the source of inspiration, again showing the influence of the art of Japan. Although Gallé was a cabinetmaker, his forte was glass. Illustrated in Figure 12.31a and b are some of the finest pieces of art glass made during that period in Nancy, by Gallé and by René Lalique (1860–1945). Lalique was able to make the transition from Art Nouveau to Art Deco, and the Lalique firm continues in business today.

Louis Majorelle (1859–1926) was the most important furniture designer of this group (Figure 12.32). Although his early career was spent in the manufacture of Louis XV–style furniture for his family business, he followed in Gallé's footsteps. However, the furnishings produced at Nancy were too expensive to be adapted to factory production. This, in addition to its eccentricity, caused many critics to argue that Art Nouveau works served style over function. The rather quick loss of interest in the style in Nancy was mirrored in Paris. By 1902, Bing's shop had closed.

Figure 12.31

Art glass: a. Lamp designed by Gallé, c. 1900; b. Lalique glass, c. 1900. *(a: Courtesy of the Minneapolis Institute of Arts; b: © Peter Harholdt/ CORBIS)*

Figure 12.32
Dining room design by Louis Majorelle. *(The Art Archive/Musée de l'Ecole de Nancy/Gianni Dagli Orti)*

Scotland (c. 1880–c. 1905)

Alternatively considered part of the British Arts and Crafts movement and a variation of Art Nouveau, the Glasgow style was named after a group of colleagues known as the Glasgow Four. The ringleader of this collaboration was Charles Rennie Mackintosh (1868–1928). Along with his wife, Margaret Macdonald, her sister Frances, and Frances's husband, J. Herbert MacNair, Mackintosh produced a body of work that is viable in either of these categories yet that might be viewed as comprising its own classification as a major, recognizable style.

Trained as an architect, Mackintosh was also an accomplished artist. He began his architectural career after attending the Glasgow School of Art, working on public buildings, including the renovation of his alma mater. He then began to receive commissions for private residences, including Hill House (1902–1904), followed by several tearooms owned by Kate Cranston, which became his signature mark. Expanding on his strong Scottish traditions in architecture, Mackintosh infused his career with new vigor through a trip to Vienna. The Glasgow Four were invited to take part in the Vienna Secession Exhibition of 1900. The white room they designed for the Secession was well received by the avant-garde architects Hoffmann, Wagner, and Olbrich (see later discussion). The Glasgow group's stylishness, which combined functionalism with restraint and elegance, appealed to the Viennese. A mutual respect developed—as well as commissions. Both sides found common ground, yet each took the Art Nouveau movement of France and Belgium in new directions.

Like works of the artist-designers of the Aesthetic and Arts and Crafts movements, Mackintosh's interiors featured cohesive, finely crafted components. Details for walls, ceilings, floors, and furniture were no more significant than those for windows, lighting, fireplaces, or carpets. Signature elements of the Glasgow style were its vertical lines, grid forms, and stylized rose. The Mackintosh color palette was mainly white, with details of pink, purple, black, and silver (Figure 12.33).

Figure 12.33
Art Nouveau, Glasgow style: Design for the Art Lover's House reception room by Charles Rennie Mackintosh, 1901. *(Mackintosh, Charles Rennie [1868–1928] Design for the House of an Art-Loving Friend: Lounge and Music Hall, engraved 1901. L.1894–1902. Location: Victoria & Albert Museum, London. Photo credit: V & A Images, London / Art Resource, New York)*

Austria and Germany (c. 1890–c. 1905)

The Secession (also called the Vienna Secession or Wiener Secession) was founded in 1897 to create a new style, breaking with the entrenched conservatism of Vienna and moving toward modernism. Among the founders of the movement were the architects Otto Wagner (1841–1918), Joseph Maria Olbrich (1867–1908), and Josef Hoffmann (1870–1956) and the artists Gustav Klimt (1862–1918) and Koloman Moser (1868–1918). The Secession's motto was "art for the times—art must be free." In 1903 it would evolve into a new group, the Wiener Werkstätte, founded by Hoffmann and Moser. The Secessionists admired Mackintosh for, among other things, his emphasis on verticality and his division of wall surfaces into zones. The work associated with these groups has a very geometric quality.

Members of the Secession designed a wide range of work, from buildings; to furniture; to enamelwork, glass, graphics, and jewelry (Figure 12.34a and b). The most important commission of the Wiener Werkstätte was the Palais Stoclet, in Brussels, for which Hoffman secured the richest materials, including marble, gold, and glass. Klimt was commissioned to complete a mosaic frieze in the dining room, an extravagance of enamel, gold, silver, and semiprecious stones (Figure 12.35a and b).

The Art Nouveau movement in Germany, notably Munich, was known as the Jugendstil, meaning "young style," after the magazine *Jugend*, which promoted the works of artists shown at the Paris Exposition. The style in Germany had roots in the work of the Belgian architect van de Velde, who moved to Germany in 1899 after many successful commissions in the new style.

By 1906 most of the Secessionist groups had formed a single design association called the DWB, or Deutscher Werkbund. This movement spread to the Netherlands and Scandinavia and became the foundation for the Bauhaus in Germany, which truly established the Modern movement.

Figure 12.34

a. Chair by Josef Hoffmann; b. Wine glass with overlay by Otto Prutscher, c. 1907. *(a: Courtesy of the Minneapolis Institute of Arts; b: © The Museum of Modern Art/Licensed by SCALA / Art Resource, New York)*

Figure 12.35

a. Dining room of the Palais Stoclet, by Josef Hoffmann, c. 1910; b. Close-up of mosaic by Gustav Klimt. *(a: The Granger Collection, New York City. All rights reserved; b: Klimt, Gustav [1862–1918].* The Embrace. *Sketch for the Frieze at the Palais Stoclet in Brussels. 1905–1909. Watercolor and pencil, 194.6 × 120.3cm. Photo: Austrian Archive. Location: Museum fuer Angewandte Kunst, Vienna, Austria. Photo credit: Scala / Art Resource, New York)*

Spain (c. 1890–c. 1910)

In 1900 Barcelona became the capital of the Catalan region of Spain and its industrial and economic center. The city retained a strong cultural and artistic identification with France. Antoni Gaudí (1852–1926), the controversial, revolutionary architect associated with the regeneration of Barcelona during this period, produced a small body of work, more exterior than interior architecture, which became a unique expression of Art Nouveau (Figure 12.36). His approach was sculptural, undulating, and organic, and it was executed with unprecedented freedom. "Art Nouveau" translated into Spanish is "Modernisme."

United States (c. 1890–c. 1910)

Known as the father of the modern American skyscraper style, the architect Louis Sullivan (1856–1924) is also credited with the expression "form follows function." However, he created many lush and intricate decorative elements, such as the Art Nouveau–

Figure 12.36

Art Nouveau, Barcelona style: Front façade detail of the Casa Batlló in Barcelona, by Antoni Gaudí, 1904–1910. *(© Fernando Bengoechea/Beateworks/CORBIS)* inspired cast-iron façade of the Carson Pirie Scott department store in Chicago, built in 1899 (Figure 12.37a and b).

There were few other contributors to the Art Nouveau style in the United States. Rather than com-plete unified interiors in the new style, the contributions were more isolated, mainly in the decorative arts. In particular, the designs and production of colored glasswork from the factories of Louis Comfort Tiffany built the legacy (Figure 12.38a and b).

Figure 12.37
Carson Pirie Scott store, Chicago, by architect Louis Henri Sullivan, featured an ornate façade. a. Exterior illustrated here and b. a close-up of the metal front of the Carson Pirie Scott store. *(a: Todd Bannor/Alamy; b: © Lee Snider/Photo Image/CORBIS)*

Figure 12.38
American Art Nouveau. a. Stained glass window and panel from 1925 by Louis Comfort Tiffany; b. Favrile glass and bronze lamp, 1892–1920. *(a: The Metropolitan Museum of Art, Gift of Robert W. de Forest, 1925. [25.173] Photograph © 1993 The Metropolitan Museum of Art; b: © Peter Harholdt/CORBIS)*

INTERNATIONAL STYLE
(c. 1917–c. 1940)

Modernism gained ground during the period between the two world wars. It transitioned from the Werkbunds throughout parts of Europe to the Bauhaus in Germany. This approach was characterized by austerity in design, abstraction, and a vehement rejection of the past. Its aim was to make no distinction between fine and applied arts. Its socialist goal was to reconcile machinery to design and to improve the standards of mass production. However, its influence was not widespread at the time. It was neither readily understood nor appreciated by any but the elite avant-garde. Therefore, it did not satisfy its expectations, at least not during its heyday.

However, these movements, along with Art Deco, helped shape the climate in the United States for the advent of **industrial design**, the practice of combining art and industry with mass production. This practice was pursued by several architects and product designers.

Holland (c. 1917–c. 1928)

De Stijl, meaning "the Style," was a group of Dutch artists in Amsterdam named after an avant-garde magazine of the same name. De Stijl was strongly influenced by the artist Piet Mondrian (1872–1944). Mondrian's theory of abstraction was to reduce art to its purest form: two-dimensional and primary. Colors were pure red, yellow, and blue. Lines were at right angles: vertical and horizontal. Gerrit Rietveld (1888–1964) joined De Stijl in 1918, producing his now famous red and blue chair around the same time. The chair was not then mass-produced but served as an expression of his philosophy (Figure 12.39a).

Germany (c. 1919–1933)

Walter Gropius (1883–1969) founded the **Bauhaus**, a school of art and design, in Weimar, Germany, in 1919. The three main areas of study were architecture, painting, and sculpture. However, many other crafts and skills were also taught, among them stonemasonry, woodcarving, weaving, ceramics, metalwork, stage design, interior design, and landscape gardening. **Functional design**, in which art was combined with engineering, new materials, and craft, was the school's aim. The basic foundation course of the Bauhaus became the cornerstone of American design education.

In 1925 the school moved to Dessau, a heavily industrialized town in Germany. Ludwig Mies van der Rohe (1886–1969) became its director in 1930. Tubular steel and glass were significant to the Bauhaus style as by-products of the technological advances of World War I. In 1933 the Nazi government forced the school to close, and many of its designers left Germany. Among those who immigrated to the United States were Gropius, van der Rohe, and Marcel Breuer (1902–1981). Many of their designs are today's classics of modernism, including the chairs illustrated in Figure 12.39b and c.

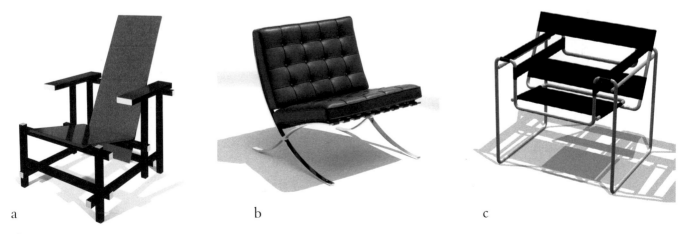

a   b   c

Figure 12.39
International style chairs. a. Gerrit Rietveld's red and blue chair, 1917; b. Barcelona chair by Mies van der Rohe, for the German pavilion of the Barcelona World Exhibition, 1929; c. Wassily chair of welded tubular steel, by Marcel Breuer, 1925–1926. *(a: Courtesy of the Minneapolis Institute of Arts; b: Courtesy Knoll, Inc.; c: Design: Marcel Breuer. Photo: Wikipedia)*

France (c. 1920–c. 1940)

Born in Ireland but immigrating to Paris in 1902, Eileen Gray (1878–1976) was perhaps the only woman architect-designer associated with the International style. She is often categorized as a designer of the Art Deco style in France, which occurred concurrently with the International style. She is perhaps best known for her design of tubular steel furniture featured along with her Bibendum chair, designed in 1917 for the rue de Lota apartment of the milliner Suzanne Talbot, also known as Madame Mathieu-Lévy. Lacquered panels and tribal art are also shown in Figure 12.40a.

Not affiliated with the Bauhaus, but pursuing a compatible vision of modernism, was Le Corbusier. Born in Switzerland as Charles-Édouard Jeanneret (1887–1965), and self-named Le Corbusier, he was a contemporary of Frank Lloyd Wright and shared similar sentiments concerning modernism. However, Corbu, as he is sometimes called, was more extreme in his vision and more austere in his use of materials. He was very much criticized at the Paris Exposition of 1925. Today, however, his furniture designs, especially the pieces in leather and chrome, are some of the most recognizable modern staples, manufactured for both residential and commercial interiors. Charlotte Perriand (1903–1999), who designed the chair shown in Figure 12.40b with Le Corbusier and Pierre Jeannert, is featured *In the Spotlight: The Influence of Japan on Western Modernism* at the end of this chapter.

Figure 12.40

a. Eileen Gray interior 1917; b. The chaise longue "pony chair" designed by Le Corbusier, Perriand, and Jeannert, 1928. *(a: rue de Lota apartment designed by Eileen Gray; b: Victoria & Albert Museum, London/ Art Resource, New York)*

Scandinavia (c. 1920–c. 1940)

By the late 1920s the functionalism touted by the Bauhaus designers had asserted itself in Scandinavia. That Scandinavia had never embraced the eclectic Revival styles popular elsewhere during the previous century made it easier for designers and artists to assimilate the modern aesthetic. This influence was evident at the Stockholm Exposition of 1930. Scandinavians followed this movement while remaining committed to the use of natural materials, in particular wood, in combination with modern technology and new materials, such as tubular steel. The use of traditional materials in more organic forms than those of the Bauhaus designers provided a greater appeal for Scandinavian design. This was instrumental in the acceptance of modernism in the United States, especially in more homogenized versions.

A key figure during this period was Alvar Aalto (1898–1976), of Finland, who experimented with tubular steel, combining it with plywood, a softer, more natural material. He also used wicker and tile (Figure 12.41a and b).

The 1930s were a time of great achievement in the decorative arts and furnishings for Scandinavian countries. They realized the Bauhaus modernist vision of producing quality through mass production.

ART DECO (c. 1920–c. 1940)

The Paris Exposition of 1925 was considered the defining moment for the style that would later be known as Art Deco, although it had been developing for at least a decade before the exhibit. The outbreak of World War I had delayed an earlier planned exhibition and thus a widespread showing of expressions of the Art Deco style. The name *Art Deco* was coined from the full name of the exhibition, Exposition Internationale des Arts Décoratifs et Industriels Modernes. Despite its name, the exhibition was more French than international. And although it intended to showcase modernity, with but a few, significant, exceptions, most of the works shown were nostalgic interpretations of the past.

Despite the exhibition's largely traditional slant, modern technology and exotic materials were incorporated. It could be said that the simplicity in form so admired by the avant-garde modernists was made extravagant through the use of expensive materials.

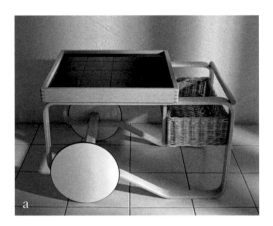

Figure 12.41

a. Aalto tea trolley of wicker, tile, and birch, c. 1937; b. Alvar Aalto, Villa Mairea, Noormarkku, Finland. *(a: Digital Image © The Museum of Modern Art/Licensed by SCALA / Art Resource, New York; b: Roberto Schezen/Esto)*

The interiors that were more traditional (and luxurious) were highly acclaimed, whereas those that were more directly aligned with the austere Bauhaus style were criticized and mocked.

France (c. 1920–c. 1935)

Design influences on France prior to the 1925 Paris Exposition included those from the theater, film, ballet, fashion, and painting. Among these were the sets and costumes created by Léon Bakst (1866–1924) for the Ballets Russes, in Paris designs marked by flamboyance, Oriental fantasy, and saturated, jewel-tone color. This freedom and exoticism was also expressed in the clothing designed by Paul Poiret (1879–1944), who not only liberated women from the restraints of corsets, but also inspired Arabian Night–style clothing, such as the turban and harem pants. The geometry and abstraction of the Cubist painters, and the wild colors of the Fauvists, were other influences on French tastes (Figure 12.42a–d).

Figure 12.42
Early influences on Art Deco. a. Set design for *Phedre* by Léon Bakst for the Ballets Russe; b. Cubist art of Pablo Picasso; *Les Demoiselles d' Avignon* (1907) features women with African masks; c. Fauvist art of Jean Derain; d. Illustration for Paul Poiret fashions. *(a: Bakst, Léon [1866–1924]. Sketch of the setting for Rimski-Korsakov's Ballet* Sheherezade, *1910. Watercolour, pencil, and gold on paper. Photo credit: Erich Lessing / Art Resource, New York; b: Picasso, Pablo [1881–1973]. © ARS, NY Les Demoiselles d'Avignon. Paris, June–July 1907. Oil on canvas, 8' x 7' 8" [243.9 x 233.7cm]. Location: The Museum of Modern Art, New York City. Photo credit: Digital Image. Photo credit: The Museum of Modern Art/Licensed by SCALA / Art Resource, New York; c: Derain, Andre [1880–1954] © ARS, NY. L'Estaque. 1905. Photo credit: Bridgeman-Giraudon / Art Resource, New York; d: The Image Works)*

Figure 12.43

Grand Salon, designed by Jacques-Émile Ruhlmann for his Hotel du Collectionneur pavilion at the 1925 Paris Exposition. *(Grand Salon, designed by Jacques-Émile Ruhlmann, 1925 (b/w photo) by French Photographer. Private Collection/ The Stapleton Collection/ The Bridgeman Art Library)*

A leading artist-turned-cabinetmaker was Jacques-Émile Ruhlmann (1879–1933), whose interiors at the 1925 Paris Exposition featured his signature style (Figure 12.43). Based on 18th-century Neoclassical designs, Ruhlmann's pieces were characteristically slender; produced with exotic wood veneers, such as Macassar ebony; and inlaid with contrasting ivory. His most elegant pieces were less concerned with function than with artistry. The furniture produced by Ruhlmann's workshop, where he employed numerous designers and craftsmen, was expensive and exclusive. In 1935 he, along with René Lalique and others, designed the interiors of the salon on the SS *Normandie*, an ocean liner that was often described as a floating palace.

Exotic materials and techniques are featured in the French Art Deco style (Figure 12.44a–c). **Shagreen,** the skin of the stingray, became popular in this period for furniture as well as smaller decorative items. The extensive use of lacquering was a reflection of appreciation for the Oriental flavor. Mother-of-pearl and lapis were also inlaid in wood furniture. **Dinanderie** was a technique developed by the Swiss-born metalworker Jean Dunand (1877–1942) that used crushed eggshells as an inlay material for metal decorative pieces, which were then lacquered.

The shapes of Art Deco objects are strongly geometric. The colors are bold and saturated. A penchant for Egyptian motifs can be attributed to several factors, among them the discovery of the tomb of King

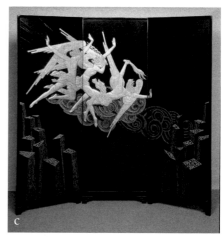

Figure 12.44

Use of exotic materials in Art Deco style. a. Ivory-inlaid Macassar ebony and shagreen coiffeuse designed by Jacques-Émile Ruhlmann, c. 1932; b. Shagreen commode, 1925; c. Eggshell lacquer by Dunand. *(a, b, and c: Image copyright © The Metropolitan Museum of Art. Image Source: Art Resource, New York)*

Tutankhamen in 1922. Stylized patterns were used in stonework for building façades and reliefs and in the ironwork of such masters as Edgar Brandt (1880–1960) as well as for decorative accessories (Figure 12.45).

Another influence on Europe, but especially Paris, was that of African culture, considered exotic at the time. This influence was twofold. Direct references can be seen between African sculptural forms and the earlier Cubist work of Pablo Picasso (1881–1973), Georges Braque (1882–1963), and others. Indirect influences occurred through the presence of Americans of African descent who chose to live in Europe, where they were generally free of the discrimination they faced in the United States. Among the most famous was Josephine Baker (1906–1975), a flamboyant and risqué entertainer who became the rage of fashion and style in Paris. The French were also fascinated by the Harlem Renaissance, a cultural movement that took place in the 1920s and 1930s in the Harlem district of New York City, home to many black artists and performers and a leading force in the new music called jazz.

The Art Deco movement gained popular appeal with the support of the leading department stores in Paris, such as the Bon Marché, which featured luxurious interior ensembles created in the style of the 1925 Paris Exposition. Although the United States did not participate in the exposition, the event was reported on and attended by many prominent American designers. Following the Paris Exposition these interiors

Figure 12.45

Iron screen by Edgar Brandt, c. 1923. *(Image copyright © The Metropolitan Museum of Art. Image Source: Art Resource, New York)*

were brought to the United States and shown in major department stores, such as Macy's and Lord & Taylor.

United States (1925–c. 1940)

During this period the United States was the leader in the development of the skyscraper. Many of the exterior façades of architecture of this time featured stylized versions of the French Art Deco style. The Chrysler Building, designed by William Van Alen and built in between 1928 and 1930 in New York City, is testimony to the American Art Deco style in architecture. It features Aztec motifs and an architectural design based on the **ziggurat**, a stepped, pyramidal-type structure (Figure 12.46).

A key designer during this period was Donald Deskey (1894–1989), who was noted for his designs of the interior spaces executed in 1932 and 1933 for Radio City Music Hall, also in New York City. His work included furniture design as well. Another was Eliel Saarinen (1873–1950), who emigrated from Finland to the United States in 1922 after winning a competition for the design of the Chicago Tribune Tower. He was commissioned to build the Cranbrook Academy of Art, an integrated artistic and educational setting that espoused total design, located outside Detroit, Michigan (Figure 12.47).

During the economic depression that followed the stock market crash of 1929, products needed to be made less expensively in order to appeal to a wider audience. Plastics and metals replaced some of the more luxurious and expensive materials in furniture design, thus making pieces more affordable. Another outcome of the Depression was the emphasis on mass production, culminating in what is referred to as **streamlined design**, implying speed and efficiency. Aerodynamic forms are characteristics of the American concept in building and furniture design as well as the design of cars, railroad interiors, and household

Figure 12.46
Art Deco Aztec-inspired design: The Chrysler Building, New York City. (© *Joseph Sohm; ChromoSohm Inc./CORBIS*)

Figure 12.47
Dining room of the Cranbrook Academy of Art, by Eliel Saarinen. (© *Balthazar Korab Ltd.*)

products, such as the radio. Streamlined design also is evident in the façades and interiors of public buildings (Figure 12.48).

Another influence on American Art Deco design was the functionalist ideas of the Bauhaus movement, promoted by an exhibit in 1934 at the Metropolitan Museum of Art in New York City. In 1933 President Franklin Delano Roosevelt had implemented a far-reaching policy, known as the New Deal, to alleviate the effects of the Depression. As part of the effort to address the widespread problem of unemployment, federal monies were given to artistic projects under the auspices of the Works Progress Administration (WPA), created in 1935 as part of New Deal policy. During the decade that followed, many public buildings were constructed that featured the talents of artists and artisans supported by this program. The government and civic buildings built during the 1930s, such as the federal post offices, illustrate the aesthetic of this period, which combined art and industry. In contrast to the esoteric abstract art of the day, much of the New Deal art incorporated stylized visions of the common man, the laborer, and symbols of the machine age, with both rural and urban references in the design.

Some New Deal artists had a sociopolitical agenda: to expose the plight of the common man (and woman) during the Depression. This theme was represented in the works of the Mexican muralist Diego Rivera (1886–1957), who was commissioned to produce public artworks in the United States. (Also see *In the Spotlight: Harlem Hospital Center Renovation* in Chapter 1 for a contemporary influence of a classic Art Deco mural.)

Although the Art Deco influence on architecture can be seen throughout the United States and in other countries, such as Cuba, there were distinct regional differences. One example can be seen in the South Beach area of Miami Beach, Florida, where Art Deco buildings that had fallen into disrepair have been restored. Upholding a preservationist approach, the buildings have been refurbished in the spirit of American Art Deco, Miami style, which included a predominance of white, pink, turquoise, and lime green (Figure 12.49).

Aspects of this style are apparent in the popular movies of the time, many of which offer a glimpse into the glamorous life (Figure 12.50). Elegant people sipping martinis; Fred Astaire in a top hat; and the elaborate, synchronized dance numbers choreographed by Busby Berkeley are just a few of the images that provided an escape from the harsh economic realities of the times.

Perhaps the culmination of art and industry for the United States was the two major World's Fairs, of

Figure 12.49
Miami tropical Art Deco. (© *Joseph Sohm; ChromoSohm Inc./CORBIS*)

Figure 12.50
American Art Deco interior: The Hollywood set from the film *The Merry Widow*, 1935. (*MGM / The Kobal Collection*)

1933, in Chicago, and 1939, in New York City. Fluorescent lighting was one of many innovations introduced at these exhibitions, which showcased collaborations among artists, architects, scientists, and designers.

Speed, streamlining, and stylization characterized the American Art Deco style. The gazelle was a popular motif, representing Africa as well as grace and speed. The pre-Columbian art and architecture of the Aztec and Mayan cultures of Mexico and Central America, and the Native American culture of the United States, also served as inspiration for many motifs and patterns. These included the sun ray, lightning bolt, zigzag, and stepped forms, which can be found during this period in the architecture of skyscrapers (see Figure 12.46) and in their interiors (Figure 12.51).

Figure 12.51
Art Deco motifs: Lightning bolts, stepped forms, and zigzags in the Chanin building in New York, designed by Jacques Delamarre in 1929. *(© Angelo Hornak/CORBIS)*

MID-CENTURY MODERNISM
(c. 1940–c. 1960)

Wartime research led to the production and application of new products, among them foam rubber for upholstery, molded plastics, fiberglass, and polyester resin. Spot welding, new uses for plywood and lamination, and extensive use of lightweight aluminum also characterized this period.

United States (c. 1940–c. 1960)

The United States saw an influx of talented designers, many associated with the Bauhaus school, who had escaped the Nazi occupation of Europe in the early stages of World War II. Some of these designers were instrumental in the construction of America's modern buildings. Others played a significant role in the merging of domestic and office furniture design and the development of the modular, cubicle approach to office design.

The office furniture company Knoll Associates formed in 1946, when Florence Schust and Hans Knoll married. Having trained at the Cranbrook Academy, studied with Mies van der Rohe, and worked for Gropius and Breuer, Schust brought with her the Bauhaus approach to furniture design. The Knoll firm searched worldwide for talented designers and nurtured them by commissioning their work and promoting their names. Among its designers were Jens Risom (b. 1916), Eero Saarinen (1910–1961), Isamu Noguchi (1904–1988) (Figure 12.52), and Harry Bertoia (1915–1978). Another far-reaching business practice associated with Knoll was the Planning Unit, which worked with clients to identify their needs in order to develop solutions. This integrated approach to corporate interior design is a model still used today.

The creations of Charles Eames (1907–1978) and his wife, Ray (1912–1988), represent a unique American interpretation of European modernism. Their work displayed a seamless integration of technology, innovation, and design. In addition to their prominence as furniture designers, they were inventors, toy makers, filmmakers, and photographers. Figure 12.53 shows their lounge chair and ottoman of laminated rosewood, anodized aluminum, and leather. The ensemble, designed for Herman Miller in 1956, became a prototype of ergonomics with its acute attention to the contours and movements of the human

Figure 12.52
Isamu Noguchi design for Knoll. *(Courtesy of Knoll, Inc.)*

Figure 12.53
Laminated rosewood and leather chair and ottoman, by Eames for Herman Miller, 1956. *(© Herman Miller, Inc.)*

Figure 12.54
Russel Wright's designs "for easy living." a. Spun aluminum ware; b. Glazed earthenware, American Modern line.
(a: © MASCA, courtesy of Manitoga/The Russel Wright Design Center; b: Wright, Russel [1904–1976] © Copyright American Modern Dinnerware, 1937, Manufacturer: Steubenville Pottery [East Liverpool, Ohio], John C. Waddell Collection, Gift of John C. Waddell, 2002 [2002.585.17a-j]. Location: The Metropolitan Museum of Art, New York City. Photo credit: Image copyright © The Metropolitan Museum of Art / Art Resource, New York)

body (see Chapter 2), integrating comfort with style. At the time, it was considered revolutionary.

The renewed prosperity that followed World War II enabled many people to build and furnish new homes. However, in contrast to their pre-Depression counterparts, most of those who made up the new middle class were unable to afford servants to polish silver, prepare formal dinners, or help around the house. Many women went to work during the war and continued after the war. This deemed efficiency in the home even more important. Also this created a need for well-designed modern furnishings characterized by low maintenance and affordability. In the 1960s the

conversation pit and sectional-style seating became common features in the informal American home.

Russel Wright (1904–1976), an American industrial designer, fused modern design and informal living while maintaining a harmony with nature. He was a precursor to today's lifestyle gurus and moguls of television and retail. His domestic lines of products, produced primarily in the 1930s through the 1950s, included housewares made of plastic, earthenware, and spun aluminum (Figure 12.54a and b). His

	Table 12.1 Color Trends: 1950s to the Present	
Decade	**Color Trend**	
1950s	Postwar prosperity in the United States creates lighthearted and youthful palette of bright pinks and turquoise, mixed with black and charcoal gray	
	Birth of rock and roll: While many homes retain conservatism of 1940s, teens incorporate the newer world of color and movement into their clothing and rooms	
1960s	Scandinavian design influences American taste: yellow-orange woods, such as teak, are popular, and analogous schemes of yellow, orange, and green hues are used abundantly	
	Fixtures and appliances shift from basic white to harvest gold, avocado and copper tone	
	Later in this decade, acidic versions of these hues take hold, often in large-scale flower power and graphic geometric prints	
1970s	Boldness, contrast, and starkness of black combined with white epitomize this high-tech decade; cold chrome is combined with black metal, plastic, and vinyl in furniture	
	Red is a popular accent to neutral colors	
	Strongly saturated, solid blocks of colors and bold patterns are powerful and popular trends	
	Countertrend emerges in use of more natural brown and earth tones, unbleached cotton, and woven textures, reflecting concern for environment	
	Mediterranean style is interpreted for American tastes in heavy, massive dark wood furniture, often offset by red textiles, including flocked wall coverings	
1980s	Softening of hue is reflected in palette reflecting the Southwestern desert	
	Colors are neutralized, toned down, muted	
	Mauve, a dull red-violet, combined with light, pickled wood is used extensively, especially by hospitality industry	
	Beige is basic	
	Teal, a deep vivid blue-green, and burgundy, a deep red-violet, relieve the neutral tones of this palette	
	Countertrend emerges in many affluent young consumers, who turn to Old World European elegance, reflected in embellished fabrics: gold becomes an important color, along with jewel tones of emerald green, ruby red, and sapphire blue *(continued)*	

furniture design represented the modern and casual lifestyle of the postwar era.

Color palettes for interiors began to change rapidly during this period, reflecting the changing tastes of American consumers. Table 12.1 summarizes these trends from the 1950s through the present day.

Scandinavia (c. 1940–c. 1960)

Although the United States was considered instrumental for much of the design of the post–World War II era, as in the decades previous, major contributions were also made by Scandinavia. That region's influence continued in the years following the war, with each Scandinavian country offering a unique statement.

In the 1950s, the U.S. and Canadian public became more aware of Scandinavian design after several exhibitions featured the award-winning entries of designers from these countries. Overall, their designs were based on functionalism and humanism. They

Table 12.1
Color Trends: 1950s to the Present, *continued*

Decade	Color Trend
1990s	Mass globalization brings vitality of faraway places: natural pigments from Asia and India form a warm palette of orange and yellow, unlike the harvest gold of a generation before
	Earth tones intensify: mustard, ochre, melon, and terra-cotta are favored
	When used, beige, black, and brown are transformed from bland neutrals by their dimensional texture: brown has casts of red or yellow (rust or copper), while beige is often a version of pale yellow-green (Chinese celadon glaze)
	With pattern less important, interest is provided with faux finishing techniques imitating textures of stone, marble, plaster, and wood
2000s	More than specific hues, the mutability and transcendence of color become significant
	Metallics and iridescent are a significant percentage of neutral colors being used
	The term *bling* is born and supports a brassy gold for a particular kind of consumer
	Layering of color is reminiscent of Renaissance frescoes, as faux finishing techniques become more sophisticated and are rendered more realistically
	A trend toward simplification and spirituality in the first years of this decade is reflected in a quiet, neutral palette, with contrast provided by large expanses of white juxtaposed with deep brown; there is an infusion of saturated, bright colors with the brown and white scheme
	The starring neutral of the latter part of this decade is neutral gray, spurred by the popularity of the TV series *Mad Men*
	The emphasis on sustainability and organic products creates demand for natural pigments
	There is a return to some of the acid colors of the 1960s, including, yellow-greens and orange
2010s	The acid version of yellow-green begins to tone down
	The predominant neutral is gray but it expands to include its warm, cool, and taupe versions
	Color blocking, like bold graphics, enlivens simple furniture forms
	Ombre, graduated tones of one hue, is used for soft coloration
	The metallic group tones down its bling and adds bronze as a favorite
	Browns become more complex, including cool red-violet and violet undertones
	Mauve is back, although called by other names, such as blush
	LED lighting is more universal, creating a digital, pulsating color palette

creatively mastered the challenge of combining good design with economy. Two major contributors in the furniture arena were Hans Wegner (1914–2007) and Arne Jacobsen (1902–1971) (Figure 12.55a and b). Alvar Aalto continued to produce his laminated wood designs and also worked in molded plastic.

After World War II Danish furniture was exported all over the world. At first, this furniture was made from the light-colored native birch. Later, darker teak imported from the East was used.

Scandinavian designers were also acclaimed for their novel use of materials and their accomplishments in many of the decorative arts. Textile prints, such as those produced by Marimekko, were bold, exciting, and colorful. The company is currently enjoying a renewed popularity and continues to produce strong graphic

Figure 12.55
Scandinavian chairs. a. Arne Jacobsen's Ant™ chair of laminated and pressed wood, steel, and rubber, produced by Fritz Hansen, Copenhagen, c. 1952; b. Walnut and cane armchair by Hans Wegner, produced by Johannes Hansen, c. 1949. *(a and b: Courtesy of Fritz Hansen)*

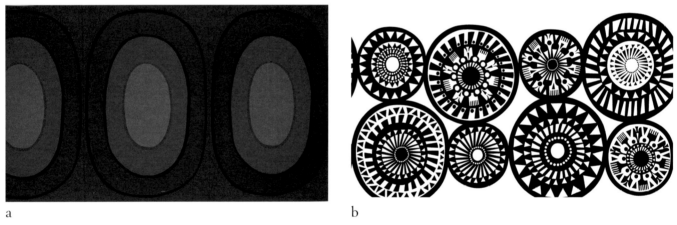

Figure 12.56
Scandinavian decorative arts, *Then and Now.* a. A printed cotton Silkkikuikka textile produced by Marimekko, Helsinski, c. 1961; b. Marimekko design for the 21st century. *(a: Cooper-Hewitt National Design Museum, Smithsonian Institution; b: Copyright © Marimekko Corporation)*

designs (Figure 12.56a and b). Glass, enamel, silver, wood, pewter, and ceramics were worked in styles that had international appeal. These designers made material and machinery compatible in a fresh and new way.

CONTEMPORARY STYLE (c. 1960–PRESENT)

Beginning in the 1960s the global marketplace began to grow, and the world began to seem a much smaller place. Today, it makes less sense to define trends by country because the Internet, made possible by technological advances, now extends around the world, allowing design ideas to be shared instantaneously. With fewer barriers, it is more difficult to know who is influencing whom.

In the United States increased affluence, combined with the baby boom of the 1940s to 1960s, led to an emphasis on youth in the latter decade. Evidence of this impact on design was seen in the emergence of specialty furniture for children and teens. The ability of this new, youth-oriented market to buy more goods spawned a new concept in retailing. With consumers no longer concerned with passing down quality goods from generation to generation, disposability became an operative concept in many industrialized countries. England's Habitat boutique shops for the home, begun by designer Terence Conran, became successful by featuring inexpensive furniture, much of it the knockdown, ready-to-assemble variety. By the 1980s mail-order catalogs and television shopping networks were providing convenient ways to furnish interiors. In the 1990s the emergence of e-commerce and e-tailing, with click-of-the-mouse technology, pushed this idea even further, creating an ease of purchasing previously unimaginable. "Consumer fever" and the expectation of instant gratification took hold as a result of these merchandising trends.

The space limitations of many consumers' interiors spurred the development of furniture systems in the 1960s. **Modular furniture**, that is, flexible, portable, multifunctional pieces, could better accommodate the needs of those living in smaller spaces (Figure 12.57a). Green design and sustainability were not topical issues then. Plastic served this concept well and became the universal language for experimental shapes (Figure 12.57b).

Popular culture, including the musical explosion led by the Beatles, Andy Warhol's pop art, and the antiwar protests of the late 1960s, cannot be underestimated for its impact on the baby boomers' sense of mainstream and counterculture design.

The American architect Robert Venturi's *Complexity and Contradiction in Architecture*, published in 1966, reopened the debate between modernism and historicism. Postmodern style in architecture developed in the 1970s. It relied on a combination of modern elements, often juxtaposed incongruously with historical references. As shown in Figure 12.58a, the AT&T Building (now Sony) in New York City, a skyscraper designed by Philip Johnson (1906–2005), boasted a broken pediment, an 18th-century furniture reference, as its crown. Venturi demonstrates Postmodernism in the whimsical chair seen in Figure 12.58b.

In the 1980s a furniture style known as Memphis began in Italy, spearheaded by Ettore Sottsass (1917–2007), whose company, Memphis, introduced

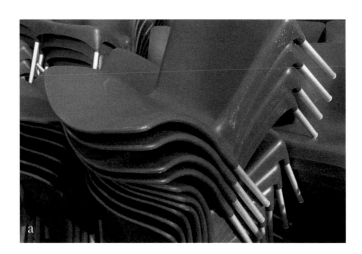

Figure 12.57
Plastic designs from the 1960s and 1970s. a. Stacking chairs designed by Joe Colombo, Sedia 4867, Kartell, Italy, 1968; b. For storage, the wall organizer called the Utensilo, by Dorothee Becker, made in Poland for the Vitra Design Museum.
(a: © Angela Bean / Alamy; b: Courtesy of the Vitra Design Museum Dorothee Becker 1970; Photographer: Andreas Sütterlin)

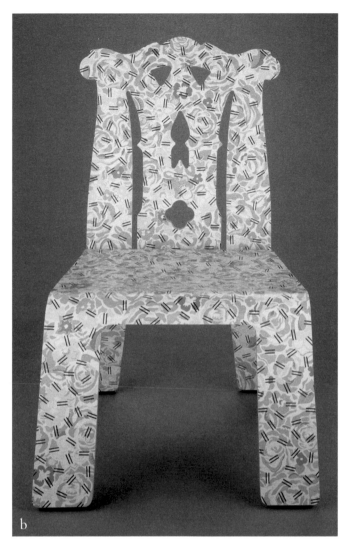

Figure 12.58

Postmodern style. a. Architecture: The pediment from Phillip Johnson's AT&T Building, New York City; b. Robert Venturi's postmodern chair for Knoll International is a satirical version of the Queen Anne style in plastic laminate. *(a: © Alan Schein Photography/CORBIS; b: The Philadelphia Museum of Art / Art Resource, New York)*

many theatrical, satirical, and impractical versions of mid-century design in bright colors (Figure 12.59). During this decade the merger of the fashion and interior design worlds became au courant. This combination, along with the prosperity of many consumers, led once again to an embracing of historic styles that touted affluence and acquisition (Figure 12.60).

Concurrently, the 1970s saw the emergence of a style featuring industrial products and materials, such as exposed heating, ventilation, and air-conditioning (HVAC) systems; interior stairs and elevators; and commercial stainless-steel kitchen appliances, as well as the use of home office furniture to define the interior space. In many urban areas, segments of the population—at first artists, then young profession-

als—began to renovate former industrial spaces and warehouses, many in the downtown districts of cities. High-tech style became fashionable as these large, open loft spaces accommodated a mixture of residential, commercial, and industrial elements in relatively raw space. Many loft-type spaces continue to be created, including as new construction as well as adaptive reuse of residential and contract projects.

Styles that featured opulence tended to be less popular after the economic downturn of the late 1980s. Budgets became leaner, resulting in a back-to-basics approach to interior design. This included a return to natural materials, combined with a denigration of synthetic counterparts. Again looking to Japan for inspiration, more minimalist design came into vogue, with

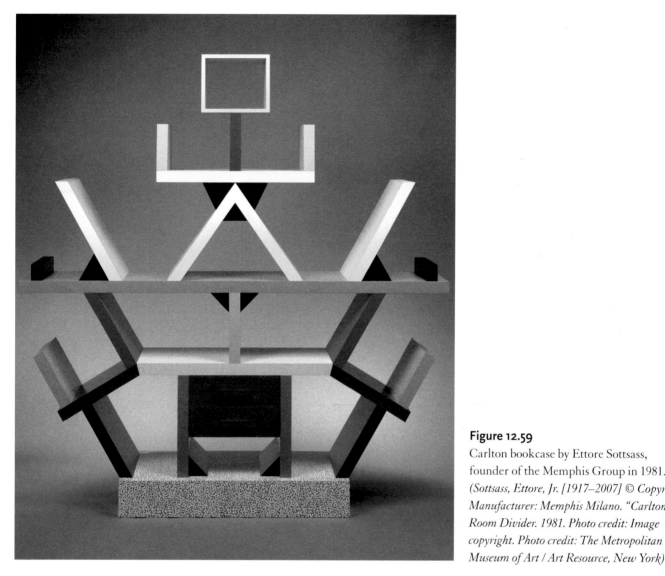

Figure 12.59
Carlton bookcase by Ettore Sottsass, founder of the Memphis Group in 1981. *(Sottsass, Ettore, Jr. [1917–2007] © Copyright Manufacturer: Memphis Milano. "Carlton" Room Divider. 1981. Photo credit: Image copyright. Photo credit: The Metropolitan Museum of Art / Art Resource, New York)*

an emphasis on simplicity, clean lines, and personal reflection (Figure 12.61). This is explored further in the *In the Spotlight: The Influence of Japan on Western Modernism* at the end of this chapter.

The 21st century began with a multitude of museum, gallery, and auction retrospectives of modern design, giving renewed zest to movements that produced, ironically, the antiques of today. Lower-priced versions of modern icons flourished and were suited for yet another economic downturn at the end of the first decade of the 21st century. Rather than approach this from a position of austerity as with the Bauhaus style, people turned to an eclectic mix of modern elements; global decoration and ornament; and a blend of old and new, machine- and handmade, as in the interior featured in Figure 12.62. Terms to describe the spaces and furnishings of the built environment today include *bespoke*, *authentic*, *artisanal*, and *the new luxury*.

Another irony for the late 20th century and beginning of the 21st century is the juxtaposition of computer-savvy, smart (computer-driven) technology and the penchant for the traditional, home-spun, and manmade approach to design. The economic gains of emerging countries in the 21st century have influenced style changes. In particular, the countries known as BRIC (Brazil, Russia, India, and China), traditionally based in the celebration of ornamentation, are driving a countertrend to minimalism. The new wealthy (known in earlier periods as the nouveau riche) have the means to build and buy homes and goods made from luxurious materials, often in very elaborate and ornate styles. Also in this century is the influence of African design based both in the region's indigenous arts as well as in designers' concepts of modern design (refer to Chapter 2 for further discussion of the relationship to sustainability). This will be explored further in Chapter 13.

Figure 12.60
Elaborate, opulent style of the 1980s. (© *Tim Lee Photography*)

Figure 12.61
Minimalist style of the 1990s. *(Richard Bryant/ Arcaid. Designed by Tsao McKown)*

Figure 12.62
Twenty-first-century design. A Manhattan apartment blends East and West, old and new, handmade and machine-made designs. *(Interior design by the Author; photo by Peter Dressel)*

Women of the International Style

The importance of architect-designer Eileen Gray and furniture designer Charlotte Perriand have been featured in this chapter. Three other women's lives and contributions to the modern movement and its influence on the built environment are featured here. They have much in common, such as coming from educated, well-to-do European families, sharing strong social and political ideologies, and an insistence on form and function. They all enjoyed long, productive lives.

Marianne Liebe Brandt (1893–1983)

Born Marianne Liebe in Chemnitz, Germany, Brandt is known as one of few women of the Bauhaus to make her reputation in design fields outside the territories associated with women such as textiles, weaving, and pottery. Her metal ware tea services (Figure a) and light fittings from the 1920s have become widely known, with a number of them produced under license from the mid-1980s by the Italian firm Alessi.

After her marriage to Norwegian painter Erik Brandt in 1919 they lived and traveled in Norway and France. She trained as a painter before joining the Bauhaus in 1923, where she became a student of Hungarian László Moholy-Nagy in the metal workshop. She advanced to become its director in 1928. After leaving the Bauhaus in 1929, Brandt worked for the studio of Walter Gropius in Berlin designing furniture for mass production and modular furniture while also working as an interior designer. Brandt was a pioneering photographer. She created experimental still-life compositions, but it is her series of self-portraits that is particularly striking.

Grete Schutte-Lihotzky (1897–2000)

Born Margarete Schutte in Vienna in 1897, she studied architecture under the eminent leaders of the Secession, notably Joseph Hoffman, later working with modern iconic architects Adolf Loos and Ernst May. Her lifelong work focused on affordable design through efficient planning to improve the living conditions in post–World War I Europe, in particular the daily work of the housewife.

Her work as an architect, along with May, for the Municipal Housing Department in Frankfurt, Germany, led to the development of a standardized kitchen that was installed in 10,000 housing units. These kitchens, inspired by railroad dining cars, were later referred to as fitted, efficiency, or galley kitchens (see Chapter 6). They incorporated an understanding of ergonomic principles based on focused study of human movements during food preparation. They were also designed to incorporate prefabricated fixtures.

She spent several years as a political prisoner in Europe until her release after World War II. Barred from work as an architect because of her affiliation with the Communist Party, she served internationally as a consultant on kitchen and kindergarten space design, and lived to be 103.

Schutte-Lihotzky's iconic Frankfurt Kitchen designed in 1926–1927 (Figure b) was recently given prominence at the exhibit in New York entitled *Counter Space: Design and the Modern Kitchen,* held at MOMA (Museum of Modern Art) from September 15, 2010 to March 14, 2011. An unusually complete example was installed for this exhibit.

In the aftermath of World War I, thousands of these kitchens were manufactured for public-housing estates being built around the city of Frankfurt-am-Main in Germany. Schütte-Lihotzky's compact and ergonomic design, with

a

Figure a
Brandt teapot. *(a: Brandt, Marianne [1893–1983] © ARS, NY. Tea Infuser and Strainer. c. 1924. Photo credit: The Metropolitan Museum of Art / Art Resource, New York)*

(continued)

Women of the International Style, *continued*

Figure b
Frankfurt Kitchen by Grete Schutte-Lihotzky, 1926.
("Frankfurter Küche, 1926" in Die Deutsche Wohnung der Gegenwart *Digital Image © The Museum of Modern Art/ Licensed by SCALA / Art Resource, New York)*

its integrated approach to storage, appliances, and work surfaces, reflected a commitment to transforming the lives of ordinary people on an ambitious scale. Previously hidden from view in a basement or annex, the kitchen became a bridgehead of modern thinking in the domestic sphere— a testing ground for new materials, technologies, and power sources, and a spring board for the rational reorganization of space and domestic labor within the home.

Eva Stricker Zeisel (b. 1906–2011)

Born Eva Stricker in Budapest in 1906, she was one of the most respected ceramicists and industrial designers of modern times. Although a centenarian, she remained active in the world of design, lending her eye for form and technical expertise to contemporary potters and manufacturers. Her recent works included designs for Crate and Barrel and The Rug Company (Figure c) in the United States and firms throughout the world. The Museum of Modern Art, in addition to the Metropolitan Museum, issued new releases of some of her early designs in new glazes and colors, which were always supervised by Zeisel.

She began her training at age 17 in traditional pottery techniques, at the time considered a more acceptable trade for a woman than architecture. She then moved to Germany, where she acquired skills in all phases of industrial production and became one of the first to move the ceramic arts into contemporary mass production, creating beautiful, useful objects for everyday living. Later after traveling in Russia, she was imprisoned, mainly in solitary confinement, having been accused of plotting to kill Stalin, and was eventually released. She married Hans Zeisel, who had waited for her for eight years. In 1938 they went to New York, where they settled permanently. In 1939 she created the department of ceramic arts and industrial design at Pratt Institute in Brooklyn, where she taught until 1952. Among her many awards was the 2005 Cooper-Hewitt National Design Award for Lifetime Achievement. In 2007, Pratt Institute Gallery celebrated her life's centennial with an exhibition of her works.

c

Figure c
Zeisel's early ceramic work, reincarnated for Crate and Barrel's Classic line dinnerware. *(c: Courtesy of Crate and Barrel)*

The Influence of Japan on Western Modernism

In both Chapters 11 and 12 many examples were given of the influence of the East on the West. In looking at themes of Western design, both in Europe and America over the centuries, we noted significant regional differences. Likewise, the various regions in the East differed then and now. We have identified influences from the East, from the Near East to the Far East on both Asian and African continents. Contributions from Egypt, Morocco, Iran, Turkey, India, China, and Japan, among others, have been noted.

This Spotlight focuses on the influence Japanese culture and design have had and continue to have on modern and contemporary design in the West.

Although most of the Revival styles and Aesthetic movement may be characterized as a nostalgic look at the past, strands of reform begin to emerge at the same time. In the latter half of the century, the aesthetic of Japan, a more restrained approach to design, captivated the minds of some designers, who would steer their course in a different direction. As noted in the text, the Aesthetic movement is sometimes referred to as Anglo-Japanese style, representing a resolution between art and machinery.

Also as discussed in the text, many designers and artists were influenced by the Arts and Crafts movement, including Frank Lloyd Wright, who studied art in Japan in 1905. He employed a mix of traditional materials and techniques, in particular related to joinery, yet his use of space was adventurous. His approach to design was to break down the barriers of tradition, expressing the freedom of America. Wright admired what he described as "the elimination of the insignificant."

Another attendee of the Centennial Exhibition in Philadelphia in 1876 was Maria Longworth from Cincinnati, Ohio, a dabbler in pottery. Japan's exhibition of ceramics impressed her so that she established a factory (or "art studio," as she preferred) at her family's estate Rookwood upon her return, where a team of artists explored new and traditional glazing techniques and patterns. The vase in Fig-ure a captures the Japanese influence with the chrysanthemum motif, a highly symbolic natural form.

International Style and Art Deco (c. 1917–c. 1940)

Eileen Gray, the architect-designer associated with the International style, studied under Japanese lacquerer Seizo Sugawara in 1906 and exhibited her lacquered furniture, screens, and objects in 1913.

Charlotte Perriand (1903–1999) spent time living in the Imperial Hotel, built by Frank Lloyd Wright, in Tokyo. It is there the chaise longue she designed with Le Corbusier and Pierre Jeannert, among other pieces, was translated into wood and bamboo, indigenous materials crafted by local Japanese artisans.

Built in the 17th century in Kyoto, Japan, the Katsura Imperial Villa influenced well-known modernist architects in the 20th century, among them Walter Gropius, who visited Japan in 1953 and found inspiration in the minimal and orthogonal design. It is considered to be the synthesis of tradition and modernity

Isamu Noguchi (1904–1988), the son of an American mother and a Japanese father, started creating furniture and lamp designs for Herman Miller in 1947. His namesake table, the Noguchi, designed in 1944, for Knoll, is a remarkable blend of both cultures (Figure d).

George Nakashima (1905–1990), a Japanese-American architect turned woodworker, was born in Spokane, Washington, and also studied, worked, and lived in France and Tokyo. His renowned crafted wood furniture business under the direction of his daughter Mira since his death continues his philosophy. From extraordinary lumber the making of useful objects to fulfill man's life begins, in a disciplined manner, the way nature produces a tree or a flower.[1] It is at an instinctual level that Nakashima interprets what he believes the wood is asking to reveal. In 2010 Mira introduced The Keisho Collection, which pre-

(continued)

The Influence of Japan on Western Modernism, *continued*

serves the methods and techniques embraced by her father. *Keisho,* a Japanese word, translates as *continuance* or *succession*.

Contemporary Style (c. 1960–Present)

With the 1980s economic downturn, more minimalist design, again looking to Japan for inspiration, came into vogue. It emphasized simplicity, clean lines, and personal reflection. The urban landscape of Japan is densely populated; compactness is therefore critical to design. (Refer to the capsule hotel type presented in Chapter 10, Figure 10.53c). The appeal

of Zen Buddhism, organic architecture, urban gardens, sanctuary, and meditation has infiltrated the design of both residential and hospitality spaces in the United States. Designers, among them Clodagh, have been greatly influenced by these themes.

The Japanese aesthetic celebrates the transcendence of nature, its random natural imperfections, and the beauty in everyday objects and rituals of living. A term *wabi sabi,* loosely translated as the beauty of imperfection as well as the importance of meditation to the built environment, is discussed further in Chapter 13.

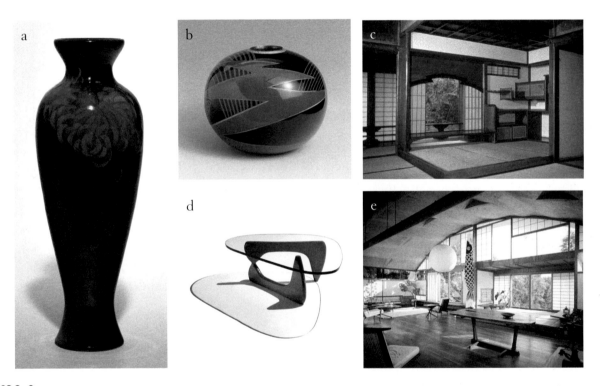

Figures a–e

a. The chrysanthemum, a symbolic motif in Japanese design, is featured in this Rookwood art pottery, 1905; b. Dinanderie Art Deco vase by Jean Dunand. c. Katsura Imperial Villa, Kyoto, Japan; a 17th-century interior inspires contemporary design. d. The Noguchi table for Herman Miller remains a classic. e. George Nakashima's woodworking tradition continues under the direction of daughter Mira. Interior of the Nakashima studio. *(a. Rookwood Pottery [1880–1960]; Amelia Browne Sprague [1887–1903]: Vase with Chrysanthemums, 1899. Ceramic, Earthenware, Height: 14 1/2 in. [36.83cm]. Photo credit: Digital Image © Museum Associates / LACMA / Art Resource; b: Dunand, Jean [1877–1942] © ARS, NY Vase, c. 1925. Photo credit: Image copyright © The Metropolitan Museum of Art. Image source: Art Resource, New York; c: © Sakamoto Photo Research Laboratory/CORBIS; d: Courtesy Knoll, Inc.; e: © Ezra Stoller / Esto. Nakashima House/Studio, Location: New Hope, Pennsylvania, Architect: George Nakashima)*

1. Adapted from Nakashima's website: "Philosophy"

Summary

This chapter introduces not only the styles resulting from the Industrial Revolution (Revival), but the resulting reform movements, specifically the early seeds of modernism.

Important highlights of the Industrial Revolution included: the inventions of cast iron, plate glass, and synthetic dyes; mass production; increase in the middle class; influx from rural areas resulting in the expansion of urban and suburban clusters; and accompanying lifestyle changes, and changes in interior design reflecting those changes.

The Revival styles, notably Gothic, Renaissance, and Rococo, were readily available with mass production (machine-made techniques). However, after some time, quality was sacrificed, with speed, low cost, and mass production taking priority. Eventually, this led to the subsequent demise of the age of Revival and planted the seeds of modernism.

Early seeds of Modernism, focusing on a return to the handmade and nature, included the Aesthetic, Anglo-Japanese, and Arts and Crafts movements particularly in England and America. The Art Nouveau movement originating in France and Belgium featured the handmade as well, but incorporated more exotic and costly materials than the other reform movements noted above. Individualistic versions of Art Nouveau appeared in Spain, and to a lesser degree in Italy, the United States, and other places.

Other movements of this period fall under the International style, such as the Vienna Secession, de Stijl, and the Bauhaus movements, particularly in Austria, Germany, and Holland.

The influx of Bauhaus-trained architects, artists, and designers to other areas as a result of World War II in Europe was to have an enormous influence on modern design on a broad scope, especially in the United States. The contribution of these early modernists, at first not universal in its appeal, would become a legacy throughout much of the industrialized world.

The contributions of Scandinavian artisans were significant; in particular, their inventive use of new and traditional materials and emphasis on the affordability, and functionality, of good design.

Design issues during the modern period have included the relationship of form to function, historicism to innovation; the interplay of traditional ideals with new materials and manufacturing techniques; the handmade versus the machine made; and the extent to which design can be innovative, good, and accessible to a broad audience. Although somewhat differentiated by movement, time frame, and region, these themes were played out through the many revival styles, the Aesthetic movement, Arts and Crafts, Art Nouveau, Art Deco, International style, and the later Modern and Postmodern movements. By the 21st century the coexistence of the machine produced and the handcrafted returned with perhaps greater resolution than it did in the throes of the early modernism of the 19th century, where this chapter began.

Vocabulary

anaglypta	functional design	revivalism (eclecticism)
Anglo-Japanese	historicism	settle
art furniture	indiscret	shagreen
Bauhaus	industrial design	streamlined design
British Raj (Anglo-Raj, Anglo-Indian)	japanning	tufting
	Japonism	twig furniture
companion chair	lincrusta	Victorian
cozy (cosy) corner	mauve	whatnot
De Stijl	modular furniture	whiplash curve
dinanderie	ottoman (pouf)	ziggurat

Exercise: Characteristics of Modernism

Create a sketch journal to document three key features of each of the eight major styles described in this chapter. Choose among architectural features, furnishings, fabrics, colors, or motifs typical of the periods and styles. For example, for Art Nouveau, to demonstrate architectural features, you might draw the bold curves of Gaudí's architecture or sketch a vignette of a Mackintosh room, including wall treatments. Examples of Art Nouveau motifs might include a sketch of the stylized rose of the Glasgow style, the plant tendrils of the French style, or the grid forms used in the Secessionist's decorative art pieces. Label these drawings and features to reinforce the vocabulary and concepts explored in this chapter.

Exercise: Using the CD-ROM

Take advantage of the contents of the CD-ROM to increase your understanding of notable designers and architects from a global perspective. Follow the instructions for Starting the CD-ROM on pages xix–xx and click on Chapter Twelve: Period Design Styles: Revival Styles (c. 1830–c. 1880)–Contemporary Style (1960–Present).

Contemporary Style: Today's designers and architects who have made a name in furniture design come from all over the world. Among them are:

The Campana Brothers
Patricia Urquiola
Phillipe Starck
Ron Arad
Zaha Hadid

Select one of the above and explore that person's sources of inspiration. Use readings from magazine articles, online profiles, biographies, or design philosophy statements. Select a piece of furniture you find intriguing, and describe how it demonstrates the designer's inspiration.

CHAPTER 13

Forecasting and Trends

Now that we have surveyed the history of design from early times to the present, we turn our attention toward the future. Because historical trends are often repeated, interior designers must learn from both the past and the present. "Trend watching is more than spotting the next new color, fabric, or hot designer. It's about observing change and understanding how to transform change into opportunity," says Patty Bouley, the owner of Bouley Design Inc., an international product development and trend service.[1] How that knowledge is then used to anticipate the future is the subject of this chapter.

There are many reasons why forecasting is important to the interior designer. As with any career, it is critical to keep pace with changes that affect employment and business. Interior designers inform and educate their clients. Increasingly, laypersons, including the increasing numbers of **DIY (do-it-yourself)** consumers, have access to a myriad of information and resources, for both retail and trade options (see later discussion). This treasure trove makes the designer's role as curator and editor of information even more important. Designers hold a competitive edge when they are able not only to introduce and explain new design perspectives to clients, but also to filter the array of choices available. Additionally, it is crucial for the designer to be aware of what is available and what is on the horizon—and, perhaps more challenging, to have a good sense of what might soon become dated or even obsolete. The success of today's designer is, in part, measured by his or her ability to understand consumer desires and needs while drawing the fine line between up-to-date and trendy.

Forecasting is defined as a prediction or calculation of future events or conditions. It is based on a rational study and analysis of available, pertinent data. Forecasting is not based on a sixth sense, magic, or esoteric astrological charts. Perception, observation, fact gathering, and analysis are skills not equally possessed by all. However, they may be honed once a person recognizes their importance and learns what to look for. This chapter examines some of the factors that are studied to forecast directions significant to interior design—that is, directions that make sense for the present and that are also adaptable for the future.

A **trend** is a general direction or movement, a prevailing tendency or inclination. One trend seen today is a closer connection between the interior and exterior. Much of this direction reflects a renewed appreciation for being part of the larger, natural world. Organic architecture and other design styles, such as Arts and Crafts, employed this connection a century ago, perhaps fashioned, or expressed, differently from how it is today. An emphasis on the livability of outdoor space expands the role of the interior designer.

Presume that for every trend there is a countertrend. The preference for the new, machine-made goods during the late 19th century was counterbalanced by the emerging Arts and Crafts movement, with its emphasis on the handmade. This dichotomy is expressed again in contemporary conversations.

International style, in the period between the two world wars, expressed a trend toward simplification. This trend, known

as modernism, could be seen through several styles that included distinct, yet overlapping, expressions of reduced ornamentation (see Chapter 12). The end of the 20th century again saw an overriding trend toward simplification of design and away from excessive ornamentation.

Fashion, like style, can be viewed as the specific choices of those who regard themselves (or are regarded by others) as being up-to-date. Although the Bauhaus designs of the 1920s and 1930s were too severe to be readily and completely accepted by most people, one expression, the use of white for interiors, became a fashionable statement, partly because of the efforts of interior designers such as Syrie Maugham (see Chapter 1).

Motifs or symbols can become, in a sense, shortcuts to understanding a particular style or movement. In the 20th century the gazelle became a symbol of the age of speed and streamlining. Many motifs are nearly universal, relating to familiar forms found in nature. Both ancient and contemporary civilizations have used some representation of the horizon, the sun, the earth, the mountains, fire, or changes in seasons in their decorations. The motif may be as simple as a horizontal line, a circle, or a triangle—or, it may be more complex, such as a maze, a symbol that depicts the part of the human spirit that is bewildered by the mysteries of life and death. In Figure 13.1a–c we can see how a symbol, in this

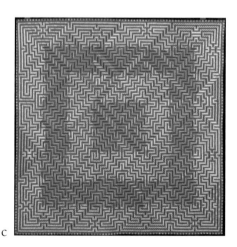

a b c

Figure 13.1
The maze: A motif through time and space. a. Ancient Roman mosaic; b. Renaissance tile; c. Modern quilt. *(a: Theseus kills the Minotaur. Detail from the "Theseus mosaic," floor mosaic from a Roman villa at Loigersfelder near Salzburg, Austria. 4th CE. Photo credit: Erich Lessing / Art Resource, New York; b: Maze design, from the ceiling of the Sala del Labirinto (photo), Italian School (15th century) / Palazzo Ducale, Mantua, Italy / Alinari / The Bridgeman Art Library International; c: Smithsonian American Art Museum, Washington, DC / Art Resource, New York)*

case the maze, has been transformed by different cultures at different times.

It is only hindsight that tells us which style is a **classic** and which is merely a **fad**. Generally, a classic has stood the test of time. Although there may be some variations over time, classics reflect the more universally accepted standards of beauty (i.e., aesthetics; see Chapter 3). Thus, the principles of geometry that governed proportion in designs from the golden age of Greece (see Chapter 11) continue to be used by architects and designers today. In contrast, the desktop waterfall, meant to create a sense of well-being through the healing properties of water, was not well received and was short lived (a fad).

TIME FRAMES AND CYCLES

Trends overlap. A new style is often considered avant-garde when introduced. It then undergoes a gradual period of acceptance, usually with substantial revision, before eventually being discarded. Sometime later, however, it may be revisited, as in the case of Bauhaus-style furniture. In modern times the cycles of style have become increasingly shorter, measured in decades, even years, not centuries. Advances in technology, manufacturing, and communication are responsible for expediting change.

The two worlds of fashion, for the person and the built environment, have moved closer together and at times appear to be concurrent. In general, however, trends affect personal fashion in shorter spurts than they do fashions for interiors. Much of this difference is due to economics. It is much less costly to change the style of one's trousers than it is to redesign a home or a public space. The correlation between fashion and interiors is explored later in this chapter.

A product (a subset of style) has a shelf life, or a life cycle. Although the life cycle of a successful product or style varies, all life cycles follow the same basic stages:

- Introduction
- Growth
- Maturity
- Stagnation
- Decline
- Reincarnation[2]

THE ROLE OF RESEARCH GROUPS, EXHIBITIONS, TRADE SHOWS, AND SHOW HOUSES

There are both formal and informal ways to gather the data needed for forecasting. Formal research resulting in detailed statistics, a snapshot of the habits and tastes of a population at a given time, may be referred to as an **environment scanning report**. Organizations such as the American Society of Interior Designers (ASID), the International Furnishings and Design Association (IFDA), and the American Institute of Architects (AIA) periodically conduct those extensive surveys.

Having a basic curiosity about people, places, and things is helpful when forecasting trends in a less formal way. Following current events and global news and people watching are helpful techniques. Some firms use focus groups, hire consultants to conduct market research, or they may rely on professional trend spotters to predict consumer buying habits and tastes. One renowned marketing expert is Faith Popcorn, founder of BrainReserve, who coined the term **cocooning** in the 1980s to describe the stay-at-home trend. This trend resurfaced in the early 21st century first in response to terrorist attacks in the United States and again later as a result of a weakened economy.

Forecasters of Color Trends

Color forecasting plays a significant part in the prediction of trends influencing the textile and interior design industries (see Chapter 4). The textile industry generally requires two years in lead time, the time between the beginning of the process and their appearance, for color picks to be incorporated into production and sales.

Most forecasters will describe several trends, often taking four or more different approaches, recognizing the complexity and variety of domestic and international consumer markets. The Color Association of the United States (CAUS), the International Color Authority, the Color Marketing Group, Pantone, Doneger, and Color Box are some prominent color forecasting groups. These groups generally forecast color for several industries, among them fashion, architecture and interior design, and automotive. Or, forecasts may be tailored to specific market niches or for individual clients. Annual forecasting reports are compiled by various trade publications, such as *Home Accents Today*.

Committees are formed that bring together industry experts from the various sectors. Representatives may include designers, manufacturers, retailers, and educators. Brainstorming sessions result in defining overarching themes, common threads that are then translated into style directions. These forecasts typically project trends for several years to come, with annual or semiannual adjustments. Many major manufacturers of paint products also produce color forecasts, generally on a yearly basis.

It is the exception for a forecasting group to limit its reports to either fashion or interiors or even to color alone. The intertwining of the design elements observed, such as texture and materials, is critical for enhancing its forecasts. Inspiration for product development is shaped by forecasting (Figure 13.2).

Exhibitions and Trade Shows

The great historic exhibitions over the years have showcased many new and up-and-coming styles. The Crystal Palace, in London, and the Exposition Inter-

nationale des Arts Décoratifs et Industriels Modernes, in Paris (see Chapter 12), both played critical roles in changing tastes in interiors (Figure 13.3a). These events helped demonstrate the use of new materials and construction techniques and offered a peek at the work being done by the best designers and manufacturers, both near and far. They were an opportunity to bring new designs to a wider audience.

Today, new ideas are introduced at trade shows in which merchandising, the selling of products, is paramount. At furniture fairs in cities such as Milan, Paris, and San Francisco, and the Merchandise Mart in Chicago, vendors introduce their new lines of merchandise (Figure 13.3b and c). The Heimtextil show, in Frankfurt, Germany, features fabrics, window fashions, and carpets. The NeoCon shows in Chicago, Baltimore, and Toronto feature products more specifically oriented toward contract interior design but have recently increased attention to residential design. Other shows relate to more specific sectors, such as sustainable design, kitchen and bath design, hospitality, and facilities management. At these shows an interior designer has the opportunity to find the unexpected among the expected, selecting from the enormous array of products. What might be of interest in certain areas may not be mass-marketed for several years in others.

Show Houses

Many charitable organizations collaborate with interior designers, architects, and landscape designers, among others, to produce show houses whose tours serve as fundraisers. Many of these events are held annually, with the site of the event and designers used changing each year. Generally, high-profile or up-and-coming designers contribute their time, expertise, labor, and furnishings to fabricate a vignette or a room in an existing building. This is an opportunity for designers, suppliers, and subcontractors to show their work to the community at large (Figure 13.4). The rooms are temporary, and designers are free to approach design solutions that touch upon fantasy because no one is expected to live in these spaces as designed. These interiors provide yet another venue at which design students and practitioners can be inspired by design ideas and spot new trends.

Figure 13.2
Design inspiration and trends. Patti Carpenter, Carpenter and Co., a global artisan manufacturer of home and personal accessories, also forecasts trends. This is a color board prepared for spring 2012. *(Courtesy of Patti Carpenter)*

a

b

c

Figure 13.4

A room by interior designer Eve Robinson for the Annual Kips Bay Show House 2010 demonstrates two trends that year: the color purple and the use of wallpaper. *(Trevor Tondro for the New York Times/*Redux)

Figure 13.3

Trade shows, *Then and Now*. a. The Great Exhibition held in the Crystal Palace, London, 1851; b. The Merchandise Mart, Chicago; c. Maison & Objet September 2010 Show, Paris. *(a: © CORBIS; b: Courtesy of Fairchild Publications, Inc.; c: Provided by the Author)*

INFLUENCING FACTORS

As we saw in Chapters 11 and 12, many factors affect how a design style progresses and how it is applied through time and interpreted for different markets. Some of the catalysts for change over the years have included the collapse of empires; inventions, such as the printing press; trade restrictions and tariffs; advances in manufacturing; religious freedom or persecution; and immigration patterns.

Among the factors that influence trends of significance for interior design are the following:

- Technology
- Communication
- Transportation
- Economy
- Demographics
- Environment and resources

- Geography and region
- Politics
- Spirituality and religion
- Popular culture

Technology

Technology has been a catalyst for change in interior design throughout the centuries. Consider the ramifications of the advances noted in Chapters 11 and 12, such as the ability to carve wood by machine, the use of larger and more complex looms to construct textiles and carpets, the production of plate glass, the casting of iron, and the creation of synthetic dyes. Over the course of the 20th century, technological advances in lighting resulted in improved color rendering that is closer to natural daylight and greater efficiency.

From the late 20th century to the present, the dominant technological influences on modern life have involved computers, their hardware and software. There is no hint of this influence's diminishing any time soon. Computerization has had an impact on the practice of interior design in many ways. It is difficult to imagine plans for virtually any interior space without considering how and where computer equipment will be installed. Space planning and product specification are dependent largely on how an organization uses computer technology. Today, the advent of mobile Internet devices (MIDs), such as iPads, smartphones, and netbooks, is making desktop and laptop computers obsolete. Supported by wireless technology, these full-featured devices offer a host of customizable services available anytime, anywhere. Cloud computing, in which third-party, or host, services process and store the user's files, results in less hardware (and therefore less desk space). Again considering that for every trend there is a countertrend, we can expect a shift away from the automated multitasking of everyday life that reduces face-to-face human contact. Like the banning of smoking in public places, cell phone use might also be restricted in the future.[3]

Chapter 7 discussed the creation of visual presentations, from floor plans to virtual tours through space, via the use of technology. Product and textile designers now have the tools to create elaborate patterns, make customized changes, and revolutionize their designs with greater speed and complexity because of advances in computer software (Figure 13.5).

Figure 13.5
Karim Rashid and his digital designs. (© *Randy Krisp*)

Computers are also used to manage and control heating, ventilation, and air-conditioning (HVAC) systems, security systems, and audiovisual media in contract and residential spaces.

Ultimately, flexibility is key to the interior designer's success. One test is the responsiveness of a design to changes that are needed as technological systems advance.

Communication

The spread of ideas—written, graphic, and oral—influences how innovations are adapted in society. The invention of the printing press meant that the plans for Palladio's architecture and Chippendale's furniture could be communicated to, and therefore copied by, many others. Increasingly, the media play a role as purveyors of style and taste. The speed with which ideas are spread has affected the cycle of trends, reducing the time span considerably over recent years.

Instantaneously, a large portion of the world's population is able to see what others wear and how they live and can compare similarities and differences. The concept of trickle-down fashion, as from royalty to the masses, is approaching obsolescence. In fact, fashion is often directed upward, not the reverse, as expressions of "street fashion" influence high fashion, or haute couture.

Transportation

The speed and accessibility of travel influences the importation and exportation of products and services. Improved transportation has made it easy to use furnishings and materials from distant sources. As more people have the ability to travel, and transportation becomes less costly and more accessible, taste and consumption levels are expanded. Throughout history, ships, trains, planes, automobiles, and other, more primitive modes of transportation have played a role in interior design.

Conversely, because transportation is often energy dependent, goods coming from a distance may not be considered desirable. This, in turn, causes a countertrend. Although faraway goods are readily transported, this is done at significant cost to the environment. Thinking globally yet buying locally is a consideration for today's designer and consumer. Sustainable thinking can be seen in the motto "closer is better."

The extent of people's movements—that is, whether they are nomadic, transient, or permanent—dictates the architecture and furnishings of their homes. For example, lightweight, packable furnishings are more suitable than heavy, solid furniture when one moves constantly.

In other circumstances, such as employment relocation, divorce, and retirement, people may anticipate moving from one location to another fairly frequently. Portability in furniture design is more highly prized under these transient situations (Figure 13.6). Historically, an emphasis on the portability of furniture was seen in the use of campaign furniture by British colonists during the Victorian era and in the development of modern, modular furniture (see Chapter 11, *FYI . . . Non-Western Influences on Design: China*).

Economy

Fluctuations in the price of goods, levels of prosperity, and amount of disposable income have all played major roles in determining design styles. For exam-

Figure 13.6
This hospitality cart from Peter Pepper Products is an example of portable furniture. *(Courtesy of Peter Pepper Products, Inc.)*

ple, as was seen in Chapter 12, the lifting of the tax on glass a century ago reduced the price of large glass installations, making curtain wall construction possible. Later, American prosperity after World War II resulted in growth in housing, suburban expansion, and more disposable income, leading to conspicuous consumption. No longer was it important to have furniture pass down from generation to generation; instead, consumers purchased less expensive furniture, which they could replace more frequently with new pieces, and spent more money on other goods and/or services instead.

During the past three decades, boom-and-bust economic cycles have led to corresponding patterns of the consumption of goods. During the stock market boom of the early 1980s, one way in which interior designers responded to rising client income was in the design of window treatments and upholstered goods consisting of multiple layers of fabrics, valances, and trims. Years later the stock market bust and ensuing downfall of many technology companies resulted in sleeker (and less costly) looks more appropriate to the leaner times. Once people felt more confident, however, luxury items and grand scale flourished again, only to be met with a backlash—again—during the worldwide economic recession in the first years of the 21st century. Figure 13.7a and b show shifts in home décor over two decades.

Supply and demand, as well as production costs (influenced by labor and resource issues), tariffs, taxes, and boycotts affect style and consumption. If goods are rare, they are prized and therefore more expensive.

Demographics

The variables that divide broad populations into more homogenous segments include age, sex, education,

Figure 13.7
Window fashions. a. Multilayered look of the 1980s; b. Simple look of 2000. *(a: Courtesy of and designed by Jamie Gibbs; b: © Winfried Heinze/Recover.com. Designed by Annie Stevens)*

income level, race, ethnicity or nationality, and region. Many market segments have been targeted for study of their consumption patterns. Of particular interest have been differences among generations (Table 13.1).

Many members of the baby boom generation, people born between 1946 and 1964, have recently retired or will soon retire in unprecedented numbers. They represent the consumer who expects a long and quality lifestyle during active retirement years. They have disposable income, appreciate quality, and expect good customer service. In recent years, researchers have begun to distinguish between earlier and later baby boomers. A goal of many younger boomers is to achieve a balance between the pursuit of material goods and the deeper meaning of life. Both groups represent a viable market for today's interior designer.

Younger demographic groups, such as **Generations X** and **Y** (born between 1965 and 1994), have been thought of as closer in taste to their grandparents (the parents of the boomers) than to their own parents. These markets often look to purchase investment-quality homes and furnishings. The older Generation Ys and those born after the mid-1990s are often called **Millennials**. The impact of social networking and the continued development in personal and micro-multimedia devices have had a multipronged influence on consumer decisions. The way in which different age groups work and play obviously impacts the planning of spaces.

Medical advances during the past century have resulted in increased life expectancy, and the proportion of the population that is older than 65 continues to grow. The concept of aging in place (see Chapter 2) is a direct outcome of this trend. Design that is adaptable to multiple life stages is thus inevitable.

Another trend relating to demographics is gender neutrality. A market research study by Rosenthal & George, published in 1999, reported that 72 percent of furniture purchases involved men.[4] Men are comfortable shopping in gender-neutral retail environments, such as Pottery Barn and Crate and Barrel, as well as surfing the Internet.

Environment and Resources

The plentitude of a material also influences the style in which houses are built. For example, in Renaissance England the typical Tudor-style home was constructed

Table 13.1
Demographics of American Generations: World War II to the Present

*Market research groups attempt to define generations in order to target consumer patterns and project buying habits and trends. A generation translates into approximately 20 to 25 years. No generation is a homogenous group, so labels must be used with caution. However, the names given to groups based on certain common characteristics provide a shortcut to understanding important demographics and how they influence lifestyle.

Generation	Description
Can-dos (born 1901–1924)	Many were GIs who returned from World War II with a civic concern for others and an affinity for teamwork. They value family, appreciate familiar brands, tend to be conservative, and look for good customer service. This generation survived the Depression and witnessed the boom in science and technology that landed a man on the moon.
Silent generation (born 1925–1945)	Currently enjoying retirement, this generation is prosperous. Many have second homes. A fringe group included the "beat generation" of the 1950s. Many were less "silent" and more active in the civil rights and feminist movements of the 1960s and 1970s. They were among the first to benefit from advances in medicine and increased longevity.
Baby boomers (born 1946–1964)	Also called the "me generation," boomers were raised by stay-at-home mothers and television. They witnessed (or experienced) the heyday of sex, drugs, and rock and roll, and many are approaching retirement in record numbers or have already retired. Quality of life with aging is expected. This group emphasizes its youthful level of activity and seeks creative change. Subgroups include the more socially conscious and activist former hippies and yippies, many of whom work in nonprofit organizations or serve in an elected office and are noted for their philanthropy. People in this group tend to long for a life that balances meaning and purpose with financial success.
Generation X (born 1965–1981)	This multicultural, street-savvy group survived as children of divorce and has seen much violence. Feeling that the generation before them made a mess of things, they are returning to basics, creating new lifestyles. They often look for support from groups of friends, not family. This generation is accustomed to visual stimulation, quick images, and computerization. Both genders are more likely to be equal partners and to share in purchasing decision and child-rearing duties. A small, yet significant, portion of this group is the "dot-commer," a young professional in the technology field, particularly the Internet, who acquired wealth in a very short time and lost much of it equally fast in the stock market bust of the late 1990s. Many have reinvented themselves successfully in both the business and political arenas.
Generation Y (born 1981–1994)	Children of baby boomers, they are sometimes referred to as "echo boomers." They relate more to the traditional values of their grandparents than to those of their parents and tend to be civic-minded and globally connected. They are loyal to brands and established companies, appreciate quality, and begin purchasing collectibles at an early age.
Millennials (born 1995–present)	The older Generation Ys and those born after the mid-1990s are often called Millennials. The impact of social networking and continued development in personal and micro-multimedia devices have had a multipronged influence on consumer decisions. Those with significant disposable income (the new affluents) are redefining the term *luxury,* favoring less conspicuous consumption and focusing more on quality, value, uniqueness, and authenticity.

with oak framing because oak was readily available in that country, whereas dwellings amid the deserts and mesas of the Americas were made of adobe, a combination of clay and straw or dried earth. The native woods indigenous to the Americas and the British Empire inspired the Age of Walnut and the Age of Mahogany (see Chapter 11). The French Art Deco style used more exotic woods from Africa and Asia (see Chapter 12). When woods are rare, too costly for mass production, or considered endangered, ordinary or inferior woods are used and are then finished with techniques such as painting, stenciling, antiquing, and faux finishing, camouflaging their imperfections. Substitutions of synthetics, such as vinyl with a wood-grain surface design, may also become more prevalent. Recent concern for endangered resources, including tropical woods, has spurred a trend toward alternative treatments, such as veneering techniques (Figure 13.8a–d).

Use of other products, such as types of paint, has changed as concern for the environment has grown.

a

b

c

d

Figure 13.8
Different woods for different times: a. Carved oak chest. England, c. 1640–1670; b. Carved and veneered walnut and oak card table. England, 1700–1725; c. Oak cabinet veneered with kingwood and enriched with marquetry, shown at the Paris Exhibition, 1900; d. Recycled tropical hardwoods used today. *(All images: V & A Images/ Victoria & Albert Museum)*

For example, water-based paints, which are less toxic, have virtually replaced oil-based paints for furnishings and interiors.

Colors are created by both natural and synthetic means. Dyes and pigments from natural resources, indigenous or imported to a region, play a role in which colors are widely used, especially for textiles and carpets. Natural dyes are derived from plant, animal, and mineral sources. The popularity of the color blue in the United States is a direct result of the role played by the blue dye that comes from the indigo plant, imported from the West Indies. Its continuing influence can be seen in Americans' long-standing affinity for denim, a heavyweight indigo-dyed fabric popularized during the California gold rush by Levi Strauss & Co. The color blue and the use of denim and indigo-colored textiles (whether produced naturally or synthetically) remain popular.

Several African textiles originally produced for use in clothing have gained in popularity for furnishing interiors. They include a group of textiles composed of neutral colorations, largely black, white, and browns derived from indigenous natural resources. One group of textiles, commonly referred to as mud cloth, is composed of hand-spun cotton that is soaked in a solution made from pounded leaves. A brown dye made from fermented pond mud is then applied. Another African textile, known as **kuba**, after the Central African tribe that produces it, is made from raffia that is appliquéd or embroidered with abstract patterns and colored with local plant dyes, typically black, yellow, and red (Figure 13.9a and b).

Geography and Region

There are several ways in which geography and region influence design styles. Throughout history, architecture, interior, and furniture design styles of city inhabitants have generally differed from the styles evolving in rural areas, provinces, or colonies (see Chapters 11 and 12).

Regional differences also play a role in the media's coverage of trade shows and the highlighting of specific products in regional markets, including those in the United States, where preferences for modern, transitional, and traditional still differ by region.

Climate also obviously affects design. In warmer climates open-air structures serve as transitions

a

Figure 13.9
Traditional African textiles used today. a. Kuba, etc.; b. Textiles by Aboubakar Fofana, Mali weaver. *(a: Provided by the Author; b: Courtesy of Aboubakar Fofana, Mali Weaver; Photography by David Ross, www.amaridianusa.com)*

between exterior and interior. In many regions these spaces become the center of daily activities in order to take advantage of the natural air-conditioning provided by breezes. These structures may be porticos, loggias, courtyards, verandas, porches, or galleries, depending on the architectural style and the origin (Figure 13.10a). Today's emphasis on energy conservation has resulted in more buildings with skylights, glass-enclosed rooms, which provide light and warmth in cold climates, as well as outdoor activity areas in warmer areas.

Moreover, heavy fabrics and tapestries are useful bed furnishings in colder climates, such as that of northern Europe. Lighter versions are more appropriate for warmer climates, as seen in the use of mosquito netting on a four-poster bed from the West Indies, featured in Figure 13.10b.

Politics

A region's style of government, whether democratic, militaristic, or autocratic, will influence design. Undoubtedly, being at war or peace influences how people live. In addition, a society that prizes art and design only for an elite class is very different from one that makes art and design accessible to many. Freedom of expression was curtailed in Germany in the 1930s; this repression of ideas and views led to the exile of many Bauhaus designers to other countries. The influence of these designers on architecture and interior design in the United States was discussed in Chapter 12.

Attitudes toward other countries also change with war. For example, during the American Revolution the colonists turned from the British to the French for artistic inspiration. Changes in political stances and policies resulted in Japan's open-trade policy in the 19th century and America's ban on Japanese imports after World War II. The end of apartheid in South Africa helped free that country to show off its traditional and visionary design ideas to much of the world. These are just a few examples.

Spirituality and Religion

Inspiration for art and design is often derived from personal or cultural spirituality or religious belief. In many cultures these beliefs have been manifested through a reverence for the sacredness of nature. Ear-

Figure 13.10
Caribbean design. a. Veranda; b. The use of mosquito netting on a four-poster tester bed is an example of regional adaptation of style. (a: © Ken Hayden/Redcover.com; b: © Marcus Wilson-Smith/ Redcover.com)

lier chapters, in particular Chapter 12, have cited the strong connection to nature in Japanese art and design as well as the Japanese respect for form and simplicity. Asian sensibilities have been continuous threads of inspiration for artists and designers in the Western world (Figure 13.11). The same value system is seen among Native Americans, who often acknowledge the presence of spirits in everyday objects.

Figure 13.11

Asian design for modern taste: table designed by Chinese-American Robert Kuo in yumu wood and copper. *(Courtesy of McGuire Furniture Company)*

The dominant religion of a country or a people will influence the type of architecture in which rituals, worship, meditation, or prayer is performed, that is, *sacred design*. Such design may be found in the form of large-scale architecture in the temples of ancient Greece and Rome; in enormous, dome-ceiling mosques and spire-topped cathedrals; and in smaller-scale spaces, such as a village hut, garden, sanctuary, or special area or niche in a home (Figure 13.12).

Places of worship are furnished according to the rites, rituals, and symbols associated with their religious affiliation. Furnishings may include simple or elaborate pews, altars, tables, prayer books, commemorative candles, and statues (of deities, saints, and demons) as well as other religious artifacts, such as masks, stones, flowers and plants, fetishes, amulets, offering bows, and crosses. Colors carry religious meanings (see Chapter 3). For example, in the Catholic Church red may symbolize the blood of Christ and purple repentance.

Islamic design is characterized by the use of intricate geometric patterns rather than figural motifs. This is dictated by the tenets of the Muslim faith. The use of figures is more prevalent in other religions, such as

Figure 13.12

Santeria, which merges elements of Catholicism with beliefs of the Yoruba and Bantu people of Africa, involves the creation of altars to specific deities. *(© Robert van der Hilst/CORBIS)*

Judeo-Christian faiths. Figure 13.13a and b shows several examples of such differences in pattern and motif.

The practice of Feng Shui, which combines spirituality, art, and design, has gained popularity in the West. Today, many interior designers and architects complement their traditional training and education with courses of study in Feng Shui. Expanding beyond the residential interior design market, Feng Shui consultations also are being sought by companies for new commercial construction or renovations.

Perhaps due more to worldview and philosophy than to religion, more Americans appear to be seeking a purposeful way of living than in previous decades. They are reassessing what it means to be successful and how they can contribute to making the world a better place.[5] Do well by doing good, is a Millennial mantra.

Popular Culture

Popular culture denotes the ideas, attitudes, and practices shared among a majority of people in a culture or society. Gathering information about cultural phenomena may entail rigorous research or simply a perusal of the shelves at a local bookseller. Over time, shifts can be observed by changes in location and quantity of titles, indicating the interests of readers (and browsers). For example, one year Feng Shui titles took center stage at a book shop; the next year that topic was relegated to a smaller, more remote section of the store.

The tastes of royalty and celebrities often influence styles for both personal fashion and interior design. The kind of bed Empress Josephine slept in and the way Jackie Kennedy renovated the White House are just two examples.

Movies and television shows are an important influence on popular culture worldwide. The glamorous fashions and furnishings depicted in films of the 1930s were unreachable for most, yet desired by much of the Depression-era population in the United States. The series of Austin Powers movies, with their exaggerated, over-the-top expressions of the late 1960s and early 1970s, helped define the **retro market** 30 years later. The 21st-century television series *Mad Men* caters to that same retro market; set a few years earlier, however, the show's American fashions and lifestyle have a very different sensibility.

Putting all these factors together, we have a perspective of a way of life, or lifestyle. Lifestyle choices are of concern to designers of residential, commercial (or contract), and hospitality interiors. Knowledge of the way people work, play, and interact and the extent of leisure time they have available is vital for interior design planning. Understanding how these factors influence issues related to privacy, mixed usage, multi-

a

b

Figure 13.13

Pattern in different cultures. a. Geometric Islamic patterns: the Mausoleum of Akbar, Sikandra, India, 16th century; b. Figural and plant forms are featured in Guatemalan textiles. *(a: © Arthur Thévenart/CORBIS; b: Provided by the Author)* tasking, recreation, and socialization is essential to interior design solutions (see Chapter 2).

Changes in lifestyle have redirected the way in which buildings and interiors are shaped and configured. Issues of common areas, such as the great room or family den, for personal and public activities; sizes of rooms; arrangements for privacy; and behavioral settings are some examples of this relationship. Interior layouts must meet the need for comfortable social distances in behavioral settings (the focus of proxemics; see Chapter 2).

Knowing whether a client's lifestyle is casual or formal, or alternates between the two, assists the designer during the space and furniture planning process. This distinction applies to individuals as well as corporations and other organizations. In more casual residential environments there is generally a shift away from en suite, or matching, furniture groups, such as the dining room set, and toward a mix-and-match approach. In office situations movable workstations and furnishings allow for adaptation, enabling a space to be configured for either a formal conference or a more casual brainstorming session among colleagues (Figure 13.14).

Lifestyle is also linked to entertaining style. This plays a significant role in how the hospitality sector handles space allocation. Layouts may be geared to fixed seating arrangements or more flexible groupings that can adapt to changing entertaining and socializing combinations. Hotel room accommodations may provide for strictly private quarters or combine areas that allow for other activities, such as business meetings, conferencing, or extended stay, to include areas for food preparation and dining.

Figure 13.14
Computerization requires flexible design approaches. Collaborative work is fostered in an environment not confined by cubicles. *(Courtesy of Idea Couture Inc.)*

CURRENT MOVEMENTS INFLUENCING INTERIOR DESIGN

Among the broad movements that have a direct bearing on interior design today are an increased focus on design in the public interest, design as a business model, the **do-it-yourself (DIY)** consumer, and the correlation between fashion and interiors. These four overarching movements underpin trends (and countertrends) that translate into styles of interior design in the 21st century.

Design in the Public Interest

Influencing Factors: Environment and Resources, Geography and Region, Transportation The role played by today's interior designer increasingly is concerned with the health, safety, and welfare of people and resources (see Chapter 2). Interior designers may play a role in the design and choice of surveillance and security systems as part of the overall design scheme, addressing the need for physical security. Natural disasters, such as hurricanes, floods, tsunamis, and earthquakes, have serious effects on the built environment and lives, often resulting in displacement of people. War and political policies may also lead to devastation and displacement. Many individuals and organizations, including government, nonprofit groups, and businesses, have responded to these needs on domestic and global levels. Some are mentioned in Chapter 2. "Prevention is the best medicine" is an apt adage here and has proven to be less disruptive and costly over the long term. Building and furnishing housing, schools, businesses, and other public spaces that may withstand the gravity of any of these circumstances should involve the unique skills of the interior design community. Providing temporary shelter that is humane, readily available, and affordable is an area to which the interior design community has much to contribute.

Sustainability includes the sustenance and preservation of human life and traditions. **Fair trade practice** is a social and business model whereby goods are made by local artisans with traditional techniques, under safe and nonexploitative conditions, and balanced with profitability. This movement is often a response to the limitations of conventional trade to deliver sustainable livelihoods to people in poor or isolated regions of the world. *Fair trade* typically denotes the cycle of goods from developing countries to industrialized countries but may also relate to issues such as minimum wage standards, working conditions, and ownership of designs. These are concerns of great interest to producers and designers in the developed world. Fair trade in several industries, from coffee bean production to carpet weaving, is important to many consumers now.

The design styles resulting from this movement reveal a respect for heritage and the handmade. Words often used to describe these products and designs are *artisanal* and *authentic*. Designers embracing this approach have achieved personal and financial success not only for themselves, but also for others, while helping produce and market attractive products (Figure 13.15).

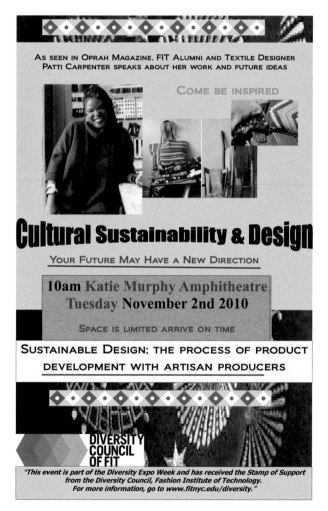

Figure 13.15
2010 Fashion Institute of Technology's Sustainability Conference, organized by the college's Diversity Council, included featured speaker Patti Carpenter, who discussed the cycle for goods. *(Poster created and photographed by Deborah Hernandez, rug designer and adjunct assistant professor, Textile and Surface Design, F.I.T., S.U.N.Y.)*

Affordability for both producer and consumer is intrinsically related to the concept of design in the public interest. If good design is universal design, it can only be accomplished for "the other 90 percent" when it is affordable. This may be achieved by making these goods and services available at low cost or pro bono. Perkins + Will's commitment to social needs in the built environment is detailed *In the Spotlight: Perkins+Will's Social Responsibility Initiative.*

Today, design in the public interest is characterized by smaller, more efficient spaces and products. Smaller, more flexible homes are growing in popularity. Today, traditional single-function rooms, such as formal dining rooms and living rooms, are being replaced by rooms that can serve multiple purposes for the household.

In Hong Kong, where apartments are small and expensive, architect Gary Chang designed a 344-square-foot apartment that can be configured into 24 different designs just by sliding panels and walls. He calls this the "Domestic Transformer" (Figure 13.16).

Design as a Business Model

Influencing Factors: Economy, Technology, Communication
Decision-makers in the artistic and creative design fields are looking at how the business world thinks. Concepts such as the bottom line, added value,

customer satisfaction, and ROI (return on investment) arc being explored by creative minds to see how these issues can help make their businesses more profitable. Conversely, the business world is looking at the creative process and how *that* can increase profitability. **Design thinking** is gaining traction in the business community as a problem-solving process. Although somewhat in its infancy, design thinking is defined as "a discipline that uses the designer's sensibility and methods to match people's needs with what is technologically feasible and what a viable business strategy can convert into customer value and market opportunity."[6] One way to think of this cross-pollination between the creative and business worlds is the combining of art and science.

With the field of interior design maturing, expanding more into health, safety, and welfare issues, increased knowledge and skills are critical. One way to attain and further develop these is through collaboration, in which people or organizations connected by a common goal come together to share ideas and skills (Figure 13.17). According to Susan S. Szenasy, the editor of *Metropolis* magazine, we can look to interior design students as natural collaborators, calling upon biologists, psychologists, artists, and engineers to help define the complex issues of sustainability.[7]

Figure 13.16
A small, high-rise apartment in densely populated Hong Kong was designed with flexible panels by architect Gary Chang. *(Photo: Marcel Lam for the* New York Times/Redux)

Figure 13.17
A collaborative approach to working is aided by the use of a round table, promoting egalitarian decision making. *(© Ocean/Corbis)*

The importance of the role of research becomes more evident in the quest to incorporate a more businesslike approach to the practice of interior design. Professional practice issues are explored in the next chapter. Traditionally, research has been conducted at the onset of a project (the programming phase) and at its conclusion (postoccupancy stage) (see Chapter 5). A growing trend is to deepen and expand the role of research throughout the design process. The trend has been most dramatic in the growth of evidence-based design) in the health-care environment. In evidence-based design, decisions about the built environment are based on credible research in an effort to create the most efficient outcomes, with improved care, lower costs, and added value. The role of evidence-based design, or informed design, is not limited to health care, however; in Chapter 5 we saw how corporate workplace studies found that well-designed spaces create opportunities for social interaction and thereby increase productivity (see Chapter 5, *In the Spotlight: Research Studies in Commercial Design: Workplace Design*).

The need for increased skills founded in a **body of knowledge (BOK)** has also resulted in a number of graduate programs with interior design at their core. In addition to providing an opportunity for specialization, such as health care, social justice, sustainable design, and design education, skills in research are honed through graduate education.

The DIY Consumer

Influencing Factors: Economy, Technology, Communication, Popular Culture Do-it-yourself home improvement, decorating and redecorating projects, and makeovers have been popular subjects of books, magazines, and television shows for decades (Figure 13.18a–c). A myriad of interior design blogs now exist—some (few) developed and managed by professionals in the design community, others not. This proliferation of information in recent years has exposed more people than ever to the concept of interior design. But it has also created unrealistic expectations that interior spaces can be quickly, cheaply, and easily designed by the layperson.

Another example of this trend, and a reaction to economic downturn, is the blurring of the lines between retail and trade. Many companies, such as Ralph Lauren Home and Baker Furniture, operate both trade showrooms and retail stores. Formerly, there was a rather rigid distinction between sources that were available to the trade, that is, those engaged in the business of architecture and design, and those available at retail, that is, to end users, clients, and cus-

a

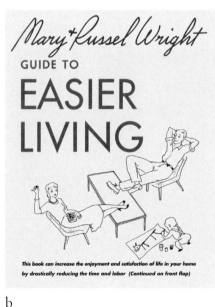
b

c

Figure 13.18
Publications for the DIY. a. *House & Garden;* b. Mary & Russel Wright's *Guide to Easier Living,* 1950; c. *Domino* magazine cover, "the guide to living with style," 2008. *(a: Woodruff/Condé Nast Archive; b: Mary & Russel Wright's* Guide to Easier Living, *1950; c: Courtesy of Domino/ Condé Nast Publications)*

tomers. Increasingly, providers of products and service are loosening their restrictions and allowing more direct access to end users. Major design centers are opening up to the public for special events or on weekends. Alternatively, these centers take an intermediary role, offering designer services, at varying levels, to on-site customers who come in on their own (Figure 13.19). Moreover, retailers offer visually appealing and user-friendly websites that DIYs can access (Figure 13.20a and b).

Figure 13.19

The Design Center at the Merchandise Mart, Chicago, provides opportunities for walk-in customers to be referred for on-site interior design services. *(Courtesy of MMPI)*

Figure 13.20

a and b. Dining room settings from Ethan Allen. The retailer promotes free design sales assistance for end users and a style quiz to help customers find the right products by "lifestyle." *(a and b: Courtesy of Ethan Allen)*

Large chain retailers, such as Crate and Barrel, Pottery Barn, and Target, feature attractively merchandised, well-designed, moderately priced products, many by respected designers, such as Michael Graves, Karim Rashid, and Philippe Starck, to market a more upscale image. Other retail stores feature living space vignettes, images of spaces that appear to be totally designed.

Inevitably, all these changes have significantly affected the interior design community. Rather than taking a stance of resistance or surrender, it makes better sense to work within this new paradigm, by working more collaboratively to find effective design solutions: "Good design helps people find the information they want while surprising them with fresh and unexpected thinking."[8]

Correlation of Fashion and Interiors

Influencing Factors: Popular Culture, Communication, Economy Throughout history there have been designers trained in one area who have worked in many media, somewhat like Leonardo da Vinci, centuries ago. Among them are Émile-Jacques Ruhlmann, Paul Poiret, Ray Eames, and Yves Behar. Crossing boundaries among fashion, architecture, interiors, graphic, and product design has proven successful for many. As retail and trade distinctions are blurring, so too are merchandise categories. One leader in this one-stop shopping approach is the retailer Anthropologie, owned by Urban Outfitters, with its youthful, eclectic array of apparel, accessories, furniture, and found objects (Figure 13.21).

Perhaps no other contemporary designer expresses the fusion of clothing and interiors better than Ralph Lauren (Figure 13.22). Decades after he established his apparel company, Ralph Lauren Home was created. The television talk show host Oprah Winfrey summed up Lauren's success as a stylemaker this way: "Ralph Lauren sells much more than fashion: He sells the life you'd like to lead." Lauren was not the first lifestyle guru, but perhaps along with Martha Stewart he is the most commercially successful. Years earlier, after World War II, product designer Russel Wright and wife Mary helped define the perfect middle-class American suburban, casual lifestyle, epitomized by the buffet dinner (Figure 13.23).

One of the threads that bind architecture and interiors to fashion and other design disciplines is a shared

Figure 13.21

Anthropologie, a division of Urban Outfitters, has successfully bridged fashion, home décor, and found objects in its youth-oriented retail stores. (*Stefanie Keenan/WWD*)

language regarding texture, color, form, ornament, proportion, and scale—the elements and principles of design (see Chapter 3). Additionally, technological advances, both digital and manufacturing, have brought the material worlds of fashion, architecture, and interiors even closer together. Ironically, preindustrial techniques, such as weaving, felting, and linking (e.g., knitting, basketry, and printing), have gained the attention of many modern designers (Figure 13.24). Finally, for both fashion and the built environment, materials help define status. For instance, both gold jewelry and gold-leaf ceilings signify luxury.

Consider the great exhibitions referred to in Chapters 11 and 12. They each sought to bring together the best and newest in all forms of art and design.

Figure 13.22
Ralph Lauren's flagship store on Madison Avenue, New York City. The historical Gilded Age mansion's exterior, interior, and Lauren's merchandising all evoke a luxurious yet tasteful lifestyle. *(Robert Mitra/WWD)*

Figure 13.23
Wright's guidelines for setting the buffet dinner, a new American way of entertaining, epitomized the casual and informal way of life after World War II in suburban America. *(Art Resource / Dinnerware by Russel Wright. Photo by Anita Calero. Copyright © Cooper-Hewitt National Design Museum)*

Figure 13.24
Knitting technique is executed here on a very large scale for these contemporary chairs. *(David Benque, davidbenque.com)*

Designers find inspiration from similar sources and are impacted by similar influences. For example, economic downturns or insecurity may lead to higher hemlines and more minimalist silhouettes, that is, less fabric, in both apparel and furnishings.

The production of furnishings for interiors by fashion designers began with home fashion, with Bill Blass's bed linens in the 1970s and Vera Wang's tableware for Waterford and Wedgwood and later mattresses for Serta. Roche Bobois partnered with Jean Paul Gaultier for the Mah Jong sofa series. Many fashion designers create textile and wall covering designs for use in interiors, among them Vivienne Westwood and Rodarte (Figure 13.25a–d).

Figure 13.25

Fashion design icons design interior furnishings. a. Vera Wang, known first for her high-end wedding dress designs, for the mattress company Serta. The "Comfortably Ever After" advertising campaign attempts to bridge the two career directions; b. Jean Paul Gaultier wearing his signature French sailor stripe mimicked in the seating designed for Roche Bobois; c. Vivienne Westwood, avant-garde British designer, teams up with the British company Cole & Son to create wallpapers based on her clothing designs; d. Relative newcomers, Rodarte, the Los Angeles–based Mulleavy sisters, teamed up with the new division from legendary Knoll named Knoll Luxe, to produce a line of textiles for interiors. *(b: © Roche Bobois; c: © Cole & Son Vivienne Westwood Collection; d: © Fairchild Archive)*

Interior spaces created by iconic fashion designers are perhaps most evident in the hospitality sector. Among these are Diane von Furstenberg, for Claridge Hotels, Betsey Johnson, at the Plaza Hotel, and Giorgio Armani (Figure 13.26a and b).

Generally, fashion has led the way for trends in interiors (Figure 13.27a and b). There are, however, some examples of the influence moving in the opposite direction. Coco Redfield found inspiration in the work of the architect Frank Gehry for the design of

Figure 13.26
Fashion designers and the world of hospitality. a. Diane von Furstenberg designed a series of suites for the landmark London hotel Claridge; b. In 2010 Giorgio Armani, already involved with the world of interiors through his Armani/Casa line of products, expands further into the built environment. His first hotel venture is the Armani Hotel in Dubai's Burj Khalifa, the world's tallest building.
(a: Courtesy of Claridge; b: Courtesy of the Armani Hotel Dubai)

Figure 13.27
Contemporary home furnishings are influenced by traditional African clothing for women. a. Chair Karmelina Martina's snail-shaped Helix chair for Moroso's *M'Afrique* collection; b. Senegalese traditional clothing inspires the Wolof carpet collection of Malene b.
(a: Photo: Alessandro Paderni for Helix Chair by Karmelina Martina for Moroso; b: Lionel Aurelien Photography)

Figure 13.28
Coco Redfield, an edgy, Manhattan-based fashion designer and stylist, is inspired by Frank Gehry's titanium architecture. *(Photo courtesy of Coco Redfield, www.millionsofroses.com)*

a metallic dress (Figure 13.28). Toile, associated with the French interiors of the 18th century, has become fashionable for apparel and accessories. The influence of William Morris and the Arts and Crafts style can be seen in Prada's resort collection (Figure 13.29a and b).

A more significant divergence from the norm has been in the sustainable movement, in which innovations in the built environment preceded the eco-fashion of today. The designer Alabama Chanin describes her approach to style as "slow design" incorporating more handwork such as stitching, and organic food production and consumption (Figure 13.30).

On a whimsical note, designs at the Sidewalk Catwalk, held in New York, held in the spring of 2010 (Figure 13.31a and b), portrayed the correlation, even symbiosis, between fashion and the built environment, by use of building materials to dress the mannequins. That same year the "It's So You" advertising campaign for Crate and Barrel played on the sameness of a person's style sensibility for his or her clothes and home.

Figure 13.29
Arts and Crafts style, *Then and Now*. a. William Morris's *Tulip and Net* cloth; b. Prada 2010 Resort Collection. *(a: Dearle, John Henry [1860–1932]. Tulip and Net. Jacquard woven wool. England, 1888–89. Photo credit: V & A Images, London / Art Resource, New York; b: © Fairchild Archive)*

Figure 13.30
Fashion designer Alabama
Chanin's lines for apparel and
home accessories incorporate
recycled materials and other
sustainable crafting techniques.
(Photo: Robert Rausch for the
New York Times/Redux)

Figure 13.31
Sidewalk Catwalk, New York City 2010, along Broadway featured a series of mannequins. Here are two paying homage to building
materials. a. Brick fireplace by Yeohlee Tang; b. Stone mannequin by Emily Saunders and Niyati Karwat. *(a and b: Sidewalk Catwalk is
a project of the Fashion Center Business Improvement District. Mannequin dressed by Yeohlee Teng [a] and Mannequin by Emily Saunders and
Niyati Karwat from Parsons New School of Design. Both photographs by Tajar P. Eisen for the Fashion Center)*

Perkins + Will's Social Responsibility Initiative

In 1935, Perkins + Will was established as an architectural design firm, and it now employs approximately 1,600 employees around the world.

"There is nothing quite like pro bono work." Although individuals throughout the firm had donated time and expertise individually, the official call for firm-supported, team-based philanthropy work materialized in 2007 during a working retreat in New Orleans of principals and associate principals. The Social Responsibility Initiative (SRI) was born of that effort, with the following mission: "Perkins+Will is committed to engage its professional resources and leadership to benefit the social needs in the built environment where design can make a difference. While encouraging volunteerism by our employees in our local communities, Perkins+Will will donate 1 percent of its time and unique intellect to initiate and execute projects and buildings that serve the broad society who otherwise would not have access to our professional services."

SRI efforts have produced the equivalent of a 15-person firm working full time on pro bono projects undertaken by 22 offices. One early initiative was for the Arlington Free Clinic (AFC), a nonprofit, volunteer-based health-care provider for uninsured adults in Arlington County, Virginia. An entire corridor of the clinic was dedicated as a portrait gallery of the 500-plus volunteers.

In May 2010 the SRI Annual Report was published, highlighting the numerous connections with nonprofit groups in Canada and the United States. The renovation of the Diabetes Health and Wellness Institute of Juanita Craft, in partnership with the City of Dallas, is featured in Figure a.

The organization's commitment to society through social responsibility was recognized with a Civic Innovation Award from the National Building Museum in Washington, D.C., in May 2010. The CEO, Phil Harrison, and firm-wide leaders gathered with 1,000 attendees, including the New Orleans Habitat Musicians Village Founder. "Social responsibility is not an option or an afterthought in our work, but a necessary investment in our world and integral to our daily practice."

Figure a
Diabetes Health and Wellness Institute of Juanita Craft, Dallas, Texas. (© CDS)

Source: Adapted from Jamie C. Huffcut, "Design for Health: Altruism in the Profession—the Implementation of Social Responsibility," Contract, *October 25, 2010, www.contractdesign.com/contract/Designing-for-Health-3421.shtml.*

Summary

A trend is a general direction or movement. A style is the manner in which a trend is expressed. A savvy interior designer benefits from trend forecasting. In addition to market research, designers are aided by studying history, paying attention to current events and world news, and people watching. Forecasting trends is based on an analysis of available, pertinent information. Some expressions may be fads, or fleeting fancies; others—the classics—withstand the test of time.

The great exhibitions of the past showcased many of the styles still in use today. New materials and applications continue to be featured at trade shows each year. Although the life cycle of trends has shortened over the years, a lead time of several years is still necessary before a trend is evidenced in mass marketing.

The factors that influence design and consumption patterns are numerous and interrelated. They include technology, communication, transportation, economy, demographics, environment and resources, geography and region, politics, spirituality and religion, and popular culture.

Overriding themes that pervade today's lifestyle are design in the public interest, design as a business model, the DIY consumer, and the correlation between fashion and interiors. All strongly impact interior design style.

Vocabulary

body of knowledge (BOK)	DIY (do-it-yourself) consumer	forecasting	Millennial
classic style	environment scanning report	Generation X	retro market
cocooning	fad	Generation Y	trend
design thinking	fair trade practice	kuba	

Exercise: Living/Working Environment of the Future

You are an interior designer hired to create an environment that will be used in the future as a studio for a forward-thinking young artist. In essence, you have been asked to plan for the design of a space five years out. The space is approximately 15 feet by 20 feet, with a ceiling height of 8 feet.

Using what you have learned about historical styles, the influences that have an impact on design, current trends, and lifestyle themes, prepare a preliminary presentation for this client. Choose from the various graphic techniques you have learned to convey your concept for the space. These techniques, either hand or computer drawn, may include sketches of the floor plan with furniture layout, perspective drawings or sketches, elevations, or models. Prepare a one-page summary of your plans for the space, including the design concept; key architectural features; fixtures, furnishings, and equipment; and color.

Exercise: Exploring the CD-ROM

Take advantage of the contents of the CD-ROM to increase your understanding of how a designer can help to solve problems and enhance a public space. Follow the instructions for Starting the CD-ROM on pages xix–xx and click on Chapter Thirteen: Forecasting and Trends.

Design in the Public Interest: Write an essay of approximately 250 words to describe a project you would like to propose in your local community (such as your college, a local hospital, day care center, bus stop shelter, or store that would be in the public's best interest). Explain how interior design can help to solve problems and enhance the public's experience in that space. Describe the space, its occupants, and use. Explain what you would like to see changed or improved and how you might accomplish this. For instance, you observe that at your school many people do not practice proper recycling as instructed on bins for paper, plastic, and so on. Another example to consider: Many materials used by students, often at faculty's instruction, are not eco-friendly. How would you propose raising awareness of these issues; who would you see becoming involved; and how?

CHAPTER 14

Professional Practice

As you take the first exploratory steps on your career path in interior design, a preview of the business aspects of the profession will prepare you for what lies ahead. Like some students, you may be apprehensive about dealing with issues that seem opposed to the artistic and creative possibilities that attracted you to this field. If so, keep in mind that business constraints, such as budgets, time frames, and building codes, may actually bring out your creativity and resourcefulness. Remember, too, that reality checks and problem solving are part of any design process.

This concluding chapter explains the world of work for the interior designer. It outlines some of the day-to-day business activities of the designer, working as an employee of an organization or as an entrepreneur. As first introduced at the start of this text, and reinforced throughout, the complexity and serious nature of the work of the interior designer continues to increase. With responsibility for health, safety, and welfare comes the demand for even higher standards and qualifications in terms of education, experience, and examination (i.e., higher credentials).

CAREER PATHS OF THE EMERGING DESIGNER

You face many choices about the direction of your career. Besides different styles of design, such as traditional or contemporary, eclectic or minimalist, there are the distinctions between residential and contract work, small and large projects, new construction and renovation. Perhaps one of the earliest and most significant decisions for the interior design student is the organizational context in which he or she will begin to work. There are basically two ways to start: either independently or by working for someone else. For each of these paths, there are pros and cons, assets and liabilities. Deciding how to get started as an interior designer is a complex process not to be taken lightly.

In earlier chapters you were introduced to some issues and facts concerning the business of interior design. Chapter 1 introduced the types of educational preparation and licensing and the professional organizations with which interior designers affiliate. Various industry sectors and related fields were outlined. Chapter 2 featured many examples of socially responsible design resulting from the efforts and input from various disciplines, including science and urban planning. Chapter 5 presented the various duties of interior designers and the phases involved in residential and contract projects. Several documents prepared throughout these phases were illustrated, among them examples of construction drawings and schedules. Chapter 6 demonstrated the ways in which interior designers use hand- and computer-generated visualizations to present design concepts and solutions. Chapter 13 featured trends in the way design firms are structured, such as collaborative and integrated design services. The changing dynamics in the relationship between the interior designer and client, partly based on shifts in economic trends, was also introduced in Chapter 13.

The objective of this final chapter is to provide a framework from which you can begin to establish personal and professional goals—a process that begins during school and that will continue throughout your career. Most students completing an interior design educational program get their start at an existing firm.

This chapter presents an introduction to the types of employment available to the beginning interior designer and the skills required. Also discussed is the impact of legislation on the profession. Practical considerations for most effectively obtaining employment are presented. With all that has been said so far, it is advisable for most emerging interior designers to consider seeking employment at an established firm. As one begins this professional journey, following the tracks outlined by the National Council for Interior Design Qualifications (NCIDQ) is a wise course. Seeking employment under the supervision of an NCIDQ certificate holder remains the most optimal career path.

Some students begin an interior design program as a career change. Many of these students have earned postsecondary degrees in subjects other than interior design and may have significant work experience. With proven skills in business, the mature student may wish to start his or her own company or do freelance work upon graduation. Various scenarios for

getting started in the workplace are introduced in this concluding chapter, including the nature of entrepreneurship (Figure 14.1). The traditional student entering an interior design program fresh from a secondary school will also benefit from learning how businesses work. He or she may chose to work independently at some point or be asked by an employer to assist with tasks relating to aspects of business, such as project management, purchasing, or meeting with vendors or clients. Various relationships among the designer, the client, and third parties, such as architects, consultants, suppliers, and general contractors, are introduced.

Deciding whether to go it alone or work for or with other designers is often a tough decision. Most people in all fields of employment would agree that owning a business is risky and would suggest learning from the experiences of others before taking on the responsibilities of starting and running one's own business. According to the U.S. Bureau of Labor Statistics, designers of all types are nearly four times as likely to be self-employed as people in other specialties. *FYI . . . Is Entrepreneurship for You?* includes key questions for you to consider for running your own business.

LEGISLATIVE IMPACT ON INTERIOR DESIGN

As introduced in Chapter 1, increasingly governmental law and policy influences the way in which interior design may be provided and by whom. Regulations exist governing all aspects of the profession, including conditions for starting a business, purchasing from

Figure 14.1

An independent practitioner at work, drafting. *(Image Source/GettyImages)*

FYI . . . Is Entrepreneurship for You?

Key Questions

1. Are you a self-starter and a go-getter? Do you have the drive and motivation to constantly market yourself, sell your skills and talents, and generate work?

2. How are your people skills? Will you be able to handle the working relationships involved with clients, staff, consultants, and contractors, among others? Do you have, or can you develop, a network of reliable resources?

3. How well do you plan and organize your time? Do you need to have someone else establish schedules and set deadlines? Are you capable of managing details, paperwork, inventory, and financials?

4. Do you have the physical and emotional stamina to run a business? Are you (and your family) prepared for the many long hours you will need to spend at work?

5. Are you able to withstand an unsteady flow of income (or lack of income) during lean times?

trade resources, and choosing how to define your occupation. Various statutes exist that regulate licensing, certification, registration, and title acts. Consumers ("the public") of services and products of all categories are protected by many governmental agency codes, at local, state, national, and international levels.

Professional, trade, and voluntary associations, such as LEED (Leadership in Energy and Environmental Design), establish criteria for membership. These organizations have rules of ethics and professional conduct. NCIDQ, on its Website, posts six different career tracks. Credits are awarded to applicants through various combinations of education, employment, and supervised work in order to qualify to take the association's exam. These regulations and standards change often.

According to the brief *Interior Design Legislation 101*, by the American Society of Interior Designers (ASID), 26 U.S. states and jurisdictions and eight Canadian provinces have laws recognizing interior designers. "Recognizing" is acknowledgment, in order to raise public awareness, that a person has met the criteria established for the minimum level of competency to practice the profession safely. It is the right of the states to determine those regulations, and they often disagree on what criteria be established and how.[1] Figure 14.2 is IIDA's view of interior design legislation in North America as of 2011.

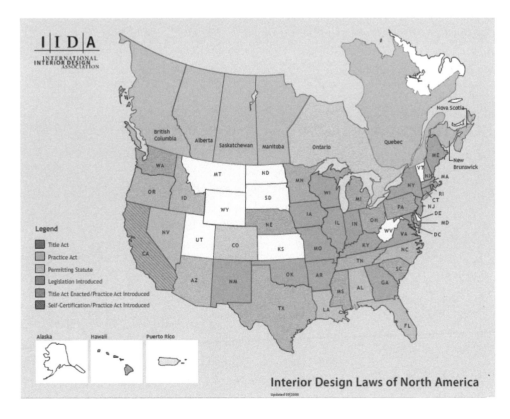

Interior Design Laws of North America

Figure 14.2

Map depicts a snapshot view of current legislative impact on North America. (© 2011 *International Interior Design Association, www. iida.org/content.cfm/advocacy*)

FYI . . . Types of Interior Design Legislation

Certified Interior Designer A person who has met certain education, experience, and examination requirements and is registered with the interior design board in his or her state. Usually this title is reserved for states with title acts.

Licensed Interior Designer A person who has met certain education, experience, and examination requirements and is registered with the interior design board in his or her state. Usually, this designation is reserved for states with practice acts.

Permitting Statute Colorado's interior design law is classified as a permitting statute. There is no state board and there is no title that is regulated. The law is an amendment to the architectural statute, adding an exemption that allows interior designers who have met the education, experience, and examination requirements to submit plans for a building permit.

Practice Act A type of law that requires an individual to have a license in order to practice a profession. Practice acts prohibit the performance of professional services by anyone not licensed by the state agency charged with the duty of regulating that profession.

Registered Interior Designer A person who has met certain education, experience, and examination requirements and is registered with the interior design board in his or her state. This title can be used with either a title act or a practice act.

Title Act Regulates the use of a title, such as "registered interior designer," and is enacted in order to raise public awareness of the qualifications of professional interior designers in a particular state. Title acts do not require individuals to become licensed in order to practice interior design, nor do they restrict an individual from providing the service of interior design. A person cannot, however, advertise or represent him- or herself as a "registered" interior designer unless he or she meets the minimum education, experience, and examination requirements established in that state and fully applies for use of the state-regulated title with the proper state board.

Source: "Legislative Terms for Interior Designers," ASID, www.asid.org.

INTERIOR DESIGN LEGISLATION

At the time of this writing, the NCIDQ exam is the universally accepted examination. Also administered through NCIDQ is a program called **Interior Design Experience Program (IDEP)**, which documents the work experience required by legislation, helpful to the entry-level designer. When a state implements a new law, it generally provides a window of opportunity for candidates to qualify to take the exam and what is referred to as a grandfather clause for practitioners who have met specific criteria prior to the passage of the new law. It should also be noted that there are many groups who oppose legislation to recognize interior design as a profession, for many different reasons (see *FYI . . . Types of Interior Design Legislation*).

PROFESSIONAL ETHICS

In addition to abiding by federal, state, provincial, and local laws, interior designers, like any business person, are expected to adhere to ethical standards. All the professional organizations mentioned in this text have a written list of standards of conduct for their members, which the organizations make available on their Websites. For example, the ASID *Code of Ethics and Professional Conduct* outlines responsibilities to four different groups: the client, other interior designers and colleagues, the profession, and the employer. In its preamble, it states: "Members of the American Society of Interior Designers are required to conduct their professional practice in a manner that will inspire the respect of clients, suppliers of goods and services to the profession and fellow professional designers, as well as the general public."[2]

TYPES OF EMPLOYMENT

According to the *U.S. Bureau of Labor Statistics Occupational Outlook Handbook*, about three out of ten interior designers are self-employed—four times the proportion for all professional and related occupations. About two out of ten wage and salary interior designers work in specialized design services. Another one out of ten worked in firms offering architectural and landscape architectural services. The remainder of interior designers provide design services in furniture and home furnishings stores, building material and supplies dealerships, and residential building construction companies. Many interior designers also perform freelance work in addition to holding a salaried job in design or in another occupation.[3]

Although just getting hired is often the primary goal of the beginning interior designer, finding a comfortable fit within a firm requires some research. Your role as a designer will vary not just in work performed, but in terms of growth potential, depending on the firm. Throughout your college days, stay ready to collect information from placement officers, guidance counselors, instructors, internship mentors, recent graduates, designers, and professional association members. Attend career fairs at your school or in your community. Use the resources of the library as well as the Internet to research companies—their mission, their leaders, and their projects. Request the latest annual report of companies whose work you admire and respect.

An **informational interview** is a more informal communication than one required of a job applicant. It is a way for you to call upon any of the above resources and request some time, either in person or on the phone (perhaps a half-hour), for you to learn more about that firm and about the interior design business in general. Plan ahead to maximize your contact's time by preparing concise and insightful questions and talking points.

Generally speaking, the larger the firm, the larger the scale of the projects and the greater the likelihood

that it competes for various types of jobs, such as hospitality and health care or possibly residential projects. Many of these big firms are both architectural and interior design firms, often headed by architects with a design division. Some firms expect their experienced designers to specialize, such as in health care; others expect generalists. Some firms are structured as studios, with each studio responsible for a complete project from start to finish; other firms are structured by department, with a project moving from one department to the next through the project stages. In that context you may be hired as a CAD operator and perform that function on various projects at one time. In a small firm, the structure is often more informal. The new employee may be afforded the chance to work in a variety of capacities. In a large firm you may find yourself with more repetitive tasks on a daily basis.

Although residential designers need to understand the personality and culture of an individual client, as an employee or prospective employee you should be aware of the corporate culture of any firm you consider working for. The atmosphere of some offices appears relaxed, whereas in others it may seem rather confined (Figure 14.3a and b). Based on trends of the 21st century (see Chapter 13), collaboration is a key office dynamic. Steelcase, a major office furniture company, finds solutions to collaboration with its Campfire and media:scape series (Figure 14.3c and d).

A range of jobs exist for the beginning interior designer or student looking for work. Some involve a specialty; others, more general duties. Among them are the following:

Intern
Many opportunities are provided for students through school-supervised work/education programs. These often mean that the student receives academic credit for successful completion of the internship; sometimes a small salary or stipend is included. Although many of the tasks you may be asked to perform may seem like "chores," there should also be a significant portion of meaningful work and learning taking place.

Junior Designer or Design Assistant
As interns, the employer may expect you to perform tasks you do not consider creative or

Figure 14.3
a. A small interior design firm; b. A large firm with cubicle arrangement for offices; c. Steelcase collaboration series known as the "Campfire Series"; d. Steelcase's videoconferencing collaboration through its media:scape series. *(a: © Jupiter Images; b: Nicolas Russell/ Getty/Images; c and d: Courtesy of Steelcase)*

truly "design." However, this work may indeed be meaningful. You may be given a variety of both administrative and design tasks, including sourcing for furnishings, space planning, drafting and drawing, and perhaps meeting with clients.

CAD Operator
Proficiency in the various programs for computer-aided drafting and design is a competitive advantage, yet so, too, is skill in other applications, such as social networking; word processing; publishing; and data management and analysis, including bookkeeping and inventory management.

One caveat is that often jobs that imply "computer specialist" may mean that other tasks will not be assigned to you. Therefore, opportunities to work with staff, clients, and vendors may be limited.

Renderer / Model Builder
Although many CAD programs include rendering and modeling, firms may want to hire someone with exceptional hand-rendering and model-making skills. In addition to architecture and design firms, real estate agencies and developers and manufacturers may employ interior design graduates to execute these designs. A similar title may include many visual presentation techniques (see Chapter 6).

Resource Librarian
Large firms, particularly those taking on contract projects, maintain a physical library of brochures, catalogs, and material samples (Figure 14.4). Responding to sustainability issues, more and more companies are now relying on Internet resources or CD or DVD catalogs and also flash drives to remain up-to-date on furniture, fixtures,

Figure 14.4
Resource library. *(Trinette Reed/Getty Images)*

and equipment (FF&E) rather than maintaining print materials. Either way, or in combination, this is an opportunity for a new designer to develop expertise regarding products, specifications, and regulations concerning product and services and to have contact with suppliers.

Showroom Assistant
Both trade and retail resources look to interior design students and graduates to assist with product or service sales. This type of employment may entail on-site visits to clients to measure and evaluate existing conditions. Working in a showroom offers the opportunity to understand better the relationships between client and designer and designer and supplier (see later discussion) as well as specifications, merchandising of product, and market trends. It is also a way to enhance interpersonal skills.

Sample Desk Receptionist
Most trade showrooms specializing in textiles or wall coverings, or both, maintain a library of samples, referred to as memos (see later discussion), to be loaned to designers. Many hire emerging designers or student interns to carry out the task of loaning out these samples. As a student, you may already be familiar with this job if you have visited a trade showroom for a school project and requested a sample of fabric for your presentation. The position provides many opportunities to meet experienced designers

(perhaps a prospective employer) as well as to gain product and trend knowledge.

MARKETING AND PROMOTION

Whether you are looking for an internship or part-time employment during your school years, applying for a job upon graduation, or seeking out clients to secure your services, you will be engaged in many of the same activities. In each of these endeavors, you will be marketing yourself; the big question is, *to whom?* You should be prepared to tailor your marketing approach based on your research of the companies you'd like to work for.

Marketing encompasses promoting and selling services and products to buyers. Obviously, if you are involved in a service industry, such as interior design, you will primarily be presenting your skills, talents, and personal attributes to potential buyers, be they clients or employers. Not only do you need to have something people want to buy, but you must be able to present that something to your potential customers as well. Communication, as we have seen, takes many forms—graphic, oral, and written. Matching the type of communication, including the choice of presentation materials, logo, website, and business cards, to your intended audience will depend on the results of market analysis, even if it is your own informal research. The term **branding** is often used to describe this comprehensive way of presenting a clear and consistent message of what you have to offer. Your brand speaks to the experience you, your services, and your products provide, what makes that experience relevant and unique. It also speaks to your style, not only of your work, but also of the way you work and how you wish you and your company to be perceived.

The way in which people hear about your product or service is through promotion. One method is paid advertising. Other methods of getting the word out may require more of an expenditure of time and effort than of actual dollars. Social networking is a major example of this. Many designers, including large-scale firms, believe strongly that producing blogs and having a strong presence on multiple social networking sites is a must for keeping visible and competitive in the current business climate. Professional affiliations, participation in related industry events, volunteering, and internships are some of the other ways you can promote your abilities. Yet another method is to use your school's resources, such as the college newsletter or alumni communications, to let people know of contributions you have made to academic, business, or civic activities.

Having your work published or displayed at school and industry events also promotes your talents and potential to prospective buyers. Responding to requests for entry in competitions offers another opportunity for people to see your work.

The basic tools used to promote one's self for employment with a firm are the résumé, cover letter, portfolio, interview, and referral. Many resources are available to assist you in writing your résumé, arranging and preparing for interviews, and presenting an effec-

tive portfolio. Referral, however, is considered to be the most effective method of promotion; interior designers often tell of business coming from repeat customers, their families, their friends, and collegial referrals.

Increasingly, it is expected that you have a website that is maintained on a consistent basis. Hiring someone to develop and maintain your site, including keeping images of project work current, may be necessary. There are also many user-friendly sites and software programs to help those who choose to develop their own site. The principles behind building and maintaining an effective site are closely aligned to the other promotional tools outlined here, especially the portfolio.

FYI... Tips for Preparing Your Résumé includes tips and reminders for effective résumés and cover letters.

FYI... Tips for Preparing Your Résumé

- *Include a targeted cover letter.* Do your homework by researching the company and the job for which you are applying. This is the appropriate place to summarize your career goal and express briefly how you might be an asset to this specific company (Figure a). This is also the place where you may show your graphic design skills, with the creation of a logo, a signature that identifies you on all correspondence. This logo may be used on thank-you notes following interviews as well as your job offer acceptance letter. Remember to keep it simple.

- *Choose the best format.* Functional or chronological (Figures b and c). For job hunters lacking related experience, a functional résumé may be preferable. This highlights broad categories of skill sets, such as communication skills, problem solving, design strengths, and interpersonal relationships. If your résumé is chronological, always start with the most recent experience and work backward.

- *Keep it short and simple.* Most résumés, especially for job applicants in early stages of their careers, should be limited to one page, two at the

most. Avoid overly designed or idiosyncratic layouts. This is a business document that may be reviewed by a non-design-oriented person, such as a human resources manager. It should be legible, with sufficient margins and spacing. Avoid elaborate or tiny fonts that cause eyestrain (and annoyance) for the reader.

- *Be descriptive.* Consider the value and impact of each word used. Avoid jargon that may not be understood if someone hasn't studied interior design. Rely on action words, such as *managed, coordinated, developed,* and *organized,* when describing duties you have performed. Include concise descriptions of your past projects, including studio projects, with facts, such as scope and budget, and accomplishments, such as problems you have solved.

- *Stay focused.* Avoid extraneous information about yourself that has no bearing on your strengths as a future employee. However, do not shortchange yourself on skills you have mastered through your education, those you have learned on your own, and the people skills you have used in volunteer or other related experiences.

JOSE LONDANO
4006 Highland Street
Sacramento, CA 95800
jose7@isp.com

April 30, 2012

Ms. Joni Klee
Human Resources Department
Brace & Norwich, Inc.
6073 Connecticut Avenue, Suite 502
Washington, DC 20000

Dear Ms. Klee:

The opening for a position as a junior designer advertised in the *Washington Post* appears to be an ideal
fit for my talents and interests. I am planning to move to the Washington area after my graduation next
month from California State University, Sacramento, where I am an interior design major. The comprehensive curriculum has provided a broad introduction to residential and contract design, and I am eager
to apply what I have learned.

In addition to classroom and studio instruction in subjects such as space planning, lighting,
color and materials, universal design, sustainable design, and survey of design, I gained valuable
experience through two summer internships. My internship at Chan & Logan Design in Alameda was
an especially beneficial opportunity to hone my drafting skills using a variety of CAD programs.

I pride myself on being a team player with a strong customer service attitude, and I would be pleased to
begin my career on your team, serving your clients. The variety of services provided by your firm has
special appeal for me as a way to explore the many facets of an interior design practice. I believe I can
provide strong support to Brace & Norwich's designers as I grow on the job.

I hope you will give my application further consideration, and I would welcome a personal interview.
You can reach me by phone at (916) 555-1234 or (916) 555-5678 or by e-mail at jose1@isp.com.
Within the next two weeks, I will be in touch with you. Meanwhile, I am enclosing my résumé.

Sincerely,

Jose Londano

Jose Londano

a

Figure a

a. Sample cover letter by an applicant for a first full-time job.

(continued)

JOSE LONDANO
4006 Highland Street
Sacramento, CA 95800
(916) 555-1234
(916) 555-5678 (cell)
jose1@isp.com

SUMMARY

Self-starting interior design college student seeking an entry-level designer position in a prestigious design firm. Eager to learn from others and contribute as a team member in residential or contract projects.

ASSETS

- Graphic Communication
  Redlining and drafting various CAD drawings
  Constructing presentation boards for contract projects
  Designing creative graphics solutions for business clients
  Arranging retailers' window and interior displays

- Interpersonal Skills
  Arranged for guest speakers and cochaired meetings for Student Interior Design Club
  Served meals as a volunteer in men's homeless shelter

- Leadership Skills
  Vice-president, Student Interior Design Club
  Student Representative, International Interior Design Association, California Chapter

- Special Skills
  AutoCAD, form.Z Revit; Adobe Photoshop, PageMaker, and Illustrator; InDesign 3D Studio VIZ and MAX
  Drafting construction documents and preparing presentation boards
  Fluent in Spanish

PROFESSIONAL EXPERIENCE

- Chan & Logan Design, Alameda, CA
  Summer intern, 2010
- Allan's Corporate Graphics, Sacramento, CA
  Summer intern, 2009
- Farrell's, Carmichael, CA
  Part-time employee in menswear boutique, September–May, 1995–1999

EDUCATION

California State University, Sacramento, CA, B.A., May 2011
Interior Design Major, GPA 3.6

b

Figure b

b. Functional résumé of a college senior seeking a first full-time job.

(continued)

JESSICA BENJAMIN, ASID

8823 Colesville Road, NW, Suite 11F
Washington, DC 20000-4823
(202) 555-0000 (phone and fax)
(202) 555-9999 (cell)
jbenjamin@isp.com

SUMMARY

With more than ten years of experience in interior design, seeking more specialization in the hospitality sector. Highly organized in business and project management with technical skills in AutoCAD, hand drafting and rendering, Excel and PowerPoint. An experienced supervisor of professional and support staff.

PROFESSIONAL EXPERIENCE

Senior Designer

Brace & Norwich, Washington, DC – a residential and contract interior design firm.
June 2010 – present

- Headed project team for renovation of Bramblett Inn dining room and kitchen in Bramblett Historical Park, Malden, VA. Responsible for space planning, lighting design, color schemes, and an FF&E selection to reproduce colonial atmosphere in 60-seat dining room with modern amenities.
- Supervise student intern program involving two local area colleges.

Interior Designer

K. A. Max Villages, Rockville, MD – builder of planned communities.
March 2005 – June 2010

- Designed and supervised installation of luxury model home at Falstaff Estates, Gaithersburg, MD
- Designed communal dining room at Conway Convalescent Home and Rehabilitation Center, Arlington, VA. Responsible for space planning, color schemes, and FF&E selection.

Office Manager

K. A. Max Villages, Rockville, MD
January 2004 – March 2005

- Developed standard office procedures for office headquarters.
- Generated and maintained all project documents, contracts, and client files.

PROFESSIONAL AFFILIATIONS

NCIDQ Certificate #2934
American Society of Interior Designers (ASID)
National Kitchen & Bathroom Association (NKBA)
Network of Executive Women in Hospitality (NEWH)

EDUCATION

School of Visual Arts, New York, NY, B.F.A. Interior Design 2004, magna cum laude
Northern Virginia Community College, Alexandria, VA, A.A.S. Accounting, 2000

c

Figure c

c. Chronological résumé of an experienced interior designer.

The development of a portfolio, which will be shown to prospective employers or clients, should begin at the onset of the interior design student's journey. The work completed for classes, in particular studio projects, may be suitable for inclusion. The format of a portfolio varies, as does the cost, and these factors need to be considered when creating your portfolio (Figure 14.5a and b).

First, it is important to decide on the purpose of the portfolio. The format you choose may differ, depending on whether you plan to use the portfolio to obtain your first job with a design firm or as a competitive edge in securing a prospective project. A portfolio can be a valuable tool for self-assessment, to identify your strengths and weaknesses. It may also be reviewed as part of an assessment for your entrance into an educational program, such as graduate school. The size of

the portfolio will depend, in part, on whether it will be transported for interviews with prospective clients and employers or mailed.

Portfolios may also be categorized as traditional or digital. A traditional portfolio is a collection of your work in printed format, such as drawings, sketchbooks, presentation boards, and materials boards. Although many prospective employers (even clients) may enjoy the tactile experience of these materials and appreciate the authenticity of original drawings, the traditional portfolio is often cumbersome (Figure 14.6a). A traditional portfolio may also include photographic images of three-dimensional work, such as models. A digital portfolio, also known as an electronic portfolio or a multimedia portfolio, can be a very efficient and dynamic communication tool (Figure 14.6b). It may combine a PowerPoint presentation and a web-

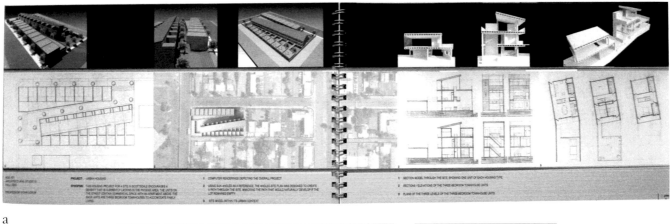

a

b

Figure 14.5

Portfolio types. a. Book format with digitally created images printed on paper; b. Easel portfolio allows work to be viewed in an upright position, either in portrait or landscape format, on a stand. *(a: Courtesy of Jeremy M. Gates; b. Courtesy of Lauren Maitha; LindsayMiller)*

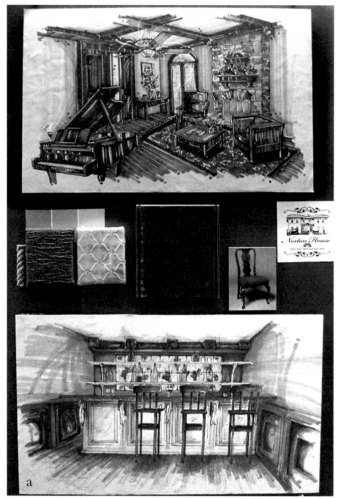

Figure 14.6

A project, especially showing materials, appears (and feels) very differently traditionally and digitally. a. This photo is of a large-scale presentation board with perspective renderings and samples of materials used, while b. is a digital composition of the intended material samples. *(Images from* Design Portfolios: Moving from Traditional to Digital, *1st Edition, by Diane Bender, Fairchild Books, © 2008)*

site, employing imagery, animation, text, and sound, or perhaps even a video. A note of caution: keep it simple, as often the relative ease of creating these multimedia productions can lead to a creation that detracts and distracts more than it informs.

As with any other tool, such as the résumé and interview, knowing something about your reviewer is helpful. Despite the ubiquitous nature of technology, there remain some generational differences concerning acceptance and understanding of digital presentations.

The cost of developing a portfolio varies significantly and includes not just expenses related to the actual presentation folder or media, but also the cost for reproduction of images, in black and white or color. Often the boards and models developed for school projects are too cumbersome to be included in their original state and need to be reproduced. (For a snapshot checklist for creating your portfolio, see *FYI . . . Tips for Creating a Portfolio.*)

OPERATING A DESIGN BUSINESS

Improved chances for success start with good planning and preparation. As the Spanish proverb advises, *saber es poder* (knowledge is power). A general rule of thumb is to secure the advice of an attorney and accountant before embarking on starting your own business of any kind.

There are many positives to being on your own. Among them is that you are your own boss (although clients may feel that they own you and, in many ways,

FYI . . . Tips for Creating a Portfolio

- *Retain copies of all your work as a student.* Include research, bubble diagrams, sketches, final drawings, working drawings, schedules, color studies, and samples boards.
- *Decide on the purpose of your portfolio.* You may need to develop more than one. For example, you may want to have one portfolio for a prospective employer that's a large architectural or interior design firm and a different portfolio for a small, independent employer. Or, you may wish to have a portfolio to use in garnering your own clients as a freelance designer.
- *Photograph all work as effectively as possible.* Even tight shots of details show your style and competence. You may choose to do this on your own or with the help of another student, someone with photography or styling experience. Hiring a professional photographer is costly but may be very worthwhile, especially to capture the best lighting effects (Figures a and b).
- *Decide on a consistent size, format, and organization to represent your work.* As much as possible, try to orient visuals in one direction, either vertically or horizontally. Keep borders and text consistent among images.
- *Review the design elements and principles* discussed in Chapter 3 and Chapter 6. They are all used to develop a well-composed portfolio.

- *Organize your work by either project or skill set,* such as hand drawing, including sketching and concept development, computer drawing, inspirations, etc.
- *Include a table of contents and introductory page* with your contact information, including a logo (if developed) and perhaps a statement of your design philosophy. Remember the concept of branding and the importance of putting your best foot forward.
- *Take advantage of services available at your school.* These may include photography, scanning, and other imaging tools; photo enhancing; duplication; and professional advice on portfolio development from instructors or the career counseling office.
- *Include only the projects you are proud of.* Is it self-explanatory, or might you need to expand on the graphics personally?
- *Put yourself in the place of the person who will review your work.* Enlist the assistance of someone you know, such as an instructor or a fellow student, to evaluate how well your portfolio material reads.
- *Consider your portfolio as a work in progress.* Keep the format flexible for revisions, additions, and substitutions.
- *Develop a digital portfolio or portfolios* to supplement, substitute, or use in combination with your traditional portfolio.

Figures a and b

Professionally photographed interiors enhance portfolios and websites, especially when lighting poses challenges or is critical to the design concept. a. Contract project. b. Residential project. *(a: Photography by www.robertlowellphotography.com; b: © TOMI Studio)* they do). Your talent and hard work can pay off to benefit you directly rather than someone else. The growth potential is virtually limitless, as are the opportunities for creativity and challenge. The U.S. Small Business Administration is a helpful source of information for start-up businesses (its start-up kit was used as reference for this chapter).

Business Structures

Businesses may be structured in several different ways. The most typical are sole proprietorship, partnership, and corporation.

Sole Proprietorship Perhaps the easiest and least costly way of starting a business is to form a **sole proprietorship**. The sole proprietor, as owner, has absolute authority over all business decisions as well as all the liability, meaning that although all profits may go to you, any monies owed, such as the result of a lawsuit, are yours as well. Personal assets, such as your home, are also your business assets.

As an interior designer, you may apply to the local government authorities to become a business entity, using either your own name or a **DBA (doing business as)**. So, if your name is Jane Doe, you may establish your business under that name or Doe Designs or any name you choose, once it is cleared with the local authorities, ensuring no one else is using it.

Partnership The most common types of partnerships are general and limited. A general partnership can be formed by an oral agreement between two or more persons. This collaboration may be especially suitable on a project-by-project basis with someone with whom you believe you can have a comfortable joint working relationship. It is recommended that a legal partnership agreement be drawn up by an attorney because partners are responsible for the other partners' business actions as well as their own. Profits may be split, but so, too, is liability. A limited partnership is a formal written contract prepared by a lawyer that clearly states the rights and responsibilities of each partner. A **joint venture** is a temporary association of two or more persons or firms for the purpose of completing a project. Again, a written agreement reviewed by or written by an attorney is recommended.

Corporation It is strongly recommended that legal counsel be involved in developing a corporate structure. There are several different varieties, but they are all made up of shareholders, directors, and officers. One of the main advantages of establishing a corporate identity is that personal assets are not at risk, because the corporation is a separate legal entity. However, on the downside, start-up costs and complexity of taxes are greater, as are the number of government regulations and the paperwork involved.

Examples of corporation types include the **subchapter S corporation** (also known as the **S Corporation**) and the **PC (professional corporation)**. The particulars about all types of corporations may vary from state to state; they relate to liability, profits, and losses.

Two hybrid business entities that combine features of corporations and partnerships are the **limited liability company (LLC)**, which has a sole proprietor, and the **limited liability partnership (LLP)**, in which there is more than one proprietor. The taxes are less complex than a corporation's, and the liability is limited to a member's investment.

Independent Contractor Another way in which a designer can operate is to become an **independent contractor**. Essentially, this means being self-employed and working on a freelance basis (rather than for one employer). The firms that hire independent contractors do not control the contractors' work. The benefits generally extended to employees, such as unemployment insurance, worker's compensation insurance, paid leave, pensions, and health insurance, do not apply to independent contractors. It is recommended that you consult Internal Revenue Service booklets and instructions as well as an accountant before you consider this category of self-employment.

Business Plan

No matter how you structure your business, a business plan is an essential tool for managing it. This formal document explains, in detail, your plans for developing a financially sound business. In addition to serving as an assessment tool, a business plan will be requested by any outside financial resources you may need to approach for start-up loans. It will also help track the progress of your business after it begins operation.

Table 14.1	
Highlights of a Business Plan	
Section	**Contents**
Introduction	Description of the business and its goals
	Legal structure and ownership
	Skills and experience you bring to the business
	Your advantages over the competition
Marketing	Products and services offered
	Customer demand for your services
	Target market
	Advertising and marketing plan
Financial management	Source and amount of start-up funds
	Method of compensation and accounting method
	Monthly operating budget for the first year
Operations	Day-to-day management practices
	Hiring and personnel procedures
	Insurance
	Lease or rent agreements for space and equipment
Executive summary	Highlights from each of the above sections

Figure 14.7
A designer and client meeting: Ideally, a written summary of issues and decisions should be prepared by the designer for his or her files. (© *Veer*)

Table 14.1 highlights the components of a basic business plan.

PROFESSIONAL RELATIONSHIPS

Whether you work independently or as part of a business structure, you will be engaged in a number of different kinds of working relationships. To a large degree, most of these relationships will be referred to in a letter of agreement or contract between the designer and the client.

The Designer and the Client

For every interior design project, big or small, there is someone referred to as the designer and another referred to as the client. These parties establish a working partnership, that is, a business relationship. If you have established yourself as an entrepreneur working independently, the designer will clearly be *you*. If you are working within the context of a firm established by someone else, it is most likely that a *principal* (owner or senior person) in the firm will be the designer representing the firm. In those cases you would most likely be expected to assist him or her (or the firm) in carrying out the agreed-upon responsibilities, but you would not officially be the designer.

Although specifics of the designer-client relationship are explained in a letter of agreement, there are often less clearly defined interpersonal dynamics. Particularly with residential work, the designer and client often spend much time together, enjoy each other's company, and may become friendly. However, this more personal side of the relationship should not impact the ground rules outlined by written agreement concerning the job at hand (Figure 14.7).

Third-Party Arrangements

In addition to the client and designer, other parties may be involved in the project, among them architects; engineers; general contractors; subcontracted labor; specifying agents; and consultants, such as art, media, or lighting specialists. The role of the interior designer often includes assisting the client in obtaining and overseeing the services provided by others, such as these third parties (Figure 14.8).

Most interior designers furnish their clients with the names of general contractors. The clients then interview these contractors, as well as others they may know of, and decide which one to use. Clients are advised to enter into separate agreements with third parties.

As lawyers experienced in this area emphasize, when designers also wear the hat of contractor they are exposing themselves to certain risks. If a designer were to actually employ a general contractor, or pay for contracted services directly, the designer would be liable for any of the contracted work. For example, if a worker were injured on the job, the designer would be held liable for any damages or costs incurred. There are also issues of insurance for property damage and guarantees

Figure 14.8
Third-party arrangements for a specific project are often appropriate between the designer and architect and the general contractor, pictured here on-site. As with significant meetings with clients, designers should prepare written summaries of the discussions. (*Jon Feingersh Photography Inc./Getty*)

for workmanship. Interior designers are encouraged, required in some jurisdictions, to maintain liability insurance, often referred to as malpractice or errors and omissions insurance, as well as other types of insurances. Contractors are required to have their own insurance to protect against claims of personal and property damage. Furthermore, certain localities may prohibit an interior designer from acting as a general contractor unless the designer holds a contractor's license.

Vendors and Suppliers

As an interior design student, you should collect information about suppliers, showrooms, manufacturers, products, and artisans for future reference. Collecting and cataloging this information can be accomplished in many ways. Networking with other people in the field, through professional affiliations and attendance at markets, trade shows, and forums and reviewing pertinent trade journals and magazines should be a part of your ongoing education. Visiting factories and workrooms is another way to learn about reliable companies you would feel confident working with. Social networking is yet another viable alternative for introducing you to potential qualified vendors and learning of their products and services.

Once you are established as an authorized business entity, you will want to formalize relationships with trade resources, generally showrooms. The requirements for establishing accounts are discussed later in this chapter.

LETTERS OF AGREEMENT AND CONTRACTS

The written statement of agreed-upon conditions between the designer and the client is either a **letter of agreement** or a **contract**. For all intents and purposes, these have the same implications, as they both serve to set forth a series of promises between parties. Regardless of the nature or scope of the project, the terms of an agreement should be in written form, not merely oral. It is for the protection of both the designer and the client that a written agreement is executed. This format can also be a useful way for both parties to communicate in a clear fashion throughout the process.

Professional organizations, such as the ASID and the American Institute of Architects (AIA), offer template versions of contracts and letters of agreement that may be purchased and, as boilerplates, they can be adapted to specific conditions. These forms offer the designer the benefit of having been reviewed by legal counsel and tested over time. However, many designers feel that the style of these forms is too cumbersome, legalistic in its jargon, and overwhelming or intimidating for residential clients. Hence, many prefer to create their own versions. In either case, it is highly recommended that the contract or letter of agreement be thorough, clear, and reviewed by an attorney familiar with the field. Any changes to an existing format should be routinely reviewed prior to execution.

The clearer the language and the more specific the clauses, the less risk there will be that terms of the agreement will be argued by either party. Certain elements are basic to these agreements, whether they apply to residential or contract projects. These common elements are outlined in *FYI . . . Basic Elements in a Letter of Agreement or Contract.*

There are subtleties to each of the elements in the list. Each project and situation brings different nuances to the terms. Beginning with item 1, scope of the project, it is not sufficient to begin the agreement by describing this only in terms of location. In addition to the specific site or address (including apartment, office, or suite number), it is important to state whether the services described will be performed for the entire space or only part of it.

Although it may seem apparent who the *designer* is, it is not always clear who the *client* is (and there may be more than one). In residential design, if there is more than one head of household it is advisable that each be considered the client. For contract projects the client may not be the occupant of the space, but rather the chief financial officer or another person with executive or fiduciary responsibility.

The description of services to be rendered by the designer and of the role the designer plays concerning the services of others should clearly state that the interior designer will assist or facilitate and visit the premises as needed but will not be held responsible for the means, methods, techniques, sequences, or procedures of construction. The designer is also not responsible for fabrication or procurement of goods; their construction, shipment, or delivery; or installation of construction or furnishings. The designer is also not

---

---

responsible for job-site safety or the acts or omissions of the contractors, subcontractors, or suppliers.[4]

Design firms differ in how strictly they apply the terminology discussed in Chapter 5 for the design services to be performed. The formal language is generally retained for contract projects but often altered for residential projects. Or, the scope of a project may deem different language more suitable. For instance, the phrases *contract documents* and *contract administration* may be replaced or eliminated in agreements for residential projects or even small contract projects.

The issue of purchasing goods is as complex as the issue of securing services from other parties. Often, it is the interior designer who writes a purchase order (see later discussion) for merchandise (i.e., goods) to be supplied by a vendor and delivered to the client. Minimally, three parties—the client, the designer, and a vendor—are involved. Add in the shippers (often two companies, from point of manufacture and from warehouse to customer), and the trail becomes convoluted. Technically, the interior designer is purchasing the goods and then reselling the merchandise to the client, in effect becoming a merchant.

To purchase on behalf of a client, an interior designer files an application with the tax authority branch of his or her state to collect sales tax. The document issued granting such permission is generally called a **certificate of authority**. It is often referred to as a **resale number** because it authorizes the holder (the designer) to do just that—resell goods to a buyer and collect the applicable taxes on behalf of the government. The designer must then pay the sales tax to the government on a regular basis. As you can imagine, when goods are defective it is not always clear who is responsible because of the number of parties involved. The safest route is to discuss this issue with an attorney who is experienced with the various commercial codes, in particular the **Uniform Commercial Code (UCC)**, which is a group of laws that govern commercial transactions between U.S. states and territories.

It makes sense for you, as the designer, to expedite the interior design project as efficiently as you can. However, there is little you can control absolutely in the entire process. A time schedule for a contract project may need to be agreed upon if the premises can be vacated only during certain times or if occupancy must be guaranteed. Otherwise, it is not advisable to state a project completion date in your contract. Nonetheless, it *is* wise to include a limit on the terms of the agreement. For example, suppose you have entered into an agreement for which you quote an hourly fee for your services. This rate is based on what the market will bear and what your skill level can command. Your firm will likely be situated competitively in the marketplace and command certain fees in certain times and certain locations. However, over time, the market may change, or your firm may relocate to an area with higher operating expenses. Finally, keep in mind that as you become more experienced, you can command higher fees. In any of these situations, you would not want to be left with an open-ended agreement regarding rate of compensation for a limitless, undefined period. Therefore, it makes sense to state the terms of limitation in your contract. You can always prepare an addendum with new terms to take effect after the original expiration date.

It is for the designer's protection that he or she retains rights to the design concept, solutions, and schematics. This is another gray area, subject to interpretation, essentially the purview of intellectual property law. At what point does a design solution go from being a specific designer's idea to an idea within the public domain? As with other aspects of a contract, the goal is risk reduction. It is better to have a clause concerning the rights of the designer than not to have one. However, you can easily give away the store, so to speak, and deem yourself secondary to the process, thereby allowing a client to take your ideas and run with them. It is here that the designer's people skills come into play. Essentially, your ability to convey the notion that you and your company are crucial to the execution of the design and plans can strongly determine how effectively this clause will play out.

FEE STRUCTURES

Interior design can be a lucrative career, but in addition to being labor-intensive, it is dependent on the economy. For many creative people, business strategy, money, and time management do not come easily. Appreciating the adage "Time is money" is part of this process (Figure 14.9).

There are many ways in which interior designers as individuals and as firms can charge clients for their services. All are considered ethical and may be profitable under certain circumstances. Whichever method(s) a

Figure 14.9
"Time is money" visualized. (© *Shutterstock*)

designer uses, the fee structure must be clearly stated in the letter of agreement or contract and understood by all parties. Some individuals and firms approach fee structures in only one way; others consider the pros and cons of each situation and charge accordingly. The most common fee structures (or a mix of these categories) are hourly fee; per diem, or daily, fee; flat, or fixed, design fee; square footage, or area, fee; cost-plus, or cost plus percentage; and retail basis. All but the last two structures may be considered fees based on professional services; the last two relate more to the payment of goods (furniture and equipment).

Hourly Fee

In both residential and contract design, charging an hourly fee is a widely used approach. The results of an online survey in late 2009 confirmed that for design firms, this is the most popular method of billing clients, at 66 percent.[5] Many interior designers favor the hourly fee because it is the way many other professionals, including lawyers and accountants, charge for their services. An **upset fee**, or *ceiling*, may be established in writing, specifying an amount not to be exceeded. Excellent records must be kept when charging on an hourly basis to ensure credibility with the client. Although there does not appear to be any norm for the hourly rate, the interior designer Mary Knackstedt, an expert in the field, offered a witty guideline during one of her many professional presentations at a trade showroom. Never charge more than the amount the local psychiatrist charges as his or her hourly fee-for-service!

One way to calculate the hourly rate is a formula known as the **DPE (direct personnel expense)**. As a rule of thumb, a protocol used by companies of all types over the years has been to estimate fees to clients that are based on a multiplier between 2.5 and 3.0. This approach factors in the costs involved not only for salary, but also for fringe benefits to staff, such as health, disability, and life insurance, and paid time off. These costs often amount to an additional 30 percent above the cost of the salary. In addition to the design staff, firms employ support personnel who are not assigned to any specific project, such as receptionists, secretaries, and bookkeepers.

Besides these personnel costs, there is **overhead**, the cost of doing business, which also needs to be factored into compensation. Overhead costs include leasing, renting, or buying space and equipment; insurance; utilities; maintenance; advertising; marketing, including website development and maintenance; computer software; professional dues; and office supplies. When these costs are **indirect**, meaning they cannot be assigned to any one project or client, they are not charged directly to a client. However, these costs need to be factored into the decision of how much to charge clients in order to keep the firm in the black and earning profits for each job. For example, if you wish the gross salary for an employee (including yourself) to be at a rate of $50 per hour, your firm is probably spending $125 to $150 per hour, two-and-a-half to three times $50, counting all direct and indirect expenses. If you are able to maintain your business with lower overhead, the multiplier could be less and still garner a profit.

If you are an employee of a firm, it is likely that your hourly salary is significantly less than the **billable rate** charged to the client. Using the previously mentioned ratio, if you are earning a salary of $30 per hour as a junior designer, your employer may be billing the client at a rate of $75 to $90 per hour. It should also be noted that not every minute of the design staff's time actually get billed to the client. Large-scale contract firms may have a tighter rein than smaller firms regarding billing the client for their designer's time.

Per Diem, or Daily, Rate

Charges for a day's work may be appropriate when an interior designer accompanies a client on a shopping trip, such as a day of antiquing. Sometimes these expeditions are made at the request of the client. Or, for the designer who has a particular specialty, this arrangement may be appropriate as a consultation fee. Although the per diem amount charged by interior designers varies, the daily rate is generally calculated on the basis of the equivalent of the designer's hourly rate, multiplied by seven hours, a typical workday.

Flat, or Fixed, Design Fee

A common practice, particularly for residential projects, is to charge a lump-sum fee for the services provided prior to purchasing, essentially covering the basic design concept. For example, a design fee might be charged for the initial presentation to the client. The tangible deliverables for the client (see Chapter 5) may include the programming phase conducted by the designer, the concept developed, and the preliminary design and schematics prepared, including floor plans, color and materials boards, and other drawings.

An interior designer may also charge a flat fee for more complete design services on a room-by-room basis, such as a lump sum of $10,000 to complete the renovation or design of a space (exclusive of the cost of products).

Square Footage, or Area, Fee

Charging on a square footage (or area) basis is more common for contract projects for which a firm has a substantial history of similar work and can predict fairly accurately how the project will proceed. This approach simply consists of a dollar amount charged for each square-foot area of the project. The fee for different types of projects and different locations varies significantly. The scope of services must be clearly defined.

Cost-Plus, or Cost Plus Percentage

A common way to charge for residential projects in which purchasing, especially furniture from trade resources, is an important part of the designer's role is **cost-plus**, or **cost plus percentage**. This approach essentially provides a way of being compensated based on the dollar amount spent by the client on these purchases. For contract jobs this sum may be a percentage of the total project cost. Although the cost-plus approach may be profitable, many in the field believe it is not suitable because it portrays the designer as a merchant or furniture salesperson rather than as a design professional.

The cost of the item is determined by the price that the supplier, or vendor, charges the interior designer. In many cases, goods that are sold through trade showrooms, such as furniture, are offered at a discount to the trade, that is, interior designers and architects. For example, a desk is priced by the trade showroom at a **list**, or **retail**, price of $2,000. A trade discount of 40 percent is offered. Therefore, the desk will be sold to the trade (the interior designer or architect) at **cost**, or the **net price**, of $1,200. Let us say that the designer decides that the markup, service fee, or commission (all variations of the same concept) is 30 percent above cost. The client would then be charged $1,560 for the desk, that is, the net cost price of $1,200 plus the 30 percent fee of $360.

Although there is no set standard for this markup, for most projects, designers charge a percentage, gen-erally between 25 and 35 percent. In this way, clients usually feel that they are still getting a fair deal using a designer, and designers feel that they are being appropriately compensated, not only for their time, but also for their expertise and for the service that goes into every purchase. (Many clients do not truly comprehend how much expertise and service *do* go into these purchases.)

For contract projects, which often involve multiples of specific purchases, it is often appropriate to lower the percentage above cost. Consider the earlier example of the desk that retails at $2,000 for a residential project. It may have cost the interior designer a total of 3 hours to plan, select, and handle paperwork related to this purchase. If the charge to the client were 30 percent of the net cost of $1,200, the compensation to the designer would be calculated as an equivalent of $120 an hour. If the same desk were to be specified and ordered by an interior designer for a contract project that required 10 such desks, and the same 3 hours of the designer's time were involved in planning, selecting, and completing paperwork, the 30 percent fee would reap $1,200 an hour. Of course, such multiple orders also entail different responsibilities for the contract designer, such as on-site oversight of installation. Nonetheless, when a designer is ordering multiples for a client it may still be profitable for the designer to work on a lower cost plus percentage, perhaps 10 percent for the example described.

Retail Basis

With this method, merchandise is sold to the client at list price. The client is not informed of the trade discount to the designer, which, in fact, may vary from one supplier to another. This arrangement may be a palatable fee structure for a client who considers it a good investment to rely on the designer's expertise and access to the most appropriate sources.

Retail stores that sell furniture and other home furnishings may retain interior designers on staff. As an incentive to shoppers, retailers may offer the services of their design employees to prospective buyers. The salary for the designers is built into the product costs. It is not always clear from the retailers' promotional materials what they actually mean when referring to the "design professionals" they have on staff. There is also a growing cadre of well-known interior designers who are now also product designers, at least to a certain degree. Some sell their designs through their own retail shops or through other stores (Figure 14.10a and b). Some have established retail stores from which they sell not only their products, but also other product lines they represent or simply carry, and combine retail with interior design consultation and workroom services. Others have licensing agreements with manufacturers for products whose design they have been involved with.

Similar to these retail situations are purchases by interior designers that are then stocked as inventory to

Figure 14.10
Interior designers who are also retailers. a. Bunny Williams' BeeLine is sold in various retail stores; b. Vicente Wolf's VW Home products line is sold in various retails stores and his own stores. *(a: BeeLine Home by Bunny Williams, photo by Edward Addeo; b: Vicente Wolf, Photographer: VW Home Showroom, New York City)*

be sold to clients, for example, antiques that a designer finds on a trip. Although the designer may not have a particular client in mind when he or she locates the items, they are thought to be a good buy to store for a future project. To handle such situations, a designer may include in the letter of agreement that inventory may be purchased by a client at **fair market price**, essentially what the product may be sold for elsewhere in the consumer market at that time.

Choice of a Fee Structure

So, how does one decide on which fee structure to use? The key to this decision is largely based on experience. Whether you are a one-person operation or work for a large organization, it is important to develop a knowledge base from which to estimate time and monies spent per project. Every project should be evaluated in this regard. It is critical to keep detailed records of information for each project. Whether this is a (daily) log kept by hand or via a software program, it is crucial to know not only how much money is spent, but also how much

time is invested. How many hours were involved, and by whom? In addition to face-to-face meetings (among staff and with vendors, consultants, and clients), what time was involved for phone calls, e-mailing, travel? How much time was spent, and by whom, on research, sourcing, drafting, preparing presentations, and conferring with architects or other third parties? A sample time log is illustrated in Figure 14.11.

It is a common and acceptable practice to charge clients using a combination of two or more approaches. One should be mindful of the client's perception of the compensation method(s) as well as the profitability margin expected by the firm. Particularly for residential clients, it is important not to make the terms of the letter of agreement—particularly the compensation clauses—too cumbersome. The following scenario illustrates a situation in which a designer might choose to use a mixed-fee structure.

Preliminary meetings between a designer and client have been held, but it is not clear how far the project will go. The designer decides to charge a

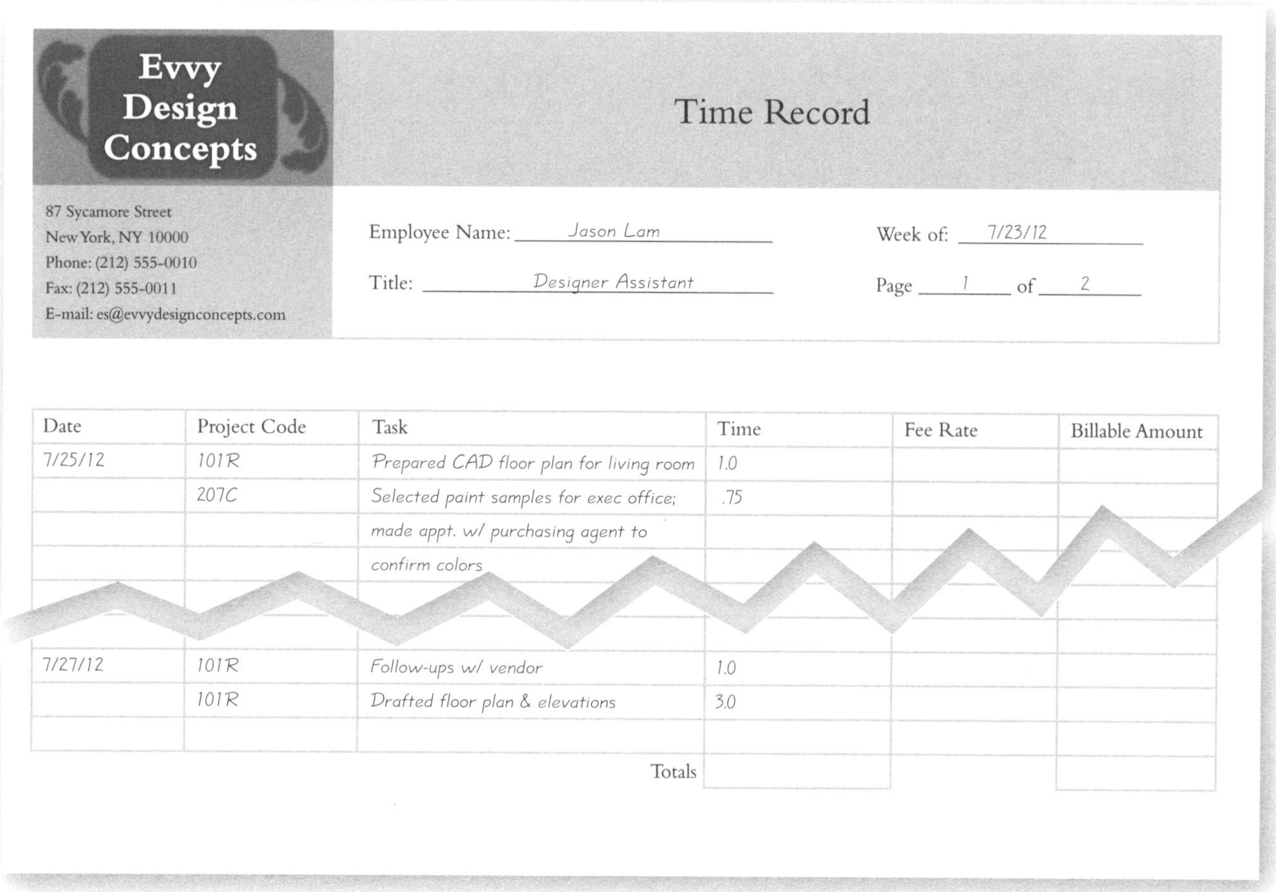

Date	Project Code	Task	Time	Fee Rate	Billable Amount
7/25/12	101R	Prepared CAD floor plan for living room	1.0		
	207C	Selected paint samples for exec office;	.75		
		made appt. w/ purchasing agent to			
		confirm colors			
7/27/12	101R	Follow-ups w/ vendor	1.0		
	101R	Drafted floor plan & elevations	3.0		
		Totals			

Evvy Design Concepts

Time Record

87 Sycamore Street
New York, NY 10000
Phone: (212) 555-0010
Fax: (212) 555-0011
E-mail: es@evvydesignconcepts.com

Employee Name: _____Jason Lam_____

Title: _____Designer Assistant_____

Week of: _____7/23/12_____

Page _____1_____ of _____2_____

Figure 14.11

Example of a time activity log.

consultation fee for the initial design concept but to include in the agreement a cost-plus arrangement for the purchasing and contract administration phases.

In this example, the designer will be paid for tangible services even if the client decides not to purchase with the designer's help or terminates the contract for any other reason. If the designer had chosen only a cost-plus basis, he or she might not have been compensated for what could turn out to be a significant amount of time and, possibly, expense.

How rosy (or pale) is the current financial state of interior design, and what is the outlook for the future? *FYI . . . The Financial Health of Interior Design and Job Outlook* provides a forecast.

FYI . . . The Financial Health of Interior Design and Job Outlook

As discussed in Chapter 13, trends evolve over time. And although no one has that perfectly clear crystal ball, we do look to the future as we make choices along the way. One major American organization that analyzes the present in order to forecast the future is the U.S. Bureau of Labor Statistics. Like the preferred time frame used by the U.S. Census Bureau, a decade is often used by this organization to demarcate trend directions.

According to the Bureau, employment of interior designers is expected to grow faster than average for all occupations, estimated at 19 percent by 2018—yet competition will be keen. Increased interest in interior design and awareness of its benefits will cause a growing demand for designers, as businesses realize the improvements that can be made to worker and customer satisfaction through good design. Businesses will look to use interior designers to redesign their offices and stores.

The services of interior designers are used by homeowners when they plan additions, remodel kitchens and bathrooms, create year-round outdoor living spaces, and home theater systems, and generally update the décor of their homes.

Demand from the health-care industry is expected to be high due to the need for facilities that will accommodate the aging population. Designers will be required to make these facilities as comfortable and homelike as possible. There will also be demand from the hospitality industry (hotels, resorts, and restaurants), for which good design work can help attract more business.

Some interior designers choose to specialize in one design element to create a niche in an increasingly competitive market. The desire for kitchen and bath design is growing in response to the surging interest in home remodeling. Designs using the latest technology in home theater, conference facilities, and security systems are expected to be especially popular. In addition, requests for home spas, indoor gardens, and outdoor living space should continue to increase.

Extensive knowledge of ergonomics and green design are expected to be valuable assets. Ergonomic design has gained in popularity with the growth of the elderly population and implementation of workplace safety requirements. The public's awareness of environmental quality and the increasing number of individuals with allergies and asthma are creating a need for designers with a knowledge of green practices.

The mean annual wage for an interior designer employed in a specialized interior design firm in 2008 was $51,202 and slightly more at $52,360 in an architectural and engineering service firm. Interior design salaries vary widely with specialty, type of employer, years of experience, and geographic region.

Sources: Adapted from the U.S. Bureau of Labor Statistics, U.S. Department of Labor, Occupation Outlook Handbook, *2010–2011 editions, www.bls.gov/oco/pdf/ocos293.pdf. Adapted from ASID Enviro Scanning Report 2010.*

BILLING PROCESS FOR DESIGN SERVICES

Billing is a significant part of the business process, no matter the fee structure. There is a schedule for payment of services provided, as well as a schedule for payment of goods to be purchased. The first of these payments to the designer, called the **retainer**, is a down payment for services to be rendered. Generally, before beginning the design process the designer will want to have a signed agreement in hand—as well as some funds with which to work. These funds are not designed to purchase products for the client, but rather to compensate the designer for his or her time.

Remember, *Time is money*.

Experience and judgment in estimation are critical. The beginning steps of a design project are often the most labor-intensive, especially when there is great enthusiasm for a new project. The question then becomes how much of a retainer is warranted? This fee should be high enough that the designer does not essentially work for free before billing the client for additional compensation, but not so high that the client is frightened away by the prospect. Determining the amount is easier said than done.

Standard business practice is to state in the contract, and to comply with the statement, that clients will be billed on a regular basis. Particularly when services are charged on an hourly basis, a practice of monthly billing is sound. It is not wise to allow charges to accumulate for a long period, thus risking a surprise factor for the client and cash flow problems for the designer. With other types of fee structures, such as a flat fee, a different type of schedule is in order. If a fee for a preliminary design concept or a specific consultation is provided in addition to the retainer, the client is generally expected to pay upon receipt of the presentation or consultation. When projects, especially contract projects, are structured for square footage fees or a flat fee for a space, installments of the total fee calculated are routine. For example, if the designer charges a fee of $10,000 for the completion of an office renovation (exclusive of the cost of furnishings), the retainer might be $3,000, with another $3,000 due at the conclusion of the schematic phase, a third $3,000 payment at occupancy, and a balance of $1,000 to be paid after the punch list is completed.

The designer may impose penalty fees for late payment, if included as part of the letter of agreement. This is generally a percentage comparable to other payment penalties, such as those issued by credit card companies.

Reimbursable, or **out-of-pocket, expenses** are another category of charges made to clients. These are incidental costs, such as for travel expenses, long-distance telephone calls, or blueprinting, related specifically to a project and therefore billed to the client, generally after the fact. Alternatively, the letter of agreement may state that because these costs are incurred, often at the request of the client, they will be billed at periodic intervals. Design firms differ in their handling of these expenses. Some firms charge them to the client; others plan for them as part of the overall cost of doing business. Out-of-pocket charges may be included as a separate category on the invoice listing fees or billed separately.

Figure 14.12 illustrates an example of an **invoice**, a bill for payment, sent to a client. The example shows a mixed-fee structure approach: a flat fee for design consultation, combined with a cost-plus-percentage fee.

RELATIONSHIP WITH SUPPLIERS

Interior designers develop a cadre of resources from which to secure goods and services. Today's designers often include in this cadre a mix of trade and retail sources. Students often have the opportunity to meet suppliers while in school, through either organized trips to design centers or guest speakers or career fairs on campus. Not only might you remember their product line after graduation, but also how you were treated. The converse is also true, so make sure you approach these sources as professionally as possible in your demeanor, dress, and courtesy.

Establishing an Account

The requirements for opening a genuine trade account—a showroom that does not sell retail, that is, directly to the consumer—vary. As seen by the example in Figure 14.13, some companies expect the designer to be affiliated with professional organizations. For others, this is unnecessary. The extent and nature of credit checks range from cursory to extensive.

Two common ways in which an account may be established are **pro forma** and **open (net 30)**.

Invoice

87 Sycamore Street
New York, NY 10000
Phone: (212) 555-0010
Fax: (212) 555-0011
E-mail: es@evvydesignconcepts.com

Bill To: Nathan Gatto
3706 Amsterdam Ave., Apt. 52
Aspen, NJ 20100

Date 7/31/12

Purchases at Net Cost

Qty	Vendor	Description	Cost	Total
1	Ranger furniture	Table and 10 side chairs w/ seat labor COM		$ 9,549.60
1	Carver	Altar table	$ 800.00	$ 800.00
10 yds	Westland fabric	Pickwick plaid fabrics for DR chairs	$ 60.50	$ 605.00
10 yds	Bravet	Laura Ashley fabric for wicker	$ 20.00	$ 200.00
1	Clifton	Coffee table sample sale	$ 300.00	$ 300.00
1	Potter Galleries	Arts and Crafts bench	$ 400.00	$ 400.00
1	Etoile	Chandelier	$ 1,500.00	$ 1,500.00
set	Norato	Dishes, handpainted, service for 12	$ 600.00	$ 600.00
1	Macon	Crystal lamp	$ 400.00	$ 400.00
			Subtotal	$ 14,354.60
		Sales tax	8.875%	$ 1,273.97
		Service fee	25%	$ 3,588.65
		Shipping and handling		$ 1,200.00
		Total		$ 20,417.22

Design Consultation Services

Hours	Hourly Rate	Description		Total
20	$ 100.00	Period covered: 7/1 – 7/31/12		$ 2,000.00
		Sourcing, purchasing, meeting w/ client		
			Subtotal	$ 2,000.00
			Total	$ 2,000.00

Make all checks payable to Evvy Design Concepts.
Thank you for your business.

Total Balance Due $ 2,000.00

Figure 14.12

Two-part invoice to a client: cost plus percentage and flat hourly fee for design consultation.

890 West 37th Street, New York, NY 10000
Tel: (212) 555-1800 Fax: (212) 555-1801
info@A&BCOHENFABRICS.com

Account Application Form

Contact Information

Name of firm _____   Telephone _____

Address _____   Fax _____

City/State/Zip _____   E-mail _____

Contact _____   Resale No.* _____

Attach copy of Resale Certificate

Business Classification

Interior Designer ☐

Contract Specifier ☐

Architect ☐

Workroom ☐

Professional Organization

ASID ☐

AIA ☐

IIDA ☐

IFDA ☐

Type of Business

Sole Proprietorship ☐

Partnership ☐

Corporation ☐

LLC ☐

Bank

Name _____   Account No. _____

Address _____   Telephone _____

_____   Contact _____

Type of Account Requested

Open - net 30 days ☐   Proforma ☐

Trade References

List companies with whom you have an account. Continue list on an attached sheet if needed.

Name _____   Account No. _____

Address _____   Telephone _____

_____   Contact _____

Name _____   Account No. _____

Address _____   Telephone _____

_____   Contact _____

Name _____   Account No. _____

Address _____   Telephone _____

_____   Contact _____

Applicant signature

I/We confirm that the information given herein is accurate and confirm that I/we agree to the Terms of Business and Conditions of Sale of A&B Cohen Fabrics.

Name _____   Title _____

Authorized signature _____   Date _____

WE RESERVE THE RIGHT TO REFUSE AND CLOSE ACCOUNTS

Credit approval - for internal use only

Account Number _____   Comments _____

Credit Limit _____   Account Type _____

Date _____   Approval _____

Figure 14.13

Application for a trade showroom account.

Pro Forma Pro forma is a kind of account for which payment in full is expected before processing the order for the goods. A designer's account is often first set up with a supplier in this manner until a good credit rating is established.

Open, or Net 30 Open, or **net 30**, refers to a type of account in which the supplier has confidence in the credit of the purchaser, in this case, the designer. This means that the order is accepted without advance payment for the goods. Most companies then send a bill to the designer, requesting payment within 30 days from the date the order is placed.

In recent years, there has been an increase in the number of retail chains that offer a small discount and other services to attract qualified interior designers to apply for a trade account with them. Williams-Sonoma Home, for example, through its Designer Marketplace program, increases the percentage off retail prices to qualified designers, depending on volume of sales (see Figure 14.14). Others offer a standard 10 percent off retail price for their trade customers.

Not all showrooms sell directly to designers, but a showroom may be a resource for designers to see and learn about the products. Particularly for contract trade resources, showrooms may then refer designers to **dealerships** for purchasing and installation services. These companies are authorized sales representatives for manufacturers. A dealership for office furniture may represent only one manufacturer for modular systems, and not that company's direct competitor, but may represent various manufacturers for lighting fixtures, audiovisual systems, and other noncompeting products.

Quotations, Estimates, and Samples

Trade resources follow several established practices that are helpful to the designer. Many trade resources offer the convenience of showing a wide array of products in a well-designed and comfortable showroom setting with trained sales staff (some of whom have interior design education and experience). Other resources have sales representatives or manufacturer's representatives who visit the interior designer's office, bringing catalogs and samples for the designer's resource library.

Although showrooms accommodate visits by the client, they prefer that designers accompany them. When that is not feasible, designers are encouraged to contact the showroom manager beforehand to dis-

Figure 14.14

Application for a trade account with a retail organization. *(Courtesy of Williams-Sonoma)*

cuss the client's unaccompanied visit. Because of the relationship between the trade showroom and the designer, including discount practices, the salespeople should not discuss pricing with the client. The goods are marked with the list price described earlier.

Discount policies vary by type of goods, by company policy, and often by volume. A common trade discount for furniture is 40 percent. However, for fabric and accessories it may be less. Some fabric suppliers use another type of discount, known as the **5/10 code** (Figure 14.15). Rather than taking a percentage off the price, they use a different calculation, as demonstrated by the following example:

A designer wishes to purchase fabric from a supplier who uses the 5/10 code as a discount to the trade. The fabric is tagged with the list price of 60.20. The designer deducts 5 from the first number and 10 from the second number, to yield a net price to the trade of $55.10 per yard.

The designer's request for price information for goods is handled by way of a form that is variously called a quote (quotation), an estimate, or a memorandum (Figure 14.16). Quite simply, this is an estimate of what the goods will cost, with the disclaimer that the price is subject to change. In addition, the pricing may be based on a generic specification, such as standard fill for an upholstered piece. It is wise at this stage to obtain an estimate of the delivery costs. If the client is expected to pay all delivery charges incurred, and the product is coming from a distance, such as overseas, this cost may be prohibitive. Sometimes, the client incurs the local delivery charge from the point of the warehouse to the client. Reliable vendors should be able to refer you to local delivery sources and may even obtain the estimate for you.

Additional aspects of estimating the costs of goods involve the concepts of **COM (customer's own material)** and **COL (customer's own leather)**, frequently during the purchasing phase of projects. Most upholstered goods specified by designers, in both contract and residential projects, rely on a furniture manufacturer or workroom *and* a fabric or leather source. Pricing is calculated without consideration of the fabric or leather cost, in other words, as a base price (Figure 14.17).

A **restocking charge** is a fee that is applied by the supplier to the buyer for the inconvenience of accepting overage goods, usually fabric or wall covering. It is often as high as 50 percent of the cost of the goods. Some designers state in their purchase orders that the client will bear this responsibility; others accept this as a part of their responsibility.

Acquiring estimates for goods and services is a process that provides the designer with the opportunity to prepare a preliminary, then more refined, budget for the client (see Chapter 5).

The designer also requests either a sample of the goods, such as a piece of the fabric or, if a sample is unavailable, a picture of the item, along with the price information (Figure 14.18). Fabric pieces are generally provided in one of two sizes. The first, called a **cutting**, or **swatch**, is a small piece that does not have to be returned to the showroom. A larger piece, called a **memo**, must be returned by the designer, generally within a specified time frame, for example, 30 days. When a large repeat (see Chapter 10) is featured on a textile, wall covering, or carpet, a memo is preferred over a cutting. Showrooms often will not provide memos on loan unless the designer has an active account with them.

A **cutting for approval (CFA)** is a crucial part of placing an order when the color or texture of goods is important, as is often the case for fabrics. When the designer selects a fabric at the showroom and is given a cutting or memo to show to the client, there is no guarantee that the piece will be representative of the fabric

890 West 37th Street, New York, NY 10000
Tel: (212) 555-1800 Fax: (212) 555-1801

Name of fabric:	Love in Bloom
Color:	Orchid
Style Number:	541110-06
Width:	54″
Repeat:	7″ vertical repeat, 10″ horizontal repeat 100% Polyester Dry Clean Only
Price:	$60.20

Figure 14.15
Sample 5/10 code on a fabric price tag.

Figure 14.16
Supplier quotation.

Quotation

893 West 37th Street
Suite 1634
New York, NY 10022
Tel (212) 555-0700
Fax (212) 555-0707
j@jlights.com

Name/Address
Evvy Design Concepts
87 Sycamore Street
New York, NY 10000

Date	Quotation No.
02/17/12	QU8626

List or Net	Telephone	Project	Fax
Net	212-555-0010	Foster Office	212-555-0011

Item #	Description/Finish	Quantity	Unit Price	Total
74230S	Dorian pendant (Steel) 30" Dia.
Platinum
or Silver Leaf

Note: Dorian pendant also available in translucent body
pricing available upon request | | 1,398.00 | 1,398.00 |
| 72631A
098
NSF | Channell Pendant, 31" Dia.
White Haze/Silver Leaf Patina to Detail
White on White alabaster/Silver leaf
antique to detail | 1
1 | 2,330.00
2,634.00 | 2,330.00
2,634.00 |
| 58134R
NSF | Wright Table Lamp, 34" H.
Silver leaf or Platinum finish | 1 | 710.00 | 710.00 |
| S393N | Lamp Shades: 8 × 24 × 14
White Linen/Nickel Spider | 1 | 142.00 | 142.00 |
| | Pack & shipping are additional charges

Lead time approx 10 wks from date of deposit | | | |

Thank you for your interest in June Lights. We look forward to working with you.

Figure 14.17
Supplier tag for COM.

Alice McGarry, Inc.
1440 Hudson Street • New York, NY 10000

Style name:	Charleston Club Series
Available as shown:	Fabric: Club cotton
Standard leg finish:	Ash, cherry, or mahogany stain
Net Price:	$2,500
COM:	$2,400–7 yds. For 54" fabric, no repeat
Upcharge:	5% for premium leg finish

FABRIC MEMO AND CUTTING ORDER

Designer / Specifier	Sue Evvy		Date 2/28/12

Firm Name	Evvy Design Concepts

Address	87 Sycamore Street

City	New York	State	N Y	Zip	10000

Account # 0805-3266   [X] Samples Taken   [ ] To Be Mailed

Memos	Cuttings
Love in Bloom	Circle String
541110-06	674-23
	Unicorn Faux Leather
	648-25

Figure 14.18
Supplier pad for use in requesting memos and cuttings.

to be shipped. The swatch may have been altered in the showroom over time by environmental conditions, such as fading, dirt, or abrasion. Furthermore, the dye lot of the bolt of goods from which the order is placed may have changed.

For these reasons, the purchase order should specify that the order is contingent on approval of the CFA. In this way, an actual sample of the fabric from the specific bolt of goods being ordered is requested and approved before the order is placed. The supplier then sends a cutting from the bolt of goods to the interior designer. For custom-colored fabrics, the interior designer may request a CFA **strike off**; that is, a sample of the specific way in which the colors for a textile will be customized for a particular order.

For other products, it is helpful to request a picture, which may be a **tear sheet**, or **catalog cut**, formerly a reprint of a page taken from the vendor's catalog or brochure but more likely now a screen print from the company or manufacturer's website. Alternatively, the vendor may take photographs of floor items or provide the designer with a complete binder showing these items.

A key question posed by the designer when selecting products for a client's review and approval is,

"What is the **lead time**?" This asks about the amount of time estimated between placing the order and receiving the goods. For custom-upholstered goods, this time frame begins upon receipt of the fabric ordered by the workroom. It is not uncommon for the response to be 12 to 16 weeks, even for domestically manufactured goods. This information will be critical for project scheduling and may affect the decision to purchase. In recent years in order to stay competitive, many companies have reduced their lead time in order to satisfy client demand.

Placing Orders

Placing orders on behalf of clients is a major responsibility. The previously mentioned forms merely begin what will be a long paper trail to the point of merchandise acceptance. Many firms employ either design assistants or administrative support personnel to stay on top of the paperwork. There are also software programs designed to provide this service as well as other data management, personnel, and inventory control functions.

A **purchase order** is, in effect, yet another contract among parties. It is executed at a minimum between the designer as the buyer of goods or services and the supplier as seller of goods or services. It should also serve as an agreement between the designer and the client and, therefore, should be signed by the client as acceptance of the terms. Because the rules concerning the parties are complex, the letter of agreement should stipulate limitations on the designer's liability to the client concerning purchases. In some cases, design firms that purchase on behalf of clients will enter into separate agreements for this purpose. Others add clauses for terms and conditions that relate to the Uniform Commercial Code (UCC), mentioned previously. As with the letter of agreement, an attorney should review the designer's purchase order form before it is executed.

The rule of thumb for a purchase order is specificity. Although the style and format may vary, certain elements need to be included. Remember, too, that for custom-upholstered goods, there may actually be two purchase orders: one for the fabric and one for the manufacturing of the piece. Examples of purchase order forms that contain these basic elements, including cross-referencing, are shown in Figure 14.19a and b.

Purchase Order

87 Sycamore Street
New York, NY 10000
Phone: (212) 555-0010
Fax: (212) 555-0011
E-mail: es@evvydesignconcepts.com

Vendor:	Amy Butler	Bill To:	Ms. Sue Evvy	Ship To:	Alice McGarry, Inc
	A&B Cohen Fabrics		Evvy Design Concepts		Workroom
	890 West 37th St.		87 Sycamore St.		1440 Hudson Street
	New York, NY 10000		New York, NY 10000		New York, NY 10000
	212-555-1800		(212) 555-0010		(212) 555-6789

Payment Method

Check		Amount Enclosed		P.O. Number	R0403–D01–1
Credit Card	x	VISA/MC/AMEX	Visa	Substitutions Allowed	NO
		Card No.	0000-8141-7777-0000	Backorder Allowed	NO
On File		Account No.		Ship via	UPS Ground
COD				FOB Destination	High Point, NC
Est. Delivery Time / Lead Time		3–5 days		Date Ordered	05/02/12
Resale		Resale No.	NYS 066-66-0000ES		

Purchases

Qty	Vendor	Description	Cost	Total
28 yds	A&B Cohen Fabrics	Name: Circle String	$ 46.00 per yd	$ 1,288.00
		Color: 674023 Antique Brass		
		Width: 54"		
		Repeat: 1 1/10" V x 3/4" H		
10 yds	A&B Cohen Fabrics	Name: Unicorn faux leather	$ 51.00 per yd	$ 510.00
		Color: 648–25 Pecan		
		Width: 54"		

Subtotal		$1,798.00
Tax Rate	8.875%	$159.57
Shipping Charges		$ 175.00
Handling Charges		--
Insurance		--
Total		$2,132.57

sofa

chair

Special Instructions

Fabric with pattern to be used for the "English Standard" sofa

Fabric in solid color to be used for the "Fanfair" chair

Cross Reference P.O. # $0403–D01–5

Approved by:

Client: *Nathan Giatto*

Designer: *Eve Evvy*

a

Figure 14.19

Purchase orders for custom-upholstered goods showing cross-referencing. a. For fabric showroom; b. For workroom.

Evvy Design Concepts

Purchase Order

87 Sycamore Street
New York, NY 10000
Phone: (212) 555-0010
Fax: (212) 555-0011
E-mail: es@evvydesignconcepts.com

Vendor: Alice McGarry, Inc.	Bill To: Ms. Sue Evvy	Ship To: Mr. Nathan Gatto
1440 Hudson Street	Evvy Design Concepts	3706 Amsterdam Avenue
New York, NY 10000	87 Sycamore St.	Apt 52
212-630-5000	New York, NY 10000	Aspen, NJ 20100
	(212) 555-0010	

Payment Method

Check		Amount Enclosed		P.O. Number	R0403–D01–5
Credit Card	x	VISA/MC/AMEX	Visa	Substitutions Allowed	NO
		Card No.	0000-8141-7777-0000	Backorder Allowed	NO
On File		Account No.		Ship via	Freight Truck
COD				FOB Destination	High Point, NC
Est. Delivery Time / Lead Time		8–10 weeks		Date Ordered	04/25/12
Resale		Resale No.	NYS 066-66-000DES		

Purchases

Purchases

Qty	Vendor	Description	Cost	Total
1	Alice McGarry Inc.	English Standard sofa	$ 4,150.00	$ 4,150.00
1	Alice McGarry Inc.	Fanfair chair	$ 2,700.00	$ 2,700.00
		Dark walnut legs		

	Subtotal	$ 6,850.00
Tax Rate	8.875%	$607.94
	Shipping Charges	$ 400.00
	Handling Charges	--
	Insurance	--
	Total	$7,857.94

sofa   chair

Special Instructions

For English Standard sofa, see cutting. 28 yards required.

COM A & B Cohen, Circle Shadow, 674023 Antique Brass, 54" W

For Fanfair chair, see cutting. 10 yards required.

COM A & B Cohen, Neither Hide Nor Hair, 648–25 Pecan, 54" W

Cross Reference P.O. # R0403–D01–1

Approved by:

Client: *Nathan Giatto*

Designer: *Eve Evvy*

b

Summary

A career in the interior design profession is unique, exciting, and challenging. In addition to the skills acquired through education and experience, many personality traits come into play. Although its focus is creative, interior design is a business endeavor. Administrative, organizational, managerial, and financial expertise play significant roles in the successful execution of any design project, large or small, simple or complex, residential or contract.

It is generally advisable for the traditional graduate of an interior design program to begin working for an established firm. There are many different types of employment for the emerging professional in both residential and contract firms.

On the other hand, nontraditional students, generally more mature, with previous work experience, may choose to work independently as an entrepreneur or as principal in a partnership or corporation.

Whether an interior designer seeks to be hired by a firm or attempts to acquire projects independently, thoughtful research and planning are in order. It is important to survey what one has to offer as a participant in a service industry, and to whom it should be offered. Many tools are available to help the beginning designer get started with marketing and promotional activities. Four key tools are the résumé, either functional or chronological, cover letter, portfolio, and website. The concept of a consistent brand about you, your firm, and your product and services is increasingly important in promoting yourself as an interior designer.

Each type of business structure has both pros and cons. With any business start-up, legal and accounting consultation should be obtained.

The interior designer, whether working alone or as part of a team, builds working relationships with clients, vendors, suppliers, and other third parties, such as architects, engineers, consultants, and general contractors. Letters of agreement and contracts are formal documents that spell out the terms for these relationships as well as other conditions for the work provided by the designer to the client.

Compensation for design services can be structured in several different ways, depending on the nature of the project and the inclination of the design firm. Typical fee structures include hourly or daily rates, flat fees, square footage fees, cost-plus percentage, and retail basis, or various combinations of these methods.

The contract administration, or purchasing, phase of a project can be lucrative. It does, however, involve a lengthy and complex paper trail requiring diligence, follow-up, and overall attention to detail.

Vocabulary

billable rate	independent contractor	PC (professional corporation)
branding	indirect cost	permitting statute
certificate of authority	informational interview	practice act
certified interior designer	Interior Design Experience	pro forma account
COL (customer's own leather	Program (IDEP)	purchase order
COM (customer's own material)	invoice	registered interior designer
contract	joint venture	reimbursable (out-of-pocket) expense
cost (net price)	lead time	resale number
cost-plus (cost plus percentage)	letter of agreement	restocking charge
cutting for approval (CFA)	licensed interior designer	sole proprietorship
cutting (swatch)	limited liability corporation (LLC)	strike off
DBA (doing business as)	limited liability partnership (LLP)	subchapter S (S Corporation)
dealership	list (retail) price	tear sheet (catalog cut)
DPE (direct personnel expense)	memo	title act
fair market price	open (net 30) account	Uniform Commercial Code (UCC)
5/10 code	overhead	upset fee

Exercise: Self-Promotion: The "30-Second Elevator Pitch"

Consider that you are about to launch your interior design career. You have been given the opportunity to promote yourself to either a potential employer or a client. You will have 30 seconds to get your message across and make that first impression. Consider what you would say about your passion for design, creative and design talent, people skills, and professional goals. Prepare your statement in writing, and present it to someone else for feedback.

Exercise: Exploring the CD-ROM

Take advantage of the contents of the CD-ROM to increase your understanding of how to develop yourself as a "brand." Follow the instructions for Starting the CD-ROM on pages xix–xx and click on Chapter Fourteen: Professional Practice.

Beginning to Brand: Whether you are planning to acquire an internship, summer employment, or full-time employment position upon graduation, developing yourself as a brand begins during your student years. Start now by drafting a sample cover letter and résumé directed toward one of the above career goals. In addition to the actual content, consider how you want these documents to look. Think about the various typefaces and fonts, color, weight, and texture of the paper, letterhead, and a logo. It is also helpful for interior design students to have business cards designed and printed. Instead of a company name, use your own name, student status, and student membership affiliation as appropriate.

Professional Organizations, Research Resources, Interior Design Blogs, and Government Agencies

Professional Organizations

(Note: All URLs were accurate as of publication.)

American Academy of Healthcare Interior
   Designers (AAHID)
   http://www.aahid.org/
American Society of Interior Designers (ASID)
   http://www.asid.org/
Association of Registered Interior Designers of
   Ontario (ARIDO)
   http://www.arido.ca/
British Institute of Interior Design
   http://www.biid.org.uk/
China National Interior Decoration Association
   (CIDA)
   http://218.247.4.32/english/Associations/38.htm
Council for Interior Design Association (CIDA)
   http://www.accredit-id.org
The Design Association (UK)
   http://www.design-association.org
Interior Design Society
   http://www.interiordesignsociety.org/
Interior Designers of Canada (IDC)
   http://www.idcanada.org/
International Federation of Interior Architects/
   Designers (IFI)
   http://www.ifiworld.org/#Homepage
International Furnishings and Design Association
   (IFDA)
   http://www.ifda.com/

International Interior Design Association (IIDA)
   http://www.iida.org/

Affiliated Professional Organizations

Acoustical Society of America (ASA)
   http://acousticalsociety.org/
American Design/Digital Drafting Association
   (ADDA)
   http://www.adda.org/
American Institute of Architects (AIA)
   http://www.aia.org/
American Institute of Graphic Arts (AIGA)
   http://www.aiga.org/
American Society of Furniture Designers (ASFD)
   http://www.asfd.com/
American Society of Landscape Architects
   (ASLA)
   http://www.asla.org/
Energy Design Resources
   http://www.energydesignresources.com/
GreenerBuildings
   http://www.greenbiz.com/buildings
Illuminating Engineering Society of North
   America
   http://www.iesna.org/
Industrial Designers Society of America (IDSA)
   http://www.idsa.org/
Institute of Store Planners (ISP)
   http://www.ispo.org/

Interior Redesign Industry Specialists (IRIS)
http://www.irisorganization.org/

International Association of Home Staging
Professionals (IAHSP)
http://www.iahsp.com/

International Association of Lighting Designers
(IALD)
http://www.iald.org/

International Council of Societies of Industrial
Design (ICSID)
http://www.icsid.org/

International Facilities Management Association
(IFMA)
http://www.ifma.org/

National Association of the Remodeling Industry
(NARI)
http://www.nari.org/

National Kitchen & Bath Association (NKBA)
http://www.nkba.org/

New Buildings Institute
http://www.newbuildings.org/

Organization for Black Designers (OBD)
http://www.core77.com/OBD/welcome.html

Retail Design Institute
http://www.retaildesigninstitute.org/about.php

Society for Environmental Graphic Design
(SEGD)
http://www.segd.org/

Affiliated Academic Professional Organizations and Research Resources

AARP
http://www.aarp.org

Abledata
http://www.abledata.com

Adaptive Environments
http://www.adaptiveenvironments.org

Alliance to Save Energy
http://www.ase.org

Allsteel Knowledge Center
http://www.allsteeloffice.com/AllsteelOffice
/Knowledge+Center/

American Lung Association
http://www.lungusa.org

Association of University Interior Designers
(AUID)
http://www.auid.org/

Carnegie Mellon Green Design Institute
http://www.ce.cmu.edu/GreenDesign/

Carpet and Rug Institute Publications
http://www.carpet-rug.org/index.cfm

Center for Inclusive Design and Environmental
Access
http://www.ap.buffalo.edu/idea/Home/index
.asp

Center for the Built Environment
http://www.cbe.berkeley.edu/

Center for Universal Design
http://www.ncsu.edu/project/design-projects
/udi/

Council for Interior Design Accreditation
(CIDA) (Formerly FIDER)
http://www.accredit-id.org/

Design Exchange
http://www.dx.org/

Environmental Design Research Association
http://www.edra.org/

GREENGUARD Environmental Institute
http://www.greenguard.org/en/index.aspx

Haworth Knowledge
http://www.haworth.com/en-us/Pages/Home
.aspx

Herman Miller Research
http://www.hermanmiller.com/

IIDA's Knowledge Center
http://knowledgecenter.iida.org/Index.aspx

InformeDesign
http://www.informedesign.org/

Interior Design Educators Council (IDEC)
http://www.idec.org/

Intypes (Interior Archetypes)
http://intypes.cornell.edu/

Knoll Research
http://www.knoll.com/research/index.jsp

National Association of Schools of Art and
Design (NASAD)
http://nasad.arts-accredit.org/index.jsp

National Council for Interior Design
Qualifications (NCIDQ)
http://www.ncidq.org/

National Trust for Historic Preservation
http://www.nationaltrust.org

Research Design Connections
http://www.researchdesignconnections.com/

Rugmark Foundation
http://www.goodweave.org

Steelcase 360 Research
http://www.steelcase.com/en/Pages/Home
page.aspx

The Center for Health Design
http://www.healthdesign.org/
The Center for Real Life Kitchen Design
http://www.ahrm.vt.edu/center_for_real_life
_kitchen_design/index.html
The Centre for Sustainable Design
http://www.cfsd.org.uk/
Universal Design Learning Lab
http://www.hdfs.hs.iastate.edu/centers/udll/

Interior Design Blogs

Art That Fits
http://blog.artthatfits.com/
Benjamin Moore–Living in Color
http://www.livingincolorwithsonu.typepad
.com/
CATALYST–Strategic Design Review
http://catalystsdr.wordpress.com/
COLOURlovers
http://www.colourlovers.com/
Contract Magazine–Talk Contract
http://www.talkcontract.com/
CoolBoom
http://coolboom.net/
Design Thinking
http://designthinking.ideo.com/
Design Spotter
http://www.designspotter.com/
Designing Better Libraries
http://dbl.lishost.org/blog/
Dialog
http://dialog.paulettepascarella.com/
Dwell Studio
http://www.dwellstudio.com/blog
Health Care Design Magazine–Blogs
http://www.healthcaredesignmagazine.com
/blogs
IDesign Arch
http://www.idesignarch.com/
Interior Design Magazine–Design Green
http://www.interiordesign.net/blog/Design
_Green/index.php
Kravet–Inspired Talk
http://kravet.typepad.com/inspiredtalk/
Make Studio
http://makestudio.blogspot.com/
Restaurants by Design
http://www.restaurantsxdesign.blogspot.com/

The Design Hub
http://thedesignhub.wordpress.com/
The Design Observer Group–Design Observer
http://designobserver.com/
The Design Traveller
http://designtraveller.blogspot.com/

Government Agencies and Standards

American Society for Testing and Materials
(ASTM)
http://www.astm.org/ABOUT/overview.html
Americans with Disabilities Act (ADA)
http://www.ada.gov/
Federal Trade Commission (FTC)
http://www.ftc.gov/
Internal Revenue Service (IRS)
http://www.irs.gov/
International Code Council
http://www.iccsafe.org/Pages/default.aspx
International Organization for Standardization
(ISO)
http://www.iso.org/iso/home.html
Leadership in Energy and Environmental Design
http://www.usgbc.org/DisplayPage
.aspx?CategoryID=19
National Fire Protection Association
http://www.nfpa.org/index.asp?cookie_test=1
U.S. Bureau of Census
http://www.census.gov/
U.S. Copyright Office
http://www.copyright.gov/
U.S. Department of Commerce
http://www.commerce.gov/
U.S. Department of Health and Human Services
http://www.hhs.gov/ocr/privacy/
U.S. Department of Housing and Urban
Development
http://portal.hud.gov/portal/page/portal/HUD
U.S. Department of Labor
http://www.dol.gov/
U.S. Department of State
http://www.state.gov/
U.S. Environmental Protection Agency (EPA)
http://www.epa.gov/
U.S. General Services Administration
http://www.gsa.gov/portal/category/100000
U.S. Green Building Council (USGBC)
http://www.usgbc.org/
U. S. Small Business Administration (SBA)
http://www.sba.gov/

Names to Know
Interior Designers, Architects, and Furniture Designers

Aalto, Alvar (1898–1976) Finnish architect and furniture designer.

Aarnio, Eero (1932–) A Finnish architect and designer noted for his molded fiberglass furniture.

Adam, James (1732–1794) and Robert (1728–1792) Scottish architects practicing in England; these brothers were known for taking on the role that general contractors assume in modern times.

Ashbee, Charles Robert (1863–1942) An English craftsman-designer and disciple of William Morris and the Arts and Crafts movement. He was a "medievalist" and in 1888 founded the Guild and School of Handcraft.

Audran, Claude, III (1658–1734) A French painter, decorator, and designer, who created wall murals and tapestries.

Baldwin William (Billy) (1903–1984) An American interior designer and decorator. He was known for his dark glossy walls and pattern mixing.

Baughman, Milo (1925–2003) A furniture designer who combined fine craftsmanship and mass production, often using steel and chrome with wood, and producing interesting textures and colors.

Belter, John Henry (1804–1863) German–born American furniture manufacturer; patented a laminating process used to make furniture that was carved into Rococo Revival style.

Bérain, Jean (1637–1711) French designer and decorator working in the Regence style. He designed furniture, tapestries, wood, and metal accessories.

Bernini, Gian Lorenzo (1598–1680) Italian architect and sculptor; designed portions of the Vatican.

Bing, Siegfried (1838–1905) German entrepreneur whose shop, Maison de l'Art Nouveau, sold furnishings that gave the style its name.

Boulle, André Charles (1642–1732) French craftsman who perfected a marquetry technique then named boullework after him.

Breuer, Marcel (1902–1981) Hungarian–born architect and designer, Bauhaus instructor; after the close of the Bauhaus in 1933, practiced in the United States and Europe.

Briseaux, Charles Étienne (1680–1754) A French Rococo architect and interior designer. In his boiserie panels he preferred straight sides with a moderate amount of curvature.

Brunellschi, Fillippo (1377–1446) The first great architect of the Italian Renaissance. Famous for his use of a series of arches supported by columns.

Chippendale, Thomas (1718–1779) British cabinetmaker and author of *The Gentleman and Cabinet–Maker's Director* (1754); his name is associated with a dominant 18th-century furniture style.

Churriguera, Jose (1665–1725) A Spanish architect who introduced the Baroque style into Spanish architecture.

Clodagh (active in New York since 1983) Irish-born interior designer and author of *Total Design*.

Cochin, Charles Nicholas (1714–1790) A French designer and engraver who opposed the Rococo style and worked in the classic tradition.

Codman, Ogden, Jr. (1868–1951) American architect, designer of Rockefeller estate in Pocantico Hills, New York, and co–author with Edith Wharton of *The Decoration of Houses* (1897).

Conran, Terence (b. 1931) British designer, retailer, and author specializing in home furnishings and lifestyle products.

Deskey, Donald (1894–1989) American designer in Art Deco style.

de Wolfe, Elsie (1865–1950) Author of *The House of Good Taste* (1913); considered the first professional interior decorator.

Draper, Dorothy (1889–1969) American society decorator noted for her oversized architectural details and upholstered furniture in bold colors.

Dresser, Christopher (1834–1904) English designer of silverware; brought Aesthetic movement to the United States when he attended the Philadelphia Centennial Exposition in 1876.

Dunand, Jean (1877–1942) Swiss-born metalworker; developed technique of dinanderie.

Eames, Charles (1907–1978) and **Ray** (1912–1988) American husband and wife furniture design team; also produced films, photography, inventions, and toys.

Eastlake, Charles Locke (1836–1906) British furniture designer and author of *Hints on Household Taste* (1868); noted for introducing the term *aesthetic style* to characterize handcrafted furniture using light–colored woods and less ornamentation than earlier styles; his name is often used to identify this furniture.

Eckhardt, Anthony George (18th century) An English manufacturer of printed fabrics and wallpapers who had a patent for printing designs on silk, cotton, muslin, calicos, and wallpapers.

Fontaine, Pierre–François Leonard (1762–1853) French architect; with Charles Percier redesigned the Chateau Malmaison with Etruscan and Egyptian decorative motifs to reflect the increased interest in archaeology.

Gallé, Émile (1846–1904) Founder in 1901 of L'Ecole de Nancy, an industrial arts alliance that revitalized marquetry.

Gaudí, Antoni (1852–1926) Spanish architect; noted for distinctively personal expression of Art Nouveau style.

Gibbons, Grinling (1648–1721) Master Carver to the Crown in England; known for large woodcarvings of vegetables, fruits, flowers, and birds.

Girardon, François (1628-1715) A French sculptor whose work was used to enhance the Louvre, Grand Trianon, Versailles.

Godwin, E. W. (1833–1886) British colorist and designer of furniture, wall coverings, and textiles showing a Japanese influence; coined the term *art furniture;* designer of the Peacock Room in collaboration with architect Thomas Jeckyll and painter James A. M. Whistler.

Gray, Eileen (1878–1976) Irish-born architect and designer active in Paris.

Greene, Charles (1868–1957) and Henry (1870–1954) American architects; noted for their Shingle or Bungalow style, which combined Japanese and American influences.

Gropius, Walter (1883–1969) German architect and a founder of the Bauhaus in Weimar in 1919.

Guimard, Hector (1867–1942) French architect–designer; noted for creating Art Nouveau interiors as ensembles.

Hadley, Albert (1920–2012) American interior designer; joined firm of "Sister" Parrish in 1962.

Harrison, Peter (1716-1775) Considered to be the first American architect in that he prepared sketches for others to build from.

Hepplewhite, George (d. 1786) British furniture designer and author of *The Cabinet-Maker and Upholsterer's Guide,* published posthumously in 1788.

Herter, Christian (1840–1883) and Gustav (1830–1898) German-born brothers, American furniture manufacturers; noted for bringing Eastlake style to the United States.

Hoffmann, Joseph (1870–1956) Austrian designer, co–founder in 1897 of the Vienna Secession movement with Otto Wagner and Joseph Maria Olbrich.

Hope, Thomas (1769–1831) British furniture maker and author of *Household Furniture and Decoration,* (1807), which popularized the Regency style.

Horta, Victor (1861–1947) Belgian architect and designer working in Art Nouveau style.

Jacobsen, Arne (1902–1971) Danish furniture designer.

Jacquard, Joseph-Marie (1752–1834) The Frenchman who, in 1801 created the Jacquard loom, which revolutionized the production of figured woven textiles.

Jeckyll, Thomas (1827–1881) British architect influenced by Japanese style; collaborator with designer E. W. Godwin and painter James A. M. Whistler in the Peacock Room.

Jones, Inigo (1573–c.1652) British architect noted for classical style.

Kent, William (1685–1748) British painter, architect, and landscape and interior designer; developed an all-encompassing approach to design.

Knoll Bassett, Florence Schust (b. 1917) and Knoll, Hans (1914–1955) American architect and German-born American furniture designer; principals of Knoll Associates, designers of modern furniture and interiors, especially known for office furniture, respectively.

Lalique, Rene (1860–1945) French designer of glass whose work bridged the Art Nouveau and Art Deco styles.

Le Brun, Charles (1619–1690) French painter in charge of the Gobelins factory, which produced tapestries for the royal residences of King Louis XIV.

Le Corbusier (Charles-Édouard Jeanneret) (1887–1965) Swiss-born French architect, noted for modernist design.

Lee, Sarah Tomerlin (1911–2001) American interior designer; known for hotel designs.

Le Vasseur, Etienne (1721–1798) A furniture designer and cabinetmaker in the styles of Louis XV and Louie XVI.

Lepautre, Jean (1617–1682) An interior designer and clockmaker. He published several works on decorative furniture which had a great influence on English styles.

Loewy, Raymond (1893–1986) An American industrial and interior designer, who created singular and evocative design.

Mackintosh, Charles Rennie (1868–1928) Scottish architect, interior designer, and furniture designer; designed the Glasgow School of Art, several tea rooms, and residences in Scotland.

Majorelle, Louis (1859–1926) French Art Nouveau furniture designer.

Marot, Daniel (1661–1752), Dutch architect–designer; his engravings served as templates for decorative details of interior design and spread a French design influence.

Maugham, Syrie (1879–1955) British society decorator.

McMillen Brown, Eleanor (1890–1991) American interior designer; founder, in 1923, of what is considered the first full-service interior design firm in the United States.

Meissonier, Juste–Aurèle (1693–1750) French artisan working in the Regence style.

Michelangelo (Michelangelo Buonarroti) (1475–1564) Italian painter, sculptor, and architect; among his best known works are the frescoes in the Sistine Chapel of the Vatican.

Mies van der Rohe, Ludwig (1886–1969) German architect and a founder of the Bauhaus; became its director in 1930.

Morgan, Julia (1872–1957) American architect and designer, best known for the Hearst Castle in California; the first woman to earn a degree in civil engineering.

Morris, William (1834–1896) British designer of textiles, wall coverings, and books; poet and writer; a leader of the Arts and Crafts movement.

Nash, John (1752–1835) English architect who became best known for his town planning abilities. His bold execution of the Marylebone region in London is one of his greatest accomplishments.

Oberkampf, Christopher-Philippe (1783–1815) The founder of the fabric factory at Jouy near Versailles, and the creator of "Toile de Jouy," a particular type of printed cotton fabric.

Olbrich, Joseph Maria (1867–1908) Austrian designer, co-founder in 1897 of the Vienna Secession movement with Joseph Hoffmann and Otto Wagner.

Palladio, Andrea (1508–1580) Italian architect and author of *The Four Books of Architecture* (1570).

Parrish, Dorothy "Sister" (1910–1994) Self–taught American decorator.

Paxton, Sir Joseph (1801–1865) British architect; builder of the Crystal Palace for the Great Exhibition of 1851.

Percier, Charles (1764–1838) French architect; with Pierre Fontaine redesigned the Chateau Malmaison with Etruscan and Egyptian decorative motifs to reflect the increased interest in archaeology.

Phyfe, Duncan (1768–1854) Scottish-born American cabinetmaker; popularized styles of Chippendale, Hepplewhite, and Sheraton in the United States.

Poiret, Paul (1879–1944) French fashion designer who extended his career into furniture design.

Pugin, Augustus Welby Northmore (1812–1852) British architect and designer; noted for reviving medieval ecclesiastical architecture and furnishings and for rebuilding the Palace of Westminster.

Putman, Andrée (b. 1925) French interior designer noted for hotel, restaurant, and retail designs.

Richardson, Henry Hobson (1838–1886) Most influential American architect of his generation, the first to influence European architecture.

Rietveld, Gerrit (1888–1964) Dutch furniture designer; noted for de Stijl movement, influenced by the painter Piet Mondrian.

Rubens, Peter Paul (1577–1640) A great Flemish painter. He decorated the Luxembourg Palace in Paris for Marie de Medici.

Ruhlmann, Jacques-Émile (1879–1933) French cabinetmaker known for craftsmanship and use of exotic materials.

Ruskin, John (1819–1900) British professor and philosopher; a founder of the Arts and Crafts movement.

Saarinen, Eliel (1873–1950) Finnish-born American architect and designer.

Sheraton, Thomas (c. 1751–1806) British designer and author of *Cabinet-Maker and Upholsterer's Drawing Book*, issued in four parts between 1791 and 1794.

Sottsass, Ettore (1917–2007) Austrian-born Italian furniture designer, founder of the Memphis style.

Starck, Philippe (b. 1949) French interior designer noted for hotel designs.

Stickley, Gustav (1858–1942) American furniture designer; noted for the Morris chair, named for William Morris.

Sullivan, Louis Henri (1856–1924) The founding father of modern American Architecture. He evolved the skyscraper design, and combined new technical means with aesthetic ideals.

Thonet, Michael (1796–1871) Austrian furniture designer; noted for bentwood designs using new process with lamination.

Tiffany, Louis Comfort (1848–1933) American designer of works in glass in Art Nouveau style.

van de Velde, Henri (1863–1957) Belgian designer noted for designing total environments; served as a link between Art Nouveau in France and Belgium and the Vienna Secession movement.

Viollet-le-Duc, Eugene Emmanuel (1814–1979) A 19th century French architect, archaeologist, and writer who is noted for his dictionary of architecture. He was enamored with the Gothic style, and he engaged in restoring important buildings like the Notre-Dame in Paris.

Vitruvius (active 1st c. B.C.) Roman architect and author of *De Architectura,* which influenced later architects who were inspired by the classical style.

Wagner, Otto (1841–1918) Austrian designer, co–founder in 1897 of the Vienna Secession movement with Joseph Hoffmann and Joseph Maria Olbrich.

Wegner, Hans (1914–2007) Danish furniture designer.

Wharton, Edith (1862–1937) American novelist, among the 19th-century "society decorators," and co–author with Ogden Codman, Jr., of *The Decoration of Houses* (1897).

Whistler, James (1834–1903) American painter living in London; collaborated with architect Thomas Jeckyll and designer E. W. Godwin on the Peacock Room.

Wood, Ruby Ross (1880–1950) American society decorator; managed the first interior decoration department in a department store.

Wren, Sir Christopher (1632–1723) British architect credited with rebuilding London after the Great Fire of 1666; brought the influence of French Baroque design to England.

Wright, Frank Lloyd (1867–1959) American architect, famed also for his interiors, textiles, and furniture, is associated with the principle of organic architecture. Included in his repertoire of well known projects are Fallingwater in Pennsylvania and the Guggenheim Museum in New York.

Zeisel, Eva (1906–2011) Hungarian-born industrial designer, known for her sensuous forms and organic approach to modernism. Her designs have included rugs, teakettle, ceramics, furniture, dinnerware, and so on. She developed and taught the first course in Ceramics at the Pratt Institute in New York.

Interior Design's Hall of Fame

Interior Design magazine's Hall of Fame was established to recognize individuals
who have made significant contributions to the growth and prominence of the design field.
The following designers have been inducted:

Marvin B. Affrime	Barbara D'Arcy	Mark Hampton
Kalef Alaton	Joseph P. D'urso	Antony Harbour
Davis Allen	Thierry W. Despont	Hugh Hardy
Stephen Apking	Orlando Diaz-Azcuy	Gisue Hariri
Pamela Babey	Angelo Donghia	Mojgan Hariri
Benjamin Baldwin	Jamie Drake	Steven Harris
Barbara Barry	Jack Dunbar	David Hicks
Louis M. S. Beal	Tony Duquette	Mariette Himes Gomez
Ward Bennett	Melvin Dwork	Richard Himmel
Maria Bergson	David Anthony Easton	Howard Hirsch
Deborah Berke	Rand Elliot	William Hodgins
Bruce Bierman	Henry End	Malcolm Holzman
Laura Bohn	Mica Ertegun	Franklin D. Israel
Joseph Braswell	Edward A. Feiner	Carolyn Iu
Robert Bray	Bernardo Fort-Brescia	Eva Jiricna
Don Brinkmann	Billy W. Francis	Jed Johnson
Thomas Britt	Neil Frankel	Melanie Kahane
R. Scott Bromley	Michael Gabellini	Ronette King
Denise Scott Brown	Frank Gehry	Robert Kleinschmidt
Mario Buatta	Arthur Gensler	Florence Knoll Bassett Krueck
Richard A. Carlson	Richard Gluckman	Gary L. Lee
Arthur Casas	Jacques Grange	Naomi Leff
Francois Catroux	Margo Grant Walsh	Debra Lehman-Smith
Steve Chase	Michael Graves	Joseph Lembo
Tony Chi	Bruce Gregga	Lawrence Lerner
Antonio Citterio	Charles Gwathmey	Neville Lewis
Clodagh	Albert Hadley	Sally Sirkin Lewis
Celeste Cooper	Victoria Hagan	Christian Liaigre
Robert Currie	Anthony Hail	Piero Lissoni
Carl D'Aquino	Mel Hamilton	Nick Luzietti

Eva Maddox
Stephen Mallory
Edith Mansfield Hills
Peter Marino
Ingo Mauer
Patrick McConnell
Margaret McCurry
Zack Mckown
Kevin McNamara
Robert Metzger
Lee Mindel
Juan Montoya
Frank Nicholson
James Northcutt
Sergio Palleroni
Henry Parish II
John Pawson
Gaetano Pesce
Norman Pfeiffer
Charles Pfister
Warren Platner
Donald D. Powell
Gwynne Pugh
William Pulgram

Glenn Pushelberg
Andree Putman
Chessy Rayner
Lucien Rees Roberts
David Rockwell
Lauren Rottet
John F. Saladino
Lawrence Scarpa
Michael Schaible
Annabelle Selldorf
Peter Shelton
Julius Shulman
Robert Siegel
Paul Siskin
Ethel Smith
William Sofield
Laurinda Spear
Jay Spectre
Rita St. Claire
Andre Staffelbach
Philippe Starck
Robert A. M. Stern
Rysia Suchecka

Takashi Sugimoto
Louis Switzer
Rose Tarlow
Michael Taylor
Matteo Thun
Stanley Tigerman
Adam Tihany
Sarah Tomerlin Lee
Calvin Tsao
Billie Tsien
Carleton Varney
Robert Venturi
Lella Vignelli
Massimo Vignelli
Kenneth H. Walker
Sally Walsh
Kevin Walz
Gary Wheeler
Bunny Williams
Tod Williams
Trisha Wilson
Vicente Wolf
George Yabu

D

Architectural Digest's Top 100 Interior Designers and Architects

This list represents a selection of the top architects and interior designers whose work has been featured in *Architectural Digest* over the past several years.

Marco Aldaco
Charles Allem
Marc Appleton
Howard J. Backen
Penny Drue Baird
Bannenberg and Rowell
Javier Barba
John Barman
Bill Bensley
Marcos Bertoldi
Karin Blake
Count Benedikt Bolza
Samuel Botero
Peter Roy Bowman
Geoffrey Bradfield
Thomas Britt
Mario Buatta
Diane Burn
Candy and Candy
Timothy Corrigan
Savin Couëlle
Elissa Cullman
Wallace E. Cunningham
Joanne de Guardiola
Mark de Reus
Douglas Durkin
David Easton
Steven Ehrlich
Mica Ertegün
Ferguson & Shamamian
Norman Foster
Linda Garland
William T. Georgis
Mariette Himes Gomez

Alexander Gorlin
Michael Graves
Allan Greenberg
Robert M. Gurney
Victoria Hagan
Mona Hajj
Alexa Hampton
Hariri and Hariri
Nicholas Haslam
Thad Hayes
Hendrix Allardyce
Ann Holden
Laura Hunt
Terry Hunziker
Ike Kligerman Barkley
Hugh Newell Jacobsen
David Jameson
Jim Jennings
Stephen Knollenberg
Richard Landry
Martyn Lawrence-Bullard
Michael Lee
Donna Livingston
London Boone
Ron Mann
Peter Marino
Marmol Radziner + Associates
Margaret McCurry
Mary Philpotts McGrath
Richard Meier
Miró Rivera Architects
Juan Pablo Molyneux
Juan Montoya

Moore Ruble Yudell
Katherine Newman
Sandra Nunnerley
Olson Kundig Architects
Thomas Pheasant
Campion Platt
Alex Pössenbacher
Jennifer Post
Antoine Predock
Bart Prince
Chakib Richani
Jaquelin T. Robertson
Jacques Saint Dizier
Nina Seirafi
Annabelle Selldorf
Stephen Shadley
Shelton, Mindel
Shope Reno Wharton
Marjorie Shushan
Michael S. Smith
Scott Snyder
José Solís Betancourt
John Stefanidis
Robert A. M. Stern
Emily Summers
Ken Tate
Roger Thomas
Suzanne Tucker
Edward Tuttle
Wang Ta-Chun
Paul Vincent Wiseman
Craig Wright
Pierre Yovanovitch

Basic Metric Conversion Table

Distances	
English	**Metric**
1 inch	2.54 centimeters
1 foot	0.3048 meter / 30.38 centimeters
1 yard	0.9144 meter
Metric	**English**
1 centimeter	0.3937 inch
1 meter	3.280 feet
Weights	
English	**Metric**
1 ounce	28.35 grams
1 pound	0.45 kilogram
Metric	**English**
1 gram	0.035 ounce
1 kilogram	2.2 pounds

General formula for converting:
Number of Units × Conversion Number =
New Number of Units

To convert inches to centimeters:
[number of inches] × 2.54 = [number of centimeters]

To convert centimeters to inches:
[number of centimeters] × 0.3937 =
[number of inches]

To convert feet to meters:
[number of feet] × 0.3048 = [number of meters]

To convert meters to feet:
[number of meters] × 3.280 = [number of feet]

To convert yards to meters:
[number of yards] × 0.9144 = [number of meters]

To convert ounces to grams:
[number of ounces] × 28.35 = [number of grams]

To convert grams to ounces:
[number of grams] × 0.035 = [number of ounces]

To convert pounds to kilograms:
[number of pounds] × 0.45 = [number of kilograms]

To convert kilograms to pounds:
[number of kilograms] × 2.2 = [number of pounds]

Glossary

A (arbitrary) lamp The lamp (in layperson's terms, light bulb) had been the standard especially in residential settings until the 21st century. Typical wattages are 25 W, 40 W, 60 W, 75 W, 100 W, and 150 W. (Chapter 7)

Accent color scheme A color scheme built on a related, contrasting, or achromatic scheme. It may involve introducing an accent color or a neutral to offset an established scheme and make it less predictable; introducing a hue in a monochromatic scheme; introducing a color into an achromatic scheme; or adding a small amount of a complement to an analogous or a monochromatic scheme. (Chapter 4)

Accent lighting A type of lighting that creates an emphasis or focus used to highlight a painting, objet d'art, or sculpture; also called key lighting. (Chapter 2)

Accessible (barrier-free) design Design that is in compliance with the Americans with Disabilities Act (ADA). (Chapter 2)

Accommodation The ability of the eye to focus at different distances (near and far vision) under normal conditions. (Chapter 4)

Achromatic color scheme A color scheme composed of white, black, and/or gray, with no hue. One that is related includes a series of grays that are close in value; one that is contrasting is composed of only black and white or grays of very different values. (Chapter 4)

Acoustics The science that deals with the production, control, reception, and effects of sound. (Chapter 2)

Acrylic impregnation A technique used to add strength to wood floors through the injection of acrylic into the wood. (Chapter 9)

Active solar energy A system in which solar energy is mechanically harvested and converted into electricity. It includes rooftop devices, greenhouses on urban rooftops, wind turbines, and hydroelectric devices. (Chapter 8)

ADA building code compliance plan A component of the contract documents package for a project that demonstrates barrier-free requirements according to the Americans with Disabilities Act (ADA) as part of, or in addition to, the construction plan. (Chapter 5)

Adaptation The normal process by which the eye adjusts to changes in the brightness of light. (Chapter 7)

Adaptive reuse An interior design approach that focuses on converting obsolescence into relevance by designing through change, not demolition. (Chapter 2)

Additive theory of color A theory regarding property of color originating from light. Mixing the three primaries of light in various combinations can produce any other color; combined in equal quantities they add up to white, or colorless, light. (Chapter 4)

Adjacency study A relationship study that depicts the organizational and hierarchical structure of a company, as well as space requirements, operational flow, and circulation patterns. It is used to develop a plan that accommodates the functions users must carry out and indicates where these are to be accomplished. (Chapter 5)

Advancing and receding colors Warm hues that appear to advance, or move closer to the viewer, and cool colors that seem to recede, or move farther away. (Chapter 4)

Aesthetics The study or theory of beauty and our responses to it; the branch of philosophy that deals with art—its creation, forms, and effects—derived from the Greek word relating to perception. (Chapter 3)

Afterimage (successive contrast) The phenomenon whereby the perception of color is altered when colors are viewed in sequence (i.e., successively), rather than simultaneously or side by side. (Chapter 4)

Aggregate A type of stone manufactured in combination with other substances, such as resin and epoxy. (Chapter 9)

Aging in place People remaining in their own homes as long as possible rather than moving, as their needs change, to less independent situations. (Chapter 2)

Alkyd paint Oil-based paint. (Chapter 9)

All-wood construction In flooring, denotes the use of veneer in contrast to solid hardwood; also called engineered or laminated flooring. (Chapter 9)

Ambient lighting Diffuse, uniform illumination that provides for safe movement; also called general lighting. (Chapter 3)

American Society of Interior Designers (ASID) An organization formed in 1975 by the merger of the American Institute of Decorators (AID) and the National Society of Interior Designers. (Chapter 1)

Americans with Disabilities Act (ADA) A national law passed in 1990 that provides civil rights protections to individuals with disabilities concerning accommodation in public facilities, employment, transportation, state and local government services, and telecommunications. (Chapter 2)

Anaglypta A lighter-weight version of lincrusta that is used to provide textural variation for ceiling and walls. (Chapter 12)

Analogous color scheme An approach to color harmony that combines hues adjacent to each other on the color wheel. It can be further specified as a range of adjacent hues that remain in one temperature zone (warm or cool, not both). (Chapter 4)

Anglo-Japanese An aesthetic movement popular in late 19th-century England that mixed the notion of craft with an interest in Japanese design. (Chapter 12)

Anthropometrics The study of and documentation of human body measurements that belong to different populations, such as adult males and females. (Chapter 2)

Applied pattern A pattern that is achieved by applying the design to a surface, as when printing a fabric. (Chapter 3)

Arabesque A typical Renaissance motif consisting of an intricate pattern of interlacing plant tendrils. (Chapter 11)

Arcading A woodcarving design reflecting a succession of Roman arches. (Chapter 11)

Architectural scale A triangular scale, with a total of 12 scales, ranging from the largest, in which 3 inches represents 1 foot, 0 inches, to the smallest, in which 1/8 inch represents 1 foot, 0 inches. (Chapter 6)

Armoire A French cupboard designed to store clothing. (Chapter 11)

Armoire à deux corps A cupboard in two parts used for storage. (Chapter 11)

Aromatherapy A therapeutic approach based on the healing potential of smell. (Chapter 2)

Art furniture The idea that furniture should be built as a form of art, epitomized by the Aesthetic movement. (Chapter 12)

Artificial light See Electric light.

Ashlar Finished, or hewn, stone used for exterior walls. (Chapter 8)

Assisted living A residence within a larger facility for persons who require help with activities of daily living, often seniors. (Chapter 1)

Association of Contract Textiles (ACT) A not-for-profit trade association that addresses issues related to contract textiles and provides for uniform labeling in terms of five performance standards: flammability, abrasion resistance, colorfastness under light and when wet, and dry crocking. (Chapter 10)

Asymmetrical balance The achievement of equilibrium through equal visual weight of nonidentical elements around an axis, resulting in a composition that is flexible, dynamic, and informal. (Chapter 3)

Aubusson A type of finely woven tapestry or rug from France. (Chapter 9)

Auditory The sensory experience of hearing, through which our ears perceive sound in the form of vibrations. (Chapter 2)

Autism spectrum disorder (ASD) A range of complex neurodevelopment disorders, characterized by social impairment; communication difficulties; and restricted, repetitive patterns of behavior. (Chapter 2)

Axis The centerline of an arrangement or design. (Chapter 3)

Bachelor chest A small chest used at the bedside. (Chapter 11)

Backlighting The technique of lighting an object from behind, producing a silhouette; the object is blackened while the background is illuminated. (Chapter 7)

Bagua An ancient Chinese tool for understanding how the environment relates to life. (Chapter 4)

Baize A type of wool felt. (Chapter 10 and Chapter 11)

Bargello Intricate, rhythmic patterns created through weaving techniques for textiles popularized during the Renaissance; now often a pattern style created through computer generation; similar to flame stitch. (Chapter 11)

Barrier-free design See Accessible (barrier-free) design.

Batik A type of resist printing that originated in Indonesia in which hot wax is applied to parts of a cloth, preventing dye from being absorbed and creating a characteristic pattern. (Chapter 10)

Batting Filling material, used in upholstered furniture. (Chapter 10)

Bauhaus A school of art and design, in Weimar, Germany, founded in 1919 by Walter Gropius. (Chapter 12)

Beam spread The distribution of light from a lamp, often enhanced by the use of reflectors. (Chapter 7)

Behavioral setting (behavioral mapping) A concept of space planning that distinguishes spaces according to activity. Boundaries and objects are delineated according to prescribed, predictable patterns of behavior. (Chapter 2)

Bergère An upholstered armchair typical of the Rococo style in France. (Chapter 11)

Bid package See Contract documents package.

Bid procurement A process of soliciting bids (usually at least three) for work to be done; also known as request for proposals. (Chapter 5)

Billable rate The rate at which a firm bills a client, which takes into account professional time, overhead, and other expenses of doing business. (Chapter 14)

Binder A substance used to harden liquid paint. (Chapter 9)

Biomass energy Energy from plant and animal wastes that can serve as fuel resources. (Chapter 8)

Biomimicry Established by the biologist Janine Benyus (b. 1958), this concept uses nature as a model to inspire designs and processes that solve human problems. The belief that studying nature will uncover effective and sustainable solutions to issues such as thermal comfort, indoor air quality, and acoustical privacy. (Chapter 2)

Block flooring See Parquet flooring.

Block style A style of lettering that is wide and square in shape and usually done in uppercase (capital) letters. (Chapter 6)

Body of Knowledge (BOK) Documented abstract knowledge relating to a particular field of study that serves as a basis for persons within a specific profession to effectively carry out their practice. (Chapter 13)

Boiserie A form of millwork consisting of raised carved wood panels often in themes to represent specific room functions, typical of the 18th century. (Chapter 11)

Bombé A French chest typical of the Rococo style featuring a curved surface. (Chapter 11)

Bonheur-du-jour A French ladies' desk consisting of a fall-front cabinet on slender legs, typical of the Rococo and Neoclassical periods. (Chapter 11)

Boullework A marquetry technique, featuring brass and tortoiseshell inlay, perfected by André Charles Boulle (1642–1732). (Chapter 11)

Branding Often used to describe a comprehensive way of presenting a clear and consistent message of what a person, company, or products have to offer. (Chapter 14)

British Raj (Anglo-Raj, Anglo-Indian) A furniture style that includes ornately carved and pierced pieces made from local woods that were often from Bombay, now Mumbai, India, popular during the Victorian period. *British Raj* refers to a contemporary version of this blended style. (Chapter 12)

Broadloom A type of carpeting that includes both 12-foot and wider rolled goods. (Chapter 9)

Brown A general term describing a hue that may include a mixture of hues between red and yellow that is of medium to low lightness and of moderate to low saturation; also referred to as a neutral. (Chapter 4)

Bubble diagram A diagram that depicts overall zones, or areas of space by type of activity. It may also refer to a more detailed diagram, indicating the location and proportional sizes of areas depicted. (Chapter 5)

Buffet A storage piece that also functions as a dining server. (Chapter 11)

Building Information Modeling (BIM) A digital representation of the building life-cycle process from design, analysis, documentation, construction, and facility management. (Chapter 6)

Building-related illness (BRI) Any of a group of illnesses that result from deficiencies in the design of the built environment with respect to heating, ventilation, and air-conditioning (HVAC); structural defects; and interior surface problems. (Chapter 2)

Bureau plat A French writing table, typical of the Baroque and Rococo styles. (Chapter 11)

Burlap A rough material woven from jute, a grass, and used in the construction of upholstered furniture. (Chapter 10)

Cable system A type of ceiling lighting system consisting of flush-mounted or suspended cables with attached fixtures that may be movable. The system may be curved, creating a sculptural effect. See also Track system. (Chapter 4)

C and S curve A swirling, delicate, and asymmetrical curvilinear design typical of the Rococo style and named for the letterforms it simulates. (Chapter 11)

Cabriole leg A curved furniture leg modeled on that of an animal, characteristic of Rococo style. (Chapter 11)

CAD An abbreviation for computer-aided drafting and design (also CADD or CAD/D); a computer program that enables a designer to generate many different types of drawings and plans. (Chapter 6)

Canapé A French sofa, to seat two or three persons, typical of the 18th century. Equivalent to the settee in England and America. (Chapter 11)

Cane Thin woven strips of plant materials, typically used for seats in lieu of cushions. (Chapter 10)

Caquetoire A gossip chair, popular during the French Renaissance and meant to accommodate the width of a woman's skirt; equivalent to the farthingale in England. (Chapter 11)

Carpet Used in very large quantities and represents the major use of synthetic fibers, such as nylon, as delineated. (Chapter 9)

Caryatid A sculptured female figure ornament used as the basis of the design for a column or support. (Chapter 11)

Cascade See Jabot.

Case good Nonupholstered furniture, whether for residential or commercial use. (Chapter 10)

Casework Built-ins or furniture that is attached to walls, whether prefabricated or custom built. (Chapter 10)

Casing The trim for a window. (Chapter 8)

Cassapanca An Italian Renaissance chest/bench with arms and a back used for storage and seating; forerunner of the modern sofa. (Chapter 11)

Cassone A marriage chest of the Italian Renaissance, in which a bride would hold her dowry. (Chapter 11)

Catalog cut A picture of a product, requested from a manufacturer. Also called tear sheet. (Chapter 14)

Cathedra An ancient Roman chair used primarily by women and resembling the Greek klismos, but heavier in proportion. (Chapter 11)

Cathedral ceiling A type of structural ceiling in an expansive triangular shape that evokes the grand scale of religious edifices. (Chapter 8)

Certificate of Authority A document issued by the appropriate tax authority to grant permission for the resale of goods and services. It is required for a designer to purchase on behalf of a client. (Chapter 14)

Certified Aging in Place Specialist (CAPS) A designation program offered through the NAHB (National Association of Home Builders) that teaches the technical, business management, and customer service skills essential to the residential remodeling industry for modifications for the aging-in-place population. (Chapter 2)

Certified bath designer (CBD) A specialty credential indicating that a designer has achieved a level of proficiency in bath design through a combination of education and experience. (Chapter 5)

Certified interior designer A person who has met certain education, experience and examination requirements and is registered with the interior design board in his or her state. (Chapter 14)

Certified kitchen designer (CKD) A specialty credential indicating that a designer has achieved a level of proficiency in kitchen design through a combination of education and experience. (Chapter 5)

Chair rail A strip of wood placed about 4 feet above the floor on an interior wall. (Chapter 9)

Chaise longue A long, reclining chair similar to the resting bed or day bed of ancient civilizations and popular during the Empire period. (Chapter 11)

Change order An authorized change to the contract documents package. (Chapter 5)

Chesterfield A type of tuxedo seating, often upholstered in leather, in which the back and inside of the arm rests are quilted and buttoned. (Chapter 10)

Chest-on-stand A two-part wood storage piece, often highly decorated with *marquetry*, typical of the William and Mary style of the 17th and 18th centuries. (Chapter 11)

Chiffonier A tall, narrow French chest of drawers on legs, typical of the Neoclassical period. (Chapter 11)

Chinoiserie French Rococo interpretations of Chinese and other Eastern motifs. (Chapter 11)

Chintz A finishing treatment for cotton fabric known as glazing; also commonly, but less accurately, used to refer to a large-scale flower pattern. (Chapter 10)

Chroma The purity, saturation, or intensity of a hue; adding gray to a hue or a hue's complement lowers its chroma. (Chapter 3)

Chromatherapy A therapeutic technique based on the healing properties of color. (Chapter 4)

Chromaticity Way to describe the appearance of light through categorizing it by its apparent temperature (warmth or coolness). (Chapter 7)

Circadian rhythms Term given to the internal biological clock regulating sleep–wake patterns. (Chapter 7)

Circulation pattern How people move around an interior space, including inside to outside, the direction of door swings, and the widths of corridors, hallways, and stairs. (Chapter 5)

Cladding The use of masonry, metal, ceramic, glass, wood, solid-surfacing, and laminate materials as a wall finish. (Chapter 9)

Clerestory Window or opening in the upper portion of a wall. (Chapter 8)

Cloisonné A technique to decorate metal objects with patterns by creating separate compartments with wire metals to separate differently colored fillers, or inlays, generally enamel; then fired in a kiln. (Chapter 11)

Cocooning A term coined by forecaster Faith Popcorn as a trend to spend leisure time at home in preference to going out. (Chapter 13)

Coffered ceiling A ceiling made up of sections of recessed panels, typically of wood. (Chapter 9)

Colonnade A series of regularly spaced columns, typical of the ancient Greek interior. (Chapter 11)

Color blindness (color deficiency) A genetic condition, more common among men than women, in which the cone receptors are diminished, causing the person to have difficulty distinguishing the values of certain pairs of colors, generally red and green, both of which appear to resemble tones of gray. (Chapter 4)

Color constancy The phenomenon by which the eye adapts to varying conditions such as lighting, correcting differences in color, so that red is still perceived as red, green as green, and so forth. (Chapter 7)

Color rendering index (CRI) An international system for comparison developed to rank light sources with respect to color representation or rendering, with 0 as the lowest rating and 100 as the highest. The CRI rating system is applied to various types of lamps, styles, and manufacturers. (Chapter 7)

Color wheel A circular graphic tool used to illustrate the organization of hues by adjacencies; generally the 12 hues to include the primary, secondary, and tertiary hues. (Chapter 4)

Commercial design See Contract (commercial) interior design.

Commode A low, wide chest of drawers, typical of the 18th century. (Chapter 11)

Compact fluorescent A type of energy-efficient fluorescent lamp replacing incandescent lamps and many older types of fluorescent lamps. (Chapter 7)

Companion chair A Victorian-style circular seat inspired by the Turkish ottoman, typically seating three persons. (Chapter 12)

Competitive bid process The process of securing several bids (usually at least three) from competing sources that is recommended for projects that involve construction and/or demolition; see also Bid procurement. (Chapter 5)

Complementary color scheme An arrangement of color that creates harmony by using complementary (contrasting) colors, a combination of warm and cool hues. (Chapter 4)

Computer-aided drafting and design See CAD.

Concrete slab system A system used to construct buildings with multiple floor levels in which concrete, either poured or prefabricated in slabs, is reinforced with steel rods. (Chapter 8)

Cone of vision In a perspective drawing, the angle of view that represents the range of sight of the viewer. (Chapter 6)

Coniferous See Softwood.

Console A table similar to a large bracket against a wall, often with a mirror placed above it. (Chapter 11)

Construction drawing See Working drawing.

Construction plan A component of the contract documents package that shows walls, partitions, columns, doors, and windows. (Chapter 5)

Contador A Portuguese version of the cabinet-on-stand; typical of the Baroque period. (Chapter 11)

Continuing care retirement community (CCRC) An approach to accommodate varying needs, generally of an elderly population, in a clustered environment to ease transition from independence to a more super-vised facility. It generally incorporates the categories of independent living, assisted living, and specialized nursing or dementia units. (Chapter 1, Chapter 2)

Continuing education unit (CEU) An accredited unit (generally one hour per unit) assigned to professional education programs often required for interior design and other professional practitioners, post formal academic training. (Chapter 1)

Contract An agreement between parties that sets forth a series of promises between the parties; see also Letter of agreement. (Chapter 14)

Contract administration phase The final phase of an interior design project. It involves the execution of the design plans, including oversight of work performed by tradespeople to see that they are consistent with the design concept. (Chapter 5)

Contract (commercial) interior design A category of design in which a company, rather than individuals, is contracting for the services; also called commercial design. Within this broad category are several subspecializations, including office design, hospitality design, retail design, health-care design, and facilities management. (Chapter 1)

Contract documents package A group of documents that serves as the basis for construction and installation of a design project (e.g., plans, schedules, and specifications); also called bid package. (Chapter 5)

Contract documents phase The fourth phase of an interior design project, in which documents describing both interior construction and furnishings are prepared for the client's written approval; the designer may also assist the client with the bidding, procurement, and selection process for contracted goods and services. (Chapter 5)

Contrasting color scheme An arrangement of colors derived by focusing on the differences among the selection of hues. It is considered more dynamic and active than a related color scheme. (Chapter 4)

Cool gray A gray that has some blue or violet mixed in. (Chapter 4)

Corinthian A style of ancient Greek capital featuring ornate carvings of the acanthus leaf. (Chapter 11)

Cork A material extracted from the bark of the cork oak tree; a green product used for interiors, such as for flooring. (Chapter 9)

Cornice A type of window top treatment consisting of a wooden frame that may be upholstered with fabric (Chapter 10); also, molding or a contrasting painted demarcation at the top of a wall. (Chapter 10)

Coromandel A type of lacquered and decorated screen featuring Oriental motifs and scenes and named after the type of ebony used to construct it; named from its regional origin in Southeast Asia. (Chapter 10)

Cost (net price) The discounted price at which an item is sold to the trade. (Chapter 14)

Cost-plus (cost plus percentage) A fee structure whereby an established percentage for design service compensation is added based on the dollar amount of these purchases. (Chapter 14)

Council for Interior Design Association (CIDA) Association that has been formed to advance education and practice standards. The association reviews educational programs against established criteria in order to accredit the programs accordingly. CIDA is an independent, volunteer organization that sets standards for interior design programs, culminating in a minimum of a bachelor's degree at the postsecondary level in the United States and Canada. (Chapter 1)

Court cupboard An English case piece of the medieval period designed to display and store possessions, either the vestments or ceremonial objects of the Church or the secular possessions of the wealthy. (Chapter 11)

Cove lighting An architectural lighting system used to distribute light evenly across a ceiling. A cove is a channel that may be constructed from many different types of materials (e.g., wood molding at the juncture between wall and ceiling). (Chapter 7)

Cozy corner (cosy corner) A Victorian-style type of banquette resembling a railway compartment. (Chapter 12)

Cradle to cradle The notion that products be developed with the potential for continuous renewability, that is, to live on forever in some form, without doing harm to the environment. (Chapter 2)

Credenza An office work surface and storage piece similar to the server or buffet used in residential dining spaces. (Chapter 10)

Criteria matrix A technique for condensing and formatting many of the programming requirements of an interior design project, including square footage needs and adjacencies, when developing preliminary design schematics. (Chapter 5)

Cup and cover See Melon (cup and cover).

Curio cabinet A type of cabinet used to display accessories ("curiosities"), dating from the Victorian era. See also Whatnot. (Chapter 10)

Curtain wall A fixed glass structure consisting of a wood or metal frame sheathed with glass. (Chapter 8)

Curule A curved, X-shaped stool used by the ancient Romans. (Chapter 11)

Curvilinear line A bent line—one that deviates without a sharp angle. (Chapter 3)

Customer's own material (COM)/Customer's own leather (COL) An added cost for fabric or leather that is not included in the price for upholstering furniture. (Chapter 14)

Cut line A horizontal slice taken through a plan at a specific height, usually 4 feet up from the floor, for a floor plan. (Chapter 6)

Cut pile A tufted carpet or rug with a surface in which the yarn loops are cut. (Chapter 9)

Cutting for approval (CFA) A request for an actual sample of a fabric from the specific bolt of goods being ordered, to be approved before the order is in place. (Chapter 14)

Cutting (swatch) A small sample, such as a piece of fabric, that does not have to be returned to a showroom. (Chapter 14)

Dado See Wainscot (dado).

Dais In a medieval great hall, the raised platform at one end of the room where the landowners dined, while others of lower station sat below. (Chapter 11)

Damask A particular type of weave; also commonly, but less accurately, used to refer to a two-tone floral, no matter how it is manufactured. (Chapter 10)

Dante chair An X-shaped chair typical of the Italian Renaissance featuring four heavy legs curving up to the arms. (Chapter 11)

Daylighting Synonymous with *skylight*. Daylight enhances visual acuity for reading and writing. (Chapter 7)

DBA (doing business as) The name under which a business entity operates, as listed with government authorities. (Chapter 14)

De Stijl Translated to: The Style. Represents a movement in the Netherlands of a group of Dutch artists in Amsterdam named after an avant-garde magazine of the same name. (Chapter 12)

Dead load The relatively fixed weight of a building's structure and equipment. (Chapter 8)

Dealership A company that is an authorized sales representative for a manufacturer, such as for office furniture. (Chapter 14)

Deciduous See Hardwood (deciduous tree).

Deck The platform, steel springs, and padding structures that support the seat cushions in upholstered furniture. (Chapter 10)

Delftware A Dutch or Flemish ceramic popular in the Baroque period and often decorated with Oriental motifs. (Chapter 11)

Deliverables Floor plans and other drawings pertaining to an interior design project. (Chapter 5)

Demolition plan A component of the contract documents package that demonstrates existing conditions to be eliminated prior to renovations that involve construction of structural components. (Chapter 5)

Design concept A generalized idea or vision not only of how an interior will look but also of how it will serve the users. (Chapter 5)

Design development phase The third phase of an interior design project, in which drawings and other documents are refined and executed to scale, with greater detail for client approval, and preliminary budget estimates may be revised. (Chapter 5)

Desk audit A review of a company's organization chart, policies, practices, and procedures. (Chapter 5)

Detail A drawing of a specific element of a design that helps to define the design concept. (Chapter 5, Chapter 6)

Dhurrie A type of flat woven rug from India. (Chapter 9)

Diagonal line A line that is at an angle. It denotes a more pronounced dynamic motion than a horizontal or a vertical line. (Chapter 3)

Diffuse lighting Lighting that provides an overall uniform illumination to a space rather than illuminating a specific object. (Chapter 7)

Digital photo editing The manipulation of photographic images. (Chapter 6)

Dimensional stability The ability of a material to hold its shape. (Chapter 9)

Diminution in size The phenomenon by which objects appear to become smaller as they move farther away from the viewer. (Chapter 6)

Dinanderie A technique in which crushed eggshells are used as an inlay material for metal decorative pieces, which are then lacquered; it was developed by the Swiss-born metalworker Jean Dunand (1877–1942); popular in Art Deco period. (Chapter 12)

Direct complementary color scheme A contrasting color scheme consisting of two hues that appear in direct opposition on the 12-hue color wheel, such as red and green. See also Complementary color scheme. (Chapter 4)

Direct lighting A technique in which light strikes its primary target first before illuminating secondary objects. (Chapter 7)

Direct solar gain A well-insulated, airtight house with large insulating windows that face the sun. (Chapter 8)

DIY (do it yourself) A term used to describe a layperson who takes on the activities of home improvement, decorating and redecorating projects, and makeovers. (Chapter 13)

Doing business as See DBA (doing business as).

Door and window schedule A component of the contract documents package that typically is presented in a format that includes the number, size, material, and hardware for interior doors and windows. (Chapter 5)

Doric A style of ancient Greek capital featuring a simple horizontal plane at the top. (Chapter 11)

Double complementary color scheme A contrasting color scheme that uses two pairs of complementary colors, such as red and green with violet and yellow. (Chapter 4)

Double rubs A method of scoring, the Wyzenbeek tests for fabric abrasion; the higher the number, the more abrasion-resistant the fabric. (Chapter 10)

Down lighting Lighting that is cast downward onto an object or objects. (Chapter 7)

DPE (direct personnel expense) A protocol used by firms to determine fees to clients, often based on a multiplier of 2.5 to 3. This approach factors in costs involved for salary and fringe benefits of staff (e.g., health, disability, life insurance, and paid time off). (Chapter 14)

Drafting The term used to describe the preparation of technical drawings based on measurements, whether manually or computer-generated. (Chapter 6)

Drop ship The location at which a delivery company agrees to leave goods that have been ordered, such as the client's location rather than the designer's location or warehouse. (Chapter 14)

Drywall construction A system of construction in which building walls are framed with panels made of gypsum. (Chapter 8)

Duchese A typical sofa of the Rococo period composed of two pieces, typically a chaise longue or large upholstered chair and an ottoman. (Chapter 11)

Dynamic load A load, in addition to the dead load and live load, that may affect a structure; it includes wind, vibrations, and shock waves, possibly of seismic or earthquake proportions. (Chapter 8)

Ebeniste The French term applied to a highly skilled cabinetmaker specializing in veneers and marquetry. (Chapter 11)

Efficacy The amount of brightness a lamp source provides in comparison with the energy used. (Chapter 7)

Eight-way hand-tied coil spring construction The traditional upholstery method in which cords are intertwined or knotted to stabilize the construction. (Chapter 10)

Electric light A type of lighting that includes incandescent, fluorescent, neon, high-intensity discharge, and LED (light-emitting diode). Also called artificial light. (Chapter 3)

Electrochromatic Fire-rated glazing material. (Chapter 8)

Element Any of the six singular components that serve as the building blocks of a design composition: line, pattern, texture, light, scale, and color. (Chapter 3)

Elevation A scale drawing that shows a vertical slice of a space; for an interior, it shows one wall with elements such as millwork on the wall surface or furniture in front of the wall. (Chapter 5)

Enamel A high-gloss paint coating. (Chapter 9); also a hard glossy coating baked on metal, glass, or ceramic ware; see Cloisonné. (Chapter 11)

End user The intended occupant or occupants of a space, whose needs, wants, and intended purpose for using the space must be considered in designing it. (Chapter 5)

Energy Star ratings A joint program of the U.S. Environmental Protection Agency and the U.S. Department of Energy; a volunteer labeling system of energy efficient products and practices. (Chapter 7)

Enfilade A layout consisting of a succession of rooms through which one can pass (and view) directly, popularized during the French Renaissance. (Chapter 11)

Engineered flooring See All-wood construction.

Engineered (laminated) Thin layers of wood bonded together with the grains running in different directions. Considered more dimensionally stable than solid hardwood and more resistant to the effects of moisture. (Chapter 9)

English Palladian (Anglo-Palladian) English design that was influenced by the Europeans. During the early to mid-18th century, it retained much of the muscular Baroque flavor in a rather unique style. (Chapter 11)

En suite A grouping of matching pieces for a particular area. (Chapter 11)

Entourage Representations of people, plants, vehicles, and other everyday items, either ready-made templates or individually constructed, that are used in 2D and 3D drawings and dropped into a model. (Chapter 6)

Environmental stewardship The responsibility of global citizens to manage and preserve our natural resources. (Chapter 2)

Environment scanning report Formal research resulting in detailed statistics, a snapshot of the habits and tastes of a population at a given time. Organizations such as the American Society of Interior Designers (ASID), the International Furnishings and Design Association (IFDA), and the American Institute of Architects (AIA) periodically conduct those extensive surveys. (Chapter 13)

Ergonomics An applied science that is concerned with designing and arranging things people use so that people and things interact most efficiently and safely. It combines anthropometric data and an understanding of body mechanics, or physiology, with product and equipment know-how; see Human engineering. (Chapter 2)

Evidence-based design A process of design based on extensive methodical research to achieve an expected outcome; originating from the field of medicine, it is applied to health-care design and to other types of built environment design. (Chapter 1)

Existing conditions A term used to describe the architectural features of a site, such as its windows and doors. (Chapter 5)

Face yarn See Pile.

Fair market price A monetary amount assigned to goods based on the estimated price it would command in an open market; based on factors such as sale of comparable goods and expert opinion. (Chapter 14)

Fair trade practice A social and business model whereby goods are made by local artisans with traditional techniques, under safe and nonexploitative conditions, and balanced with profitability. (Chapter 13)

Farthingale An English chair of the 16th and 17th centuries, constructed without arms to accommodate the hoop skirts worn by women in this period. Equivalent to the caquetoire in France. (Chapter 11)

Fauteuil A version of the bergère (an upholstered armchair typical of the Rococo period), but with open sides. (Chapter 11)

Faux finishing Fake renderings of various natural materials (e.g., wood, stone, and gems) or surface patinas (e.g., old painted plaster or distressed finishes). Faux bois mimics wood; faux marbre mimics marble. (Chapter 9)

Fenestration A door or window opening in a building. (Chapter 8)

Festoon See Swag (festoon).

FF&E An abbreviation for fixtures, furnishings, and equipment. (Chapter 5)

Fiber A natural or synthetic thread or filament that is capable of being sewn, woven, or spun into yarn. (Chapter 9)

Fiberboard A material consisting of compressed fibers of wood bonded together in sheets. (Chapter 8)

Fiber optic lighting Uses a remote source for illumination. The light source is housed in a box, and the directional lamp is usually metal halide or tungsten-halogen. (Chapter 7)

Field measurement (field survey) A measurement of a space, including doors and windows, that is taken on-site. (Chapter 5)

Finish plan A component of the contract documents package that notes the surface coverings. It may include several schedules, such as a plan for all wood finishes and another for paint finishes. (Chapter 5)

Five/ten (5/10) code A discount offered to the trade by some suppliers of fabric. The buyer subtracts five from the first number on a tag, and ten from

the second number, to calculate the discount price. (Chapter 14)

Flame stitch Intricate, rhythmic patterns created through weaving techniques for textiles popularized during the Renaissance; now often a pattern style created through computer generation, similar to bargello. (Chapter 11)

Float glass A process of glass production in which molten glass moves out of the furnace along a flat molten metal, producing a glass that is freer from distortion with better heat insulation properties than its predecessors. (Chapter 8)

Flokati A traditional handwoven, long-pile woolen rug from Greece; similar to more contemporary shaggy rugs. (Chapter 9)

Flood beam spread A beam spread angle of more than 25 degrees. (Chapter 7)

Floor plan A plan for how furniture and equipment should be laid out; also called furniture layout plan. (Chapter 5)

Fluorescent lighting A lamping type that consists of a glass tube filled with a low-pressure mercury vapor, which produces an invisible ultraviolet radiation that activates white phosphorous crystals inside the lamp. The phosphorus glows or fluoresces, converting the ultraviolet energy into visible light energy, casting diffuse lighting with few shadows. (Chapter 7)

Flush-mounted fixture A fixture in which a lamp is affixed to the ceiling or wall so that the lamp and its housing are revealed; also called surface-mounted. (Chapter 7)

Fly ash A waste product from processing coal used as an alternative to cement as an ingredient for concrete; less impact on the environment. (Chapter 9)

FOB (free on board) A term used in purchase orders to specify that a shipment is without charge for delivery to and placing on board a carrier at a specified point; also called freight on board. (Chapter 14)

Foot-candle (fc) A measurement of light level; the metric equivalent is lux. One footcandle equals 10 lux. (Chapter 7)

Footing The part of a foundation that extends below the soil to provide stability by distributing the load. (Chapter 8)

Forecasting Predicting or calculating future events or conditions on the basis of a rational study and analysis of available pertinent data. (Chapter 13)

Form The basic line, shape, and configuration of an object that serve to distinguish one object from another. (Chapter 33)

Fossil fuel A fuel (e.g., coal or oil) made from buried deposits of decayed plants and animals that have been exposed to heat and pressure in the earth's crust over hundreds of millions of years. (Chapter 8)

Framing wall system A system of wall construction that uses vertical posts or beams attached to a top plane and a bottom runner; it requires fewer posts than stud construction. (Chapter 8)

Fresco The technique of painting on wet plaster. (Chapter 11)

Frieze A type of cut pile in which the yarns are twisted, forming a curly, textured surface; also, in classic interior architectural style, a decorated area between the cornice and dado. (Chapter 11)

Fullness In a window treatment, the ratio of fabric width to window width, such as triple fullness, where three widths of a fabric are used for one window width. (Chapter 10)

Full-spectrum light White light or light that contains the full spectrum of light waves. (Chapter 7)

Functional design Where art is combined with engineering, materials, and craft. (Chapter 12)

Functionalism An early 20th-century style that sought to create designs appropriate for modern industrial society. Its proponents believed that good design should be readily available to all classes and would improve the standard of living. (Chapter 2)

Furniture and equipment plan A component of the contract documents package that consists of one or a series of floor plans that identify all "movable" furnishings as well as built-in cabinetwork, fixtures, and appliances, such as for kitchens and bathrooms. It may be accompanied by elevations and details to depict customized units. (Chapter 5)

Furniture layout plan See Floor plan.

Fusion (optical mixing) When a color from a distance reduces its apparent scale. For example, a carpet that appears to be made up of small green and red fibers when viewed up close will read as muddy brown when experienced from a realistic distance and installed in the actual space. (Chapter 4)

Gable The triangular shape achieved when a roof structure is not a horizontal plane. (Chapter 8)

Galley kitchen A term derived from the kitchen areas on naval ships; for residential use, to describe kitchens generally with no dining area designed to maximize limited space and minimize inefficient activity. Typically cabinets are built-in along two opposing walls, making use of vertical storage. First mass-produced for public housing after World War I in Germany, it became known as the Frankfurt Kitchen. (Chapter 5)

General lighting See ambient lighting.

Generations X and Y Persons born between 1965 and 1994 are in this generation. (Chapter 13)

Geometric shape A category of shape, whether straight or curvilinear, that is regular (e.g., square, rectangle, triangle, or circle). With knowledge of one dimension, a mathematical formula can be used to calculate other dimensions. (Chapter 3)

Gestalt psychology The study of perception and behavior that purports that humans naturally perceive things as a whole, as complete and therefore comprehensible to them. (Chapter 3)

Glare Brightness that is more than the eye can naturally adapt to. (Chapter 7)

Glazing The use of glass as a construction material or the process of fitting glass into frames as a construction method. (Chapter 8)

Glulam (glue a laminated timber) A type of structural timber product composed of several layers of smaller pieces of timber laminated together to form vertical columns or horizontal beams as well as curved, arched shapes. (Chapter 8)

Golden mean See Golden section (golden mean).

Golden section (golden mean) A formula used by the ancient Greeks that was thought to approximate the best proportions, producing the most universally appealing relationship among parts. The ratio of the larger to the smaller of two parts is the same as the ratio of the whole to the larger part. (Chapter 3)

Gondola chair A chair shaped to follow the contours of the body, popular during the Empire period. (Chapter 11)

Gray good See Greige good (gray good).

Graywater Domestic (non-toilet) wastewater that can be treated for nonpotable (nondrinkable) use, such as landscaping. (Chapter 8)

Great hall A large room in a medieval house or castle that provided space for the many serfs (peasants who worked the land) maintained by the landowner or lord. (Chapter 11)

Great room A contemporary term to describe a large, open interior space that is multifunctional, such as for dining and entertaining; a derivative of the communal great hall of the medieval castles in Europe. (Chapter 5)

Green Building Certification Institute (GBCI) An organization that provides independent oversight of professional credentialing and project certification programs related to green building design; see LEED. (Chapter 1)

Greige The way a textile's color is described when in its natural form, not dyed or finished; also a term to describe a hue that is a mixture of the ranges of brown with gray; sometimes called taupe. (Chapter 4)

Greige good (gray good) Fabric that retains its natural color or is left uncolored if synthetic. (Chapter 10)

Grille The outlet opening in an interior that connects to a duct in a forced hot air heating system; also called register. (Chapter 8)

Grisaille A technique that was developed during the Renaissance for painting in gray scale. (Chapter 11)

Grotesque Monstrous and fantastical creatures that are typical Renaissance motifs. (Chapter 11)

Grout The filler used between tiles, generally a mortar or cement mixture. (Chapter 9)

Gueridon A small table or stand to hold a candelabrum or other small articles. (Chapter 11)

Guild A type of organization that had its heyday in feudal society in the 13th century, in which members practiced a craft associated with a similar pursuit, advancing from apprentice to master artisan. (Chapter 1)

Gypsum wallboard (GWB) See Gypsum wall partition (GWP). (Chapter 8)

Gypsum wall partition (GWP) A panel made of the mineral gypsum, a calcium sulfate over metal lath, used in drywall construction; also called Sheetrock or plasterboard. (Chapter 8)

Halogen A subcategory of incandescent lighting, more accurately called tungsten-halogen or quartz-halogen, depending on its casing. Halogen lamps render colors better than A lamps and burn at a continuous rate or level of brightness, making them more predictable in effect. (Chapter 7)

Hand A term used to describe the feel of a fabric to the touch. (Chapter 10)

Hard flooring Flooring made from materials such as wood, bamboo, stone, ceramic, and glass. (Chapter 9)

Hardwood (deciduous) tree Wood from trees that bear broad leaves in an annual cycle of growth and decay. (Chapter 9)

Hieroglyphics A pictorial script painted or carved on the walls of ancient Egyptian structures that offers details about their civilization, customs, religion, and technical skills. (Chapter 11)

Highboy (tallboy) A tall version of a chest-on-chest, typical of the Chippendale style and Queen Anne period in England and America. (Chapter 11)

High-intensity discharge (HID) lamp A type of lamp that relies on passage of an electric current through a gas or vapor under high pressure. The three basic categories are mercury vapor, high-pressure sodium, and metal halide. (Chapter 7)

High key (color range) A choice of hues in the high-value (lighter) range. (Chapter 4)

Historicism The replication of a period style through strict and studied references. (Chapter 12)

Homeostasis A feeling of equilibrium and well-being. (Chapter 2)

Horizontal line A line that is parallel to the plane of the earth, its horizon. This type of line denotes stability, ever-present nature, rest, and repose—qualities that represent our perception of the earth's horizon. (Chapter 3)

Horizon line In a perspective drawing, the viewer's eye level. The standard convention is for this to be approximately 5 feet, 0 inches. (Chapter 6)

Hue The family of a color or the way in which one color (e.g., red) is distinguished from another (e.g., yellow); often used interchangeably with the word *color*. (Chapter 3)

Human engineering The way in which humans and things interact effectively; see ergonomics. (Chapter 2)

Human scale A recognizable, constant range of expected human size, used in comparison with an object or a structure. (Chapter 3)

HVAC Heating, ventilation, air-conditioning (Chapter 2, Chapter 8)

Hydronic A cost-effective, energy-efficient radiant heating system that utilizes heated water as the medium to transfer uniform heating. (Chapter 8)

Ikat A resist printing technique that originated in Indonesia; produces a distinguishable blurred pattern. (Chapter 10)

Incandescence The temperature at which an electric filament begins to glow, producing light. (Chapter 7)

Incandescent lighting A type of electric lighting produced by the application of electric energy to a thin wire filament until it reaches the point of incandescence, which causes the filament to glow. It is perceived as more yellow than natural light; is less energy efficient than newer lamps; becoming obsolete in usage. (Chapter 7)

Independent contractor A person who is self-employed and working on a freelance basis rather than for one employer or, strictly speaking, as a business entity. (Chapter 14)

Indigo A natural plant dye from the indigo plant, generally an inky blue color (Chapter 10)

Indirect cost A cost of doing business that cannot be assigned to a particular project; for example, rent of a designer's office space. (Chapter 14)

Indirect lighting A technique that directs light toward a secondary object before striking the primary object. (Chapter 7)

Indiscret A conversation sofa, popular during the Second Empire period in France. (Chapter 12)

Industrial design The practice of combining art and industry with mass production. (Chapter 12)

Informational interview A more informal meeting than one required of a job applicant. It is a way to learn more about a firm or business before applying for employment and/or to learn more about an industry or product. (Chapter 14)

Intergenerational design The design of environments where persons of different age groups have the chance to interact and learn from each other. (Chapter 5)

Interior architect A term used, especially in Europe, to describe the occupation taken up by several 18th-century men who employed cabinetmakers, painters, and sculptors to execute their designs for interiors. (Chapter 1)

Interior decoration Decoration of an interior through ornamentation that enhances the space, adds to its individuality, and may provide psychological and symbolic comforts, but is not required to meet the most basic universal human needs of safety and protection. (Chapter 1)

Interior decorator An individual who works only with surface decoration, such as paints, fabrics, and furnishings. (Chapter 1)

Interior design The planning and design of architectural interiors and their furnishings, including the necessities of the space relating to issues of safety and protection. As a specialty profession, it began to develop separately from architecture in the 18th century. (Chapter 1)

Interior designer An individual who works with both the interior architecture and the furnishings of a space and whose preparation for the profession includes education and/or certification. (Chapter 1)

Interior Design Continuing Education Council (IDCEC) A volunteer organization whose mission is to review courses for approval to be counted as continuing education units (CEUs) for several of the interior design organizations and educational conferences. (Chapter 1)

Interior Design Educators Council (IDEC) An organization primarily composed of college educators and researchers in the field of interior design. IDEC's mission is the advancement of interior design education and scholarship by promoting recognition of the contribution of interior design education, scholarship, and practice to the advancement of quality of life within the built environment. (Chapter 1)

Interior Design Experience Program (IDEP) Administered by the NCIDQ to provide a structure for the entry level interior designer to transition from formal education to professional practice. Components include preparation for the NCIDQ examination and documentation of employment experience. (Chapter 14)

International Interior Design Association (IIDA) An international organization founded in 1994 to represent interior designers worldwide and created by the merger of the Institute of Business Designers (IBD), the International Society of Interior Designers (ISID), and the Council of Federal Interior Designers (CFID). (Chapter 1)

Intimate distance The shortest of the four distance zones identified by the American sociologist Edward T. Hall (1914–2009); it corresponds to a space up to 18 inches between individuals. See also Proxemics. (Chapter 2)

Invoice A bill for payment. (Chapter 14)

Ionic A style of ancient Greek capital featuring volutes or spirals. (Chapter 11)

Iridescence A lustrous effect of light and color mixing, resulting in a rainbow-like array of colors. It may be created when natural or artificial light refracts off a surface that is slick, either as a natural condition or in a manufactured product designed to cast that effect. (Chapter 4)

Isometric projection A drawing that relies on the use of three axes, each at 30 degrees. (Chapter 6)

Jabot A folded fabric that hangs down the sides of the window; also called cascade. (Chapter 10)

Jacquard loom The name of a specific loom invented in 18th-century France that assists in the production of weaving large, complex patterns, rather than one particular print pattern. (Chapter 10)

Jamb The frame for a door or window. (Chapter 8)

Japanning Black finish that is lacquered in the style of the Orient. (Chapter 12)

Japonism The influence of the arts of Japan on those of the West; popular in the late 19th century. (Chapter 12)

Jasperware A type of porcelain object known for its matte glaze, used by Josiah Wedgwood (1730–1795) in the Neoclassical style. (Chapter 11)

Joinery The technique of connecting wood members together. See also Spline and Tongue and groove. (Chapter 9)

Joint venture A temporary association of two or more persons or firms for the purpose of completing a project. (Chapter 14)

Joist system A system of construction in which wood or concrete beams (joists) are spaced close together, horizontally, to support load-bearing walls. A deck (or platform) made of either wood or concrete is then applied. (Chapter 8)

Jute Derived from a grass, and considered a green product, is used to create burlap, a material used in the construction of upholstered furniture and as the backing, or lining, for carpet and linoleum. (Chapter 10)

Kaolin White clay; an essential part of the Chinese recipe for hard-paste porcelain. (Chapter 11)

Kast (or kas) Of Dutch origin. Similar to an armoire, but wider, at times measuring 8 feet high and 8 feet wide. (Chapter 11)

Kelvin scale A scale used to determine the warmth or coolness of light (i.e., the ratio of red to blue). Lower Kelvin values represent warmer temperatures; higher values, cooler temperatures. (Chapter 7)

Key lighting See Accent lighting.

Kilim A category of a flat woven rug attributed to Central Asia and Turkey; similar to Navajo rugs in the United States. (Chapter 9)

Kline An elongated version of the throne chair of ancient Greece; an early form of couch. (Chapter 11)

Klismos An ancient Greek chair featuring a curved back (yoke) and legs that sway backward, concave, (referred to as saber legs); and woven seat. (Chapter 11)

Kuba An African textile. After the Central African tribe that produces it, is made from raffia that is appliquéd or embroidered with abstract patterns and colored with local plant dyes, typically black, yellow, and red. (Chapter 13)

Lambrequin A structure generally made of wood and upholstered with fabric, which frames the sides as well as the top of a window treatment. (Chapter 10)

Laminate A generic term used to describe several products, including flooring and doors, created by high-pressure lamination techniques; it implies a multilayered product. (Chapter 9)

Laminated flooring See All-wood construction.

Lamp The technical term for what is generally referred to as a light bulb by lay persons. (Chapter 7)

Lamp life The average rated life span of a lamp (i.e., how long before it is expected to burn out). (Chapter 7)

Landing A resting area in a staircase. (Chapter 8)

Lateral load Includes wind loads and earthquake loads, planned for in the original design of the building. (Chapter 8)

Latex paint Water-based paint. (Chapter 9)

Lath A wood strip used as a building material, such as for wall construction. (Chapter 8)

Lawson A type of seating in which the arm height is lower than the back height. (Chapter 10)

Lead time The amount of time estimated between placing an order and receipt of the goods. (Chapter 14)

LEED An acronym for Leadership in Energy and Environmental Design; an internationally recognized voluntary green building certification system developed by the U.S. Green Building Council (USGBC) to establish a variety of rating systems for the residential and commercial building and construction industries. (Chapter 1)

Legend In a plan, the explanation for a list of symbols. (Chapter 6)

Letter of agreement A written document that serves as a contract between parties and spells out the scope of a project, the parties and their responsibilities, the services to be rendered, terms for payment of goods, compensation for services, ownership and rights, and termination and arbitration clauses. (Chapter 14)

Licensed interior designer A person who has met certain education, experience, and examination requirements and is registered with the interior design board in his or her state. (Chapter 14)

Life-cycle cost A calculation of cost relative to the product's life expectancy. (Chapter 8)

Light-emitting diode (LED) An electrically charged lighting source derived from digital technology in which a microprocessor color chip is used to program a full range of color at steady or random intervals. (Chapter 7)

Lighting plan A component of the contract documents plan that includes all fixtures (e.g., portable table and floor lamps, wall sconces, and dimmer and switching controls). It may be combined with a reflected ceiling plan or be a separate plan. (Chapter 5)

Light primaries The three colors of light that, when combined, produce white light: red, green, and blue. (Chapter 2)

Light reflectance value (LRV) A measurement that uses a scale from 0 to 100 percent. At 0 percent, no light is reflected; at 100 percent, all light is reflected. (Chapter 7)

Limited liability corporation (LLC) A type of hybrid business entity that combines features of corporations and partnerships. LLC has a sole proprietor. (Chapter 14)

Limited liability partnership (LLP) A type of hybrid business entity that combines features of corporations and partnerships. In LLP there is more than one member. (Chapter 14)

Lincrusta An invention from the Victorian period, a heavily embossed wall covering that could be painted or varnished to resemble leather, wood, or plaster. (Chapter 12)

Line A one-dimensional unit, either straight or curvilinear, that gives dimension to a space and is created by connecting two points. (Chapter 3)

Linenfold A type of carving suggesting fabric folds and used to adorn walls, chests, and chair backs in the medieval period. (Chapter 11)

Line voltage Standard voltage, usually 120V in the United States, which is carried through electrical transmission lines. (Chapter 7)

Linoleum A processed mixture of natural substances that contains solidified linseed oil from the flax plant, cork and wood flour, limestone, and pigments. It is backed with jute, installed in sheets or tiles for flooring, and has a long life cycle. (Chapter 9)

List price The price at which an item is offered for sale in a showroom or retail facility; also called retail price. (Chapter 14)

Lit bateau A boat-shaped bed, typical of the Empire period, that was draped with fabric and placed with one side against the wall. (Chapter 11)

Lit de repos A type of French sofa of the Renaissance, inspired by the ancient Greek couch. (Chapter 11)

Live load The weight of the occupants and furnishings in a building. (Chapter 8)

Local lighting See Task lighting.

Long gallery A long, narrow room, often running the length of a house's frontage; typically used for exercise, games, and social events and to display collections, such as Chinese porcelains. (Chapter 11)

Loop pile A tufted carpet or rug surface in which the yarn loops are left uncut. (Chapter 9)

Lowboy A short chest of drawers on legs, typical of the Chippendale style and Queen Anne period in England and America. (Chapter 11)

Low key (color range) A choice of hues in the low-value (darker) range. (Chapter 4)

Low voltage Voltage that has been stepped down, usually through a transformer, to 12V for use by residential and commercial customers. (Chapter 7)

Lumen The international unit used to measure the quantity of light; sometimes referred to as luminous flux. (Chapter 7)

Lumen per watt (LPW) A measurement of the efficiency of a lamp. (Chapter 7)

Luminaire The technical term for a complete lighting unit or fixture. (Chapter 7)

Luminance The level of brightness of a lamp. (Chapter 7)

Luminosity The inherent ability of a hue to reflect light; yellow is the most luminous, violet the least. (Chapter 4)

Luminous flux See Lumen.

Lux The metric equivalent of *foot-candle;* used in measuring light level. One foot-candle equals 10 lux. (Chapter 7)

Marquise A small sofa or wide upholstered armchair (bergère), typical of the French Rococo style. (Chapter 11)

Masonry The term used to describe certain building materials, including concrete, brick (kiln-fired clay), and stone (various types of rocks). These materials are generally bonded together with mortar, a mixture of water and cement. (Chapter 8)

Mass The spatial dimensions of a three-dimensional form; the property that gives it weight. (Chapter 3)

Material board See Sample board.

Mauve A term coined to describe a purple color produced synthetically beginning in 1859. (Chapter 12)

Melon (cup and cover) A term used to describe furniture legs with bulbous turnings, typical for English Renaissance style. (Chapter 11)

Memo A large sample, such as a piece of fabric, that is loaned to the designer and is to be returned to a showroom, generally within a specified time frame, such as 30 days. (Chapter 14)

Menuisier The French term for a cabinetmaker or joiner who specializes in solid wood and carving. (Chapter 11)

Metamerism The phenomenon in which colors under different lighting situations do not appear the same. (Chapter 7)

Mid-value scheme A term often used to describe contrasting color schemes with hues of medium lightness. (Chapter 4)

Millennial Persons born after the mid-1990s are often called Millennials. (Chapter 13)

Millwork The term used to describe woodwork, including wall and ceiling panels, molding, door finishes, window trim, cabinetry, mantels, and built-in furniture. (Chapter 9)

Mirror reflector (MR) halogen lamp A type of halogen lamp that uses a reflector, operates on low voltage, and is often part of a track or cable system suspended from the ceiling. (Chapter 7)

Modular furniture Furniture that is flexible, portable, and composed of separate pieces. (Chapter 12)

Monochromatic color scheme A color scheme derived from the use of only one hue. It may include different values and chroma levels to avoid monotony. (Chapter 4)

Mortise and tenon A type of wood joinery for furniture that combines a projection inserted into an opening. (Chapter 11).

Motif Distinctive feature or element of a design or ornament; a theme. (Chapter 3)

Mullion A thin vertical member that divides the components of a door or window. (Chapter 8)

Multidirectional lighting (omnidirectional lighting) A type of diffuse lighting that provides an overall uniform illumination to a space rather than illuminating a specific object. (Chapter 4)

Muntin A strip separating panes of glass in a sash. (Chapter 8)

Nanometer (nm) One billionth of a meter. Wavelengths of light are measured in nanometers (nm). (Chapter 4)

National Association of Schools of Art and Design (NASAD) Organization that reviews college level educational programs in the fields of art and design against established criteria in order to accredit the programs accordingly. (Chapter 1)

National Council for Interior Design Qualification (NCIDQ) An organization that serves to identify those interior designers who have met the minimum standards for professional practice by passing an examination. NCIDQ continually updates the examination to reflect expanding professional knowledge and design development techniques. (Chapter 1)

Natural light A type of lighting that includes daylight, flame, candle, and skylight. (Chapter 3)

Neon lighting A type of colored light produced as a result of different gases or vapors and commonly used in commercial signs and billboards. (Chapter 7)

Net price See Cost (net price).

Net 30 account An account for which payment is required within 30 days from the date an order is placed; see also Open (net 30) account. (Chapter 14)

Neutral color scheme A color harmony scheme produced with various values and tones of the brown family. These hues usually fall into the warm side of the color wheel. (Chapter 4)

Neutral gray A mixture of black and white only in various ratios. (Chapter 4)

Neutralization A process whereby hues are toned down to result in a grayish, muddy brown or black, depending on the particular hues and their ratios. (Chapter 4)

Nonesuch A type of paneled chest used in 16th-century England. (Chapter 11)

Occasional furniture Lightweight, movable furniture. (Chapter 10)

Off-gassing The process by which volatile organic compounds (VOCs) are released into an interior environment. (Chapter 2)

Olfactory The sensory experience of smell, delivered through the nose. (Chapter 2)

Omnidirectional lighting See Multidirectional lighting (omnidirectional lighting).

Open (floor) plan A concept of interior design that eliminates walls between rooms. (Chapter 8)

Open (net 30) account An account for which orders are accepted without advance payment for the goods. (Chapter 14)

Organic architecture A theory of architecture utilized by Frank Lloyd Wright (1867–1959) that proposes that the core of a home should extend outward into the landscape. (Chapter 8)

Organic light-emitting diode (OLED) A lighting device based on organic (carbon-based) materials which emit light in response to an electric current. (Chapter 7)

Organic shape A shape that is based on nature and living objects, whether in the animal (and human) or plant kingdom. It includes amorphous or amorphic (i.e., without a definitive shape), biomorphic or zoomorphic (i.e., representing human or animal components), and botanical shapes (i.e., representing the plant world, including vines, leaves, flowers, and fruits). (Chapter 3)

Ormolu Gilded or golden brass or bronze used for decorative purposes (e.g., furniture mounts); typical of French furniture in the 18th century. (Chapter 11)

Ornament Visual detail that is purely decorative, not functional. (Chapter 3)

Orthographic drawing A drawing that consists of a two-dimensional projection of a plane, like a vertical or horizontal slice through the space. It includes the different types of plans, elevations, and sections used to convey a proposed design. (Chapter 6)

Ottoman (pouf) A type of low, upholstered seating, inspired by Turkish design, typical of the Victorian period. (Chapter 12)

Out-of-pocket expense See Reimbursable (out-of-pocket) expense.

Overhead The cost to a firm for doing business, which includes leasing, renting, or buying space and equipment; insurance; utilities; maintenance; advertising; professional dues; and office supplies. (Chapter 14)

Pagoda Was first built as a temple and was believed to ward off flood, deter winds, and improve the prosperity of the people. (Chapter 11)

Paisley A plantlike motif from India. (Chapter 10)

Parabolic aluminized reflector (PAR) lamp A type of reflector lamp, widely used in outdoor applications, that is made of two pieces of glass fused together: one is the reflector and the other the lens. (Chapter 7)

Paraline drawing The simplest and most accurate of the three-dimensional drawings, which uses the same scale and width and length measurements for furnishings as those used on the floor plan but includes height for walls and for each piece of furniture and architectural element (e.g., windows and doors). (Chapter 6)

Parallel rule (straightedge) A drawing tool that consists of a bar the same width as the drafting table, and attached with screws, that slides up and down by a pulley. (Chapter 6)

Parquet (block) flooring Flooring composed of blocks of hardwood, generally in the form of squares of smaller pieces that may be applied in various patterns; also called block flooring. (Chapter 9)

Partition An interior wall that separates rooms and may be floor-to-ceiling height or a partial height. (Chapter 8)

Passementerie A French word that describes the array of ornamental trimmings used for soft window treatments, upholstered furniture, and textiles for bed, bath, and tabletop. (Chapter 10)

Passive solar energy Systems that capture and store direct solar energy to heat buildings and water without the use of mechanical devices. (Chapter 8)

Pattern The repetition of a specific shape, theme, figure, or motif that is discernible as a distinct entity; it may be either applied or structural. (Chapter 3)

Pelmet A type of top window treatment with a frame made of fabric that is stiffened with buckram, a type of jute or cotton. (Chapter 10)

Pendant A lighting fixture that is suspended from the ceiling on a stem or chain; a large-scale pendant is commonly known as a chandelier. (Chapter 7)

Performance specifications Expectations for products, such as how well they will perform (or last) under specific conditions (e.g., heavy-duty traffic). (Chapter 5)

Personal distance The second shortest of the four distance zones identified by the American sociologist Edward T. Hall (1914–2009); it corresponds to a space of 18 inches to 4 feet between individuals. See also Proxemics. (Chapter 2)

Personalization The efforts of human beings to make their environments reflect individuality. (Chapter 2)

Perspective drawing A drawing that adds volume or three-dimensionality to the concept for the design of an interior space. Interior designers typically produce one- or two-point perspective drawings. (Chapter 5)

Photobiology A science that examines the interaction of light and the human experience with those lighting choices. (Chapter 7)

Photo linear system A method of one- or two-point perspective drawing that may be used on-site. It involves supplies for measuring a sidewall of the interior, as well as photo imaging and print capability. (Chapter 7)

Phototherapy A therapeutic technique that uses full-spectrum lighting and lighting box devices to simulate natural light; helpful in alleviating seasonal affective disorder (SAD). (Chapter 2)

Photovoltaics (PV) Solar cells that convert sunlight into electrical energy; an energy efficient system often installed in panels. (Chapter 8)

Pictorial drawing A drawing that provides a more realistic view of a space through use of a singular graphic. It may be further categorized as either paraline or plan oblique. (Chapter 7)

Picture plane An imaginary transparent plane, like glass, through which an area to be drawn is viewed. (Chapter 6)

Picture window A large expanse of glass, generally fixed. (Chapter 8)

Pietre dura The technique of creating a mosaic of colored stones forming a pattern, typical of the Italian Baroque style. (Chapter 11)

Pigment Natural or synthetic coloring matter. (Chapter 9)

Pilaster A column-like feature projecting slightly from a surface such as a wall or façade. (Chapter 11)

Pile The face yarn of a tufted carpet or rug. (Chapter 9)

Plain weave A type of weaving pattern in which rows of crosswise yarn passing over and under lengthwise yarn alternate with rows of crosswise yarn passing under and over lengthwise yarn to produce a checkerboard. (Chapter 10)

Plan In the contract documents package, any of several types of drawings depicting proposed layouts on a particular plane (e.g., the floor or ceiling). (Chapter 5)

Plane A flat surface, often rectilinear in shape, such as those of floors, walls, and ceilings. (Chapter 3)

Plank-and-beam system A system of construction that is similar to a joist system that spaces the joists or beams farther apart. (Chapter 8)

Plan oblique A type of paraline drawing that is a projection from an existing plan rotated to the angle the designer selects; the most common choices are 30/60 degrees or 45/45 degrees. The total degrees of each choice always add up to 90 degrees. (Chapter 6)

Plantation shutters A type of window shutter with wide blades. (Chapter 10)

Plasterboard See Gypsum wall partition (GWP).

Plenum A space above a suspended ceiling that can accommodate heating ducts and wiring. (Chapter 8)

Plush (velvet) pile A type of cut pile carpet or rug in which the pile is deep. (Chapter 9)

Plywood Thin sheets of wood glued together. (Chapter 8)

Poché From the French for "pocket"; the designer fills in the two lines of the wall to create its thickness on a floor plan. (Chapter 6)

Polychrome Application of more than one pigment color. (Chapter 11)

Pop-up retail A retail approach to supplement their ongoing retail establishments to test out the viability of selected locations, to test-market new products, or for seasonal merchandising; a temporary installation. (Chapter 5)

Porcelain ceramic A type of high-quality ceramic tile used for flooring. (Chapter 9)

Portico A roofed porch held up by columns. (Chapter 11)

Post and lintel (post and beam) A system of construction comprised of vertical (post) and horizontal supports (lintel or beam). (Chapter 11)

Postcompletion step The final step in the design process during which the interior designer and client evaluate the end results; also called postoccupancy evaluation (POE). (Chapter 5)

Postoccupancy evaluation (POE) See Postcompletion step.

Pouf See Ottoman (pouf).

Powder room (half-bath) Contains a toilet and sink area, with no bathing facilities. (Chapter 5)

Power and communications plan A component of the contract documents package that includes telephone and electrical wiring information for computers, and electrical wiring for acoustical equipment, security, intercom systems, and so on. (Chapter 5)

Practice act A type of law that requires an individual to have a license in order to practice a profession.

Practice acts prohibit the performance of professional services by anyone not licensed by the government agency charged with the duty of regulating that profession. (Chapter 14)

Preproject step The first step in the design process, during which the relationship between a prospective client and the interior designer is established. (Chapter 5)

Presentation model A more finished three-dimensional model than a study model, done to scale to show the interior of a space. (Chapter 6)

Press cupboard Similar to a court cupboard, but with more closed space for storage; typically used in England in the 16th and 17th centuries. (Chapter 11)

Primaries of color The three primary color pigments that, when mixed together, produce black: red, yellow, and blue. (Chapter 3)

Primaries of light White light is composed of the three primaries of light: red, green, and blue. (Chapter 3)

Primer The first coat applied to a substrate to prepare it for subsequent finishing coats. (Chapter 9)

Privy In the medieval house, the private quarters for the lord and his important guests and consisting primarily of a bed and sitting area, chapel, and kitchen. (Chapter 11)

Professional corporation (PC) A type of business organization often used by licensed professional such as doctors, lawyers, and accountants; varies from state to state. (Chapter 14)

Pro forma account An account for which payment in full is expected prior to processing an order for goods. (Chapter 14)

Programming phase The first phase of an interior design project in which, through data gathering and analysis, the designer determines the requirements that need to be met, culminating in a design concept to describe the proposed character of the space. A written program or plan of action, preliminary budget estimates, and projected time schedules are then developed. (Chapter 5)

Project manager A person assigned to manage the phases of an interior design project to ensure not only that a prescribed work plan is developed, but also that the project is executed according to that plan and in a timely manner. (Chapter 5)

Proxemics The study of the nature of spatial distances maintained by persons under different circumstances pioneered by the American sociologist Edward T. Hall (1914–2009) in the 1960s. (Chapter 2)

Public distance The longest of the four distance zones identified by the American sociologist Edward T. Hall (1914–2009); it corresponds to a space of 12 feet or more between individuals; see also Proxemics. (Chapter 2)

Puddling A formal drapery treatment in which the hemline falls below floor level so that the excess fabric is arranged on the floor. (Chapter 10)

Punch list A list that outlines outstanding or deficient items at the final stages of installation for a project. (Chapter 5)

Purchase order An order for goods, which serves as a contract between the designer as the buyer of goods or services and the supplier as seller of goods or services. (Chapter 14)

PVC Polyvinyl chloride; see Vinyl.

Qi (chi) The philosophy of the ancient Chinese thought to be the breath that created the universe. (Chapter 11)

Quartz-halogen A type of halogen lamp that uses quartz for its casing. (Chapter 5)

Quaternary level When all the tertiary colors are mixed with either a primary or secondary hue a 24-color wheel or extended color wheel is created. (Chapter 4)

Radial balance An equilibrium that relies on a center point, which serves as the axis around which elements of equal visual weight are arranged. (Chapter 3)

Radiant air heating Heating accommodated within a raised structural floor used for newer commercial buildings and in many contemporary residential interiors. (Chapter 8)

Rafter A beam used to support a roof. (Chapter 8)

Railroading A method of constructing fabric patterns so that they may be laid horizontally rather than vertically. (Chapter 10)

Rattan A type of plant stem that is bent into shapes and used to construct furniture. (Chapter 10)

Rebar (reinforced bar) An addition of steel rods to reinforce concrete foundations. (Chapter 8)

Recamier A version of the resting or day bed, usually a backless couch with a high curved headrest and a low footrest, popular during the Empire period. (Chapter 11)

Recessed fixture A lighting fixture that is essentially hidden in the architecture, often the ceiling. (Chapter 7)

Reflect Wavelengths that are not absorbed into the wall's surface or transmitted through it are bounced back, carrying information about the color. (Chapter 4)

Reflected ceiling plan A component of the contract documents package that includes all architectural elements that interface with the ceiling. It may detail the types and locations of lighting and ceiling fan fixtures; ceiling materials; sprinkler, smoke detector, and air temperature control systems; and partitions that touch the ceiling. (Chapter 5)

Refract bend The bending of a light wave as it penetrates a surface to produce varying wavelengths and thereby hues. (Chapter 4)

Register See Grille.

Registered interior designer A person who has met certain education, experience, and examination requirements and is registered with the interior design board in his or her state or province. (Chapter 14)

Reimbursable (out-of-pocket) expense An incidental cost, such as for travel expenses, long-distance telephone calls, or blueprinting, related specifically to a project and therefore billed to the client. (Chapter 14)

Related color scheme A color scheme derived by focusing on unifying or similar attributes of the selections. It is considered more calming and stable than a contrasting color scheme. (Chapter 4)

Rendering The term applied to the various hand or computer-assisted drawing techniques used to flesh out designs so that they ring true to life. (Chapter 6)

Renewable A term describing a resource that is not endangered or threatened as it is easily renewed within a fairly short time, such as bamboo. (Chapter 5)

Repeat The repeat of a pattern is the distance from the start of the pattern to the end of the pattern. This measurement needs to be considered for both horizontal and vertical directions. (Chapter 10)

Request for proposals See Bid procurement.

Resale number An identification number issued by governments to persons such as interior designers that authorizes a person to resell goods to a buyer and collect and pay the applicable taxes on behalf of the government. (Chapter 14)

Residential interior design A category of design that focuses on the planning and specification of interior materials and products used in private residences. (Chapter 1)

Resilient flooring A type of flooring that provides greater shock absorption and more give than hard flooring surfaces. It includes natural and synthetic surfaces such as vinyl, rubber, linoleum, cork, asphalt, combinations, and laminates. (Chapter 9)

Resin A natural, yellowish, translucent substance usually formed from plant secretions or a synthetic variety with similar properties. (Chapter 9)

Restocking charge A fee that is applied by a supplier to a buyer for the inconvenience of accepting overage goods, usually fabric or wall covering. (Chapter 14)

Retail price See List price.

Retainer A down payment or deposit for services to be rendered. (Chapter 5)

Retro Something retro is a style, trend, or fashion modeled on something from the past. (Chapter 13)

Return The distance of a drapery from the wall. (Chapter 10)

Revivalism The revival of aspects of a previous period style; typically associated with the Victorian period; not necessarily based on accurate historic representation. (Chapter 12)

Riser The height of a stair. (Chapter 8)

Rose window Stained glass windows primarily found in churches and cathedrals. (Chapter 11)

Rough plumbing The stage in which the placement of pipes and drains for a building is planned. (Chapter 8)

Rubble Rough stone used for exterior walls. (Chapter 8)

Rug A term generally used for fiber finished flooring that is loosely laid over an area rather than installed, or affixed wall-to-wall. (Chapter 9)

Rush A thick reed-like plant with a hollow stem used in weaving chair seats and other furniture. (Chapter 10)

Rya A type of woven rug from Scandinavia. (Chapter 9)

Saber leg A furniture leg that curves backward, as seen in the Greek klismos. (Chapter 11)

Safety glass A glass that is produced by laminating a sheet of transparent plastic between sheets of clear glass. It is similar to tempered glass in its resistance to impact. (Chapter 8)

Sample board A presentation prepared to illustrate the types of materials and furnishings being considered to carry out a design concept; also called material board. (Chapter 5)

Satin weave A type of weaving pattern in which lengthwise (or sometimes crosswise) yarns float over several yarns before interlacing to give a smooth feel and lustrous appearance. (Chapter 10)

Savonarola chair An X-shaped chair typical of the Italian Renaissance; similar to the Dante chair but with additional supports. (Chapter 11)

Savonnerie A type of finely woven tapestry or rug from France. (Chapter 9)

Saxony A type of cut pile that has more twist to the yarn than plush and is considered less formal than the plush style. (Chapter 9)

Scale A comparison of the relative size of two or more objects; often a comparison of an unknown sized object to the known dimension of the human scale. (Chapter 3)

Scalloping A wall lighting technique that spaces fixtures in such a way as to create overlapping pools of light shaped like a scallop; essentially a form of accent lighting. (Chapter 7)

Schedule In the contract documents package, a document that provides supplementary notes (e.g., a recommended type of fixture and its location). (Chapter 5)

Schematic A diagrammatic representation of the framework for a plan. (Chapter 5)

Schematic design phase The second phase of an interior design project in which drawings and other documents are prepared to depict the design concept and solutions, including the formulation of ideas for space allocation, layouts for furniture and equipment, and the types of finishes to be used. (Chapter 5)

Sconce A wall-mounted lighting fixture. (Chapter 4)

Seasonal affective disorder (SAD) A psychological condition in which depression occurs as daylight decreases during the fall and winter seasons. Various therapies, often utilizing full-spectrum lighting, are employed to alleviate the symptoms. (Chapter 2, Chapter 7)

Secretaire-à-abattant A type of fall-front desk that combines a writing surface with drawers, popular during the Neoclassical period. (Chapter 11)

Section A drawing that shows a vertical slice of a design that illustrates wall thickness in addition to other elements. (Chapter 5)

Sedia A Renaissance-style armchair with a tall back and high, upholstered seat. (Chapter 11)

Selective absorption When white light falls on an opaque object, the surface of the object, such as Newton's wall, absorbs certain wavelengths of the light and reflects others. (Chapter 4)

Semainier A French term for a tall, narrow chest of seven drawers, one for each day of the week, typical of the Neoclassical period. (Chapter 11)

Semiflush fixture See Semi-recessed (semifllush) fixture.

Semi-recessed (semiflush) fixture A lighting fixture that is suspended only slightly. (Chapter 7)

Settee A lightweight, rather delicate sofa on legs, typically seats two or three persons; often distinguished by a carved back and front legs spaced according to the number of people it was intended to seat. (Chapter 11)

Settle A version of a wood bench with back and arms, based on seating of the medieval period derived from a storage chest; it was popularized during the Arts and Crafts movement. (Chapter 12)

Sgabello Italian Renaissance wooden side chair with small seat and three legs. (Chapter 11)

Shade A lower value of a hue created by adding black, developing a darker version. (Chapter 3)

Shagreen The skin of the stingray, popular as a covering for furniture in French Art Nouveau and Art Deco styles. (Chapter 12)

Shape A two-dimensional unit, such as a square, created as a line shifts direction, developing both length and width. (Chapter 3)

Sheathed In a wall framing system, to be wrapped with a layer, usually of plywood or fiberboard. (Chapter 8)

Sheen level A term that refers to the reflectance of light by a surface layer; used in describing paint. (Chapter 9)

Sheetrock See Gypsum wall partition (GWP).

Shim space A space around a window unit that helps to stabilize the unit. (Chapter 8)

Shop drawings Drawings, diagrams, illustrations, schedules, and other documents prepared by contractors that illustrate how specific portions of the work on an interior design project will be fabricated or installed. (Chapter 5)

Sick building (office) syndrome A term coined to reflect the situation in which worker absenteeism or lack of productivity is attributed to vague, hard-to-diagnose complaints, including dizziness, faintness, and fatigue, caused in most cases by inadequate air circulation exacerbating the negative effects of pollutants (e.g., paints, stains, synthetic chemicals, and adhesives). (Chapter 2)

Sidemark (tag) An identifying remark (e.g., Smith dining room) affixed to a purchase order for an item that accompanies it during shipping; also called tag. (Chapter 14)

Simultaneous contrast The way in which colors influence each other, by attributes of hue, value, and chroma, when placed next to each other or simultaneously viewed. (Chapter 4)

Singerie A French Rococo motif featuring humorous, playful depictions of monkeys, often in European dress. (Chapter 11)

Sited The manner in which a property is located or positioned (e.g., northern or southern exposure). (Chapter 5)

Sketch A rough drawing outlining the key features of an object, space, or concept. It often serves as a preliminary study for the designer or as a quick way to communicate ideas to others and is based on approximations, not exact measurements. (Chapter 6)

Sketch model See Study model.

Skim coat An extensive preparation of walls that are in poor condition prior to finishing with a paint coating. (Chapter 9)

Skylight A window placed in a roof or ceiling. (Chapter 8)

Social distance The next to the longest of the four distance zones identified by the American sociologist Edward T. Hall; it corresponds to a space of 4 feet to 12 feet between individuals; see also Proxemics. (Chapter 2)

Socially responsible design An interior design approach that focuses on designing for the present with current resources while planning for and anticipating the future. It is mindful of preserving natural resources, including human resources, land resources, and energy. (Chapter 2)

Softwood Wood from evergreens, such as pine and fir that bear needle-like leaves; also called coniferous. (Chapter 9)

Sole proprietorship A business structure in which the owner, as sole proprietor, has absolute authority over all business decisions as well as all the liability. (Chapter 14)

Solid A structure that is formed by the addition of the third dimension, depth or volume, to a two-dimensional object. (Chapter 3)

Solid surface A category of synthetic material (a polymer) often used to simulate marble, granite, stone, and other natural materials. (Chapter 9)

Solvent A liquid vehicle for the pigment in paint. (Chapter 9)

Specifications A component of the contract documents package that provides clarifying information further detailing specific recommendations, such as a manufacturer's brand and model number for a product. (Chapter 5)

Spectral theory of color Sir Isaac Newton (1642–1727), an English mathematician and physicist, is credited with developing the spectral theory of color. In the late 1660s, Newton demonstrated that when a beam of daylight is passed first through a window and then through a triangular glass prism onto a wall, the light refracted, at different angles to the wall. (Chapter 4)

Splat (vase) back chair A type of chair characterized by a central panel (the splat) that serves as a back rest; associated with the Queen Anne style in America. (Chapter 11)

Spline A method of joinery in which a thin strip forms a key between two boards to lock them together, used in flooring and millwork. (Chapter 9)

Split complementary color scheme Rather than using two hues that are directly opposite each other on the color wheel, as in a direct complementary scheme, three hues are chosen, softening the effect of the con-

trast. Geometrically, the choices form a triangle on the color wheel in which two of the sides are equal in length, and the third is shorter. (Chapter 4)

Spot beam spread A beam spread angle of less than 25 degrees. (Chapter 4)

Stackback The amount of space taken up by draperies when they are open. (Chapter 10)

Stacking diagram A schematic drawing that may be used to represent the locations of major components within the space. (Chapter 5)

Station point In a perspective drawing, the location from which the space is viewed. (Chapter 6)

Straightedge See Parallel rule (straightedge).

Streamlined design Implies speed and efficiency. Aerodynamic forms are characteristics of the American concept in building and furniture design as well as the design of cars, railroad interiors, and household products, such as the radio, façades, and interiors of public buildings. (Chapter 12)

Strike off A sample of a specific way in which the colors for a textile will be customized for a particular order. (Chapter 14)

Structural pattern A pattern that is achieved by arranging the elements of a structure or its surface, as when weaving a fabric or arranging rectangular shapes of bricks. (Chapter 3)

Stud wall A typical flexible wall system that may be constructed in either wood or metal using small, upright elements known as studs; these systems may be prefabricated in panels that are brought to the construction site. (Chapter 8)

Study model A three-dimensional model used to explore design ideas; also called sketch model. (Chapter 6)

Subchapter S (S Corporation) A type of business entity whereby the corporation's income or losses are divided among and passed through to its shareholders. (Chapter 14)

Subfloor The structural floor, which often is not the finished floor surface. (Chapter 8)

Subtractive theory of color The way colors of substances are produced from the primaries red, yellow, and blue. (Chapter 4)

Successive contrast See Afterimage (successive contrast).

Suite Adjoined rooms with related functions. (Chapter 5)

Surface-mounted fixture See Flush-mounted fixture. (Chapter 7)

Suspended fixture A lighting fixture that hangs, usually from the ceiling; see also Pendant. (Chapter 7)

Sustainable (green design) Socially responsible design that considers the needs of future generations to preserve the natural environment and its resources. (Chapter 1)

Suzani A traditional woven textile crafted in Central Asia, particularly in Uzbekistan;. often colorful with large scale medallion patterns. (Chapter 10)

Swag (festoon) A semicircular-shaped fabric top window treatment, which may be fixed or draped loosely and is often used with a jabot. (Chapter 10)

Swatch See Cutting (swatch).

Symmetrical balance A formal, static, and traditional type of balance achieved with identical elements situated on either side of an axis. (Chapter 3)

Tabouret A type of stool used by ladies in the Rococo period when in the king's presence. (Chapter 11)

Tactile The sensory experience of touch, which receives perceptions of pressure or traction, usually through the skin. (Chapter 2, Chapter 3)

Tag See Sidemark (tag).

Tallboy See Highboy (tallboy).

Task lighting A type of lighting that illuminates certain areas of a space to facilitate specific activities, such as reading; also called local lighting. (Chapter 3)

Taupe A mixture of the ranges of brown, such as beige, with gray. (Chapter 4)

Tear sheet (catalog cut) A picture of a product, requested from a manufacturer. (Chapter 14)

Tempered glass Glass that has been strengthened with the addition of other ingredients to prevent breakage. (Chapter 8)

Terra-cotta From the Italian for baked earth, a type of often reddish-brown ceramic tile that generally requires a penetrating sealer and topcoat sealer to protect its surface from moisture. (Chapter 9)

Territoriality A behavioral trait that involves attachment to a territory. It expresses a basic need for protection from harm and freedom from danger. (Chapter 2)

Tête-à-tête An S-curved seat made for two for courting couples, typical of the French Rococo period. (Chapter 11)

Tetrad color scheme A variation of the double complementary color scheme. It also uses four hues, but the hues are equidistant from each other on the color wheel, geometrically forming a square (e.g., violet, yellow, blue-green, and red-orange). (Chapter 4)

Textile Any cloth or fabric manufactured in various ways, but usually woven. (Chapter 10)

Texture The features of a surface, comprising both its construction and its finish. (Chapter 3)

Thermal The perception of heat through the skin when it absorbs air or touches an object. (Chapter 2)

Threshold A plank-like element customarily placed under a door and constructed from any of several materials, among them wood, metal, or stone. (Chapter 8)

Throw distance of light How far and with what intensity illumination will reach. As the throw distance increases, the pool of light increases, causing the intensity of the light to diminish. (Chapter 7)

Tint A variation of a hue created when white is added, thus heightening the value, creating a lighter version. (Chapter 3)

Title act Regulates the use of a title, such as "registered interior designer," and is enacted in order to raise public awareness of the qualifications of professional interior designers in a particular state. (Chapter 14)

Title sheet (or page) A cover sheet for the contract documents package, which includes the name and location of the project, a list of all drawings and documents included in the package, the title block (i.e., the letterhead and logo of the person or firm preparing the documents, including license, registration, or certificate number and stamp mark, if appropriate), and lines on which the client will indicate his or her approval with signature and date. (Chapter 5)

Toile de Jouy A fine cotton fabric, generally white and printed in one color with a scene, typically a pastoral image. It was popularized during the Rococo period in France and is named after the factory outside of Versailles at Jouy, where it was produced. (Chapter 11)

Tone A muted version (lower chroma) of a hue, created by adding gray or a hue's complement. (Chapter 3)

Tongue and groove A method of joinery in which a joint is formed by fitting a projection cut along the edge of one board, the tongue, into a recess carved along the edge of another, the groove. (Chapter 9)

Torchiere A standing floor lamp generally used to provide uplighting. (Chapter 7)

Tracery Carved openwork ornamentation, typically used on the tops of windows and doors in the Gothic style. (Chapter 11)

Track system A type of ceiling lighting system consisting of flush-mounted or suspended tracks with attached fixtures that may be movable. (Chapter 7)

Tread The depth of a stair. (Chapter 8)

Trend A general direction or movement; a prevailing tendency or inclination. (Chapter 13)

Trestle A large table consisting of a wood or marble board atop lateral supports. (Chapter 11)

Triadic color scheme A color scheme created by use of hues that are equidistant from one another on the color wheel, forming a triangle in which all three sides are equal. Typical schemes are the primary colors of red, yellow, and blue; more subtle variations include the three secondary colors or tertiary colors. (Chapter 4)

Triangle kitchen design An approach to kitchen design that considers the location of the three primary workstations: sink, refrigerator, and cooktop. (Chapter 5)

Tripartite In three parts; a typical layout of the ancient Egyptians that divides a house into three main sections: a reception area, a columned central hall or living room, and private quarters. (Chapter 11)

Trompe l'oeil An artistic technique that tricks the eye so that the viewer imagines a two-dimensional plane as having three-dimensionality rather than being flat; a decorative painting technique that simulates a material such as marble or details so realistic that they do not appear to be painted. (Chapter 3)

Trumeau A mirror and painting, used as a decorative feature over a door, mantel, or cabinet typical of the Rococo period. (Chapter 11)

Truss A triangular bracing configuration in either wood or metal that serves to distribute load evenly;

it is used as a framework for supporting a roof. (Chapter 8)

Tufted Description of carpeting produced by thrusting a face yarn through a primary backing, applying an adhesive, and then bonding a secondary material to it. (Chapter 9) Also, description of an area of an upholstered piece that is quilted and buttoned, typical of Revival-style furniture. (Chapter 10)

Tufting The buttoning of upholstered fabric. (Chapter 12)

Tungsten-halogen A type of halogen lamp that uses tungsten for its casing. (Chapter 7)

Tunnel test A test that rates the response of a textile to heat and flame. (Chapter 10)

Turkey work A heavy fabric that imitated Eastern carpet design and was used to cover seating during the Renaissance. (Chapter 11)

Tuxedo A type of seating in which the arm height is the same as the back height. (Chapter 10)

Twig furniture Furniture pieces made of branches, popularized in early 20th-century American Adirondack style. (Chapter 12)

Twill weave A type of weaving in which crosswise and lengthwise yarn intersects in a way that forms a diagonal pattern. (Chapter 10)

Two-by-four (2 × 4) A wooden stud that is actually $1\frac{1}{2}$ inches deep by $3\frac{1}{2}$ inches wide and may be of various lengths. (Chapter 8)

Underdrapery A drapery panel, often of lighter weight, such as a sheer, that hangs closer to a window than an outer drape. (Chapter 10)

Underlayment The backing and padding to be used with a floor covering. (Chapter 9)

Unidirectional lighting Light that is directed to illuminate specific objects and surfaces. (Chapter 7)

Uniform Commercial Code (UCC) A code that has been adopted as statutory law in nearly every U.S. state and territory and governs numerous areas of commercial law involving business, commerce, and consumer transactions. (Chapter 14)

Universal design Based on a distinct body of knowledge that relates to both human and design factors. This approach fosters opportunities for as many people as possible to have access to good design. (Chapter 1)

Upholstery A combination of textiles as the covering and the fill to surround a frame of another material, generally wood. It may be used for furniture or cladding of walls, partitions, and window top treatments. (Chapter 10)

Up lighting Lighting that is cast upward onto a surface or object. (Chapter 7)

Upset fee A ceiling amount for an hourly design fee not to be exceeded on a project. (Chapter 14)

Valance A stationary, soft top window treatment, usually pleated or draped in some fashion, that may or may not hide the hardware. (Chapter 10)

Value The degree of lightness or darkness of a color. (Chapter 3)

Vanishing point In a perspective drawing, the point at which lines converge to a shared spot on the horizon. (Chapter 6)

Vargueño A Spanish writing cabinet of the Baroque period. (Chapter 11)

Vase back chair See Splat (vase) back chair.

Veiling reflection Glare produced indirectly by light bouncing off of a reflective surface. (Chapter 7)

Velvet See Plush (velvet) pile.

Venetian blind A horizontal slat window treatment, originally made from wood but now also of vinyl, and similar to a louver door, that can be angled in different ways to control light and allow privacy. (Chapter 10)

Vernis martin A rich green-colored varnish developed by the Martin brothers of France during the Rococo period. (Chapter 11)

Vertical line Lines that are perpendicular (at a right angle) to the horizon. (Chapter 3)

Vibrating color A phenomenon that occurs when strong contrasts of color with high saturation are juxtaposed. The eye does not adequately focus on the two, causing the edges of each hue to blur and shift. It is most apparent in bold striped patterns, particularly in small spaces, where the stripes appear to move. (Chapter 4)

Victorian A term applied to the period of Queen Victoria's reign (1837–1901), as well as the Revivalist styles that were common in England and the United States during this period. (Chapter 12)

Vinyl Any of a variety of manufactured products created from the family of chemicals known as polymers, specifically polyvinyl chloride (PVC). It may be solid or a composite. (Chapter 9)

Visible spectrum The spectrum of light that humans are able to see (from red to violet). (Chapter 4)

Visual weight The visual emphasis given to a component as part of an arrangement in a composition. It may be influenced by size, shape, texture, color, complexity, and position. (Chapter 3)

Void A form that is composed by negative areas (hollow spaces). (Chapter 3)

Volatile organic compound (VOC) A potentially harmful compound found in many products, such as solvents and adhesives, that produces toxic fumes and gases that dissipate with time. (Chapter 2)

Volume Used to describe complete and encased spatial dimensions. (Chapter 3)

Wainscot (dado) A treatment used on interior walls, generally consisting of wood panels that cover the lower part of the wall and run to a point approximately 4 feet above floor level. (Chapter 9)

Wall bracket fixture (sconce) A wall-mounted fixture. (Chapter 7)

Wall grazing A lighting technique used to emphasize the texture of the wall with a higher level of illumination if desired. (Chapter 7)

Wall washing A technique used to provide a smooth distribution, or wash, of light over a vertical surface or plane, usually an entire wall. (Chapter 7)

Warm gray A gray that has some warm hue such as one in the red to yellow range mixed in. (Chapter 4)

Warp Lengthwise yarns on a loom. (Chapter 9)

Watt The unit used to measure the consumption of electrical power; symbolized by the letter W, such as a 60 W lamp. (Chapter 7)

Wavelength A method of measuring light in which bands of light are measured as pulsations or electromagnetic energy. (Chapter 4)

Webbing Strips of material woven in a basketweave pattern and laid over the springs in an upholstered piece to prevent the springs from penetrating the batting. (Chapter 10)

Weft The filling (widthwise or crosswise) yarns in a woven material. (Chapter 9)

Whatnot Any of a range of collectibles, usually displayed in curio cabinets, or the cabinets in which these items are displayed; popular in the Victorian period. (Chapter 12)

Whiplash curve A sinuous and thin line that is a typical motif in Art Nouveau style. (Chapter 12)

White noise A mixture of sounds in wide frequencies that are considered neutral sound. (Chapter 2)

Wicker Furniture, usually casual in style, made by the weaving of twigs or vines. (Chapter 10)

Wilton Wool carpet composed of a limited number of colors woven on a specific type of loom called a Jacquard loom. (Chapter 9)

Wire glass A type of glass in which a metal mesh system is infused into the glass to resist shattering. It is used for windows requiring fire resistance. (Chapter 8)

Working drawing The plans, schedules, and specifications developed during the contract documents phase; also known as construction drawing. (Chapter 5)

Work-related musculoskeletal disorder (WMSD) Symptoms such as stiff neck, fatigue, lower back pain, stress on joints, and carpal tunnel syndrome, resulting from a poor fit between humans and machines and produced when muscles are kept in a prolonged static contraction, inhibiting blood flow and causing fatigue. (Chapter 2)

Workroom The factory or work site where furniture is upholstered or draperies fabricated. (Chapter 10)

Woven Description of rugs or cloth produced by interlacing yarns or strands of fiber in a pattern that combines warp (lengthwise) and filling (widthwise, crosswise, or weft) yarns; it may involve the use of knots. (Chapter 9)

Wyzenbeek test A test that evaluates the ability of a fabric to withstand abrasion. (Chapter 10)

Xenon test A test that measures how well the color of a fabric resists fading when exposed to light. (Chapter 10)

ZEB (Zero Energy Building) A residential or commercial building in which energy needs have been greatly reduced through efficiency gains, such that the balance of energy needs can be supplied with renewable technologies. (Chapter 8)

ZEH (Zero Energy Home) A classification given to single, private homes. This type of building uses efficient construction and appliances with commercially available renewable energy systems (often photovoltaic), such as solar water heating and solar electricity. (Chapter 8)

Ziggurat A stepped, pyramidal-type structure. (Chapter 12)

Zone An area of space designed to be used for a particular type of activity. (Chapter 5)

End Notes

Chapter 1

1. Martin Thorpe, *Roman Architecture* (Wiltshire, UK: The Cromwell Press, 1995).
2. John Barrington Bayley and William A. Coles, introduction to Edith Wharton and Ogden Codman, Jr., *The Decoration of Houses* (originally published, 1897), The Classical America Series in Art and Architecture (New York: W. W. Norton, 1978).
3. Charles L. Eastlake, *Hints on Household Taste* (New York: Longmans, Green, 1878).
4. U.S. Department of Labor, Bureau of Labor Statistics, *Occupational Outlook Handbook,* 2010-2011 edition, "Interior Designers," http://www.bls.gov/oco/ocos293.htm
5. John F. Pile, *Interior Design* (Englewood Cliffs, NJ: Prentice Hall, 1988).
6. Wharton and Codman, *The Decoration of Houses*, Introduction and 10.
7. Sir Hugh Casson, *Inscape: The Design of Interiors* (London: Architectural Press, 1968).
8. *Merriam-Webster's Collegiate Dictionary,* 10th ed. (Springfield, MA: Merriam-Webster, 1993).
9. *Encyclopaedia Britannica Online,* s.v "Interior Design," http://www.britannica.com/EB checked/topic/290278/interior-design (accessed May 1, 2012).
10. U.S. Department of Labor, Bureau of Labor Statistics, *Standard Occupational Classification,* "27-1025 Interior Designers," http://www.bls.gov/soc/2010/soc271025.htm
11. *A Study of Interior Design: Analysis of the Needs of Practice and Implications for Education* (Chicago: IIDA Foundation and E-Lab, 2001), 49.
12. The American Society of Interior Designers (http://www.ASID.org) and the International Interior Design Association (http://www.IIDA.org).
13. Load-bearing structures, the purview of architects and engineers, are differentiated from non-load-bearing structures by being intrinsic to the essential foundation of a building's structure rather than structural divisions related to space planning.
14. ESR2009/Environmental scanning report, ASID (American Society of Interior Designers), prepared December 2008 by Michael Berens, Director of Research and Knowledge Resources for ASID, 13.
15. The American Society of Interior Designers (http://www.ASID.org) and the International Interior Design Association (http://www.IIDA.org).
16. American Society of Interior Designers, *The Interior Design Profession: Facts and Figures* (Washington, DC: ASID, 2010), 40.
17. L. Capirsello, S. Filkins, C. Burke, and M. Berens "Preparing Students to Enter the Interior Design Profession: Results of an Employer Survey," *Innovation in Technology and Design,* IDEC 2006 Conference Proceedings, Scottsdale, AZ, March 12–April 2, 2006, 192–198.

Chapter 2

1. Mary Knackstedt, "The Unique Value." *ASID ICON*, January/February 2008, 28.

2. *Working Draft for Discussion,* "Socially Responsible Design (SRD)," IDEC, March 30, 2006.

3. Architecture for Humanity, ed., *Design Like You Give a Damn: Architectural Responses to Humanitarian Crises* (New York: Metropolis, 2006).

4. The Center for Universal Design, North Carolina State University, http://www.ncsu .edu/www/ncsu/design/sod5/cud/about_ud /udprinciples.htm

5. Clodagh, *Total Design: Contemplate, Cleanse, Clarify, and Create Your Personal Spaces* (New York: Clarkson Potter, 2001), 34.

6. R. D. Chin, *Feng Shui Revealed: An Aesthetic Practial Approach to the Ancient Art of Space Alignment* (New York: Clarkson Potter, 1998).

7. The Occupational Safety and Health Administration (OSHA) was established by the federal government in 1971 to develop standards for employers regarding ergonomic protection.

8. Dr. Marvin J. Dainoff, *The Effect of Ergonomic Worktools on Productivity in Today's Automated Workstation Design* (Oxford, OH: Miami University Center for Ergonomic Research, not dated).

9. Press release, Humanscale, New York, NY, www.humanscale.com

10. Census Brief CENBR/97–5, U.S. Department of Commerce, Economics, and Statistics Administration, Bureau of the Census, Washington, DC, December 1997.

11. Centers for Disease Control National Center for Health Statistics, Division of Data Services, Hyattsville, MD.

12. Susan Behar, *The ASID Report*, January–February 1991.

13. U.S. Department of Health and Human Services, National Institute of Diabetes and Digestive and Kidney Diseases. http://www2 .niddk.nih.gov/

14. Centers for Disease Control National Center for Health Statistics, http://www.cdc.gov/nchs/

15. *Ibid.*

16. Samantha McAskill, "Designing for Acoustics, Hearing and Aging," http:// www.asid.org/designknowledge/aa /inplace/active/Designing+for+Acoustics _Hearing+and+Aging.htm

17. National Institute on Aging, Bethesda, MD, http://www.nia.nih.gov/alzheimers

18. Interview conducted with Debbie Schwartz and Kevin Woods, Color Association of the United States (CAUS), 2002.

19. National Institute of Neurological Disorders and Strokes, NIH, http://www.ninds.nih.gov /disorders/autism/autism.htm

20. Valerie Fletcher, Institute for Human Centered Design, presentation at the ICFF Metropolis Conference, May 2010.

21. Census Brief CENBR/97–5, U.S. Department of Commerce, Economics, and Statistics Administration, Bureau of the Census, Washington, DC, December 1997.

22. United Nations Commission on the Status of Women, 54th session, March 1–13, 2010.

23. National Aging in Place Council, Washington, DC, http://www.ageinplace.org/

24. American Society of Interior Design, *Aging in Place—Aging and the Impact of Interior Design* (Washington, DC: ASID, 2001), 2.

25. Edward T. Hall, *The Hidden Dimension* (New York: Doubleday, 1966).

26. David Kent Ballast, *Interior Design Reference Manual: A Guide to the NCIDQ Exam,* 4th ed. (Belmont, CA: Professional, 2007), 13.

27. Julie Stewart-Pollack and Rosemary Menconi, *Designing for Privacy and Related Needs* (New York: Fairchild, 2005), 1.

28. Clodagh, *Your Home, Your Sanctuary* (New York: Rizzoli, 2009), quoted at http://www .clodagh.com/book/book.php (accessed May 24, 2010).

29. Susan Winchip, *Sustainable Design for Interior Environments* (New York: Fairchild, 2007), 4–5.

30. Keri Luly, "EnvironDesign Notebook: H$_2$O: The Next Big Green Issue Is Blue," *Interiors and Sources,* September 1, 2009, http://www .interiorsandsources.com/tabid/3339/Article ID/8855/Default.aspx

31. Mary Ann Lazarus, "EnvironDesign Notebook: Inviting Nature In," *Interiors and Sources,* 1 July 2009, http://www.interiorsandsources.com/tabid/3339/ArticleID/8664/Default.aspx

32. Cara McCarty, Ellen Lupton, Matilda McQuaid, and Cynthia Smith, *Why Design Now? National Design Triennial* (New York: Cooper-Hewitt, National Design Museum, Smithsonian Institution, 2010), published in connection with the exhibition *Why Design Now? National Design Triennial* shown at Cooper-Hewitt, May 14, 2010–January 9, 2011.

33. "The Universe Study," *Interior Design*, March 1, 2010, 98.

34. C. Jaye Berger, "Environmental Law and the Design Profession," *The ASID Report*, May–June 1993.

35. Dr. Paul Polak, quoted on the website of the exhibition "Design for the Other 90%," Smithsonian Cooper-Hewitt National Design Museum, 2010, http://other90.cooperhewitt.org/

36. About the Exhibition "'Why Design Now?'" National Design Triennial exhibition, Smithsonian Cooper-Hewitt National Design Museum, 2010, http://exhibitions.cooperhewitt.org/Why-Design-Now/about

Chapter 3

1. David Kent Ballast, *Interior Design Reference Manual: A Guide to the NCIDQ Exam,* 4th ed. (Belmont, CA: Professional, 2007), 43.

2. *Merriam-Webster's Collegiate Dictionary,* 10th ed. (Springfield, MA: Merriam-Webster, 1993).

3. Tim Brown, *Change by Design: How Design Thinking Transforms Organizations and Inspires Innovation* (New York: HarperBusiness, 2009), 4.

4. Ballast, *Interior Design Reference Manual*, 43.

5. *Ibid.,* 23–32.

6. *Ibid.,* 43.

7. Patricia A. Rodemann, *Patterns in Interior Environment: Perception, Psychology, and Practice* (New York, John Wiley & Sons, 1999), 7.

8. "Design Daily: Beauty, Proportion May Be Instinctual," *Los Angeles Times,* January 6, 2010.

9. Tony Chi and Associates official website, "About Us," http://www.tonychi.com/main.html

Chapter 4

1. Donald Kaufman and Taffy Dahl, *Color: Natural Palettes for Painted Rooms* (New York: Clarkson Potter, 2002), 13.

2. *Merriam-Webster's Collegiate Dictionary,* 10th ed. (Springfield, MA: Merriam-Webster, 1993).

3. Jim Long and Joy Turner Luke, *The New Munsell Student Color Set,* 2d ed. (New York: Fairchild, 2001), 60.

4. *Merriam-Webster's Collegiate Dictionary*.

5. There is a lack of consensus regarding the perceived temperatures of yellow-green and red-violet, and they are sometimes placed in the categories opposite to those described here.

6. Long and Luke, *The New Munsell Student Color Set.*

7. *Ibid.,* 5.

8. *Merriam-Webster's Collegiate Dictionary*.

9. John A. Brabyn, Gunilla Haegerström-Portnoy, Marilyn E. Schneck, and Lori A. Lott, "Visual Impairments in Elderly People under Everyday Viewing Conditions," *Journal of Visual Impairments and Blindness* 94, no. 12 (2000): 741–755.

10. *Merriam-Webster's Collegiate Dictionary*.

11. Leatrice Eiseman, *Colors for Your Every Mood: Discover Your True Decorating Colors* (Sterling, VA: Capital, 1998).

12. R. D. Chin, *Feng Shui Revealed* (New York: Clarkson Potter, 1998).

13. Antonio F. Torrice and Ro Logrippo, *In My Room: Designing for and with Children* (New York: Fawcette Columbine Ballantine, 1989).

14. Linda L. Nussbaumer, *Evidence-Based Design for Interior Designers* (New York: Fairchild, 2009), 201.

15. Ronald L. Reed, *Color + Design: Transforming Interior Space* (New York: Fairchild, 2010), 47.

16. *Ibid,* 47.

17. The Color Computer, produced by M. Grumbacher, is a 12-hue color wheel that demonstrates analogous schemes, including up to 5 hues; therefore, 1 hue will be in the opposite temperature zone.

Chapter 5

1. National Council for Interior Design Qualification, "About Us: Definition of Interior Design," http://www.ncidq.org/AboutUs/AboutInterior Design/DefinitionofInteriorDesign.aspx

2. David Kent Ballast, *Interior Design Reference Manual: A Guide to the NCIDQ Exam,* 4th ed. (Belmont, CA: Professional, 2007), 29.

3. Mark Karlen, *Space Planning Basics* (New York: Van Nostrand Reinhold, 1993), 57.

4. National Council for Interior Design Qualification, "About Us: Definition of Interior Design," http://www.ncidq.org/AboutUs/AboutInterior Design/DefinitionofInteriorDesign.aspx

5. *Ibid.*

6. Cyril M. Harris, ed., *Dictionary of Architecture and Construction* (New York: McGraw-Hill, 2000).

7. National Council for Interior Design Qualification, "About Us: Definition of Interior Design," http://www.ncidq.org/AboutUs/AboutInterior Design/DefinitionofInteriorDesign.aspx

8. Jerrold M. Sonet and Alan M. Siegel, "Contract Administration," *Interior Design,* December 1985.

9. As defined by the National Kitchen and Bath Association (NKBA), certified kitchen designer (CKB) and certified bath designer (CBD) credentials include a combination of education and experience (see Appendix A).

10. Maureen Mitton and Courtney Nystuen, *Residential Interior Design: A Guide to Planning Spaces* (Hoboken, NJ: John Wiley & Sons, 2007), 96.

11. Stacy Straczynski , "Designer Perspectives: Future Corporate Design Trends," *Contract,* May 19, 2010, http://www.contractdesign.com /contract/Designer-Perspective-1925.shtml

12. *Ibid.*

Chapter 6

1. Douglas R. Seidler and Amy Korté, *Handrawing for Designers: Communicating Ideas through Architectural Graphics* (New York: Fairchild, 2010), 2.

2. Francis D. K. Ching and Corky Binggeli, *Interior Design Illustrated,* 2nd ed. (Hoboken, NJ: John Wiley & Sons, 2005), 68.

3. David Kent Ballast, *Interior Design Reference Manual: A Guide to the NCIDQ Exam,* 4th ed. (Belmont, CA: Professional, 2007), 65.

4. Eddy Krygiel, Greg Demchak, and Tatjana Dzambazova, *Introducing Revit Architecture 2008: BIM for Beginners* (Indianapolis, IN: Wiley, 2007).

5. Suining Ding, *Modeling and Visualization with AutoCad* (New York: Fairchild, 2009), 3–4.

Chapter 7

1. Susan M. Winchip, *Fundamentals of Lighting,* 1st ed. (New York: Fairchild, 2008), 24.

2. Alice McKeown and Nathan Swire, "Vital Signs," *WorldWatch Institute,* October 15, 2008, http://vitalsigns.worldwatch.org/vs-trend/strong-growth-compact-fluorescent-bulbs-reduces-electricity-demand

3. U.S.Department of Energy, "Energy Efficiency and Renewable Energy," *Solid-State Lighting: R&D Challenges,* 2011, http://www1.eere .energy.gov/buildings/ssl/sslbasics_randd.html

4. Susan M. Winchip, *Fundamentals of Lighting,* 1st Edition (New York: Fairchild, 2008), 46.

5. Winchip, *Fundamentals of Lighting*, 138.

6. *Ibid.,* 33.

7. *Ibid.,* 30.

8. *Ibid.,* 149.

9. "A 'Light Bulb' Moment for People with Dementia," *Think Magazine,* Case Western University, May 12, 2009, http://www.case.edu /think/breakingnews/Lightbulb.html

10. Jean Nayar, "Healing Light," *Contract,* October 2008.

11. Winchip, *Fundamentals of Lighting.* 12.

12. *Ibid.,* 30, 94, 95.

13. *Ibid.,* 105.

Chapter 8

1. *Fabrick* is the archaic word for "fabric," or the structure of a building.
2. Andrea Palladio, *The Four Books of Architecture* (New York,: Dover Publications, 1965), 1.
3. Stanley Abercrombie, *A Philosophy of Interior Design* (Harper and Row, 1990), 2–3.
4. Edith Wharton and Ogden Codman, Jr., *The Decoration of Houses* (originally published, 1897), The Classical America Series in Art and Architecture (New York: W. W. Norton, 1978).
5. Susan M. Winchip, *Sustainable Design for Interior Environments,* 1st ed. (New York: Fairchild, 2007), 170–176.
6. Francis D. K. Ching, *Building Construction Illustrated* (New York: Van Nostrand Reinhold, 1975), 7.
7. David Kent Ballast, *Interior Design Reference Manual: A Guide to the NCIDQ Exam,* 4th ed. (Belmont, CA: Professional, 2007), 314–315.
8. Nancy Keates, "Ceilings Come Down to Earth," *The Wall Street Journal,* May 23, 2008.
9. Abercrombie, *A Philosophy of Interior Design*, 5–10.
10. Wharton and Codman, *The Decoration of Houses*, 64.
11. Palladio, *Four Books,* 30.
12. *Ibid.,* 30.
13. Ballast, *Interior Design Reference Manual: A Guide to the NCIDQ Exam,* p. 171.
14. Palladio, *Four Books,* 34.
15. Ballast, *Interior Design Reference Manual,* 346.
16. Cynthia A. Leibrock and James Evan Terry, *Beautiful Universal Design* (New York: John Wiley & Sons, 1999).
17. Ballast, *Interior Design Reference Manual,* 325.
18. NREL, National Renewable Energy Laboratory, U.S. Department of Energy.
19. Ballast, *Interior Design Reference Manual,* 337–340.

Chapter 9

1. National Council for Interior Design Qualification, "About Us: Definition of Interior Design," http://www.ncidq.org/AboutUs/AboutInterior Design/DefinitionofInteriorDesign.aspx
2. The Hardwood Council. "American Hardwood Information Center." "How Selecting Materials Impacts Our Lives." http://www .hardwoodinfo.com/articles/view/pro/22/283
3. Alison Zingara, "Medium Award for Material of the Year 2009," *Matter.* 6.4: 23–25, adapted from *Matter,* a publication of Material ConneXion.

Chapter 10

1. Amy Willbanks, Nancy Oxford, Dana Miller, and Sharon Coleman, *Textiles for Residential and Commercial Interiors,* 3rd ed. (New York: Fairchild, 2010), 68.
2. Frank Theodore Koe. *Fabric for the Designed Interior* (New York: Fairchild, 2007), 28.
3. Willbanks et al., *Textiles for Residential and Commercial Interiors,* 10, 80.
4. TOTO USA, Inc., press release, www.toto usa.com
5. Edith Wharton and Ogden Codman, Jr. *The Decoration of Houses* (originally published, 1897), The Classical America Series in Art and Architecture (New York: W. W. Norton, 1978).

Adapted from and for further reading:

- Lisa Godsey, *Interior Design Materials and Specifications,* 1st ed. (New York: Fairchild, 2008).
- Frank Theodore Koe, *Fabric for the Designed Interior* (New York: Fairchild, 2007).
- Phyllis G. Tortora and Robert S. Merkel, *Fairchild's Dictionary of Textiles,* 7th ed. (New York: Fairchild, 1996).
- Amy Willbanks and Sharon Coleman, *Textiles for Residential and Commercial Interiors,* 3rd ed. (New York: Fairchild, 2010).

Chapter 11

1. Jeannie Ireland. *History of Interior Design.* (New York: Fairchild, 2009), 41–59.
2. *Ibid.,* 83–95.
3. *Ibid.,* 117.
4. *Ibid.,* 122.

5. *Ibid.,* 111.
6. *Ibid.,* 165.
7. *Ibid.,* 269.
8. *Ibid.,* 295.

Adapted from and for further reading:

- Mark Hinchman, *History of Furniture: A Global View* (New York, Fairchild, 2009).
- Jeannie Ireland, *History of Interior Design* (New York: Fairchild, 2009).
- Martin M. Pegler. *The Fairchild Dictionary of Interior Design,* 2nd ed. (New York: Fairchild, 2006).
- Susan Winchip. *Visual Culture in the Built Environment: A Global Perspective* (New York: Fairchild, 2010).

Chapter 12
Adapted from and for further reading:

- Mark Hinchman, *History of Furniture: A Global View* (New York: Fairchild, 2009).
- Jeannie Ireland, *History of Interior Design* (New York: Fairchild, 2009).
- Martin M. Pegler, *The Fairchild Dictionary of Interior Design,* 2nd ed. (New York: Fairchild, 2006).
- Susan Winchip, *Visual Culture in the Built Environment: A Global Perspective* (New York: Fairchild, 2010).

Chapter 13
1. Bouley Design Inc. website, "Philosophy," http://bouleydesign.squarespace.com/philosophy/
2. Patti Carpenter, "Cultural Sustainability and Design" (Presentation to the Diversity Council, Fashion Institute of Technology, New York, November 2, 2010).
3. American Society of Interior Designers. *Environmental Scanning Report,* 2010, 5, 7, 8.

4. "IFDA's Vision for the Future," *20/20* (ABC Newsmagazine), IFDA website for release, March 5, 2001.
5. *Environmental Scanning Report,* 8.
6. Tim Brown's official website, "Definitions of Design Thinking," September 7, 2008. http://designthinking.ideo.com/?p=49#content
7. Susan S. Szenasy. "The Growing Need for Creative Problem Solving through Design Thinking," American Society of Interior Designers, *The State of the Interior Design Profession.* eds. Caren S. Martin and Denise A. Guerin. (New York: Fairchild, 2010). 78–82.
8. Ellen Lupton, "Communication," in *Why Design Now? National Design Triennial,* Cooper-Hewitt, National Design Museum, Smithsonian Institution, 2010, 140–167, published in conjunction with the exhibition "Why Design Now? National Design Triennial" shown at Cooper-Hewitt, May 14, 2010–January 9, 2011.

Chapter 14
1. American Society of Interior Designers. *Interior Design Legislation 101,* 2012.
2. American Society of Interior Designers, in "Preamble 1.0," eds. Cara McCarty, Ellen Lupton, Matilda McQuaid, and Cynthia Smith (New York: *Code of Ethics and Professional Conduct*) 1, 2012.
3. Kenneth G. Roberts. "The Fundamentals of Finding a Job in Any Economy," American Sociey of Interior Designers, 2012. http://www.asid.org/career/jobs/The+Fundamentals+of+Finding+a+Job+in+Any+Economy.htm
4. David Kent Ballast, *Interior Design Reference Manual: A Guide to the NCDIQ Exam, 4th ed..* (Belmont, CA: Professional 2007), 447.
5. "The Universe Study by Research Results Inc." *Interior Design Magazine,* December 2009, 40.

Index